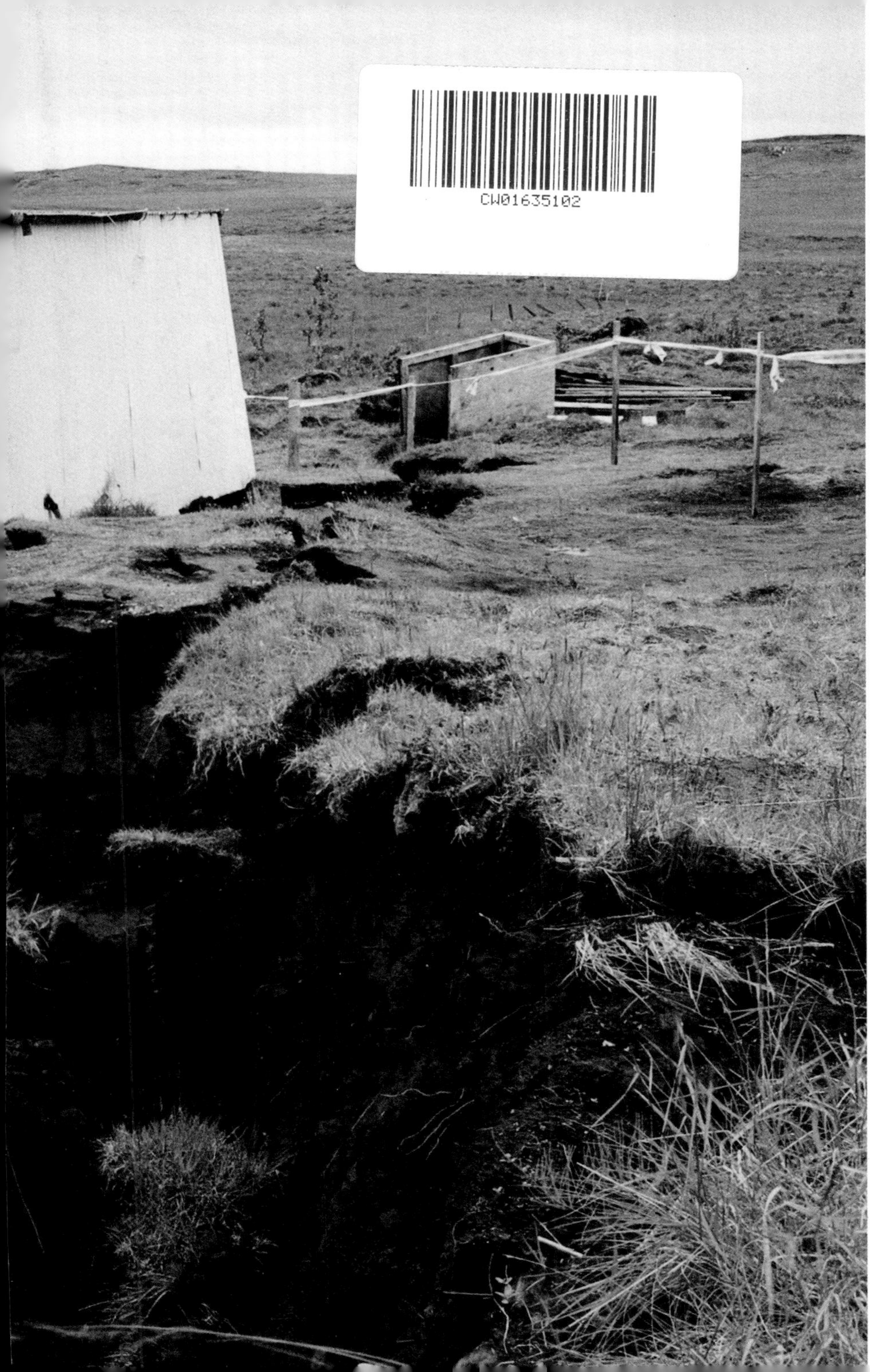

su
sur ro

r
und ings
ed

Neue Galerie am Landesmuseum Joanneum
Graz, Austria

ZKM | Center for Art and Media
Karlsruhe, Germany

The MIT Press
Cambridge, Massachusetts   London, England

Olafur Eliasson: Surroundings Surrounded

Essays on Space and Science

Edited by Peter Weibel

A publication by the
Neue Galerie, Graz,
ZKM | Karlsruhe and
The MIT Press, Cambridge
on the occasion of the exhibition:

Olafur Eliasson:
Surroundings Surrounded
Neue Galerie am Landesmuseum
Joanneum, Graz, Austria
March 30 - May 21, 2000
ZKM | Center for Art and Media
Karlsruhe, Germany
May 31 - August 26, 2001

The book

Editor: Peter Weibel
The selection of the authors and texts, by Peter Weibel in cooperation and in discourse with Olafur Eliasson

ZKM | Karlsruhe
Publication Program
Ursula Frohne, editor

Editorial Assistance:
Monika Lahrkamp, Timo Linsenmaier, Stephanie Lüke, Ina Scholl, Thomas Zandegiacomo Del Bel

Manuscript Editors:
Charlotte Eckler and Lisa Rosenblatt

Editorial Support:
Caroline Eggel,
Burkhard Riemschneider

Design Concept and Layout:
Jürgen Betker, Beate Kamecke,
Achim Römer

Translations:
Ian Balfour, Pauline Cumbers, Anna Elkins, Dan Marmorstein, Anthony Maxwell, Martin Wawrzynczak

With special thanks to the authors and the publishing houses.

This book was printed and bound in Karlsruhe by Engelhardt & Bauer

ISBN 0-262-73148-7

The exhibition

Neue Galerie, Graz

Curators:
Christa Steinle and Peter Weibel

Project Manager:
Günther Holler-Schuster

Technical Realization:
Andreas Hochegger, Nikolaus Vodopivec, Alois Weitzer, Kasimir Werschitz, Franz Zollner

Public Affairs:
Karin Buol-Wischenau, Margot Goettsberger

Education Program:
Birgit Laback and Team

ZKM | Karlsruhe

Curator:
Peter Weibel

Project Manager:
Sabine Himmelsbach

Assistance:
Katrin Kaschadt

Registrar:
Gina Linder

Technical Manager:
Martin Häberle

Assistance:
Volker Becker, Claudius Böhm, Martin Boukhalfa, Silke Fehsenfeld, Mirco Frass, Gregor Gaissmaier, Jürgen Galli, Ronny Haas, Werner Hutzenlaub, Gisbert Laaber, Thomas Linder, Christiane Ostertag, et. al.

Public Affairs:
Sonja Bichsel, Christiane Gerhold, Sabine Peters

Education Program:
Bernhard Serexhe

Assistance:
Dorothee Rosenbauer

Website:
Tom Fürstner, Lydia Lindner

Special thanks to:
Elke Cordell, Hans H. Diebner, Anna Reiss, Marco Sonntag, Bonnie Teut

Studio Olafur Eliasson

Installation:
Tomski Binsert, Ralf Brög, Jeppe Hein, Patrick Kalt, Martin Kern, Emil Tomasson

Logistics and Development:
Tomski Binsert, Caroline Eggel, Patrick Kalt, Martin Müller, Emil Tomasson

Contents

The only thing we have in common is that we are different

Your inverted veto

Editorial

During the 1996 group exhibition "Remote Connections," Olafur Eliasson, whose work we had become aquainted with in Berlin's neugerriemschneider gallery, showed for the first time at the New Gallery of the State Museum of Joanneum.[1] He chose one of the most privileged and most difficult rooms of the New Gallery: the Mirror Hall. Produced relatively simply, yet to great effect, his light installation, *The Organic and the Crystalline Description*, constituted a central work of this group exhibition and was later reproduced repeatedly in diverse publications. After that we followed his astonishing international career, and by 1998, we decided to invite him to stage his first major solo exhibition in a museum. Up until this time, those interested in his art only had the chance to see individual works included in prominent group shows. It seemed important to us to display the large ensembles and groups of works by the artist in their totality, in order to better present Olafur Eliasson's intentions to the public. Owing to construction problems in the New Gallery, the exhibition was delayed for a year, which gave the artist the opportunity to produce many new works expressly for this show. The minute details of the exhibition were conceived during numerous conversations in Graz and Berlin. The precision of Olafur Eliasson's planning, as well as his operational competence, was already striking and evident in the way he invented this comprehensive exhibit with its logistical and technical difficulties.

This exhibition offered an introductory *parcours* through all the fields of work and the methods that Olafur Eliasson deals with in his installations: the factors of human perception in an age of technology and the laws of nature from the perspective of their anthropological relativity. His work addresses the question of our conception of nature and the technical aids that we use to observe, construct, and measure it.

Nature has long been a testing ground, even a battlefield for human beings. Romanticism wanted to rescue nature from mankind by anti-scientific means. The ecology movement wants

1. *Remote Connections. Media Art in the Era of Displacement*, ed. Ammon Barzel, Neue Galerie Landesmuseum Joanneum, steirischer herbst 96, Graz, Austria.

2. Bruno Latour, *Science in Action*, Harvard University Press, Cambridge, Mass., 1987.

to do this in scientific fashion. Olafur Eliasson takes up both impulses and develops a new artistic strategy by displaying nature as the testing ground and the construct of science. His foil is not reality but natural science. Instead of addressing a pre-scientific or premediated perception of nature, his installations deal exclusively with phenomena of nature as natural science has made them analytically accessible to us. He displays nature as artificially constructed by natural science under laboratory conditions in the laboratory of the museum. It is not just a case of a science exhibition in a "science center," but rather the artistic observation of science at work. This scientific labor in the laboratory (in the sense of Bruno Latour[2]) is astonishingly attractive. The laboratory emerges as a place not only of knowledge but also of enjoyment. In the individual cabinets of the museum, the observer experiences a sequence of perplexing phenomena, unexpected sensations, and impressions. The scientific laboratory within the museum is a place of

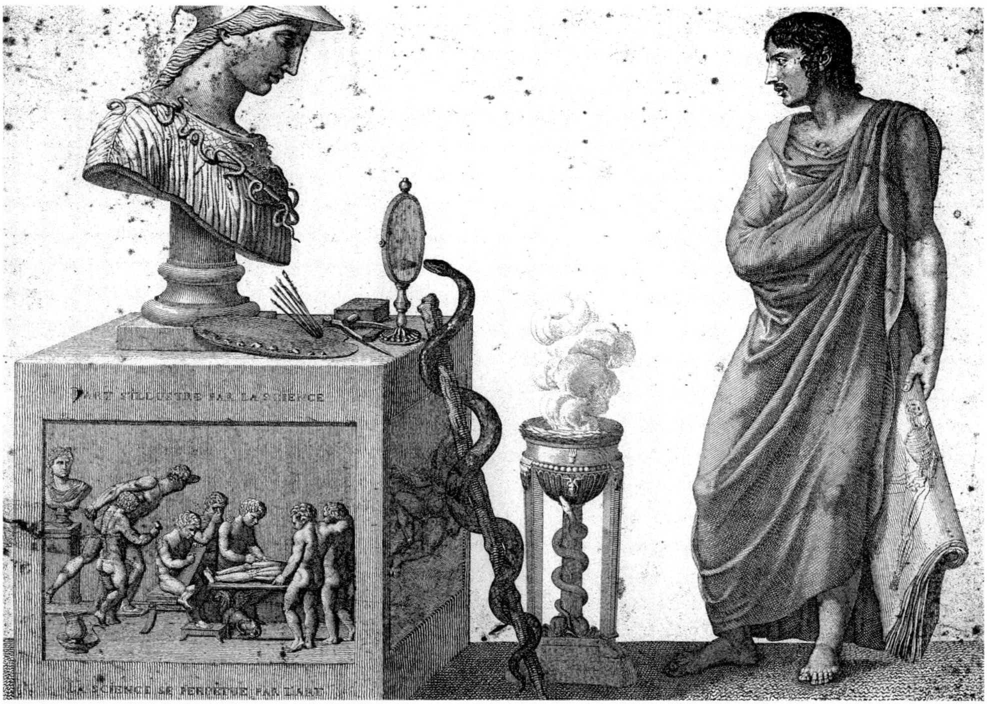

L'art s'illustre par la science, la science se perpetue par l'art (Art illustrated by science, science perpetuating itself through art)

Engraving by Jean Marie Leroux after a drawing by Jean Galbert Salvage, *Anatomie du Gladiateur Combattant, applicable aux Beaux Arts, ou Traité des os, des muscles, du mécanisme des mouvements, des proportions et des caractères du Corps Humaine*, Paris 1812, Neue Galerie am Landesmuseum Joanneum, Graz, Austria

wonder and desire. Museum halls become rooms for experience, in which the observer witnesses nature under scientific conditions. Nature appears as a kind of anthology of special effects, transposed from the virtual world back into the world of our natural senses.

Our constructions of nature change throughout the course of history, parallel to social, ideological, technical, and other changes. Physical structures themselves are not free from social determinations and socialized possibilities, because the apparatuses of perception and measurement determine which physical structures we recognize, as well as what we recognize as physical structures. Often, cultural models appear natural to the individual, such that they are falsely believed objective characteristics of our natural environment. The apparently purely physical experiments with the four elements – water, fire, earth, and air, and the light and color that derive from them – are thus, in reality, also experiments with our patterns of perception, and our models of the environment, our social structures. Via his apparatuses for perceiving reality, Eliasson establishes empirical connections among reality, perception, and represented reality in a straightforward way. By means of cultural techniques, he transforms natural processes (the waterfall flows upward instead of down). In this way, nature becomes, hypothetically, a product of civilisation. The difference between a natural environment and an anthropomorphic system is not differentiated from within, but from the outside. Surroundings are not folded inward, but rather encircled from the outside. The environs become a system. "Surroundings" are "surrounded." The traditional difference between nature and culture, and the drawing of their boundaries, is questioned.

Eliasson succeeded in transposing his artistic universe into the circumscribed topography of Graz's New Gallery in the twelve first-floor rooms and in the inner courtyard. He transformed the *parcours* through the New Gallery and the inner courtyard into one of his favorite *topoi,* almost into a *torus.* The first room was a curtain of sprayed water whose drops appeared to the viewer, through stroposcopic light-projection, to be transformed into crystals, suspended in the air. The last room was a wind installation with sixteen ventilators, *Your windless arrangement* (1997) (Malmö Museum of Art, Malmö, Sweden), which seemed to suck the visitor not only into the inner room, but also out of it. The exit door remained open during exhibition times so that the staircase led one to the ground floor and worked like a wind tunnel. When visitors left this wind tunnel and walked out of the exhibition into the open air of the courtyard, they stood in front of a giant, artificial waterfall, whose tumultuous thunder could be heard throughout the entire tour of the exhibition. Thus, the path led through the four elements with their configurations of material and light (solid, liquid, gaseous), from water to water.

One year later, in his significantly expanded major solo-exhibition in Karlsruhe's Center for Art and Media (ZKM), Eliasson similarly charted a new concept for exhibiting, which involved the topography of the building. In this show, which stretches throughout the entire exhibition space in atrium 8 and 9, the Center for Art and Media (ZKM) presents Eliasson's copious work to the public. The artist, who has appeared at the Venice Biennale in 1999, was nominated for the prize in Contemporary Art by the National Gallery in Berlin in 2000. Shown together with early works are works created especially for this exhibition. A system of denser and dissipated alternating zones leads the observer in a periodic fashion through Eliasson's work-fields. The exhibition of these new fields of action and communication platforms, as well as other larger individual pieces, is made possible by the size of the Center's atriums. On display, for example, are an artificial ice-field, *The very large ice-floor* (1998), the circle of color, *Tell me about your miraculous invention* (2000), the horizon line, *360 degree expectations* (2001), a cover of light, *Yet untitled* (2000), and a mirrored cathedral, *Wonderland Dome* (2000). Eliasson planned this exhibition, too, with his customary precision.

The question of the catalogue was open for discussion at the very start of exhibition planning. Early on, Eliasson expressed the wish to publish not a conventional catalogue documenting his work but rather to have his work surrounded by scholarly commentaries. Together with Peter Weibel, he produced a list of the various spheres of work and possible authors. By the end of this process, it emerged that Eliasson actually did not want any art-historical commentaries; instead, the work should remain without commentary and function as an insert or interface to the individual chapters. An anthology of scholarly texts, partly already published, partly written for this publication, intended to provide insights into the ways in which Eliasson operates. The scholarly texts are to constitute the foil, a kind of material collection of the horizon, in light of which a deeper understanding of Eliasson's work would be possible. This book is an innovative project, because the exclusivity with which art theory and art criticism are renounced renders possible a new alliance between science and art, and documents how the two, as parallel worlds, cross over into each other with equal justification and do not exist as divided cultures (C. P. Snow, *The Two Cultures,* 1959). It is indeed Olafur Eliasson's art which allows for an optimal intersection of science and art, because he does not take nature as his point of departure but rather science, which explains nature for us, namely, natural science. His art is a kind of meta-science, which appropriates and reflects the findings of natural science, and transforms them into art, into aesthetic experience, and into sensual experience. This new alliance between science and art is the manifest element of a paradigm shift which introduces entirely new paths and options for twenty-first century art. As a result, you have in front of you a book which not only offers an almost encyclopaedic insight into science and the terrains of its problems such as space, but also into the implicated problematics of the most topical contemporary art, which is oriented to the future. It thereby also provides an overview of Olafur Eliasson's artistic universe. The singularity of this book is this: scientists speak for art, and thus we provide a retort to the Science Wars.[3]

The gauntlet thrown in the face of artists and philosophers by the science warriors responsible for igniting Science Wars is now disarmed. This disarmament is taking place, because it has been demonstrated that art and science can share the same terrain, even though their products are different. A new alliance resides in this sharing.

The brilliance of the contributions by significant authors and their readiness to cooperate on this unusual project not only fills our two institutions with gratitude and admiration, it also confirms for the art and science communities that they are not strangers to one another: on the contrary, they are reliant upon one another. Thanks to the generous efforts of the authors, an extraordinary volume of materials and a book has come into being that is unparalleled in the context of art or science. What holds is not *ars gratia artis,* but rather "*scientia sine arte nihil est - ars sine scientia nihil est*" (Jean Vignot, 1392).

Christa Steinle,
Peter Weibel

3. Alan Sokal and Jean Bricmont, *Fashionable Nonsense: Postmodern Intellectuals' Abuse of Science,* Picador, New York, 1988; *Science Wars,* Andrew Ross (ed.), Duke University Press, Durham and London, 1996.

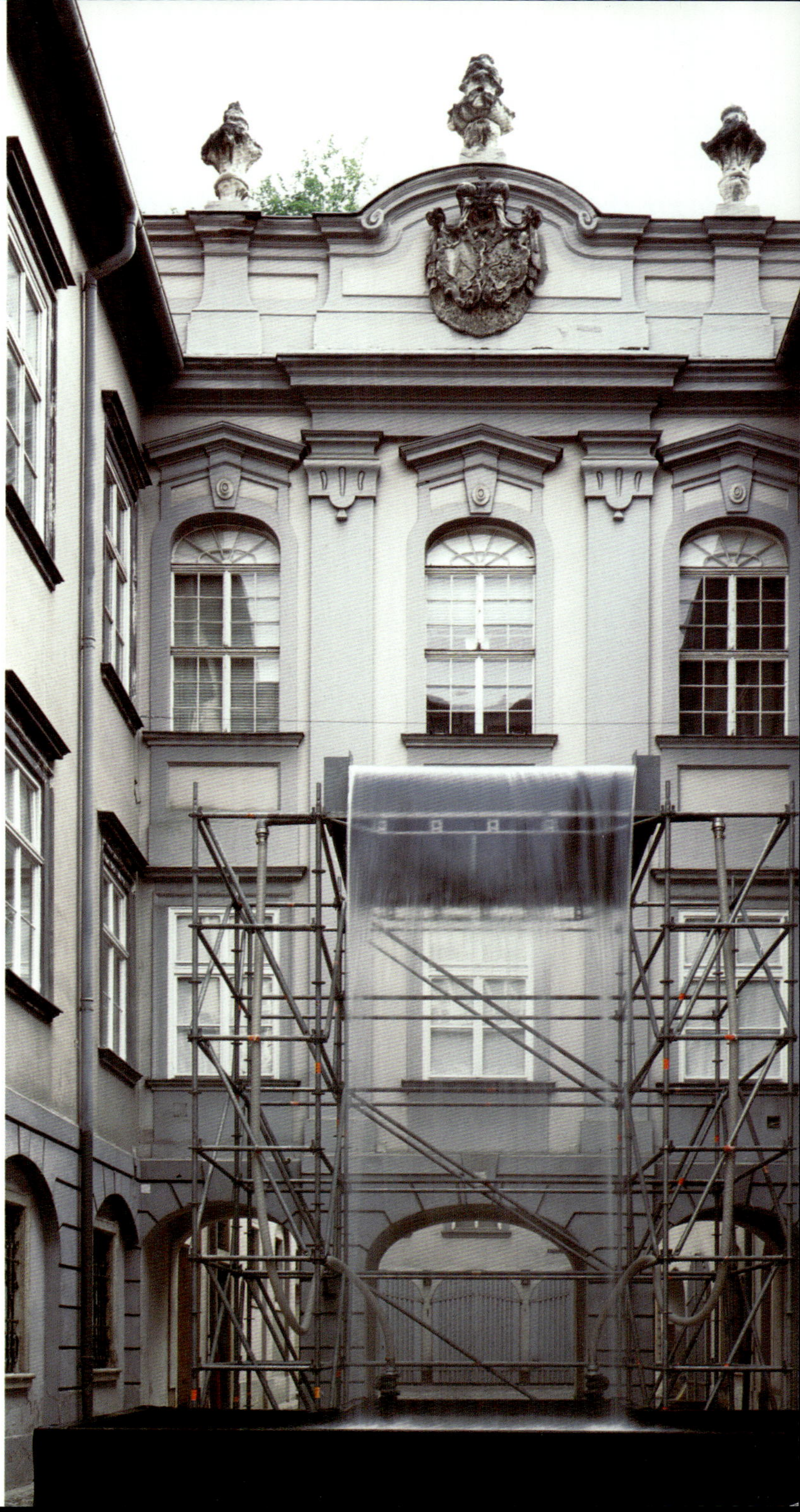

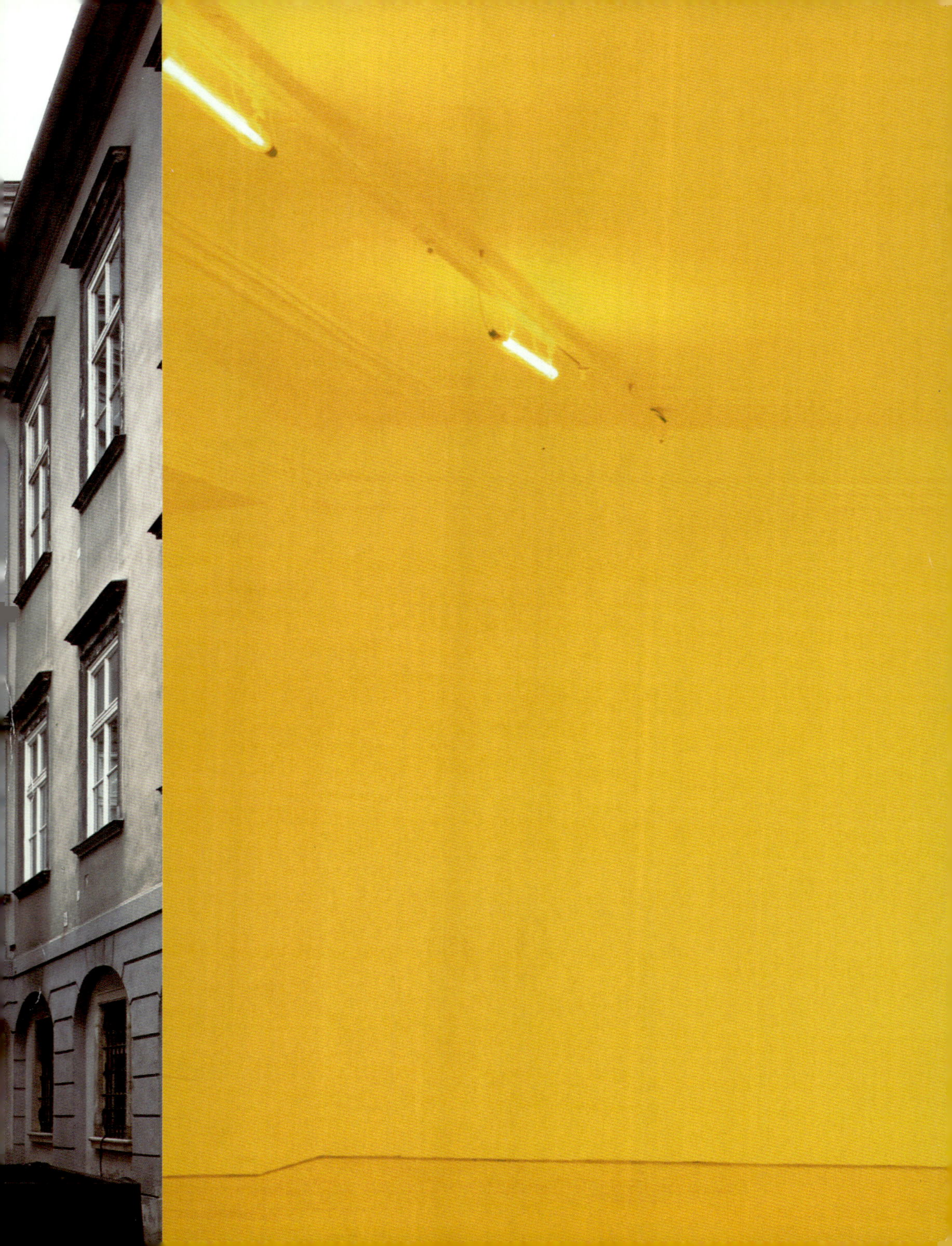

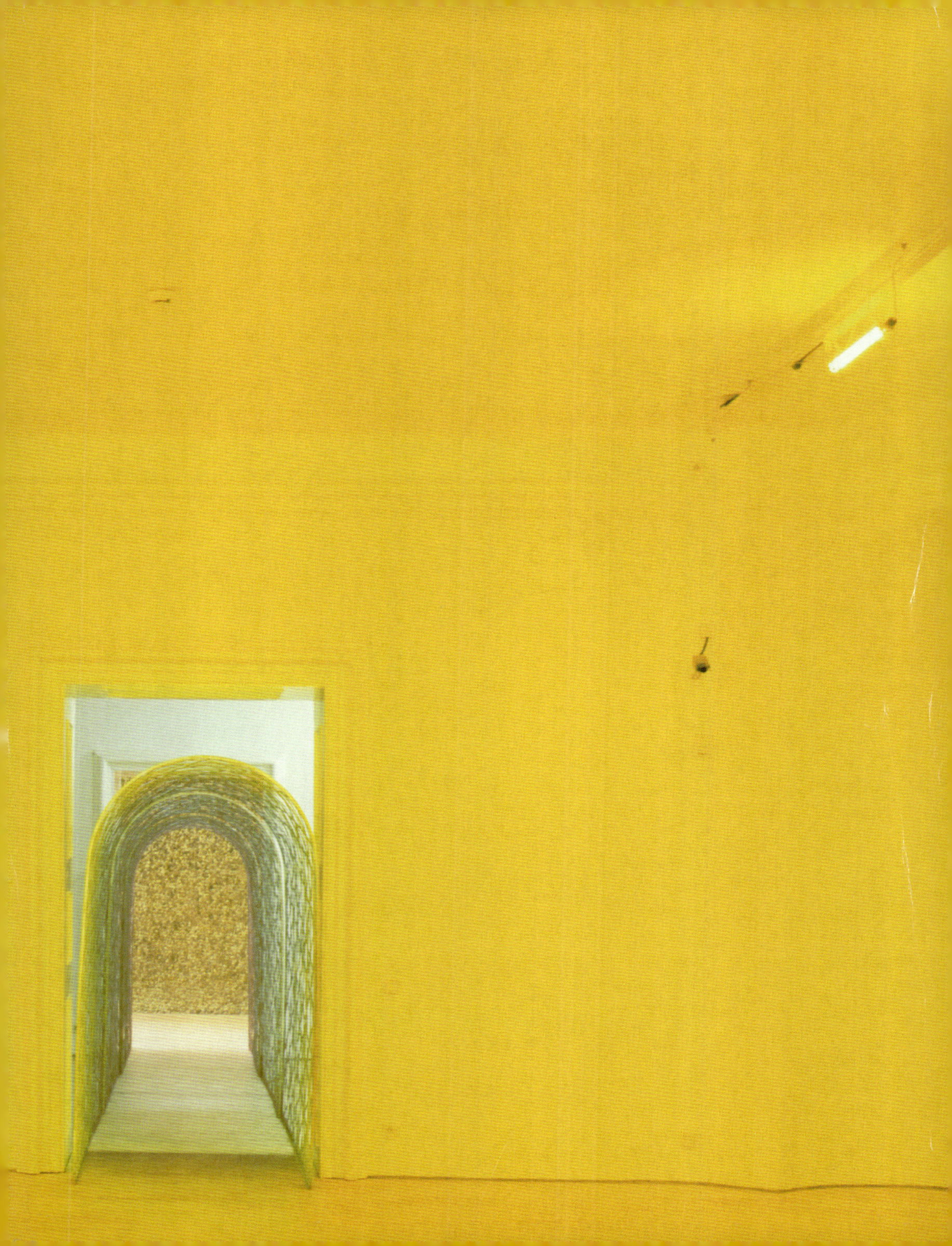

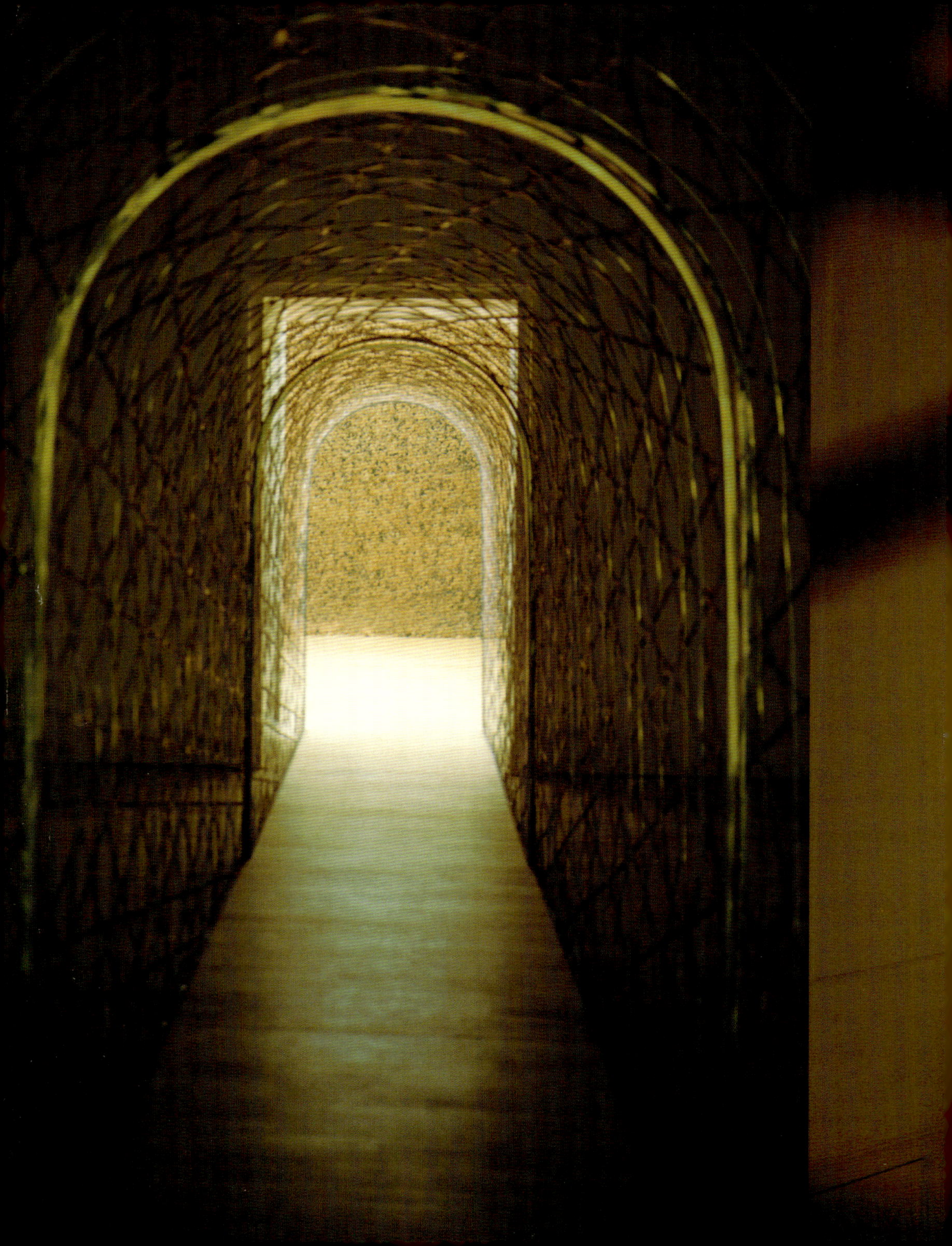

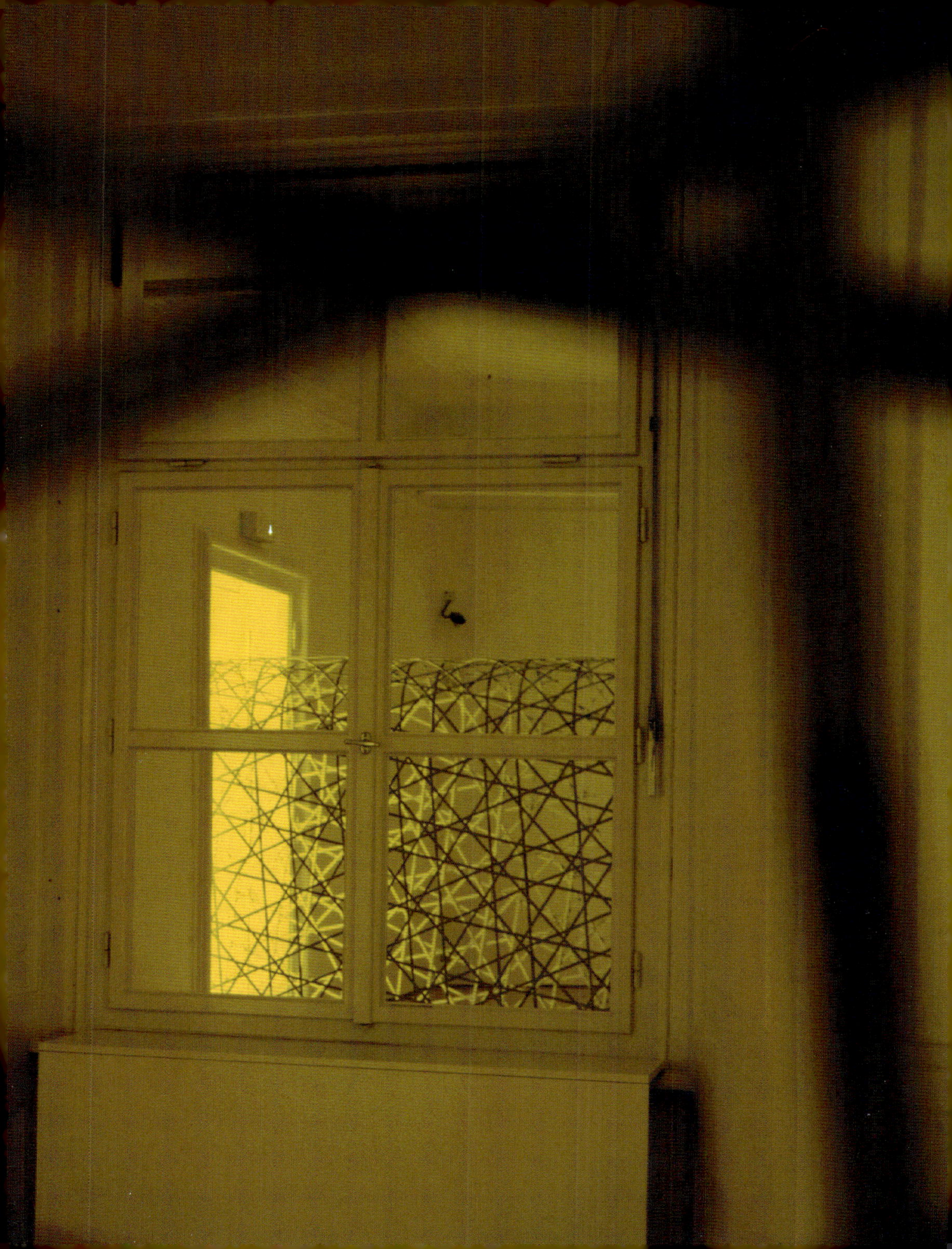

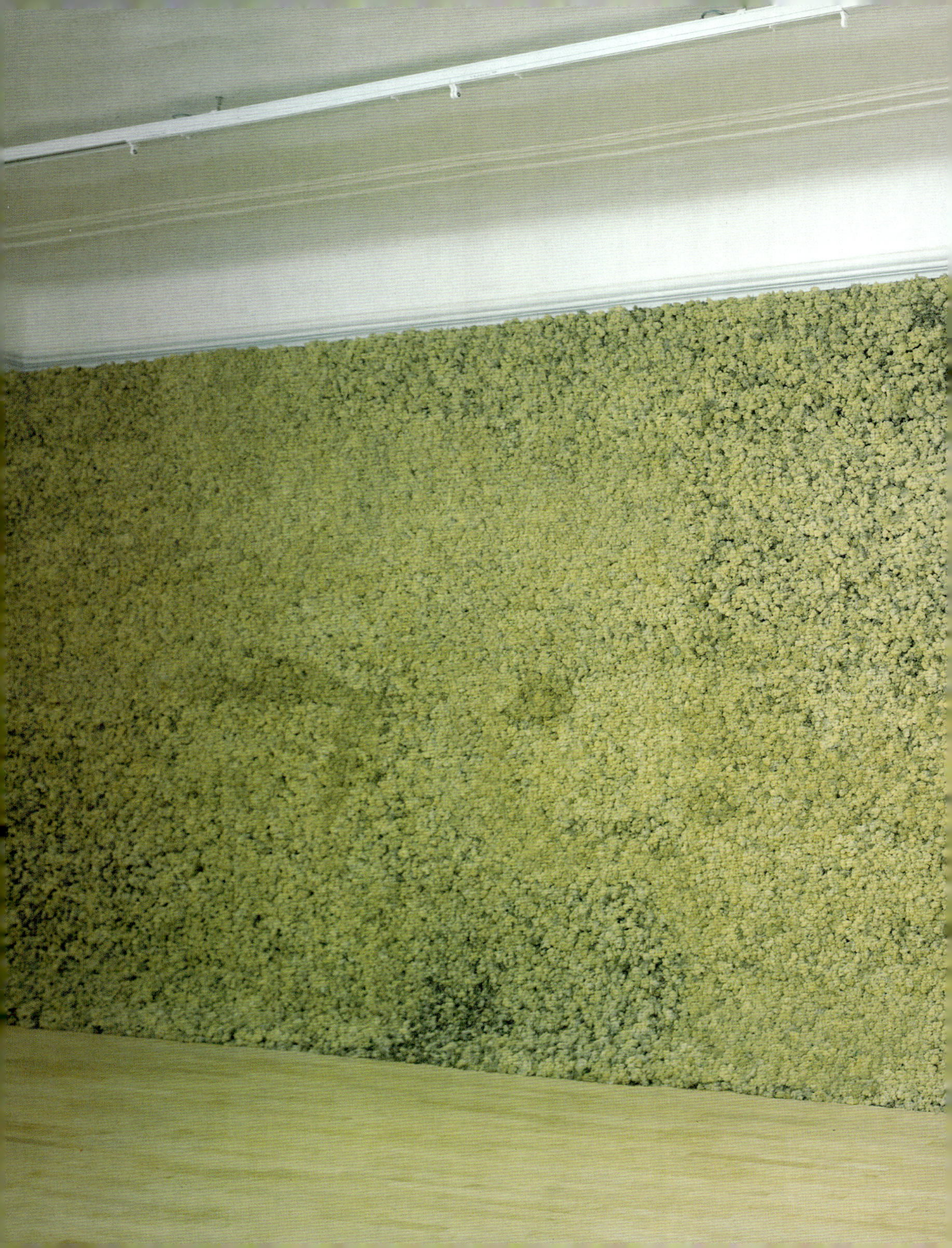

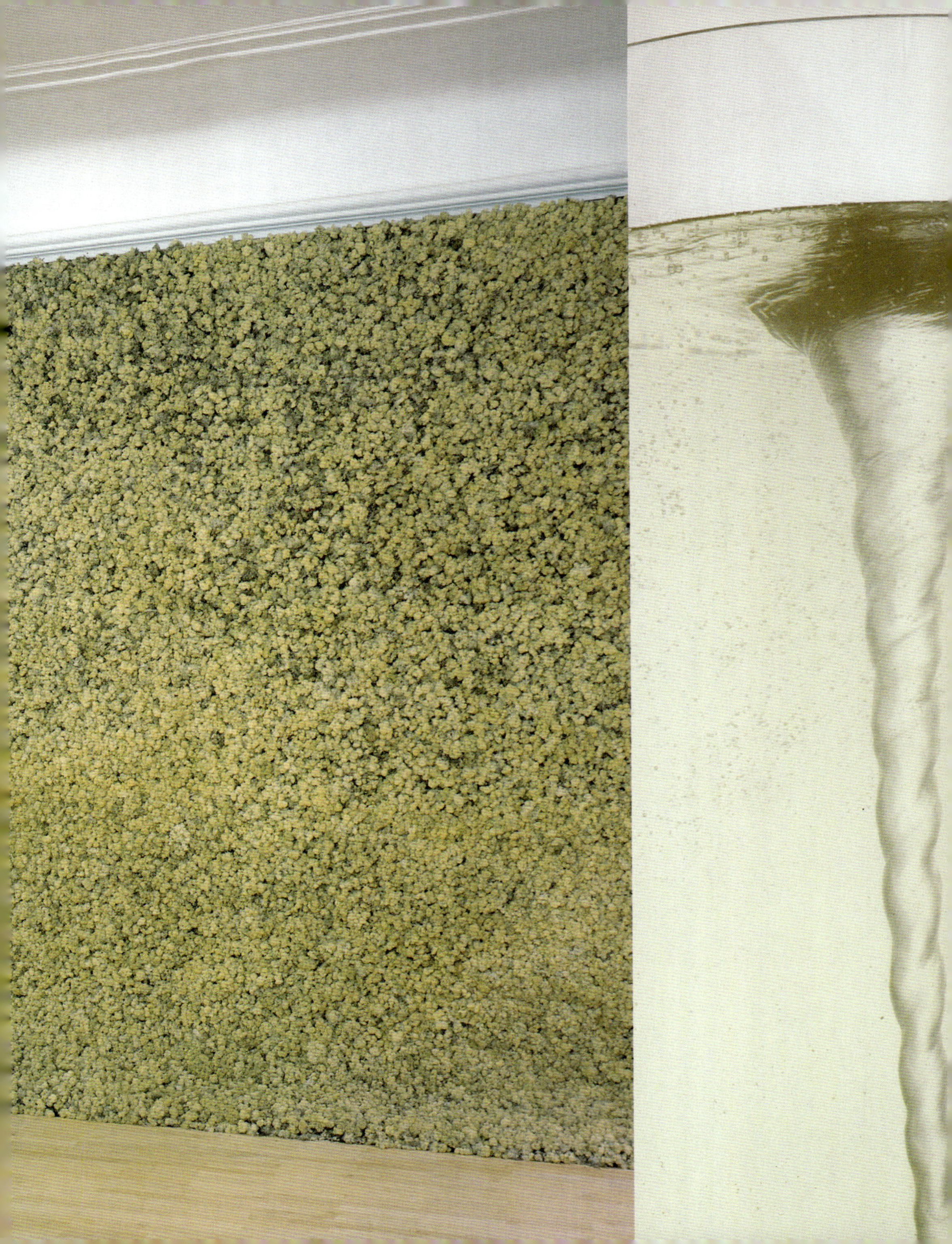

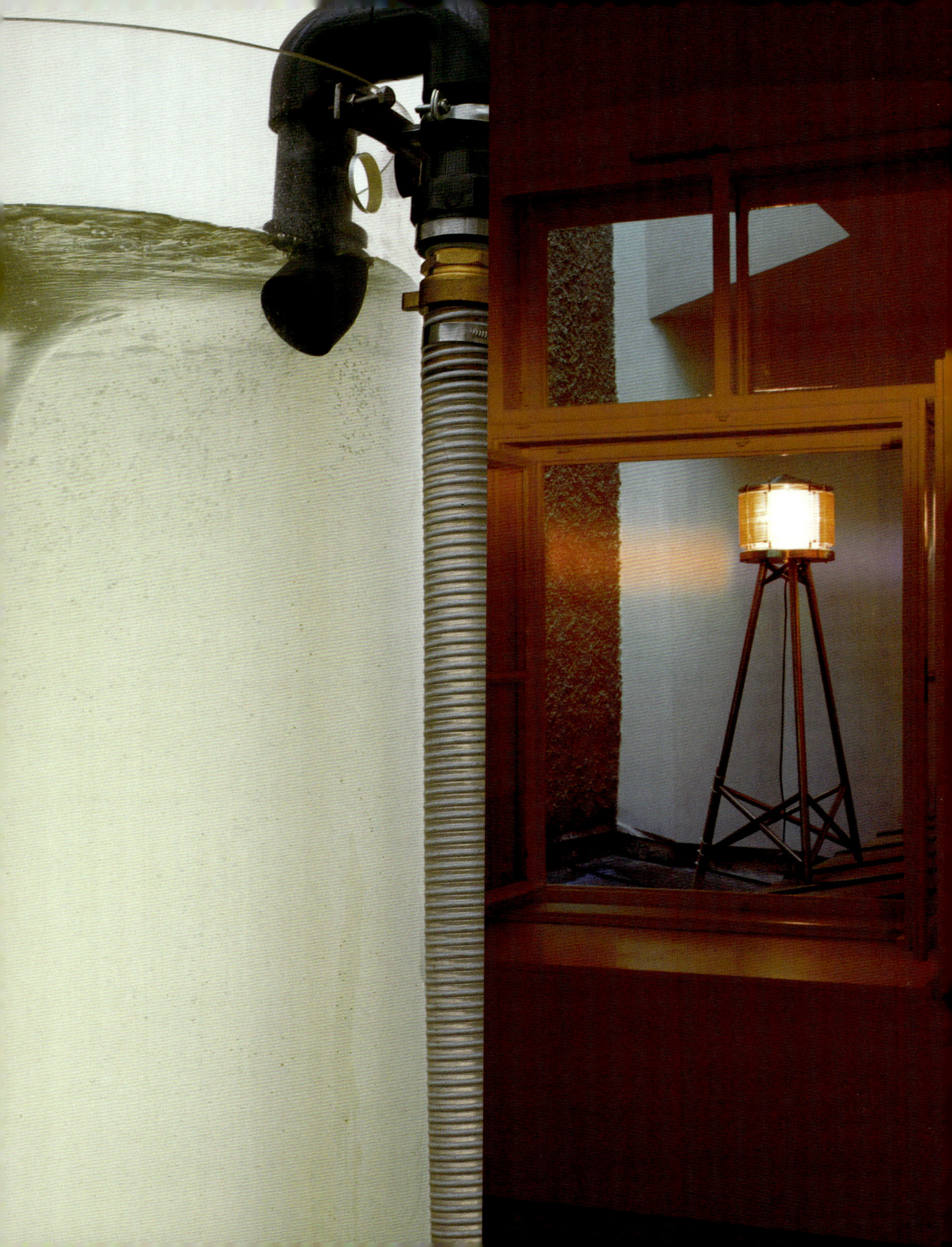

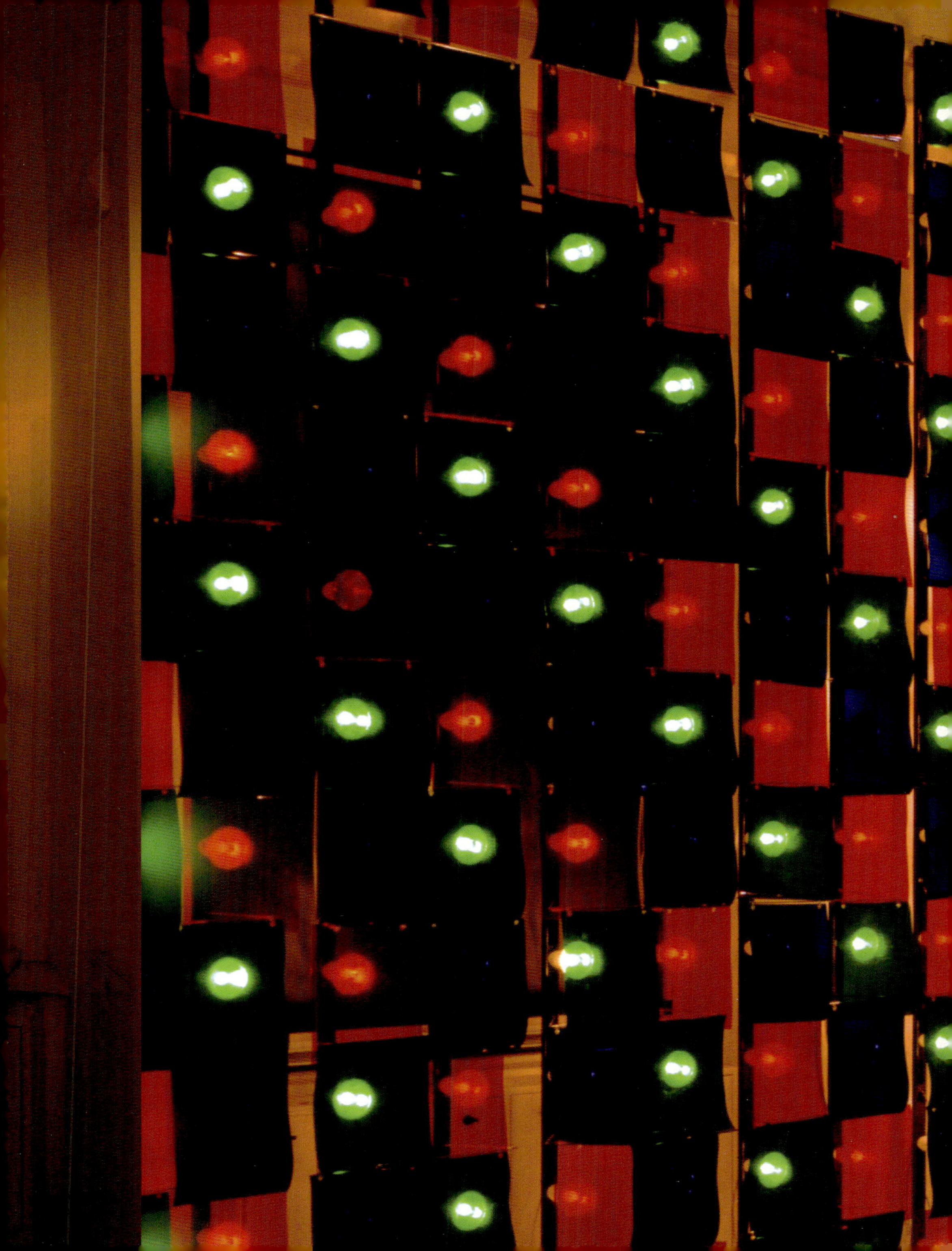

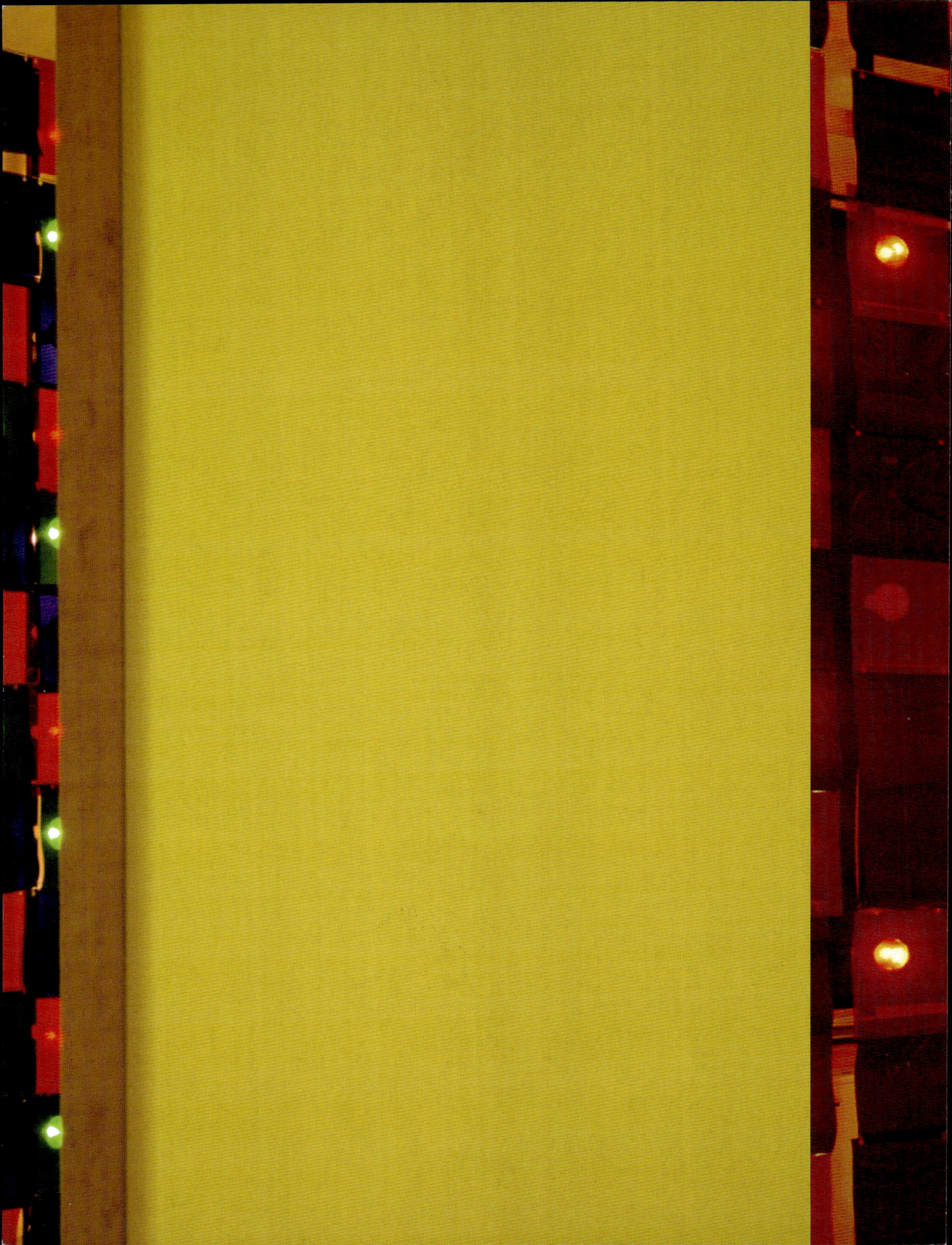

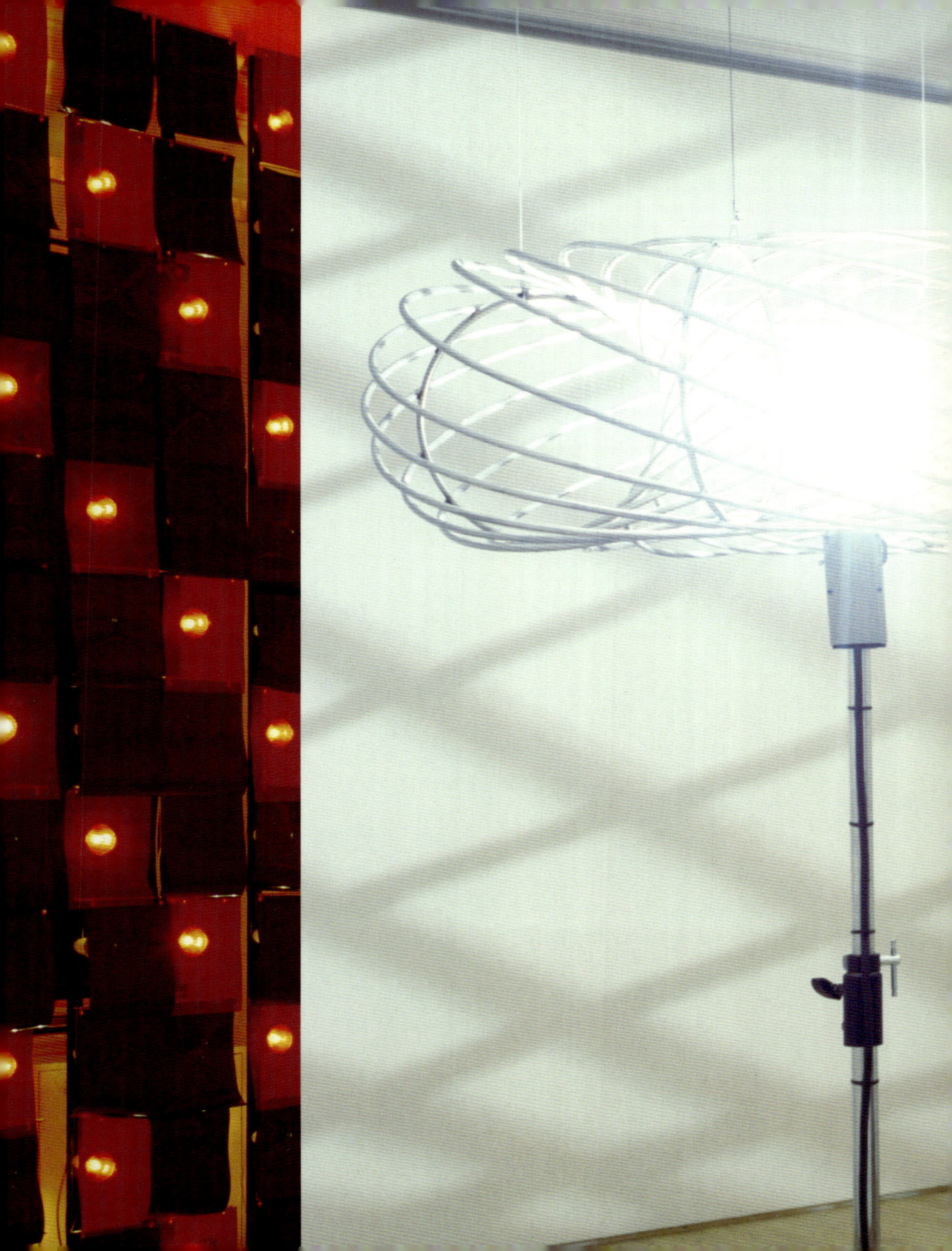

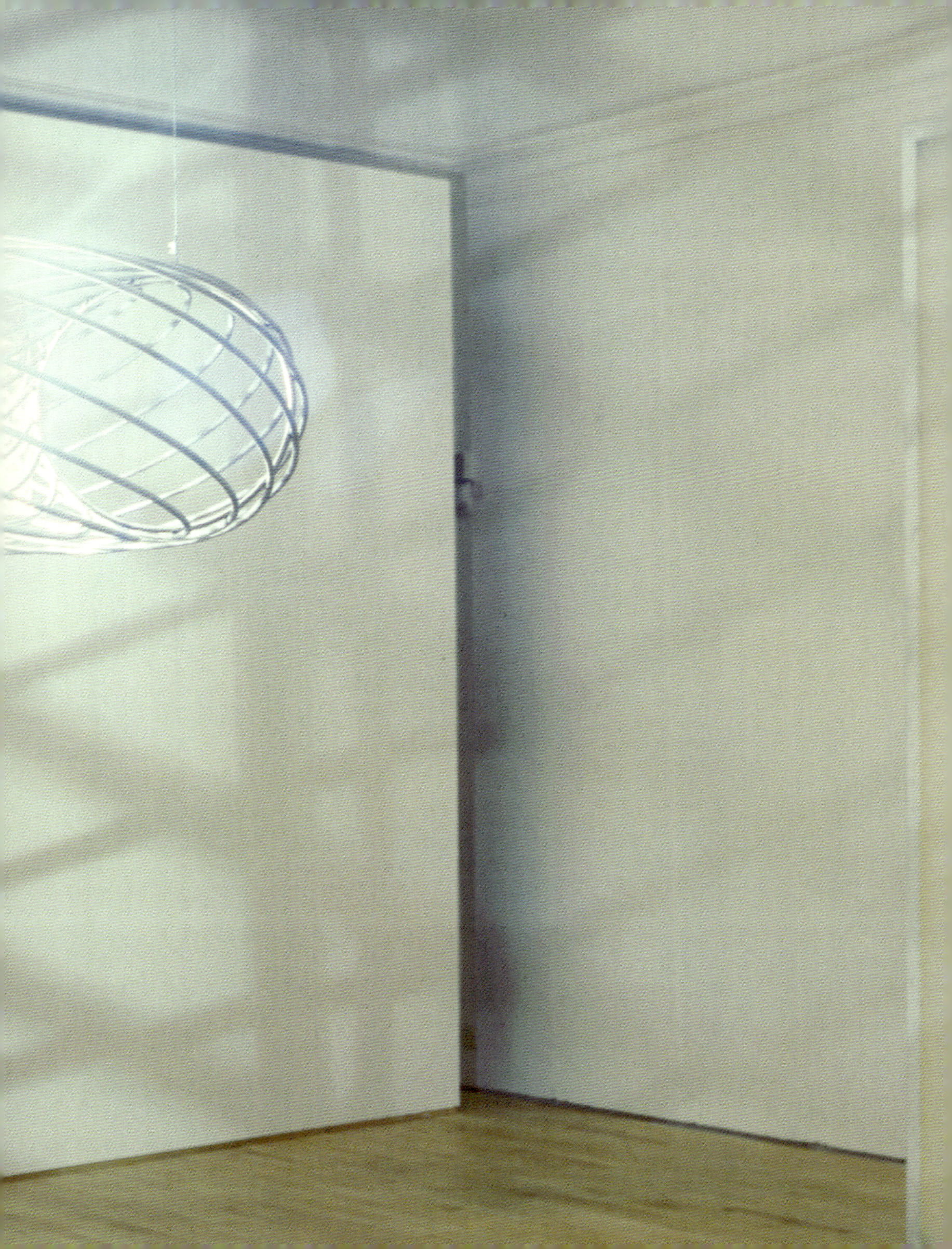

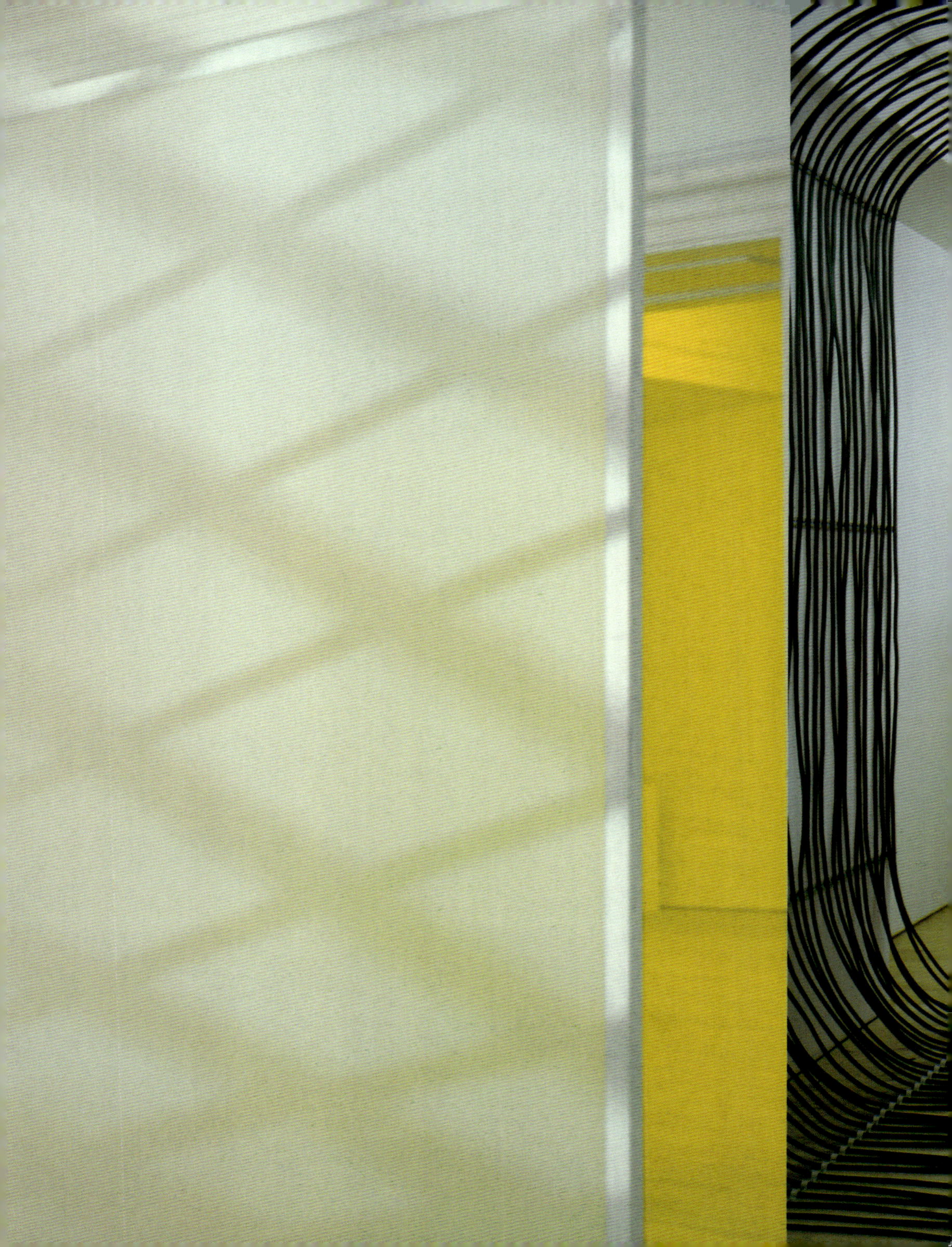

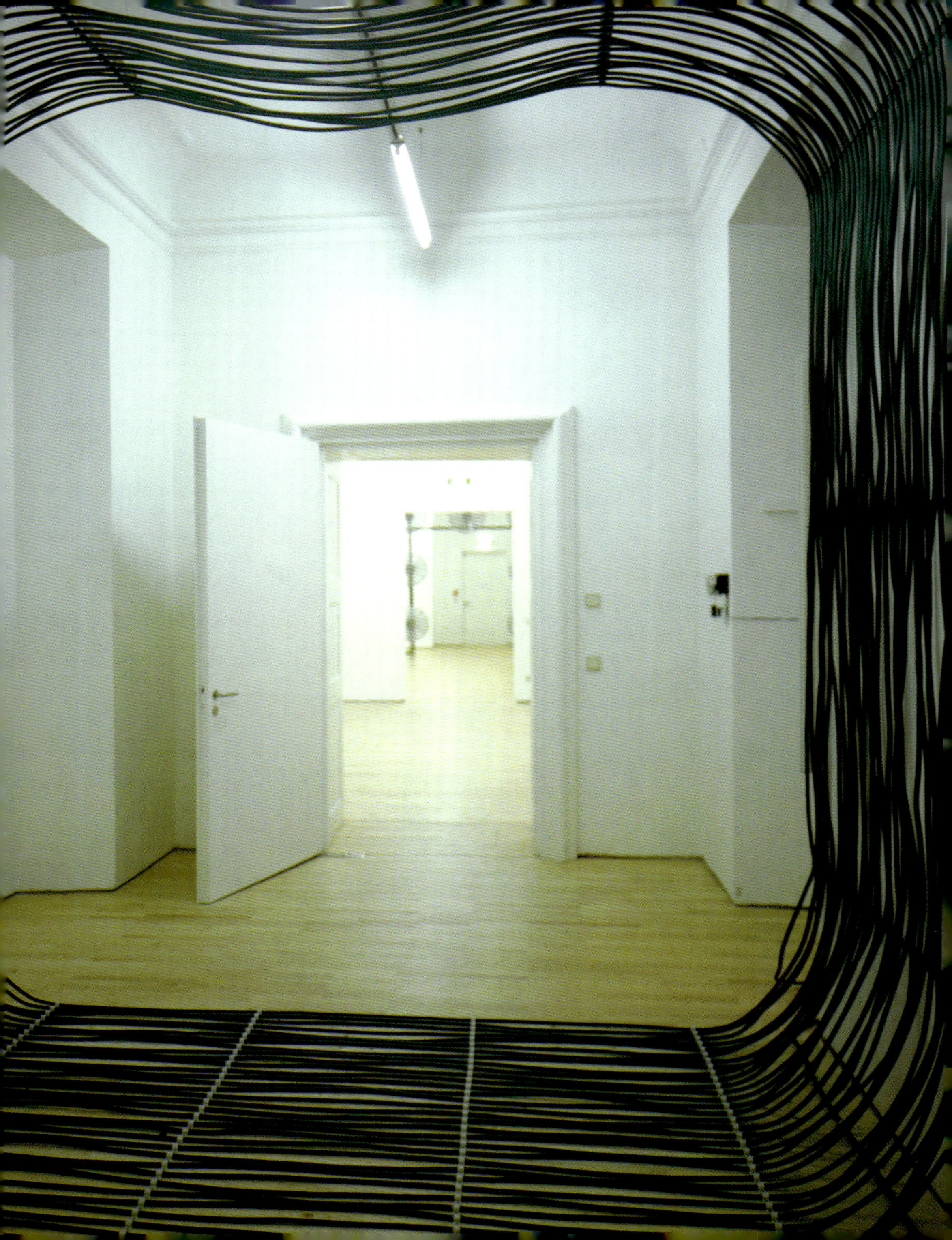

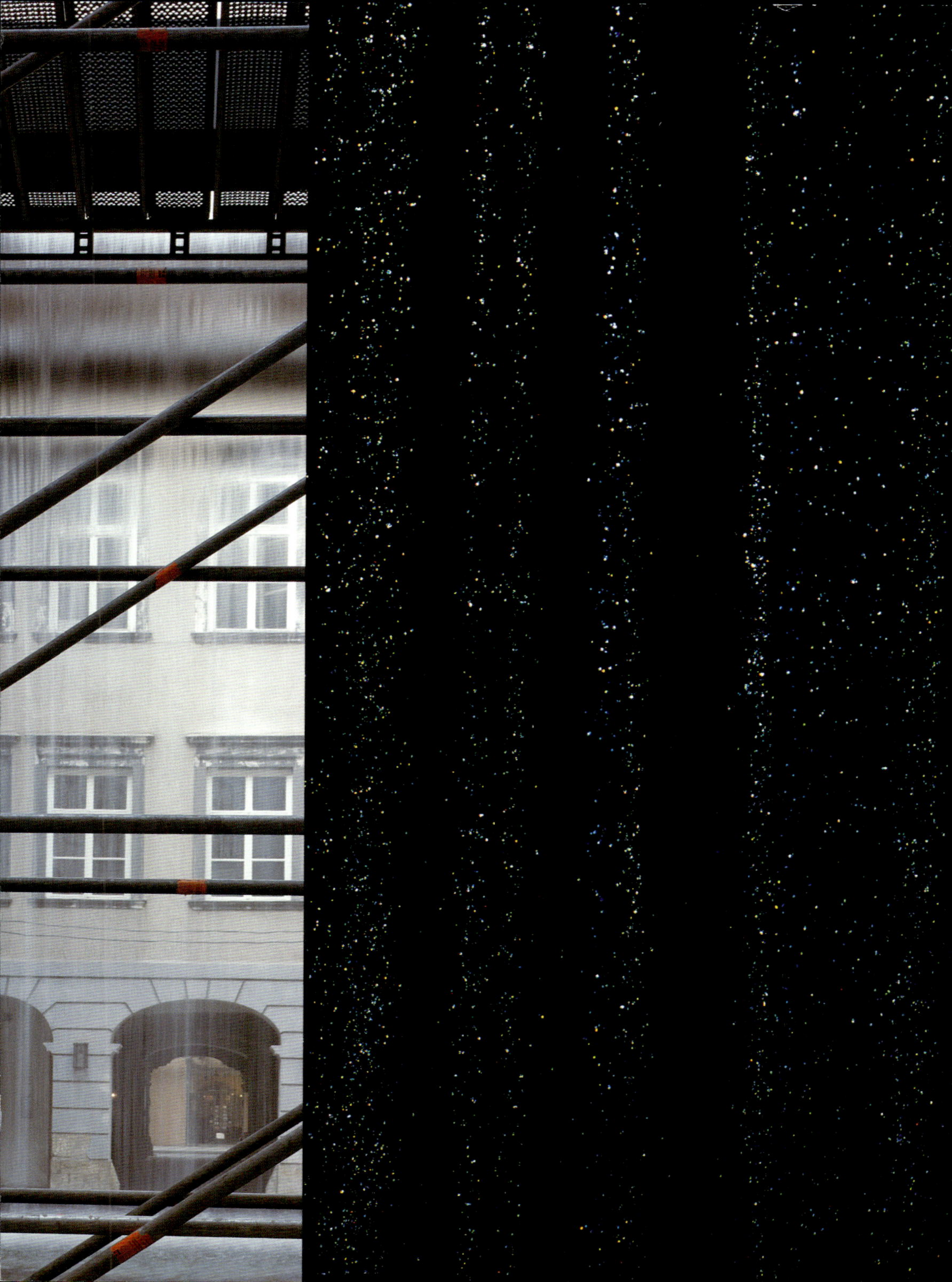

1 **Waterfall**, 1998	Size varies with installation; scaffolding, pump, water; installation view: Neue Galerie am Landesmuseum Joanneum, Graz, Austria
2 **Room for one color**, 1998	Size varies with installation; light, control panels; installation view: Neue Galerie am Landesmuseum Joanneum, Graz, Austria
3 **Fivefold tunnel**, 1998	11 x 1,1 x 2,2 m; stainless steel; installation view: Neue Galerie am Landesmuseum Joanneum, Graz, Austria
4 **Fivefold tunnel**, 1998	11 x 1,1 x 2,2 m; stainless steel; installation view: Neue Galerie am Landesmuseum Joanneum, Graz, Austria
5 **Moss - wall**, 1994	Size varies with installation; wood, moss; installation view: Neue Galerie am Landesmuseum Joanneum, Graz, Austria
6 **Vortex for Lofoten**, 1999, detail	220 x 120 cm; water, plexiglass, hose, metal, pump
7 **5 orientation - lights**, 1999	200 x 70 x 70 cm; light, steel, color filter; installation view: Neue Galerie am Landesmuseum Joanneum, Graz, Austria
8 **Room for all colors**, 1999, detail	Size varies with installation; light, dimmer, control unit; installation view: Neue Galerie am Landesmuseum Joanneum, Graz, Austria
9 **Room for all colors**, 1999, detail	Size varies with installation; light, dimmer, control unit; installation view: Neue Galerie am Landesmuseum Joanneum, Graz, Austria
10 **Doughnut**, 2000	Size varies with installation; light, steel; installation view: Neue Galerie am Landesmuseum Joanneum, Graz, Austria
11 **Blitzableiter-Induktionsspule**, 2000	Size varies with installation; cable; installation view: Neue Galerie am Landesmuseum Joanneum, Graz, Austria
12 **Waterfall**, 1998, detail	Size varies with installation; steel, pump, water; installation view: Neue Galerie am Landesmuseum Joanneum, Graz, Austria
13 **Your strange certainty still kept**, 1996, detail	Size varies with installation; strobe lights, water, pump, basin

Hans C. von Baeyer

Impossible Crystals

I do not know what I may appear to the world but to myself I seem to have been only like a boy, playing on the seashore. Thus Sir Isaac Newton, the patriarch of modern physics, defined his life's work. And in so doing he revealed a truth about his vocation that is rarely apparent to nonscientists. Too often the playful child in the center of the enterprise is hidden by a wall of abstruse theory and an impenetrable welter of technology. But occasionally we see a little face peeking out from behind the mask of profundity, and from such rare glimpses we gain a better insight into the true nature of science than from volumes of erudite explanation.

The vital role of scientific playfulness is vividly illustrated by the story behind the discovery of a new class of materials known as quasicrystals. Quasicrystals are three-dimensional structures, but their antecedents exist in two dimensions, in the plane. The story begins in January 1977, when Martin Gardner devoted his Mathematical Games column in *Scientific*

American to the question of how to cover a plane with tiles. It's a problem as ancient as Greek mosaics, yet Gardner's essay sparked a flurry of research that brought tiling to the forefront of modern physics.

The mathematical analysis of tiling begins with the observation that a plane – a bathroom floor, for example – can be covered, without gaps, by tiles in the shape of rectangles, triangles, or hexagons, but not by circles or stars or even, significantly, regular pentagons. No matter how you try to join pentagonal tiles, they will always leave gaps. To convince yourself of that, just cut out a pile of identical pentagons and play with them on your desk. You will soon develop a distinct antipathy toward the five-sided monsters.

A regular pentagon has fivefold symmetry, which means that if you rotate the pentagon about its center, it looks the same after every one-fifth of a rotation. Similarly, a square has fourfold symmetry, a hexagon sixfold, and so on. Any shape that tiles a plane can impart its symmetry to the whole tiling pattern: you can rotate a hexagonal tiling about the center of any hexagon, for example, and see that the whole pattern has sixfold symmetry. If you could use a pentagon to tile a plane, then the tiling could exhibit fivefold symmetry. But, of course, pentagons are prohibited.

Using two tile shapes instead of one, however, Gardner reproduced intriguing tiling patterns that did indeed display fivefold symmetry: whole regions could be rotated so that the arrangement of tiles within looked the same every one-fifth of a rotation. One pattern, for example, contained groups of tiles that looked like five-pointed stars. It was as if pentagons were defining the rules without actually being present.

Gardner learned how to construct these puzzling tilings from Roger Penrose, a British mathematical physicist. Penrose has a knack for playing tricks with geometry. In his youth he and his father drew an impossible object, the "Penrose staircase," which spirals round and round without getting higher or lower. The Dutch artist M.C. Escher used their mind-boggling concept in a famous lithograph, *Ascending and Descending*, which shows a line of men going both up and down the stairs simultaneously.

"Penrose tiles" are equally intriguing. Neither of the two basic shapes is a pentagon, and they do not combine to form a pentagon. But the shapes are like mischievous pentagonal offspring: they have angles and proportions that can be found in a pentagon and its diagonals, and when assembled

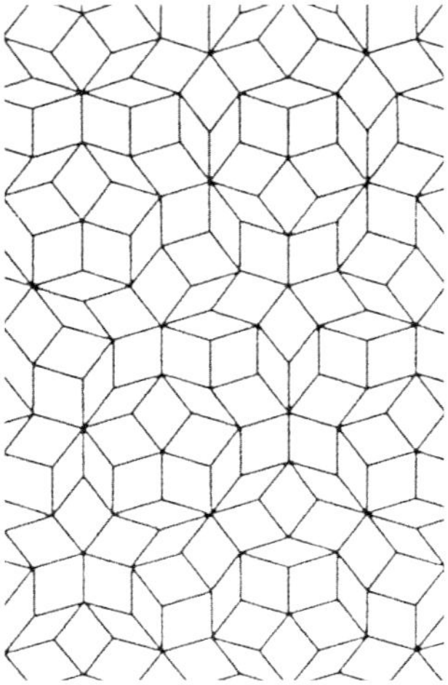

Fig. 1
Penrose tiles

on a plane the two proudly display the fivefold symmetry of their parent.

The simplest Penrose tiling uses two diamond shapes, one fat and the other skinny. The fat shape has interior angles of 72 and 108 degrees, the interior angle of a regular pentagon.

The skinny shape has interior angles of 144 and 36 degrees, an angle formed by the pentagon's diagonals. While all the tile edges are of equal length, the ratio of the area of the fat tiles to that of the skinny tiles is $(1+\sqrt{5})/2$ which equals approximately 1.618. This happens to be the ratio of the length of a diagonal to that of a side of a regular pentagon. It is also the famous "golden ratio," a measure revered as a standard of harmony by both the ancient Greeks and a legion of Renaissance painters and architects. As we shall see, the golden ration and pentagonal symmetry are embedded in the design of Penrose tilings in many wondrous ways.

Any Penrose tiling can be constructed in an infinite variety of patterns. Every variation is nonperiodic, and therein lies its allure. Unlike the individual bricks in a wall or the pickets in a fence, no group of one or more tiles can be repeated indefinitely to generate the whole pattern. At first glance Penrose tilings may look periodic. Groups of tiles do form such repeating motifs as five-pointed stars. But a more careful look reveals that the spacing between these motifs is irregular, and some are rotated with respect to others.

Naturally, when researchers saw these patterns balance teasingly between order and chaos, they were drawn to them like children to a brand-new toy. Over the next half-dozen years many Penrose tilings were generalized to three dimensions, using solid polyhedrons that fill space without gaps. Like their counterparts in the plane, the three-dimensional tilings were also nonperiodic.

One of the enchanted players was Paul Steinhardt, a physicist at the University of Pennsylvania who is well aware of the research value of playthings. Steinhardt's office is filled with toys. Scattered among the books and computers that are the standard trappings of the scholar's craft is every conceivable kind of model, from the crudest cardboard cutouts untidily held together with tape to expensive computer graphics. Anything at hand is pressed into service: coat hangers, foam balls, dice from the game Dungeons and Dragons, acetate sheets, Tinkertoy pieces, toothpicks, construction paper. Steinhardt is a natural victim for the kind of game that can be played with three-dimensional nonperiodic tilings.

Indeed, in 1984, he and one of his graduate students, Dov Levine, became so caught up in the game that they took the analysis one step further: they programmed their computer to calculate the diffraction patterns these theoretical structures would produce if the building blocks were real atoms instead of imaginary tiles.

Diffraction patterns are the windows physicists use to peer inside materials. When beams of electrons or X-rays pass through a solid material, they are diffracted, or scattered, by the atoms inside. The diffracted beams can be photographed head-on, and the images they form on the film reflect the atomic architecture of the solid. By themselves, diffraction patterns are not much to look at. They consist of mysterious arrangements of dots and streaks that bear little resemblance to the solids they portray. But to the initiated they are as recognizable as family snapshots.

The most distinct diffraction patterns contain sharp, isolated dots. These are the portraits of crystals, and they owe their clearly defined spots to the periodicity of the underlying structure. When the beams hit the atoms in a crystal, they scatter in all directions; but in a few preferred directions, depending on the arrangement of atoms, the diffracted beams reinforce one another, producing bright spots on the film. A crystal is a little like an orchard planted in a rigid geometric grid. Most lines of sight are blocked by trees, but you can see right through to the other side in a few directions.

In another class of diffraction patterns, the dots are either spread out into fuzzy rings or altogether absent. These are the images formed by glassy materials. Glasses, in contrast to crystals, are made of atoms or molecules stuck together randomly; they are more like random forests than well-planned orchards. Because they offer no preferred directions for diffraction, the patterns they produce contain no sharp dots.

Until the discovery of quasicrystals, it was thought that there were only these two classes of solid materials, corresponding to these two types of diffraction patterns. If the pattern contained sharp dots, the material was a crystal, if the dots were fuzzy or absent, the material was a glass. Every pure solid in nature, from gemstones to metals to DNA, was either crystaline or glassy.

Levine and Steinhardt called that neat scheme into question when they aimed a simulated X-ray beam at one of their imaginary solids. The computed diffraction pattern contained a surprise: unmistakable sharp points. Since the atomic arrangement of their solid was nonperiodic, it should have produced the fuzzy diffraction pattern characteristic of glassy substances.

This contradictory result required an explanation, of course, and to understand what was going on, the two physicists went back to the source of their computer model: the two-dimensional Penrose tiling. They also consulted Robert Ammann, a recreational mathematician. Ammann's work led them to the discovery that the spacing between the tiles was neither periodic nor random but something in between, an order called quasiperiodic.

This is a subtle kind of order, which is revealed, Ammann found, only by reference to a pentagonal grid. In this grid the rulings are not perpendicular, like those of normal graph paper, but parallel to the five sides of a pentagon. The five sets of intersecting lines, each set rotated 72 degrees from the next, produce a graph paper with fivefold symmetry.

The tricky part of Ammann's procedure was to draw one of these fivefold grids over a Penrose tiling so that a line from each of the five sets passed through each and every tile; it's a tough thing to do on a nonperiodic tiling. But Ammann figured out how to draw such a grid by adjusting the spacing between parallel lines to correspond to an order with an old mathematical pedigree: The distance between "Ammann lines" is one of two lengths, either a longer length, a, or a shorter length, b. The ratio of the longer to the shorter is the golden ratio. And the two lengths succeed each other in a predictable, fixed order – an infinite series known as the Fibonacci sequence.

Just as a Penrose tiling contains no group of tiles that can be repeated to generate the entire pattern, the Fibonacci sequence contains no shorter string of a's and b's that can be repeated to generate the whole. Yet the sequence can be produced by following two simple rules. Leonardo Fibonacci, a thirteenth-century mathematician, defined those rules when he considered the idealized propagation of rabbits. The first rule: Start with one adult rabbit, a, and assume that at the end of every year each adult has a baby, b, which you record right after its parent. Second rule: Every baby grows into an adult the year after it is born. (Fibonacci, a realist, made each letter stand for a pair of rabbits. Steinhardt and many others simplify by pretending that a single parent can have a baby, and we follow the simpler description here.)

To get the first term of the sequence, you start with one adult: a. In the second year the adult has a baby, and the sequence goes to two terms: ab. In the third year the original adult has another baby, which is recorded after the adult, and the first baby grows up, to give you aba. In the fourth year you add a baby after each adult, and change the baby that was already there to an adult, getting abaab. If you keep going year after year, you get abaababa, abaababaabaab, and so forth. Another way to generate the sequence is to add the sequences of the two previous years, writing last year's sequence first. And so the sequence does not change from year to year; it just grows longer. If you write down the total number of rabbits in each year (1 in year one, 2 in year two, 3 in year three, 5 in year 4, and so on), you get a string of integers that make up the famous Fibonacci sequence (1, 2, 3, 5, 8, 13, 21, 34, 55, 89 ...), in which each term is the sum of the previous two. And again the golden ratio rears its beautiful head. As the series progresses, the ratio of any two successive terms approaches 1.618.

Obviously Fibonacci was onto something. Nearly eight centuries ago he invented a sort of one-dimensional Penrose pattern, a sequence that while not periodic is not random either. There is a perfectly rigorous prescription for predicting what the next member of the sequence will be. Thanks to the recreational mathematics of the Middle Ages, Steinhardt and Levine were onto something, too. They finally had an explanation for the diffraction pattern of their imaginary solid. Their discovery amounted to the demonstration that, contrary to established belief, periodicity in three dimensions was not necessary for producing diffraction spots – quasiperiodicity was quite sufficient.

But their quasiperiodic solid had an awkward feature: the dots in the diffraction pattern were arranged with five-fold symmetry. To traditional crystallographers, such a pattern is simply unacceptable. It is a fundamental tenet of their science. Crystals cannot produce diffraction patterns with five-fold symmetry because the underlying arrangement of atoms cannot have pentagonal symmetry any more than bathroom floors can be tiled with pentagons.

So whatever Steinhardt's imaginary solids were, they were not crystals. But the discrete spots in the diffraction patterns showed they were not glasses either.

Their underlying structure combined properties of crystals with those of glasses; the theoretical substances were like mammals that lay eggs, the platypuses of physics. Steinhardt decided to call them quasicrystals, and added them to the growing list of amusing ideas that sprang from Penrose's mathematical recreation.

But then the incredible happened. In the fall of 1984 Steinhardt was on leave at the IBM research center in Yorktown Heights, New York. One day a colleague, Harvard physicist David Nelson, came into the office with exciting news. He put on the table a small copy of a diffraction image made with a real alloy of aluminum and manganese. Nelson explained that a team of researchers at the National Bureau of Standards had made the picture, and he pointed out the unusual appearance of the pattern of dots: an obvious fivefold symmetry.

Steinhardt's pulse quickened. The picture looked amazingly similar to a computer simulation he and Levine had produced and not yet published. Levine happened to be visiting from Philadelphia that day. Immediately the three scientists, as excited as boys playing on the seashore, set to work measuring the spacing between dots on an enlargement of the real photograph and comparing the result with the computer printout. Steinhardt recalls that he knew what the answer would be even before the measurements confirmed it. The two pictures agreed with each other.

The moment of truth, in science, comes when theory confronts experimental evidence. Agreement between the two is the ultimate arbiter of validity. Nothing else matters. The comparison of data with calculations usually proceeds in bits and pieces, and truth emerges gradually from the confusion that surrounds all creative effort. But when the moment of truth arrives in an unexpected flash, as it did that day at IBM, it illuminates and energizes the scientific enterprise for years to come.

Thus a new field of solid-state physics, the science of quasicrystals, was born. It grew up quickly. In short order more than a hundred alloys with fivefold symmetry were discovered; sevenfold, ninefold, elevenfold, and other previously forbidden symmetries proved to be possible; scholarly symposia were convened, and fat monographs were published.

But in the closet there lurked a skeleton – a potentially fatal flaw in the whole scheme. While researchers were beginning to understand the architecture of two- and three-dimensional quasiperiodic tilings, no one could think of a mechanism by which millions upon millions of real atoms could arrange themselves spontaneously in those intricate patterns.

Anyone who tries to assemble Penrose tilings quickly realizes that it's not easy. You have to think ahead, and keep the whole pattern in mind when adding a tile; otherwise there is trouble. If you make a mistake, you have to undo a lot of work that has gone before. The problem is that while there are local rules, or instructions for fitting a tile into a particular niche, these rules are not sufficient to build the entire pattern. It seems necessary to augment them with global rules that force you to plan ahead and check the configuration of tiles at far distant points. And between 1984 and 1988 the conviction grew that perfect quasiperiodic tilings could not be constructed with local rules alone.

Local rules for adding tiles are analogous to forces that attract and hold new atoms to the surface of a growing quasicrystal; they are plausible ingredients in the growth mechanism. Global rules are not. The atoms on a growing surface do not plan ahead, and they do not check the orientation of distant surfaces. They respond only to the interatomic sticking force – which is electrical in origin – of their immediate neighbors. If quasiperiodic patterns could be constructed only with the help of global rules, they could not be assembled by real atoms in real alloys, and quasicrystals could not exist in nature.

The problem was so serious that researchers began shifting their attention to more conventional explanations of the observed diffraction patterns. The two-time Nobel laureate Linus Pauling, for example, championed an arrangement of ordinary crystals called twinning. Twinned crystals grow from separate origins and penetrate each other at odd angles, such as 72 degrees. This might produce a diffraction pattern with spurious fivefold symmetry, even though the underlying structure was conventional. Other researchers, including Steinhardt himself, studied glassy structures with tiny embedded crystaline fragments. These fragments, it was thought, might produce a diffraction pattern with spots almost as sharp as the dots from crystals, even though the overall structure was glassy.

But then, in 1988, playfulness paid off once more. George Onoda, an IBM ceramics expert, started toying with about 200 Penrose tiles. Unconvinced by the claims that he wasn't supposed to be able to do it, he learned how to assemble flawless tilings of any size he wished using strictly local rules. "I approached it as a puzzle," he says, "as a challenge to try to prove the naysayers wrong."

Onoda showed Steinhardt his procedures, and the two of them fiddled around with the tiles for a couple of hours. Steinhardt simplified Onoda's insights to a set of rules that force the vertices of the tiles into one of the eight possible combinations found in a perfect Penrose tiling. With the help of two other researchers, he then hammered out a mathematical proof, corroborated by a computer simulation of a million tiles, that quasiperiodic structures can indeed grow naturally – at least in two dimensions.

Following these rules, you can build a Penrose tiling by adding tiles to a growing boundary. The rules specify which type of vacancy to fill first and to choose randomly if there is more than one equivalent vacancy, which of the two tile shapes you should use in every case, and which way it should be turned. You don't have to pay attention to any distant part of the pattern to assemble a tiling, any more than an atom has to know what's going on somewhere else before it decides which way to turn and attach to its neighbors.

For the complete theory of quasicrystals the local rules must be generalized to three dimensions, and they must be shown to correspond to actual atomic forces. Neither of these tasks has been achieved yet, but Steinhardt, for one, believes they will be.

In the meantime, experimentalists have been busy. They continue to report bigger, more perfect quasicrystals and are diligently measuring their physical properties. No one knows what to expect, for none of their vast experience with crystals and glasses permits them to make confident predictions about quasicrystals. Quasicrystalline alloys, because of the intricate interlocking of their constituents, might turn out to be harder than crystals and therefore might be used as replacements for industrial diamonds. Or they might end up at the heart of novel electronic devices as yet undreamed of. Who knows? Researchers are going to have to play around with them a bit and see what they can do.

Per Bak

The Science of Self-Organized Criticality

Self-organization of earthquakes

I first heard about the Gutenberg-Richter law in 1988 during a Gordon conference on fractals, soon after our discovery of SOC. Gordon conferences are informal, private conferences where scientists in many different areas can present and discuss their most recent results. The Gordon conference is a magnificent institution that has served science very well. They take place in the summer at a few small colleges near the beautiful lakes, forests, and mountains of New Hampshire, and offer an opportunity to combine scientific discussions with a variety of recreational activities. As we have seen before, the environment plays a large role in human scientific creativity.

Scientists in general, and physicists in particular, are quite enterprising when it comes to selecting sites for their communal activities. My career as a physicist has allowed me to visit some of the most fantastic places on Earth, such as Aspen, Colorado (the Aspen Center of Physics), Santa Barbara (the Insti-

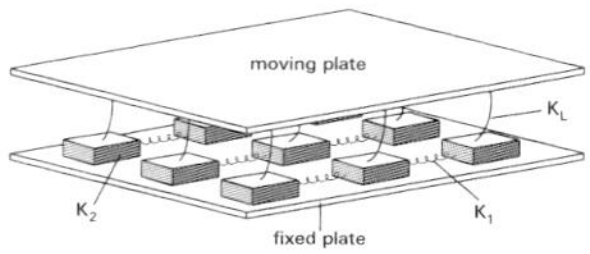

Fig. 1
Block-spring model of earthquake fault. The blocks are also connected with slowly moving plate leaf springs. They are also connected with each other by springs. Parameters K_1, K_2, and K_L specify the strengths of the springs. The blocks are moving on a rough surface. A blocked slide when the force on it exceeds a critical value.

tute of Theoretical Physics), New Hampshire, Venice, the Great Wall of China, Moscow (the Landau Institute), Santa Fe (the Santa Fe Institute), and the Alps (the Physics Institute in Les Houches, near Chamonix). You don't get rich from doing physics, but you do get an opportunity to go to all the places the rich would go to if they had the time.

The Gordon conference was on fractal structures in nature. It was particularly stimulating because it brought together scientists from many different fields. More typical scientific conferences deal with narrow esoteric subjects about which all the participants are experts. One of the speakers of this conference was Yakov Kagan of UCLA, who addressed the importance of scale-free behaviour of earthquakes and earthquake zones. He pointed out that faults form fractal patterns, and presented worldwide earthquake data showing power law behaviour of earthquake magnitudes over seven decades. This was the first time I had heard about the Gutenberg-Richter law.

Kagan gave a sharp rebuttal to much of the folklore surrounding the earthquake business, such as "characteristic earthquake" sizes. I had never been involved professionally in geophysics and knew little about the subject. Nevertheless, I was fascinated by his talk. Were earthquakes like the sand slides in our sandpile model? Tectonic plate motion, providing the energy for the earthquakes, would correspond to tilting the sandpiles in the ramp version of the model. The ruptures would correspond to toppling grains. Just as the increased force on the grains from the slow tilt would necessarily sooner or later cause the sand to topple somewhere, the slowly increasing pressure from the tectonic plates grinding into one another eventually must cause rupture somewhere. Just as toppling grains can affect one another in a domino process, one rupture can lead to another by the transfer of force, and sometimes lead to a large chain reaction representing a large earthquake. In a larger perspective, one might think of the plate motion as the source of "landscape upheaval" and the earthquake as the "erosion," whose combined effects organize the crust of the earth to the critical state, using Rinaldo's "landscape out of balance" picture.

I returned to my laboratory and, together with Chao Tang, did some further computer simulations of the sand model. We studied the continuous, deterministic version in which the sandpile is slowly tilted.

What we had in mind was a block-spring picture of earthquake generation (fig. 1), in which the fault is represented by a two-dimensional array of blocks in contact with a rough surface. In the real world, one cannot localize the earthquakes to single preexisting faults. The Gutenberg-Richter law concerns the statistics of earthquakes over an extended region like California. Of course, we cannot construct a realistic computer model of California and follow its evolution through hundreds of millions of years, as we would like to do. In the block-spring model, the blocks are connected to a constantly moving plate by leaf springs. The leaf springs represent the pressure on the material near the fault due to the tectonic plate motion. The blocks are also connected with each other by coil springs. Each element sticks to the surface when the sum of the spring forces is less than a threshold. The leaf springs exert a constantly increasing force on all the blocks. When the force on a particular block becomes larger than the threshold, the block slips instantaneously in the direction of the moving rod. Because of the coil springs, this increases the force on the four neighboring springs, and might cause the force on one or more of those blocks to exceed the critical value, so that they, too, would slip. This could lead to the chain reaction representing the earthquake. This type of model had been introduced years before, in 1967, by Burridge and Knopoff at UCLA.

It was payoff time for our work on the rotating pendulums. The arithmetic of the block-spring model was very much the same as for the coupled pendulums. Pulling the blocks by the leaf spring was like slowly winding up all the pendulums simultaneously, until one of them would make a rotation, initializing an avalanche. The slip of a block corresponds to the rotation of a pendulum. In turn, we knew that the rotation of a pendulum is equivalent to the toppling of a grain of sand in the sand model. Thus, the three models are mathematically identical; if you have studied one, you have studied them all. Indeed, it was at that point we found that the continuous, slowly driven deterministic sandpile model provided the same power law as the initial stochastic version, driven by adding sand randomly. Thus, the Gutenberg-Richter law is the fingerprint that the crust of the earth has self-organized to the critical state.

Soon after, other groups independently discovered that earthquakes could be thought of as a SOC phenomenon. Didier and Anne Sornette, a married couple at the University of Nice, presented their results in a short article in Europhysics Letters; they pointed out the analogy between sandpile models and block-spring models. Didier Sornette may be the most imaginative of all geophysicists – maybe even too imaginative, if that's possible. Every six months he comes up with another general observation or theory of some geophysical phenomenon. His batting average of being right may not be perfect, but in science that does't matter, as long as just once in your lifetime you say something important and correct. Keisuke Ito and Mitsuhiro Matsusaki of Japan published a much more detailed account in the *Journal of Geophysical Research*. These authors also studied the possible origin of aftershocks, which also were known to follow a power law distribution known as Omori's law. Amazingly, all three groups chose essentially the same title: "Earthquakes as a Self-organized Critical Phenomenon."

A fourth group, Jean Carlson and Jim Langer of the Institute for Theoretical Physics, Santa Barbara, made much more laborious calculations on a more detailed model in which the blocks did not slip instantaneously to their new positions, as represented by the toppling of a grain of sand in the sand model, following Newton's law. They kept the inertia of the blocks, in contrast to the sandpile versions. This type of calculation is very slow, so only small systems can be studied. It was precisely to avoid such calculations that we introduced the simpler sand models instead of the messy rotating pendulums, which supposedly would behave in the same way. Another justification for the simpler sand model is that we really don't know the forces, including the friction, to insert into the block-spring model, so the model is not realistic under any circumstances. Carlson and Langer found a power law for small earthquakes, and they found more or less periodic huge earthquakes, a distribution not found for real earthquakes. Their simulation gave a much better description of the early sandpile experiments performed by the Chicago group, where inertial effects take over and prevent intermediate size avalanches. Recall that, in contrast, the Norwegian group had reduced inertial effects by using long sticky grains of rice.

We were ambitious, and sent an account of our earthquake ideas to the world's most prestigious journals, first to *Nature* and then to *Science*. Our article was rejected by both journals, by geophysicists who did not understand what it was all about. The idea of having a general theory of the phenomena of earthquakes was unacceptable. However, the referees should be given credit for revealing their identity, which is not required in the normally anonymous refereeing process. To appreciate the pain and annoyance that one might feel because of such a decision, it should be pointed out that essentially anything can be published, no matter how insignificant, even in *Nature*. Most published material sinks like a rock and never surfaces again. It is precisely when you have something potentially new and interesting that you get in trouble. Ironically, dozens of articles applying our ideas to various natural phenomena have since appeared with great regularity in those same journals.

Soon after, I presented our ideas at a conference on earthquakes in Monterey, California, a place with a spectacular view of the surf of the Pacific Ocean. I couldn't help noting in my talk that our article had been rejected for publication in *Nature* by Professor X who is sitting to the left, and for *Science* by Dr. Yo who is sitting to the right. Both flushed. But at least everyone became aware of our ideas at that point. At the same conference, Jim Langer presented calculations on the more detailed Carlson-Langer one-dimensional blockspring models.

Eventually, our article was published in the *Journal of Geophysical Research* by its editor, Albert Tarantola, who took the matter in his own hands and published the article despite its rejection by his referees. By 1995, there were more than 100 articles in the literature supporting the view of earthquakes as a Self-organized Critical Phenomenon.

Our model was immensely oversimplified and wrong in one respect. Our original sand model was conservative, that is, all the sand that topples ends up at the neighboring sites. There is no sand lost in the process. That is quite reasonable for sandpiles. For earthquakes, on the other hand, a careful analysis of the block-spring model shows that there is no reason for conservation of forces. The amount of force that is transmitted to the neighbors may be less than the release of force on the sliding block. As soon as the condition of conservation was relaxed in the sand model, by letting not one grain of sand arrive at the neighbor sites, but, say only 0,9 grains, the Gutenberg-Richter law would be obeyed only up to a cut off magnitude that would depend on the degree of conservation. There would be only small earthquakes. The blockspring model would not be critical! (...)

The brain

The human brain is able to form images of the complex world surrounding us, so it might seem obvious that the brain itself has to be a complex object. However, it is not necessarily so. We have seen that complex behavior can arise from models with a simple architecture through a process of self-organization. Perhaps the brain is also a fairly simple organ.

Starting from a native state with little structure, the information about the surrounding environment is coded into the brain by a process in which the brain self-organizes into a critical state. In analogy with the sandpile, a "thought" may be viewed as a punctuation, i.e., a small or large avalanche triggered by some minor input in the form of an observation, or by another thought.

The brain contains trillions of neurons. Each neuron may be connected to thousands of other neurons. The firing mechanisms of individual neurons are fairly well understood, but – how do trillions of neurons work together to form the emergent process we call thinking? Comparing with the way computers work, the function of the computer is not apparent from the properties of the individual transistors making up the computer. Those who construct computers do not even have to know how transistors work. The function of the computer comes from the way these interconnected transistors work together.

There is at least one major conceptual difference between the computer and the brain. The computer was built by design. An engineer put together all the circuits and made it work. No engineer – no computer. However, there is no engineer around to connect all the synapses of the brain. Even more to the point, there is no engineer available to make adjustments every time the outer world poses the brain with a new problem. One might imagine that the brain is ready and hard-wired from birth, with its connections formed through biological evolution, with all possible scenarios coded into the DNA. This does not make any sense. Evolution is efficient, but not that efficient. Indeed, the amount of information contained in the DNA is sufficient to determine general rules for neural connections but vastly insufficient to specify the whole neural circuitry. While there is some hard wiring – a lobster brain is different from a human brain – the functionality has to evolve during the lifetime of an individual. This means that the structure has to be self-organized rather than designed. Brain function is essentially created by the problems the brain has to solve.

Thus, to understand how the brain functions it is important to understand the process of self-organization. It is not enough to take the brain apart at some given instant and map out all existing connections, just as we don't understand the sandpile by just making a map of all the grains at some given point in time. Essentially all modeling of brain function from studying models of neural networks has ignored the self-organized aspects of the process, but has concentrated on designing a working brain model by engineering all the connections of inputs and outputs. This is good enough if the system is going to be used for some engineering purpose, such as pattern recognition, but it is basically misguided when it comes to understanding brain function.

Why should the brain be critical?

One may argue at least two different ways that the brain must be critical. First, consider a brain that is exposed to some external signal, representing for instance a visual image. The input signal must be able to access everything that is stored in the brain, so the system cannot be subcritical, in which case there would be access to only a small, limited part of the information. Grains dropped on a subcritical sandpile can only communicate locally by means of avalanches. The brain cannot be supercritical either, because then any input would cause an explosive branching process within the brain, and connect the input with essentially everything that is stored in the brain. This can be seen in a different way. Consider a neuron somewhere in the brain, and an output neuron at a distance from that neuron. By changing the properties of the neuron, for instance by increasing or decreasing the strength of its connection with a neighbor neuron, it should be possible to affect the output neurons in the brain; otherwise that neuron would not have any meaningful function. If the brain is in the frozen subcritical state, there will be only a local effect of that change. If the brain is in a chaotic disordered state with neurons firing everywhere, it is not possible to communicate with the output neuron, and affect its signal properly, through all the noise.

Hence, the brain must operate at the critical state where the information is just barely able to propagate. At the critical state the system has a very high sensitivity to small shocks. A single grain of sand can lead to a very large avalanche. We say that a critical system has a large susceptibility. Of course, the avalanches at the critical state in the sandpile do not perform any meaningful function, so our problem is to teach the avalanches to connect inputs with the correct outputs.

How does the brain organize itself to the critical state? In the sand model, the criticality was ensured by adding grains of sand at a very slow rate, one grain at a time.

In the last couple of years I have been working on this problem together with Dimitris Stassinopoulos. Stassi had been working with Preben Alstrom at the Bohr Institute on neural network models of steering processes, such as tracking a flying target. The network was kept at a critical state by a

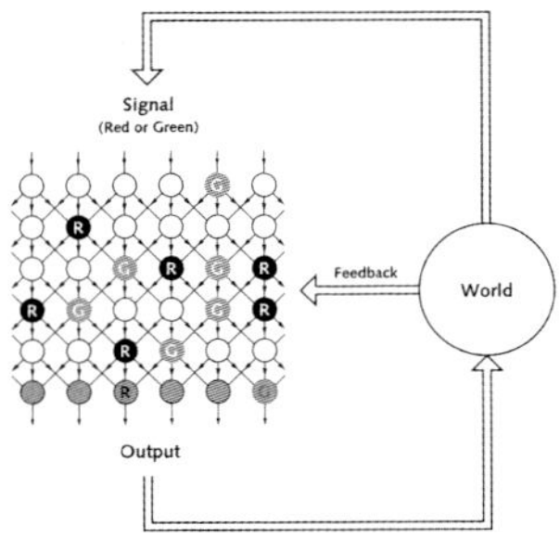

Fig. 2
Block diagram of brain interacting with the outer world. The world shows a red or green signal to the brain. The signal is fed into the brain at arbitrary neurons. The bottom row represents the action resulting from the processes going into the brain. This is transmitted to the environment, which provides a feedback. If the response is not correct, the environment does not provide food.

feedback mechanism that would keep the output, rather than the input, low.

It occurred to Stassi and me that maybe one could construct a toy brain model using ideas from that work, so I invited him to visit Brookhaven for a year.

The monkey problem

One of the problems in describing brain function is the uncertainty in determining what exactly is the problem that the brain is actually "solving." What, precisely is the function of the brain? It isn't enough to simply say that it is "thinking." A good deal of brain research traces the location of the activity of the brain when a person is subjected to various stimuli, but gives next to no insight on general principles. Before constructing a model, we found it important to define a specific problem that the brain was to solve.

A hungry monkey is confronted with the following problem. To get food, it must press one of two levers. At the same time it is shown a signal that can either be red or green. If the red signal is on, it has to press the left lever; if the green signal is on, it has to press the right lever. The signal switches back and forth between the red one and the green one. If the correct lever is pressed, the monkey will get a couple of peanuts.

A block diagram of the situation is shown in (fig. 2). The outer world sends a signal to some of the neurons in the brain, through the eyes of the monkey. The resulting action of the monkey is fed back to the outer world, which in turn provides feedback to the monkey and its brain by either giving or denying food. After a number of wrong tries the monkey learns to perform properly.

The fact that the function of the brain has to be self-organized puts severe constraints on any brain model. In our model, neurons were arranged on a two-dimensional grid. The neurons in each row are connected with three neurons at the row below that neuron, as indicated by the arrows in the block diagram. We have also studied a network where the connections were completely random. This network functions almost as well, but is more difficult to illustrate graphically. The firing signal from the environment is represented by pulses that are fed into a number of random neurons, the red ones if the signal is red, the green ones if the signal is green. It is a simple matter to define the initial network. It took only a couple of sentences to specify the geometry. Not much more information is needed to specify a larger network. The brain model "at birth" is a simple structure.

At each step, each of the neurons are either in a "firing" state or a "non-firing" state, according to whether their input voltage, or potential, exceeds a threshold. Firing neurons send electric signals to other neurons, driving their potentials closer to the threshold. This is very similar to the sand model, in which a toppling occurs if the height exceeds a threshold. The signal from a firing neuron is sent to the inputs of the three neurons in the layer below. The input of each neuron depends on the strengths of the connections between that neuron and the one that fired. In addition, a small amount of noise was added to all the inputs.

The output is given by the neurons in the bottom row. Say, for instance, that for the red signal, neurons # 10 and # 15 counting from the left must fire, and for the green signal, neurons # 7 and # 12 must fire (fig. 3).

In the beginning, the strengths of the connections between neurons were chosen arbitrarily. The red [here dark grey] and green [here grey] inputs were switched every 200 time steps, or whenever the output was correct. The feedback from the environment was sent to all the neuron connections in a totally democratic way. This could represent some hormone, or some other chemicals fed into the brain. In this sense, our model is fundamentally different from most other neural network models in which an amount of outside computation, not performed by the network itself, has to be carried out to update in detail the strength of the connections.

If there is a positive feedback signal, that is, the proper output neurons fired, all the connections between simultaneously firing neurons are strengthened whether or not they were responsible for the favorable result. If there is a negative signal, all these firing connections are weakened slightly. All other non-firing connections are left alone.

This type of scheme has been tried before without much success, precisely because of the weak communication between inputs and outputs, which makes learning prohibitively slow. Also, whenever the red [here dark grey] signal is on, the pattern that is favorable for the green [here grey] light is forgotten, and vice versa. An extra ingredient is needed. If there are too many output cells firing, all thresholds are raised. The function of this mechanism is to keep the activity as low as possible, and it results in setting up the brain in a critical state. To think clearly, you have to keep cool! If the activity becomes too low,

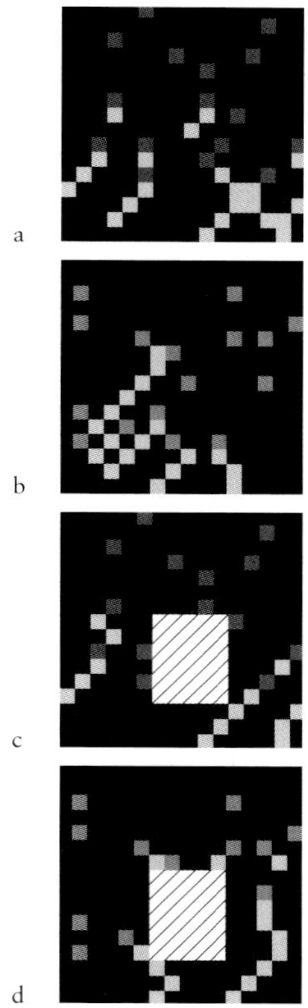

Fig. 3
Successful firing patterns in the fast switching phase. The two sets of input neurons are colored red [here dark grey] and green [here grey], respectively. For (a) the red input in the cells #10 and #15 of the bottom row must be triggered; for (b) the green signal in the output cells #7 and #12 must be triggered. The yellow [here light grey] squares show which outputs are firing for the two inputs. Successful patterns after the removal of a block of thirty neurons (c) and (d).

for instance if the brain is asleep with no output, the thresholds of all neurons are lowered and more neurons fire. The monkey becomes hungry and activates the brain. Note that all of these processes are biologically reasonable; they can be performed by chemicals being sent around in the brain without a specific address.

Fig. 4a shows the performance, measured as the relative number of output neurons that are firing correctly. After an initial period of very erratic response, which we call the learning period, the toy brain eventually learns to switch quickly back and forth between the correct responses. The transition is very sharp. Fig. 3 shows the successful firing patterns as yellow [here light grey] squares for the two different inputs.

Note the difference from the original response (D. Stassinopoulos and P. Bak, "Democratic Reinforcement. A Principale for Brain Function," in *Physical Review*, E 51, 1995, p. 5033.)

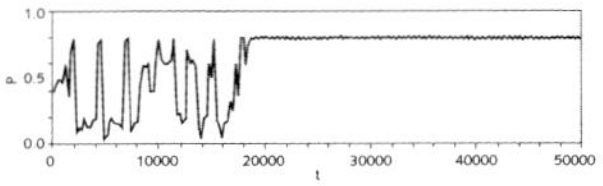

Fig. 4a
Performance vs. the number of time steps. The performance is defined as the relative number of correct output cells that are firing. Note the transition where the brain has learned to switch quickly between the two patterns.

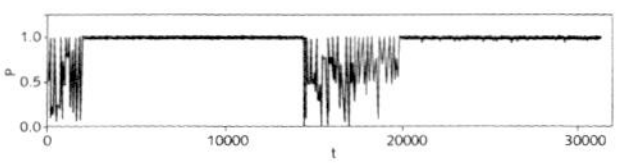

Fig. 4b
In (b) a five by six block is removed after 15,000 time steps. After a while, the brain has learned again to switch correctly between the two outputs.

The brain and river networks

What happens inside the network during the learning process? Through a complicated organizational process, the system creates internal contacts or connections between selected parts of the input signal and the correct output cells. The process can be thought of as the formation of a river network with dams (thresholds). When the output is incorrect the riverbeds are raised (the firing connections are weakened) and the dams are lowered (the thresholds are lowered), which causes water to flow elsewhere; this is the process of "thinking." During that period there is an increased activity in the brain.

If at some point the response happens to include the correct cells, the riverbeds are deepened but all the dams are raised, which prevents the signal from going elsewhere. The system tries to lower the activity as much as possible while still connecting with the correct output. At some point the thresholds will become too high and the output becomes too low (the monkey loses concentration), but the system immediately responds by lowering the threshold. The small amount of random noise prevents the network from locking into wrong patterns, with too deep riverbeds from which it cannot escape. It allows the network to explore new possibilities.

The process is somewhat similar to the mechanism for the evolution model. During periods of low fitness (improper connections with output) there is a relatively great activity where the system tries many different connections until it finds a state with correct connections (high fitness), in which most of the neurons are passive, just as the species in the evolution model have fitnesses above threshold in the periods of stasis, in which they have "learned" to connect properly with the environment.

The ability of fast switching is related to the system operating at the critical point. The signal is barely able to propagate through the system. The flow pattern is very similar to Andrea Rinaldo's critical river networks, and does not look like a flooded system with large lakes. A traditional neural network model corresponds to a flooded system with roughly half the neurons firing at all times, resulting in poor communication. At the critical point, the system can easily switch from a state in which one system of rivers is flowing to a state in which another system of rivers is flowing to a different output. We exploit the high susceptibility of the critical state.

The network is robust to damage. After 150,000 steps, a block of thirty neurons was removed from the network as shown in fig. 3c and d. After a transient period the network had relearned the correct response by carving new rivers in the network. The performance is shown in fig. 4b. In other words, instead of using some features of the input signal, the system learns to use other features. Think of this as replacing "vision" with "smell."

Our toy brain model is not a realistic model of the brain. Its sole purpose is to demonstrate that aspects of brain function can be understood from a system starting with a minimum amount of structure. The ability of the brain to function is intimately related to its dynamics, which organize knowledge about the outer world into critical pathways of firing networks in an otherwise quiet medium. The criticality allows for fast switching between different complicated patterns without interference. The memory is encoded as a network of riverbeds waiting to be filled up under the relevant external stimulus.

The feedback between reality and the individual through perception of the physical world determines the interconnected structure of the brain.

Cecil Balmond

Powers

The Elders could just about bring themselves to admit that addition and subtraction fitted neatly within the logic of a set of circles, derived from adding up the integers of numbers by applying the sigma code. But powers? Those exponentially jumping values of doubling, tripling, quadrupling… Could that escalation of numbers have set patterns, even though the numbers grew so rapidly beyond simple calculation?

Enjil had gone too far, they whispered amongst themselves as the boy gave them his crooked smile and picked up the chalk again. To their mind his voice was cheeky, arrogant, and insolent, announcing that the power expansion of numbers unfolded in set ways and was not open ended as they may have thought. The sun, shining on the young Master, threw sharp shadows into the holes of his ravaged pock-marked face. The black spots made him look sinister. Were they in the hands of a demon, they asked, as some of them feared?

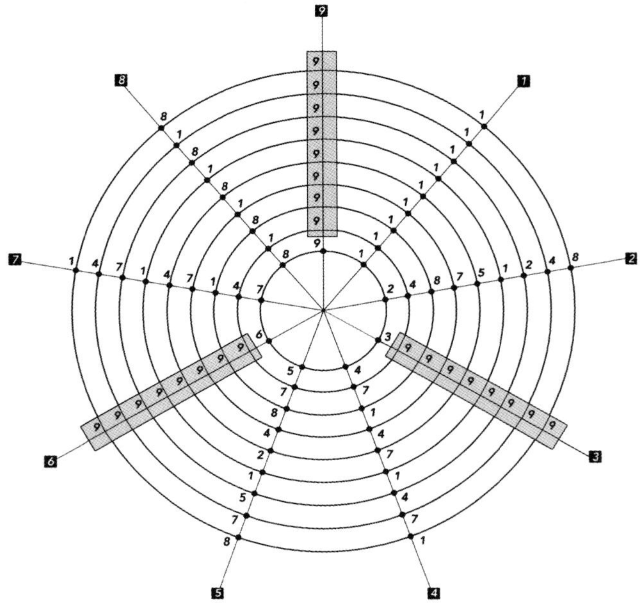

Then Enjil began his demonstration by writing out the numbers, adding the digits to reduce the powers to one number only, and revealing the patterns to the astonished Elders. The adoring crowd who by now had accepted him as the light of the Academy settled down and went quiet, awaiting the demonstration as when a new comet comes into a black sky.

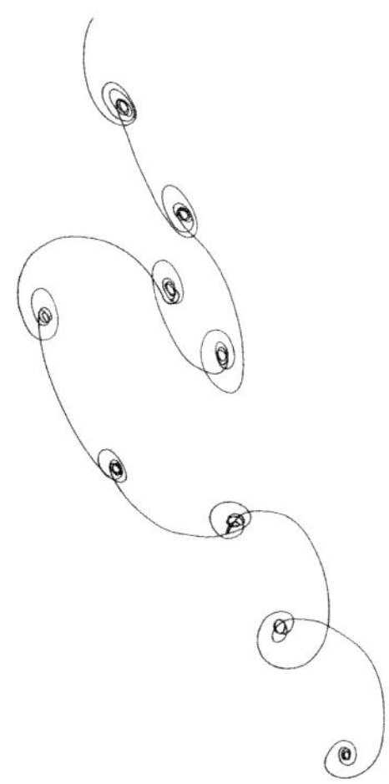

Though this time the concept of the powers of numbers was beyond their daily arithmetic, the way Enjil reduced the problem to simple numbers made the crowd believe they had been shown a great mystery, that unto now had been hidden; and even though they may never use doubling and quadrupling in their everyday affairs, the fact that even such big jumps were controlled in set ways, underneath the surface of numbers, was something they found extraordinary.

The world and the huge jumps to the stars were perhaps then not so great and unbelievable – perhaps even invisible ways were all around, if only they knew how to look. So they willed the young Master success. They watched him limp from one end of the blackboard to the other as he wrote out his belief in the expansion of numbers in an elegant way. And they began clapping when they saw the fun of it all.

Enjil wrote out his workings in a neat hand.

The workings

The sequence for N^2 where N=1, 2, 3... is

1^2	2^2	3^2	4^2	5^2	6^2	7^2	8^2	9^2...
1	4	9	16	25	36	49	64	81...

If the integers of the numbers in the second row are added and reduced to one number, then we have

1 4 9 7 7 9 4 1 9...

As the expansion continues from 102 to 182 we have

10^2	11^2	12^2	13^2	14^2	15^2	16^2	17^2	18^2
100	121	144	169	196	225	256	289	324

The same rule is applied to reduce these numbers to one value

1 4 9 7 7 9 4 1 9

In fact, as the square powers are plotted further, the code numbers keep repeating. Every third, sixth, and ninth value in the sequence is 9.

Similarly the expansion N^3 for N = 1 to 9 gives

1 8 27 64 125 216 343 512 729

which reduces, according to the sigma code as

1 8 9 1 8 9 1 8 9

Here the rhythm is 1, 8, 9 with the third, sixth and ninth values acting as anchor points, just as in the sequence for N^2.

Similarly the expansion of N^4 is

1	16	81	256	625	1296	2401	4096	6561
1	7	9	4	4	9	7	1	9

Again the pattern emerges here of every third value being 9, and the sequence being nine numbers, beginning with one and ending with nine.

If the calculations are continued to higher values of N and the code sequences are written out from N^1 to N^9 we arrive at:

N^1	1	2	3	4	5	6	7	8	9
N^2	1	4	9	7	7	9	4	1	9
N^3	1	8	9	1	8	9	1	8	9
N^4	1	7	9	4	4	9	7	1	9
N^5	1	5	9	7	2	9	4	8	9
N^6	1	1	9	1	1	9	1	1	9
N^7	1	2	9	4	5	9	7	8	9
N^8	1	4	9	7	7	9	4	1	9
N^9	1	8	9	1	8	9	1	8	9

These sequences can help find other relationships between the powers of numbers. Because the arithmetic is reduced to single values, it is easy to test various speculations about how numbers relate to each other. I found interesting patterns very quickly using the code values rather than carrying out the actual multiplication. All one has to do is obtain the sigma value, the rest is easy.

The interesting feature is that each of the sequences of nine values, when added up horizontally, gives the rhythm 9 – 6 – 9 – 6 – 9... That is the row for N^1, in the above table adds up to 9, the row for N^2 adds up to 6. The row for N^3 adds up to 9 and so on.

If each sequence of the power expansions is written out in a circle of nine values, we obtain a picture of concentric orbits say for N^2 and N^3, the following is then true:

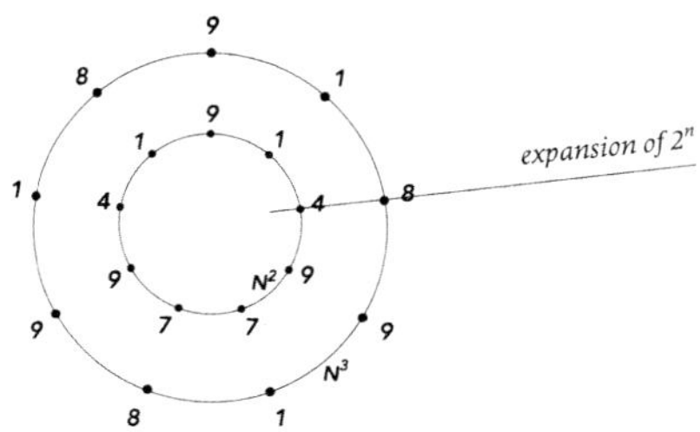

The inner circle is the sequence for N^2. This means the whole expansion of N^2, sits along this inner circle with values 1 – 4 – 9 – 7 – 7 – 9 – 4 – 1 – 9 spinning around the circumference.

And the outer circle is the sequence for the expansion of N^3, with the values 1 – 8 – 9 repeating. Because the sequences have only nine values they fit around each other neatly, just as in the first Mandala. There is also a flow outwards along radiating arms of the powers of a given number. The line for 2^n is shown, i.e. 22 = 4, 23 = 8, etc.

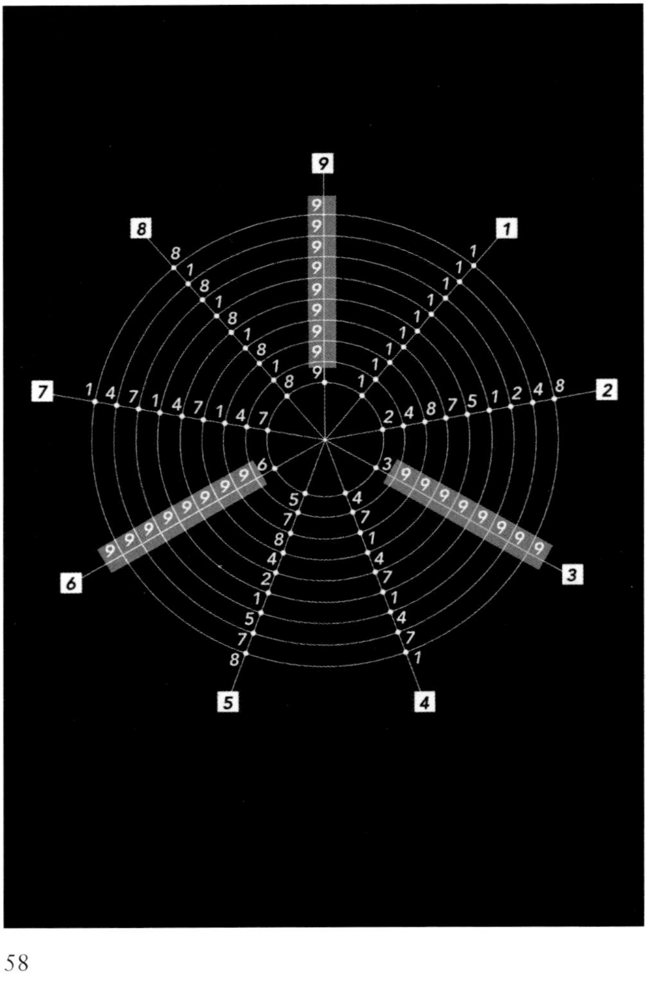

Power Mandala

The innermost circle is the expansion of N^1, the sigma code itself, the numbers 1 – 9.

The second circle relates to N^2. The third circle relates to N^3 and so on, where N = 1, 2, 3,...

But each radiating arm is the sigma sequence of a fixed number being raised successively to higher powers.

For example, the arm starting at number 2 in the innermost circle shows the sequence

2 4 8 7 5 1 2 4 8

which is the sigma value of the power expansion of

21 22 23 24 25 26 27 28 29

Each radiating arm sums up to a multiple of nine and successive orbits have the sigma patterns 9 – 6 – 9 – 6 – 9 – 6... when the values of each orbit are added up, starting from the innermost circle.

The strong radiating lines of 9 divide the Mandala into three sections.

It can also be seen that along each radiating arm some patterns are short, before they repeat, like that for number 4. Numbers 2 and 5 have longer sequences before they are repeated. But the numbers 3, 6 and 9 raised to successive powers are held by the fixed value of nine.

The patterns that repeat are:

1^N	–	1...					
2^N	–	4	8	7	5	1	2...
3^N	–	9...					
4^N	–	7	1	4...			
5^N	–	7	8	4	2	1	5...
6^N	–	9...					
7^N	–	4	1	7			
8^N	–	1	8...				
9^N	–	9...					

The power circles show that though a number seemingly jumps rapidly as it is raised to higher powers, underneath the surface there is a set of repeating cycles.

There is conservation at work, in secret.

So we go back in time to that first circle of the compound in the Academy, with the sun shining down on the blackboard and on Enjil as he draws his power circles. Not only have additions, subtractions, multiplications and divisions been held in the power of just nine orbits, now he demonstrates how all the possibilities of expanding numbers in squares, cubes, and quadrupling and so on are also held around the circumference and radius of just nine circles, one within the other.

As Enjil adds the numbers within each sector, along each curve, and outwards along each radius, he shows them how nine and its stepping stones of three and six run through the whole construction of this newest Mandala. The mathematics of the powers of numbers are beyond the humble village folk who keep arithmetic simple, to bartering for grain and livestock, but they still smile and cheer for they understand how complicated things can be broken down and made simple. The Elders are different; they are clever and know all about numbers – or so they thought until this fateful day of the Examination, which turns into an examination of themselves. Now they have to look again at how they see the dust of arithmetic after what Enjil has shown them, the reflections that turn in the precious mirrors, visions, covered with numbers in secret...

...Enjil showed them that numbers were more than just counters in calculations. They had a secret life. If anything, these hidden reflections were more exciting than the actual images of arithmetic. For on the surface every calculation was a forced answer with one outcome only; and the possible outcomes were a million times a million and more in all the calculations one could do. But it was not just the outer event that mattered, that was nothing if an inner life could not be guessed at.

In this way Enjil argued for the jewels he had found, hidden in the dust of calculations. As he said, if calculations and all the sums we do are just patterns of an untamed wind, blowing any which way it pleases, what cannot change is the character that seeds the wind, the fixed points which structure and raise shape and whose force always gives direction.

The powers of numbers jumped like those ghosts in a storm, growing larger and more frightening every time. But in the leaps, a rhythm, a pulse that no one could see turned, in repeating ways, never changing no matter how big the jumps. No one need be afraid, he said.

Enjils proposal was that his Mandalas were fixed orbits which gave the essence of all the movements of numbers. In secret mirrors, they held the inner reflections.

Like with people, numbers had a hidden nature. And even though we may do so much in the outward appearance of our lives, what mattered was the inside shape of a person, he argued, that gave character to everything else.

Even though people were all different in various circles of power and influence, underneath it all they shared a set of values, love of family and fear of God. People everywhere held to some sort of secret code. Even if they did not talk about it their actions were governed by an inner faith. In the same way Enjil said numbers were blown this way and that by the fate of calculation and worldly actions, all appearing to be different; but underneath it all a hidden mantra turned, holding sway in a myriad world of change.

He said the Mandalas of nine were but the fixed points in a set of beautiful meditations, on the meaning of numbers.

Lise
Bek

Creating Reality by Sight
A Contribution to the History of Man's Visual Relation to his Surroundings

Conditions of sight and reality

"Let there be light!"

Upon this command of the Divine Creator, so we are told in the Biblical myth, the foremost condition for man visually relating himself to his natural surroundings was set forth.

But as history shows, the ways in which he managed over time to interpret what he saw into terms of reality seems to be a cultural rather than a natural matter. It presupposes an ability to make distinctions of a far more conscious kind than that involved in the purely visual process.

In fact, in order to come into existence, reality must be apprehended in opposition to what is not real, and which, consequently, cannot be seen. It is a question which has undoubtedly haunted man ever since his exit from his primordial symbiosis with nature to enter the stage of culture. And the answer will, in its turn, determine the way in which the visual data perceived by the human eye are selected and ordered to transmit them to the mind for comprehension.

In our research into the interdependence of modes of vision and concepts of reality of bygone ages, we have to trust the artists of those days as the eye-witnesses to the constant process of change undergone by the general conceptual ideas and visual conventions. But in the obligation to capture the essence and appearance of things and matters before or even without their being made conscious to people in general, the artist will, in his work, often be at odds with the ideas and conventions of his contemporaries.

The process of visual impressions being formed and providing information, for its part, results in two basically different modes of vision. One is characterized by the viewer's concentration on the concrete object seen either as solid form or as planar image occupying his vertical field of vision. The main feature of the other one is sight as travelling through the horizontal field of spatial extension, in which the objects seen are located. The two modes, moreover, differ inasmuch as the first one originates in the immediate visual sensation of the things seen, whereas the other implies a mental reflection in calculating and measuring spatial intervals and distances.

Given the character of the respective visual models it cannot be surprising that the one concentrating upon the thing seen has been predominant from the very beginning, exemplified as it is already in the way in which the prehistoric cave painters configured their prey on the rough walls of their rocky sanctuaries, in its tactile appearance as huge, shaggy-haired animal bodies close at hand. And it is equally significant that it was not until the Renaissance when a new state of man as a rational, thinking being was proclaimed that the other mode gained ground. In the Renaissance, for the first time, man and his surroundings became part of a reality related to physical existence in space and time.

Another question to be discussed, then, is whether this mode has been superseded, in turn, by yet another mode of organizing the surroundings in visual terms – that of modernity – and furthermore, if this mode also has reached its end.

1. From objectness to image of vision

Object, surface, form

In the ancient Mediterranean high cultures, especially that of Pharaonic Egypt, visual interest was still attached to the front side of the object in its surface character, as expressed in the flat or negative relief with its twisted figures and the block-like statue barely carved or chiselled on each of its four sides. Both seem to echo, in the vertical plane, the way in which the scanty elements of significance in the planar void of the desert sands are unconsciously perceived: the steep sides of the Nile valley, the smooth river band, the square pattern of the fields of crops, and the dusty-grey, flat-roofed houses, hardly discernible, not to be interpreted by present day eyes, in their quasi non-perspectival uniformity, as a spatial continuity.

The only things which had any claim to reality were those of a higher cosmic order. And to obtain this privilege, so it seems, not only the durability of material but far more the submission to geometry were indispensable qualities able to elevate the things of the visible world from their earthly state of fluctuating uncertainty to a higher sphere of eternity. In art, the frail object was thus hardened into stone or metal and endowed with geometric form, so to speak, to withstand the power of time.

The furtherance of such elevation of the divine Pharaoh in life and death was the main function of official art and architecture, from the statues and temples to the erection of his prismatic pyramid tomb, not to mention the mummification of his dead body. But at the same time, the works of art thus formed, not only made up the landmarks in man's field of vision, but collaborated, as it were, to form the model for the pattern that he imposes on the visual impression, drawn from his daily-life observations of the surroundings.

In archaic and classical Greece, the role played by geometry in making things suited to reality, was in some respects a different one. In fact, it acts as the force immanent in objects through which a higher degree of existence and, hence, of visual certainty is allotted to them. But at the same time, it was only the things pertaining to the sphere of the living, and among them especially those related to man and to civilized human life in community, that could aspire to existence at all, as opposed to the non-existence of wild, untamed nature, of the world of death and the dead.

In Greek culture, furthermore, the object, to the beholder, tended to become more and more individualized, just as it gained solidity as form. The silhouetted figure was shaded in painting, and sculpture evolved into full plastic volume: the statues of divinities and athletes standing as free columns in their surroundings.

It was not only through their visibility as form, however,

that the objects seen received existence as real against an indefinite background. It was thanks to proportioning and measure, just as much, that the human figure was detached from the randomness of nature.

Already the mathematician Pythagoras confirmed that the world's essence consisted of numbers and geometry, and it was upon this thesis that the sculptor Polyclete built his theory of the proportioning of man.

This proportioning was regarded, on the other hand, as a general scheme having relevance for all objects in their pretention to become part of reality, a pretention to which architecture responded in turn. So the compact blocks of temples stood proudly on their mountain peaks or promontories as the fixed and firm points in the middle of the nowhere of natural elements, the shining goal to which the wanderer might direct his sight and steps.

How different these temples look today in their ruinous airiness and how seemingly situated to command the magnificent view over the surrounding landscape so highly appreciated by every beholder since the Romantic era! But to the ancient Greeks, it was not the view outward from the temple, the dwelling of unapproach-able divine power, but the temple itself as the all-attracting viewpoint and clearly defined solid form that had preference.

The Athenian Acropolis, with its many and various monuments, illustrates this situation perfectly. Scattered around the irregular ground of the plateau, the temples, altars, and statues are each positioned so as to afford the most splendid and awe-inspiring view to the people entering the Propylaea. But the amount of space lying between the building blocks to them remained an indefinite fluid as can be deduced from modern archaeological endeavours to transpose the non-geometrical formation of the open area to the same geometric order as that of the buildings there, laid out according to a scheme of geometrical symmetry.

Upon entrance to the plateau, the beholder would instantaneously turn his eyes to the right – the good or right side. And here he saw the main sanctuary, the Parthenon, presenting itself not on an axis, but in an overedge view, as a towering mass of architectonic elements, columns, architraves, etc. Furthermore, it was only its upper part that was to be seen above the tall temenos wall in much the same way, in fact, as was the case a couple of centuries later, in the illusionistic prospects in Pompeian wall painting.

The duality between geometry and optics

At the turn of the fourth century, the scene was changing radically. Reality was no longer thought to be found in the human world of the senses, but had withdrawn to a higher sphere of existence in the perfect world of ideas, to use Plato's philosophical formulation, an abstract universe ruled by the order of geometry. The earthly world, for its part, was reduced to a sheer illusion, a faint shadow of the true reality, again in Plato's words.

Consequently, things seen were no longer comprehended in their objectness as form but rather faded into shallow images of vision. This new concept of reality, on the other hand, resulted, it seems, in people becoming more alert to the momentariness, the ever-changing aspects of shape, movement, light, and color, in short the sense-appealing values that characterized what they saw in contrast to the immobile order of a higher reality, to be comprehended intellectually only.

As an indication of this alteration of the visual convention, the ideal timelessness of the statue was given up in Hellenistic sculpture and the human figure was brought into motion – bodily as well as mentally – plunged into dramatic action or upset by passion as exemplified in the Pergamon altar. Sculpture even rivalled the painted picture in its sparkling liveliness. In architecture, form was likewise manipulated to evoke, from a given position, a harmonious visual impression of sight despite any irregularity of form. So all the large temple complexes from Kos to Pallestrina were laid out according to this rule of optical symmetry.

It was the great natural scientist of the epoch and true Platonist, Euclid, who, in his *Optics* codified this new mode of vision as a correlate to his definition, and, in the *Elements,* the universal principle of structure as based upon the five regular geometric figures.

The Euclidean optical theory presupposed the beholder's visual confrontation with the surroundings as a tapestry which covered his vertical field of vision, and in which the things seen were turned into image one by one, each occupying its bunch of visual rays focused in the eye, but without any mutual interrelation or spatial location.

In art, this theory was turned into an aesthetic ideal as it appears from the work *On Architecture,* written in the early Augustan period by the Roman architect, Vitruvius. Following the Aristotelian distinction between truth and the only seemingly true, Vitruvius contrasts the ideal essence or absolute measurements of the building, its symmetria, in his terminology, with its appearance in the likeness of this truth or, what he calls Eurythmia, the visible beauty.

In painting, too, he favors the illusionistic concurrence with nature in representing "things that exist or might be in existence," as he puts it. And again, the illusionistic effect is brought about by means of a plasticity formed in light and shadow as well as by the elaboration of the surface texture in the objects shown. Especially in the still life genre of Pompeian painting this is apparent.

At any rate, the illusion sought is, however, one of things, not of space, and in the same way the purpose of the manipulation of architectural elements in the building and of natural ones in their views towards the surroundings is that of bringing to the eyes of the beholder a pleasant picture rather than to insist upon their space relations, the eye and not the horizontal being his only focus of reference.

The advent of Christianity did not cause any difference in the general mode of vision, since the Christians made the same distinction between a higher reality of Divine order and the disorderly human world. Thus Euclidean optics remained valid as the theory of vision for yet another millennium.

But there was a difference, nevertheless. In fact, the visible world was upgraded from its idleness as a shadow of reality to a significance as its sign. From the proposal of this doctrine by St. Augustine in the fourth century A. D., it was upheld and developed through generations of theologians until the end of the Middle Ages.

In this new capacity the singular object came to be a reflection of the Divine, however dim it might be. And even as the natural surroundings were visually trawled for those distant glimpses of heavenly order, it was embodied in the layout and proportioning of architecture to the point where Vitruvian symmetria prevailed over eurythmic beauty of sight. A peak in this respect was reached in the Gothic cathedral.

The bodily illusion of freestanding sculpture was equally repressed, and so was the figure carved in a flat relief or painted on a uniform golden or coloured background. Subtly geometrisized in form and proportioning though they were, these figures were still to be beheld, however, in the Euclidean manner as optical images in the vain depthlessness, if not in the transparency, of the stained glass windows.

Illusionism as a whole was abolished as a vain if not sinful temptation to the senses. And instead, all skill was exercised to render things and events as faithfully as possible, not in the mimetic sense of the ancients, but in order to secure their symbolical function as signs referring to the matters of Divine reality – a weighty issue in an age in which you were not even allowed to eat an apple without reflecting upon the Fall of Man. As symbolic forms, then, it was essential that they should be identifiable to the beholder not primarily in their individuality, but as types.

2. The spatial revolution

The centrally focused view

But from the visualization in Gothic architecture of heavenly reality and its Divine order as a mathematical abstraction, the conclusion was easily drawn that the same ordering principle was to be found in Divine Creation, inherent in the natural surroundings though hidden behind their imperfect form of appearance. And in addition, it was considered to be within the capacity of man, now raised from his previous low state as a sinful earthly creature to the position of a rational being and as such a participant in Divine rationality, to visually reveal this truth.

Sight was consequently no longer regarded as a fallacious tool for man's orientation in the world of senses, but was privileged to function as the exact scientific instrument for measuring the geometric scheme not only of the immediate surroundings, but of the whole universe. The diminution of size, blurring of form, and fading of colours with the augmenting distance were no longer considered distortions due to the weakness of sight. They were classified, instead, as accidental features of the visible world that man would be able to compensate for intellectually through comparison and judgement.

Such was the opinion held among scholars, to whom mathematics was a theological discipline aiming at the comprehension of the universe as God's creation. It was the case, not least, among those members of the Franciscan order who to that end had specialized in optical studies or what was in the late Middle Ages called perspectiva.

The artists likewise began to believe in what they saw with their own eyes and endeavoured to represent everything, faithful to both the order of inward structure and casualness of outward appearance. And in directing the attention towards the comparison of objects nearby and far away they happened to get frustrated by the intervals between the various objects present in the field of vision. And in their efforts to submit these areas of insubstantiality to order and measurement, the concept of space originated as an equally three-dimensionally defined container of three-dimensional objects.

But as a further result of this preoccupation with space the focus was shifted from the eye of the beholder to the line of relation from eye to horizon, which in its turn, caused the field of vision to revolve by 90 degrees. Sight, then, was not interrupted by the image configured in the vertical field of vision by the object seen, but might follow its course through spatial extension to its farthest point on the horizon.

It was in Florence of the early Renaissance, in the 1420s, that this new visual approach was demonstrated in practice. The first to realize the significance of the central fugal point as the point of convergence for all lines running parallel to the axis of vision was the architect Fillippo Brunelleschi who invented the method of linear perspective as a device to construct a convincing architectonic prospect. But already a decade later, his method was improved and also provided with a theoretical foundation by his younger contemporary, the learned humanist, Leon Battista Alberti. From his little treatise *On Painting,* it appears that to him the picture was a small-scale representation of the visible world, fictitiously rendering everything in its true geometric form. So, within the three-dimensional coordinate system of linear perspective, the individual objects are located exactly on the geometrically laid out ground plane as pawns on a chessboard.

Very soon, perspective was taken over by the painters as the basic scheme of organization of the picture. And as pictorial art at that time is likely to have made up the mode and model of vision in general, just as the flow of diverse pictures does for us today, this central perspective gradually became the chief organizing principle for both the planning architect and the observing beholder. And for both the key element was the central line of force, which functioned as the axis of symmetry as well as of vision.

Neither the layout of the building in long flights of spacious rooms nor the cityplan with its straight broad roads, flanked on either side by rows of rhythmically columned building facades, might have been planned like this, or lent themselves to perception as visually calculable, without people having the compasses of perspective in the eye.

Even the views obtained from inside the building outwards, from its windows or balconies, were cunningly designed to suit perspective. And people in general or at least those of the cultural elite for whose benefit architecture was projected and the great works of art produced, diligently exercised their eyes to cope with the demands of the new visuality.

But to return to things seen, their embeddedness as individual objects in the three-dimensionality of space meant to them that their own three-dimensionality of form acquired a more tangible character for the beholder than the things seen had had to the ancient Greek. For although they were apprehended in their objectness, they still appeared as hovering before an indefinite ground of vision. Neither was the structuring principle of the universe and consequently of the individual object, to be regarded by Renaissance man as an abstract force, but rather as a concrete stereometric skeleton upholding the object as form. And it was a stereometry that could readily be made directly accessible to sight, as it happened in architecture and not least in the geometrically laid out garden, with its trimming of vegetation devised to expose its true form.

The new way to conceive the universal order of geometry on the part of Renaissance humanists became apparent in their reception of Plato's regular figures structuring the elements. For to them these figures were not merely intelligible ideas, but concrete bodily forms that could be hewn in stone or drawn in perspective as had been done, incidentally, by Leonardo da Vinci.

This practical attitude in respect to the philosophical heritage has to be seen, certainly, in the light of the humanistic redefinition of Divine order to be an all pervading principle of Creation embodying the whole universe in geometric form. Reality, in other words, had descended from the heavenly sphere to become part and parcel of the human world, and it was a reality of form and space, made recognizable to man thanks to his rationality.

The widening of the scope of vision

But to the people of the age of Humanism it occurred, moreover, that by means of perspective a hitherto unthought of functional and visual domestication of the natural surroundings through their systematization came within the reach of man. And right from the outset in the sixteenth century, it was both practiced strategically in surveying the territorial extension of land possessed and fruitified aesthetically through the invention of the category of landscape.

In the first case, perspective was made the instrument for measuring large entities of land by a system of triangles. But from this practice a desire to physically mark off the domination of the ground to the limits of one's possessions ensued. This was done by spinning a web of geometric order around the building which formed the centre of the residence, finely meshed in its immediate neighbourhood, in the tiny patterned beds and paths and of the parterre garden successively enlarged to embrace the far away fields and roads. In the Versailles of Louis XIV this concept of domination through geometry was driven to extremes, the ordering principle seemingly overstepping the reach of vision.

In fact, the whole idea of the widely extended gardens laid out from the sixteenth century onwards to accompany the detached villas and palaces was to visualize the dramatic struggle between nature and art, in which the first one entering the garden domain in its raw form in forest trees, cascades, and rocks is gradually tamed to succumb, at last, to the geometrization of the latter.

In Versailles the battle has come to an end, one might say, and the natural elements are all inscribed in the same geometrical order of art. But also the dark wilderness of huge forests could be drawn into the pattern of domination by tracing the long straight deer paths through their tree masses. In the same way, the systems of royal high roads laid out in the various countries during these years were a means to signify the potency of the ruler rather than to facilitate communication.

As far as the notion of landscape is concerned, it has its background in the same perspectival definition of the natural surroundings as a certain section of spatial extension, in which the totality of natural elements, hills and valleys, plains, forests, rivers, and lakes, are unified by means of a common ordering principle in accordance with the mathematical laws of sight and appropriate to be taken in by the beholder in a single view.

In a certain sense, the garden of Versailles, to return to it once more, with its open grass lawns, shining waters, and domed groups of trees can be seen as a compromise between the traditional geometric order of art and the new concept of landscape in an idealised form. But long before that, landscape had invaded the pictorial universe as a motive nearly superseding that of the human figure. And thus, it fell upon the painters, as it seems, to procure the model for the new way of visual experience related to landscape.

For as the field of attention was moved from the scene of architecture, for whose formal and visual setting central perspective had been instrumentalized, to that of landscape, the scope of vision was considerably widened. The eyes of the beholder would now have to find their own way, so to speak, in the field of open space spread out before them like a fan. Besides, the location of elements, indicators of distance in landscape, would be less regular than in architecture and, consequently, less reliable as measuring posts.

The face-to-face confrontation between man and the visible surroundings, which had been determinant right from primordial times for his visual attitude whatever his mode of vision might have been, was thus abandoned in favour of a freer wandering of sight in a scanning movement all over the area.

For the first time in the history of sight, there was no axis of relation, whether optically or geometrically fixed, from eye to object or, as in central perspective, to horizon. And so the horizon became the line of fixation for the eye to follow. In the garden of Versailles, the tension between the axially focussed composition in layout and the size of the elements making them more apt for scanning, can thus be noticed.

In the scanning operation the beholder did not, evidently, take his point of departure from the right – the traditionally good side – but would reverse the process so as to go from left to right. The inspiration for doing so might have come from the procedure of reading, a skill that had been more commonly diffused as a result of the invention of printing.

The described alteration of the visual procedure did not remain without effect upon the landscape itself. The scanning view appeared to be more readily adaptable for those wanting to take in large, undifferentiated quantities, be it of mountain ranges, forest masses or sandy shores and open sea, and equally for the enumeration of a variety of juxtaposed details. So new types of landscapes as opposed to axially balanced ones, the ideal representation of which was the Versailles garden, were drawn into the field of aesthetic attention as distinguished by the Romantics as categories of the sublime and the picturesque.

By the way, a new kind of order was substituted for the Divine one: that of nature, an organic principle for the geometric one – a fact, which had consequences for the mode of vision as well.

But it was not only landscape that was made legible in this way. Also the towns with their skylines of variegated architectonic forms were read in a transversal scanning as cityscapes. And in the layout of streets and squares, the long lines and wide spatial entities, the uninterrupted sequences of building facades were preferred over the long processional streets of Sixtus V's papal Rome in the sixteenth century or the broad boulevards of nineteenth century Paris as replanned by Baron Haussmann.

And it was through this Parisian urbanity that the stage was set for "modern life" as the French advocate of modernity par excellence, Charles Baudelaire phrased it.

3. Sight and modernity

Man as the organizer of reality

The actor of the play thus staged was man. And man's role was that of organizer, not only of an appropriate mode of vision tuned to modern life, but of reality itself.

Since the Age of Reason, reality had been identical with the physically present world as sensed by man. It therefore became of vital importance to investigate how the senses functioned, and as far as sight is concerned, during the eighteenth century, a lively discussion on optics was underway.

With geometry having been abandoned as the structuring principle in favor of organity, sight also had to be defined as an organic function. But at the same time, the static order that had been imposed by geometry upon the surroundings in terms of their quality as the perfect work of Divine creation, was dissolved. And so the perspectival mode of sight, deduced as it was from such preexistent order, lost its impetus. The cubists' halfhearted endeavour, on the threshold of the previous century, to accomodate the swiftness of changing visual impressions designated as typical of modern life to a multiperspectival scheme, marked its end as a means of grasping reality, although not as a commonplace and comfortable convention.

Left alone, then, in the face of a surrounding world governed by the dynamics of physical forces and the everchanging development of organic life, man had to mobilize what was believed to be his innate disposition for order, to come to terms with it.

The first opportunity for the exercise of this newly discovered faculty was offered by the landscape garden. Here, at every turn of the winding path, the garden wanderer was meant to stop to admire the artfully composed illusion of "nature's neglectible beauties" to quote from the letter by Pliny the Younger translated and widely read in eighteenth century England. The recipe for these compositions as well as for the beholder's visual organization of them was borrowed, incidentally, from the classical French landscape painting of the previous century.

With the Romantics' enthusiasm for the ruinous decay of the built and natural form, however, the inclination for asymmetry and the disorderly rudeness of form was also imposed upon architecture. Thus Gothic architecture from Wolfgang Goethe's Straßburg Cathedral to John Ruskin's Stones of Venice was made the touchstone of the new mode of vision. And new architecture was built, likewise, to satisfy this mode.

There was but a short distance, however, from the perception of organic order to that of abstract form, from the view across the Thames to the Houses of Parliament in London of the mid-nineteenth century to the guessing of concrete form in the ink blot of the Rorschach test in the psychological laboratory of the 1820s. In both, the resulting visual effect is dependent upon the beholder himself, caused as it is by his search for "the good Gestalt."

A prerequisite for the success of such an enterprise was the total disentanglement on the part of the beholder from the burden of any cultural tradition or visual convention to give way to an unprejudiced openness of mind and eye. But with modern perceptual psychology, Ruskin's Romantic concept of "the innocent eye" is converted into what Rudolph Arnheim termed "the creative eye." Thus, rather than being the passive recipient of his surroundings, man became their creator through his activity of organizing them visually. The word creators would also apply to the modernist avant-garde in their originating a new world of abstraction, a world in which space has substantialized into a plasma of space-volume interacting with the bodily mass of form on equal terms just as figure and ground in the perceptual process of beholding.

However reluctantly this modernist idea, if not illusion, of pure sight and abstract form was accepted as an aesthetic doctrine, it has nevertheless, in the long run, profoundly influenced the general way of seeing of the twentieth century. The lead, here, was taken by commercial designers, who utilized the reduction of forms and forces of the physical world to their essential minimum, a reduction undertaken by Paul Cézanne, Piet Mondrian, or the architects of the white international style to bring before the eyes of the beholder-buyer an impressive image of the stainless reality to be created through the possession of material things. But from the world of advertising, abstraction diffused into the real world as the main principle of its being ordered visually.

Despite his activity as an organizer of his surroundings, man is standing motionless, in front of what is seen. His only movement, in principle, would be that of his eyes and their visual oscillation between figure and ground reflecting the dynamic interplay of form-masses and space-volume within his field of vision. Thus, man is still, so it seems, the fixed point of reference for the surroundings as they are exposed to his view at a given moment.

As argued above, this had been the case as long back as we are able to trace, through artistic evidence and the changing modes of vision, whether they concentrated upon the objects themselves, their visual image, or were directed towards the spatial extension containing the objects.

The beholder communicating with his surroundings

But a difference there is, nevertheless, for in the modern way of seeing, the eyes have been brought into motion – a characteristic also of the widescope visual scanning. The specific feature of the modern understanding of man's visual relation to his surroundings is that also the surroundings are conceived of as being visually apprehended not in their quality of constant phenomena, but as caught by sight, in an ongoing process of movement and change.

In art, consequently, movement likewise came into focus. The futurists, in taking over from the impressionists their inspiration in photography, tried to arrest movement in their painting and sculpture. In their celebration of modern age technical inventiveness, they exalted speed – in trains, cars and the like.

Although it was in the cinema, in the movies, more than anywhere else, that the art of motion found its own expression, movement and change was also the keynote in other fields of art. Thus in dance and performance, movement was reactualized as an element of significance. Especially in the genre of happening, initiated as an art form by Dada, new forms of movement were experimented with. In the happenings, the improvised and unpredictable confrontation of people with their surroundings and with one another that had puzzled artists from Impressionism onwards, was exploited as a real phenomenon.

In the exploitation of man's confrontation with the surroundings in reality, then, the problem was to become a major issue. So Maurice Merleau-Ponty, in his updating of perceptual psychology, inserted the beholder in the world of things seen instead of letting him keep up his earlier privileged position as the observer standing outside. Besides, he evolves a theory of the relation between the beholder and the surrounding world as one of mutual visual exchange, in which the overlapping of things, one behind the other, functions as an indication of depth, the most vital dimension in man's acknowledgement of being placed in a reality of things in space.

One might see the use, from the 1960s onwards, of reflecting and mirroring building materials as well as the interactive installations with their TV cameras as a kind of miming of this attitude to the world of sight.

Parallel to Merleau-Ponty, on American ground, James J. Gibbson undertook a similar redefinition of the psychology of perception. In his view, man was not only part of his surroundings, but he was moving about in space among the various elements, some of which are of a movable kind like himself, whereas others, such as buildings, trees, and mountains, are stationary – the mountain and other huge elements to a degree, even, where people are accustomed to seeing them only from one side. This mode of beholding things when moving in the surroundings is termed by Gibbson "the ecological" mode as opposed to the "primitive" or the "perspectival" mode of the immobile beholder.

In fact, this way of seeing appears to be the adequate mode for the Baudelairian hero of modernity, the dandy strolling about in the city mingling in the anonymous mass of people in their busy activities. But it might as well be an attitude symptomatic of the beholder in his spatial relation of himself to the elements of the installations or "sculpture in the expanded field" to use Rosalin Krauss's definition.

In the same way one might conceive of those large-scale projects of land art situated in deserts, lakes, and other regions of a grandiose nature as man-made counterparts to the big steadfast elements in the moving and movable world of sight – the world of which the beholder is, according to Gibbson, but an unprivileged part.

So the enormous void of Michael Heizer's *Double Negative* in the Nevada desert would appear to be a reversion of this type of visual experience in its insistance on being the only element of the surrounding desert landscape to remain firm and unapproachable like the mountains of earlier days. A plausible interpretation in terms of sight would be, then, that in present times, when all mountains have been climbed and all their secrets disclosed, the non-existence of the void will be the only lasting element. It is an element. On account of its size, this void seems, moreover, just like the mountain, to be seen only in Gibbson's perspectival view.

Cyberspace – the end of reality or a fresh start

In recent days, concern with reality appears to have concentrated upon another void, that of cyberspace existing only in the void of the monitor and in the minds of people. This virtual reality, nevertheless, in its incorporeal transparency has already left its mark upon the way in which the surrounding world is experienced and upon the surroundings themselves in as much as the same incorporealness of virtuality is to be recognized when one walks in streets fronted by the flickering images of reflecting mirror-clad facades or overlooking the endless fields of monoculture crops. So, in architecture, the same paper-thin forms, the same subdued colors have made their appearance like those developed in the screen imagery. And at the same time, smog has managed to suck from the urban and natural surroundings, all dimensions and all volume of form and space. Due to this state of affairs, it might seem that we will increasingly experience our surroundings in a kind of underwater mode of vision, as if living in a wrapped-in and consequently ungraspable reality, a gigantic project in the manner of Christo. It is a reality, moreover, in which the organic order conquered by modernism has conceded to the digital computer systems and the dynamics of physical movement to the flux of web communication. This mode of vision tends to be cherished by people who consider themselves to be living in the hurricane's eye of present day events, notably in the commercial and economic centres. It is inevitable, one might say, as a prerequisite of making virtual reality inhabitable as a human place of living.

But at the same time, evidently, an equally urgent need has emerged for man to regain a firm grasp of his surroundings in their capacity as a physical reality undergoing the processes of natural life as thematized in the art projects in which the changes caused by nature and time are typified. It is a need primarily felt, it seems at first glance, by the inhabitants of the periphery of the metropolitan culture, be it in the suburbs or on the outskirts of the cities or in villages in the countryside, as well as by the adepts of ecological movements.

One may ask, in conclusion, if two such modes of experiencing the visible surroundings really exist today, or if the dualism is to be found in modern man and the dual attitude to life and the world. And one may add that to find a possible solution to this dilemma, art might play a vital role in as much as it is through artistic distillation that our general ideas or reality and modes of vision are either reinforced or weakened.

Ben van Berkel, Caroline Bos

Interactive Instruments in Operation Diagrams

Architecture still articulates its concepts, design decisions, and processes almost exclusively by means of *a posteriori* rationalizations. The compulsive force of legitimizing arguments still dominates contemporary debate, even though it only represents a limited interpretation of the complex web of considerations that surrounds each project. Yet, for the most part, we cannot bear to analyze our own internal discourse for fear of disrupting the notion of the eminent utility of our projects and thus precipitating their disappearance.

The dependence of architects on being selected for work should not be underestimated. Inevitably, our strategies, our formulations and the ways in which our interests evolve are related to this dependence. Since architecture – at least in the open, democratic, Western society in which we work – now results from a highly institutionalized, cooperative process in which clients, investors, users, and technical consultants all take part, it is natural and right that architects strive to be reasonable, responsible partners in this process and condition themselves to think and to present themselves in a way that will persuade others that large investments can be safely entrusted to them. The frustrating result is that there is hardly any real architectural theory to be found, despite the diversity of practices at work today and despite a hugely expanded volume of architectural publications. There is only after-theory.

The pressure of rationality is such that architectural theory is streamlined toward a moment of compelling logic, in which factors of location, programme, routing, construction, and anything else that plays a role in the origination of a design are directed toward the triumphant conclusion that the particular design under discussion is the only objectively justifiable one. The demand to present the "right" solution, even when the contents of that concept have become very uncertain, propagates architecture's dual claims of objectivity and rationality. Like a door slamming shut, the barricade of retrospective justification roughly blocks the view of what went on behind it.

Architecture as social discursive practice

Looking into diagrammatic procedures is one way to partially open that door and to dislocate the protective and constrictive barriers that architecture has raised to hide its vulnerable centre. As one of the many techniques used by architects to advance their ideas within the development of a design, a diagrammatic technique presents an opportunity to examine the social-discursive aspect of architectural practice from within.

Discourse analysis is a relatively new approach being used in the humanities. As a method it combines insights from text analysis, argumentation analysis, and historic research.[1] Discursive practices have been defined as persistent patterns of discourse management. Their function is to regulate production, consumption and distribution of texts within a particular field of interest. Discursive practices cannot very well be seen as separate from the social framework in which they take place, which is why we refer to them as social discursive practices. The dependent positions of architecture within the economic system generally put a disproportionate emphasis on arguments of persuasion, which are only a small, externally orientated part of the social-discursive practice of architecture. The challenge for the next generation of architects is to acknowledge and analyze the internal discourse, which from a social-discursive viewpoint is far more comprehensive than the

1. We are indebted to Jaap Bos for drawing our attention to the social-discursive approach in his doctoral thesis *Authorized Knowledge*, Utrecht, 1997, which deals with the discursive history of Freudian psychology. See also N. Fairclough, *Discourse and Social Change*, Polity Press, Cambridge, 1992.

methodological process that is the basis of current design practice and to find a theory of the real in that.

Dismantling the scaffolding of rationality and objectivity is risky. The process might appear to imply a renunciation of all claims to any measurable, quantifiable worth. If we reject the predictable, rational interpretation of "winning schemes" as competitive fictions, what standards do we then apply to judge architecture if we don't want to end up with a lame "anything goes" conclusion? The answer must lie somewhere in the vast field between the poles of objectivity and subjectivity, between relativity and rigidity. The method by which architecture makes use of the intense fusion of information within a diagram is located somewhere between those poles. It would seem that it is not even fixed in one specific place, as the meaning of the diagram is not unequivocal. There are different interpretations of the diagram, which occupy different positions on the sliding scale between subjectivity and objectivity. Some of the interpretations explored most thoroughly in recent times have been the philosophical implications of the diagram, its imagery and the ways in which it instrumentalises concepts of organization.[2]

The meaning of the diagram

The specific meaning of the diagram in relation to architecture has been colored by our knowledge of Bauhaus methods. But let's forget about this; the modernist diagram has nothing to do with our subject, as a quick glance at the diagrammatic practices of Gropius, Mies van der Rohe and their students makes clear. To see architecture as a built line diagram is practically the reverse of our position. More to the point is the general understanding of the diagram as a statistical or schematic image.

In its most basic and historical definition, the diagram is understood as a visual tool designed to convey "as much information in five minutes as would require whole days to imprint on the memory."[3] Diagrams are best known and understood as reductive machines for the compression of information. When the informed reader consumes a specialist diagram, the effect is like that of a self-inflating life jacket: a small package that grows to full size in the time it takes to exhale a breath of air. But diagrams can also be used as proliferating machines. This is how architecture today interprets their use, thus transforming the diagram's conventional significance. When read archi-

2. Examples: Gilles Deleuze, *Foucault*, trans. Sean Hand, University of Minnesota Press, Minneapolis; Gilles Deleuze, *Francis Bacon: Logique de la Sensation*, Edition de la Différence, Paris, 1981; Greg Lynn, "Forms of Expression," in *El Croquis,* no. 72 (1), 1995.

3. J. Krausse, "Information at a Glance: On the History of the Diagram," in *Oase*, SUN Nijmegen, 1998. Krausse here quotes William Playfair, architect of the contemporary diagram, whose book *The Commercial and Political Atlas* (1786) introduced economic curve diagrams and bar charts.

tecturally, the diagram, which is often a bland, blank, blinding image, is never fully understood or rather, its full meaning is not allowed to break through. A diagrammatic practice pursues a proliferating, generating, and open instrumentalization in architecture.

Architecture focuses more on the reading and consumption of diagrams than on their labor-intensive production. The condensation of knowledge that is incorporated into a diagram can be extracted from it regardless of the significance with which the diagram itself was originally invested. The specific information contained in the diagram is discarded; that is not what architecture is after. For architecture, the diagram conveys an unspoken essence, disconnected from an ideal or an ideology, that is random, intuitive, subjective, not bound to a linear logic, that can be physical, structural, spatial or technical. In this regard, architecture has been encouraged by the writing of Gilles Deleuze, who described the virtual organization of the diagram as an abstract machine.

Deleuze's abstract machine

Deleuze helps us understand ideas by giving examples: thousands of them, so that our minds continuously swing back and forth between the abstract and the real. Architecture similarly oscillates between the world of ideas and the physical world, thus his writings seem to hold a highly specific meaning for architecture. We make extensive use of Deleuze's writings for this text, but are not out and out Deleuzians; our reading is specifically architectural.

Deleuze offers at least three versions of the diagram: via Michel Foucault, via Francis Bacon and via Marcel Proust. We do not make a distinction between the three diagrams in order to demonstrate some disparity between them, for there is none. Instead of recognizing three "versions" of the diagram, we should instead speak of moods or tonalities, for what strikes us is that three deeply significant aspects of the diagram are conveyed in three very different modes. In each case, the diagram has a different meaning and corresponds to a different stage in the process of understanding, selecting, applying, and triggering Deleuze's abstract machines.

The first stage of the diagram is associated with Foucault, through whom we learn to understand how the figure of the diagram is not representational; this is the crisp, dry, intellectual argument. In the second stage, through Bacon, we live through an artistic struggle; as we mentally take up the paint-

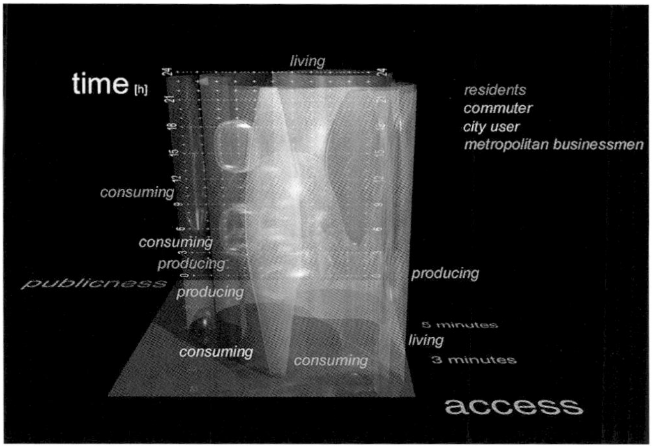

brush, we simultaneously engage in an earthy and lighthearted, playful debate about the selection and application of the diagram. In the third stage of the diagram, through Proust, the interaction of time and matter is introduced without which there can be no transformation. Here the argument takes a literary and musical turn; refrains in music, literature and psychology are taken to create a lengthy and intricate narration culminating in the invention of faciality.

For Foucault, Jeremy Bentham's 1791 plan for the Panopticon is "the diagram of a mechanism of power reduced to its ideal form (...), a figure of political technology."[4]

It conveys the spatial organization of a specific form of state power and discipline. The arrangement of the Panopticon is the expression of a number of cultural and political conditions that culminate in a distinctive manifestation of surveillance. It incorporates several levels of significance and cannot be reduced to a singular reading; like all diagrams, the Panopticon is a manifold. Typically, when a diagram breeds new meanings, these are still directly related to its substance, its tangible manifestations. Critical readings of previous interpretations are not diagrammatic. Put in the simplest possible terms, a diagram is a diagram because it is stronger than its interpretations. Although Foucault introduced the notion of the diagram as an assemblage of situations, techniques and functionings made solid, he put the emphasis more on the strategies that form the diagram than on its actual format. He isolated the "explicit programme" of the Panopticon in the

4. Michel Foucault, *Discipline and Punish: The Birth of the Prison*, Vintage Books, New York, 1979.

context of his concept of repressive hypothesis; the concept of repression was his real protagonist. Deleuze reverses the agenda and zooms in on the configuration and working of the diagram itself.

Deleuze recommends that Foucault be read not as an historian but as a new kind of mapmaker. For him, the diagram is interesting not as a paradigmatic example of a disciplinary technology, but as an abstract machine that "(makes no) distinction within itself between a plane of expression and a plane of content."[5] Diagrams are distinguished from indexes, icons and symbols, their meanings are not fixed. "The diagrammatic or abstract machine does not function to represent even something real, but rather constructs a real that is yet to come."[6]

Without this crucial intervention, Foucault's diagram quickly deflates under pressure. The explicit programmes selected by Foucault were never directly or completely realized as institutions because the diagram is not a blueprint. It is not the working drawing of an actual construction, recognizable in all its details and with a proper scale. No condition will let itself be directly translated into a fitting or completely corresponding conceptualization of that condition. There will always be a gap between the two. For the same reason, concepts such as repression and liberation can never be directly applied to architecture. There has to be a mediator. The forward-looking tendency of diagrammatic practice is an indispensable ingredient for understanding its function; it is about "the real that is yet to come."

Tools against typologies

Deleuze has contributed to the insight that the relentless intrusion of signs and significations can be delayed by the diagram, which thereby allows architecture to articulate an alternative to a representational design technique. Previously, if the concepts of repression or liberation, for example, were introduced into architecture, a complex formal expression of this concept would be reduced to a sign with one clear meaning, which would subsequently be translated back into a project.

This reductive approach excluded many possibilities in architecture. While concepts are formulated loud and clear, architecture itself waits passively, as it were, until it is pounced upon by a concept. A representational technique implies that we converge on reality from a conceptual position and in that way fix the relationship between idea and form, between content and structure. When form and content are superimposed

5. Gilles Deleuze, *A Thousand Plateaus*, trans. Brian Massumi, University of Minnesota Press, Minneapolis, 1987, p. 141.

6. Gilles Deleuze, *Francis Bacon. The Logic of Sensation*, trans. Daniel W. Smith (unpublished manuscript), p. 55.

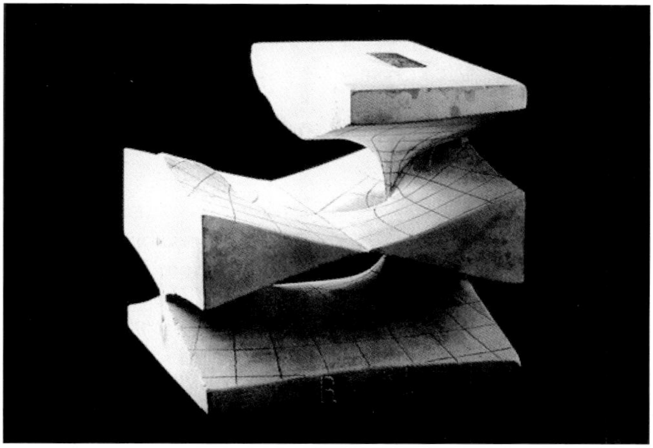

in this way, a type emerges. This is the problem with an architecture that is based on a representational concept: it cannot escape existing typologies.

An instrumentalizing technique such as the diagram delays typological fixation. An experimental or instrumental technique does not proceed literally from signs. If aspects such as routing, time, and organization are incorporated into the structure using an instrumentalizing technique, concepts external to architecture are introduced into it rather than superimposed. Instances of specific interpretation, utilization, perception, construction, and so on unfold and proliferate application on various levels of abstraction, liberating the design from a tendency toward fixed typologies.

How this is done is a trivial question for many techniques, but a vital one for what we call an instrumentalizing technique. The role of the diagram is to delay typology and advance a design by bringing in external concepts in a specific shape: as figure, not as image or sign. How do we select, insert and interpret diagrams? This is where Deleuze's second diagram comes in, the diagram of the painter that "is a violent chaos in relation to figurative givens, but is a germ of rhythm in relation to the new order of painting."[7]

Where architecture seeks to resist building typology, painting confronts the perpetual fight against "clichés, clichés!" as Deleuze exclaims, seemingly as desperate as any of us at the ludicrous inevitability of triteness, "not only has there been a multiplication of images of every kind, around us and in our

7. Ibid.

heads, but even the reactions against clichés are creating clichés."[8] Deleuze describes how to escape this, Bacon works random smears into his paintings, blind marks that insert into the work another world: a zone of the Sahara in a mouth, somewhere else, the texture of a rhinoceros skin found in a photograph.

The selection and application of a diagram has a certain directness. It involves the insertion of an element that contains, within, dense information, something that we can latch onto, that distracts us from spiralling into a cliché, something that is "suggestive." In architecture, instead of a smear of paint we use technical manuals, photocopies of paintings or random images that we collect to suggest a possible virtual organisation. These diagrams are essentially infrastructural; they can always be read as maps of movements, irrespective of their origins. The diagram is not selected on the basis of specific representational information. It is essentially used as a proliferator in a process of unfolding.

Instrumentalizing the diagram

It is significant that Bacon did not apply his diagrams to his paintings in an unmediated way, as in the collage, but rather instrumentalized or effectuated them in the medium of paint. At this point the third meaning of the diagram, which confirms and facilitates the previous two, emerges: the triggering of the abstract machine. The abstract machine must be set in motion for the transformative process to begin, but where does this motion originate? How is the machine triggered? What exactly is the principle that effectuates the changes and transformations that we find in real life and real time? Furthermore, how can we isolate this principle and render it to the dimensions that make it possible to grasp and use at will?

Deleuze offers an indication by pointing at the novelistic treatment of time. Through Proust's novels run, for instance, long lines of musicality, passion, picturality and other narrative lines that coil around black holes within the story. The black holes are a literary construction that enables change. If there were no black holes for the protagonist to fall into, the landscape of the narrative would be an unrealistically smooth and timeless plane, which would make it impossible for the hero, whose character and adventures are formed by this landscape, to evolve. The landscape of the story, the black holes, and the character become one – neither completely subjective nor objective – in order for the story to move forward. The

8. Ibid., p. 49.

narrative is constructed and read like a face, its intensity, passion and expressiveness fused into an indissoluble composition. Together, the black holes and the landscape form the abstract machine of faciality.

Faciality: The operational dream

The question is: how could this novelistic device to propel things into motion be meaningful in architectural practice? Can architecture also use the concept of the black hole/surface to develop an apparatus for triggering the effect of transitions in time? One of our current projects is structured as a diagram of faciality. The master plan for the station area of Arnhem consists of a bus terminal, an underground car park, office buildings and a train station, all parcelled out to different owners. Previous urban designs for the location have proved the impossibility of accommodating all of the programmatic needs in a cumulative manner. Our research therefore focuses on finding the holes, that is, the overlapping areas of shared interests where one layer off the landscape falls into another one. In the Arnhem project, pedestrian movement, which is the one element shared by every party, forms these holes. Movement studies form a cornerstone of the proposal. The analysis of the types of movement includes the directions of the various trajectories, their prominence in relation to other forms of transportation on the site, their duration, their links to different programs and their interconnections.

From these motion studies, the station area gradually begins to emerge as a landscape of interrelated movements. The holes in this landscape create a system of shortcuts between programmes, a hybrid of a centralized system and an exhaustive pattern of all possible connections. A year into the project, the topology of relations finally demands the introduction of a diagram that encapsulates the technical/spatial organization. A diagram is never a totally serendipitous find; as part of our search for a new way of understanding the station area we had begun to study mathematical knots with the idea that a landscape with holes could also be perceived as a knot of planes. The diagrammatic outcome of this is a Klein bottle, which connects the different levels of the station area in a hermetic way.

The Klein bottle is as deeply ambiguous as it is comprehensive; it stays continuous throughout the spatial transformation that it makes to go from being a surface to a hole and back again. As the ultimate outcome of shared, motion-based relations, the Klein bottle is an infrastructural element in two respects: pragmatically and diagrammatically. As a concept, the Klein bottle has come about as a result of studies of shared, interactive, local conditions. As a diagram, the Klein bottle becomes an actor in the interactive process as it begins to evoke new, more specific meanings at, for instance, structural and spatial levels.

Focusing the design on shared concerns means that relations form the parameters of the project, instead of the optimization of individual data. This generates new possibilities that no single, individual interest could have engendered. The project is pragmatic in the sense that it deals emphatically with real social, economic, and public conditions, but, crucially, this is an interactive pragmatism. Utilitarian needs are not met in a reactive way but are drawn together and transformed, which inevitably leads to the renegotiation of the relations between the parties. This approach implicitly endorses a certain policy by centering on collective interests. The project is not an unprincipled opportunist response to what is being asked, which is in any case impossible in a large-scale, multi-client project of considerable complexity. Neither, however, is there a preconceived idea of urbanism that precedes the specificities of location, programme or users. Instead, the project emerges interactively.

The abstract machine in motion is a discursive instrument; it is both a product and a generator of dialogical actions which serve to bring forth new, unplanned, interactive meanings. Discourse theory introduces the notion that meanings are not transferred from one agent to another but are constituted in the interaction between two agents. Likewise, the architectural project is created in this intersubjective field. Diagrams, rich in meaning, full of potential movement, loaded with structure, turn out to be located in a specific place after all. Understood as activators that help trigger constructions that are neither objective nor subjective, neither before-theory nor after-theory, neither conceptual nor opportunist, the location of the diagram is in the intersubjective, durational, and operational field where meanings are formed and transformed interactively.

Aaron Betsky

Let it Rain: The Art of Code

The point of revelation at the end of the science fiction film *Matrix* is the moment when the hero finally sees things clearly: not as part of an ordered universe, the result of God's plan or true love, but as data. The completely mundane reality he has been inhabiting, one which resembles the one we inhabit today, melts away to show him an endless shower of zeros and ones. He seems to stand in this deluge, realizing that he is no more than a bit of meat and processing power harnessed by machines. It is a frightening, and yet beautiful moment, for many of us suspect that not only is that blandness now the future, but the future of the *Matrix* is now.

We live in a world defined by codes. Computer codes, those vast amalgamations of zeros and ones that control so many of the objects we use and constitute the flow of information that flows all around us, are the most obvious results of the system of combination. They reduce more and more of our reality to a system that is not so much semantic as recursive: meaning and action come not out of signification, but out of the abstract relationship of those two digits. Beyond such binary logic, more and more of the scenes of everyday life are defined by codes. The buildings we design appear as a result of codes of construction, life safety codes, codes that are meant to open spaces up to larger groups of people, codes that protect us from possible hazards inherent in materials. Then building regulations come into play, meant to protect the world in which the building appears: zoning regulations, maximum allowable floor-area ratios, codes that limit the materials we can use. Finally, there are the codes of behavior that tell us what spaces we can use and how we can use them. These range from restrictions enforced with locked doors opened only through security codes to the elaborations of signage we have come to know as "information architecture," to the way in which we walk on the right side of a corridor and always, of course, walk, don't run.

These seem like banal concerns, but they are the generators of banality. It is because of codes that the environment we inhabit has fewer and fewer clues as to how it was made, is less and less specific to a place, and seems to most of us more and more alien to our bodies, our experiences, and our expectations. The one thing codes are, is that they are not experiential. They have reduced the way things work to a level of abstraction we can comprehend, but not truly know. They have leached all sense of meaning out of how things appear, and they replace the logic of how we make things, including the human-made environment, with a sameness that has the glassy surface produced by the chemical codes of refining and recombination. Our future is plastic, which is to say that it is an infinitely malleable result of programmed materials and forms produced on computers. Ironically, we have found out that we ourselves are the results of codes, and thus we can alter ourselves. The body and how we know the world is no longer an unalterable fact at the core of our existence, but just another conceit of codes.

Codes do not have to produce banality – after all, DNA has resulted in the variety of human existence. Certainly designers and planners have, for the last few centuries, thought that codes could be liberating. The codification of language, of laws and mores, and, more directly, of building practices, might have removed the originary power from those constructs, but it was also meant to make it easy for us to communicate, build, and engage in social relations. Our freedom to act was to be guaranteed by codes. In their reductive force, codes clarified, opened up and grounded a new form of knowledge. Modern art and architecture sought to give shape to this liberating new reality by reducing itself to systems of proportions and manipulations of material without meaning or image. In the end, modernism could present only the silence of the sign that was now silent. Architecture and art both threaten to disappear into codes for its constructions – for which neither a single artwork or a single creator is necessary.

Yet something persists. The survival of art should be a clue that codes meet resistance. We continue aspiring to knowledge and to the experience of who and where we are. We tend to still think of ourselves as bodies existing in a space in which we want to be at home. The world does not appear to us as a rain of data as it did in *Matrix*, but as "meatspace." We do not see what we make as code, but as something real.

Increasingly, the core of art is to confront the code. While Hollywood chooses to show it in the most literal manner possible, artists are trying to use codes in such a manner that they reveal themselves. The fascination with the banality, the "inform" and the "quotidian assemblage" are all related in this effort, not as a desire to glorify the ordinary, but to confront and picture it on its own terms. When such art manages to be critical without losing the logic of the codes it confronts, its power is that of the mirror that doubles the code's effect without recourse to its original structure, thus liberating it from its mathematical tyranny. Whether in the bombast of Damien Hirst's work or in the pleasure of the ordinary, revealed and typified in the work of Andreas Gursky, such embrace of the code is rescuing the ancient art of making beautiful objects.

Other artists are working directly with code, redirecting it to produce results that are not "logical," intended or even salutary to the system. Exploiting the inconsistencies that occur in any system, they produce forms that dance alive the chaos, rather than order that codes can also produce. Their mistakes, viruses, and algorithmic programs confront us continually with the unknowability of codes. The internet provides many opportunities for such mischief, as artists such as Mark Lafia are discovering.

Finally, there are those artists, and Olafur Eliasson is one of them, who use codes to produce effects that, though a logical result of codes, can amaze us by altering our perceptions and understanding of what we think of a physical reality. As a counter to the projected and themed realities that seem to be the cultural productions most proper to codes, these forms of art produce effects that retain the abstraction, malleability and lack of materiality proper to codes, but do give back to us a new reality. It is science fiction, perhaps, but one that reveals both its science and its fiction.

This is how we can confront codes. By utilizing and revealing both its inherent logic and its artificial nature in a manner that redeems us as witnesses to what is otherwise unpresentable, such an art will make it possible to maintain the sense – if even for a moment and if even in the rarified context of the museum – that code is not only recursive, but discursive as well. The art of the code might shower us with a realization of our reality.

Daniel
Birnbaum

The Hospitality of Presence
Problems of Otherness in Husserl's Phenomenology

The limits of presentation

Perception, according to Husserl, is distinguished from all other intentional acts by the intuitive givenness of its object. There is no mediation by means of signs or other re-presentations. Instead, the object is given corporeally in originary *presence*. If temporally extended objects are given perceptually, as Husserl claims, then what does that imply for the concepts of presence and *perception*?

The groundbreaking aspect of Husserl's phenomenology of time-consciousness is its attempt to extend the concept of presentation beyond what is given in the now. In order to grasp the Husserlian notion of presentation, it is important to understand the distinction between presentational and re-presentational consciousness:

Perception in this case is the act that places something before our eyes as the thing itself, the act that "originally constitutes" the object. Its opposite is re-presentation ("Vergegenwärtigung, Re-Präsentation"), understood as the act that does not place an object itself before our eyes, but represents it (X, 41/43).

What is original in Husserl is the way he distinguishes between presentational and re-presentational consciousness. Concerning our experience of the past, the line is not drawn between perception on the one hand and memory on the other, but between two different forms of the latter: primary and secondary memory. By primary memory, Husserl understands the immediate consciousness of "just-having-been" (X, 165/169). It is the ability of consciousness to retain phases that have just elapsed, but have not yet entirely disappeared from consciousness. By secondary memory, on the other hand, Husserl means the re-presentation of something that previously was given through presentation. It is through primary memory – what Husserl after 1909 will call *retention* – that the past is originally constituted. Primary memory can therefore rightly be said to be a condition of the possibility of secondary memory.[1] In an analogous way, the future is given in primary expectation. Only that which has been constituted presentationally (in impression, primary memory, and primary expectation) can be given re-presentationally through secondary acts.

Primary memory and primary expectation are parts of ongoing experience. As parts of the basic segment of actual consciousness, they remain continuous with impressional consciousness. And the phases of the object they intend, are, although not present in the sense of the now, given in intuition. Does that mean that these phases are perceived? Initially, Husserl has problems making up his mind on this point. He sometimes wants to restrict the scope of perception to the now:

Now if we relate the use of the word "perception" to the difference in givenness with which temporal objects present themselves, the antithesis of perception is the primary memory and the primary expectation (retention and protention) that occur here; in which case, perception and nonperception continuously blend into one another. In the consciousness that belongs to the directly intuitive grasp of a temporal object – of a melody, for example – the measure or tone or part of a tone now being heard is perceived, and what is momentarily intuited as past is not perceived (X, 39f/41).

1. The essential difference between primary and secondary memory is, however, not to be sought in the temporal distance of the intended object from the primal impression. Husserl even admits the possibility of something being re-presented in secondary memory while still being given presentatively. Rather, the difference is to be found in the forms of intentionality: primary memory (retention) is not a self-sufficient act, but a moment of the basic "cross section" of consciousness, to which corresponds the presentational givenness of the past, present, and future phases of the object. Secondary memory, on the other hand, is a full-blown act, which represents not only an elapsing phase, but an entire section of what was previously given presentationally.

Here Husserl clearly seems to suggest that the term "perception" applies only to the part of the object which is given as now; the other phases are not perceived, they are even "the antitheses of perception." That, however, seems to contradict Husserl's general claim that succession and temporally extended objects are in fact perceived. How would that be possible if only the now-point is given in perception?

In the very same paragraph, however, Husserl problematizes the initial claim. The now, to which perception was previously restricted, is nothing but an "ideal limit, something abstract, which can be nothing by itself" (X, 40/42). Even if we reduce the now to an idealized presence, we are, according to Husserl, not able to rid it of certain traces of absence. On this level of experienced time, presence and absence penetrate each other in an irreducible way: "Moreover it remains to be said that even this ideal now is not something *toto coelo* different from the not-now but is continuously mediated with it. And to this corresponds the continuous transition of perception into primary memory" (X, 40/42). In the last instance it may be considered nothing but a question of terminology, but it is still interesting to see how Husserl in the following paragraph explicitly widens the concept of perception to encompass not only the impression but also primary memory. The distinction is no longer drawn between now-impression and memory, but, as was indicated above, between the two different types of memory. Primary memory is direct intuition of the past, and must therefore be considered a form of perception:

But if we call perception the "act" in which all "origin" lies, the act that "constitutes originally," then "primary memory is perception." For only in primary memory do we see what is past, only in it does the past become constituted – and constituted presentatively, not re-presentatively. The just past, the before in opposition to the now, can be directly seen only in primary memory (X, 41/43).

The reluctance with which Husserl extends the concept of perception to the non-presence of the elapsed phases of experience is a sign of what has been called the "subversive aspect" of embracing a "solidarity between the living present and retention."[2] If the non-presence of primary memory is included in the extended now, why then are other forms of non-presence, that of secondary memory and other forms of re-presentation, excluded?

2. P. Ricoeur, *Time and Narrative*, vol. 3, trans. K. Blearny and D. Pellaner, The University of Chicago Press, Chicago and London, 1988, p. 283, n. 12.

We will, more than once, return to these questions concerning the ultimate limits of presence. Accepting primary memory (and primary expectation) as perception does not, however, amount to blurring the crucial distinctions within to the broadened concept of presence. The whole point of Husserl's "diagram of time," as it is introduced in § 10 of the lectures, is to highlight the essential aspects of the temporal flow. The "movement" illustrated in this diagram is the continuous "sinking down" of primal impression into primary memory or, in the later terminology, into retention.[3]

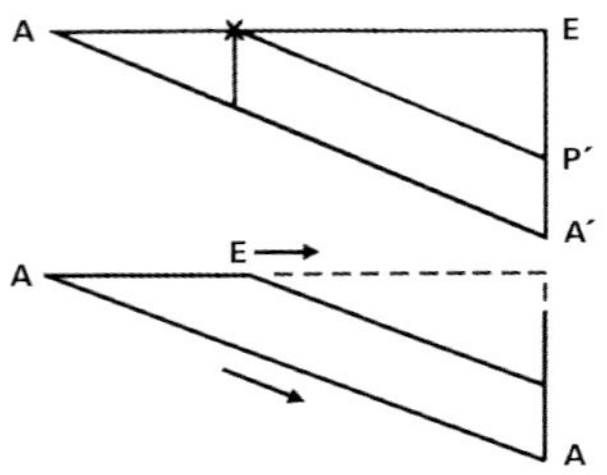

AE – The series of now points.
AA´ – Sinking in to the past.
EA´ – Continuum of phases (Now-point with horizon of the past).
E→ – The series of nows perhaps filled with other objects.

As shown in the diagram, every now-point is succeeded by now-points, creating a series, represented by the line AE. Every experience has its beginning in the "source-point" of impression, but immediately starts sinking downwards into pastness. The impression P, for instance, sinks down along the line PP, and by the time E is experienced in the mode of the now, i.e., as an impression, P has been modified into the retention P. As long as the temporal object is presented in ever new impressions, the object is still perceived as present. When the impression E elapses and sinks down into the past, the temporal objects stretching from A to E is no longer present and from that point on continuously sinks deeper into the past.

The sinking down into pastness of retention is not a disappearance into oblivion. On the contrary: Husserl's model accounts for the fact that the elapsing phases are not absent from the scene of consciousness, but retained as being past. He is not surreptitiously trying to transform what is past into something present. The retention is not a "pictorialization," "after-image" or "echo," (X, 32/33) i.e., a presence signaling something which is absent in a mediated way. There is no mediation here. Husserl insists: "The intuition of the past cannot itself be a pictorialization. It is original consciousness" (X, 32/33). The point is exactly that what is past gives *itself* as something being past: "Here, in the unity of the consciousness that gives us something itself, the past pretends to be given itself only as past; the now, only as now. We state this honestly, just as we see it and have it" (X, 344/355).

This givenness of the past *as* past still is a givenness; it is not a complete absence. Had it not been for this givenness of the past in retention, the flow of consciousness would have been a one-dimensional flux, in which every now would have appeared momentarily, only to disappear immediately afterwards into the abyss of irretrievable pastness. It is retentional

3. Although the change of terminology from "now-perception," "primary memory," and "primary expectation" to "primal impression," "retention," and "protention" does not take place until 1909, the latter terms were inserted later in the early text, so that the two terminologies are used side by side in the version of the lectures published in 1928. If not explicitly stated, we will treat the terminologies as synonymous. The general implications of the shift of terminology will be discussed in connection with Husserl's critique of the "apprehension – content of apprehension" schema.

consciousness that makes possible the experience of duration; had it not been for retention, we would not have been able to look back towards past phases of experienced objects, or, for that matter, past phases of consciousness itself. As Husserl points out: "We therefore owe it to retention that consciousness can be made into an object" (X, 119/123).

Even if Husserl is willing to extend the concept of presentation beyond the now-point, to encompass primary memory and expectation as well, he still ascribes a certain priority to now-consciousness. Retention is nothing but a modification of impressional consciousness, and retention would therefore not be possible were it not preceded by the direct perception of the now: "It is precisely this primal consciousness that passes over into retentional modification – which is then retention of the primal consciousness itself and of the datum originally intended in it" (X, 119/123). To stress its dependency, retention is described as the "comet's tail," the comet being the perception of the now. The primal impression itself, on the other hand, is not dependent upon anything but itself; it is the "source" from which all experience is "produced:"

The primal impression is the absolute beginning of this production, the primal source, that from which everything else is continuously produced. But it itself is not produced; it does not arise as something produced but through "genesis spontaneo" it is primal generation. It does not spring from anything (it has no seed); it is primal creation (X, 100/106).

The priority and self-sufficiency of impression has been problematized by commentators, who have pointed to a tension in Husserl's discussion of the primal impression: On the one hand impression is described as an autonomous source-point, out of which all other temporal determinations spring forth; on the other hand the now is "nothing by itself," and is only conceivable in its continuous mediation with the not-now of retentional and protentional phases.[4] Could one not conclude from the latter fact that impression is just as dependent upon retention and protention as they are upon impression? Some critical commentators have been willing to go even further: "It is tempting," Wood claims, "to treat retention as the primal phenomenon, with impressional consciousness as extrapolated or derived from it, or perhaps as only one of its abstract phases."[5] If we were to adopt such a view, the privilege of now-consciousness over retention and protention which Husserl postu-

4. Although retention and protention are often presented as symmetrical, and as equally important for the constitution of the flow, undeniably Husserl pays much more attention to the givenness of the past. Since Husserl has comparably little to say about protention, the critical literature is small as well. See, however, the chapter "Protention," in K. Held, *Lebendige Gegenwart. Die Frage nach der Seinsweise des transzendentalen Ich bei Edmund Husserl, entwickelt am Leitfaden der Zeitproblematik,* Nijhoff, The Hague, The Netherlands, 1966, pp. 29 ff. The asymmetry is, in fact, an interesting characteristic of Husserl's thought, and could be the point of departure for a confrontation with other positions, notably Heidegger's, where the asymmetric relation appears to be the exact opposite. For a comparison between Husserl, Heidegger, and Dilthey with respect to the privilege of different modes of temporality, cf. D. Carr, *Interpreting Husserl. Critical and Comparative Studies,* Kluwer, Dordrecht, Boston and London, 1978, pp. 197 ff.

5. D. Wood, *The Deconstruction of Time,* Humanities Press, Atlantic Highlands, N. J., 1989, p. 94.

lates, would be difficult to uphold: impression would appear as a "modification" of retention, rather than the other way around. Such a reversal would have dramatic effects not only on this single point, but on Husserl's conception of givenness and presence as such.

Regardless of how one is inclined to interpret the alleged priority of impression over retention and protention, it is important to keep in mind that all of these phases, according to Husserl, contribute to presentational consciousness. This means that the "diagram of time," illustrating the sinking down of impression into retention, renders nothing but the intuitionally given, i.e., presence in the extended sense of the term. How large is the scope of presentation? How deep can something sink into pastness without disappearing into oblivion? Since retention is original consciousness through which the past is constituted, it makes no sense to answer these questions in a manner that already presupposes what is constituted by the mode of intentionality under discussion. To say, for instance, "the scope of retention is three seconds," would be a vain attempt to apply units of objective time to a level where these cannot unproblematically be applied. So what terminology are we to use when stating the limitation of retention? As Husserl pointed out, the diagram itself draws no limit to the retentionally, and thus presentationally, given: "The limitation of the temporal field is not taken into consideration in the diagram. No ending of retention is foreseen there, and *idealiter* a consciousness is probably even possible in which everything remains preserved retentionally" (X, 31/32). Nothing in the diagram explains why retention is not infinitely extended. At the same time there is no doubt that Husserl took it as a self-evident fact that the scope of primary memory is limited:

Thus a pushing back into the past continually occurs. The same continuous complex incessantly undergoes a modification until it disappears; for a weakening, which finally ends in imperceptibility, goes hand in hand with the modification. The original temporal field is manifestly limited, precisely as in perception's case. Indeed, on the whole, one might dare to assert that the temporal field always has the same extension. (X, 30 f/32)

How does Husserl account for this limitation and for the possibility of forgetting? Since a consciousness in which nothing ever disappears into oblivion seems possible to Husserl – and the diagram in fact seems to represent such a limitless field of presentation – one has to inquire into the nature of the limitations of human consciousness. Is it a question of an empirical limitation inherent in the human psyche, or is it an essential feature of finite subjectivity?[6]

What interests us here is the fact that Husserl does not regard the concept of an infinite retention as self-contradictory, which implies that the presentational character of retention does not necessarily limit this intentionally to what has just elapsed into pastness. What distinguishes retention from secondary memory is not primarily the fact that the intentional object is closer in time. The crucial difference is, rather, the very mode of givenness of the object. While retention is a presentational mode of consciousness, secondary memory re-presents its object.

References

Husserl's Collected Writings, *Husserliana;* vol. X, *Zur Phänomenologie des inneren Zeitbewußtseins 1893-1917,* ed. R. Boehm, Nijhoff, The Hague, The Netherlands, 1966; vol. XI, *Analysen zur passiven Synthesis. Aus Vorlesungs- und Forschungsmanuskripten 1918-1926,* ed. M. Fleischer, Nijhoff, The Hague, The Netherlands, 1966.

6. If, in principle, the span of retention could be unlimited, then why do we ever forget anything? In vol. XI, we find a theory of "empty retentions" which purports to explain how each new *Urimpression* continuously disappears into the night of oblivion. See Mishara, 1990, for an analysis of this theory and the notion of the unconscious on which it is founded.

Ina Blom

Too Close to the Real[1]

I

If some future art historian wanted to sum up the art of the last half of the twentieth century in a few snappy sentences, she might describe it as a persistent fantasy about accessing the real. This fantasy might be seen to oppose various older notions of "realism," now reduced to a mere question of artistic representation, that is, of style. The new notion of the real was, on the contrary, anchored in different types of interpretations of the relation between image and reality. On the one hand, a fantasy about "some" real was generated by the seemingly totalitarian complicity between the illusions of art and the society of the spectacle, where the condition of images and appearances has come to govern the relations of production and thus all other social relations. Debord's *La Société du Spectacle* opens symptomatically with a quote by Feuerbach that opposes image to thing and representation to reality, complaining that "the summit of illusion has now

1. Elements of this essay have previously appeared in Ina Blom, *The Cut Through Time. A Version of the Dada/Neodada Repetition*, Acta Humaniora, University of Oslo, 1999.

become the summit of sacredness." On the other hand, an exploration of the continuity between artistic processes and process "in the real world" was generated by an awareness of the mediated nature of reality itself – i.e. an awareness of a real that is not simply given, but continually produced through signifying processes for which (certain types of) artistic creation could even seem to provide powerful conceptual models.

However, both modes of thinking could support fantasies about an art that would be somehow vested in the "concrete," an art that would gain in relevance or radically sharpen its affective modalities by an appeal to various vernacular or "non-artistic" languages or by implicating itself in "actual" social scenarios. The phenomenological turn to the concrete was, so to speak, literalized as an aesthetic imperative that applied to the work of art itself – given that this work was now primarily understood as a relational and situational structure and not as an aesthetic "object."

Obviously, the term "fantasy" would be a product of hindsight. At the time of high concretism it could not have seemed less relevant. Art was not illusion, not fantasy, not escapism, not exoticism. Concretist art was simply "of this world," in the sense that it opened itself to the phenomena of one's most immediate surroundings, without prejudice, framing or filtering. It paid attention to any material scratches, marks or recordings made by the real on itself, as evidenced for instance by the technological processes of phonography and photography. However, a closer look at certain developments in the late 1950s and early 1960s – arguably the years when the notion of the concrete developed its most single-minded and literalist edge – gives us, perhaps, an image of a reality that is already fissured by doubts and ambivalence. It was a doubt that could (and can today) only be felt indirectly and in quick glimpses, for it was soon enough buried under the overly persuasive formal language of minimalism, which did a lot to turn the appeal of the concrete from strategy of rupture to artistic doxa.

From this perspective it is interesting to note how this instance of ambivalence interrupted the concretist scenario at the precise moment when its appeal to the real was at its most optimistic and self-assured. At the moment when "everyday life" and "material reality" were posited as the key concepts for a new art practice, the meaning of these terms was also questioned in a quite radical way. In the late 1950s and early 1960s, the most influential advocate of the new appeal to the real was notably the composer John Cage, who posited the radical ideal that any sound – or indeed any phenomenon of the world – could be understood as music or as art. He was, in other words, the most explicit propagandist for the notion that art should open itself up to the particularities of the concrete world of phenomena. But Cage's world – his radically situational and contextual reality – does in fact promote a very particular worldview. This is a view of reality which emphasizes the play of chance, while suppressing the instance of causality or contiguity – as if in complicity with Maurice Merleau-Ponty's contention that we must "recognize the indeterminate as a positive phenomenon."[2] To Cage, reality is indeterminate and indeterminacy is reality. Reality is an infinitely heterogeneous sphere of chance occurrences, a place of becoming where (as Cage put it, borrowing the words of Marshall McLuhan) "information brushes against information." If art was to align itself with this reality, it would have to obey certain basic rules. The means by which one could get access to the real world was, first of all, through the *methods of chance*. Chance used as a *method* would guarantee that the work of art would be like reality itself in its manner of operating. The work based on chance methods would then be just another piece of reality. But to access the chance play of reality, all obvious instances of cause and determinacy would have to be neglected. This was Cage's front against psychologism and surrealism: The ego and its desires is notably one significant instance which brings up questions of a radical contiguity or cause that would be at odds with his essentially *detached* perspective on the chance play of the world.[3]

From this point onwards it is also possible to see the potentially ideological nature of Cage's reality. It can become ideological precisely to the extent that it may produce "reality itself" – that is, a comprehensive and all-explanatory view of the world or what Cage calls "nature." The potentially ideological aspect of his artistic methods resides in their ability to persuade us that reality *is* essentially an indeterminate and heterogeneous sphere of infinite changes. The *methods* of chance were, in other words, produced as true and relevant to the extent that they managed to express how reality *produced itself as a totality.* The persuasiveness of Cage – his general influence on the art of the 1960s – is a well-known phenomenon. Yet what is interesting is the more particular question of *how* his followers interact with his particular notion of a chance-based reality – i.e., in what way this reality becomes a

2. Maurice Merleau-Ponty, *The Phenomenology of Perception,* Routledge, London, 1992, p. 6.

3. The 1961 publication of *Silence,* Cage's collected texts, made his aesthetics widely available as a "package" independent of the experience of his actual musical works.

world for them. For in the work of some of the artists who engaged seriously (and even passionately) with Cage's project, this opening up to reality was in fact increasingly dramatized as a *closure* – i.e., *as* a totality with particular limitations and obligations.

Here I am mainly referring to a type of work developed around 1960-61 by a handful of artists who would a few years later be associated with the Fluxus movement. Evolving out of a combination of post-Cagean aesthetics, concrete poetry and New Realism, Fluxus is typically understood as the ultimate example of the irruption of the real in the sphere of art (the famous "merging of art and life").[4] Yet it is also with this group of artists that Cage's concrete "reality" is definitely displaced. This does not amount to something as straightforward as a critique of Cage. Rather, Cage's indeterminate reality is displaced as these artists work through their own fascination with this reality, as well as the obligations it places on them. For obvious reasons, Cage's reality could not simply be taken on by a younger generation of artists as a "style" or a "working strategy." Its appeal was more far-reaching than that: it had certain precise ramifications for the constitution of artistic identity. For the potentially ideological meaning of Cage's reality-system would not simply be a result of Cage's own arguments, his own construction of an aesthetic system vested in the concrete. An ideological meaning could only be constituted retroactively – that is, when all the different elements which developed in his work over a long period of time were supplemented by a master signifier *(indeterminacy)* which gave this particular ideological field its illusion of totality and consistency.[5]

The point is that the totality of this reality-system as such only appears the moment a younger generation of artists invests it with desire – that is, the moment they identify with "indeterminate reality" as something approaching "the only true perspective for an avant-garde artist today." But at this point Cage's reality no longer appears in terms of his own insistently non-affective view on the infinite play of the world's heterogeneous objects. Reality – Cage's reality – has, like all realities, become a bind, and Cage's studied lack of affect is then also displaced by the determinacy of desire. Chance is, simply, framed by cause, and indeterminacy appears only in terms of a sublime fascination for the infinite continuities of the reality-surface. Cage's concrete reality has in fact returned as a fantasy.

4. Cage's teaching at the New School of Social Research in New York in 1958-59, and his summer course in Darmstadt were vital to the development of many of these artists.

5. As pointed out by Slavoj Žižek in *The Sublime Object of Ideology*, Verso Books, London, 1989, pp. 95-114.

II

The new type of work developed by this group of artists pays allegiance to the concept of chance, while, all the same, exploring a radical instance of cause or determinacy. To pay allegiance to the concept of chance is to emphasize production at the expense of reproduction, or to search out the new rather than the known:

Often I hear somebody say that the most important thing about a work of art is not that it be new but that it be good. But if we define good as what we like, which is the only definition of good I find useful when discussing art, and then say that we are interested in what is good, it seems to me that we will always be interested in the same things (that is, the same things that we already like).

I am not interested in good; I am interested in new – even if this includes the possibility of its being evil.[6]

Here, composer La Monte Young comments on his groundbreaking *Composition 1960* series, in which he introduced sustained sounds of interminable lengths, investing sound with a static, thing-like quality. This was one of the works that became the model for a type of work which Young and his colleagues named Events – a reference to the way in which indeterminacy produces the *new.* Yet the Event-works actually seem more focussed on the static determinacy of singular phenomena than the floating and collage-like multiplicity of Cage's compositions. The dancer Ann Halprin, who collaborated with Young around 1960, joined him in his quest for the event of the new: yet her choice of words deliberately or unconsciously undercuts the absolute singularity of this new, and invests it with a dimension of repetition. Halprin calls out for a work of "risk, exposure, and intensity," a work in which "*everything is experienced as if for the first time.*"[7] Here, her words somehow echo those of Jacques Lacan, who writes about the accident or the meaningless event that occurs *as if* by chance: the point is that the notion of chance that we ascribe to such events is but a shield for what cannot be faced in the awake state of ordinary reality. What the notion of chance covers up for us, what we cannot face, is the presence of a radical determinacy or a *cause*. And for Lacan, cause is essentially understood in terms of the beating or pulsating realm of the drives.[8] Young's search for the new may well evoke the experi-

6. La Monte Young, *Lecture 1960*, first delivered to a class in contemporary music at the Ann Halprin Dancer's workshop, Kentfield, California, 1960. Printed in *Tulane Drama Review* (*TDR*) 10, 1965.

7. Halprin, quoted in Udo Kultermann, *Leben und Kunst*, Tübingen, 1970, p. 79.

8. Jacques Lacan, *The Four Fundamental Concepts of Psychoanalysis*, W.W. Norton & Company, London, 1994, pp. 69 and 76.

ence of the "first time" as it appears to us in the awake perspective on chance events, *but only as a perspective which misses the endless repetition that is the realm of cause or desire.* At the crux of an avant-garde tradition obligated both by the concept of the everyday and the concept of chance operations, Young evokes the shock of the new only through the presence of a kind of radical *cause* or determinacy which must always remain hidden to the everyday perspective on "reality." The *as if* which is appended to both "by chance" and "for the first time" then marks the *gap* between two "realities:" the everyday reality in which any chance occurrence may take place, and the hard kernel of causality which is irreducible to such explanations, and which (in Lacanian terms) is called the real of desire.

The dramatic impact of this new perspective on the cause/chance dialectic is hardly to be missed in the early developments of Young's work. One of the first written responses to Young's statement on new-ness (submitted in a Sept. 1960 letter to Young by the artist Robert Morris) seems to take up precisely the interconnected themes of cause and repetition. In the form of an elliptic note, Morris first defines the new as an *occurring present.* But in the graphic set-up of this note, *the new* and the *occurring present* are linked by the equal sign paired with the word "must" in parenthesis: the equation does, in other words, align the actuality or the presence of the new with the presence of cause, or the inevitable "must." Right below this definition, Morris introduces the question of repetition: *"On what level is one thing not divided from another and on what level is it (make 2nd thing exactly same as 1st) without relationship to the 1st?"*[9] Because it is impossible and nameless, the encounter with cause always takes place as if for the first time: its reality, however, is that of an impenetrable *kernel or continuity* where, Morris suspects, things cannot be divided from one another.[10]

Young's response to Morris was a formulation which would become tremendously influential – and maybe even decisive – for the whole direction and meaning of the event in Fluxus. A few months after Morris' letter, Young wrote his *Composition 1960 #10 (To Bob Morris)* – which simply contained the instruction *"Draw a straight line and follow it."* No piece before it had so starkly drawn up the dumb, deaf and determinate realm of cause or the *drive* of desire: it is simply a line that must be followed forever, no matter what. The significance of this piece is demonstrated by the fact that many of the

9. Morris, letter to La Monte Young, September 7, 1960.

10. According to N. Katherine Hayles, Cage's emphasis on chance does not necessarily mean an abandonment of cause, but may be seen as the intersection between independent causal chains, each of which is deterministic on its own. The intersections, however, create unthinkable complexity and unpredictability. (N. Katherine Hayles, "Chance Operations: Cagean Paradox and Contemporary Science," in Marjorie Perloff and Charles Junkerman (eds.), *John Cage. Composed in America,* University of Chicago Press, Chicago, 1994). Here Hayles more or less reduplicates that aspect of Cage's naturalism which refuses to take questions of signification into account, other than through the general recognition that in a complex world the creation of any meaning is not only possible, but a positive precondition for artistic creation. In contrast to this view stands Lacan's description of cause as an "embarrassment" for the whole philosophical tradition, something that cannot be rationalized or given meaning, since cause is identified with the inexplicable real of desire, the presence of which we necessarily fail to recognize. And this is why cause must be distinguished from that which is determinate (or simply processual) in a chain: a certain *gap* always remains in the function of cause.

Fluxus-related artists made works that appear to be versions of it, adapted to different areas of reality. Nam June Paik's 1962 *Zen for head* is a point in case: with his hair dipped in paint, the performer traces a straight line with his head (his body necessarily following). Paik has acknowledged the influence of Young's 1960 compositions, which he received in Cologne that same year: "They were such a fresh surprise I could not sleep."[11] Other prominent examples were Arthur Köpcke's all-purpose concept *Continue*, which was materialized in terms of various kinds of obligations to follow a line or stick to a process, or George Brecht's *Direction* which simply shows a pointing hand indicating a direction to be followed.[12] Dick Higgins created a series of propositions called *Danger Music*, exploring the consequence of cause as if in response to Young's notion of the potential "evil" of the new. In more general terms, this focus on causality typifies the obligation to follow a process through all its consequences – a prominent feature of much performance art. In this context, however, it is enough to note that La Monte Young's static and obstinate focus on the singular event *reveals* the repetition of cause as the always missed dimension of the "first time" of the new.

In this context, something rather dramatic then seems to happen to the objects of the concrete world: they cease to be simply effects within the infinite chance play of the world that Cage chooses to call *silence*. Instead of participating in this (rather noisy) "silence," they evoke a fundamental *muteness:* they become hard, mystical, impenetrable, and irrevocably singular. George Brecht's 1960 assemblage called *Medicine Cabinet* is a case in point. It is a typical well-worn medicine cabinet with a glass door and two shelves. Because of its modest size, there might be some formal resemblance to Joseph Cornell's glass fronted boxes, yet the matter-of-fact constellation of diverse, banal objects within it (a tea-strainer, a child's building block, a golf ball, a seed pack, a postcard, a small cut-glass bottle, a stone egg, a bell, a cup, several boxes, etc.) does not, in itself, appear enigmatic. The coming-together of these objects is not interesting, dreamlike, paradoxical, or confrontational. Nor is it an obvious framing of a piece of ready-made household reality, as in many of the works of the New Realists. If anything, the objects of the constellation vaguely reference the kind of *extras* that gather up in certain cupboards and drawers because they do not fit in anywhere else. In this sense they could be seen as exceptions, particular cases: *singular objects*. And because of their obstinate singularity, the con-

11. Interview with Nam June Paik, New York, October 1988.

12. *Direction*, in George Brecht, *Water Yam*, New York, 1964.

stellation of these objects seems to hint at disorder or to highlight the limits of order itself – despite the fact that the assemblage does not in any way appear dramatically messy. The enigmatic character of Brecht's assemblage does not lie in a presentation of a secret, nor in an overt referencing of a piece of reality, but in its *"disappearing" totality* – that is, the mute and banal singularity of something which *refuses to stand out*. This is both their point of fascination, and the mechanism through which they complicate any point of view on reality.

In the work of La Monte Young it might seem that the hidden realm of cause is evoked not by moving further away from everyday reality but by moving closer to it – too close, in fact. Like Cage, Young insists that each sound is a "being," but rather than approaching this "being" in terms of its floating positioning within the heterogeneous totality of sounds, Young closes in on the material reality of the single sound itself. Here, the paradigmatic work was the *Composition 1960 # 7*, which posits the reality of a fifth "to be held for a long time." But ultimately this controlled closing in on sound tends to highlight less the physical or "real" properties of sound than the terms of the subjective immersion in the sound environment – what Young called "getting inside the sound itself:" *"I began to feel the parts and motions of the sound more, and I began to see how each sound was its own world and that this world was only similar to our world in that we experienced it through our own bodies, that is, in our own terms."*[13]

Two important developments result from this approach. The one is a particular and elusive spatial experience where the single sound folds itself out as an infinitely variable surface due to the positioning and moving about of the listening subject. This possibility is brought forth through Young's work with "real sound" *or just intonation*. In contrast to the equal tempered tuning system which divides an octave into twelve parts (so that a musician can play in any key and move freely from one key to another), just intonation approaches the sound in terms of its own precise frequency ratio, and not in terms of its relation to other sounds within an arbitrary system. While equal tuning has a tendency to obscure the natural harmonics in each note, just intonation can at times allow an almost prismatic experience of its overtone structure.[14]

However, as Young states, the big advantage of just intonation is that it makes exact repetition possible, because such tuning involves an exact measuring of the sound: "*Since intervals from the system of rational numbers are the only intervals*

13. Young, Lecture 1960, op.cit.

14. Kyle Gann, "The Outer Edge of Consonance: Snapshots from the Evolution of La Monte Young's Tuning Installations," in William Duckworth and Richard Fleming, *Sound and Light. La Monte Young and Marian Zazeela*, Associated University Press, New Jersey, 1996, pp. 153-189.

that can be repeatedly tuned exactly, they are the only intervals that have the potential to sound exactly the same on repeated hearing. It is for this reason that the feelings produced by rational intervals within a gradually expanding threshold of complexity have the potential to be recognized and remembered, and, consequently, develop strong emotional impact."[15]

As Young explains, the emotional impact of the exactly repeated sound derives from its ability to evoke memory and recognition – that is, to establish the continuity of a pattern through which the listening subject itself is given consistency and self-presence. Yet this consistency is precarious: Because each pitch has a different wavelength, each is reinforced at different points in a room by bouncing back on itself in phase, and canceled out at other points in the same room where the bounceback is 180 degrees out of phase. Thus every point in space has its own pattern of reinforced and canceled frequencies. The more complex the pitch structure and the smaller the spaces between the pitches, the less the ear has to move to find itself confronted with a very different harmony.[16] At this point, consistency or continuity itself turns uncanny: the encounter with the physical reality of the sound is also an encounter with one's own missing out on it.

The second development is then the occurrence of a radical mechanism of repetition in the works of Young at the very moment sound is actually approached as a concrete singular being with individual physical characteristics – as represented most radically in the work *566 for Henry Flynt,* which consists of 566 repetitions of a single sound cluster. Approached as a real physical being, sound itself stages a disappearance act – a disappearance act that takes place because its physical reality is ultimately contingent on a subjectivity whose meeting with it never exactly happens. The reality of sound – which is now "factual," determinate and causal – has also become elusive, inexplicable, pulsating, and repetitious. It was these types of experiences with the chance/cause dialectic that made Dick Higgins sum up the Eventworks in terms of *boredom* – a throwback to Baudelaire, who, in *Les fleurs du mal,* describes how boredom swallows the world in the gap of a big yawn.[17] For Higgins it was a way of describing disappearance on two reciprocal levels: how the subject disappears into an all-enveloping, confusing work/world, which, for its part, lacks any kind of consistency or hold. It was perhaps the inevitable outcome of this brief attempt to move too close to the real.

15. Young, quoted by Gann, op. cit., p. 162.

16. Gann, op.cit., p. 188.

17. Dick Higgins, "Boredom and Danger," *Something Else Newsletter,* December 1968.

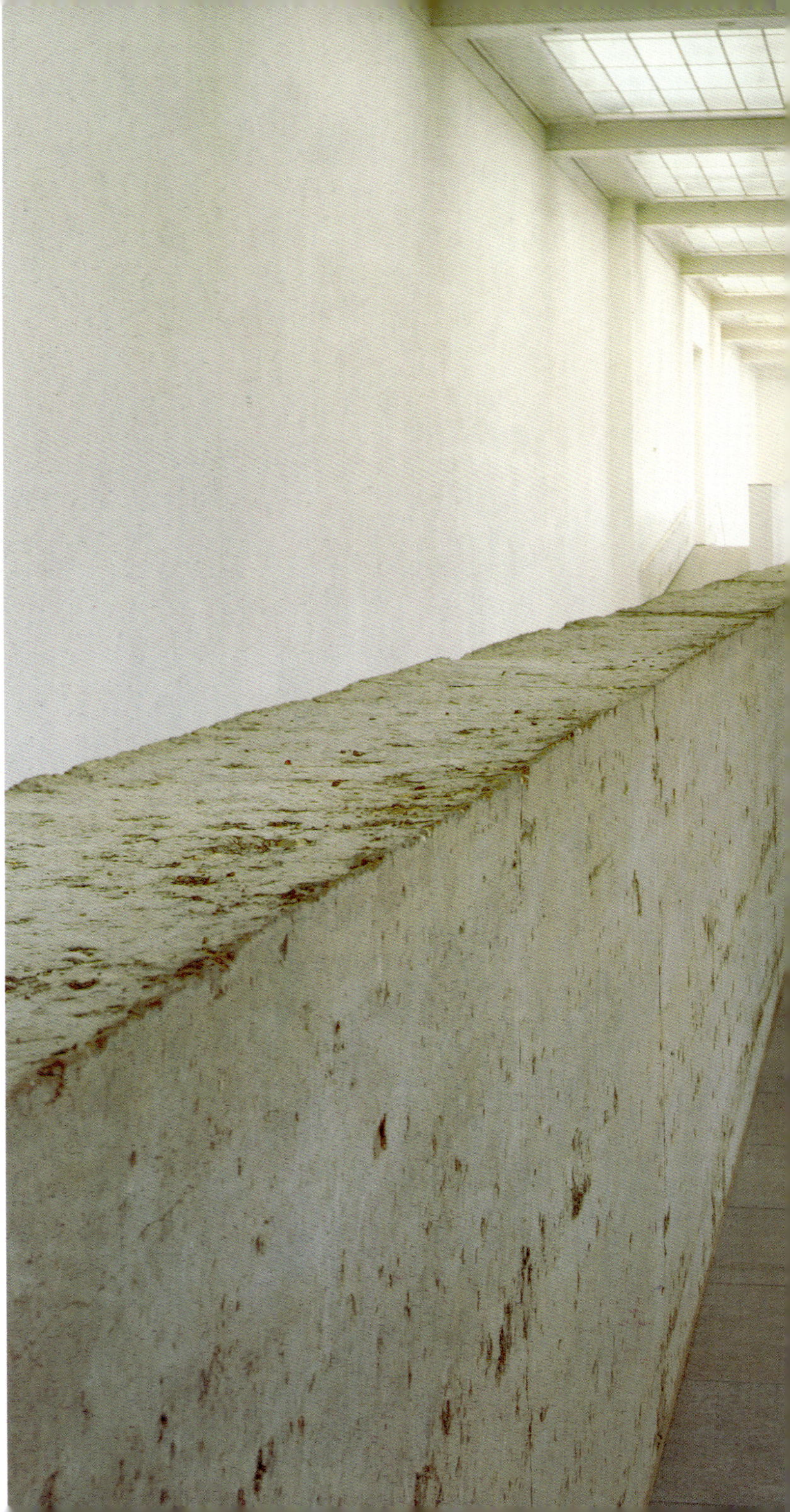

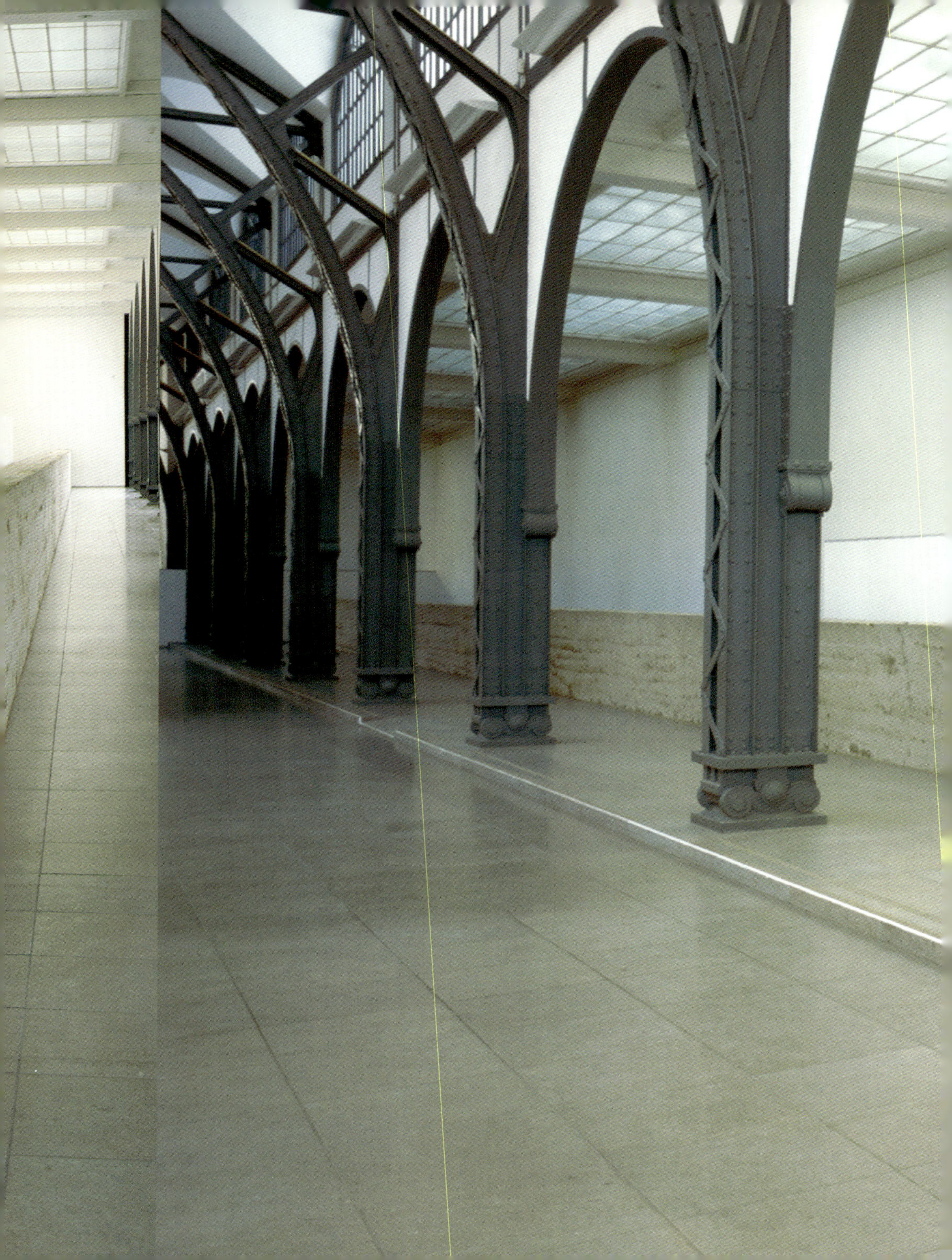

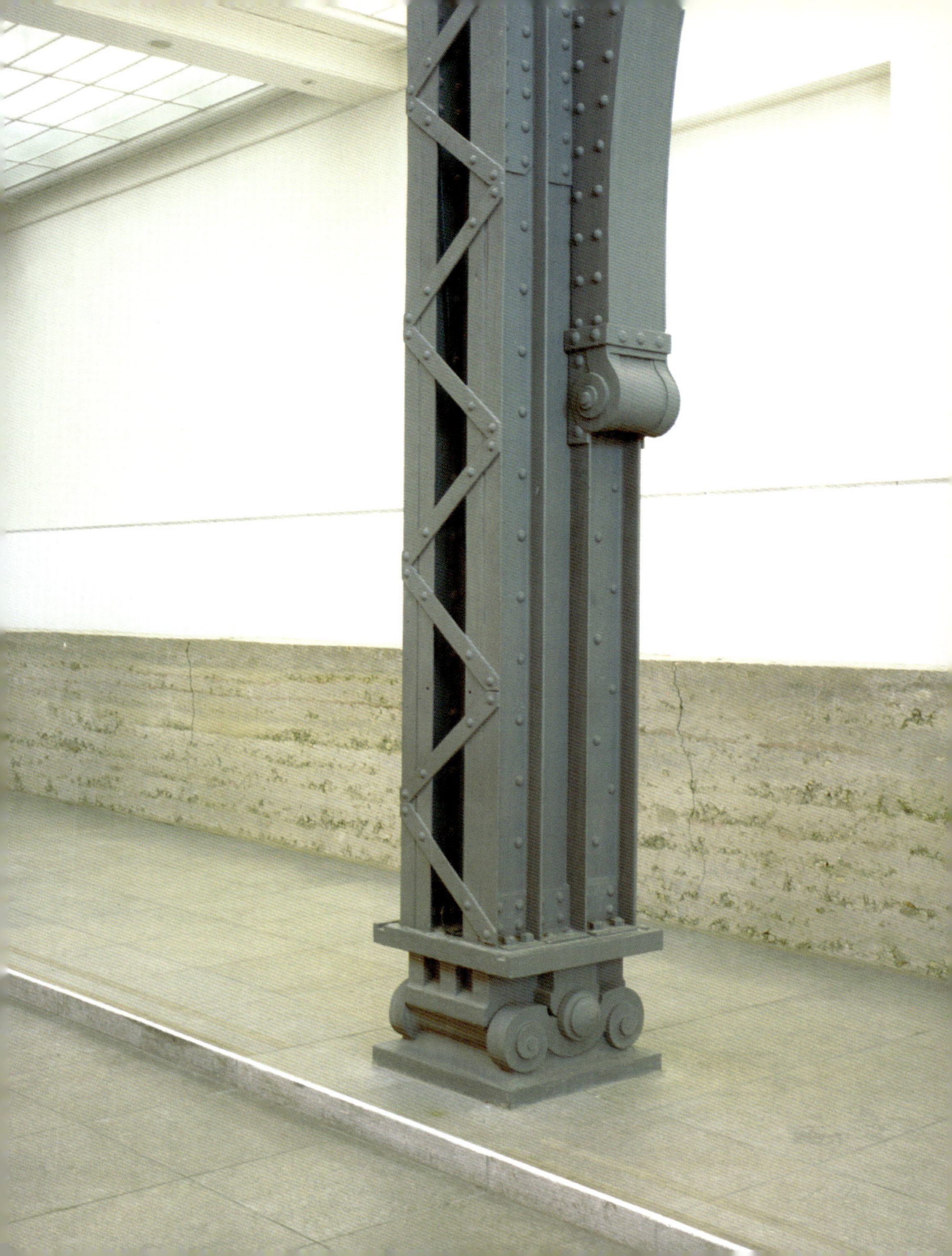

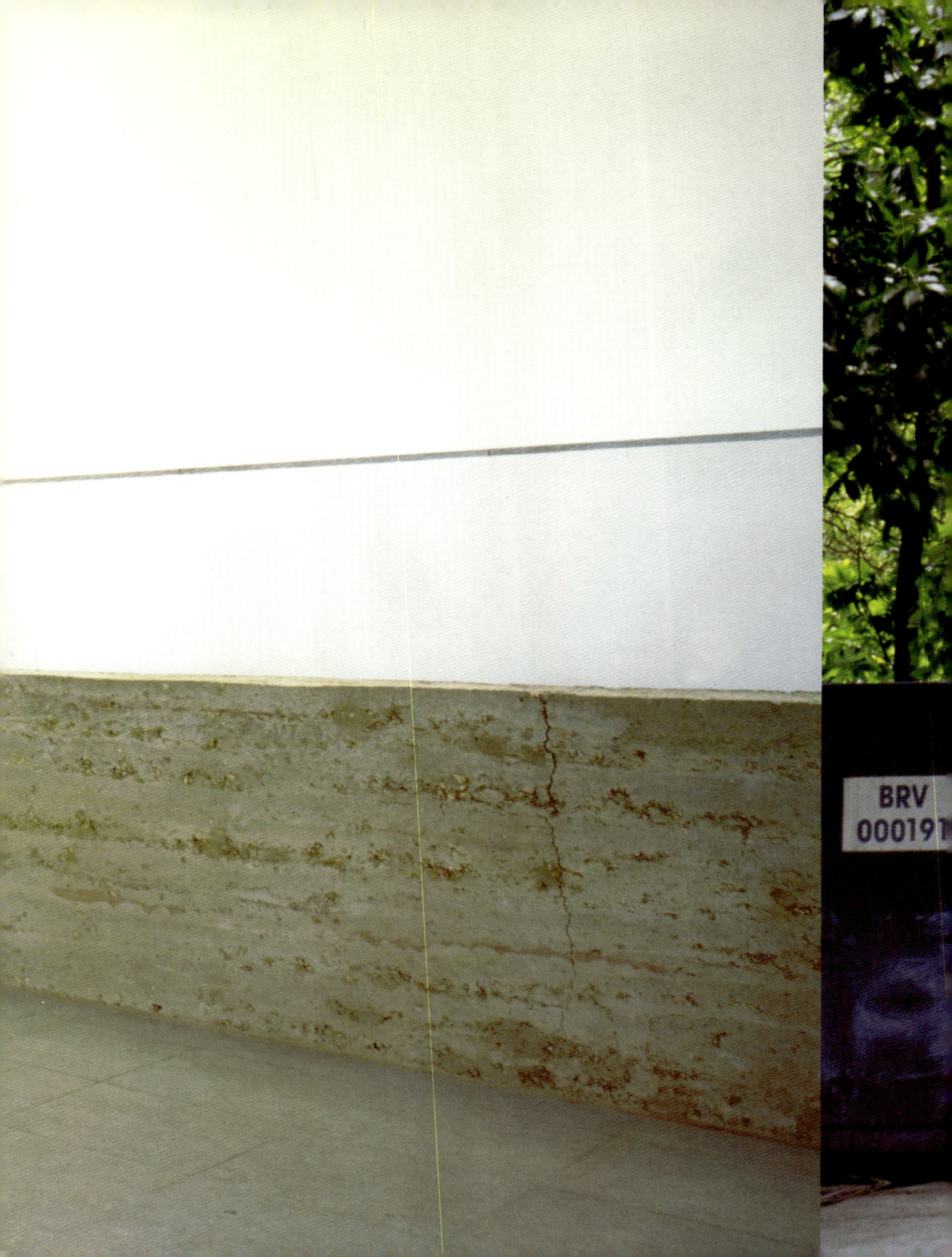
BRV
000191

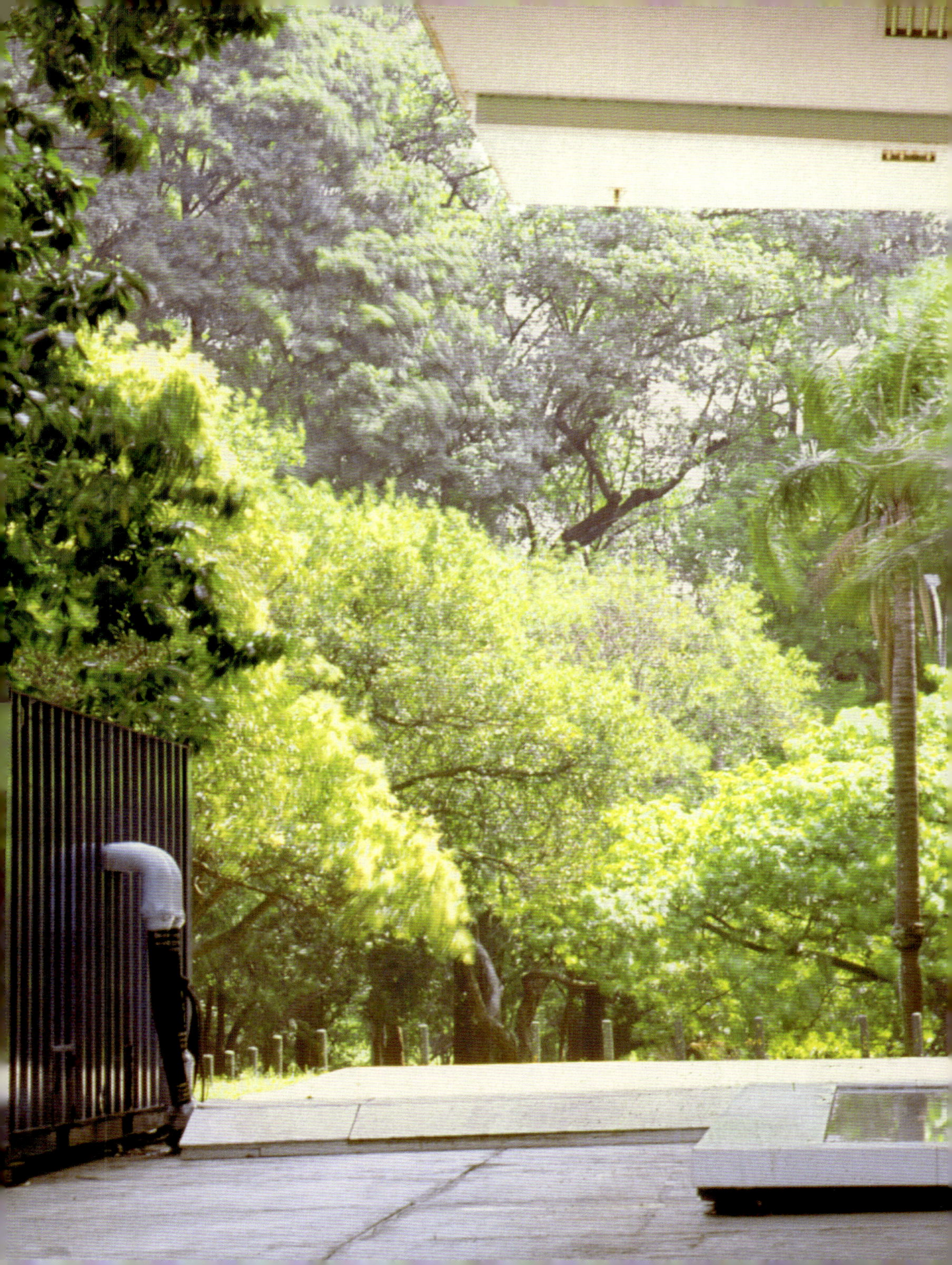

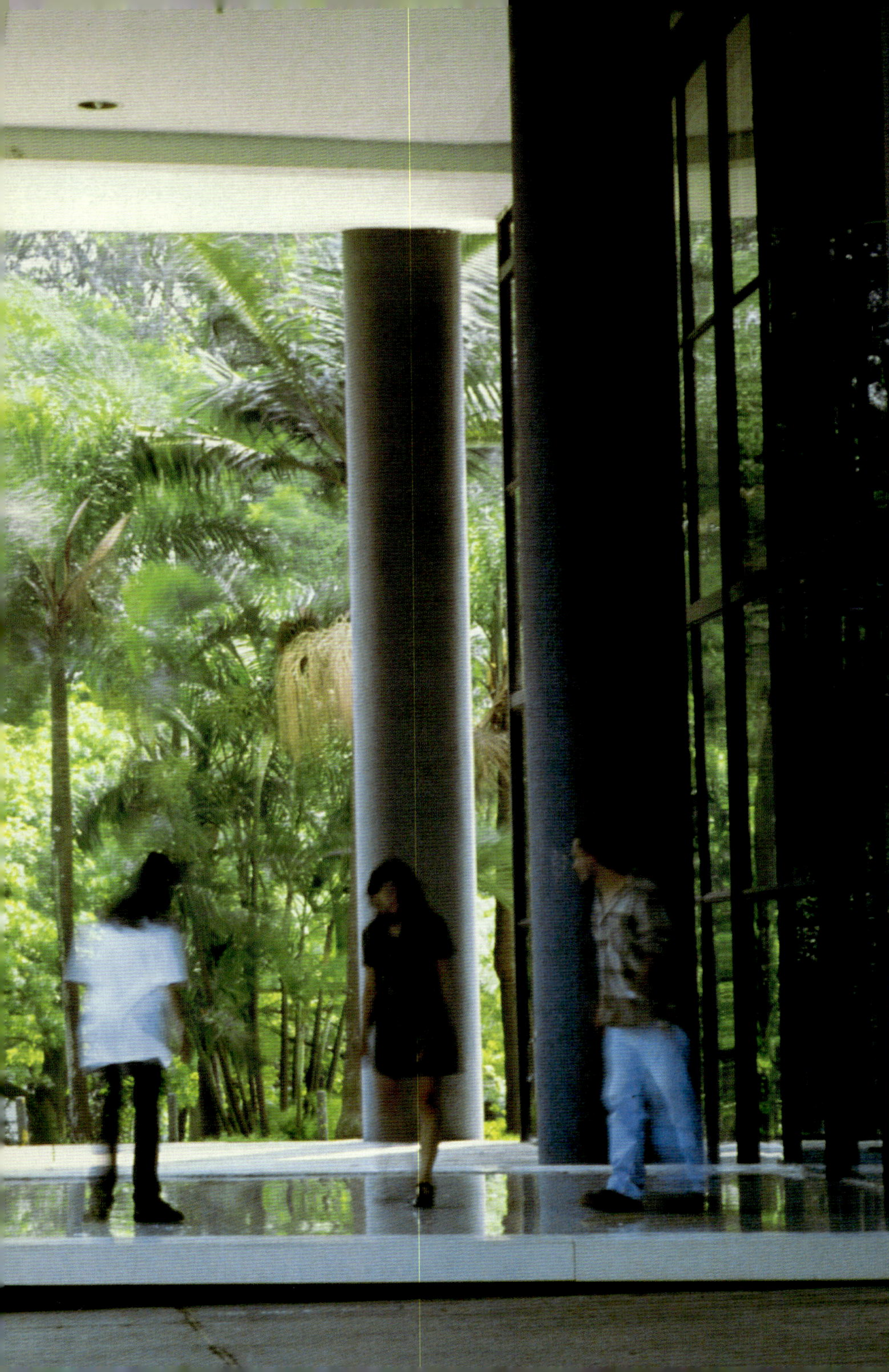
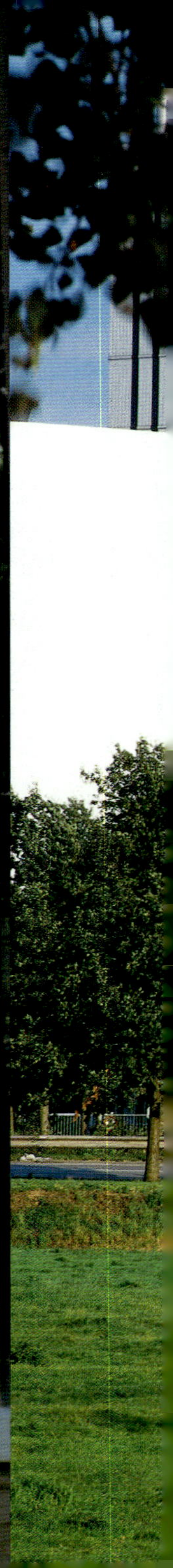

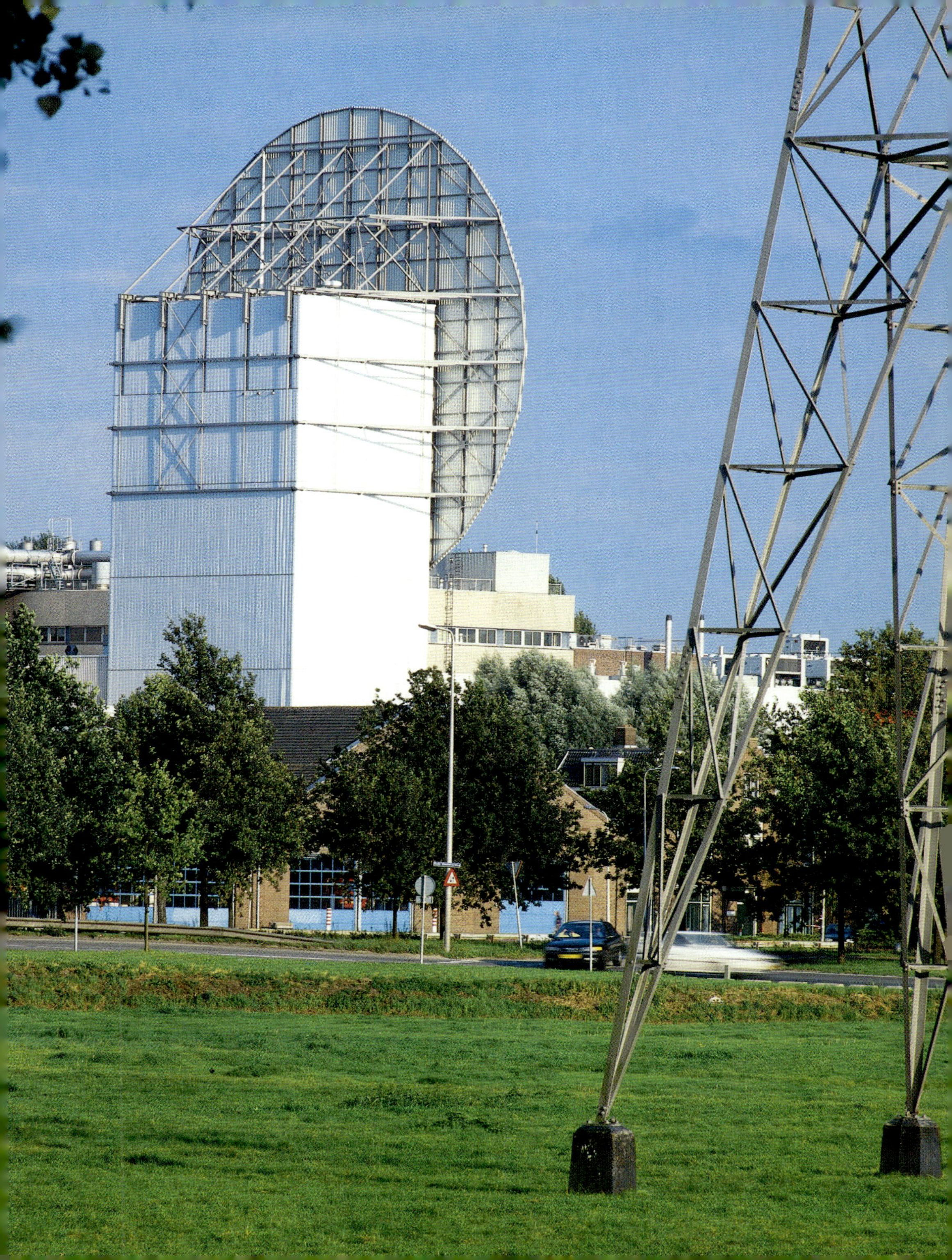

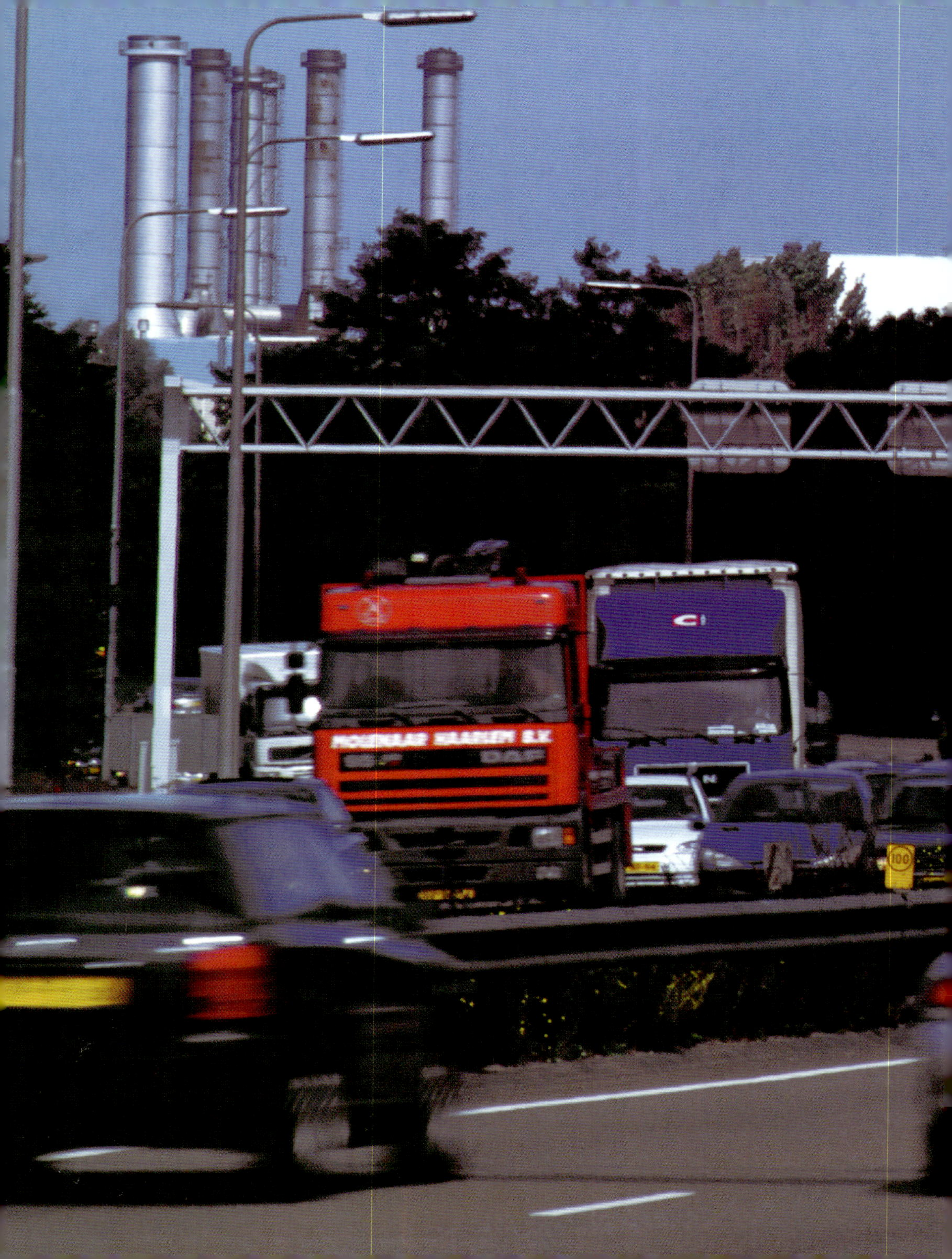
100

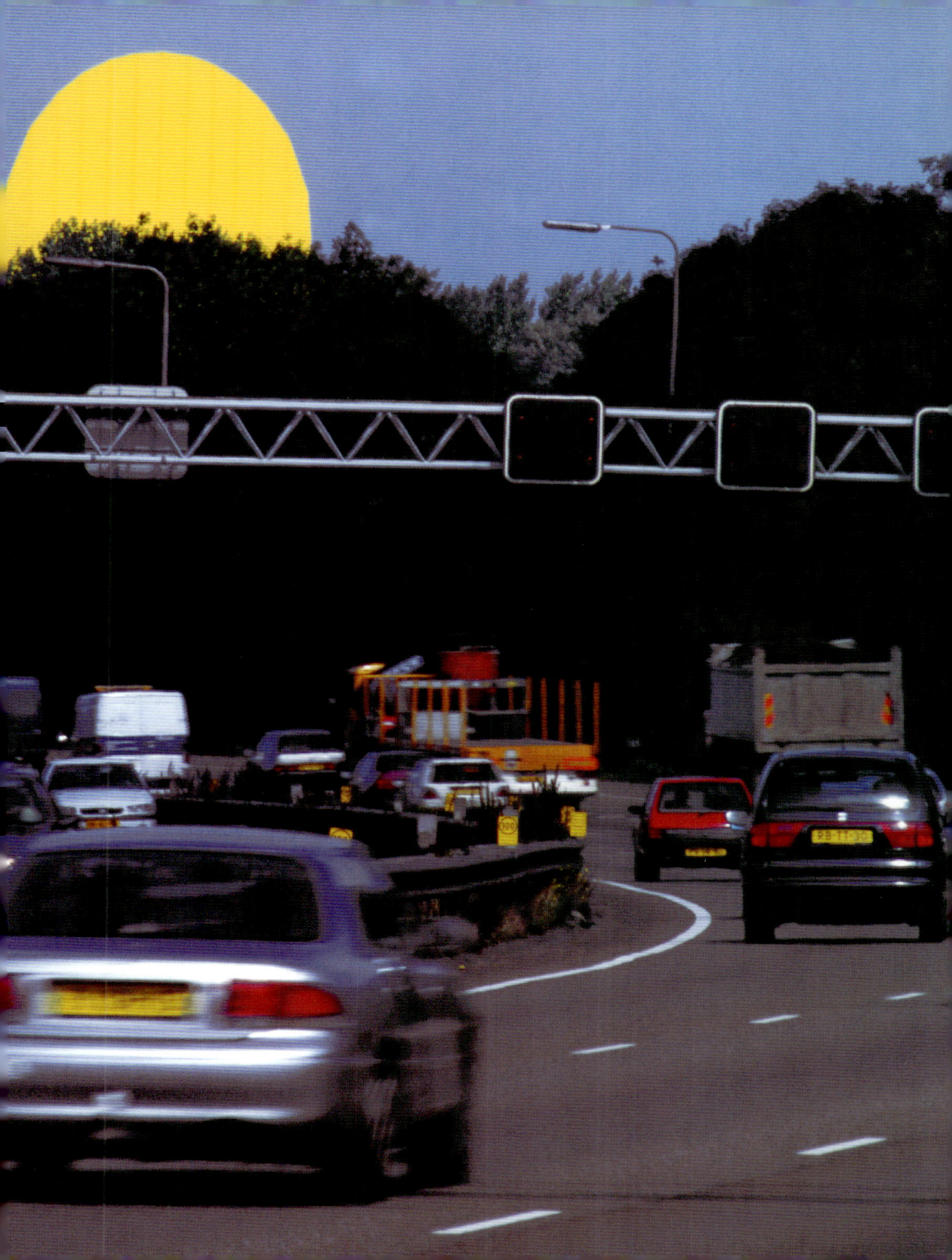

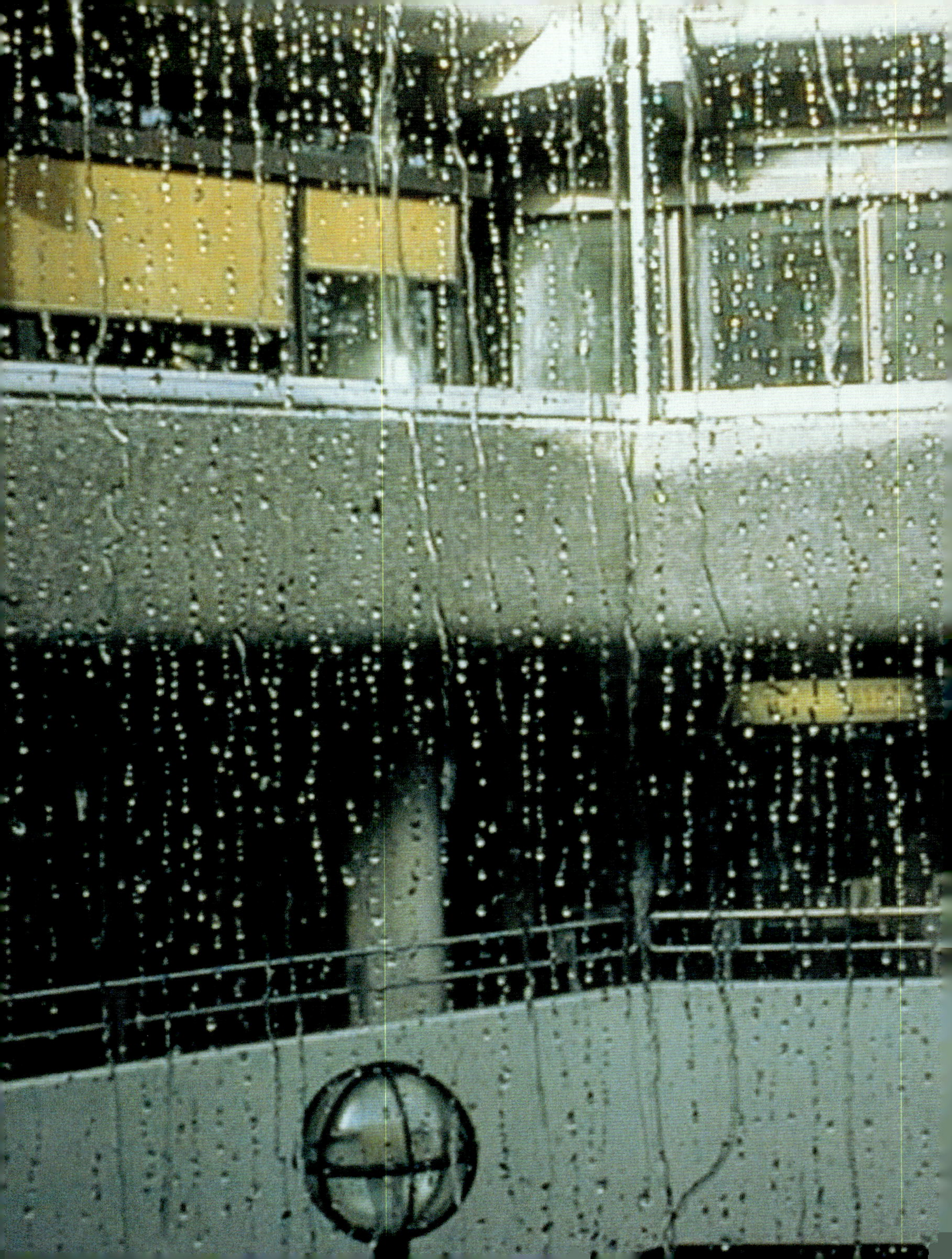

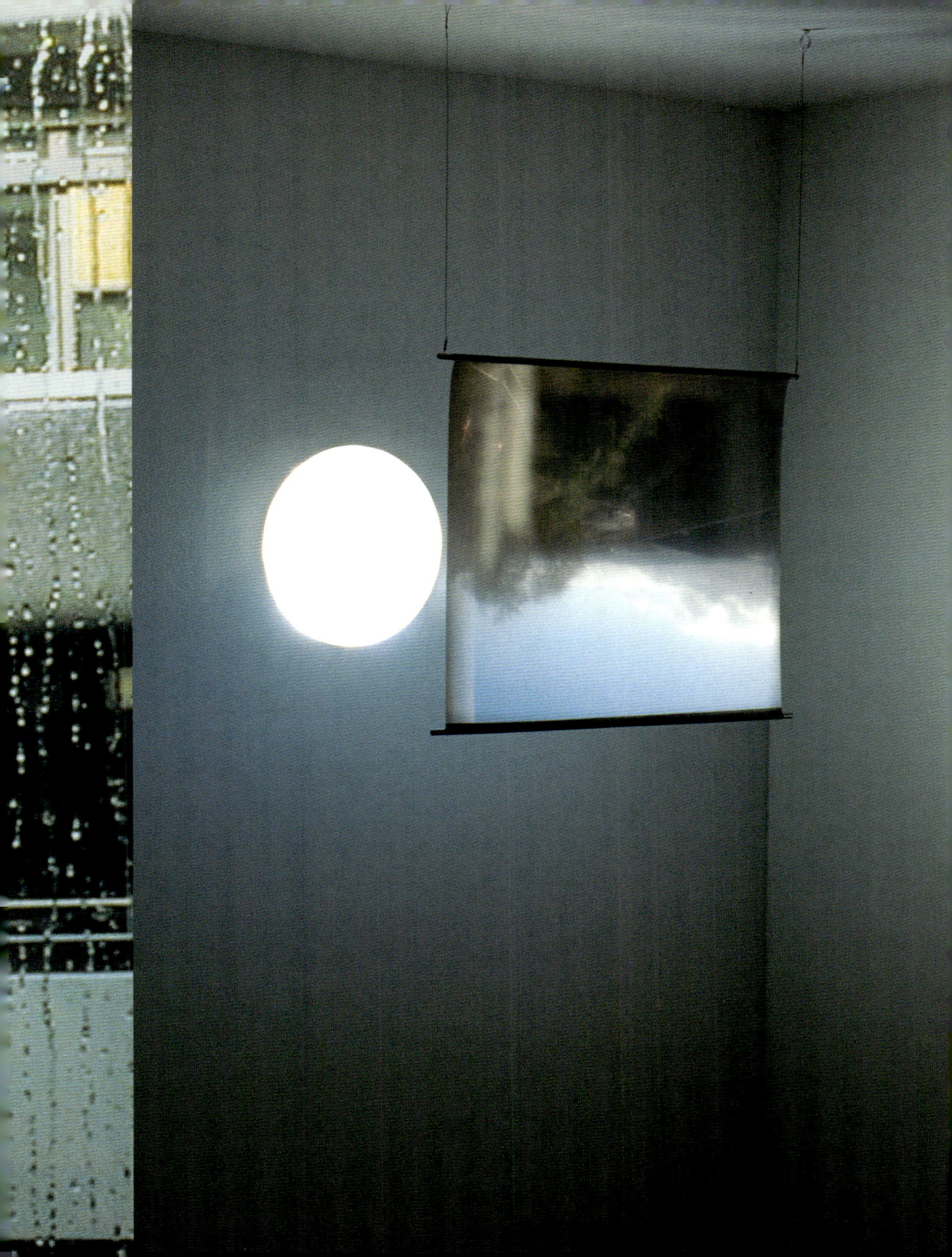

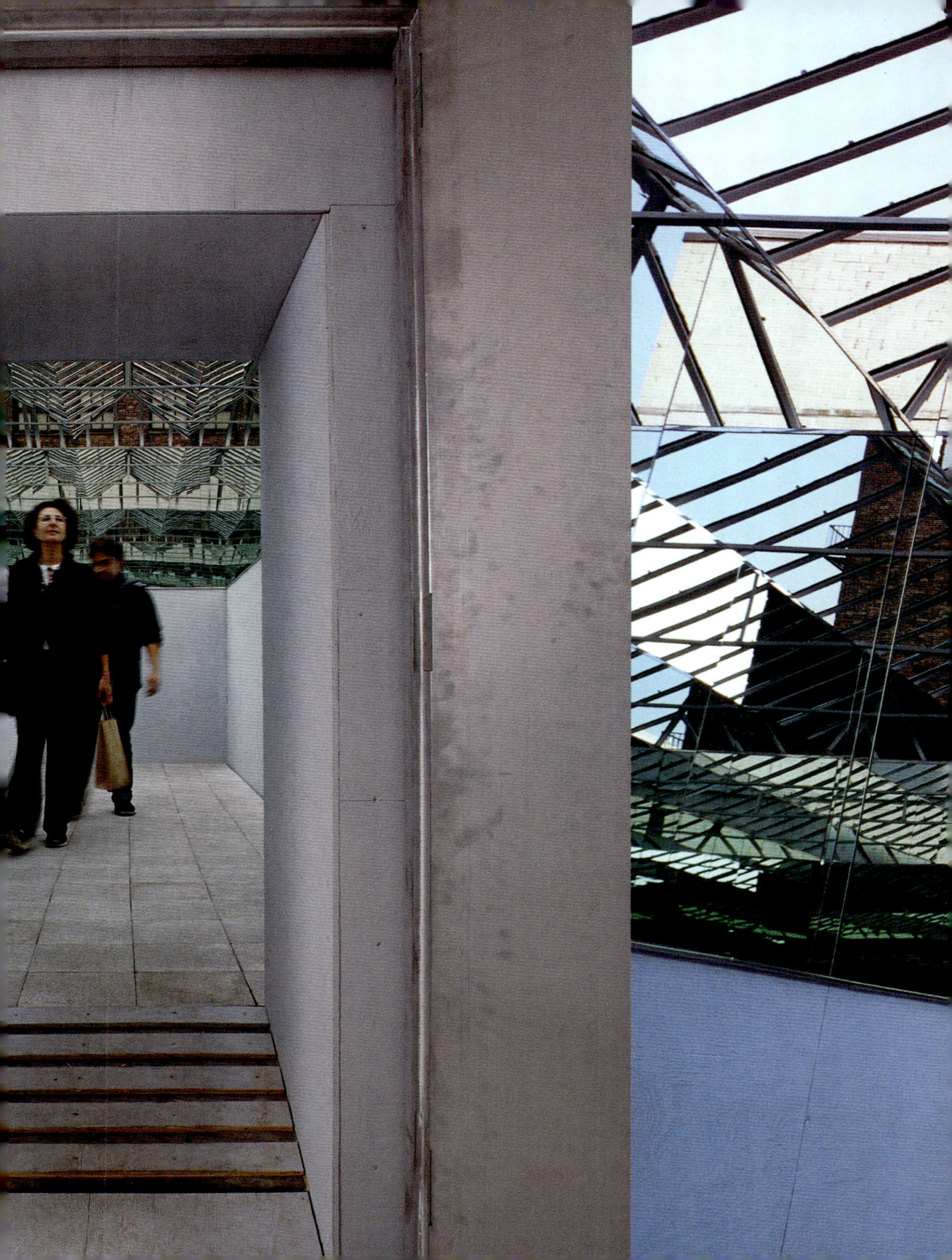

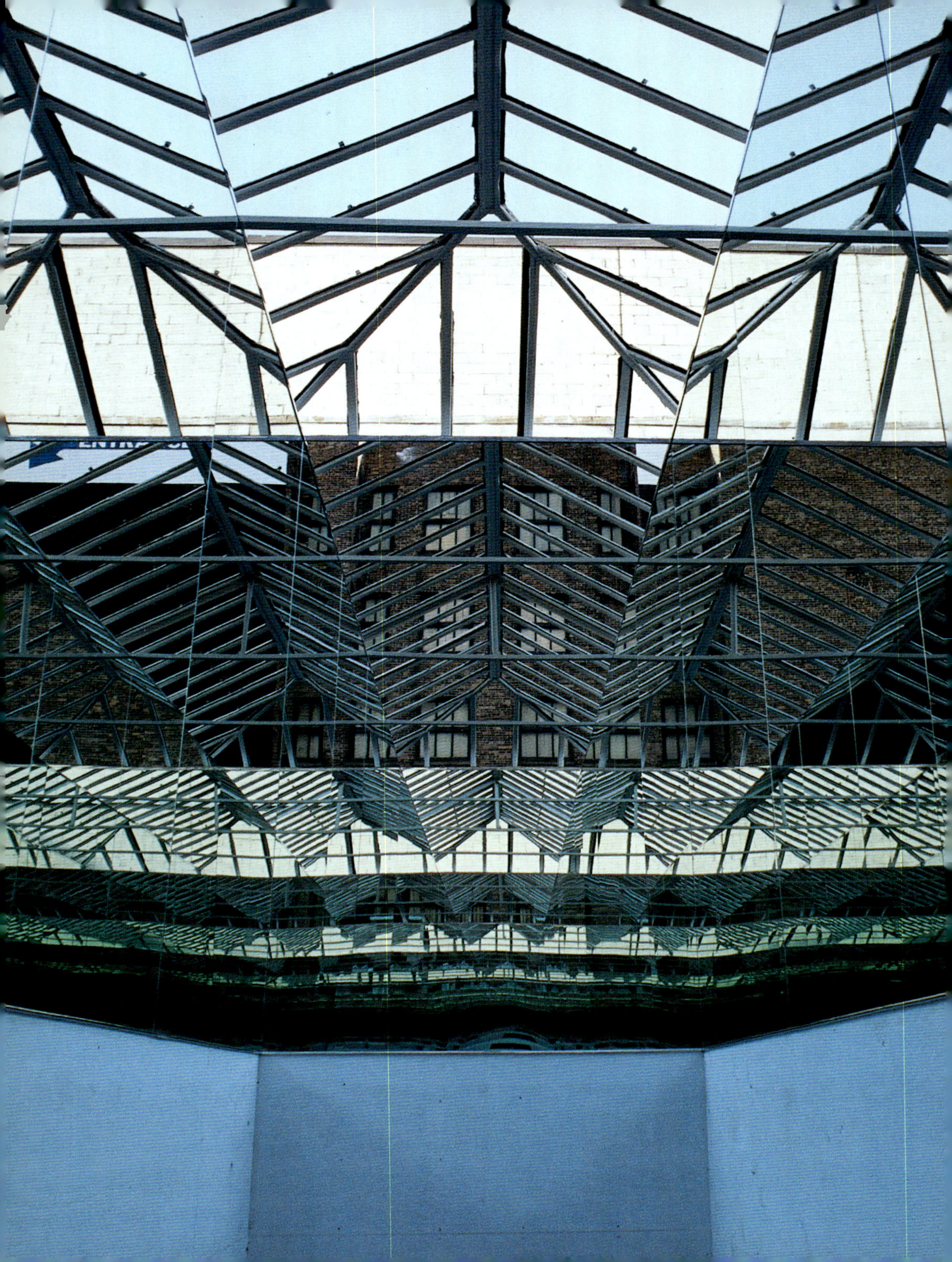

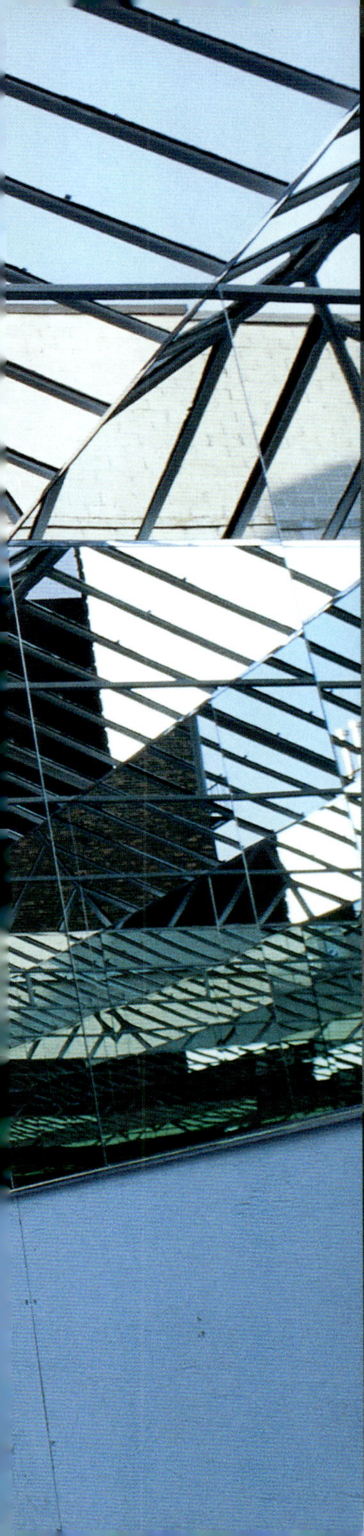
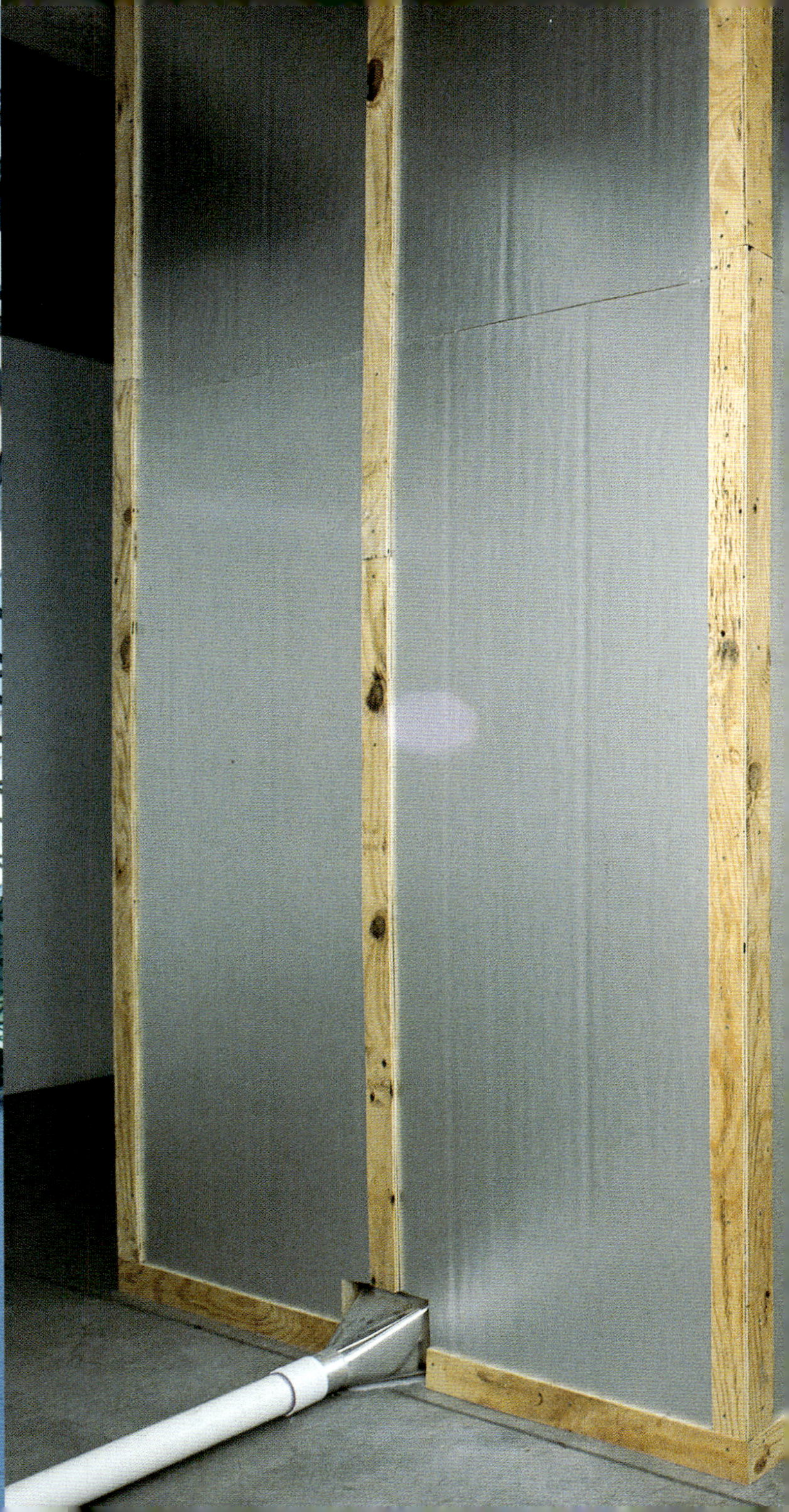

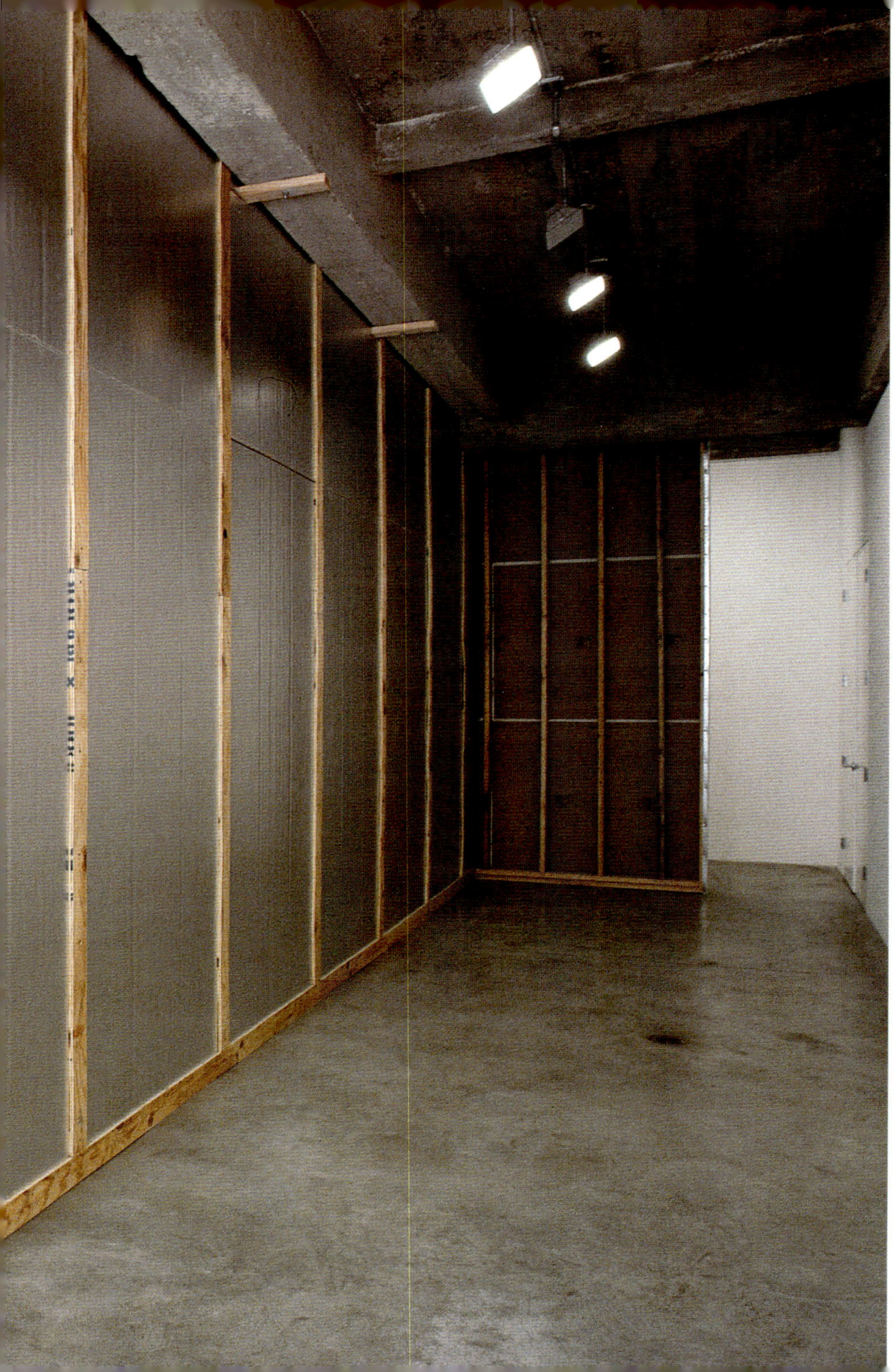

1	**Earthwall**, 2000	8000 x 120 x 40 cm; tamped earth, installation view: Hamburger Bahnhof, Berlin, Germany
2	**Earthwall**, 2000	8000 x 120 x 40 cm; tamped earth; installation view: Hamburger Bahnhof, Berlin, Germany
3	**The very large ice-floor**, 1998	Size varies with installation; water, ice-machine, basin; installation view: Sao Paolo Biennale, Sao Paolo, Brazil
4	**Double sunset**, 1998	ø 38 m; giant yellow metal sun, erected on a tower block; installation view: Utrecht, The Netherlands
5	**Double sunset**, 1998	ø 38 m; giant yellow metal sun, erected on a tower block; installation view: Utrecht, The Netherlands
6	**Regenfenster**, 1999	Size varies with installation; water, hose, glass; installation view: Frankfurter Kunstverein, Frankfurt/M., Germany
7	**Camera obscura**, 1999	Size varies with installation; lens on steel tripod, black foil; installation view: Frankfurter Kunstverein, Frankfurt/M., Germany
8	**Your now is my surroundings**, 2000	Size varies with installation; mirrors, air, metal frame; installation view: Tanya Bonakdar Gallery, New York, USA
9	**Your now is my surroundings**, 2000	Size varies with installation; mirrors, air, metal frame; installation view: Tanya Bonakdar Gallery, New York, USA
10	**Your now is my surroundings**, 2000	Size varies with installation; mirrors, air, metal frame; installation view: Tanya Bonakdar Gallery, New York, USA
11	**Your now is my surroundings**, 2000	Size varies with installation; mirrors, air, metal frame; installation view: Tanya Bonakdar Gallery, New York, USA

Jonathan Crary

Visionary Abstractions

… the nineteenth century, still the most obscure of all the centuries of the modern age up to now.

Martin Heidegger

Allergic to any relapse into magic, art is part and parcel of the disenchantment of the world, to use Max Weber's term. It is inextricably intertwined with rationalization. What means and productive methods art has at its disposal are all derived from this nexus.

Theodor Adorno

The collapse of the camera obscura as a model for the condition of an observer was part of a process of modernization, even as the camera itself had been an element of an earlier modernity, helping to define a "free," private, and individualized subject in the seventeenth century. By the early 1800s, however, the rigidity of the camera obscura, its linear optical system, its fixed positions, its identification of perception and object, were all too inflexible and immobile for a rapidly changing set of cultural and political requirements. Obviously artists in the seventeenth and eighteenth centuries had made countless attempts to operate outside the constraints of the camera obscura and other techniques for the rationalization of vision, but always within a highly delimited terrain of experimentation. It is only in the early nineteenth century that the juridical model of the camera loses its preeminent authority. Vision is no longer subordinated to an exterior image of the true or the right. The eye is no longer what predicates a "real world."

The work of Goethe, Schopenhauer, Ruskin, Turner and many others are all indications that by 1840 the process of perception itself had become, in various ways, a primary object of vision. For it was this very process that the functioning of the camera obscura kept invisible. Nowhere else is the breakdown of the perceptual model of the camera obscura more decisively evident than in the late work of Turner. Seemingly out of nowhere, his painting of the late 1830s and 1840s signals the irrevocable loss of a fixed source of light, the dissolution of a cone of light rays, and the collapse of the distance separating an observer from the site of optical experience. Instead of the immediate and unitary apprehension of an image, our experience of a Turner painting is lodged amidst an inescapable temporality. Hence Lawrence Gowing's account of Turner's concern with "the indefinite transmission and dispersal of light by an infinite series of reflections from an endless variety of surfaces and materials, each contributing its own colour that mingles with every other, penetrating ultimately to every recess, reflected everywhere."[1] The sfumato of Leonardo, which had generated during the previous three centuries a counter-practice to the dominance of geometrical optics, is suddenly and overwhelmingly triumphant in Turner. But the substantiality he gives to the void between objects and his challenge to the integrity and identity of forms now coincides with a new physics: the science of fields and thermodynamics.[2]

The new status of the observer signaled by Turner is perhaps best discussed in terms of his celebrated relationship to the sun.[3] Just as the sun described by classical mechanics was displaced by new notions of heat, time, death, and entropy, so the sun presupposed by the camera obscura (that is, a sun that could only be indirectly re-presented to a human eye) was transformed by the position of a new artist-observer.[4]

1. Lawrence Gowing, *Turner: Imagination and Reality?*, Museum Of Modern Art, New York, 1966, p. 21.

2. Turner's break with Newtonian and Euclidian models of space and form is discussed in Karl Kroeber, "Romantic Historicism: The Temporal Sublime," in *Images of Romanticism: Verbal and Visual Affinities*, Karl Kroeber and William Walling (eds.), Yale University Press, New Haven, 1978, pp. 163-165, and in Michel Serres, "Turner traduit Carnot," in *La traduction*, Paris, 1974, pp. 233-242.

3. Turner's relation to the sun is discussed in Ronald Paulson, "Turner's Graffiti: The Sun and its Glosses," in *Images of Romanticism*, pp. 167-188; Jack Lindsay, *Turner: His Life and Work*, Harper and Row, New York, pp. 210-213, and Martin D. Paley, *The Apocalyptic Sublime*, New Haven, 1985, pp. 143-170.

4. On the cultural effects of these new concepts, see Krzysztof Pomian, *L' ordre du temps*, Gallimard, Paris, 1984, pp. 300-305.

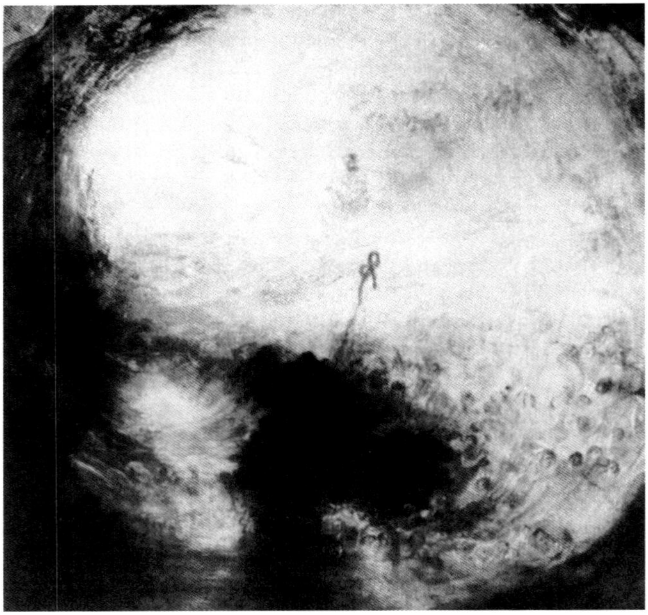

Fig. 1
J. M. W. Turner, *Light and Colour (Goethe's Theory) – The morning After the Deluge*, 1843.

In Turner all of the mediations that previously had distanced and protected an observer from the dangerous brilliance of the sun are cast off. The exemplary figures of Kepler and Newton employed the camera obscura precisely to avoid looking directly into the sun while seeking to gain knowledge of it or of the light it propagated. In Descartes's *La dioptrique,* the form of the camera was a defense against the madness and unreason of dazzlement.[5]

Turner's direct confrontation with the sun, however, dissolves the very possibility of representation that the camera obscura was meant to ensure. His solar preoccupations were "visionary" in that he made central in his work the retinal processes of vision; and it was the carnal embodiment of sight that the camera obscura denied or repressed. In one of Turner's great later paintings, the 1843 Light and Colour (Goethe's Theory – The Morning after the Deluge), the collapse of the older model of representation is complete: the view of the sun that had dominated so many of Turner's previous images now becomes a fusion of eye and sun.[6] On one hand it stands as an impossible image of a luminescence that can only be blinding and that has never been seen, but it also resembles an after-

5. See Michel Foucault, *Madness and Civilization. A History of Insanity in the Age of Reason,* trans. Richard Howard, Pantheon, New York, 1973, p. 108. "Dazzlement is night in broad daylight, the darkness that rules at the very heart of what is excessive in light's radiance. Dazzled reason opens its eyes upon the sun, and sees nothing, that is, it does not see ..."

6. The extent to which Turner was influenced by Goethe's writings on physiological optics is uncertain. That Turner was clearly aware of the physiological power of complementary colors is asserted in Gerald E. Finley, "Turner: An Early Experiment with Color," in *Journal of the Warburg and Courtauld Institute 30,* 1967, pp. 357-366. See also John Gage, "Turner's Annotated Books: Goethe's 'Theory of Colours,'" in *Turner Studies 4,* Winter 1982, pp. 34-52.

7. The suggestion that Turner's suns are self-portraits is made in Paulson, *Turner's Graffiti. The Sun and its Glosses,* p. 182, and in Lindsay, *Turner,* op.cit. p. 213.

8. Turner's personal contact with Brewster is discussed in J. A. Fineberg, *The Life of J. M. W Turner R.A.*, Oxford, 1966 (second

image of that engulfing illumination. If the circular structure of this painting and others of the same period mimic the shape of the sun, they also correspond with the pupil of the eye and the retinal field on which the temporal experience of an afterimage unfolds. Through the afterimage the sun is made to belong to the body, and the body in fact takes over as the source of its effects. It is perhaps in this sense that Turner's suns may be said to be self-portraits.[7]

But Turner was not alone in the nineteenth century with his visionary relation to the sun. Three scientific figures already mentioned in this study, Sir David Brewster, Joseph Plateau, and Gustav Fechner, all severely damaged their eyesight by staring into the sun in the course of research on retinal afterimages.[8] Plateau, inventor of the phenakistiscope, went blind permanently. Though as scientists their immediate aims obviously differed from those of Turner, on a more important level theirs too was a shared discovery of the "visionary" capacities of the body, and we miss the significance of this research if we don't acknowledge its strange intensity and exhilaration. What this work often involved was the experience of staring directly into the sun, of sunlight searing itself onto the body, palpably disturbing it into a proliferation of incandescent color. Clearly these scientists came to a piercing realization of the corporeality of vision. Not only did their work find the body to be the site and producer of chromatic events, but this discovery allowed them to conceive of an abstract optical experience, that is of a vision that did not represent or refer to objects in the world. And the work of all three, whether as technological invention or empirical scientific study, was directed toward the mechanization and formalization of vision.

Although not involved like Brewster or Plateau in the invention of any optical device, the career of Gustav Fechner is perhaps the most interesting when juxtaposed with Turner's.[9] Fechner confounds many of the conventional dichotomies on which much nineteenth-century intellectual history is founded. Standard accounts have insisted on a kind of split personality. On one hand he seemed a Romantic mystic immersed in the *Naturphilosophie* of Oken and Schelling and in a Spinozist pantheism.[10] On the other, he was the founder of a rigorously empirical and quantitative psychology, crucial for the later work of Wilhelm Wundt and Ernst Mach, providing them with the theoretical foundations for a comprehensive reduction of perceptual and psychic experience to measurable units. But these two dimensions of Fechner were always intertwined.[11]

edition), p. 277; Lindsay, *Turner,* p. 206; and Gerald E. Finely, "Turner's Colour and Optics: A New Route in 1822," in *Journal of the Warburg and the Courtauld Institute 36,* 1973, p. 388.

9. On Fechner's seminal position in the history of scientific psychology, see, for example, E. G. Boring, *A History of Experimental Psychology*, New York, 1950, pp. 275-296. For a general statement of his principles for the measurement of sensation, see Fechner, *Elements of Psychophysics,* trans. Helmut E. Adler, Holt, Rinehart and Winston, New York, 1966, pp. 38-58; *Elemente der Psychophysik,* Breitkopf & Härtel, Leipzig, 1860, vol. 1, pp. 4075.

10. On Fechner's "mystical" writings, see the "Introduction" by Walter Lowrie in *Religion of a Scientist: Selections from Gustav Theodor Fechner*, trans. and ed. Walter Lowrie, Pantheon, New York, 1946, pp. 9-81. See also Fechner, *Life After Death,* trans. Mary Wadsworth, Pantheon, New York, 1943. For Spinoza' s relation to the work of Müller and Fechner, see Walter Bernard, "Spinoza' s Influence on the Rise of Scientific Psychology," in *Journal of the History of the Behavioral Sciences 8,* April 1972, pp. 208-215.

11. See, for example, William R. Woodward, "Fechner's Panpsychism: A Scientific Solution to the Mind-Body-Problem," in *Journal of the History of the Behavioral Sciences 8,* October 1972, pp. 367-386.

His exhilarating and finally agonizing experience of the sun in the late 1830s was no less primal than it was for Turner.[12] Already in 1825 a solar preoccupation infused Fechner' s literary meditations on vision:

"Thus we may view our own eye as a creature of the sun on earth, a creature dwelling in and nourished by the sun's rays, and hence a creature structurally resembling its brothers on the sun(...). But the sun's creatures, the higher beings I call angels, are eyes which have become autonomous, eyes of the highest inner development which retain nevertheless, the structure of the ideal eye. Light is their element as ours is air."[13]

This early declaration of an emanative, autonomous vision, of a luminous and radiant eye, is part of a wider recurrence in the nineteenth century of a Plotinian model of the observer to which Turner can also be linked.[14] In 1846 Turner produced a painting titled *The Angel Standing in the Sun.* A square canvas exactly the size of *Light and Colour* of 1843, the formal structure here is also insistently circular. In both of them Turner's familiar vortex modulates into a pure spherical whirlpool of golden light: a radial conflation of eye and sun, of self and divinity, of subject and object.

In the center of the later work is the figure of a winged angel raising a sword. Turner's use of this symbol, however, is an indication less of his links to a Romantic or Miltonic tradition of such imagery than of his remoteness from the paradigm of the camera obscura. As it was for Fechner, the recourse to the angel, an object with no referent in the world, is a sign of the inadequacy of conventional means for representing the hallucinatory abstraction of his intense optical experiences. The angel becomes a symbolic acknowledgment by Turner of his own perceptual autonomy, an exalted announcement of the ungroundedness of vision. And it is in this sense that Turner's work can be said to be sublime: his painting is concerned with experience that transcends its possible representations, with the insufficiency of any object to his concept.[15]

But if Turner's work suggests the extent of experimentation and innovation in the articulation of new languages, effects, and forms made possible by the relative abstraction and autonomy of physiological perception, Fechner's epochal formalization of perceptual experience comes out of a related crisis of representation. Like Turner's art, Fechner's work is grounded in an exhilaration and delirium made possible by the collapse of the dualities inherent in the camera obscura – its split between perceiver and world. Fechner had a primal certainty

12. Fechner's so-called crisis of 1840-1843, his physical and mental problems resulting from his experiments with afterimages, is detailed by his nephew in Johannes Emil Kuntze, Gustav Theodor Fechner: *Ein deutsches Gelehrtenleben,* Breitkopf & Härtel, Leipzig, 1892, pp. 105-138. He also suffered severe eye strain due to the precise scalar readings needed for his studies of binocular vision.

13. Gustav Fechner, "On the Comparative Anatomy of Angels," trans. Marilynn Marshall, in *Journal of the History of the Behavioral Sciences 5,* no. 1, 1969, pp. 39-58.

14. Goethe gave Plotinus a place of prominence in the introduction to his optics: "We are reminded here of (...) the words of an old mystic writer, which may be thus rendered: 'If the eye were not sunny, how could we possibly perceive light? If God's own strength lived not in us, how could we delight in Divine things?' This immediate affinity between light and the eye will be denied by none (...) It will be more intelligible to assert that a dormant light resides in the eye, and that it may be excited by the slightest cause from within or without." Theory of Colors, p. III. Heidegger discusses this passage from Goethe in his *Schelling's Treatise on the Essence of Human Freedom,* trans. Joan Stambaugh, Athens, Ohio, 1985, pp. 54-56. On Plotinus and his relation to the history of art theory, see Eric Alliez and Michel Feher, "Reflections of a Soul," in *Zone 4,* 1989, pp. 46-84.

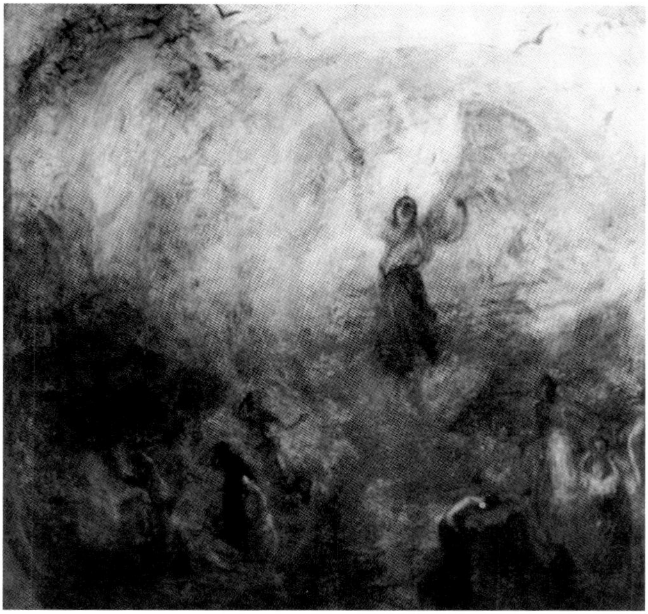

Fig. 2
J. M.W. Turner, *The Angel Standing in the Sun*, 1864.

of the interconnection between mind and matter: they were simply alternate ways of constructing the same reality. But what he wanted, and spent years seeking, was a method of establishing an exact relationship between interior sensory experience and events in the world, to situate these two domains on the same field of operations. Whatever his intentions, the end result was to relocate perception and the observer within the reach of empirical exactitude and technological intervention.

Sensation as a multiplicity of intangible psychic affects, however, was not in itself rationalizable – that is, it was not directly accessible to study, manipulation, duplication, and measurement as an empirically isolable entity. But if sensation did not lend itself to scientific control and management, any form of physical stimulus did. Thus Fechner set about rationalizing sensation through the measurement of external stimulus. Where Herbart had failed in his attempt at mental measurement, Fechner succeeded by quantifying sensations in terms of the stimuli that produced them. His achievement was the establishment of what is variously called Fechner's Law or Weber's Law, in which he proposed a mathematical equation

15. My use of the term sublime refers to the work of Jean-Francois Lyotard, *The Postmodern Condition: A Report on Knowledge,* trans. Brian Massumi, University of Minnesota Press, Minneapolis, 1984, pp. 77-79: "Modernity in whatever age it appears, cannot exist without a shattering of belief and without discovery of the 'lack of reality' of reality, together with the invention of other realities(...). I think in particular that it is in the aesthetic of the sublime that modern art (including literature) finds its impetus and the logic of avantgardes its axioms (...). The sentiment of the sublime (...) develops as a conflict between the faculties of a subject, the faculty to conceive of something and the faculty to 'present' something." See also Lyotard, "The Sublime and the Avant-Garde," in *Artforum 22,* April 1984, pp. 36-43.

that expressed a functional relation between sensation and stimulus.[16] With such an equation the inside/outside of the camera obscura dissolves and a new kind of annexation of the observer is made possible. For the first time subjectivity is made quantifiably determinable. This is Fechner's "Galilean" achievement-making measurable something that had not been so before.[17]

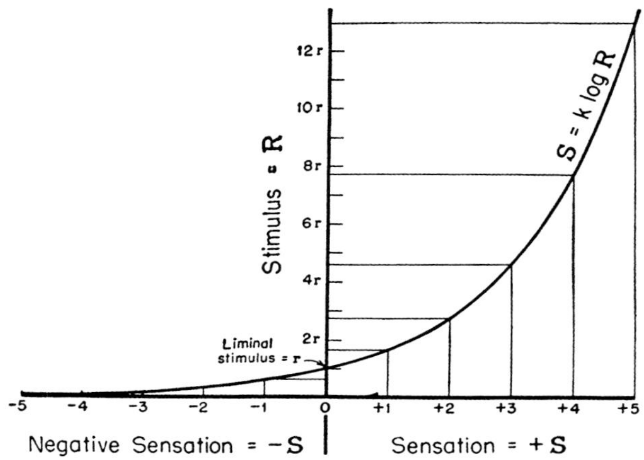

Fechner's Law: S = k *log* R.

Fechner's research furthered the realization of the arbitrary or disjunctive relation of sensation to its external cause that Muller's work on nerve energies had already disclosed.[18] For example, he found that the intensity of a sensation of light does not increase as quickly as the intensity of the physical stimulus. Thus he concluded that there was a disproportional, though predictable, relation between increases in sensation and increases in stimulation. Central to Fechner's work was the establishment of measurable units of sensation, quantifiable increments that would allow human perception to be made calculable and productive. These were derived from thresholds of sensation, from the magnitude of the stimulus needed to generate the very least noticeable sensation over and above the stimulus that is unnoticed by the human sensorium. These units were the much-debated "just noticeable differences." Thus human perception became a sequence of magnitudes of varying intensity. As Fechner's experiments with afterimages also had shown him, perception was necessarily temporal; an observer's sensations always depended on the

16. Named for Ernst Weber, Fechner's teacher, whose work between 1838 and 1846 on the sense of touch was the basis for Fechner's proposals. Foucault cites Weber's work in the 1840s as coinciding with the emergence of a technology of behavior and the "supervision of normality" in a variety of fields. *Discipline and Punish: The Birth of the Prison*, trans. Alan Sheridan, Pantheon, New York, 1979, pp. 294-296.

17. See Harald Høffding, *History of Modern Philosophy, vol. 2*, Macmillan, New York, 1955, p. 529: "The only difference between Fechner and Spinoza here is that Fechner is eager to discover a mathematical functional relation between the two sides of existence."

18. "Even when applied in the same way, one and the same stimulus may be perceived as stronger or weaker by one subject or organ than by another, or by the same subject or organ at one time as stronger or weaker than at another. Conversely, stimuli of different magnitudes may be perceived as equally strong under certain circumstances." *Elements of Psychophysics*, op.cit. p. 38.

19. Michel Foucault, *The Order of Things*, Pantheon, New York, 1973, pp. 349-351.

20. "In a sense, the power of normalization imposes homogeneity; but it individualizes by making it possible to measure gaps, to determine levels, to fix specialties,

previous sequence of stimuli. But it is segmented temporality very different from that implied in Turner, or from the kind of experience that Bergson and others later sought to champion over the scientific project initiated by Fechner. It is relevant that at the time Fechner was performing his experiments in the 1840s, George Boole was overlapping the operations of logic with those of algebra, attempting a related formalization of "the laws of thought." But as Foucault has insisted, mathematization or quantification, although important, is not the crucial issue in the human sciences in the nineteenth century.[19] Rather, at stake is how the human subject, through knowledge of the body and its modes of functioning, was made compatible with new arrangements of power: the body as worker, student, soldier, consumer, patient, criminal. Vision may well be measurable, but what is perhaps most significant about Fechner's equations is their homogenizing function: they are a means of rendering a perceiver manageable, predictable, productive, and above all consonant with other areas of rationalization.[20]

Fechner's formalization of perception renders the specific contents of vision irrelevant. Vision, as well as the other senses, is now describable in terms of abstract and exchangeable magnitudes. If vision previously had been conceived as an experience of qualities (as in Goethe's optics), it is now a question of differences in quantities, of sensory experience that is stronger or weaker. But this new valuation of perception, this obliteration of the qualitative in sensation through its arithmetical homogenization, is a crucial part of modernization.

At the center of Fechner's psychophysics is the law of the conservation of energy, an insistence that organisms and inorganic nature are ruled by the same forces. He describes the human subject: "In a way the relations are like those of a steam engine with a complicated mechanism(...). The only differences is that in our organic machine the engineer does not sit on the outside but on the inside."[21] And Fechner is certainly not alone here. All of Helmholtz's work on human vision, including binocular disparity, stemmed from his original interest in animal heat and respiration and his overriding ambition to describe the functioning of a living being in precise physiochemical terms. Thermodynamics stand behind both his and Fechner's delineation of a being that works, produces, and sees through a process of muscular exertion, combustion, and release of heat according to empirically verifiable laws.[22] Even if Fechner's dominant legacy is the hegemony of behaviorism and the myriad processes of conditioning and control, it is

and to render the differences useful by fitting them one to another. It is easy to understand how the power of the norm functions within a system of formal equality, since within a homogeneity that is the rule, the norm introduces, as a useful imperative and as a result of measurement, all the shading of individual differences." Michel Foucault, *Discipline and Punish,* op. cit., p. 184. Foucault's notion of "homogeneity" recalls its place in the work of Georges Bataille: "*Homogeneity* signifies here the commensurability of elements and the awareness of this commensurability: human relations are sustained by a reduction to fixed rules based on the consciousness of the possible identity of delineable persons and situations (...). The common denominator, the foundation of social homogeneity and of the activity arising from it, is money, namely the calculable equivalent of the different products of collective activity. Money serves to measure all work and makes man a function of measurable products. According to the judgment of *homogenous* society, each man is worth what he produces; in other words he stops being an existence for itself he is no more than a function, arranged within measurable limits, of collective production (which makes him an existence for something other than itself)." Bataille, *Visions of Excess: Selected Writings 1927-1939,* trans. Allan Stoekl, University of Minnesota, Minneapolis, 1985, pp. 137-138.

important to see how his psychophysics originally sought a delirious merging of the interiority of a perceiver into a single charged and unified field, every part of it vibrating with the same forces of repulsion and attraction, an infinite nature, like Turner's, where life and death are simply different states of a primal energy. But modern forms of power also arose through the dissolution of the boundaries that had kept the subject as an interior domain qualitatively separated from the world. Modernization demanded that this last retreat be rationalized, and as Foucault makes clear, all the sciences in the nineteenth century beginning with the prefix psycho – are part of this strategic appropriation of subjectivity.[23]

But Fechner's rationalization of sensation not only led to the development of specific technologies of behavior and attentiveness; it was also a sign of the reshaping of an entire social field and the position of a human sensorium within it. Later in the nineteenth century Georg Simmel found Fechner's formulations to be an incisive means of expressing how sensory experience had become adjacent and even coincident with an economic and cultural terrain dominated by exchange values. Simmel derived from Fechner an informal kind of calculation to demonstrate how exchange values were equivalent to quantities of physical stimulation. "Money," he wrote, "operates as a stimulus to all kinds of possible sentiments because its unspecific character, devoid of all qualities, places it at such a great distance from any sentiment that its relations with all of them are fairly equal."[24] In Simmel's account of modernity, the observer is conceivable only as an element in this flux and inexorable mobility of values: "Within the historical-psychological sphere, money by its very nature becomes the most perfect representative of a cognitive tendency of modern science as a whole – the reduction of qualitative determinations to quantitative ones."[25]

The "real world" that the camera obscura had stabilized for two centuries was no longer, to paraphrase Nietzsche, the most useful or valuable world. The modernity enveloping Turner, Fechner, and their heirs had no need of its kind of truth and immutable identities. A more adaptable, autonomous, and productive observer was needed in both discourse and practice – to conform to new functions of the body and to a vast proliferation of indifferent and convertible signs and images. Modernization effected a deterritorialization and a revaluation of vision.

21. Gustav Fechner, *Elements of Psychophysics*, op.cit., p. 35.

22. Ibid., pp. 32-33. "Accordingly the kinetic energy of a system may increase without drawing on potential energy and may decrease without a corresponding increase of potential energy as long as the kinetic energy simultaneously decreases or increases in another part of the system (...). It is impossible to be lost in external perception and to think deeply at the same time. In order to reflect acutely on something we have to abstract from something else (...) the facts are too closely connected with the previous discussion for us not to see also in them an extension of the law of the conservation of energy to the play of purely psychophysical forces."

23. Michel Foucault, *Discipline and Punish,* op. cit., p. 193. Freud's expressed admiration for Fechner's "economic standpoint" is well known, but on a more general level psychoanalysis can be seen as another operation of relocating the "interior" contents of the unconscious onto a field where they can be formalized in linguistic terms, however imprecisely.

24. Georg Simmel, *The Philosophy of Money,* trans. Tom Bottomore and David Frisby, Routledge and Kegan Paul, London, 1978, p. 267. For Simmel's extended reconstruction of Fechner's Law, see pp. 262-271.

(...) I have tried to give a sense of how radical was the reconfiguration of vision by the 1840s. If our problem is vision and modernity, we must first examine these earlier decades, not the modernist painting of the 1870s and 1880s. A new type of observer was formed then, and not one that we can see figured in paintings or prints. We've been trained to assume that an observer will always leave visible tracks, that is, will be identifiable in relation to images. But here it's a question of an observer who also takes shape in other, grayer practices and discourses, and whose immense legacy will be all the industries of the image and the spectacle in the twentieth century. The body that had been a neutral or invisible term in vision was now the thickness from which knowledge of the observer was obtained. This palpable opacity and carnal density of vision loomed so suddenly into view that its full consequences and effects could not be immediately realized. But once vision became relocated in the subjectivity of the observer, two intertwined paths opened up. One led out toward all the multiple affirmations of the sovereignty and autonomy of vision derived from this newly empowered body, in modernism and elsewhere. The other path was toward the increasing standardization and regulation of the observer that issued from knowledge of visionary body, toward forms of power that depended on the abstraction and formalization of vision. What is important is how these paths continually intersect and often overlap on the same social terrain, amid the countless localities in which the diversity of concrete acts of vision occur.

25. Georg Simmel, *The Philosophy of Money,* op.cit., p. 277.

György Darvas

Symmetry and Asymmetry in Our Surroundings
Aspects of Symmetry in the Phenomena of Nature, Physical Laws, and Human Perception

Symmetry and the lack of symmetry in phenomena

Objects and phenomena in our surroundings show signs of symmetry and the lack of symmetry at the same time. Really, the same thing is symmetric in one (or more) aspect(s), i.e. preserves its one or more property(ies) under certain transformation(s), e.g. a reflection or rotation, while it is asymmetric in other aspects, i.e. its other properties are not conserved. There is no perfect symmetry (when all properties are preserved) and no perfect asymmetry (when no single property is preserved). A very asymmetric world would be ugly, while a very symmetric world would be boring. This concerns not only our physical surroundings, but also its artistic representations.

Can a term that is not categorically applicable to a normative characterization of our surroundings serve as a useful category to make an order in the pool of phenomena around us? Of course it can. So much, that it can be applied to the characterization of fine differences observed in a scale between opposite extremities.

The concept of symmetry

The meaning of this mysterious term went through a fabulous transformation during its use over dozens of centuries. The proper translation of the Greek term *symmetria* [________] – (from the prefix *sym* [___ – common] and the noun *metros* [______ – measure]) – is "common measure." The Greeks interpreted this word as the harmony of the different parts of an object, the good proportions between its constituent parts. Later this meaning was transferred to, for example, the rhythm of poems, of music, the cosmos (the "well-ordered system of the universe as contrast of chaos"). Therefore the Latin and the modern European languages used its translations such as harmony or proportion until the Renaissance. In a wider sense, balance or equilibrium also belonged to this family of synonyms. It is not too difficult to conclude that in some ways, symmetry was always related to beauty, truth, and good. (These relative meanings determined its application in the arts, the sciences, and ethics.) Symmetry was not only related to such positive values, it even became a symbol of seeking perfection (cf. Plato).

A glance at the history of (the use of the concept of) symmetry

The first scientific analysis of the notion of symmetry (which survived) was given by the Roman architect Vitruvius, in the first century B.C. in his *Ten Books on Architecture*. This work laid the basis of the individual meaning of the notion. According to his usage, symmetry is a general term which incorporates the common features of the different meanings of the synonyms such as harmony, proportion, rhythm, etc. It was not by chance that the humanists of the *quattrocento* rediscovered Vitruvius' works for themselves. Newer and newer translations were published and the term *symmetry* (instead of translation) settled in the modern European languages (first in *Vulgare* [Italian - *symmetria*], then in German [*Symmetrie*]). It was also not by chance that this ground-gaining took place parallel to the self-consciousness of the arts, development of art theory, appearance of the application of perspective, and in general, geometry in visual arts. One must only mention the works by Lorenzo Ghiberti (*I Commentarii*), Leon Battista Alberti (*De pictura, Della Pittura*), Piero della Francesca (*De prospectiva pingendi*), Luca Pacioli (*Summa de arithmetica, geometria, proportionalita, De divina proportione*), Leonardo da Vinci and Albrecht Dürer (*Underweysung der Messung, Vier Bücher von menschlicher Proportion*). The term symmetry took on its contemporary meaning in the fifteenth century.

Following the Greek golden age (fifth century B.C.), the paths of the sciences and the arts crossed each other again in the Renaissance, to separate once more for centuries, and to meet for the third time in the cultural melting pot of the twentieth century, providing ground again for the fertile application of symmetry in both (hemi)spheres of human creativity.

Manifestations of symmetry

If one asks the general reader, what she/he means by symmetry, more than half will answer, it is something like *reflection*. Well, they are right; reflection is a very frequent (although not the most frequent) manifestation of symmetry. Let's take a shape on a plane, and a straight line on the same plane. We can reflect all points of this shape through the straight line, and we will get the mirror-shape of the original. Why do we call the two shapes symmetric? Because the mirror-shape preserved many properties of the original. The length of the lines between its corresponding points, the distance of the individual points from the reflecting straight line, the angles of crossing straight lines connecting the corresponding points, and the form of the shape did not change. Other properties can be listed, what did not change was, e.g., its color, etc. At the same time, the direction of movement about the left and right sides changed. What happened? Precisely: we first took a *geometric object;* second, made a *geometric transformation* (reflection through the straight line), which changed some properties; and third, found that certain other *geometric properties* have remained invariant under the given transformation. After two reflections in respect to the same straight line, we get back the original object. We also call reflection bilateral symmetry. Similar observations can be done by reflecting 3D objects. A relatively large portion of the readers will mention rotation. Rotation is also a frequent manifestation of symmetry. Let's take a shape on a plane, and a straight line, now perpendicular to the plane (axis of the rotation). We can rotate all points of the shape with the same (but any) angle around the straight line. The rotated shape will preserve its properties, only its placement in the plane and direction will be changed. We can say again, that (first) we took a geometric object, (second) made a geometric transformation (rotation around the straight line), which changed certain properties, and (third) found that other properties have remained invariant under the given transformation. If we choose an angle of the rotation which is an integer (n) divisor of 360°, we can get the original object back again after n transformations (rotations). In these cases we speak about n-fold symmetry. Similar observations can be made when rotating 3D objects.

Fewer readers will mention the most frequent manifestation of symmetry: *translation*. Let's take an object, a direction, and a distance. Let's move the object in the fixed direction by the given distance, and let's repeat this transformation any number of times, in principle *ad infinitum*. We will never get back the original, but we receive a series of the same object('s copies). The object preserved all its properties, but its placement in the plane (in the space). What happened? Again, (first) we took a *geometric object*, (second) made a *geometric transformation* (translation in a fixed direction by a given distance), which changed the object's placement, and (third) found that its *geometric properties have remained invariant* under the given transformation. We can translate the same object in several directions. Decorative arts prefer to apply translation of symmetric motives. Examples for translation symmetry are: frieze patterns, mosaics, windows of a building, or crystals in the sciences. Any repetition can represent symmetry, e.g. rhythm in poetry and in music, or all periodic phenomena, like periodicity in celestial mechanics or in the calender.

Conservation of further geometric properties may serve as bases for certain symmetries.

Similitude is a symmetry transformation, where the distances change between the corresponding points of two objects, but the ratio between the lengths and the angles are preserved, thus the shape of the object remains similar to the original.

Affine projection transforms straight lines into straight lines (this is the retained property), although it does not preserve the angles.

Topological symmetry leaves the neighborhood relations intact among the points of the object, although it changes the distances between them and the angles of the lines connecting them, and straight lines are not transformed as straight lines. A good example for topological symmetry is (the lattice of the points of) a squashed sponge.

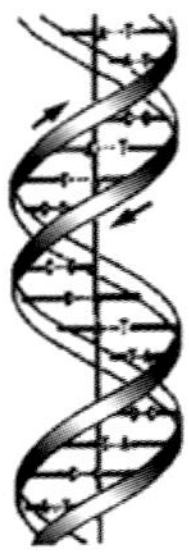

Fig. 1
Double *helix* by Watson and Crick

Combined symmetries
There are combined symmetries when we perform two or more symmetry transformations of the same object, and these leave one or more properties intact.

Let's take an object, for example, translate (glide) it in a direction at a certain distance, and then reflect it onto a straight line parallel with the direction of the glide. Then repeat these transformations any number of times. This is the so-called *glide reflection,* frequently applied in frieze patterns.

Other geometric symmetry transformations can also be combined. For example, a *helix* can be obtained by combining rotation and translation towards the axis, etc.

Let's now combine affine projection and similitude. This combination of symmetry transformations provides us with the *perspective,* widely applied in painting and graphic representation. Were it not for a symmetry transformation preserving features, we could not discern the original from the picture. *Aerial perspective* combined similitude and color change. The subject of the transformation in the case of perspective representation is the visible reality, and the transformed object is the artwork. Perspective representation is a manifestation of symmetry. From the *quattrocento* up to the end of the nineteenth century, perspective was the main tool in the hands of artists to paint real representations of our surroundings.

Developing perspective in the arts
Application of symmetry transformations was a subject of evolution ever since the centuries that perspective was in use. The single vanishing point, for example, could be doubled and even moved (translated). Development was able to represent an object from different perspective(s). Twentieth century art went further. Application of topological symmetry combined with the similitude offered new ways of seeing, new tools for artists. Thus, they could even give up the straight line, fixed direction (demanded by the affine projection), and replace it by a topology. This made it possible for them to stress certain important features of the represented object. The use of double or more centers of projection (vanishing points), or even dissolution of the fixed centers, – liberating the painter from a central perspective – opened new vistas for artists to provide the spectator with a multiple-sided representation of the delineated object. Multiple-sidedness could be understood here first in geometric terms, later also figuratively.

(*Dimensions in representation.* We should mention, at least parenthetically, that this liberation also led to the dissolution of the limits determined by the dimensions of the real world. In fact, we live in a three-dimensional world, and our physical laws do not allow any other description for the sciences. But the rationality of the sciences are not obligatory for the arts. A fourth dimension, realized by time, cannot be represented in spatial dimensions according to the rules accepted by science. However, the introduction of time as an imaginary fourth dimension in the theory of relativity activated the fantasy of artists to represent time as a separate dimension in artworks. This was the beginning of the twentieth century, when cinema developed, which opened time as a new dimension for artistic representation by series of consecutive pictures. Movies made it possible to express a series of happenings, thus extending the two dimensions of representation provided by a canvas into a third dimension, into time. Nevertheless, this development was too trivial. Traditional arts also sought to represent the course of time in graphics, paintings, and sculptures. Let's merely recall Futurism, which expressed movement in different kinds of artistic products. Movement, motion *per definitionem* incorporates the aspect of time (since one always moves "in time"). This new perspective also allowed a new way of thinking about dimensionality. The canvas is two-dimensional. Although the surface of an amphora is curved in space, one can also draw on it, taking only the limits provided by the two dimensions into consideration. Perspective – more precisely the geometrical tools, i.e. the symmetry transformations – offered the possibility for us to project real representations of the three-dimensional world onto the two dimensions of the canvas. Oh, that wonderful kit provided by symmetry of geometry! Having such a marvellous set of tools in our hands, why not apply it to project four dimensions into two? And it happened. If three dimensions (3D) can be projected to make two (2D), then four dimensions (4D) can be projected to make three, and these geometrical transformations being transitive, 4D can be projected to make 2D. And art did not stop at the representation of time as an imaginary fourth dimension in the surface. Spatial objects in 4D appeared in artworks. (For mathematically less experienced readers, 4D can be recognized in the simplest case when there are 4 directions, each perpendicular to the three others.) And even higher dimensions; why not. Symmetry transformations no longer impose geometrical limits to artistic fantasy. In many cases, multiple dimensions

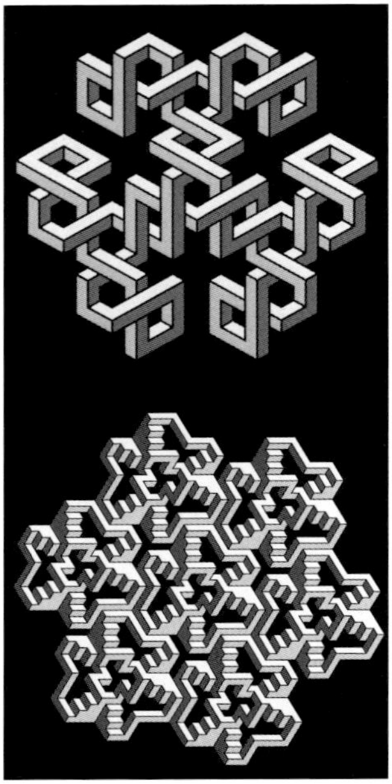

Fig. 2 and 3
T. F. Farkas

cannot be recognized, e.g. by drawing perpendicular straight lines; nevertheless one realizes that the artwork represents impossible objects. Let's recall the many drawings by M.C. Escher of Holland, or T. F. Farkas, from Hungaria. (Some of these impossible objects [i.e., not realizable in the real three dimensions] can be imagined to be "made real" in higher dimensions.)

Following this short digression, returning to our main sequence of ideas, let's realize that those pictures, deliberated from the central perspective and beyond, at first do not appear symmetric, *in the old-fashioned, everyday meaning which restricted symmetry operations to reflection, rotation, translation, and maybe allowed inclusion of similitude and affine projection, the naive spectator would be right.* Having allowed combined symmetries and included topological symmetry, our concept of symmetry was extended. This makes it possible to understand the view of artists who ruptured with conservative traditions. This allows us to find the beauty (via symmetry, i.e., the harmony of details, balance between the parts) in artworks which go beyond traditional composition. To accept this approach and go even further, we should become acquainted with ways of generalizing about the concept of symmetry.

Generalization of the concept of symmetry

All the aforementioned kinds of symmetry were geometrical symmetries. What was common to them? In all cases, we performed a certain *geometric* operation, a transformation. During this transformation *one (or more)* geometric *property(ies)* of this geometric object *did not change.* We say that this property proved to be *invariant under the given transformation.*

Let's now replace the geometric transformation with *any* kind of transformation. Let's apply such transformations not only to geometric objects, but also to *any* kind of object. Let's investigate not only its geometric properties, but allow considering *any* kind of property of the objects.

In other words: in general we can speak about symmetry if – *under any* (not necessarily geometric) *transformation* (operation), *at least one* (not necessarily geometric) *property of the* (not necessarily geometric) *object* is left *invariant* (intact). Thus we made a generalization in three respects: *any transformation, any object,* and its *potential property.*

This generalized meaning of symmetry allows the application of symmetry to materialized objects in physical and organic nature, to products of our mind, etc. Over geometric (morphological) symmetries we can discuss functional symmetries and asymmetries (e.g. in the human brain), gauge symmetries (of physical phenomena), properties, such as color, tone, shading, weight, etc. (of art objects).

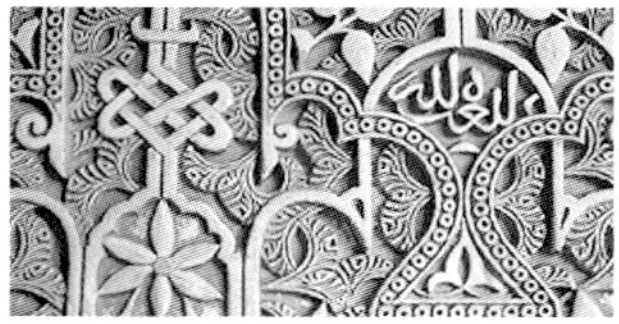

Fig. 4
Dissymmetry on an Alhambra arabesque fragment

Perfection and symmetry

With this extension of the meaning of symmetry – thus opening the door so widely to different phenomena, and being ready to admit many of them as symmetries – one can put the question: is everything around us, therefore symmetric? Before saying no, I recall that symmetry is never perfect. Objects can be invariant with respect to certain transformations, but never to all. Certain properties of objects can be invariant under a transformation, but not all. Aspiration for perfection does not mean one finds it everywhere.

Dissymmetry

Especially in the arts, symmetry often manifests itself in combined and generalized forms. Here we should emphasize the role of *dissymmetry:* this expression denotes objects which show symmetry in their general features, but this symmetry is slightly distorted. For example, a door is generally a mirror symmetric object, but the asymmetrical handle distorts this bilateral symmetry. The facade of a monumental building may show symmetry, but the curtains are pleated in different folds in all symmetrically placed windows which can be open or closed as well as decorated with different flowers. This dissymmetry shows signs of life in an otherwise inanimate building. Motifs of an arabesque show a symmetric shape, but individual leaves may differ from their symmetrically placed pair and tendrils spin around each other, which distorts perfect mirror symmetry. Nevertheless, we find dissymmetry beautiful; usually more beautiful than perfection.

Pierre Curie, the great physicist and crystallographer said over one hundred years ago: "Dissymmetry makes the phenomenon." What did he mean? The subject of a scientist's study should seek to localize where symmetry is distorted. What is there to study in a perfect object? Actually, for crystallographers the dislocations of the matter provide the most interesting phenomena. Most of our devices would not work without semiconductors. How do they function? The epoch-making discovery was that very, very small amounts of contamination can completely change the electrical conductivity of a perfect crystal. While jewellers look for perfect gem crystals and never find them, scientists produce (almost) perfect artificial crystals and 'distort' them, because they learned how to exploit the advantages of imperfection. The history of the recent half-century in particle physics was nothing other than a series of symmetry-breaking discoveries.

Reflecting reality: To what degree are pictures, obtained by symmetry transformations, true and proper mirrors of reality?

Returning to the arts, let's look for the degree to which artworks obtained by symmetry transformations are (at least in generalized terms) true and proper mirrors of reality? If I have stirred up illusions in anybody about a perfect and symmetric world, I must now disappoint them. Perfection of even the simplest mirror-images can be doubted. Make a photo of yourself (enlarge it, at least in principle to your original size), then stand in front of a looking glass and compare your two images. Both look like your perfect double. Anyway, they differ, don't they? Try to shake hands with both. If you want to shake the right hand of the photo, your hand will cross the vertical axis between the two "bodies;" you and your picture form a *rotational symmetric pair* around this axis. Your right hand is across the left hand of your picture, your mole on the right face is seen on the opposite side of the photo. And what about the looking glass? The same mole is on the right side of your image in the looking glass. Moving your right hand to the looking glass, the image hand from the left side will move to the mirror plane. You find that your image in the looking glass (contrary to your photo) is a *mirror symmetric pair* of you. Now compare your two images. You will realize that the mirror image and the photo image are 'mirror symmetric' to each other. Do you see your mole on the opposite faces of the two images and your right hand on the opposite sides of your image bodies? Right. Now, what is your real image? Which of the two represents your appearance more perfectly?

Does a perfect (bilateral symmetric) image even exist? Let's have a look at this ancient Sumerian picture (already analyzed by H. Weyl in 1952). The two figures stand almost symmetrically face to face. This symmetry is distorted, however, for both lift up their right hand, and the left figure's right hand is closer to us, while the right figure's right hand is farther from us. Would the image be more symmetric if one draws the picture again, only changing the right figure's shape to lift it closer to our hand? Graphically, by no means. However, we could say that the two figures are asymmetric again, because one of them lifts its right hand, and the other its left one. This scene cannot be drawn in a perfectly symmetric way. Our belief in the perfection of the world's symmetry is cracked up.

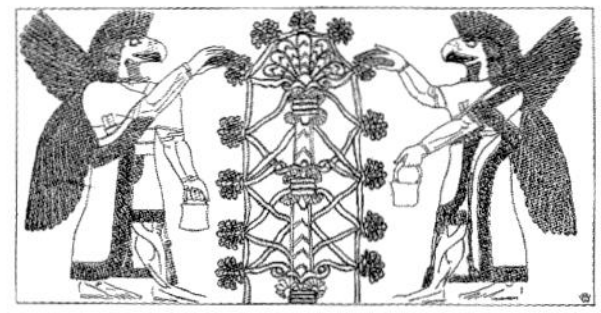

Fig. 5
Dissymmetry on a Sumerian picture

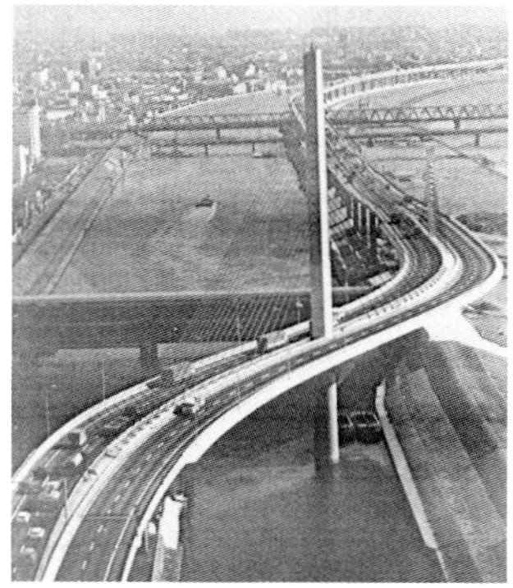

Fig. 6
Asymmetric bridge in Japan

Are our surroundings symmetric?

Do not give up! Look around in your surroundings. What do you find? A lot of symmetric objects, both natural and man-made. Whatever I was explaining to you, there is symmetry, harmony and beauty surrounding us. The world is almost perfect, well, with some distortions, let it be; but it saved at least its dissymmetry, which is, mainly symmetry. Symmetry is quite natural. All people are almost symmetric. (Who sees that our heart beats aside, that our motions are co-ordinated from our left brain hemisphere?) The butterflies are more symmetric; the flowers are symmetric, and so on.

Most bridges over the Thames, the Seine, the East River, the Rhine, the Danube, etc., are symmetrically built between the two riversides. Is it quite natural? Not at all. Look at the metro bridge in western Paris in front of the Maison de la Radio crossing the river at an oblique angle. Similarly, so does the northern highway, before leaving Tokyo. The Danube bridge in downtown Bratislava is perpendicular to the riverbanks, but its single pillar is placed asymmetrically near the southern bank. And yet, it harmonizes just as it does with the castle on the hill on the opposite side.

It seems quite natural that a tennis court is symmetric, doesn't it? It must be symmetric in two ways: firstly in geometric terms; secondly in moral terms, since both the physical conditions and the rules of the game for the two players should be identical, i.e. symmetric. Nevertheless, these conditions and rules were not always so self-evident. In the sixteenth century, when this game was formed, Henry VIII played it in his Hampton Court palace in an asymmetric room, where not only the asymmetric geometry of the room but also the rules provided an advantage for the king.

Self-evidence and naturalness of symmetry may depend on local and temporary, physical and social conditions. Something similar can be said of the acceptance of art trends, i.e. of change in the perception of beauty, harmony, symmetry.

The phenomena of symmetry in nature

Treating the symmetries of objects, we so far have considered

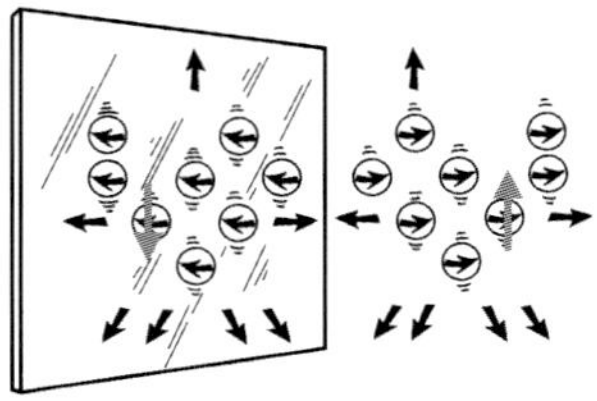

Fig. 7
Reflection of rotating spheres

their geometric shapes. Color may be subject to symmetric transformations as much as shape. It belongs to our – natural and artificial, including artistic – surroundings. Color is perceived as similar to geometric properties; it is a macroscopic phenomenon. In fact, the description of changes in discrete colors can be handled by the same mathematical tools (group theory) as geometric properties, although we know colors do not form a discrete set. We know, however, that they are macroscopically perceived microphysical phenomena: different wavelength photons reflected by the electron orbits on the surface atoms of the observed matter. Further, we know that electron orbits absorb and emit photons submitted to the laws of particle physics, quantum mechanics, and quantum electrodynamics. These theories apply not only geometric, but also – according to Eugene P. Wigner, so-called – dynamic symmetries. Dynamic symmetries do not follow from the geometry of our space and time, but, rather, from deeper invariances of the laws of nature. To mention an example for dynamic symmetries, we could recall the conservation of the electric charge.

Geometric and dynamic symmetries

Symmetries in our physical surroundings rarely appear alone. In most cases, they manifest themselves in combined forms. Often we meet a few geometric symmetries together, and dynamic symmetries always appear along with one or more geometric symmetry(ies). Combined symmetries are in most cases less perfect than singular ones.

Let's look at a very common physical phenomenon, e.g. a rotating sphere. It has spherical symmetry but also cylindrical symmetry; the axis of the rotation fixes a direction in space. Let's imagine that an arrow marks the axis of the rotation according to our right hand pointing upward. Let's now reflect this object to a mirror-plane. We will see the mirror-sphere rotating in the opposite direction. If we imagine the arrow marking the right-hand rotation axis reflected in the mirror, it should be directed downwards. This direction corresponds to the reflection of the rotating sphere. At the same time, if we place a real arrow in front of the mirror plane, it will not turn the arrow upside down. The situation is similar to our own image in the looking glass and on a photo. The difference is that, in this case we can compare the images with our experience and correct the geometric content of the mirror image.

There is a different case when the image has a concrete physical content. Let's replace the arrow with a wire conducting an electric current and the rotating sphere with a magnetic needle. They are parallel while there is no current in the wire, and the north pole of the needle fixes the direction of an arrow along the wire. As soon as we conduct an electric current "towards the north pole" in the wire, the magnetic needle will turn aside according to the fingers of our right hand. If we observe this arrangement in a mirror, we see that the needle will rotate in the opposite direction around the wire, however, the direction of the current in the wire is not supposed to be reflected. As soon as we replace the arrow with a real physical object we can not reflect it like in the case of the rotating sphere.

What is the difference? In the case of the rotating sphere we had only geometric objects and geometric symmetries. In the case of the current and the magnetic needle, the direction of the arrow was determined by moving electric charges, which caused a cylindrical magnetic field around the wire. Any reflection of the geometry did not reflect the charges, which could reflect the direction of the current and the magnetic field. In another experiment we can "reflect the charges" (i.e. replace the negative charges with positive ones, so-called charge conjugation), which will cause an opposite-direction current, and the magnetic needle will turn to the opposite direction. However, in this case we do not need a mirror to observe the geometrically reflected phenomenon.

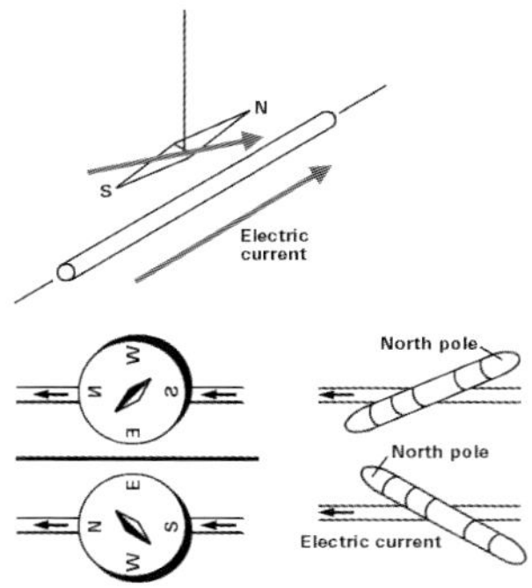

Fig. 8
Reflection of electric current and magnetic needle

Symmetries and the laws of nature

Physics identified several further properties, which "behave" similar to the electric charges, subjected to dynamic symmetries. According to a mathematical theorem, formulated by Emmy Noether (1918), all symmetries imply the conservation of a physical quantity (characterizing a property), and all conservation laws imply a symmetry. Remember, by symmetry we understood the invariance of a property under transformation. It was not by chance that Hermann Weyl, one of the greatest personalities studying symmetry in the twentieth century, stated: "The mathematical laws governing nature are the source of symmetry in nature." We have good reason to suppose (according to Wigner, 1963) that, while geometric symmetries establish correspondence between physical events, the dynamic symmetries refer to laws of nature rather than correlations between events. Although these far-reaching thoughts gained their exact formulations in physics in the 1950s, their philosophical roots look back to the seventeenth century, when modern experimental science was at the beginning stages (primarily in Bacon's *Novum Organum,* 1620, and credit should also be given to Galileo and Newton in this respect). Laws of nature were first formulated in that era. They stated, on the one hand, that events (experiments) can be reproduced independent of place and time (and will lead to the same results), and on the other hand, that the laws of nature (concluded from those experiments) are independent of place and time (where and when they were established). Please note, these were the first symmetry laws: both the events and the generalized conclusions (laws) are invariant under spatial and time translations in our surroundings.

Symmetry and human perception

The phenomena observed in the above experiments can be explained by the combination of a geometrical and a dynamic symmetry operation (mirror-reflection and so-called charge-conjugation). If an imperfection of the symmetry is visible, our eyes adding the necessary correction to the picture (see, e.g. the famous Wundt experiment in psychology). When one of the combined elements of symmetry is invisible (a non-geometric property: e.g. a charge), we can't rely on our organs of sense; we must relegate it to our mind. Here we should cross frontiers between our sensitivity and rationality, our perception of the arts and the sciences, although, the once strict borders between them are becoming blurred.

Looking around, we find several symmetry properties in our physical and biological surroundings. We can easily realize that during the evolution of matter, while more and more complex formations came into existence, step by step, matter increasingly lost symmetries, (during which new, never before existing symmetry properties appeared, along with new qualities, which would be broken again at a higher level). Let's mention the decreasing number of retained quantities caused by the weakening of the fundamental physical interactions, paying special attention to parity non-conservation (violating the mirror symmetry). The asymmetry in the presence of chiral molecules in our surroundings leads to the dominance of handedness in the molecules (amino-acids, proteins, RNA, and DNA) which plays the determining role in living phenomena. Thus, it is not surprising that living creatures show an increasing morphological asymmetry (losing first spherical symmetry, then cylindrical, and further also bilateral symmetry), later leading to functional asymmetries as well. The most apparent functional asymmetry developed in *homo sapiens,* namely the lateralisation of the brain.

Recent achievements in brain research discovered more and more functions specialized to one or the other brain hemisphere. In our case the most important ones are the following: the separation of emotions and rationality; artistic abilities and scientific thinking; holistic and detail-oriented approaches; spatial and temporal perception; sensitivity to (simultaneously existing) sets or (elements of) sequences; perception of whole melodies or separate (musical) notes; affection to manual creativity or verbal expression, etc. The list could be extended, however, further hemisphere-dependent characteristics can be deduced from the enumerated ones. Note that the first features mentioned of each pair are attributed to the right brain hemisphere, and the second ones to the left hemisphere.

Almost all humans possess a slight dominance of one or the other hemisphere in their brain functions. Although the differences are not high, even the slightest dominance can determine different perception of the stimuli from the surroundings, different affection to reflect on the surroundings, and different abilities for creativity in the arts or the sciences, depending on a right or left hemisphere dominance. The conscious application of these identified *asymmetries in human perception* involve far-reaching consequences in the development of the individual's personality, in (possible differentiation of) education, and in understanding of the individual's relation to her/his surroundings.

William Day

Motion

We perceive both physical things and their motions. Material substances with their properties give us a feeling of certainty, but motion has about it an aura of mystery. The question is: How does motion fit into the scheme of things?

Motion is nature's most fundamental variable. It is the change of an interval between two objects or positions. One object moves relative to the other as a reference. That is relative motion. It is a localized phenomenon, and is a common occurrence. On the other hand, if there is a universal reference to which everything moves, then the motion is absolute. That means it is the same everywhere in the universe. And that is unusual.

Of the two motions, relative motion is the one that is ephemeral. It floats free of any mooring with no lasting quality. Move the reference and the properties associated with it change; move it at the same rate in the same direction and they vanish.

Absolute motion, on the other hand, is anchored to something stable. It is defined by a reference that is always stationary. With absolute motion the stability of the material world is not undermined by an endless shifting of uncontrolled change.

The Greeks, who based their physics on perception, saw the earth as stationary and all things moving relative to it. Motion was absolute.

They regarded reality as an indeterminate number of static states. Everything had its place of stability in the universe, where it was at rest and strove to reach it. Motion, therefore, was a change from one position to another. It was always closed and finite. There was, however, a problem in expressing this mathematically.

Being geometericians, the Greeks thought in terms of limits, of line segments, of geometrical figures and arrangements. Their universe was one of composition, a world that was finite and closed. And in it, motion was a limited displacement from one place to another.

Geometric analysis forced the Greek mathematicians to use comparative rather than metrical definitions. They could compare distances travelled in two uniform movements when times were assumed to be the same; or the times when the distances were the same; or the ratios of distances on one hand to times on the other. But without algebra and the equal sign, they could not arrive at a velocity as a number or magnitude representing a ratio of unlike quantities, namely distance and time.

In the sixteenth century mathematicians commenced to translate the geometrical methods inherited from the Greeks into algebraic symbols.These attempts to link up the "numerical geometry" of the Greeks with the newly-developed science of algebra culminated in the "analytical" geometry of Descartes.

The immense power of Descartes' method was not merely in converting geometry to algebraic notations, but in creating a more general attitude towards space. For Euclid and other Greek mathematicians a straight line was generally thought of as having a definite length. In Descartes' geometry, a straight line represented by a definite equation had no such limits. The equation specified a particular direction with respect to the axis, but it did not set limits to its extension.

Geometry ceased to be merely a static comparison of the innate properties of shapes and took on a dynamic aspect. A circle was no longer just a plane figure bound by a line consisting of an indeterminable number of points equidistant from its center, it was a figure traced by a point moving in a plane in a way which kept it equidistant from a point.

Thinking of motion as a rate changed our conception of reality. When the universe was opened up, physics, and the algebra and calculus to express it, became open-ended. Motion lost its moorage and became a state that could exist independently and endlessly. No longer could it be identified with some definite origin. It was free to show itself only as relative motion. Force could change it, but was not necessary for it to exist.

When Copernicus allowed the earth to move he shifted the image of the universe off perception and toward a conception that made the motions of the cosmos mathematically simpler. Galileo then recognized that objects moving relative to a spinning earth meant that objects moved relative to each other, regardless of any other movement that they might have.

Galileo's conception of motion

Until the Copernican revolution the universe was geometrically closed with the celestial bodies moving on spheres encased in an Archimedean space. The sun, moon, planets and stars were not of the same substance as the terrestrial environment, but of a pure ethereal non-corruptible quality that could move without the constraints of physical laws.

In Aristotle's cosmology the universe was finite, for nothing at infinite distance could revolve around a motionless earth in twenty-four hours. By allowing the earth to move, Copernicus removed these limits that had bound the universe for 2,000 years. This shift in orientation of the cosmos transformed our conception of space. With a revolving earth, space became a boundless void with no perceivable limit to its extent. The fathomless emptiness of a Euclidian space which Aristotle believed impossible became the new image of the universe for the dawning of the scientific age.

Motion in the Greek physics was a form of change. A change of position required a force, and any sustained motion required a continual force. The perplexing question was why a thrown object should continue after it leaves the hand. The Greeks believed that the continuity of motion was caused by a commotion created in the air behind the object that propelled it forward. It was the discrediting of this theory that led to Galileo's novel conception of motion.

In experiments with trajectories and inclined planes, Galileo realized that it is not motion but the change of motion that requires a force. If all obstructions and resistances are removed, there was apparently no reason why something in motion should not go on indefinitely. Force causes acceleration, not motion, so a motion by itself remains undiminished unless obstructed or acted upon. Galileo, therefore, came to the remarkable conclusion that motion is more than change, it is a state of being, just as being at rest is a state. Once motion is instilled, unless interfered with, it persists forever.

After the heliocentric system of Copernicus, this was the most revolutionary idea to come out of the Renaissance. It changed a way of thinking and set the foundation for a new worldview. Galileo, by his conception of motion as a state, disengaged motion and set it free to fly through space unimpeded and endlessly. The effect of motion being a state was that a moving body no longer needed any participation by the space through which it travels. Space became a void, and could be nothing more.

Newton used this concept and devised a scheme to explain why the moon and planets were able to move in orbits indefinitely. He took Galileo's definition of motion and had it equivalent to rest only if it was uniform and rectilinear. Then, drawing upon the impression that it takes force to move things, he made gravity a force of attraction between masses and used it to act across space, pulling bodies from their straight line inertial motion into the perpetual fall of the orbits. This was the founding of dynamics as a physics in which it is believed that were it not for forces of nature, everything would be mired in inertia or flying off in endless directions.

Modern physics looks upon this law of inertial motion as its most fundamental law. The principle is simple: a body left to itself remains at rest; or if it is put into motion it will continue to move in a straight line indefinitely unless interfered with its movement. To us the concept is perfectly clear, plausible, and even self-evident. It seems obvious that this is the natural state of matter. But less than four hundred years ago to nearly everyone the idea seemed not only false, it seemed even absurd. The reason is that pure inertial motion does not occur in nature. It is absolutely and completely impossible.

Suppose now that motion doesn't have to be forced, that things in space move spontaneously just from reacting to their space environments. The state of being, therefore, would not be the inertial motion of things in a void, but the expected condition of objects being in a relation with their environments.

Then suppose that things in space move spontaneously until they form stable arrangements. These arrangements would be systems where one set of components encircles a nuclear body in the endless motion of orbits. These would be the known systems, the atoms and gravitational systems. Consider the apple.

Newton in the orchard saw things from a very limited terrestrial perspective. If the earth had been a point as he had to assume for his calculations, the behavior of the apple would have been quite different. When the apple dropped from the tree it would not have been stopped in its fall. It would have continued to fall at an ever increasing rate, zoomed past the earth-point at an enormous velocity, continued in its flight on the other side, decelerating as it went, then stopping momentarily, only to fall back again to complete an extremely elongated orbit and return to the tree with no net gain or loss in energy. What Newton saw was only a small slice of this potentially much larger action. The reason the apple fell to the ground was simply because the earth bulged out and got in the way.

When an object is thrown, therefore, it does not take on a continuous endless inertial motion. Any object released in space goes into an orbit, or what can be described as potentially an orbit. Any dropped object begins an orbit, and any motion added to it becomes a part of the orbit length. A thrown object adds the length of forced motion across its elongated eliptical fall and widens it on one end. To us it looks like a continuous motion that could go straight if thrown hard enough, but that is a misimpression. No more motion is created or continued than the forced displacement and the spontaneous motion of the fall.

When a batter hits a baseball, the ball is propelled against its inertia only for the instant of the hit and the distance it is accelerated. That equation is $d = vt$, or for the average velocity during acceleration: $d = 1/2v2t$. To translate this distance to the length it would add to an orbit it is the fraction of the orbital velocity of a circular orbit at that position in the gravitational field: $d = v2t/2vo$. That is the distance of motion given to the ball.

If that short distance is all that is added to the ball's orbit, why then does a slugged baseball take off for center field?

The baseball is propelled against its inertia only for an instant by the bat and then goes into what potentially would be an orbit. Because geometry is thought of as being static, we think of distance as metrical and independent of velocity and time. But in kinematic geometry distance is interrelated with velocity and time by the classic equation, $d = vt$.

Kepler's second law states that for orbiting planets, a line connecting the sun and planet sweeps out equal areas in equal times. In other words, in the kinematics of orbits where distances are related to the velocity and time, distances for equal areas are equivalent. Areas swept by an orbit are comparable because the distance covered is dependent on the velocity and time.

When the baseball is hit it gains a high velocity in a very short time and distance. That span becomes an arc of the ball's potential orbit. The ball then continues on its orbit, slowing down and taking longer. The distance it covers is considerably greater than when it was accelerated by the hit. Both distances, however, are equivalent by the equation $d = vt$. Our problem is that we think of the distance to center field in terms of static geometry, when in fact it is an arc that is equal in area swept compared to when it was being propelled. As far as the ball is concerned, it is in orbit and nothing more is changing.

The idea that an object would go in a straight line unless diverted is not reality. It is a creation of our cerebral imaging. Any object moving spontaneously or being propelled by force and then released assumes some part of an orbit, either actual or potential. Not only is motion the natural state, it is orbital motion.

An indication that the natural state is orbital motion shows itself in the way we have to go into space. If things were being held to the earth by a force of gravity one would think that it should be possible simply to move away from the earth slowly and continually. But that is not the case. To leave the earth we have to reach an escape velocity. We have to propel first into an orbit, then enlarge the orbit until it is out of the orbital structure of the earth system. Even then, however, we haven't escaped. From the earth we would go into orbit around the sun. And from there we would extend into a journey around the galaxy.

Galileo's conception of motion originated to account for the behaviour of matter when free of any obstruction. Experimentally, it seems like that is what happens. Force changes the motion, but motion itself is like a property that persists unless changed by some interference. To us it seems obvious, but that is because we have been taught that way. Motion is not something that is instilled in a body like a property which, if not given up, keeps it going forever.

The belief has no rational basis and has been assumed to be true because it just seems that that is what happens. That abstract concept, nevertheless, shaped the worldview and set the course of physics for the next three hundred years. The effect of Galileo's abstraction was that it detached motion from direct causality and put physical theories afloat in a sea of abstractions. Physics became a science of mathematical descriptions rationalized by unsubstantiated causes.

Newtonian physics was and is quite adequate for the Galilean-Newtonian worldview for which it was designed. Despite the misconceptions and abstractions the scheme gives accurate descriptions of bodies moving in space. With this scheme it seemed that a comprehensive understanding of physical reality was theoretically possible. That is, until near the end of the nineteenth century. A crisis then appeared that has haunted physics ever since.

Newton believed light to be corpuscular and moving through space the way matter moves through space. But Thomas Young, in 1803, demonstrated unequivocally that light consists of waves. Wave motion is the means by which energy is transmitted through a medium. There was evidence that light travels as waves, but there was no corroborating evidence of a medium. If a medium exists for light, why then does matter not encounter a resistance to its movement through it? Instead of solving this problem by reexamining the basic concepts, physicists kept dynamics and rationalized the inconsistencies by paradoxical theories.

The problem climaxed in 1887. In that year, Michelson and Morley tried to measure the movement of the earth through the ether by determining its effect on the velocity of light.[1] They were unable to detect any movement whatsoever. From the standpoint of Newtonian dynamics this was incomprehensible. Every school child knows that the earth moves around the sun.

This became a junction when physicists could have taken either of two courses. They could have questioned the conceptions upon which physics was founded: that the motion of matter and light are unrelated and space is not a void; or they could have kept dynamics and created conditions to make the theories consistent with it. They stayed with dynamics and gave matter variables.

Einstein's relativity theory

The Michelson-Morley experiment of 1887 showed that something is fundamentally wrong with Newtonian physics. The direct indication of the experiment is that the velocity of light

1. A. A. Michelson, and E. W. Morley, "On the relative motion of the earth and the luminiferous ether," in *Am. J. Sci.*, 34(3), 1887, pp. 333-345; *Phil. Mag.*, 24(5), 1887, pp. 449-463.

is always constant. Why it should be constant can be due to either of two suppositions:

1. Light and matter have unrelated motions, or

2. we cannot measure changes in light's velocity.

Einstein took the second supposition and used "relativistic effects" to develop his theory of relativity.

Einstein kept Newton's impression that light moves through space the same way matter moves through space. In other words, he kept the Galilean-Newtonian worldview. He believed that light is self-propagating and doesn't need a medium. He therefore dismissed Newton's absolute space as unnecessary and contended that there is only relative motion. Einstein believed that we can move relative to light, we just can't measure the difference on light's velocity. Light's velocity is always constant because anything moving relative to it changes in such a way that changes in light's velocity can't be measured. As objects approach the speed of light, time slows, lengths contract, and masses increase.

Einstein's theory of relativity was an extremely accurate way of measuring the world in motion as we see it, but it doesn't measure the objective reality. In Newtonian physics there is an objective universe that exists independent of us. To measure this universe we have to know the distance to correct for light's transmission time. Einstein dismissed the idea that this physical reality can be truly measured and contended that the only true reality is that as seen by the observer. Einstein therefore put the observer in the perpetual present and made time synonymous with the velocity of light.

It is generally assumed that Einstein resolved this Michelson-Morley paradox by his theory of relativity. The fact is, he did not. He took over earlier suggestions that attempts to measure a change in light's velocity fail because any would-be change is nullified by a compensating change in the object used to measure it.

Einstein's reasoning is similar to that originally proposed by Lorentz and FitzGerald, namely that there is a contraction of length and dilation of time in one frame of reference with respect to the length and time in another reference frame. The difference is that Lorentz and FitzGerald assumed the contraction and time dilation were caused by the earth's physical reference frame moving in interaction with an ether; whereas Einstein assumed that they were caused by the intangible relative velocity between successive reference frames of the moving earth.[2]

Einstein's assumed "causative factors," however, proved to be impossible for exactly the same reason the Lorentz and FitzGerald theories were impossible. It is not rationally possible for a contraction and time dilation in one reference frame to cause velocities of two light beams in opposite directions at assumed velocities c - v and c + v to be simultaneously converted to c. In other words, the presumed conditions to nullify a reading of the earth's forward movement simply cannot, at the same time, nullify a change in the reading of light's velocity in the opposite direction. The velocity of light is absolute, but it cannot be proven by invoking the movement of the earth.[3]

There is a non-material medium

Relativity is a modification of dynamics to make things consistent with the null result of the Michelson-Morley experiment. Just as with Newton's theory, relativity requires space to be a void. Dynamics cannot posit a medium without undermining the very premises upon which the entire science has been built. Instead of interactions being between bodies of matter, they would be between matter and the medium. The problem is: there is clear experimental evidence that the medium exists.

In 1913, Georges Sagnac, a French physicist, modified the Michelson-Morley experiment of 1887 so that instead of doubling the path of the light beam back upon itself, a split beam of light was directed around the edge of a 20-inch turntable.[4] When the table was rotated and the light beam was brought on itself there now were interference fringes. The edge of the rotating table did indeed move relative to the light waves, or more correctly stated, relative to the medium of the light waves. In 1925, Michelson, together with Henry Gale, adjusted his original experiment so that it measured the earth's rotation, and this too showed the Sagnac effect.[5] Sagnac's discovery led to advances in guidance system technology. The ring-laser gyroscopes, that guide jets such as the Boeing 757 and 767 through the skies, operate on the "Sagnac effect."[6]

Just as Newton left out light and fields to make a mechanical model in a void, his successors have left out the medium to keep explanations in terms of dynamics. In order to justify light waves and fields they contend that these waves are self-

2. A. Einstein, "Zur Elektrodynamik bewegter Körper," in *Ann. d. Physik* 17(3), 1905, pp. 891-921; English trans. W. Perrett and G. B. Jeffrey, *On the electrodynamics of moving bodies,* Methuen and Co., London, 1922.

3. R. L. Henderson, *The Return of Common Sense: The Demise of Relativity,* Common Sense Press, Sun City, AZ, 1992.

4. G. Sagnac, "L'éther lumineux demontré par l'effet du vent relatif d'éther dans un interfermetre en rotation uniform," or in *Compt. rend.* 157, 1913, pp. 708-710, 1410-1413.

5. A. A. Michelson, and H. G. Gale, "The effect of the earth's rotation on the velocity of light," or *Astrophys. J.* 61 (3), 1925, pp. 140-145.

6. D. Z. Anderson,"Optical gyroscopes," in *Sci. Am.*, 94-99, April, 1986.

propagating. Waves, however, do not exist without a medium, and nothing can propagate its own motion without an expenditure of energy.

The experiments could not show the earth moving through the medium and relative to light, but the experiments with rotational motion clearly showed movement through the medium. This actually compounded the mystery since some people accepted Sagnac's experiment as indication of the medium, but did not accept at face value the fact that the Michelson-Morley result did not show the earth moving. As we shall see, both experimental results are correct.

The problem is how to make a physical theory to reconcile the motion of light with the motion of matter. Light is nonmaterial, consists of waves, travels at an enormous velocity, and its waves are transverse.[7] To be consistent with physics, all of these conditions indicate that there must be a non-material medium of extreme rigidity. Matter, on the other hand, has motion only relative to other matter.

How then is it possible to combine the requirements for light's motion with Newtonian physics where matter has inertial motion and moves through an unreactive void called space, and still be free of inconsistencies and contradictions? The answer is: It apparently isn't possible. Everyone is trying to keep the Galilean-Newtonian worldview with its physics of dynamics and explain light and fields in terms of the physics of matter. It doesn't work. Every explanation is riddled with flaws. Einstein's answer was to ignore the requirements for light and claim there is no medium. The ether idea does no better. It ignores the conditions of light and then ignores that there can't be any interaction between the ether and matter.

There can't be an interaction of the medium with matter when it moves freely in space, otherwise there would be a resistance. There isn't any. To make the ether extremely tenuous simply begs the question and ignores the physics requirements. All rationalizations suggesting drag, entrainment, or other adjustments are dodging the issue.

So how can there be a universal medium for light that matter moves through without interaction?

The only way the conflict can be resolved is to reverse the process in solving the problem. Instead of trying to fit light into the physics of matter, we need to devise a physics of light and fit matter into it. This is reasonable because the material universe did not arise from matter, it arose from something nonmaterial.

7. Transverse waves move perpendicular to the motion of the waves. Rope waves are transverse. By moving the free end of a rope up and down quickly the wave moves down the rope but the parts of the rope making the wave move up and down in place. If the rope moves vertically or horizontally, the waves have a vertical or horizontal polarization. Only transverse waves can have a polarization.

The worldview that we inherited from Galileo and Newton has given us a false impression of space. There is no void in the strict sense of being a nothingness. The medium is space. Matter consists of motion (electromagnetism) that decoupled from the medium into self-contained particles which then organized and aggregated to become objects now suspended in the medium by their gravitational fields. The medium is exactly as it has been known it must be to be consistent with light's properties. Matter doesn't move in the medium. It has only relative motion, which is a secondary effect from individual bodies moving in direct response to the geometry imposed on the medium by other bodies.

If matter is structured on motion, this means the property that atoms and gravitational systems are based on is motion, not energy. In other words, matter has to be thought of holistically, and by its features that are absolute. Since these systems are orbital, their orbits have to be regarded in their entirety. The property of motion that defines an orbit is not its rate, not the velocity or momentum, but the total motion, which is to say, the length of the orbit. It is the total motion of the earth's orbit that is absolute, so absolute that we set our calendars by it.

Matter is structured on total motion

This is a new concept to physics and unrelated to dynamics. In physics, motion has been treated as a separate variable of matter, not as an integral part of matter's structure. It is measured as a rate. As a result, interest has been in how fast something moves, and not how far. In the kinematics of orbital systems, however, the motion is cyclical and finite. It goes the length of the orbit, then repeats itself.

Defining matter by its absolute values frees physics from a perplexing problem. If all motion were relative, then orbital systems would need an outside reference to define that motion. In dynamics, the moon and planets stay in orbit because of a fortuitous balance between the force of gravitational attraction and their natural tendency to continue in straightline inertial motion. Without an external reference, however, inertial motion does not exist and one body cannot encircle another. All systems would undergo gravitational collapse.

The theoretical basis of dynamics, therefore, makes an unusual demand on physical reality. With this physics, a galaxy alone in space would be unstable. Without a surrounding universe it could have no inertial motion and would collapse from its own gravity. Not only does Newton's theory require each galaxy to be surrounded by the universe, it requires the universe in each perspective to be spherically symmetrical.

It is possible that the universe is so precisely balanced, but this seems to be an instance of asking physical reality to stand in singular balance in order to justify an established theory. It seems that we are trying to tell nature how it should be, rather than accepting reality by its most logical interpretation.

A physics based solely on relative motion is conceptually on the wrong side of reality for defining matter's structure. It implies that atoms and gravitational systems cannot stand alone, that they have no motion without the rest of the universe. But holistically, where the motion of electrons and planets is taken in its entirety, they are self-contained and Mach's principle is unnecessary.[8]

Orbital systems are self-contained

Matter is structured on a pattern that is the same for three stages of a hierarchy. The hierarchy consists of particles, atoms, and gravitational systems. In each case there is a nucleus that creates the space environment with which the lesser components respond by moving and making the system. Each stage differs from the other by the type of nucleus, the condition of space it creates, and the kind of component that responds to it. The hierarchy results because the systems of one stage become the units for the stage that follows. Particles condense, atoms follow, and the amassing and aggregation of atoms lead to the formation of gravitational systems.

Matter is structured on orbital systems but the difference in size between a nucleus and its system is enormous. The proton has a diameter of approximately 10-13cm, while that of the hydrogen atom is 10-8cm. The atom, therefore, is 100,000 times larger than its nucleus. This is comparable to a grain of sand in the middle of a football field, far beyond the range of visibility. The other systems of matter's hierarchy show the same tremendous disparity in size.

This disproportionality strains the credibility of Newtonian dynamics. In physics it is believed that there is a force of attraction between the nucleus and the orbiting bodies that holds the latter on their courses. It is difficult, however, to imagine that a grain of sand could generate so much power that it can extend across a space of 100 yards and pull another grain of sand around it. Pluto, at the rim of the solar system, moves in an eternal twilight of a sun so distant that it appears in the sky like a star.

8. Mach believed that the motion of each individual body is determined by all other bodies in the universe.

How then to account for the formation of these systems? Nature has no forces, it follows the path of least effort. It takes no force for a body to move spontaneously in response to its environment. The nucleus influences the course of its satellites, not by forcing their motion, but by shaping the environment which guides them. The natural tendency, therefore, has been for those things which create an environment around them to be the nuclei around which systems form.

Physics has made a full turn. Just as the Greeks had a problem using geometry to express a rate, physicists have a problem combining matter and motion. The universe is not closed as the Greeks imagined, but matter doubtlessly is. The dynamics that have served so well to expand into the universe are totally inappropriate for describing the composition and geometry of matter.

In order to define a structure based on motion we need to define motion as it is related to its cause. Motion is not a state as hypothesized by Galileo. It is not an endless extension. Motion is a displacement by an applied force that goes so far and stops. When the force stops, so too does the extension of the motion. It cannot, however, simply terminate as a dead end in space. It closes on itself in a manner that gives explicit meaning to motion and the nature of matter.

The displacement by force, the suspension in the medium, and the orbital structures of matter are all interrelated. The impulse of matter is to be in the center of its gravitational field that holds it in suspension. It is under a compulsion to be centered in its gravitational field, and any displacement adds to the path followed by the body in its return to the center.

The Greeks were right. Everything does have its natural place and strives to reach it. They just had the center wrong. The natural place is actually the center of the interactive environment, and for bodies in space, that is the center of their gravitational field. It is the imbalance made in the field by the earth's strong gravity that causes bodies to fall to equalize their own fields and remain centered.

A displacement by force, therefore, does not leave the body displaced in a new space environment. The body retains the acquired motion but continues its fall. The displacement span adds to the fall from its own vector and creates an orbit of total motion that continues to repeat itself.

It is not the rate of displacement but its extent that is added as motion. That motion, that total motion, is given as a length extended to the orbit and can be changed only by a transfer from an external force.[9]

9. This is readily apparent from the space program. If a satellite in orbit is given a rocket boost, it doesn't go faster, it goes farther. It moves into a larger orbit. The length of the orbit has been extended by applying a force to the satellite. To bring a satellite down, NASA fires retrorockets and reduces the orbit.

Total motion is a structural feature of matter derived from movement through the medium and is as absolute as a wavelength of light.

There is an overlap of an object's commitment to its total motion and its compulsion to move into a gravitational gradient to equalize its field. The downward move into the gradient is superimposed by the total motion to complete the orbit. Whereas a body with no total motion will fall vertically into the gradient, one with the motion can run against it. Like a surfer, a satellite in an elliptic orbit rides to its apogee and slides to its perigee, varying its velocity and adjusting its direction within the confinement of its orbit.

The universe is a landscape of peaks and hollows, of highs and lows, mapped in the intensity of gravitational fields and the masses of matter that make them. And as bodies in space move, they ride the waves of other bodies and surf the contours of their fields.

The Copernican revolution opened up the universe and expanded the horizons. The physics that developed from it grew with the belief that rest is really only a special case of motion and it is not motion but the change of motion that results from force. This new way of thinking was eminently suitable for exploring a universe that seemed to extend toward the infinite. The problem, however, arose when the visions of theorists turned inward toward the infinitesimal, to the structure and composition of matter. Matter is not open-ended. It is finite and closed. Its properties are absolute, not relative.

Just as Copernicus mentally raised our perspective and imagined the sun and planets from a more distant position to see a simpler order to the planetary system, we need to expand our mental image even farther, toward the astronomical and the infinitesimal, to see the hierarchy upon which matter is structured.

There is a hierarchy of particles, atoms, and gravitational systems assembled solely on motion. Remove motion from each and the system collapses to the next lower level. Between atoms and gravitational systems are the combinations and aggregates of atoms from which gravitational systems form. But without motion, atoms become particles, and particles shrink to the infamous Black Hole.

What is astonishing is how unsubstantial matter really is. The volume on every level, with size delimited by only a few components in motion, is almost entirely space. Without structure there is little else. The vacuous nature of matter is made possible by moving components screening a volume from general mixing. Particles and atoms are readily penetrated by things smaller, but appear hard and impenetrable to things larger. When this house of cards collapses, the true nature of matter and its origin reveal themselves.

The residual motion that lies at the foundation of matter's structural hierarchy is what remains. It is motion without any frames of matter. It is motion at the level of electromagnetism where motion and energy are synonymous.

The inescapable conclusion is that matter arose from and expanded on motion in a hierarchy of size like an inverted pyramid. Motion defines its size and confines its action. The structural motion segregates the composition of the system from its surroundings and gives rise to the physical properties that it exhibits. The atoms, the molecules, substances, and gravitational systems act as units. Their properties are holistic, and they are absolute.

Kinematic geometry

Structures based on motion have a geometry based on motion. In dynamics, force transmutes to acceleration in relative motion by the equation $F = ma$; in the new physics, force converts to a displacement span added to orbit length, or $F = ml$. There are, therefore, the following kinematic geometry principles:

1. Distance is interrelated with velocity and time by $d = vt$.
2. All lines of motion in space are closed.
3. Orbital lengths are absolute and self-contained.
4. Force translates to orbital change by $F = ml$.

We are in a structure of matter, a stage of the hierarchy, however large it might seem, and a part of it. When we look out through space we are looking out through the skeletal frame of the material world. To move through this world we have to follow the principles to which it owes its existence. Moving freely through space is not one of them. The impression that we can fly through space the way we fly through the air is an illusion. There is no free motion. Motion in space cannot be separated from structure. It can occur only in the process of structure building.

Fields give a shape to the medium and make motion possible. It is not the object moving through the medium, but rather the medium with the imposed geometry to which the object steadies. A gravitational field weakens the tension of the medium and slows the velocity of light and equilibration of other fields in it. An object in the gradient of a strong gravitational field will experience an imbalance in the equilibration of its own field and will therefore move spontaneously into the gradient to equalize its own field by the Doppler effect and remain centered. To the object it is always in the center of its space environment, to us it is falling, and we call it gravity.

Jørgen Dehs

Sense of Landscape
Reflections on a Concept, a Metaphor, a Model

In its present day use, the word landscape is not a geographical term or a territorial judicial concept. First and foremost it signifies a space of nature where the sense of sight can spread out unhindered. We have an interest in landscape when we feel the need to stretch our legs – and stretch our eyes. Along with this common understanding – and probably because of it – the term landscape enjoys a comprehensive career as a metaphor. The concept can actually be used about any sight that extends itself, as long as it is of an adequate scale. This makes the concept a little suspicious. Every chaotic totality is assembled into a unity as soon as it is labeled a landscape. The term "urban landscape" sheds a redeeming glow upon even the most dejected neighborhood; "industrial landscape" transforms any romping ground for the ravages of industry into an object of aesthetic sensibility. Perhaps this is due to nothing more than the simple association of landscape with a peaceful mental state – even when the landscape referred to is one filled with industrial waste. Precisely this suspicious feature gives reason to consider the concept, metaphor, model "landscape" just a little closer. Perhaps there is more to it.

When we look at a landscape, we're not looking at an object that our glance is directed towards as a focal operation, rather, we see the totality of all the possibilities of focus that exist within a field of vision. We devote ourselves to the sight and not to the objects included in it. In this sense, it is the sight itself, which is the object. This makes landscape a typical case for aesthetic thinking. When one speaks of "the aesthetics of landscape," it is merely a specification of what already lies in the concept of landscape. It is not a question of the attitude of the spectator. An examination of a landscape as landscape is unavoidably an aesthetic examination. This is also true for all forms of "like-a-landscape," that is, when landscape is used as metaphor.

Pushed to an extreme, landscape means a flowing variety that is held together by the spectators glance. And perhaps every attempt at unfolding the historical and semantic potential of the concept is doomed to end in a flow – and in such a way that it escapes being assembled into a unity. But, with that, I have already anticipated one of the awkward points in that which I call: a sense of landscape.

The symbolic presence of nature

To view nature, or as it is referred to in the letters of Cézanne, to stand "face to face" with it, is not directly an account of a dialogical nature. Hermeneutics, and its tradition, is known for emphasizing the dialogical relationship between the recipient and the work of art. This model possesses the small, but entertaining problem that "dialogue" cannot be taken literally in this context either. The dialogical relation must be understood in much broader terms. Perhaps the work of art causes a process of reflection whose components are questions raised by the work, and answers one can also find in the work. In any case, it is justified to claim that the work – for example, one of Cézanne's paintings of Mont Saint-Victoire – neither formulates questions, nor provides answers. The spectator's dialogue is with himself, even when it takes place "face to face" with the work – that is, if it takes place at all.

The model can perhaps be made more literal if one transfers it to a sufficiently exclusive pattern of culture. Schopenhauer suggested on one occasion that one should imagine the dialogue with a work of art placed in a feudal context. When you confront a work of art, it is like meeting a distinguished member of the royal court: one does not speak to *them*, one waits politely to be spoken to you. Defining the form of the dialogue will most certainly end in maintaining its asymmetry. This becomes evident when the dialogue model actually appears in relation to nature. According to Kant, nature "speaks" to us through its beautiful forms. Even though the experience of the beauty of nature has to do with pleasing the senses, Kant emphatically associates it with a thoughtful state. As he writes: "The thought that nature has produced this beauty (...) must accompany our intuition and reflection."[1] Nature speaks to us and our answer is thoughtfulness.

What applies to a man-made work, apparently also applies to nature. But, if one asks if art and nature are thereby equal dialogue partners, Kant answers no. Nature has the authority in the area of aesthetics. This means that art, in order to be successful, has to resemble nature: "the purposefulness of the form must appear just as free of all arbitrary constraints of rules as if it was a product of pure nature."[2] Approximately thirty years later, Hegel also answers no, but because he means the opposite. Nature is only beautiful as "a reflection of the beauty that belongs to the spirit." This means that when we appreciate nature as an aesthetic object, it is because it reflects the governing aesthetic norms in art and in culture. In a dialogue between nature and culture, it is culture that has the first and the last word.

Even more explicitly than Hegel, the neo-Hegelian Joachim Ritter has contributed to the idea that the nature we conceive of as a contrast to culture has its own cultural history. Thanks to him, the concept of landscape has achieved a prominent position in the history of aesthetics. In his famous and controversial article from 1963,[3] Ritter conceives landscape as a key concept in the determination of the cultural function of aesthetics since the 1700s. The tradition of devoting oneself to nature is interpreted by Ritter as a pattern that lies in continuation of the Antique concept of theory, *theoria*, meaning at once: contemplation, exploration, and divine service. The object of contemplation for the Greeks was the beautiful and good order of things, ultimately nothing less than the cosmos. Such an innocent way of making the totality of nature a theme has not been in vogue since the Renaissance. More correctly, it loses its prestige as a theoretical project when the mathematically oriented sciences take over as the medium of knowledge in the field of nature. Ritter's suggestion is that the aesthetic

1. Imanuel Kant, *Critique of Judgment* (1790), trans. from *Werke in sechs Bänden,* vol. V, Darmstadt, 1975, p. 396.

2. Ibid. p. 404.

3. "Landschaft. Zur Funktion des Ästhetischen in der modernen Gesellschaft," in J. Ritter, *Subjektivität. Sechs Aufsätze,* Suhrkamp, Frankfurt/M., 1974, pp. 141-190.

relationship to nature can be understood as the bourgeois culture's compensation for this loss. In the pleasurable contemplation of a landscape, a metaphysical activity lives on – one that was originally conceived as corresponding to thought, and not to the senses.

When landscape comes into aesthetic honor and dignity as a symbolic representation of nature as a whole, it is, as Ritter maintains, not within the perspective of the farm worker. The aesthetic enjoyment of nature is a privilege for the bourgeois individual, who is removed from nature in his everyday life. The plot in Ritter's exposition suggests a fateful union between landscape and art. When we disregard the farm worker, landscape doesn't relate to our actual existence. At most, it relates to a pause, of shorter or longer duration, inserted into the daily pattern of urgent doings. In Ritter's perspective, landscape appears as a phenomenon of comprehensive cultural meaning which is due to its status as an exception. Both landscape and art can be described as paradoxical cultural institutions whose prestige is coincidental with their ability to maintain an aura of an alternative value system. In the case of landscape, this is the aura of fundamental reality in a liberating scale.

Ritter's way of thinking is, as mentioned, Hegelian. He argues for the existence of meaningful reason in the development of western culture. The wealth of modern culture and its ability to supplement itself is demonstrated in the fact that the Greek concept of theory has not been lost in the development of the technical-scientific dominance over nature. On the contrary, it is resurrected in a transformed version, as an aesthetic feeling for landscape. It is trifling to add that neither the Romantic space of nature, nor the Hegelian idea of modern culture, are intact phenomena today – if they ever were. In the meantime nature, both as a material and an aesthetic resource, has been so drastically intervened upon and so thoroughly worn down, that its ability to symbolize a fundamental reality fades in our consciousness, in favor of more complex relationships and overlaps between nature and culture. The great theoretical perspective on the concept of landscape is in the process of closing. But, even perspectives that are less spectacular than Ritter's should have their rights.

Landscape as non-work (Hegel)

Despite Ritter's proclaimed Hegelianism, he doesn't mention anywhere in his article the remarks on landscape found in

Hegel's lectures on aesthetics (1818-1829). This is likely because in the great, nature-despising, historical thinker there is very little to look for on this issue. The little there is – it mostly resembles a couple of casual remarks – is surely of interest only if one is pursuing a different path than Ritter. But, Hegel's lectures actually present a definition of the concept "landscape." This distinguishes itself by first and foremost viewing landscape in a negative contrast to the work of art and ending with a positive appreciation:

"There is another sense in which we attribute beauty to Nature, namely, when we have the collective picture and a landscape before us rather than observe the living form of a simple object. Here we have no organic articulation of parts such as is derived from their notion and is presented to us as such ideal unity in spontaneous life. We have instead a rich variety of objects both organic and inorganic, which are united together on one or more planes of vision in their distinctive features, contours of mountains, winding outlines of rivers, groups of trees, huts, dwellings, palaces, and cities of mankind, ships, roadways, heaven and sea, valley and rock-cleft. We find, in addition to this variety and proceeding therefrom, a delightful or imposing harmony (äussere Zusammenstimmung) which appeals to our senses and interests us."[4]

Landscape cannot, and for good reason, be brought into agreement with Hegel's understanding of beauty as "the sensuous semblance of the idea" (sinnliche Scheinen der Idee). The idea is lacking which means that the unifying principle under which the parts could be organically subsumed is lacking. Instead, plurality and diversity reign and will not be assembled under law-bound relations, but rather, demonstrate an *äussere Zusammenstimmung* that interests us. Landscape appears here as an ultimate limit for what could be considered a unity. Inside of this rich diversity, *äussere Zusammenstimmung* is the only positive component of form.

One could wonder if it is only as an event of form that we take interest in the *äussere Zusammenstimmung* of the elements. If *Zusammenstimmung* meant, for example, a substantial harmony, it must be added that *Nicht-Zusammenstimmung* interests us as well. Just as the quotation explicitly puts landscape in contrast to an organic unity, it (unlike the English translation) avoids the loaded classical concept of harmony. Instead, it seems to indicate a medium for our interest in the encounters between perceivable things. This means that the separate elements will appear in the perspective of *äussere*

4. G. W. F. Hegel, *The Philosophy of Art,* vol. I, trans. F. P. B. Osmaston (1920), New York, 1975, p. 182.

Zusammenstimmung as soon as we view them as parts of a landscape.

This could indicate that the concept of landscape in the Romantic era anticipated the role that the institution of art plays today; that is a frame, which provides the guarantee that any manifestation will be principally relevant to our interest in art. Even though Hegel tried systematically to release art from the binds of nature, and at nature's expense, it is obvious that the *äussere Zusammenstimmung* in this case "interests us" *because* it is not arranged – that is to say it appears ordered *without* a landscape architect having been involved in it. In this case, Hegel is principally in agreement with the Kantian formula of beauty, "purposefulness without purpose." That nature is responsible for this semblance of purposefulness is according to Kant a decisive factor for our interest in the beautiful. On all accounts, it is useful to keep Kant and Hegel together in this matter.

It is a well-known ancient hypothesis that everything in nature has a purpose. This hypothesis is intended to guarantee a higher order behind the seemingly coincidental state of things. In Kant's aesthetics, it is reduced to mean that everything in nature *apparently* has a purpose. It has become an aesthetic statement, which is further exposed in the Hegelian pattern of thought: regarded as a work of art, nature makes no mistakes. This is not an obvious point of view. It can hardly be dated further back than the Romantic era and thus to the first manifestations of a modern conception of art. But the Hegelian pattern of thought is more complex: regarded as art, landscape is neither art nor work; even still, it is through the lenses of art and culture that landscape is able to please, impress and interest us.

Kant demonstrates an aesthetic interest that is not bound to the concept of the artwork, but rather bound to nature. The work of art for him is secondary to this interest. This means that Kant still operates within the framework of the classical idea of Mimesis: art imitates nature. However, it is with a divergent semantic; it has little to do with an ideal and fundamental reality that in advance contains everything valid in the realm of art. Instead, one could speak of a dynamic pattern. The genius who has the ability to create something radically new is the instrument of nature. The liberal arts still need a legitimizing court and this court is still nature.

With Hegel, nature is no longer legitimizing anything. When others claim that everything has its basis in nature, they have, according to Hegel, ignored the fact that it is the task of the intellect to raise the question of what the basis is, and therefore it is the intellect that holds the truth about nature and not the reverse. As is summarized in his lecture compendium, *Enzyklopädie der philosophische Wissenschaften*: "in this truth nature disappears." This is not intended as a critique of truth: "The semblance that the Spirit is mediated through some other is abolished (aufgehoben) by the Spirit itself, while this has what you may call the sovereign ingratitude to abolish that which it seems mediated through."[5]

When we have an interest in nature, which is "eternally something other than the concept of it," it is under Hegelian conditions a negative print of the spirit (mind) which is the object of our interest. This is where the critical potential in his concept of nature is hidden. That which he calls our interest for *äussere Zusammenstimmung* could, for example, have something to do with a certain dead weight in the spirit's (mind's) sovereign ingratitude. This would be a sort of counter move: a slight weakening of sovereignty.

Landscape as model

I suggest that we must take seriously the idea of this dead weight when we, as Hegel, systematically conceive of the aesthetic of nature as a reflection of the way in which we see works of art. In doing so, the concept of landscape receives a noteworthy historical perspective, which concerns both the concept of beauty and the concept of the artwork. Landscape presents itself as one of the apocryphal sources of the weakened work concept in art. It seems evident that it is a painter of landscapes, Cézanne, who is commonly regarded as both the last traditional, and the first modern artist. "Face to face" with nature, he painted himself out of the figurative, and out of the work, as far as the construction of its unity (based upon a five-hundred-year-old tradition) is due to central perspective. When the artistic components have left the unity of the work and sought an alliance with nature, landscape takes over as the form of operation in painting. How, and how far we understand landscape as a kind of operational alternative to the concept of the work, can be suggestively illustrated with three models: "Identity in Transition," "The Borderless Place," and "Symbolic Landscape."

1. Identity in transition

Landscape is not just a subjectively constituted visual unity, it also represents (symbolically Kant would say) a dimension of

5. Trans. from G. W. F. Hegel, *Theorie Werkausgabe*, vol. 10, pp. 17 and 25.

reality on the other side of subjectivity. There is good reason to maintain this even though one has recognized the constitutional relationship between nature and culture. Sense of landscape is tied to the view – as well as to its physical reality. Due to this reality, the unity of landscape is an identity in transition. Landscape has its seasons and erosions; its elements have their age.

With this, the concept of the work discloses its idealistic features by only acknowledging identity – while the real work of art seldom lies about its historicity and its finite physical being. Time modifies the unique in a work of art; slowly but surely bringing it to ruin. The work of art is always on the way to sharing destiny with all other physical objects. This common fate becomes more and more apparent on its body. No matter what the picture originally stated, this, over time, erodes into a landscape. If the work of art represents an uprising against death, it is on borrowed time. The unique, which gradually fades into common destiny, cannot be restored. When the uprising against death receives technical and scientific support, it transforms the unique to its own prosthetic.

Sense of landscape means here that the unique is no longer the point of departure – which as regards landscape, is a conceptual abstraction. What is unique is the individual process – the continuum of transitions which has no witnesses. This transitory feature should not be confused with being something specifically modern. On the contrary, compared to the phenomena of *speed*, sense of landscape has to do with a slowness that could be mistaken for a complete standstill.

2. The borderless place

Landscape is a place extended to its aesthetic borders. Landscape means the maximum area of an aesthetically defined spatial unity. A continent, a country or a city, for instance, are not, unlike landscape, aesthetically defined places. Compared with the sacred aura that surrounds the concept of *genius loci,* Hegel's panoramic landscape is considerably more prosaic and sober, and rightly so: a secularized version of "the spirit of place" prior to the spirit becoming holy (Hegel is a speculative idealist with an inclination to realism).

Any space can be viewed from its potential as a landscape, or rather as a landscape in a landscape. In contrast to how we think of a work of art, landscape is something that in the final analysis, surrounds the spectator. To be face to face with a landscape also means being in it. A sense of landscape disturbs the aesthetic line of demarcation between spectator and object. The only border is the line of the horizon, which is spontaneously drawn through the spectator's view. This is true both perceptually and culturally – if one can distinguish between the two. The work, on the other hand, is extremely dependent, both perceptually and culturally (whether one can distinguish or not), on its own act of demarcation against its surroundings.

3. Symbolic landscape

Sense of landscape is a sense of other methods of reading than the linear or hierarchical. Around 1950, Marshall McLuhan noted that the frontpage of the *New York Times* had less to do with a linear text than with a "symbolic landscape." To say that newspapers address their readers in the form of a landscape of meaning, indicates an inflation compared to any rationally established hierarchy of meaning. But, there is a good reason for this inflation; everything that the paper prints is, in principal, of equal value as regards the function of media. Nothing can give the news greater meaning than that it is actually new.

The method of reading here concerns the post-Gutenbergian media culture. In this field, the landscape model is clearly not an aesthetic formula for how we reconcile ourselves with the unintentional results of our projects: if they can't be a work, they can always be a landscape. As part of an aesthetic form of production, the method of reading has nothing to do with a distinction between nature and culture. Instead, we find ourselves in a public laboratory for what Hegel called *äussere Zusammenstimmung*. In this context, sense of landscape is a major condition for survival, but also that which, in the long run, is worn upon. As long as our sense of the symbolic landscape is merely a sense of *layout,* it is difficult to speak of a counter move against the sovereign ingratitude of the spirit. It can hardly be bound to gratitude that we, in our doings, are confronted with nothing other than ourselves. A landscape, which we only read as our own text, and where we meet nothing other than our own intentions, is not on the same level as the concept of the work of art, and therefore not a potential alternative to it.

Concluding remarks

Sense of landscape can simultaneously be understood as a Romantic, a Modern and a media aesthetic (Postmodern) construction. That it contains a modification of arbitrary order may make it suspicious – possibly because it functions as a built-in corrective to an experience we narrowly connect with modernity. That the world should – with the words of a young Wittgenstein – be nothing but "everything that is the case," has through a long tradition been understood as an outrageous loss of meaning. It is a part of our understanding of our situation, that the lingering contemplation of the essential coherence of things *(theoria)* has lost its object. The essential coherence of things has, despite the phenomenological attempt at creating a resurrection, for some time been out of philosophical vogue.

Still there is wide agreement that contemplation can be melancholic, as in Walter Benjamin's portrait of "the allegorist" to paraphrase: When things are exposed to the allegorist's glance, the force of life flows out of them and they are surrendered to his mercy or disfavour; the thing is given meaning only to the extent that the allegoricist attaches meaning to it.[6]

The aesthetic corrective for a contingent world cannot create meaning where there is none. It is a corrective in the sense that aesthetic contemplation always plays the role of an extenuating circumstance. This is not in itself suspicious. A realism without extenuating circumstances is no realism. In any case, sense of landscape – in contrast to the era of Kant and Hegel – can be accused of being a fake that masks its own underlying nihilism. However, there is more to it.

6. W. Benjamin, *Ursprung des deutschen Trauerspiels* (1925), Suhrkamp, Frankfurt/M., 1972, p. 204, f. 1.

Diller + Scofidio

Blur Building

The Blur Building is a media pavilion for Swiss Expo 2002. It is situated at the base of Lake Neufchatel in Yverdon-les-Bains, Switzerland. The pavilion is made of filtered lake water, shot as a fine mist through 13,000 fog nozzles creating an artificial cloud that measures 300 feet wide by 200 feet deep by 65 feet high. A built-in weather station controls fog output in response to shifting climatic conditions such as temperature, humidity, wind direction, and wind speed. The public can approach Blur via a ramped bridge. The 400 foot long ramp deposits visitors at the center of the fog mass onto a large open air platform where movement is unregulated. Visual and acoustical references are erased along the journey toward the fog leaving only an optical "white-out" and the "white-noise" of pulsing water nozzles. Prior to entering the cloud, each visitor responds to a questionnaire/character profile and receives a "braincoat" (smart raincoat). The coat is used as protection from the wet environment and storage of the personality data

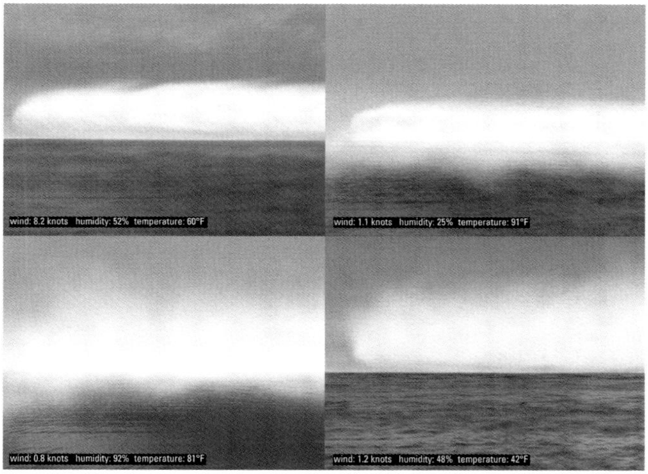
wind: 8.2 knots humidity: 52% temperature: 60°F
wind: 1.1 knots humidity: 25% temperature: 91°F
wind: 0.8 knots humidity: 92% temperature: 81°F
wind: 1.2 knots humidity: 48% temperature: 42°F

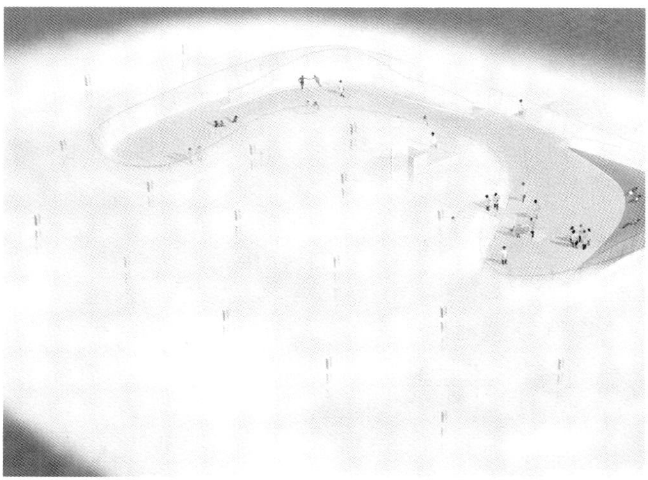

for communication with the cloud's computer network. Using tracking and location technologies, each visitor's position can be identified and their character profiles compared to any other visitor. As visitors pass one another, their coats will compare profiles and change color indicating the degree of attraction or repulsion, much like an involuntary blush. The system allows interaction among 400 visitors at any time. Visitors can climb another level to the Angel Bar at the summit. The final ascent resembles the sensation of flight as one pierces through

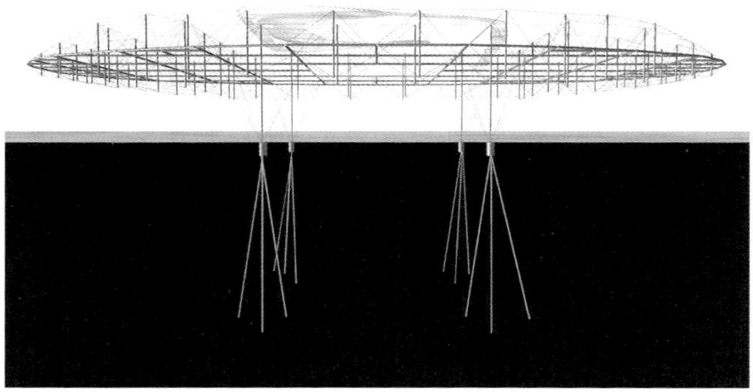

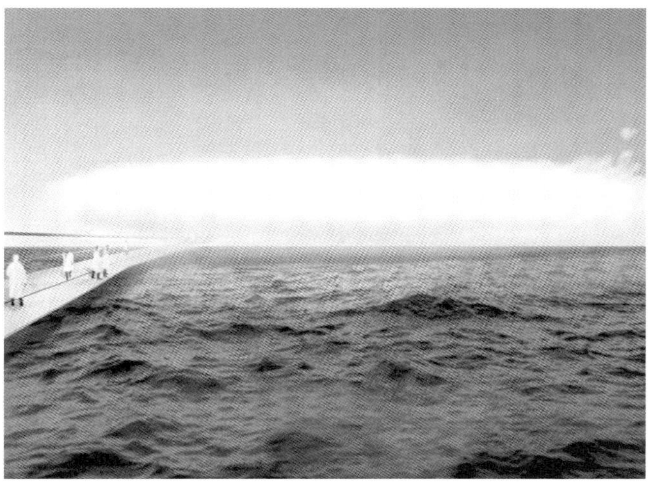

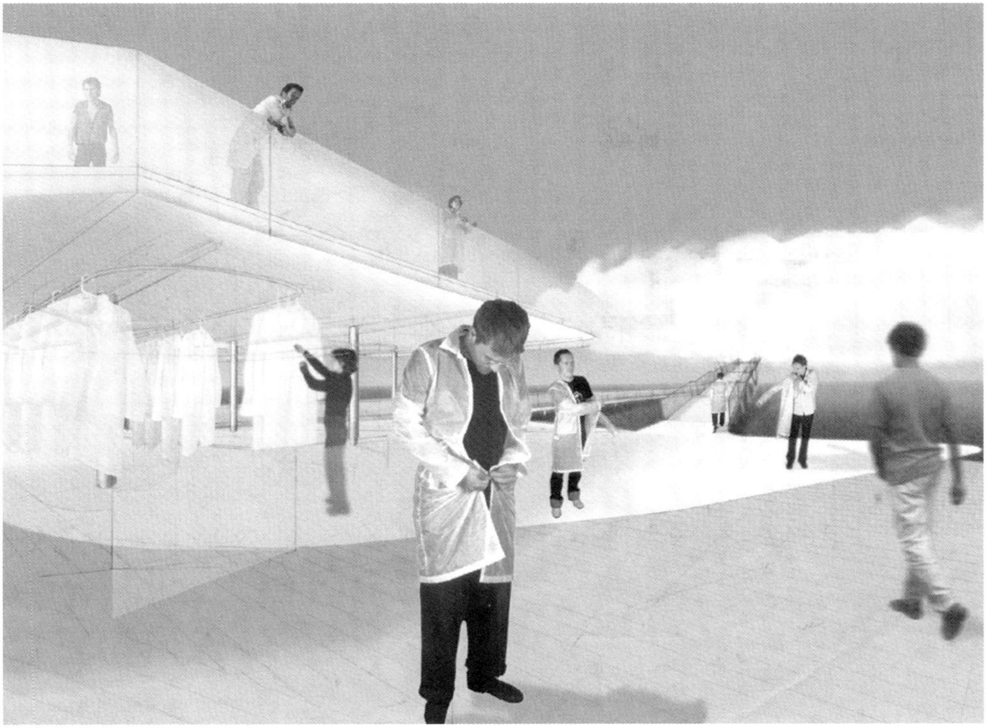

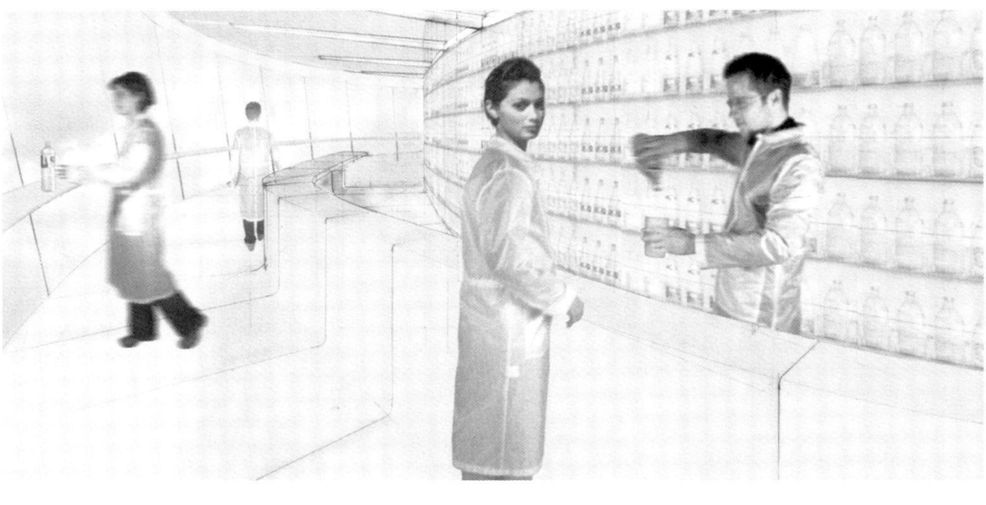

the cloud layer to the open sky. Here, visitors relax, take in the view, and choose from a large selection of commercial waters, municipal waters from world capitals, and glacial waters. At night, the fog will function as a dynamic and thick video screen.

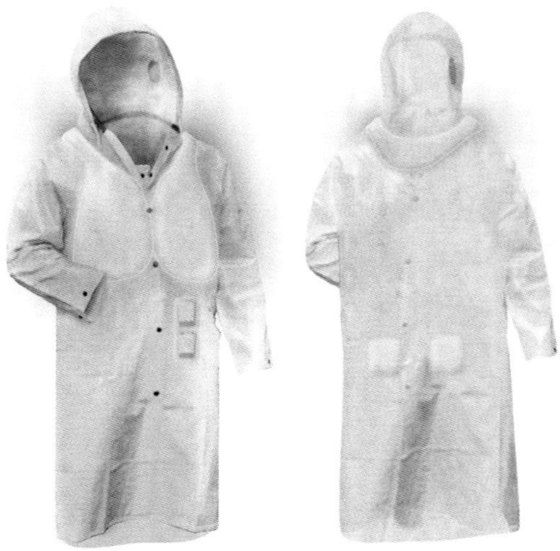

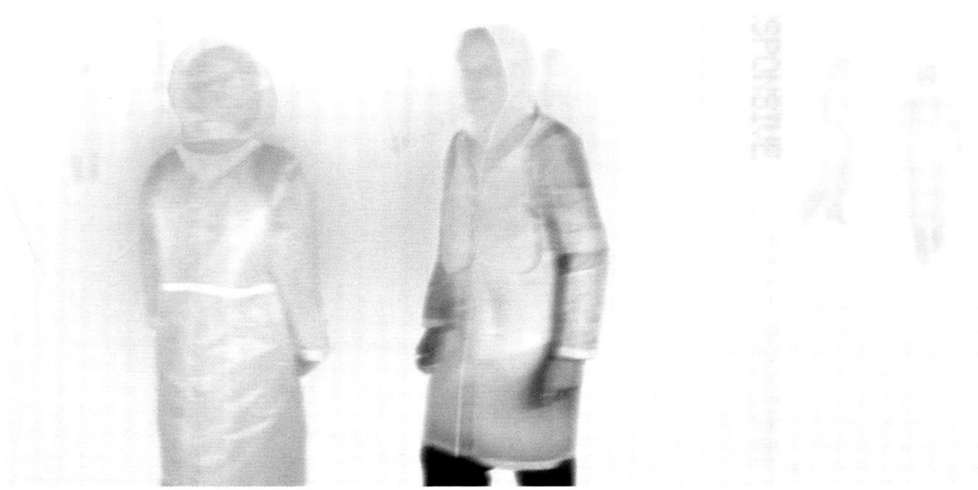

Thorleifur Einarsson

Geothermal Activity

The upper layers of the earth's crust are subject to daily, and even more so, seasonal temperature changes. Daily variations occur over depths of centimetres but seasonal variations occur from 10-30 metres downwards, though this varies according to the strata and climate in question. At the depth at which the seasonal effects die out, the temperature is close to the mean annual temperature, which in Iceland is 5°C near sea level. Below this level the temperature rises with depth. On continents where volcanism and folding have not occurred for a long period of geological time, the temperature at 1000 m depth is around 30°C. In Iceland, the temperature at 1000 m depth outside geothermal areas is generally 50-100°C while in high temperature geothermal areas it can reach the boiling point on the surface and increase by as much as 1°C/m where the increase is greatest (Fig. 1).

Water which has percolated to only shallow depths thus varies in temperature according to season, but if it goes deeper,

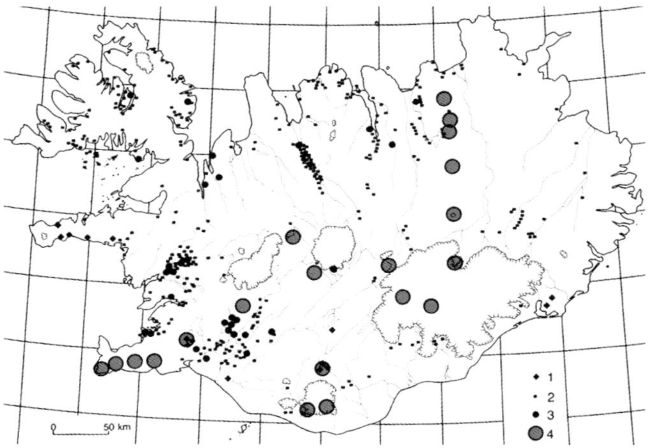

Fig. 1
Distribution of geothermal localities in Iceland. Explanation: 1) mineral springs up to 70°C, 3) hot springs 70-100°C and 4) high temperature areas.

the temperature will be the same all year, usually around the mean annual temperature of the area. Springs with water of a constant temperature are known in Iceland as *kaldavermsl*. On the other hand, water which percolates downwards to considerable depth is heated in accordance with the temperature gradient in the area. When it rises again to the surface it carries heat from within the earth. The main characteristics of such water are that it is hotter than the ground water and contains more dissolved solids. For instance, the amount of dissolved solids in Reykjavík's drinking water is around 60 mg/l while the domestic hot water in Reykjavík contains around 340 mg/l and in Hveragerdi around 1200 mg/l. The outlet vents of hot water or steam are known as hot springs (Icel. *hverir*) and the area in which they occur is a geothermal area.

For a long time it was believed that the hot water and steam in geothermal areas originated directly in cooling magma batholiths or intrusions deep within the crust. Research has now shown that most of the water is precipitation which has percolated downwards through the bedrock. Because of the high temperature gradient in geothermal areas, the temperature of the water has already reached 100°C or more at a few hundred metres depth.

Geothermal areas have traditionally been divided into low temperature areas, i.e. hot water areas and high temperature areas, i.e. steam areas with solfataras and fumaroles. This division is based on the temperature of the geothermal area. The temperature is either measured in deep drill holes or calculated from the silica content of the hot water (silica temperature). The temperature in low temperature areas is usually around 100°C at 1000 m depth and increases slowly below that, e.g. a temperature of 142°C has been measured in a 2000 m deep drill hole in Reykjavík and 160°C at 3000 m depth. The division between low temperature and high temperature geothermal areas is internationally set at 150°C measured at a depth of 1000 m. The highest temperatures measured in high temperature areas in Iceland are 340°C at a 2000 m depth in a drill hole at Krafla at Myvatn and 380°C at Nesjavellir, south of lake Thingvallavatn (Fig. 1).

The water emerging in low temperature areas is always basic[1] and is usually accompanied by precipitation of geyserite around the hot spring.

At the surface in high temperature areas, on the other hand, are acid solutions, e.g. sulphuric acid, which dissolve the rock around the vent. Drilling in high temperature areas has shown, however, that beneath the water table the water is also basic. The difference between the water in low-and high temperature areas lies in there being much more dissolved material in the latter areas, the temperature being much higher (Fig. 2). The steam in high temperature areas is formed by boiling at the water table level.

Accompanying the steam in geothermal areas are gases. In high temperature areas these are mainly hydrogen sulphide (H_2S), carbon dioxide (CO_2), hydrogen (H_2) and a few others such as nitrogen (N_2). On mixing with the atmosphere in the solfatara fumarole vent, the hydrogen sulphite combines with oxygen in the atmosphere to form sulphuric acid (H_2SO_4), which can be very strongly acidic. At the high temperatures the rock dissolves and breaks down so that certain materials are washed away while the residual materials are a mixture of clay minerals, geyserite and gypsum. Some pure sulphur usually precipitates from fumaroles but this is largely washed away by rainfall. In earlier centuries, a considerable amount of sulphur was worked in Iceland which, with Sicily, had a monopoly on sulphur for a long time. Most of the mines were at Krysuvík, Námafjall and at Theistareykir.

The gas in low temperature areas, on the other hand, is mainly nitrogen. There is also usually a little hydrogen sulphide and other gases as indicated by the smell. Around hot springs silicous material is deposited from the water as geyserite.

Hot springs generally emerge at dikes or fractures which prevent the water flow in porous beds in the bedrock while

1. Acidity (pH) is measured on a scale of 14. If greater than 7, the solution is said to be basic. Low temperature geothermal solutions have a pH of around 9. If lower than 7, the solution is acidic, acidity increasing with decreasing values. Acidity in high temperature geothermal areas can be as high as pH 1-2.

directing it upwards, for the fractures are frequently open and the rocks along the dikes disturbed.

In many geothermal areas the flow has been increased by deep drilling, which has several effects. Firstly, precipitates from the hot water fill cavities and cracks in the rock as it cools blocking the paths of flow. Impermeable sediment in the bedrock can also prevent the upward flow of hot water, for which drilling opens a pathway. Secondly, drilling can reach porous beds or fractures through which the water flows. Thirdly, the flow to the drill hole can be increased by pumping since this leads to the formation of a downdraw cone which causes greater inflow.

Before drilling for hot water is commenced in geothermal areas, detailed geophysical, geochemical and geological research is carried out to determine the main area of upward flow and the amount of hot water or steam in the area.

High temperature or steam geothermal areas

High temperature areas occur only in active volcanic zones and probably mainly where there are shallow magma chambers or intrusions cooling underneath in active volcanic areas. Thus high temperature areas are localised areas of upward pound water flow in active volcanic areas.

There are 20-30 high temperature areas in Iceland of which the main ones are: Reykjanes-Svartsengi, Krysuvík, Hengill, Kerlingarfjöll, the Torfajökull area, Grímsvötn, Dyngjufjöll, Námaskard, Krafla and Theistareykir (Fig. 2).

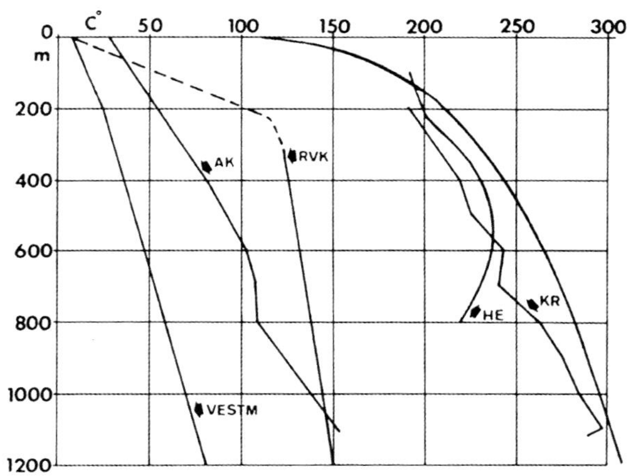

Fig. 2
Temperature in deep drillholes in Iceland, i.e. in Vestmannaeyjar (Heimaey), Laugaland in Eyjafjödur (AK), Reykjavík, Hengill (HE), SW-Iceland and Krafla (KR), N-Iceland. Boiling point curve is shown on right.

There are mainly two types of edifice in high temperature areas, fumaroles and solfataras. In fumaroles the temperature of the steam is sometimes more than 100°C, i.e. superheated steam, which emerges under considerable pressure. The water table is usually quite far below the surface so that normally very little water accompanies steam springs and what little there is forms by condensation of the steam on its way to the surface. Solfataras are common in high temperature areas. They contain blue-grey boiling clay, the color being due to sulphur compounds of iron which form when sulphuric acid dissolves the rock, the acid forming when hydrogen sulphide (H_2S) reacts with atmospheric oxygen. In the solfataras the clay splashes as gas bubbles burst and the clay builds up a rim around them. The rocks of high temperature areas are usually greatly altered as mentioned earlier.

Low temperature or hot water spring areas

There are believed to be about 250 low temperature areas in Iceland, in which there are 600-700 large or medium sized hot water springs.

The natural discharge from them is estimated to be 1800 l/sec of 75°C hot water which can be increased by drilling and pumping, though this depletes the water supply so that care must be taken when utilising the area so that colder water is not drawn in. The flow is usually subject to little change except in geysers or erupting springs which shoot water or steam jets into the air every so often. The temperature of the springs seldom exceeds boiling point. In drill holes on the other hand, the temperature is much higher while it should be borne in mind that the boiling point increases with increased pressure, the temperature being for instance 121°C at a water depth of 10 m (Fig. 1).

Unlike the high temperature areas, a minority of low temperature areas are connected to recent volcanic areas, since activity ceased in most of them during the Pleistocene or Tertiary. The hot water emerges in fractures or even along dikes in the bedrock. Deuterium isotope measurements suggest that the hot water in low temperature areas originated in inland mountain areas, such as in the active volcanic zones and has flowed from there as ground water and been heated at depth on its way to the geothermal areas over a long period. For example, the hot water in the Borgarfjördur area, W-Iceland, is believed to have come from Langjökull. Water percolates downwards easily in the active volcanic belts because of the number of open fractures and the porosity of the rocks, i.e. the water sinks downward rapidly. The low temperature areas are spread widely over almost the entire country except for the southeastern and eastern parts where there is very little geothermal activity; the majority of thermal water spring areas are on the flanks of the volcanic belt in the southwest, e.g. in Borgarfjördur and Árnessysla (Fig. 2). Hot water springs are divided into several groups, mainly according to temperature.

"Eruptive springs or geysers" are the best known of all Icelandic hot springs especially since the international term for *goshver*, geyser, is coined from the largest of them, Geysir in Haukadalur. Geysir was first recorded following a great earthquake in southern Iceland in 1294.

Geysir eruptions usually start with rumbling accompanied by much boiling and frothing in the vent, which is then followed by water jets which erupt higher and higher until the eruption reaches its maximum. At its highest, the eruption jet of Geysir reached 70-80 m. After a few minutes, the eruption decreases and is replaced by steam which escapes with a loud whistling sound, until it gradually decreases. However, the behaviour of "eruption" is very variable, even in the same spring.

Iceland has quite a number of erupting springs apart from Geysir, others being Gryta (Gryla) in Hveragerdi, Strokkur in the Geysir area and Uxahver in the Reykjahverfi area in Thingeyjarsysla. There are also *goshverir* in Kamchatka, New Zealand and in Yellowstone Park in the USA., some of which erupt very regularly and to great heights. Geysir consists of a 2 m deep basin at the top which is about 15 m in diameter. Extending downwards from this is a 20 m deep pipe which is only 1-2 m in diameter. While Geysir existed as such, the temperature was 80-90°C on the surface with a discharge of 2-3 l/sec. The temperature at the base of the pipe was 128°C, which is below boiling point at this depth. At a depth of 10 m the temperature proved to be close to boiling point, or 120°C, boiling point being 121°C at this depth and in eruptions superheating has been measured.

Several theories have been put forward as to the cause of geyser "eruptions" which can be divided into the geothermal gas and boiling theories.

Geothermal gases escape in all hot springs, the force together with that of steam sometimes being so great, that a lot of springs appear to be boiling even though the water is below the boiling point.

The gas is believed to facilitate boiling in the feeder pipes to the main spring vent. When the total pressure of gas and steam is sufficient, they erupt into the feeder pipe and cause eruption.

The boiling theory assumes that in the Geysir eruptions, 126°C hot water suddenly enters high up in the feeder vent, e.g. at a 10 m depth, where it is in fact superheated, the boiling point at this depth being 121°C. This leads to flash boiling and the resulting sudden steam formation produces an eruption.

By definition hot water springs have varying water temperatures above 70°C. The largest hot water spring is Deildartunguhver in Borgarfjördur which has a discharge of 150 l/sec of 100°C hot water and as such is the largest thermal spring in the world. Water from it is used for domestic heating in the towns of Akranes, Borgarnes and surrounding areas. The largest hot water spring areas are Reykir in Mosfellssveit near Reykjavík, the Reykholt area in Borgarfjördur, West-Iceland,

Reykhólar in Reykhólasveit and Reykjandes in Ísafjardardjúp, Northwest-Iceland, Skagafjördur and the Fljdt-area and the Reykirarea in South-Lingeyjarsysla, North-Iceland.

In the upper Arnessysla area, South-Iceland, geothermal springs are widespread, e.g. in Flúdir, at Laugarás, at Stóra-Fljót, Sydri-Reykir and Laugarvatn. In addition to these areas, there are large hot water springs in Hveravellir, at Geysir, in Hveragerdi, although the latter can be regarded as a high temperature area with ground water at the surface.

Warm springs or *laugar* are closely related to hot springs but have only small amounts of gas and no geyserite precipitation. Warm water springs or *laugar,* bridge the gap between hot water springs (*hverir*) and *kaldavermsl* and are much more common than hot water springs (Fig. 2). Many of them can be regarded as cooling hot springs since they sometimes occur on geyserite fields, e.g. at Leirá in Leiràrsveit, West-Iceland.

Warm mineral springs are closely related to warm springs. The water in them is warm but mixed with carbon dioxide (CO_2) so that they appear to boil due to rapid escape of the gas. There is usually precipitation of calcium carbonate or travertine. The largest warm mineral spring in Iceland is at Lysuhóll on Snaefellsnes.

Cold mineral springs (*ölkeldur*) are cold water springs mixed with carbon dioxide. Most of them are on Snaefellsnes, e.g. Raudamelsölkelda. Ölkelduvatn is similar to soda water in taste but with a slight iron flavour.

At the close of the Hekla eruption in 1984, carbon dioxide emission was evident in the Hekla lava above the farm

Naefurholt, while at the same time the water in the area was carbonated and hard. Such emissions are referred to outside of Iceland as mofettes and are common in ancient fold mountains and volcanic areas throughout the world.

Economic use of geothermal heat

From ancient times, geothermal water has been used for bathing and washing. The first drilling for hot water in Iceland was at the Thvottalaugar in Reykjavík in 1928. Drilling was started in Reykir in Mosfellssveit, 17 km east of Reykjavík in 1933, while the Reykjavík District Heating Authority was formed in 1943. Since then many deep drill holes have been sunk in Reykjavík, which provide a large quantity of water. The Reykjavík District Heating network now also serves the neighbouring towns of Kópavogur, Gardabaer, Mosfellsdaer, Álftanes, and Hafnarfjördur, all serving 140,000 people. The normal consumption of hot water is about 1500 1/sec which can be increased to 3000 1/sec during cold spells. In addition, the Reykjavík District Heating Authority has taken into use water from the geothermal plant at Nesjavellir, south of Thingvallavatn, where cold water is heated by steam from the high temperature geothermal area there. District heating authorities are now widespread and serve about 85% of the country. Many country schools have also been built in geothermal areas. Swimming pools which make use of geothermal heat number about 100. Geothermal heat is used for greenhouse heating, particularly in southern Iceland and vegetables, fruit and flowers are produced in considerable quantities. Electricity is generated from geothermal energy to a small extent using steam turbines at Krafla, Bjarnarflag at Myvatn, Svartsengi near Keflavík and in the near future also at Nesjavellir. Finally, geothermal heat is used in the production of diatomite at Myvatn, algal meal at Reykhólar í Reykhólarveit and salt in Reykjanes.

Geothermal energy is of no less importance to Iceland's energy budget than hydropower. It accounted for 31.3 percent of the country's energy demand.

Norman Foster

The Rainbow Cloud

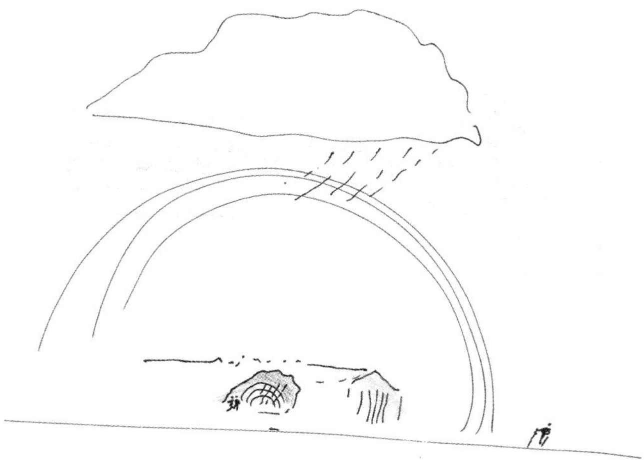

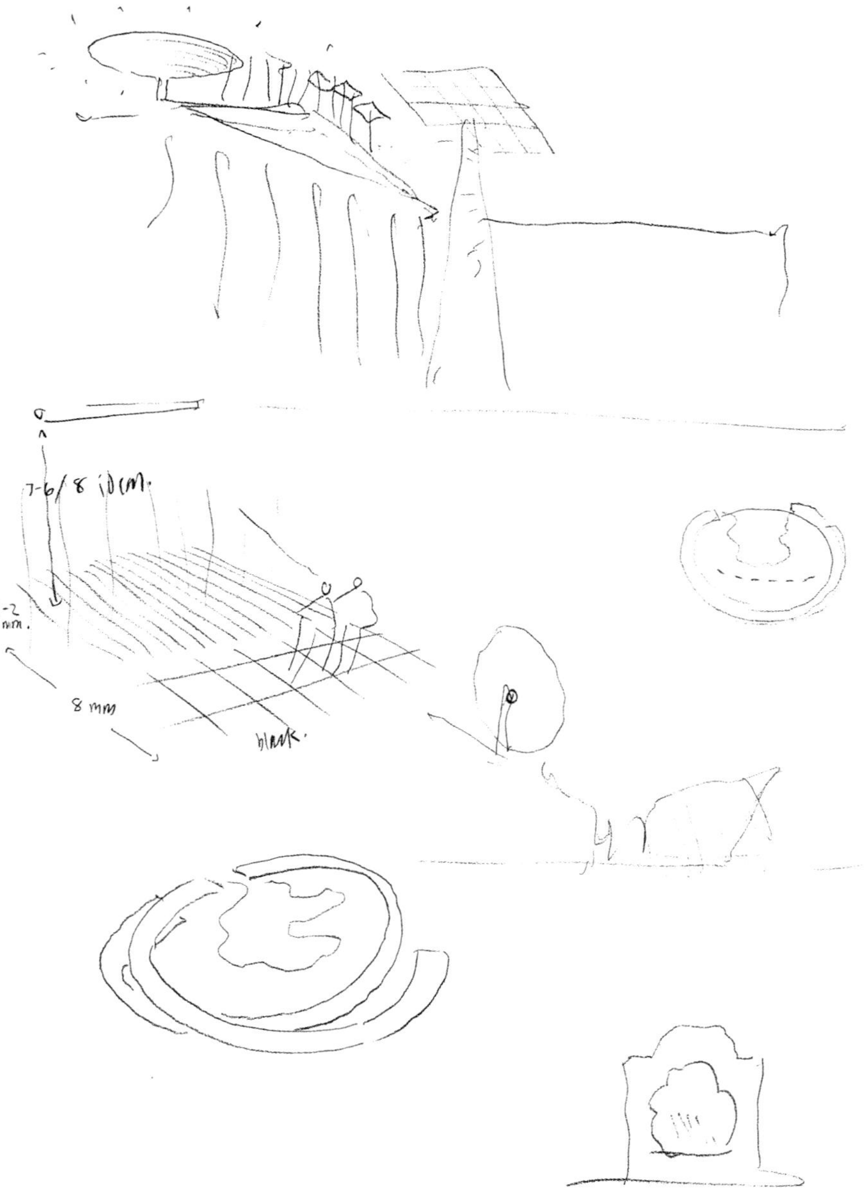

7-6/8 idem.
1-2 mm.
8 mm
black.

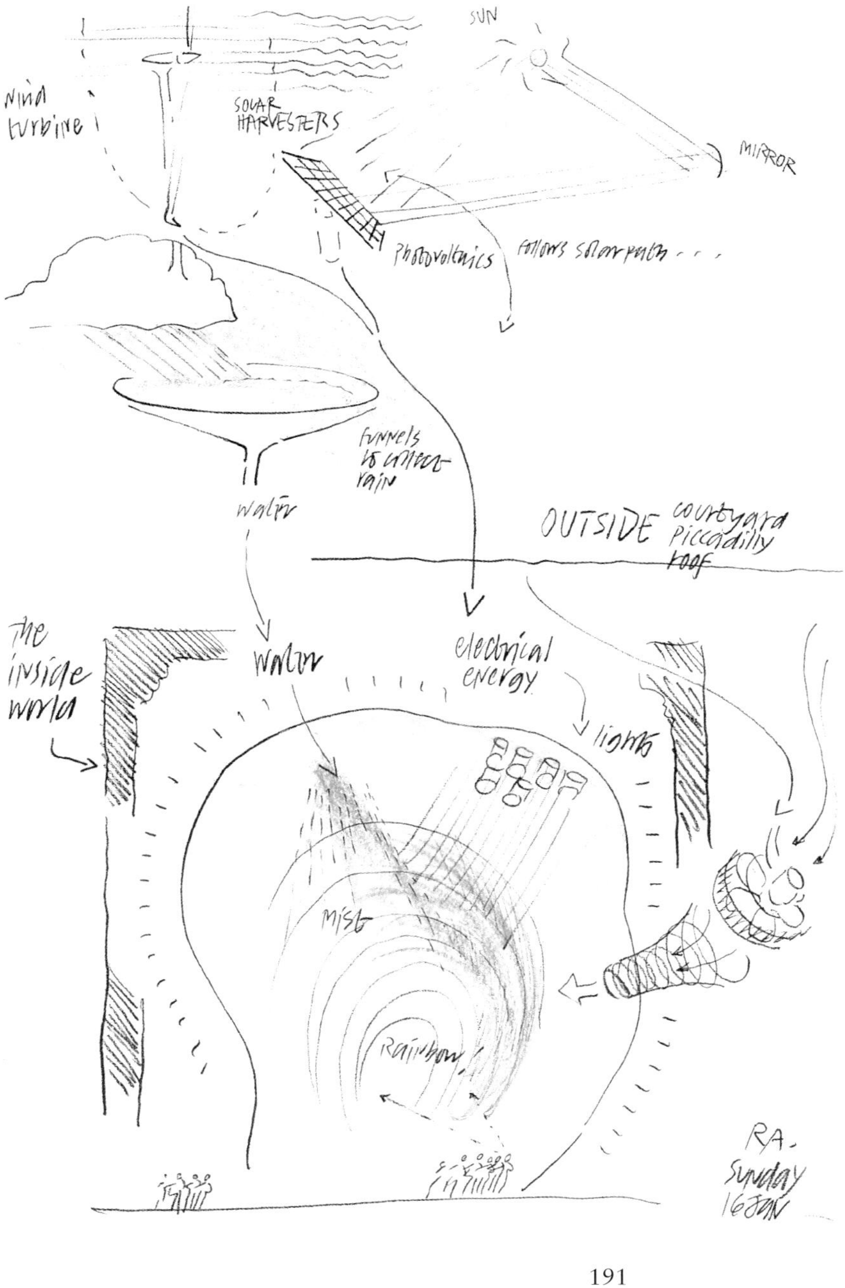
SUN
wind turbine
SOLAR HARVESTERS
MIRROR
Photovoltaics
follows solar path . . .
funnels to collect rain
water
OUTSIDE
courtyard Piccadilly roof
the inside world
water
electrical energy
lights
mist
Rainbow
RA. Sunday 16 Jan

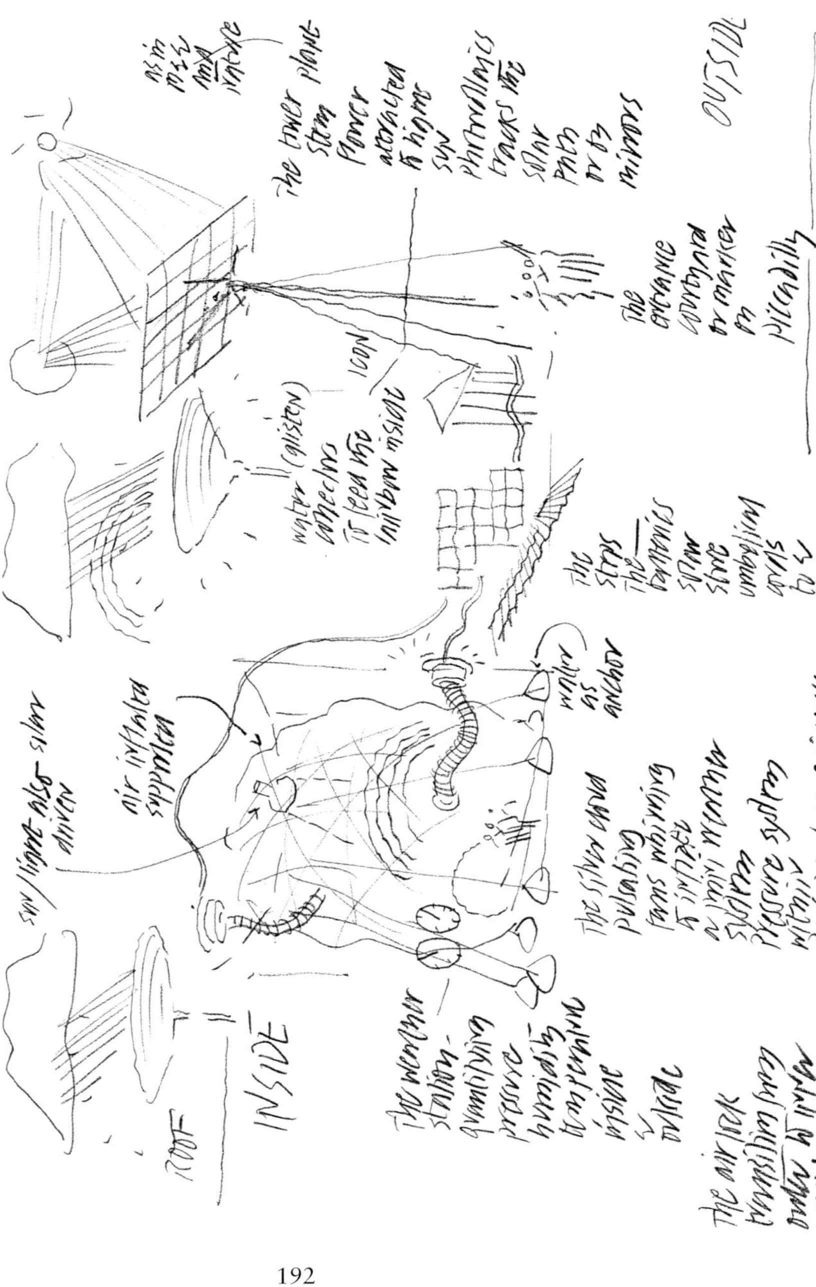

sun/light also solar driven
air inflated
ROOF
INSIDE
water (glisten) collectors to feed the rainbow inside
ICON
The tower plant stem flower attracted to higher sun photovoltaics tracks the solar path or to mirrors
The weather station - quantifying pressure humidity temperature inside & outside
The silver cloud pulsating fans whirring to inflate a mini weather system Pressure system within Rainbow as evidence
water as anchor
The steps The batteries solar store umbilical cords
The entrance courtyard or marker on Piccadilly
OUTSIDE
The air lock transition from outer to inner worlds.

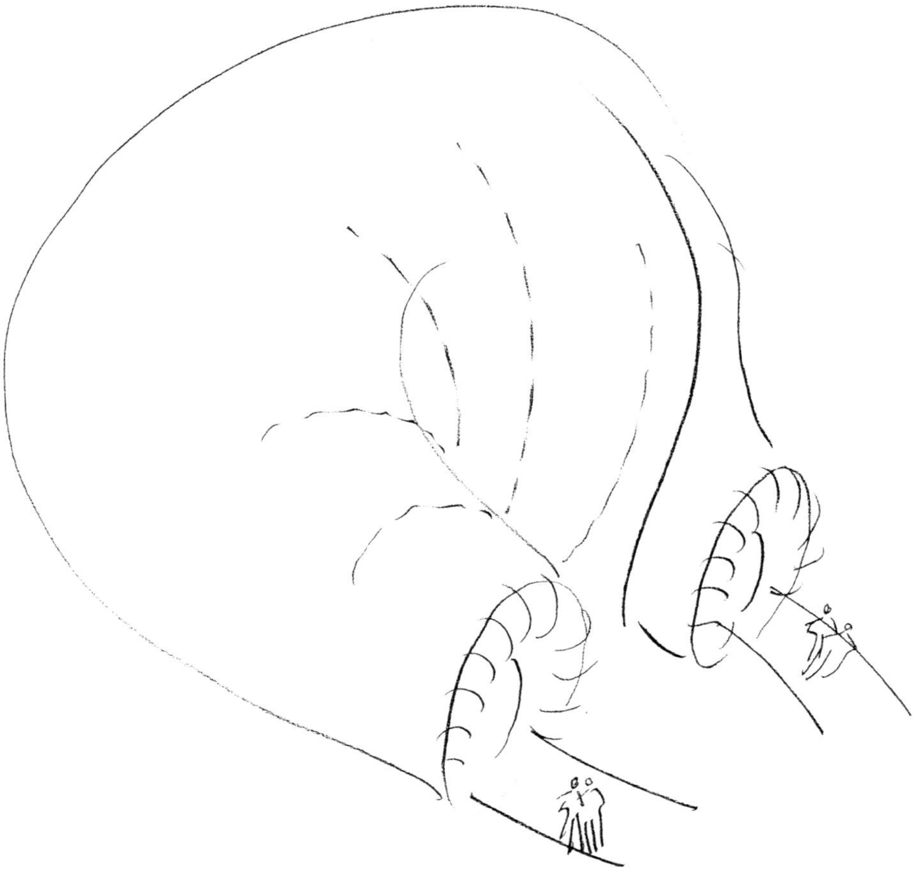

Yona Friedman

Towards a *Poor World* or How Scarcity Might Prevent the Catastrophe

The illusions

The most remarkable characteristic of the second half of our century is the sudden awareness of *poverty*. This awareness, one must note, arrives after a very short period in which we were supposed to be enormously rich.

The illusion of our wealth was produced by other illusions, more fundamental ones, and the loss of the illusion of wealth is the consequence of the loss of our *basic* illusions.

What were these basic illusions?
1) The universal belief that the world contains sufficient resources for postponing worries about scarcity to future generations. 2) We thought that the earth could nourish man sufficiently if the birth-rate does not pass a set threshold. 3) The third illusion (the one I consider the worst of all) is the one I call the *illusion about the possibility of global communication*. It means the belief which supposes that mankind as a whole

could learn to understand each other. 4) The last illusion is of not having sufficient space for a growing population.

The crisis we are now experiencing, progressing inevitably towards a *poor world*, is the result of two facts:
1) The date of exhausting resources is nearer than we thought.
2) Global communication is impossible.

Before beginning to explain the impossibility of global communication, I must first introduce a certain terminology. Observing any human group, we see an exchange of signs: a communication process between group members is established. If we don't understand their language, we can always observe that, after the exchange of signs (or words), some members of the group *behave differently*. We can thus conclude, that they were *influenced* by communication with others.

If we are keen observers, we would try to sketch the observed influences. Group members would be indicated by initialled dots, and observed influences by arrows.

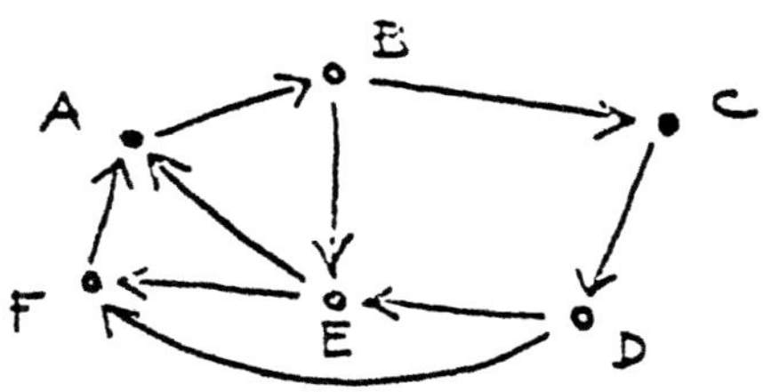

We could make another observation: influences are not necessarily *directly* exerted. Many are transmitted by *intermediaries*. We can thus conclude that a transmitted influence is weaker than a direct one, and it is weaker still if the number of intermediaries necessary to its transmission grows.

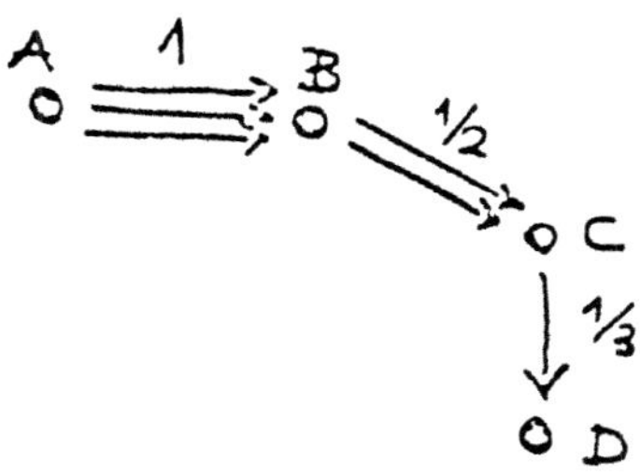

These considerations and observations, simplified as they are, enable us to find out how *hierarchy* works within a given group. We only have to compare the *sum of exerted and received influences* between all members of the group.

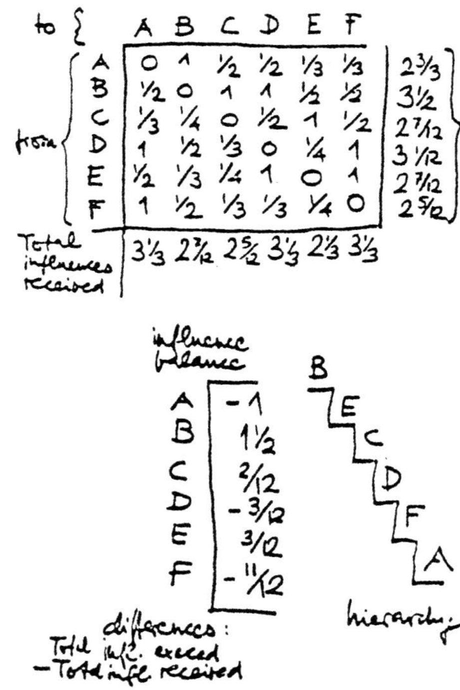

This hierarchy shows the *social structure* of the group. The sketch we mentioned indicates the *mathematical structure* of the same group. *Social structure* is a function of *mathematical structure*, which can have different forms like *egalitarian* groups, *hierarchical* groups and *oligarchical* groups. Now we have succeeded in describing internal communication structures, we can continue to find out why global communication is necessarily impossible. All the time we observe *human* groups. *Human* means individuals characterized by some specific biological properties. We will now consider some of these biological characteristics, which seem to be particularly important:

a) *Valency*, or the largest number of influences that can be assimilated by a human being during a given reference time.
b) *Transmission capacity*, what indicates a *measure of human error* in transmitting an influence received from another individual and addressed to a third one. *Valency* and *transmission capacity* are necessarily *larger* for simple messages than for complex ones.

Both characteristics have an effect on decision rapidity within a group. Conclusions about these lengthy considerations (social structure of groups, human valency, and their influence on decision rapidity) are logical and simple. A human group cannot work unless the number of its members remains below a threshold number that is dependent upon specific human valency and transmission capacity. We will call this threshold *critical group-size*.

The concept of critical group-size implies very serious and inevitable consequences for any social structure. They are inevitable because part of the factors defining the critical group-size are the biological characteristics of the human species. One of these inevitable consequences is the impossibility of global communication for mankind, as the number of individuals pertaining to it is larger than any critical group-size admissible for groups with man's biological characteristics. Considering the actual dimensions of human organizations, any attempt at communication within these organizations blocks itself. We cannot hope to bypass such blocks with sophisticated technology, as the blocks do not result from deficiencies in the technical set-up, but from those of the human brain: and we cannot bypass the human brain in any communication process concerning humans.

Let us take for example an everyday feature; a central television transmitter which, by hypothesis, could transmit influences to a quasi unlimited number of receivers.

Here is the rub. This process does not really represent a communication system, as receivers could turn down recep-

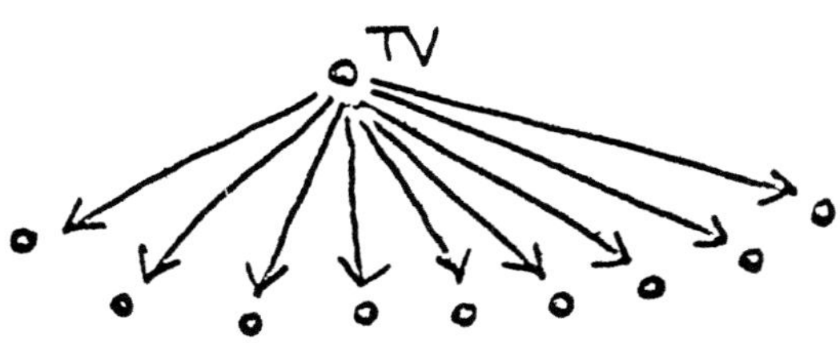

tion, or ignore the message sent, or even misinterpret it. To make this process an efficient communication system, it would have to contain some gadget to receive answers from the receivers, i.e. a feedback towards the centre.

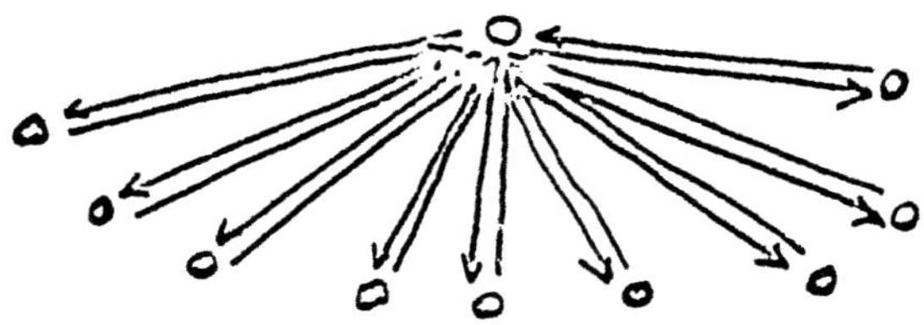

But however the centre was organized, it could never assimilate from millions of sources: the feedback mass would be larger than the specific valency of the centre. Admitting even that the valency of the machine receiving the feedback could be larger than the feedback mass, humans directing the machine would not be able to use it. (In other words, the Orwellian Big Brother cannot function.)

In my personal language, I call this the *impossibility of global communication* (resulting from the numerical constraint implied by critical group-size): the *Babel tower syndrome*. The Biblical image is perfect: an organization (the builders of the tower) grows and, growing, it represents a menace to God. God does not intervene, he simply waits for the phenomenon of the impossibility of global communication to manifest itself.

To realize this impossibility of global communication is of prime importance in our shift towards a *poor world*.

Model of the poor world

The impossibility of planetary communication makes a shift towards *global poverty* inevitable. The characteristics are:
a) *Disintegration of large organizations*. One of the typical signs of this trend is the fact that large organizations go in for more and more foreign policy and less and less domestic policy. b) *Devaluation of the tokens emitted by large organizations*. Money loses its exchange value, and the barter system is used more and more instead. c) *Reduce transportation*. Money can very easily be sent anywhere; effects or reserves drawn from a public community pool are less mobile. Communities tend to become self-sufficient because of the unreliability of central services; self-sufficiency means less from outside, more

from inside. d) *Less division of labour.* Self-sufficiency does not admit a great degree of division of labour for relatively small sized organizations. e) *Less commerce.* f) *Less competition.* g) *Less stored space.* A home is used effectively only part of the day, the same with the workplace, etc. – one waiting while the other in use. In a poor world, spaces are used more in the time sharing way. h) *Developing of one-man technologies.* This technology admits one-man teams which are less dependent upon organization. i) *Poor world.* This expression implies that, if such a trend comes about, the present, non-industrialized nations might have a better chance of survival in a world of scarcity. India, China, etc. – these big human masses which are ungovernable by central organizations – survive by small self-sufficient local organizations. Once it gets poorer, Western civilization (Russia included) will have to save itself by a reorganization which is independent of current ideologies, and is but a simple result of the obvious self-blocking of oversized organizations.

This model is not necessarily the one for the future. But, as it might become real, it would be better if we were prepared for it, and had an appropriate strategy for such an alternative.

Ursula Frohne

Re-Mapping the Virtual World
Utopian Construction versus Power Structures in Cyberspace

Men can, in short, become gods (if not God). What need then for "politics," understood as the power struggles of a materially straitened and socially decided world? The frequently noted contempt for politics in utopian theory is the logical complement of its belief in perfectibility.

Krishan Kumar[1]

The Net creates a communication society that no one can escape.

Peter Weibel[2]

My interest in the cultural impact of the emergence of new technologies has developed out of my scholarly affiliation with the ZKM | Center for Art and Media in Karlsruhe since 1995. From my practical and theoretical experience as an art historian working on contemporary image technologies in the context of visual art and its consequences for the museum, my

1. Krishan Kumar, *Utopianism*, Open University Press, Milton Keynes, 1991, p. 29.

2. Peter Weibel in his lecture given at the symposium "Wie wird Künstlichkeit wirklich?" ("How does the artificial become real?") MedienRaum Luxembourg, September 22 – 23, 2000.

focus has shifted during the past years to investigating aspects of representation in the realm of digital media, in particular the Internet and its utopian promises suspended between culture and politics. My research focuses on the rhetorical constructions of the new media culture as a sphere of unrestrained participation, also for those who belong to the non-represented parts of global society. It considers the dynamics of electronic communication technologies as an unlimited means to monitor and access the world, while at the same time maintaining distance and detachment from its social reality. For an investigation of the question of how the world is represented in the new sphere of Cyberspace and which parts of the world are screened out, I will employ trans-disciplinary methods, including (art) history, sociology, media theory, political and postcolonial theory, gender, and cultural studies.

As a global medium, the Internet is generally characterized as an historical opportunity to realize virtual universal communication. It opens spaces for hybrid discourses which are decentralized, interactive, unlimited, non-hierarchical, transmedial and intercultural, serving as a non-profit, knowledge-exchange system which creates and is accessible to the global community. As one of the earliest propagators, Nicholas Negroponte coined the popular epithet "only connect" as an idiomatic vehicle for all kinds of utopian projections on the potential of digital media and the Net as a new communication technology. These include, but are not limited to the potential to create new forums for political and cultural networking and public discourse, thus developing new dynamics and strategies of participation and raising new notions of agency and democracy in civil society. Worldwide, this optimistic rhetoric has been associated with the spirit of humanization and enlightenment, in the sense that these future-orientated technologies of representation bring the ideal of equality into reach for a collective virtual community in Cyberspace, beyond social, national, or ideological limits. We might think of Donna Harraway and Sadie Plant as two of the main voices in this choir of Network optimists who regard the imaginary space of Cyberspace as a strategic forum for a socialist-feminist culture and as a sphere free of gender roles which is opened up for experiments with alternative identity models, combining technological and human components under the premises of "pleasure" and the intended "confusion" of dominating identity expectations resulting in new mobile, polymorphic, and multi-facetted simulation models. Both in theory and in practice, Harraway and Plant view the rhizomatic structures of electronic technologies and media as specifically feminine working and communicative strategies with the potential to subvert patriarchal interests and overcome traditional gender roles by forming alternative virtual communities outside the established social systems.

According to Saskia Sassen however, those characteristics of the Internet's public image have been largely shaped by the early hacker-culture, which indeed propagated a radical decentralization of this medium and developed software programs to guarantee free access to the Net. Today's reality contrasts with those pioneering enterprises at the still open "frontier" during the medium's early phase: The Net has increasingly become a battleground for superceding power interests and segmentation. "It has turned out that the electronic space not only serves as a communication device, but has become the main scene for the accumulation of capital and operations of the global market's capital."[3] In spite of this development, the revolutionary pathos which characterizes the public notion of Cyberspace as the epitome of a new era of decentralized power structures and global democracy remains unbroken and optimistic constructions of the Net have become commonplace among users from inside and outside the cultural arena. In general, Cyberspace serves as a projection screen for nostalgic visions of a universal space for "romantic flights from suppression and poverty"[4] which in fact represents an economically desirable territory for the extremely hierarchical interests of global corporations. Fascinated by the technological possibilities of a multi-local networking system, these constructions have perpetuated the myths that seem to ignore the social, historical, political, and ethical implications that go along with the idiomatic meaning of "connectivity" and its powerful conveyance of integrative, interactive, and communicative efficiency. As artist and theorist Olu Oguibe has pointed out, "the realities and conditionalities of connectivity are, nevertheless, more elaborate and complicated" in the sense that a "digital divide" emerges between "those who belong within the network and are thus able to partake of its numerous advantages, and those who are unable to fulfil the conditionalities of connectivity."[5] Apart from a reliable telecommunications infrastructure and the basic economic and political conditions of having access to a computer and a Net-

3. See Saskia Sassen, "Digitale Netzwerke und Macht" (Digital Networks and Power), in Hauke Brunkhorst and Matthias Kettner (eds.), *Globalisierung und Demokratie* (Globalization and Democracy), Suhrkamp Verlag, Frankfurt/M., 2000, p. 330.

4. Ibid., p. 338.

5. See Olu Oguibe, "Connectivity, and the Fate of the Unconnected," in the electronic journal *Telepolis,* December 7, 1999; see also www.heise.de/tp/english/inhalt/co/6551/1.html.

connection, there are a number of obvious pre-conditions that define the privilege of participation as a social and cultural disposition.

From my perspective as an art historian and media theorist, the cultural concept of Cyberspace needs to be critically investigated as a new formation of a public sphere where social interaction and cultural encounter, including artists' concepts, find an open domain, implying the potential for emancipation from the limitations in our contemporary social reality. My approach considers modern communication and image technologies as a means to recover the meaning and experience of community in the sense that communication translates directly into communion and a vision of the electronic community as the 'good society'. In my research I am concerned with these utopian aspirations and sentiments, but instead of accepting them on their own terms, my interest will focus on their discursive status and significance in the world we presently inhabit. The utopian temptation expressed in Krishan Kumar's observations quoted at the beginning shall be discussed critically in its function as representing an alternative reality "in a world gone wrong." Also, seen historically, the recent displacement of utopian thought from time back to space includes a cultural nostalgia – not so much in the sense of a retrospective desire for a return to an "innocent" pre-technological era, but for an autonomous, technologically achieved domain. This domain is on a continuum (and almost regressive in its sentiments) with other hyperreal utopian spaces, from eighteenth century concepts to theme parks and Biosphere II.[6] However, speculations about disembodied rationality, tele-presence, interface-technology, cyborg-identity, and other models of transcending the traditional limitations of the subject and the mundane frustrations of reality cannot escape the historical and political conditions of a materially constrained and socially divided world. In as much as the institutions that develop and promote the new technologies exist solidly in this world, virtual communities inhabit this world as well. It is therefore necessary to situate representations of the virtual-technological revolution in the context of current cultural and political geographies to critically reflect the rhetoric of their prophets in relation to the global condition of our time – "ethnic conflicts, resurgent nationalism, urban fragmentation," dislocation and erosion of the social fabric.[7] By contrasting the "mythology" and "metaphysics" of Cyberspace with its sociology, a re-map-

6. See Kevin Robins, *Into the Image*, London, New York, 1996, p. 96.

7. Ibid.

ping of its dialectic status as a "virtual reality" in the true sense of the term becomes the crucial issue of my project's investigation.

As a largely language and text-dependent medium, unlike radio or television, the Internet requires a certain level of literacy (with English as the dominant communication language), and to a certain degree, also technological knowledge, which is not only to be questioned in the economically less developed regions of the world, but even in the most industrialized nations, where a great number of people are as unlikely to connect, because of their psychological disposition, age, or class. Acknowledging this "digital divide," it becomes increasingly evident that, as we connect, we become part of a "new ethnoscape, what one might call a netscape or cyberspace where information and individuals circulate and bond into a new community. And as this community broadens in scope and significance, we are effectively implicated in the relativization of those who remain on the outside of its borders."[8]

In as much as the Net represents the matrix of connectivity and the sacred corridor of seemingly limitless freedom for an increasing number of participants, the blind spot of the Network community remains the socio-political reality and its cultural implications of technological and symbolic exclusion resulting in the absence of those who are not partaking in the powerful global machinery which Marshall McLuhan called the "unified global field of awareness." A new public force such as the Net mobilizes enormous capabilities as an emergent, global social-system and forum for agency on the part of the represented, whereas the non-articulated outsiders are nearly invisible and voiceless. They inhabit the "dark continents" of our digital culture as Terry Harpold reveals in his "Critique of Internet Metageographies" in reference to Joseph Conrad's *Heart of Darkness* as one of the defining tropes of high colonialism.[9]

Harpold's analysis of the "blind spots of cartography" might, literally and symbolically, also shed light on the aspects of "darkness" in the virtual sphere of the Net. By showing how the un-networked nations appear as uniform, "framed voids," which would merge with the empty background, were it not for their faint borders, the "darkness," as the sphere of the non-represented, becomes visible. "Thus, the fusion in such

8. See Oguibe, op.cit., 1999.

9. See Terry Harpold, "Dark Continents: A critique of Internet Metageographies," in the electronic journal *Postmodern Culture,* 1999 (http://www.iath.virginia.edu/pmc/text-only/issue.199/9.2harpold.txt).

images of a tropology of presence/absence and fullness/emptiness with conventional signifiers of region and nation, encodes the traces of network activity with meanings beyond the mere (visual) registering of place-names. Viewed with an eye to their unacknowledged political valences, these images [and the cultural practice] of the wired world (that is, of the mostly unwired world) draw (...) on (visual) discourses of identity and negated identity that echo those of European maps of colonized and colonizable space of nearly a century ago."[10]

Another focal aspect of my investigation regarding the political issues of Cyberspace is the idea of the virtual community as a revitalization and renewal of collectivity, conviviality, and democratic participation, thus the notion of a return of the political into the sphere of public interest. With the construction of the "electronic agora"[11] as the unacknowledged potential of computer-mediated communication, Howard Rheingold emphasizes the importance of Cyberspace as "one of the informal public places where people can rebuild the aspects of community" to recapture the sense of a "social commons." Slavoj Žižek, on the other hand, points out that the structure of the Net promotes strategic usages for all kinds of collective interests which ultimately lead to even more explicit splittings of society into numerous factions, as a kind of tribalization and segmentation of social relations without a collective horizon of experience.[12] Through its organization in discussion forums and chat groups, the Net undergoes an ideological segregation into leftists, rightists, radicals, chatters, Cyberpunks, Cyberfeminists and so on, which originates in the nature of the medium itself and raises the question of whether certain aspects of virtual culture are not inimical to democratic structures. Based on the practice of debate in the sense of what Richard Sennett calls the "art of exposure,"[13] the idea of a democratic virtual community represents a domain of refuge and withdrawal, in spite of its disseminating capacities. The question to be raised is whether the pluralistic and communicative structure of Cyberspace results in discursive interactions or whether they are neutralized in a self-referential media play of disconnected opinions, a fake diversity of fanatic particularity factions, a mono-culture of self-display, because it remains inside the reservation of an alternative sphere. Does the "excessive freedom" (Žižek) delegated to the users of the new technologies lead to a pseudo-communication, where everything is adjustable to one's own personal standards, opin-

10. Ibid.

11. See Howard Rheingold, *The Virtual Community: Finding Connection in a Computerized World*, Secker & Warburg, London, 1994, p. 6; see also Robins, op.cit., p. 97.

12. See Slavoj Žižek, *Die Pest der Phantasmen*, Passagen Verlag, Vienna, 1997, p. 94.

13. See Richard Sennett, *The Conscience of the Eye: The Design and Social Life of Cities*, Alfred A. Knopf, New York, 1990, p. 97.

ions and limitations? Could Cyberspace therefore be regarded as a compensating projection screen for an engagement in the political?

These aspects lead back to the question of the ideological implications of Cyberspace as a utopian concept of "one network, one world." In the digital culture of the World Wide Web, neither the issue of subjectivity nor the importance of physical "place" become obsolete. According to the feminist art/theory project "Old Boys Network," virtual reality does not represent a different reality as such, contradicting the hegemonial and hierarchical conditions of reality. Extending this aspect to artists' practices, this means that to the degree that artists work with hybrid, site specific, and ephemeral methods in alternative spaces such as the Internet, they link up with strategies of the 1960s and 1970s where the physical artspace began to lose its defining power over the art work. However, neither the White Cube of the gallery space nor the digital virtual space is neutral. Both spheres are socially and ideologically defined. Therefore, neither the White Cube nor the digital artspace request or imply a political use. Conversely, hierarchical uses are as possible in the digital artspace and with electronic media as in the traditional gallery space. Thus, electronic space is not by definition neutral, but rather socially conditioned even as a site for artists' projects. The use of new technologies is neither essentially reactionary nor a realization of socio-political utopias. Although the structure of the Internet and new media in general does not intrinsically serve subversive and alternative interests, it offers a range of possibilities for subjective modes of action.

Does the World Wide Web thus provide a powerful tool for – intended or unintended – colonizing practices? Without saying that the Net is the new domain of colonialism, it nevertheless creates structural inclusions and exclusions (not so much virtual ones, as real ones, in the sense of social and political effectiveness) that cannot be separated from a world history of colonization and contemporary globalization. The crossing of boundaries inside this realm reaffirms those boundaries between the parts of the world where access to electronic media has become part of the everyday and those parts where the cultural, infrastructural and economic pre-conditions have not yet been achieved. Although the technological revolution has different effects in the industrialized nations than in the economically disadvantaged regions, its traces are no less succinct as artist and theorist Ursula Biemann shows in her video-essay *Performing the Border* (1999). She documents the production industry of the new technologies located in Mexican border towns along the Rio Grande near the American city, El Paso. Large numbers of young women work in these "maquiladoras," the "gold mills" of high-tech industry. While the capital-intensive production branches of the communication business are located on American soil, the labor-intensive factories are on the Mexican side, attracting large numbers of female workers from the rural regions. Biemann's video investigates the existential aspects of the border as a concrete and also metaphorical construction for exploitation in the realm of the new technologies. A "technology of gender" evolves, according to Teresa de Lauretis, in the context of this new international/global division of labor and represents the "constant reconstruction of gender difference and the consolidation of power, subjectivity, and identity in a world of Cyborgs."[14]

On the basis of these preliminary thoughts, a number of queries about the cultural consequences of new media politics can be articulated for the subsequent steps in my research on this project: Does technical mobility – achieved and promoted by the new media – enable an emancipation of body and language politics, which makes the asserted transcendence of boundaries viable? Or do the utopian concepts of virtual reality and Cyberspace in practice exclude a certain range of actual bodies and languages and thereby inevitably lead to political and cultural segregation. Do the inherently limiting aspects of an uncritical concept of virtuality, as it were, vanish behind the promises and general affirmation of a new media-based future? Could the effect of this development be summarized as the equation of a globalization tendency that turns out to be nothing other than the Westernization of the world and a new incarnation of colonialization? As new power structures evolve, drawing new borders around and between cultures, we might realize that these are not only a matter of re-mapping virtual space, but are increasingly reflected in real space.

14. Yvonne Volkart refers to Teresa de Lauretis in: "Kriegszonen: Körper, Identitäten und Weiblichkeit in der High Tech Industrie," in *springerin,* V, June-August 1999, pp. 40-42 .

This text evolved from a panel at the CAA 2000 conference in New York that I co-chaired with Christian Katti on the topic "Crossing Boundaries in Cyberspace: The Politics of Body and Language Since the Emergence of New Media." The contributions to this panel were published in *Art Journal,* 59/4, Winter 2000, pp. 8-37.
Special thanks to Christian Katti whose inspiring thoughts have fueled discussions on this theme.

Peter Galison

Objectivity is Romantic

Some years ago, while working with the historical documents of twentieth century particle physics, I came across a genre I had never seen before: an atlas of cloud chamber photographs. What was this object – a textbook, a coffee-table volume, a popularization? As it turned out, it was not quite any of these. Instead, physicists used these atlases to train the eyes of initiates into the cloud chamber business; experts compiled the list of known phenomena so that, when the experimenter spied something unfamiliar in the laboratory, it could be identified as a discovery. The exemplar for such a literary object was, the authors asserted, the medical atlas that for centuries had been used to train physicians to spot and identify pathologies. Medical atlases exist in the thousands. There are atlases of skulls and atlases of wrists, x-ray atlases and eye atlases, atlases of every conceivable pathology and atlases of surgical technique, atlases of instrument readouts, and even atlases of "normal deviations" that might be mistaken for pathologies.

But the story did not end there, since particle physicists were not the only scientists to seize upon the medical compendium. There were, in adjacent libraries, atlases of turtles, rocks, stars, flowers, fossils, and spectra. Far from the grand theories of nature, far from ontological debates about the reality of atoms, quarks and black holes – in short, far from science dressed up in its Sunday finest, for almost two hundred years these atlases have carried from practitioner to practitioner the assembly of known objects.

But there was more. In studying these pictorial volumes, I realized that the authors struggled long and hard to assure themselves and their readers of the quality of the images they conveyed. Many of the nineteenth century volumes proudly proclaimed that their images were, unlike their predecessors or competitors, objective. And they went on to explain, in detail, how their particularly mechanical procedures of sample collection, preservation, depiction, and reproduction underwrote that very objectivity – along with a powerful commitment to self-restraint on the scientists' part. Here, then, was an opportunity to look at scientific objectivity not so much as an abstract philosophical problem, but rather as a ground-floor view of scientific practice aimed at the working objects of science. How, over a long period and across a myriad of fields, did scientists, speaking to scientists, assure themselves that they could represent nature objectively? It was a potential gold mine: objectivity in use and across time.

Over the last years, in collaboration with Lorraine Daston, I have struggled to make sense of this cornucopia of systematically deployed pictures.[1] In an effort to delimit the problem, we are not,at least in our book in progress, aiming to capture all the meanings and uses of the term "objectivity" as, for example, it occurs in the social sciences. Nor are we surveying the sprawling array of uses to which the full range of scientific figures and illustrations have been put: this is not a history of pie charts and bar graphs, of iconic representation, biogeographical maps, high-speed photography, or particle physics displays. It is not, and it is worth insisting on the point, an account of scientific visualization in general. Instead, we are exploring systematic arrangements of images that scientists devise to capture the working objects often collected in the form called an "atlas," but just as often appearing under titles like "handbook" or "guide." What has emerged from our various studies are a periodization that divides theses image collections into three regimes; and an understanding that,

1. Lorraine Daston and Peter Galison, "The Image of Objectivity," in *Representations* 40, 1991, pp. 81-128; Peter Galison, "Judgement Against Objectivity," in Caroline Jones and Peter Galison (eds.), *Picturing Science, Producing Art*, Routledge, New York, 1998, pp. 327-59.

in each regime, the epistemic, procedural, and moral are inextricably linked.

In this brief essay, I would like to review, schematically, the outlines of the picture that we have constructed from the images of objectivity in the making. Then, rather more speculatively, I would like to point in the direction where I think one can locate the confluence of concepts, practices, and moral understandings that made possible this form of scientific knowledge, this mechanical objectivity that joined automatic procedure to the moral insistence of self-abnegation.

Objectivity and scientific image

All virtues – even all epistemic virtues – are not the same. And for the tradition of scientific atlas-makers before 1800, it was a singular good to depict the body, plants, and sky phenomena in ways that would be "true to nature." Being true to nature allowed – indeed demanded – massive intervention. In sum, before mechanical objectivity, one could not simply draw what one saw, because the Typus could not depend on any particular instance. Here is Goethe in 1792:

(A)n anatomical archetype (Typus) will be suggested here, a general picture containing the forms of all animals as potential, one which will guide us to an orderly description of each animal ... The mere idea of an archetpye in general implies that no particular animal can be used as our point of comparison; the particular can never serve as a pattern (Muster) for the whole.[2]

Not incidentally, but essentially, anyone preparing a visual representation of a natural kind must, in the search for truth to nature, select and idealize. For it is the best that stands for the truest representation of nature. Albinus, in 1749, put it this way as he explained why he put forward the skeleton that he depicted:

And as skeletons differ from one another, not only as to the age, sex, stature and perfection of the bones, but likewise in the marks of strength, beauty and make of the whole; I made choice of one that might discover signs of both strength and agility; the whole of it elegant, and at the same time not too delicate; so as neither to shew a juvenile or feminine roundness and slenderness, nor on the contrary an unpolished roughness and clumsiness; in short, all of the parts of it beautiful and pleasing to the eye. For as I wanted to shew an example of nature, I choosed to take it from the best pattern of nature.[3]

2. Johann Wolfgang Goethe, "Erster Entwurf einer allgemeinen Einleitung in die vergleichende Anatomie, ausgehend von Osteologie" (1798, 1893), in Dorothea Kuhn und Rike Wankmüller (eds.), *Goethes Werke*, 14 vols., seventh edition, Munich, 1975, vol. 13, p. 172 (slightly modified) from Douglas Miller (ed.) and trans., *Goethe: Scientific Studies*, New York, 1988, p. 118.

3. Bernhard Siegfried Albinus, *Tables of the Skeleton and Muscles of the Human Body*, London, 1749, sig. r.

But even Albinus's careful choice did not suffice. So, as he dutifully reports, he had to remove the "blemish" to make more "perfect," to alter the parts so as to render the whole more "altogether just." This genial depiction is, as we will see, a long way from the mechanical objectivity that largely displaced it.

The surprising, indeed astonishing transformation that takes place between the eighteenth century and the years after the 1820s and 1830s, involves the inversion of the values espoused by a Goethe or an Albinus. No longer is intervention by the genial author the most important feature to be prized in scientific representation; it becomes a veritable epistemic vice. Rather than by means of an improvement on nature, it was only through superhuman self-restraint that the author could aspire to let nature "speak for itself." As Hermann Pagenstecher and Carl Centus write in 1875, they "endeavored in these (pictures), to represent the object as naturally as possible. It cannot be hoped that they have always succeeded in the attempt: they are but too conscious how often in its delineation the subjective idea (subjective Anschauung) of the investigator has escaped his hand." Against the seduction of the subjective, the authors squelched their own views and "prevailing theories;" theirs was to be an endeavor that would be "purely objective." Others struggled to minimize the "personal element."[4] Technologies that aimed to automate the transfer from nature to page were many, including various forms of the mechanical trace, the direct impression of objects on the page, along with the cameras lucida and obscura. When film entered the scene, it, like other technologies before and after, was celebrated as a release from the "Artistic aids" that always threatened to make interpretation a personal, subjective feature of depiction.

Here – in this celebration of self-abnegation, in the horror at the personal, the subjective, the artistic, the interpretive, in the direct transfer of nature onto the picture – lies the ideal of mechanical objectivity: an objectivity defined by its moralized and automatic status beyond the reach of the artist's hand. What practitioners faced in the nineteenth century was, however, anything but a self-evident epistemic virtue. Objectivity may not carry with it accuracy. More than one author happily renounced the precision, the color, the sharpness, the depth of field, even the usefulness that a gifted scientific illustrator could bring to the table. In place of these lost attributes, boosters of mechanical objectivity could often produce only blurry

4. M. Allen Starr, *Atlas of Nerve Cells*, New York, 1896, pp. v-vi.

black and white photographs, incomplete tracings, or partial projections. But, they insisted, their photographs were automatic – and as such did not pass through the dreaded dark glass of interpretation. In directness, so the defenders would have it, lay the real virtue of the objective. Objectivity was not (and is not) accuracy.

Mechanical objectivity is also not to be confused with truth. An objective procedure with its restraint and automaticity might create the conditions under which the true might be encountered. But the objective would not guarantee truth and certainly could not make claim to being the only path to truth. Neither was objectivity certainty. Indeed, in contemplating the ferocious insistence on objectivity during the mid-nineteenth century, one is left with the uneasy sense that mechanical objectivity, examined close up, may well be the most peculiar of epistemic virtues. Objectivity in its mechanical guise emerges as a ferociously austere, self-denying virtue, a virtue present when all the special skills, intuitions, and inspirations of the scientist could be quieted and nature could be transferred to the page without intervention or interpretation. Like the ascetic through whom God would speak, the scientist's self-silencing, for the advocates of objectivity, would create the moral and epistemic conditions under which Nature could speak. In this hushed domain of science, the whispered voice of nature still needed to be amplified by machinery, and could only be heard against the muted background of a silenced soul.

Unlike the regime of genial depiction ("truth to nature"), the regime of mechanical objectivity bore imperfection on its sleeve as a sign of righteousness. Here are two fossil experts just after the turn of the twentieth century, proclaiming that it was

> *obviously necessary to give such figures of the fossils themselves – by mechanical means if possible – as should agree with the originals in all respects, showing their imperfections as well as their perfections, that the reader might be in a position to judge of the fidelity of the descriptions by the figures themselves, and might also be able, should the need arise, to identify the actual fossil or type specimen represented on the plates.*[5]

No improvement here, no removal of blemishes in the interest of a truth behind the appearances; in fact, blemishes signaled to the viewer that no one had inappropriately interposed interpretation between visible nature and the printed page. To those who gaze at this picture: no one has stood between you and the original object, for this is nature's own autograph.

5. Gertrude Lillian Elles and Ethel M. R. Wood, *A Monograph of British Graptolites*, London, 1901, p. 2.

There is a distal end of objectivity, a time after which it became possible to see mechanical objectivity as but one virtue among others. More specifically, atlas makers begin to be unapologetic about using expert judgment to alter, interpret, and select figures. They undertake these very un-automatic steps not in defense of a hidden nature that can be revealed only to them, but rather in a frank admission that the expertly trained eye can often sort phenomena more quickly and effectively than the rote application of a mechanical protocol. This "Judgmental objectivity," if you will, begins to displace mechanical objectivity in the 1920s, 1930s, and 1940s. For example, in 1951, Frederic A. and Erna Gibbs launched a new edition of their comprehensive *Atlas of Electroencephalography*. Unlike the library of mechanically objective atlases of the previous century, this atlas explicitly renounced the ideal of objectivity as the ultimate goal of representation. Patiently the authors explained all the ways that algorithmic, indexed, and quantitative approaches might be applied to the sorting of the electroencephalogramms. The mid-twentieth century authors understood perfectly that such automatic procedures were precisely the goal of mechanical objectivity. To make that clear, they even referred to "objective measurements" when describing the various ways one might try to create a diagnostic category, distinguishing, for example, between epileptic and non-epileptic brain traces. But objective measurements is *not* what they advocated. Instead they concluded: "Accuracy should not be sacrificed to objectivity; except for special purposes analysis should be carried on as an intellectual rather than an electro-mechanical function."[6] Encountered after the perusal of hundreds of nineteenth century atlases espousing the ideal of mechanical objectivity, a statement like that one is stunning: a deliberate renunciation of an automatic record of nature in favor of judgement.

One sees this advocacy of judgement over objectivity time and again, in absolute contrast to the myriad atlases of the mid-nineteenth century. This judgmental phase required expertise, but it is a trained expertise, not a genial leap. In *An Atlas of Star Spectra* published in 1943, for example, the authors explicitly tied the sorting of star spectra to the thoroughly integrative human judgement employed in the assessment that a particular face belongs to a specific race. (I should note, perhaps unsurprisingly, that facial-racial metaphors prospered from the late 1930s up to the end of the Second World War.) "The operation of spectral classification is similar.

6. Frederick A. Gibbs and Erna L. Gibbs, *Atlas of Electroencephalography*, vol. 1, *Methodology and Controls*, Addison-Wesley Publishing Company, Inc., Reading, Mass., 1951, 1958, pp. 112-13.

The observer must use good judgment as to the definiteness with which the identification can be made from the features available; but good judgment is necessary in any case, whether the decision is made from the general appearance or from more objective measures."[7] It was impossible, said the authors, to classify stars based on a routinized and quantified procedure.

Some precision: mechanical objectivity did not die a sudden death in the 1920s. One can find examples of mechanically objective atlases well into the 1960s or 1970s. What one does not tend to find are examples of judgmental objectivity (explicit repudiations of mechanical objectivity) in the middle or late nineteenth century.

Similarly, the older Typus (genial depiction) argument did not vanish overnight with the objectivist approaches launched in the 1820s and 1830s; and again, similarly, one does not tend to find mechanically objective atlases in the mid-eighteenth century. The important point is twofold: first, that there is a longer-term order to be ascertained here, marked by the introduction of new forms of organizing pictures to stand for and classify natural objects; and second, that the procedures, morality, image status, and even the person of the author-artist took on different forms in these regimes of representation: genial depiction, mechanical objectivity, judgmental objectivity.

At the risk of schematizing the already schematic, consider the following necessarily abbreviated chart (bearing in mind that the dates are of course only approximate):

7. W. W. Morgan, Philip C. Keenan, and Edith Kellman, *An Atlas of Stellar Spectra*, University of Chicago Press, Chicago, 1943, p. 5.

	Before 1820 **Genial Depiction**	1820-1920 **Mechanical Objectivity**	After 1920 **Judgmental Objectivity**
Persona	genius	manufacturer	trained expert
Practice	intervention	automatic transfer	conditioned judgment
Image	metaphysical	mechanical	interpreted
Ontology	universals, truth to nature	individual standing for type	families of objects

The pictorial regime before 1820, for example, carried with it a scientific persona, the genius, appropriate of unveiling nature's true face behind the veil. Necessarily that parting of appearances required massive intervention – recording merely what one saw would manifestly lead astray. Precisely because the picture produced by an Albinus or Goethe was not what one saw of nature in the raw, the image itself had a status beyond that of a mere reflection – a metaphysical image. And the ontology associated with such a world was clear: there were universal forms, skeletons for example, of which the too-thin, too-fat, or chipped examples to be found in the sub-lunary morgue or under our own skins were but imperfect realizations.

Set against the pictorial regime of truth to nature, that of nineteenth century mechanical objectivity stood in striking contrast. The scientific persona became not that of the intervening genius, but rather one at ease tending precise machines. Like the manufacturer who guarded against the faulty running of factory looms, the scientist supervised his apparatus to ensure proper functioning. When the machine moved properly, the product would be regular, precise, and independent of the skill of the operator. This mechanical transfer of nature to page produced images held to be homomorphic to the original object. Tracing, stamping, photographing, projecting (the particular method is not so important) – the mechanical transfer aimed to produce a record of an individual in nature that would stand for a type or class. Crucial is that the image is the visual signature of the natural object, *that* natural object, and not an abstracted, improved, or idealized *Urbild*.

Having understood the pictorial regime to be at once about the right kind of practical procedure, ontological commitment, and moral practitioner, one then raises the question: How can we understand the nature of the shifts from genial depiction to mechanical objectivity to judgmental objectivity? Much of this discussion will be speculative, and comes with a warning. Years ago, the physicist George Gamow wrote a widely-used book on atomic structure; when he came to difficult sections, he placed in the margins a skull crossbones to signal readers that they were on shaky ground. While the preceding remarks summarize work of which I am largely confident, that which follows is more conjectural. But although largely unmapped, I believe it to be fertile territory. (…)

This paper builds on a presentation made at the public session on "The Humanities and The Sciences" at the annual Meeting of the American Council of Learned Societies in May 1999. I would like to thank Lorraine Daston, Caroline A. Jones, my fellow panelists, and members of the audience for their helpful comments.

Manuel Gausa

Dynamic Time – (In)Formal Order: (Un)Disciplined Trajectories

I. Space-time-information and new architecture

In these pages we defend an interpretation of present-day architectural production which, in addition to being based on disciplinary references, professional praxis, or a simple chronicle of events, also takes a "transversal" look at the contemporary scene. This enables us to tolerate the definition and organization of our habitat and surroundings (the basic essence of architecture) as an interpretation – taken from scientific, social, philosophical, and artistic viewpoints – of its associated space and time. This is not a particularly new approach. It refers us back to similar attempts to connect a critical – "local" – diffusion of events (artistic or technical creation) with a cultural – "global" – understanding of reality.

"Understanding the nature of things to be able to act on them."[1] This is a "holistic" approach which runs through the recent history of criticism, from Veyne to Virilio and Kübler to Jencks. Yet, perhaps it was the paradigmatic essay *Space, Time*

1. Vincente Guallart, "House on the city limits," in *Quaderns 211*, 1996.

and Architecture, written by Sigfried Giedion in 1941, which, for its time, best reflected the desire for interaction between architecture, art, and science. When Giedion published his book in 1941,[2] it had been just 36 years since Albert Einstein had launched his famous Theory of Relativity which was to have such a major influence on our understanding of the universe. The term "space-time," used by Giedion, assumes intentionally scientific overtones which implicitly suggested a correlation between new aesthetic experimentation and new scientific theories of relativity.[3] The latter did away with the Aristotelian (and Newtonian) idea of an essential, metaphysical time – apart from space – and ended up definitively linking the two concepts: from that moment on, measurement of time depended on position in space and therefore on the relative movement of the observer.[4]

This was the substitution of a classical "absolute" order – continuous, homogeneous, compact and deterministic – by a new, more relative, discontinuous order, but none the less subject to the strict – rational – control of form and results.[5] It was in fact this idea of chaos or chance – "I cannot believe that God plays dice with the cosmos"...; his was a universe run according to generalized rules which involved the precise predictability of results.[6]

We could say, then, that modern space – that is, relativist space – meant the shift from the hierarchical idea of composition to the freer idea of position, though the latter continued to rest on the stable, coherent definition of prefigurable results. Planes, elementary Cartesian "rationalist" geometry were to become the basic mechanisms of a fragmented spatial conception, yet still in reference to strict, prefigured definitions.

Giedion wrote: "It is volumes which engender space. Today, architects have to constantly deal with the task of arranging these volumes of varying heights in reciprocal correspondence. Our new history begins with the optical revolution which did away with the hierarchical perspective of a single viewpoint. Today we are capable of perceiving the energy of volumes positioned freely in space, without relations of perspective..."[7]

II. Dynamic systems – (in) properties

We are still applying the residue of this modern conception of architecture – positional, Euclidean and linear – although, as the mathematician Peter Saunders points out,[8] *"Even physicists no longer believe in that eternal, solid, exact universe*

2. Siegfried Giedion, *Space, Time and Architecture,* Harvard University Press, Cambridge, Mass., 1941.

3. Ignasi Solà-Morales, "The construction of the history of architecture," in *Quaderns 181-182,* 1989.

4. Stephen W. Hawking, *A Brief History of Time,* Bantam, London, 1995.

5. Francis Struaven, "L'orphélinat d'Aldo Van Eyck" (Aldo Van Eyck's Orphanage), in *Bulletin 2* of the École d'Architecture de Versailles.

6. Hawking, op.cit.

7. Giedion, op.cit.

8. Peter T. Saunders, "Nonlinearity. What it is and why it matters," in *A. D. New Science=New Architecture?,* vol. 67, 9/10, September-October 1997.

which underpinned the deterministic paradigm. Instead, today we talk of a dynamic universe where space and time do depend on the observer, but where most of the properties only exist uncertainly and hardly predeterminably."

The Newtonian paradigm and, to a large extent, Einstein's paradigm are now facing the challenge of a shifting universe where most of the processes, even the apparently most stable, are extraordinarily undisciplined and end up leading to non-linear behaviour which is a result of their dynamic, interactive nature. In these processes, the global position must be combined with the considerable effect on the whole, with a continuous modification of its trajectories. The global system changes as local information varies and accumulates.

The study of dynamic systems in relation to theories of chaos and quantum mechanics has undergone a progressive development in the last 50 years, thanks to the recent technological capacity to simulate (and calculate) trajectories of complex, hard-to-define geometry by computation,[9] revealing the evidence of the "principle of uncertainty" which rules our universe, which has been another step forward in understanding it, beyond the theory of relativity.[10] Although there is as yet no complete theory in this respect, we are now aware, as Stephen Hawking points out, that quantum mechanics and the theories of chaos introduce an "inevitable randomness of science:" rather than considering precise, invariable, single results, they only announce informational possibilities. Here we could contend that classical space and modern "space-time" have been succeeded by an (interactive) "informational space-time" which gives rise to greater instability and indeterminacy in our understanding of the universe. At the same time, this has led to the definitive introduction of the influence of information (abstract and diversified, global and individual, contradictory and compatible) and its undisciplined effect on the manifestation of dynamic processes.

Our universe, our cities, our behaviour, even our time, respond mainly to dynamic, non-linear processes. The field of architecture, however, continues to trust models of order based on rigid, pre-established, implicitly inalterable structures: pure, strict, and incontestable.

In his recent writings, Cecil Balmond has more than once referred to this situation of distancing and lack of harmony between new science and "old" architecture:[11] *Chaos manifests itself as a succession of various orders, fairly different to the traditional idea we have of what we call "order." Is this a*

9. The theory of chaos emerged from a relationship between the computational instrument and mathematical analysis. I. Ekeland, *Le chaos*, Flammarion, Paris, 1995.

10. Hawking, op. cit.

11. Cecil Balmond: "New structure and the informal," in *A. D. New Science=New Architecture?*, op. cit.

new "informal" order, not necessarily random or arbitrary, based on a "series of overlapping, shifting certainties and information? In the informal there are no established rules or set patterns to be blindly copied, but rhythms of inferred relationships and interconnections between events."

Our aim as architects is to produce new mechanisms for action in keeping with the stimuli of a "new" global order in a constant state of suspense. An order in keeping with the dynamic – interactive – processes which define our understanding of contemporary space – and time. Complex processes defined by what we will call the "infactor" associated with them: high levels of information, the principle of incertitude – indeterminacy, instability, and incoherence –, infrastructural properties – immanence, intermittence, and interactiveness – the condition of incompleteness-infiniteness – and above all – as Balmond himself says – a tendency toward "informality" which can be directly associated with its apparent "indiscipline."

Their trajectories present manifold fluctuating and/or combinatory movements – possible, diverse "latent states" – which produce precarious situations of balance. They are, then, movements which, though normally based on generic schemes with a varying degree of prediction and recurrence – "islands of certainty" –, generally tracing out surprising, "spontaneous" trajectories which are, by definition, increasingly free: "Whereas linear systems almost always have a single point of balance, non-linear systems have more than one state of balance which include branching points, as well as transitions from one stable trajectory to another, giving rise to major changes at very short intervals."[12]

As opposed to the traditional idea of order established by the classical interpretation of space, that was based on the idea of composition 16, the modern ideology set up an alternative "new order," associated with a realistic interpretation of space and time, that was based on positions as a freer but nonetheless strict – measurable – system of linkage between objects. The shift in the contemporary paradigm and the new idea of time associated with it encouraged a new "informal" and "informational" order based on arrangements that are open to individuality and diversity.

Arrangements as combinations but also as tactical decisions, produced by a processed, deliberate, flexible interpretation of variable pieces of information which are capable of encouraging many and varied events. Decisions rather than

12. Saunders, op. cit.

designs. Criteria rather than representation. These criteria should be operative, though, as well as infrastructural (rather than (pre)figured responses). Versatile systems rather than orderly compositions.

In the course of this century, we have progressed from a classical conception of time and space – continuous, solid, absolute, static, exact and regulated, but also eternal, symbolic, metaphysical and ritual (based on the "harmonious" aesthetics of evocation) – to a modern "space-time" – discontinuous, fissured, relative, precise, but also rigid, inalterable and mechanical (deriving from a functional, mechanical, severe, technical, typological, precise rigor).

Contemporary "space-time," however, is presented as a landscape which is progressively freer of prejudice, more mutable and – however, more infrastructural. A "space-time" of interconnected, interactive messages which finds a new dimensional vector in information. An "information-space-time," then, which is combinatory, "open" and differential; probable rather than regulated, precise or exact; tactical and digital rather than evocative (ritual) or mechanical; opportunist rather than symbolic or dogmatic; mutable rather than eternal or positioned.

While modern space signified a shift from the idea of composition – as regulation – to that of position – as correlation –, today, contemporary space means a shift from the idea of position to that of disposition, or arrangement – as a tactical decision but also as a possible combination of information. From a predictable vision of the universe, we have progressed to one which was measurable and now to one which is differential.

This is an elastic, hybrid, fluctuating situation which translates to an "unpredictable" new order defined according to complex geometries of variable topography and freer, more direct, "extrovert" forms.

III. Spirals, loops, flashes. The triptych of time.

In the coming issues we aim to look at various approaches to this contemporary interpretation of space and time – related to a new understanding of dynamic systems favoured by new technologies – with particular emphasis on certain potential systems related to the implicit notions of order, structure, geometry and growth, but also with other, more ambiguous notions such as past and present – memory and history – or perception and appropriation.

These are approaches which take trajectories – spirals, loops, and flashes – as the basis for their formulation which, like in dynamic systems themselves, refer to events such as "generic, condensing movements:" "strange attractors," usually of fractal geometry, referring to "indeterminate pseudo-determinism"[13] in relation to certain recurrent figures or diagrams which we associate here with the inproperties defining this new "information-space-time."

Our aim here is to promote research on new approaches to design: flexible organisational systems, capable of generating more open, complex "relational" structures, but also capable of articulating the appearance of unexpected movements.

Wordings associated with the local system but which suddenly formulate "rebel trajectories" in the global system, distort their convention by articulating apparently contradictory or improper combinations; merging anciently disparate concepts (up and down, exterior and interior, in and out, figure and background, public and private, etc.) in new hybrid unions.[14]

Paradoxes. It is these wordings which are considered both "in the system and beyond it" – "serving yet transcending it"[15] – and underlie the "undisciplined" definition of the dynamic systems dealt with here. They allude both to the flexible nature of their associated form and order and to the very will implicit in the enunciation of dynamics of alteration and transgression. They are, then, operative paradoxes, as "epigrams" of "other possibles."

1. "Being one and several at once. Case and class."

The first essay, "*Open time – Fractal time (spirals)*" – *Q222* – aims to deal with the incomplete definition and the "infrastructural" nature of dynamic systems by analyzing new combinatory devices. These devices intended to promote processes of spatial organization in which the final form manifest as a one-off snapshot of interrupted development (a form in a "latent state" – on standby – can be associated with the properties of incompletion and infiniteness which define any open system).

These devices are constructed using basic evolutionary geometries (frameworks, matrixes, swirls, rhizomatous meshes) which are capable of taking on overlapping information and mutating with it. Flexible, evolutional diagrams, manifested by means of "immanent structures," however, vary their

13. The contribution of the theory of chaos has been to propose a pseudo-determinist model, leaving a space to chance, a dimension to the unpredictable, randomness. The system finds itself confined to more or less stable trajectories – strange attractors – but its movement escapes us. I. Ekeland, op.cit.

14. Manuel Gausa, "Arquitectura reactiva," in *Quaderns 219,* 1998.

15. Douglas R. Hofstadter, *Gödel, Escher, Bach un eterno y grácil bucle,* Tusquets, Barcelona, 1995.

scale, and are mutable in their development. To this, the mathematical theory of fractals can be applied, where whole and fragmental dimensions respond to open parameters of "a-scale" reproduction and self-similarity. It is, then, interesting to look at the relationship with genetics as "basic information" capable of producing complex interaction on the basis of elementary starting rules: "configurations" of variable progression which, on the basis of the creation of sequences, interaction and internal displacement – or "uncoiling" – lead to virtual growth and mutation of the form in the combining "spirals" of "open," definitively incomplete time.

2. "The effective past is the transferred here and now."

The second essay, *"Elastic time – Tangled time (loops)" – Q223* – looks at the undisciplined and apparently incoherent nature of dynamic systems applied to the ambiguous relationships that can be established between memory and action: "now" and "then," history and the present; past and present, not as solid, sealed categories, but as open coordinates which can be manipulated, compressed or expanded in unaccustomed new combinations. Beyond a linear, static reading of events, what we defend here is a possible "tactical" reading, unbiased, comprising leaps, intricacy and spiralling: a mischievous, insolent play of association and displacement in which the past always "runs into" the present, and the present is transferred to the past. The old behaviourist direction; chronological, hierarchical, purist or dogmatic, of orthodox, historiographic readings, makes way for an operative vision – activist and tactical – where dialogue does not mean reverence or respect for the past, but complicity between "cultural echoes" as harmonized pieces of information which suddenly detect and intersect each other.

Trajectories in motion – not sealed compartments – make for strange associations between "now" and "then," not as "anticipation" and "actuality," but as harmonized search sequences in which – why not? – certain images of the past could be seen as images of the present abducted "backwards;" as witnesses of an "agreed-on" action, transported along the loops of space-time with curved dimensions. Or signals – pulses of light – invisible until now and suddenly becoming evident by intersecting their trajectories with our interests and by revealing information which had until "now" been concealed. This makes it a reappearance rather than a memory, a "running into" rather than anticipation.

3. "Occupation without permanence, construction without building."

The third topic, *"Fleeting time – Precarious time" (flashes) – Q224* – deals with the impermanent quality of dynamic systems, associated with the unstable trajectories which characterize them. Temporary presences and contracts in which the construction of "precarious" mechanisms refers to a "merely instant" architectural manifestation made up of reversible constructions, fabrications, and installations. Ephemeral episodes, fleeting organizations, superposed deposits, bound up in a state between real and fictitious, constructed, and scenographic, with reference to a new, more receptive sensibility to the dematerialization of an architecture which is ultimately related to the light and evanescent manipulation of information, of construction and light.

Basically, our idea is to address the time triptych constructed around three strange "attractors:"

1. Spiral trajectories, capable of exacerbating the incomplete, infrastructural nature of dynamic systems and their associated properties (incompleteness, infiniteness, interaction) by analyzing the internal organization – matrixes – intended to generate evolutional processes which are open in time.

2. Loop trajectories, capable of pointing to the undisciplined – and apparently incoherent – quality of these systems by looking at the relationship between "then" and "now:" past and present, memory, and action, history and the present, as fluctuating states which can disclose agreed-on, overlapping, interactive sequences on the basis of unexpected tactical associations.

3. And, finally, flash trajectories, capable of synthesizing impermanence and instability on the basis of a positive relationship with the ephemeral, which describes new temporary contracts in the organization and definition of space. In short, three approaches which aim to look at the informal nature – informal in the sense of the absence of form – but also as the absence of prejudices (codes) and the presence of "information" (stimuli) – of contemporary design and its associated dynamic systems.

Brian Greene

Space, Time, and the Eye of the Beholder

In June 1905, twenty-six-year-old Albert Einstein submitted a technical article to the German *Annals of Physics* in which he came to grips with a paradox about light that had first troubled him as a teenager, some ten years earlier. Upon turning the final page of Einstein's manuscript, the editor of the journal, Max Planck, realized that the accepted scientific order had been overthrown. Without hoopla or fanfare, a patent clerk from Bern, Switzerland, had completely overturned the traditional notions of space and time and replaced them with a new conception whose properties fly in the face of everything we are familiar with from common experience.

The paradox that had troubled Einstein for a decade was this: In the mid-eighteenth century, after a close study of the experimental work of the English physicist Michael Faraday, the Scottish physicist James Clerk Maxwell succeeded in uniting electricity and magnetism in the framework of the *electromag-*

netic field. If you've ever been on a mountaintop just before a severe thunderstorm or stood close to a Van de Graaf generator, you have had a visceral sense of what an electromagnetic field is, because you've felt it. In case you haven't, it is somewhat like a tide of electric and magnetic lines of force that permeate a region of space through which they pass. When you sprinkle iron filings near a magnet, for example, the orderly pattern they form traces out some of the invisible lines of magnetic force. When you take off a wool sweater on an especially dry day and hear a crackling sound and perhaps feel a momentary shock or two, you are witnessing evidence of electric lines of force generated by electric charges swept up by the fibers in your sweater. Beyond uniting these and all other electric and magnetic phenomena in one mathematical framework, Maxwell's theory showed – quite unexpectedly – that electromagnetic disturbances travel at a fixed and never-changing speed, a speed that turns out to equal that of light. From this, Maxwell realized that visible light itself is nothing but a particular kind of electromagnetic wave, one that is now understood to interact with chemicals in the retina, giving rise to the sensation of sight. Moreover (and this is crucial), Maxwell's theory also showed that all electromagnetic waves – visible light among them – are the epitome of the peripatetic traveler. They never stop. They never slow down. Light *always* travels at light speed.

All is well and good until we ask, as the sixteen-year-old Einstein did, what happens if we chase after a beam of light, at light speed? Intuitive reasoning, rooted in Newton's laws of motion, tells us that we will catch up with the light waves and so they will appear stationary; light will stand still. But according to Maxwell's theory, and all reliable observations, there is simply no such thing as stationary light. No one has ever held a stationary clump of light in the palm of his or her hand. Hence the problem. Luckily, Einstein was unaware that many of the world's leading physicists were struggling with this question (and were heading down many a spurious path) and pondered the paradox of Maxwell and Newton largely in the pristine privacy of his own thoughts.

Here we discuss how Einstein resolved the conflict through his special theory of relativity, and in so doing forever changed our conceptions of space and time. It is perhaps surprising that the essential concern of special relativity is to understand precisely how the world appears to individuals, often called "observers," who are moving relative to one another. At first, this might seem to be an intellectual exercise of minimal importance. Quite the contrary: In the hands of Einstein, with his imaginings of observers chasing after light beams, there are profound implications to grasping fully how even the most mundane situations appear to individuals in relative motion.

Intuition and its flaws

Common experience highlights certain ways in which observations by such individuals differ. Trees alongside a highway, for example, appear to be moving from the viewpoint of a driver but appear stationary to a hitchhiker sitting on a guardrail. Similarly, the dashboard of the automobile does not appear to be moving from the viewpoint of the driver (one hopes!), but like the rest of the car, it does appear to be moving from the viewpoint of the hitchhiker. These are such basic and intuitive properties of how the world works that we hardly take note of them.

Special relativity, however, proclaims that the differences in observations between two such individuals are more subtle and profound. It makes the strange claim that observers in relative motion will have different perceptions of distance and of time. This means, as we shall see, that identical wristwatches worn by two individuals in relative motion will tick at *different rates* and hence will not agree on the amount of time that elapses between chosen events. Special relativity demonstrates that this statement does not slander the accuracy of the wristwatches involved; rather, it is a true statement about time itself.

Similarly, observers in relative motion carrying identical tape measures will not agree on the lengths of distance measured. Again, this is not due to inaccuracies in the measuring devices or to errors in how they are used. The most accurate measuring devices in the world confirm that space and time – as measured by distances and durations – are not experienced identically by everyone. In the precise way delineated by Einstein, special relativity resolves the conflict between our intuition about motion and the properties of light, but there is a price: individuals who are moving with respect to each other will not agree on their observations of either space or time.

It has been almost a century since Einstein informed the world of his dramatic discovery, yet most of us still see space and time in absolute terms. Special relativity is not in our bones – we do not feel it. Its implications are not a central part of our intuition. The reason for this is quite simple: The effects of special relativity depend upon how fast one moves, and at the speeds of cars, planes, or even space shuttles, these effects are minuscule. Differences in perceptions of space and of time between individuals planted on the earth and those traveling in cars or planes *do* occur, but they are so small that they go unnoticed. However, were one to take a trip in a futuristic space vehicle traveling at a substantial fraction of light speed, the effects of relativity would become plainly obvious. This, of course, is still in the realm of science fiction. Nevertheless, clever experiments allow clear and precise observation of the relative properties of space and time predicted by Einstein's theory.

To get a sense of the scales involved, imagine that the year is 1970 and big, fast cars are in. Slim, having just spent all his savings on a new Trans Am, goes with his brother Jim to the local drag strip to give the car the kind of test-drive forbidden by the dealer. After revving up the car, Slim streaks down the mile-long strip at 120 miles per hour while Jim stands on the sideline and times him. Wanting an independent confirmation, Slim also uses a stopwatch to determine how long it takes his new car to traverse the track. Prior to Einstein's work, no one would have questioned that if both Slim and Jim have properly functioning stopwatches, each will measure the identical elapsed time. But according to special relativity, while Jim will measure an elapsed time of 30 seconds, Slim's stopwatch will record an elapsed time of 29,99999999999952 seconds – *a tiny bit less*. Of course, this difference is so small that it could be detected only through a measurement whose accuracy is well beyond the capacity of handheld stopwatches run by the press of a finger, Olympic-quality timing systems, or even the most precisely engineered atomic clocks. It is no wonder that our everyday experiences do not reveal the fact that the passage of time depends upon our state of motion.

There will be a similar disagreement on measurements of length. For example, on another test run Jim uses a clever trick to measure the length of Slim's new car: he starts his stopwatch just as the front of the car reaches him and he stops it just as the back of the car passes. Since Jim knows that Slim is speeding along at 120 miles per hour, he is able to figure out the length of the car by multiplying this speed by the elapsed time on his stopwatch. Again, prior to Einstein, no one would have questioned that the length Jim measures in this indirect way would agree *exactly* with the length Slim carefully measured when the car sat motionless on the showroom floor. Special relativity proclaims, on the contrary, that if Slim and Jim carry out precise measurements in this manner and Slim finds the car to be, say, exactly 16 feet long, then Jim's measurement will find the car to be 15,99999999999974 feet long – *a tiny bit less.* As with the measurement of time, this is such a minuscule difference that ordinary instruments are just not accurate enough to detect it.

Although the differences are extremely small, they show a fatal flaw in the commonly held conception of universal and immutable space and time. As the relative velocity of individuals such as Slim and Jim gets larger, this flaw becomes increasingly apparent. To achieve noticeable differences, the speeds involved must be a sizeable fraction of the maximum possible speed – that of light – which Maxwell's theory and experimental measurements show to be about 186,000 miles per second, or about 670 million miles per hour. This is fast enough to circle the earth more than seven times in a second. If Slim, for example, were to travel not at 120 miles per hour but at 580 million miles per hour (about 87 percent of light speed), the mathematics of special relativity predicts that Jim would measure the length of the car to be about eight feet, which is substantially different from Slim's measurement (as well as the specifications in the owner's manual). Similarly, the time to traverse the drag strip according to Jim will be about *twice* as long as the time measured by Slim.

Since such enormous speeds are far beyond anything currently attainable, the effects of "time dilation" and "Lorentz contraction," as these phenomena are technically called, are extremely small in today's life. If we happened to live in a world in which things typically traveled at speeds close to that of light, these properties of space and time would be so completely intuitive – since we would experience them constantly – that they would deserve no more discussion than the apparent motion of trees on the side of the road mentioned at the outset of this text. But since we don't live in such a world, these features are unfamiliar. As we shall see, understanding and accepting them requires that we subject our worldview to a thorough makeover.

The principle of relativity

There are two simple yet deeply rooted structures that form the foundation of special relativity. As mentioned, one concerns properties of light. The other is more abstract. It is concerned not with any specific physical law but rather with *all* physical laws, and is known as the *principle of relativity.* The principle of relativity rests on a simple fact: Whenever we discuss speed or velocity (an object's speed and its direction of motion), we must specify precisely who or what is doing the measuring. Understanding the meaning and importance of this statement is easily accomplished by contemplating the following situation.

Imagine that George, who is wearing a spacesuit with a small, red flashing light, is floating in the absolute darkness of completely empty space, far away from any planets, stars, or galaxies. From George's perspective, he is completely stationary, engulfed in the uniform, still blackness of the cosmos. Off in the distance, George catches sight of a tiny, green flashing light that appears to be coming closer and closer. Finally, it gets close enough for George to see that the light is attached to the spacesuit of another space-dweller, Gracie, who is slowly floating by. She waves as she passes, as does George, and she recedes into the distance. This story can be told with equal validity from Gracie's perspective. It begins in the same manner with Gracie completely alone in the immense still darkness of outer space. Off in the distance, Gracie sees a red flashing light, which appears to be coming closer and closer. Finally, it gets close enough for Gracie to see that it is attached to the spacesuit of another being, George, who is slowly floating by. He waves as he passes, as does Gracie, and he recedes into the distance.

The two stories describe one and the same situation from two distinct but equally valid points of view. Each observer feels stationary and perceives the other as moving. Each perspective is understandable and justifiable. As there is symmetry between the two space-dwellers, there is, on quite fundamental grounds, no way of saying one perspective is "right" and the other "wrong." Each perspective has an equal claim to truth.

This example captures the meaning of the principle of relativity: The concept of motion is relative. We can speak about the motion of an object, but only relative to or by comparison with another. There *is* thus no meaning to the statement "George is traveling at 10 miles per hour," as we have not specified any other object for comparison. There is meaning to the statement "George is traveling at 10 miles per hour past Gracie," as we have now specified Gracie as the benchmark. As our example shows, this last statement is completely equivalent to "Gracie is traveling at 10 miles per hour past George (in the opposite direction)." In other words, there is no "absolute" notion of motion. Motion is relative.

A key element of this story is that neither George nor Gracie is being pushed, pulled, or in any other way acted upon by a force or influence that could disturb their serene state of force-free, constant-velocity motion. Thus, a more precise statement is that *force-free* motion has meaning only by comparison with other objects. This is an important clarification, because if forces are involved, they cause changes in the velocity of the observers – changes to their speed and/or their direction of motion – and these changes can be felt. For instance, if George were wearing a jet-pack firing away from his back, he would definitely feel that he was moving. This feeling is intrinsic. If the jet-pack is firing away, George *knows* he is moving, even if his eyes are closed and therefore can make no comparisons with other objects. Even without such comparisons, he would no longer claim that he was stationary while "the rest of the world was moving by him." Constant-velocity motion is relative; not so for non-constant-velocity motion, or, equivalently, *accelerated motion*.

Setting these stories in the darkness of empty space aids understanding by removing such familiar things as streets and buildings, which we typically, although unjustifiably, accord the special status of "stationary." Nonetheless, the same principle applies to terrestrial settings, and in fact is commonly experienced.[1] For example, imagine that after you have fallen asleep on a train, you awake just as your train is passing another on adjacent parallel tracks. With your view through the window completely blocked by the other train, thereby preventing you from seeing any other objects, you may temporarily be uncertain as to whether your train is moving, the other train is moving, or both. Of course, if your train shakes or jostles, or if the train changes direction by rounding a bend, you can feel that you are moving. But if the ride is perfectly smooth – if the train's velocity remains constant – you will observe relative motion between the trains without being able to tell for certain which is moving.

Let's take this one step further. Imagine you are on such a train and that you pull down the shades so that the windows are fully covered. Without the ability to see anything outside your own compartment, and assuming that the train moves at absolutely constant velocity, there will be no way for you to determine your state of motion. The compartment around you will look *precisely* the same regardless of whether the train is sitting still on the tracks or moving at high speed. Einstein formalized this idea, one that actually goes back to insights of

1. The presence of massive bodies like the earth does complicate matters by introducing gravitational forces. Since we are focusing on motion in the horizontal direction – not the vertical direction – we can and will ignore the earth's presence.

Galileo, by proclaiming that it is impossible for you or any fellow traveler to perform an experiment within the closed compartment that will determine whether or not the train is moving. This again captures the principle of relativity: since all force-free motion is relative, it has meaning only by comparison with other objects or individuals also undergoing force-free motion. There is no way for you to determine anything about your state of motion without making some direct or indirect comparison with "outside" objects. There simply is no notion of "absolute" constant-velocity motion; only comparisons have any physical meaning.

In fact, Einstein realized that the principle of relativity makes an even grander claim: the laws of physics – whatever they may be – must be absolutely identical for all observers undergoing constant-velocity motion. If George and Gracie are not just floating solo in space, but, rather, are each conducting the same set of experiments in their respective floating space-stations, the results they find will be identical. Once again, each is perfectly justified in believing that his or her station is at rest, even though the two stations are in relative motion. If all of their equipment is identical, there is nothing distinguishing the two experimental setups – they are completely symmetric. The laws of physics that each deduces from the experiments will likewise be identical. Neither they nor their experiments can feel – that is, depend upon in any way – constant-velocity travel. It is this simple concept that establishes complete symmetry between such observers; it is this concept that is embodied in the principle of relativity. We shall shortly make use of this principle to profound effect.

The speed of light

The second key ingredient in special relativity has to do with light and properties of its motion. Contrary to our claim that there is no meaning to the statement "George is traveling at 10 miles per hour" without a specified benchmark for comparison, almost a century of effort by a series of dedicated experimental physicists has shown that any and all observers will agree that light travels at 670 million miles per hour *regardless of benchmarks for comparison.*

This fact has required a revolution in our view of the universe. Let's first gain an understanding of its meaning by contrasting it with similar statements applied to more common objects. Imagine it's a nice, sunny day and you go outside to play a game of catch with a friend. For a while, you both leisurely throw the ball back and forth with a speed of, say, 20 feet per second, when suddenly an unexpected electrical storm stirs overhead, sending you both running for cover. After it passes, you rejoin to resume your game of catch but you notice that something has changed. Your friend's hair has become wild and spiky, and her eyes have grown severe and crazed. When you look at her hand, you are stunned to see that she is no longer planning to play catch with a baseball, but instead is about to toss you a hand grenade. Understandably, your enthusiasm for playing catch diminishes substantially; you turn to run. When your companion throws the grenade, it will still fly toward you, but because you are running, the speed with which it approaches you will be less than 20 feet per second. In fact, common experience tells us that if you can run at, say, 12 feet per second then the hand-grenade will approach you at (20 - 12 =) 8 feet per second. As another example, if you are in the mountains and an avalanche of snow is rumbling toward you, your inclination is to turn and run because this will cause the speed with which the snow approaches you to decrease – and this, generally, is a good thing. Again, a stationary individual perceives the speed of the approaching snow to be greater than that perceived by someone in retreat.

Now, let's compare these basic observations about baseballs, grenades, and avalanches to those about light. To make the comparisons tighter, think about a light beam as composed of tiny "packets" or "bundles" known as photons. When we turn on a flashlight or a laser beam we are, in effect, shooting a stream of photons in whatever direction we point the device. As we did for grenades and avalanches, let's consider how the motion of a photon appears to someone who is moving. Imagine that your crazed friend has swapped her grenade for a powerful laser. If she fires the laser toward you – and if you had the appropriate measuring equipment – you would find that the speed of approach of the photons in the beam is 670 million miles per hour. But what if you run away, as you did when faced with the prospect of playing catch with a hand grenade? What speed will you now measure for the approaching photons? To make things more compelling, imagine that you can hitch a ride on the starship *Enterprise* and zip away from your friend at, say, 100 million miles per hour. Following the reasoning based on the traditional Newtonian worldview, since you are now speeding away, you would expect to measure a *slower* speed for the oncoming photons. Specifically, you would expect to find them approaching you at (670 million miles per hour – 100 million miles per hour =) 570 million miles per hour.

Mounting evidence from a variety of experiments dating back as far as the 1880s, as well as careful analysis and interpretation of Maxwell's electromagnetic theory of light, slowly convinced the scientific community that, in fact, this is not what you will see. *Even though you are retreating, you will still measure the speed of the approaching photons as 670 million miles per hour, not a bit less.* Although at first it sounds completely ridiculous, unlike what happens if one runs from an oncoming baseball, grenade, or avalanche, the speed of approaching photons is always 670 million miles per hour. The same is true if you run toward oncoming photons or chase after them – their speed of approach or recession is completely unchanged; they still appear to travel at 670 million miles per hour. Regardless of relative motion between the source of photons and the observer, the speed of light is always the same.[2]

Technological limitations are such that the "experiments" with light, as described, cannot actually be carried out. However, comparable experiments can. For instance, in 1913 the Dutch physicist Willem de Sitter suggested that fast-moving binary stars (two stars that orbit one another) could be used to measure the effect of a moving source on the speed of light. Various experiments of this sort over the past eight decades have verified that the speed of light received from a moving star is the *same* as that from a stationary star – 670 million miles per hour – to within the impressive accuracy of ever more refined measuring devices. Moreover, a wealth of other detailed experiments has been carried out during the past century – experiments that directly measure the speed of light in various circumstances, as well as test many of the implications arising from this characteristic of light, as discussed shortly – and all have confirmed the constancy of the speed of light.

If you find this property of light hard to swallow, you are not alone. At the turn of the century physicists went to great length to refute it. They couldn't. Einstein, to the contrary, embraced the constancy of the speed of light, for here was the answer to the conflict that had troubled him since he was a teenager: No matter how hard you chase after a light beam, it still retreats from you at light speed. You can't make the apparent speed with which light departs one iota less than 670 million miles per hour, let alone slow it down to the point of appearing stationary. Case closed. But this triumph over paradox was no small victory. Einstein realized that the

2. More precisely, the speed of light through the *empty space* is 670 million miles per hour. When light travels through a substance such as air or glass, its speed is decreased in roughly the same way that a rock dropped from a cliff is dragged to a slower speed when it enters a body of water. This slowing of light relative to its speed through a vacuum is of no consequence for our discussion of relativity and is justifiably ignored throughout the text.

constancy of light's speed spelled the downfall of Newtonian physics.

Truth and consequences

Speed is a measure of how far an object can travel in a given duration of time. If we are in a car going 65 miles per hour, this means of course that we will travel 65 miles if we persist in this state of motion for an hour. Phrased in this manner, speed is a rather mundane concept, and you may wonder about the fuss we have made regarding the speed of baseballs, snowballs, and photons. However, let's note that *distance* is a notion about space – in particular it is a measure of how much space there is between two points. Also note that *duration* is a notion about time – how much time elapses between two events. Speed, therefore, is intimately connected with our notions of space and time. When we phrase it this way, we see that any experimental fact that defies our common conception about speed, such as the constancy of the speed of light, has the potential to defy our common conceptions of space and time themselves. It is for this reason that the strange fact about the speed of light deserves detailed scrutiny – scrutiny given to it by Einstein, leading him to remarkable conclusions.

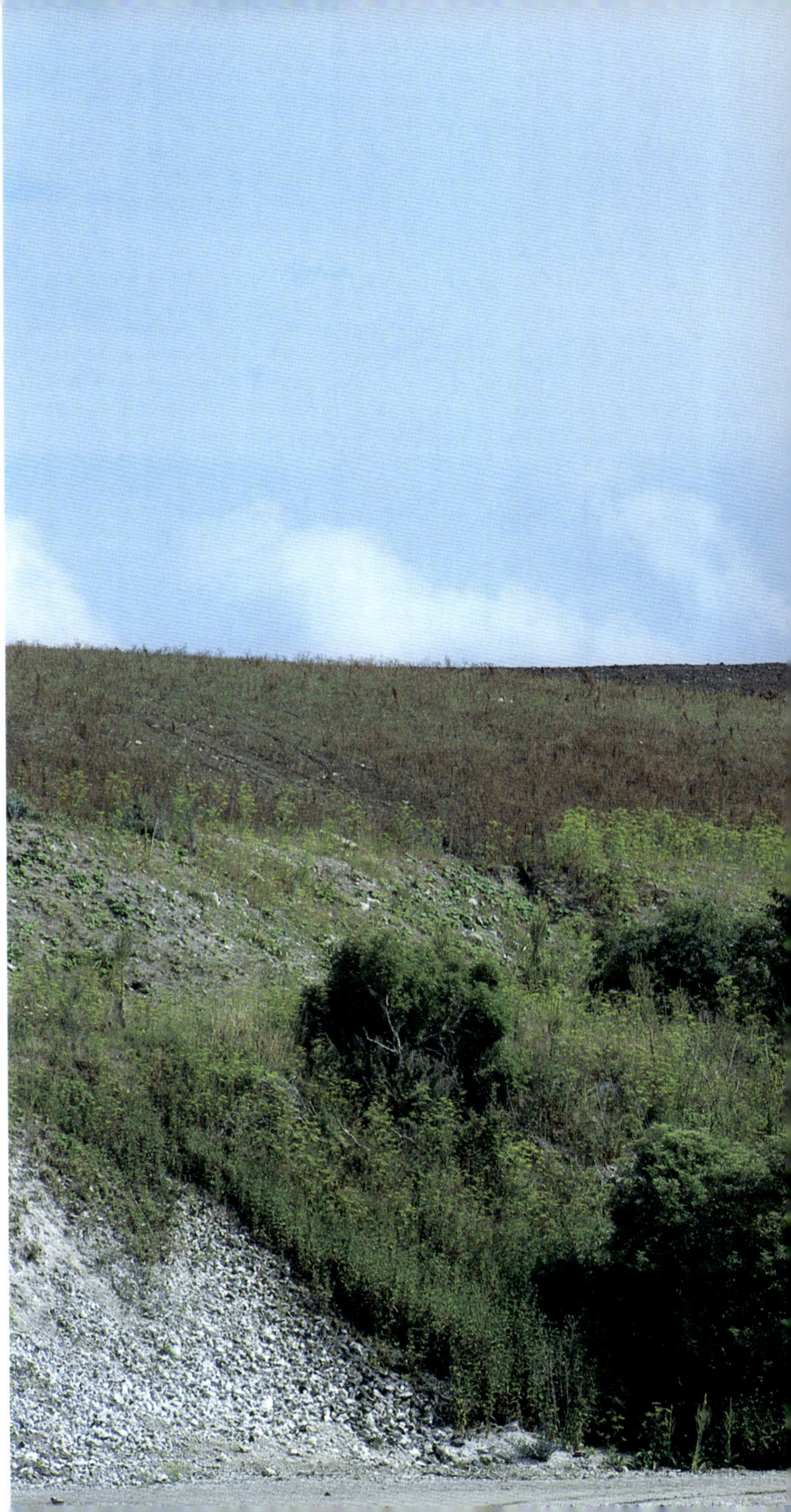

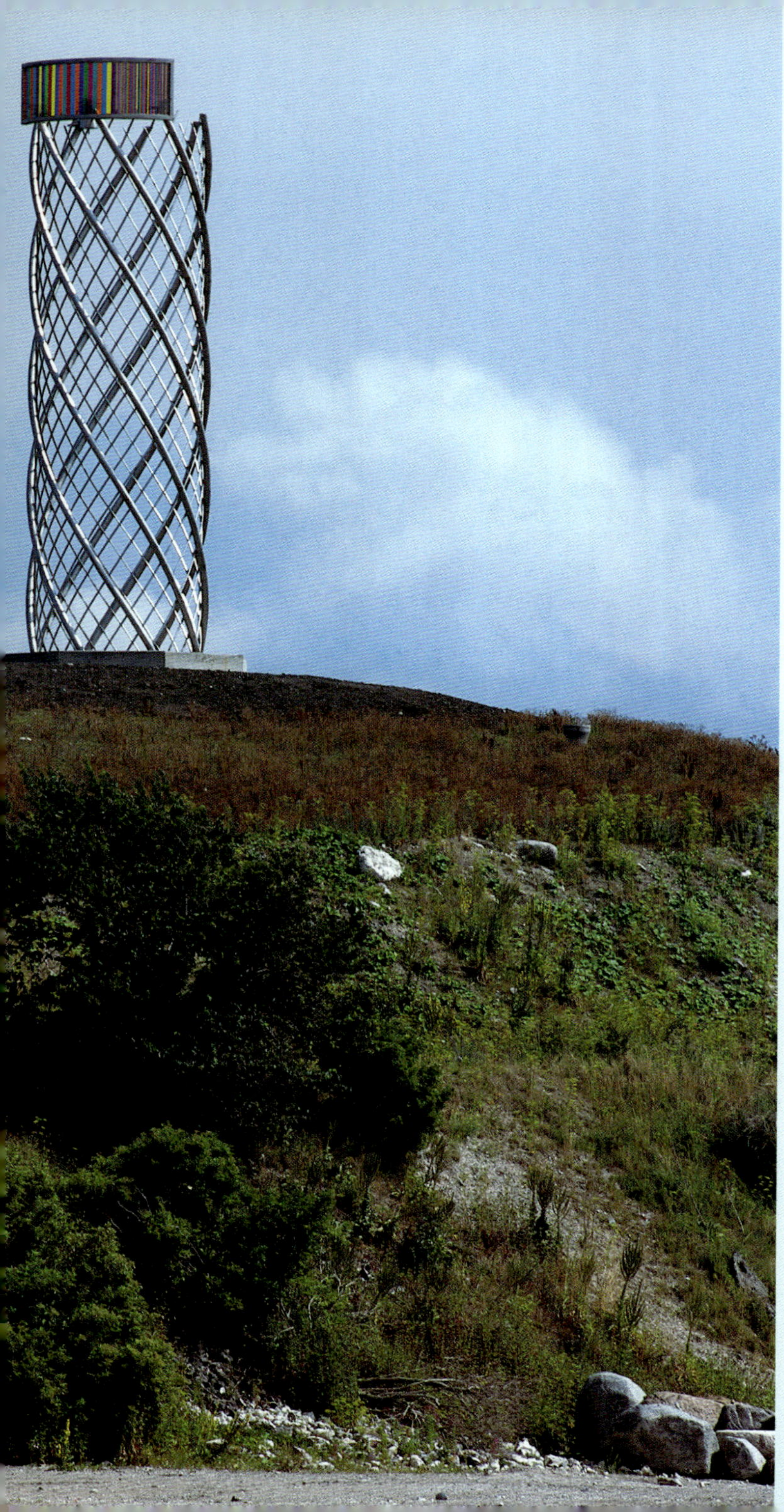
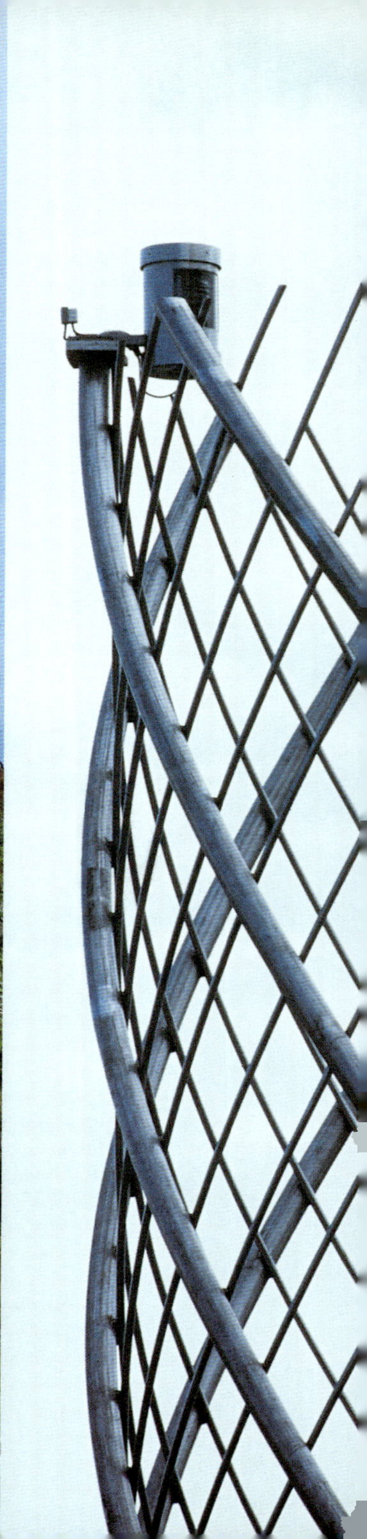

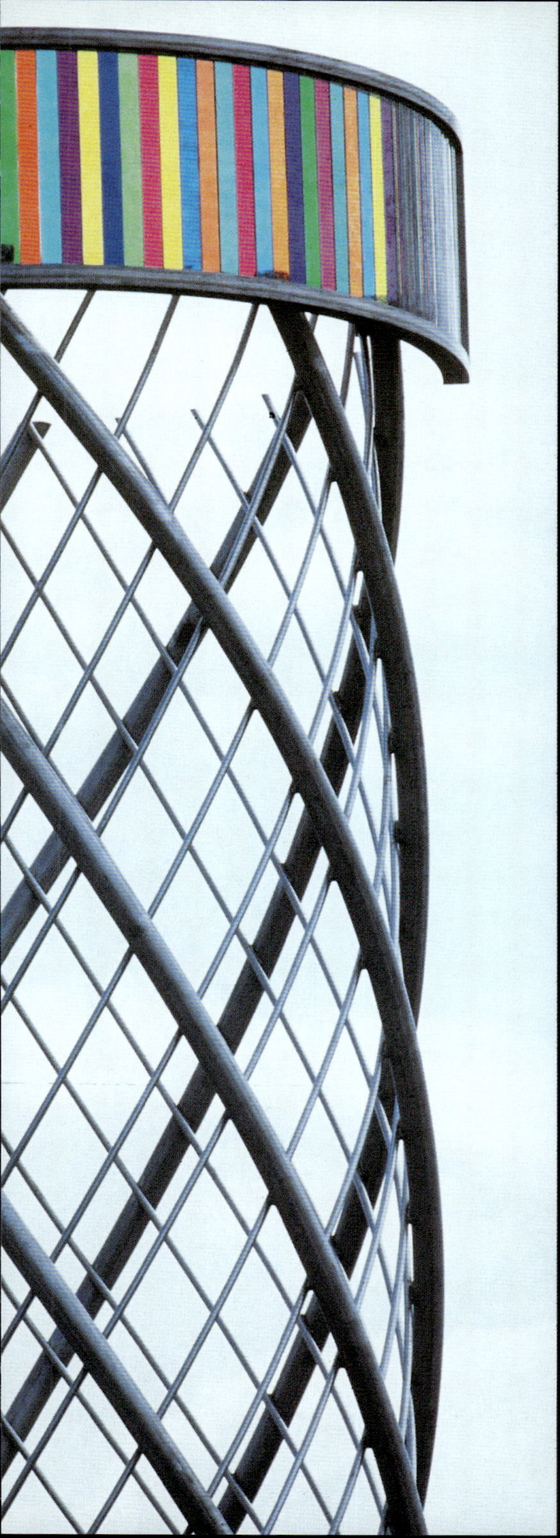
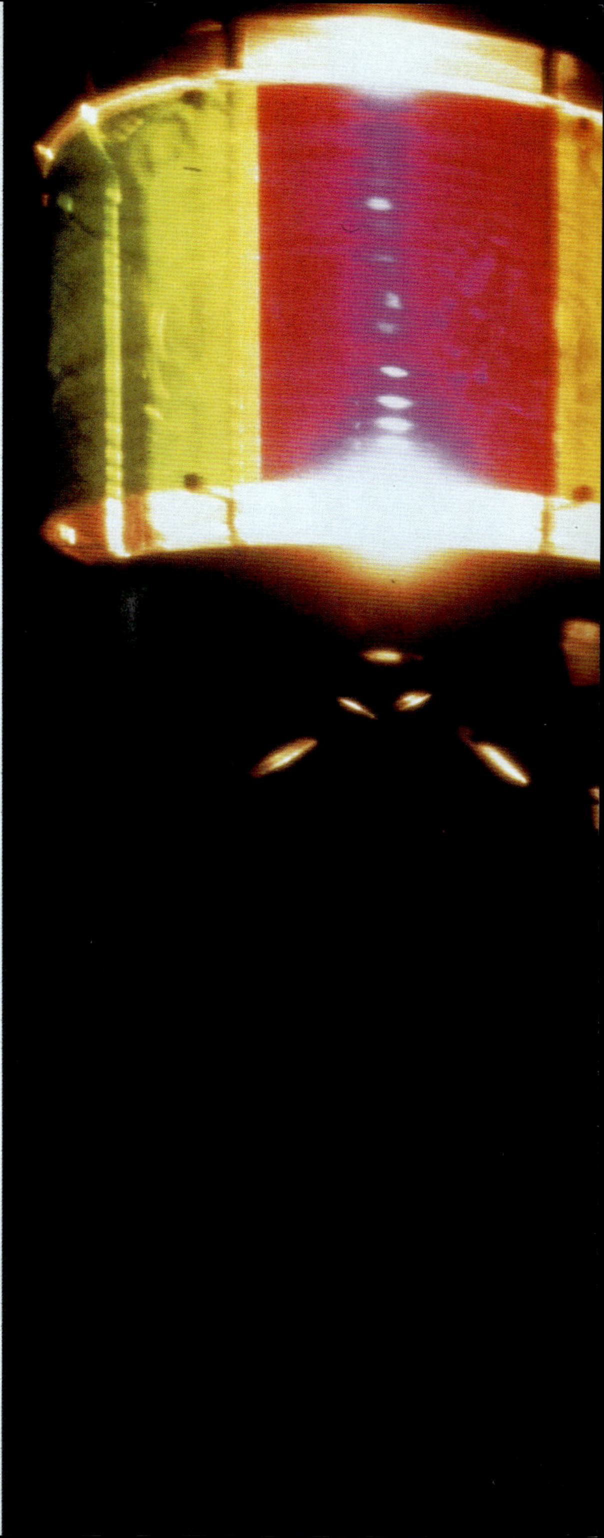

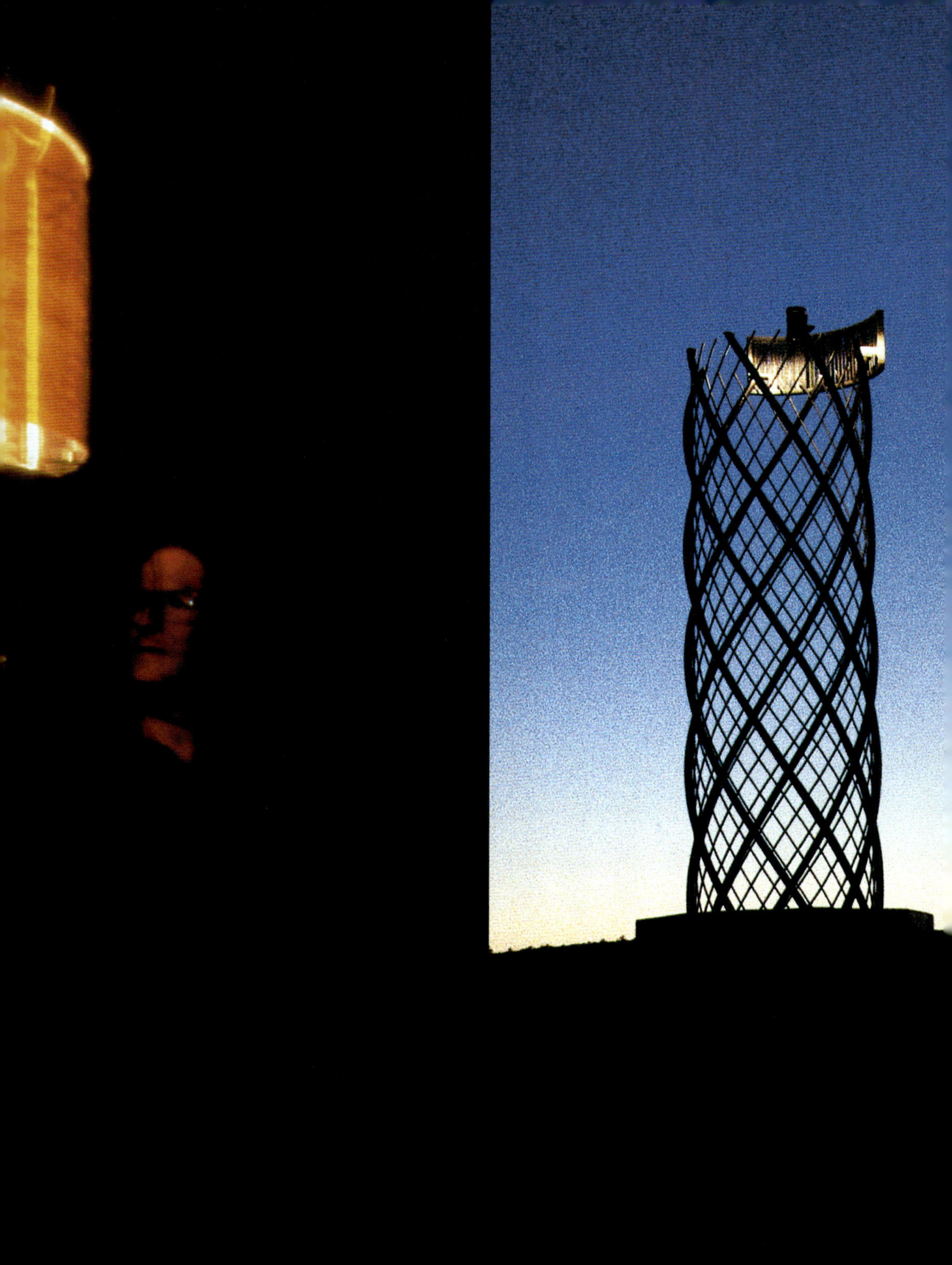

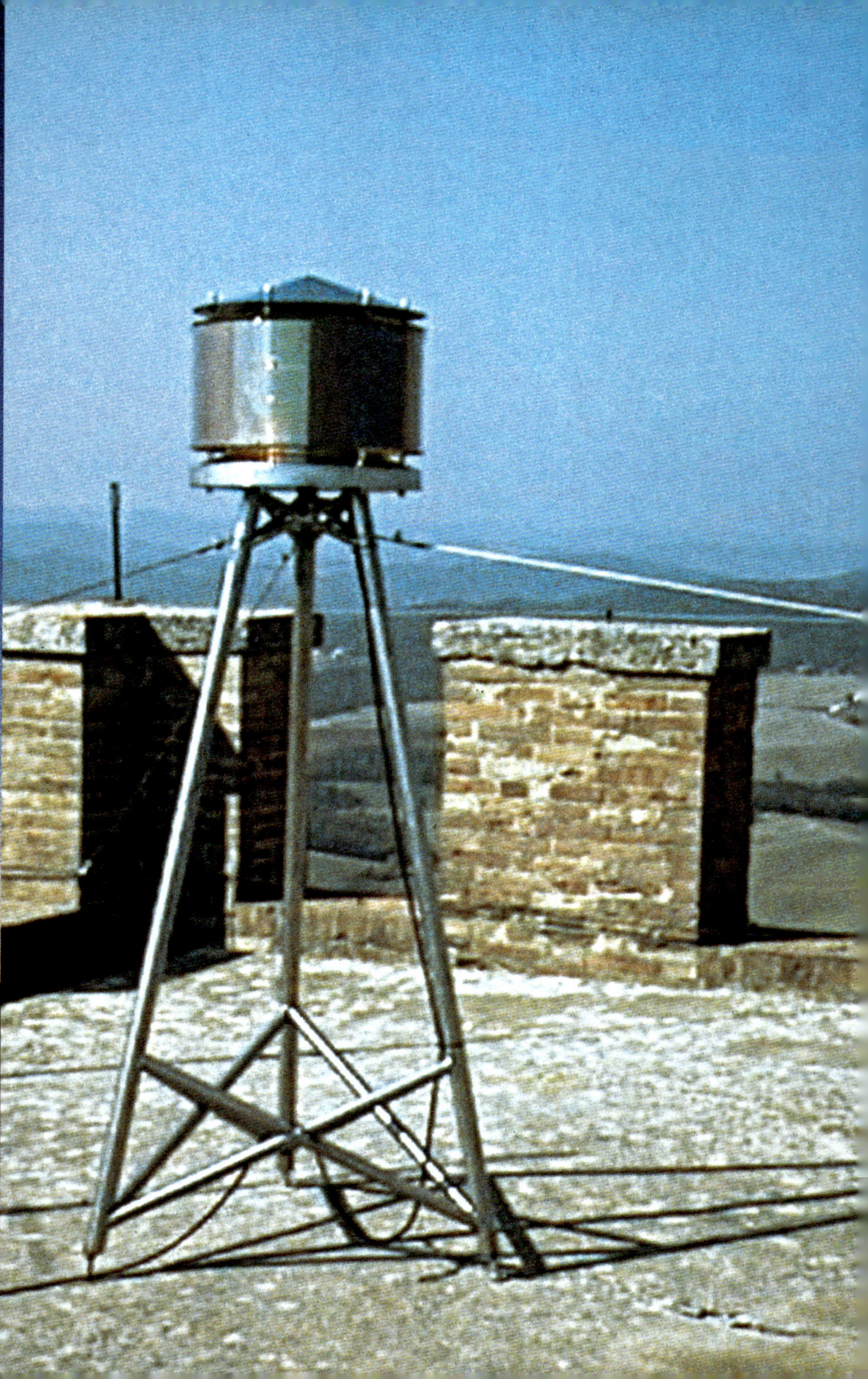

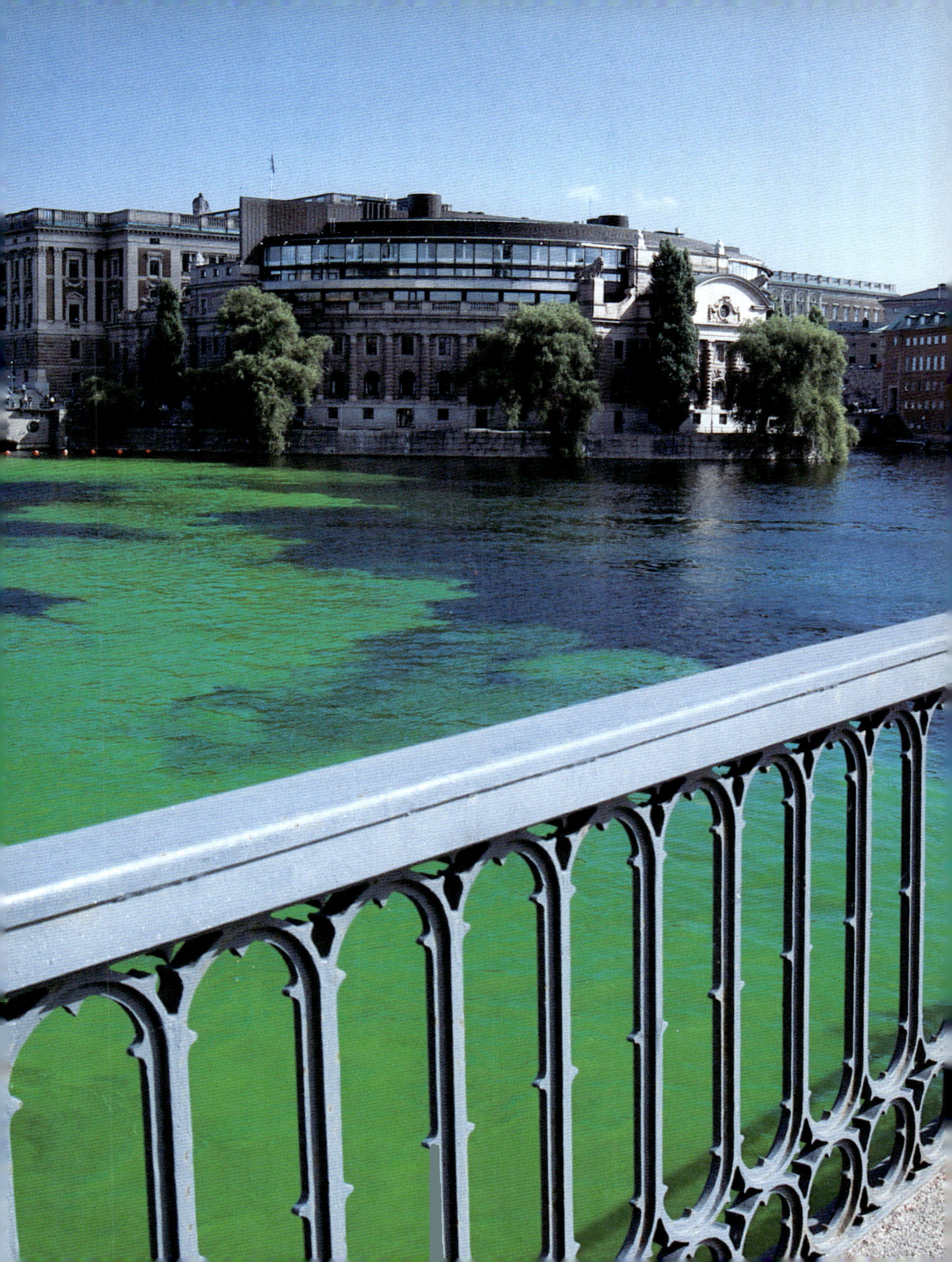

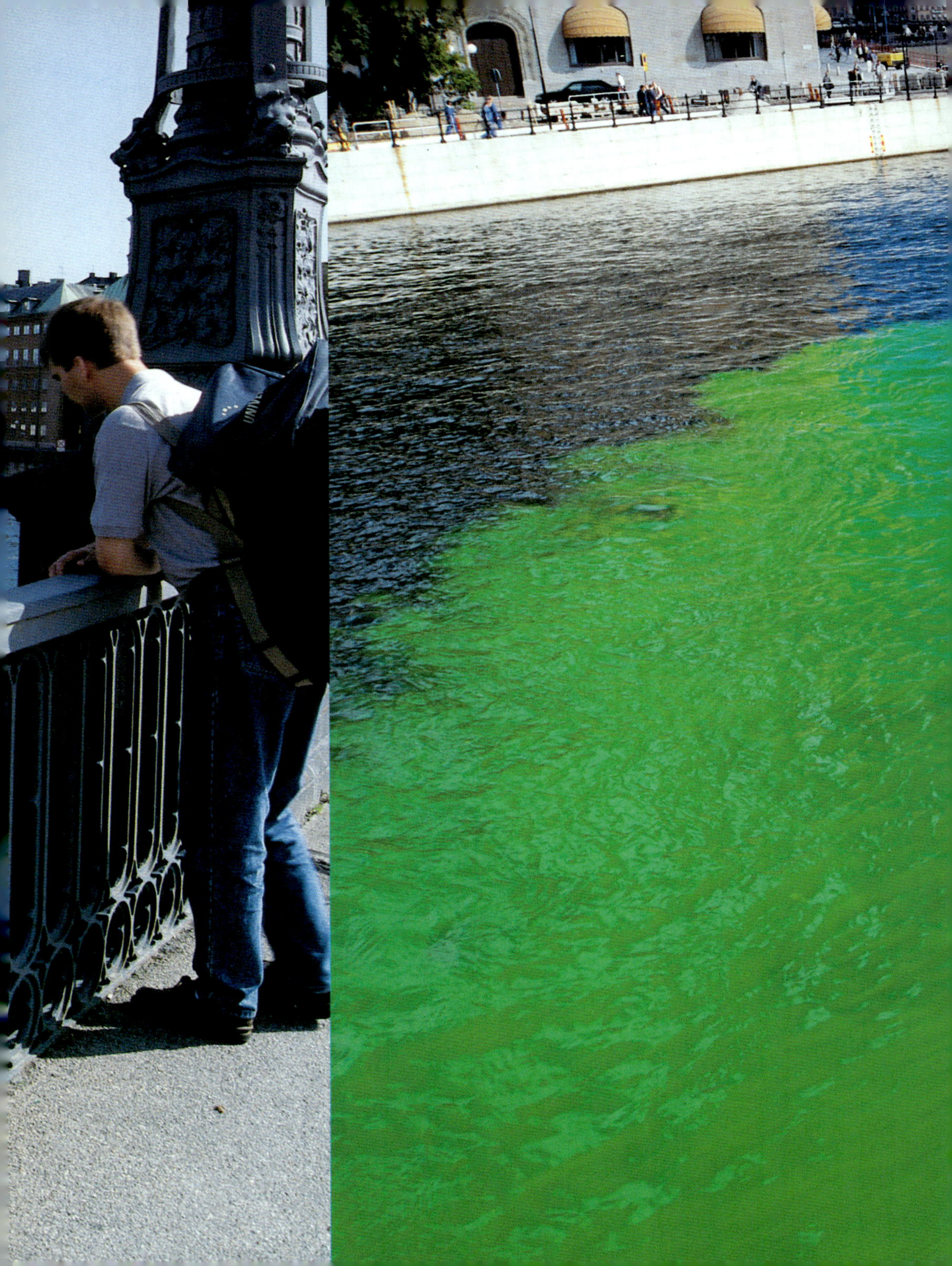

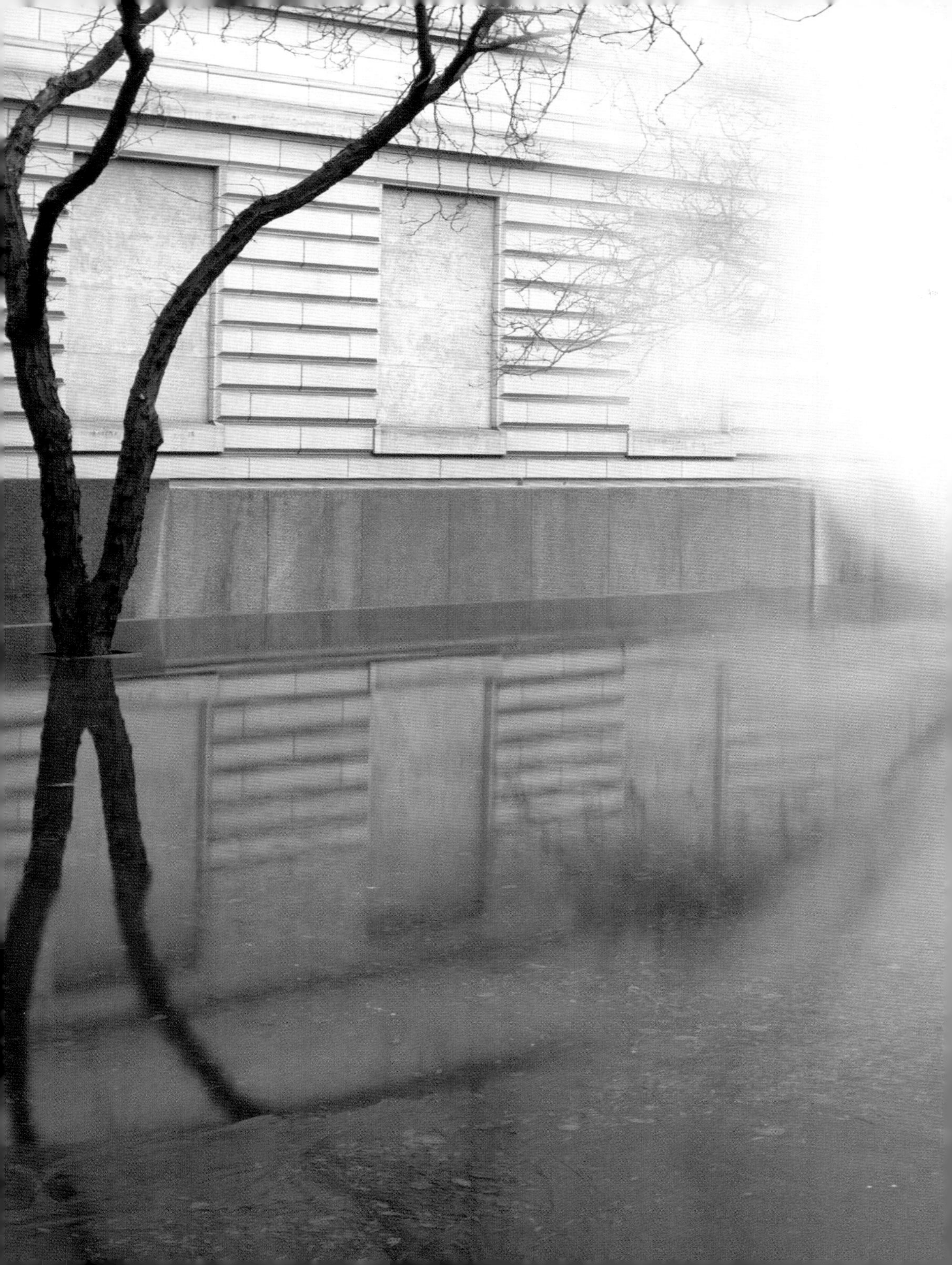

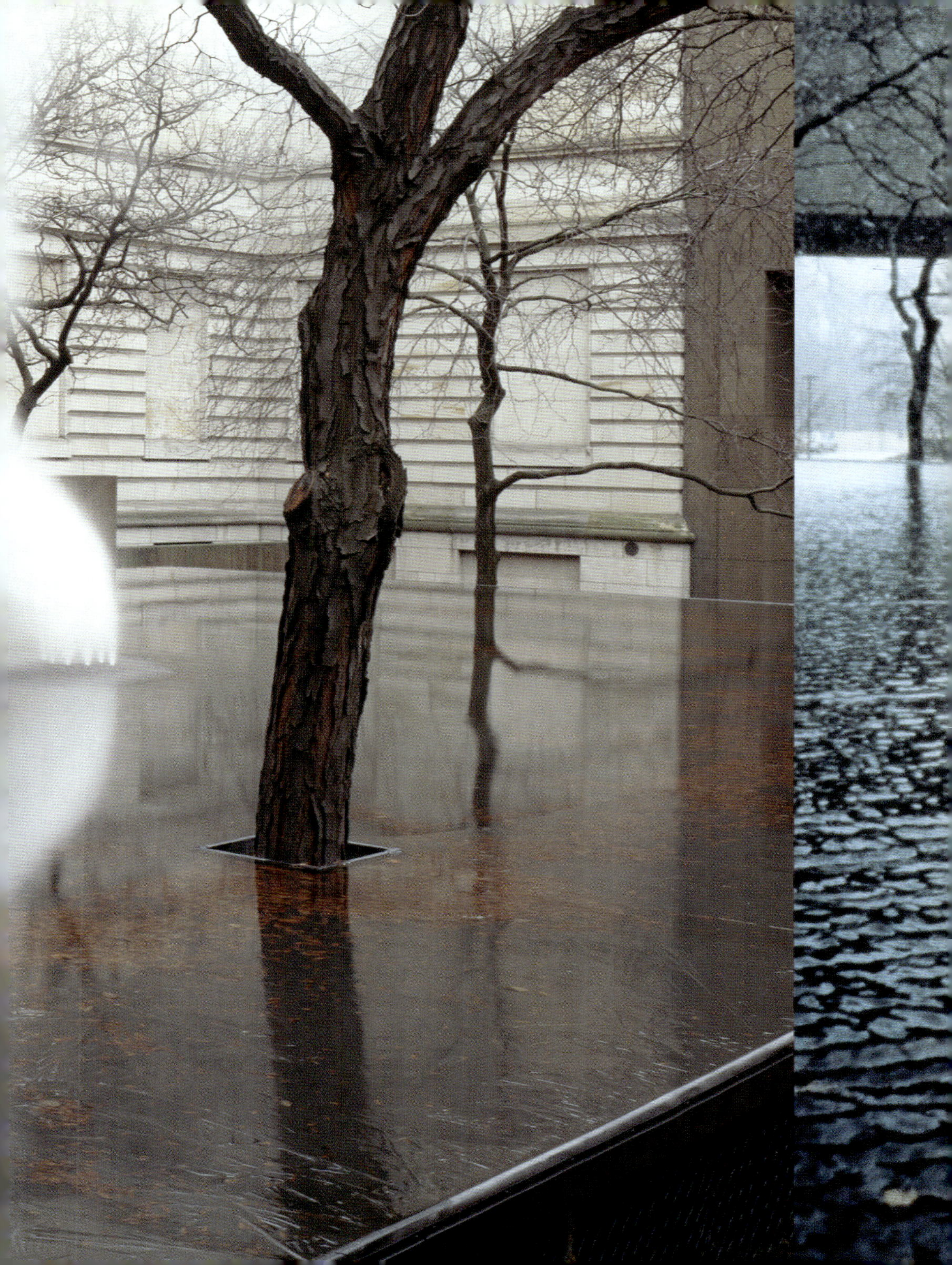

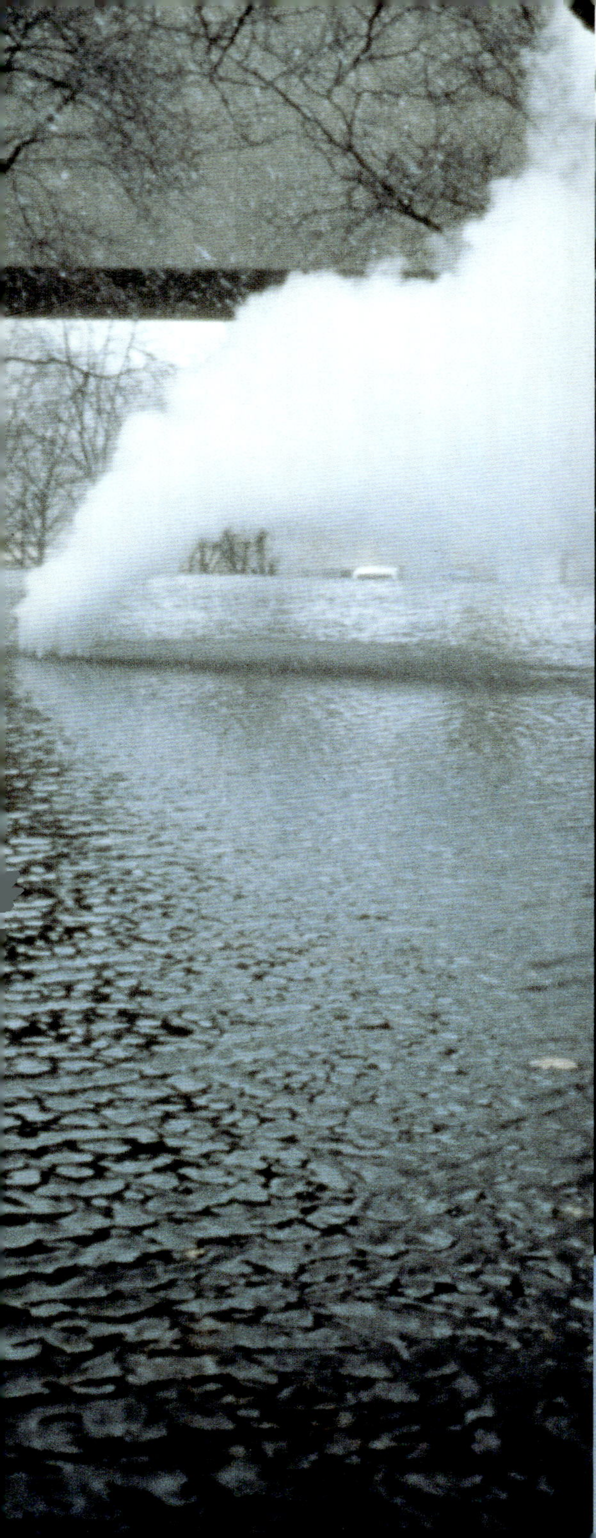
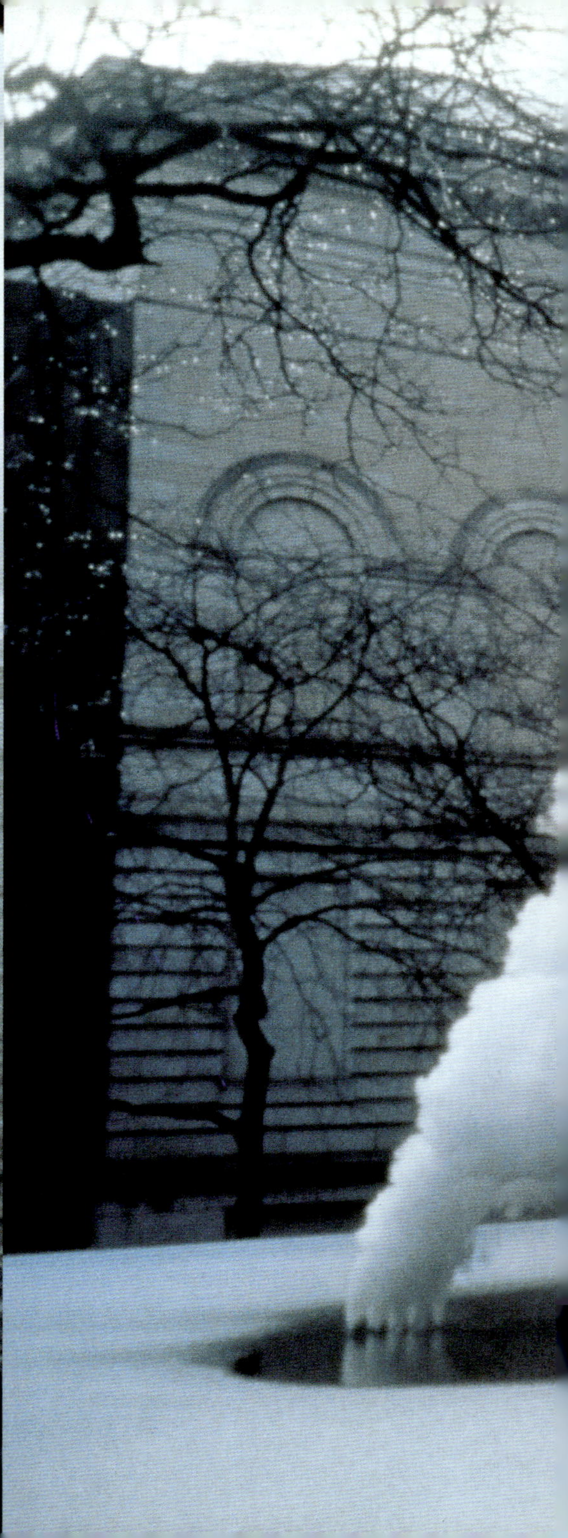

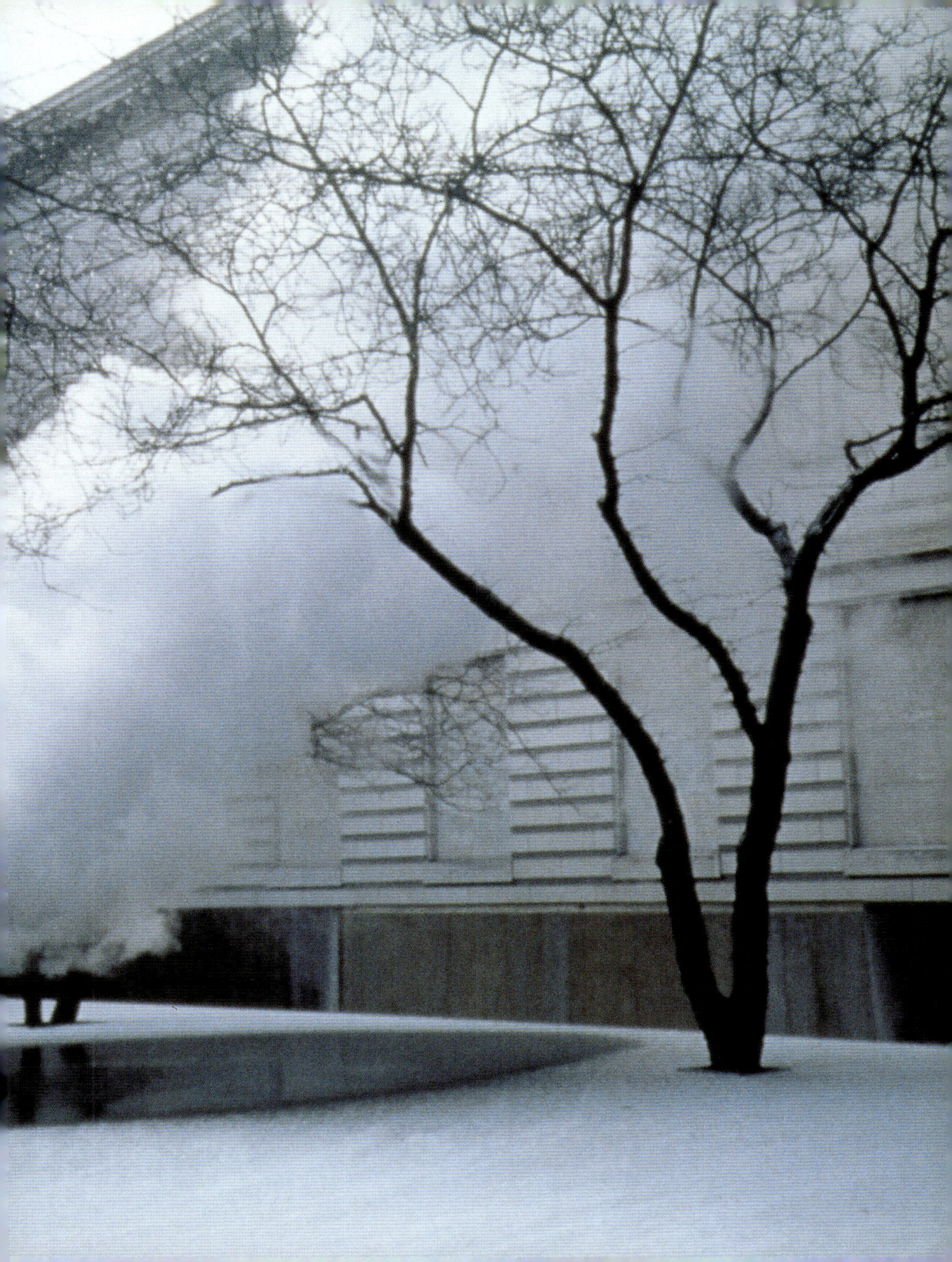

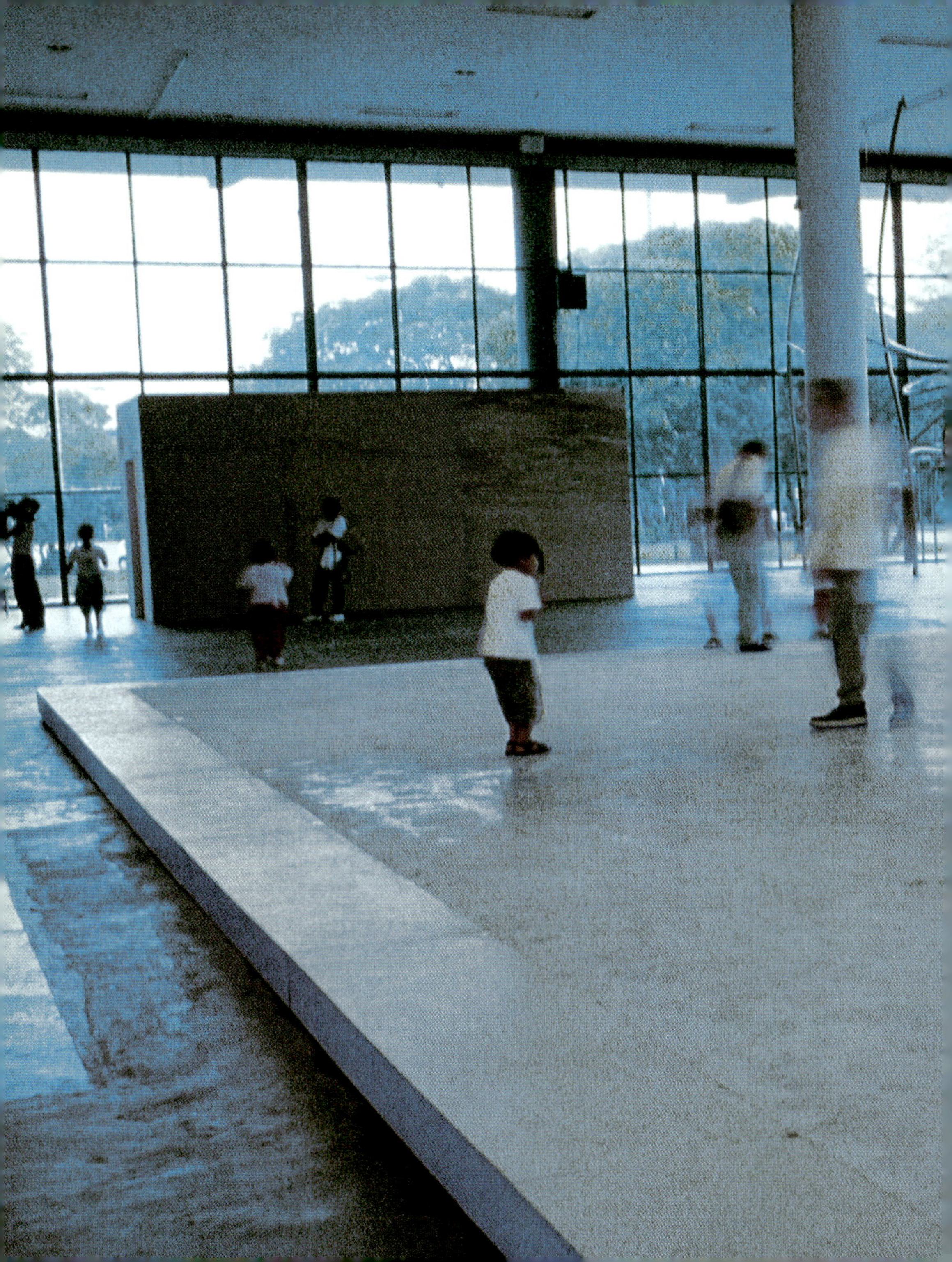

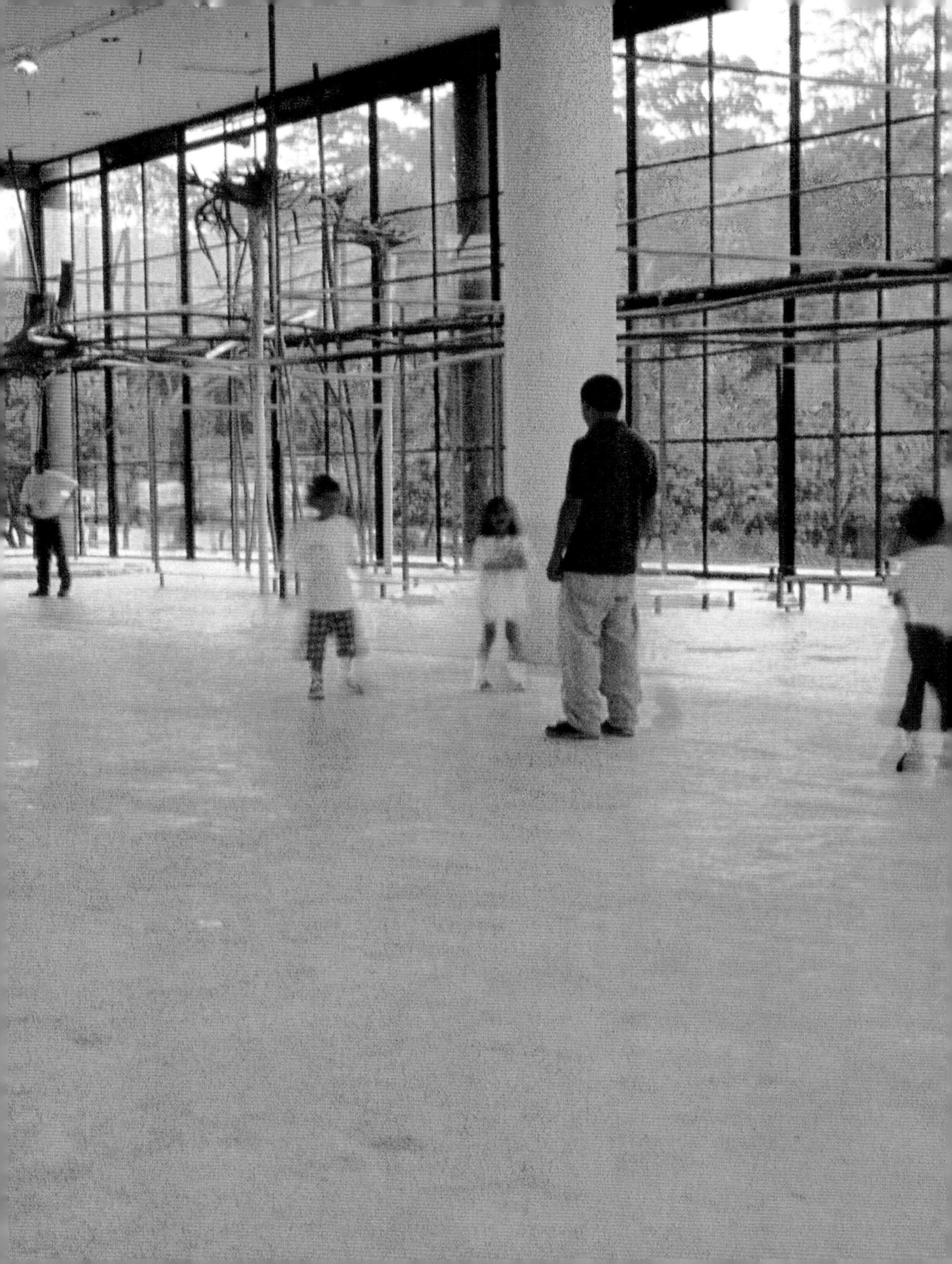

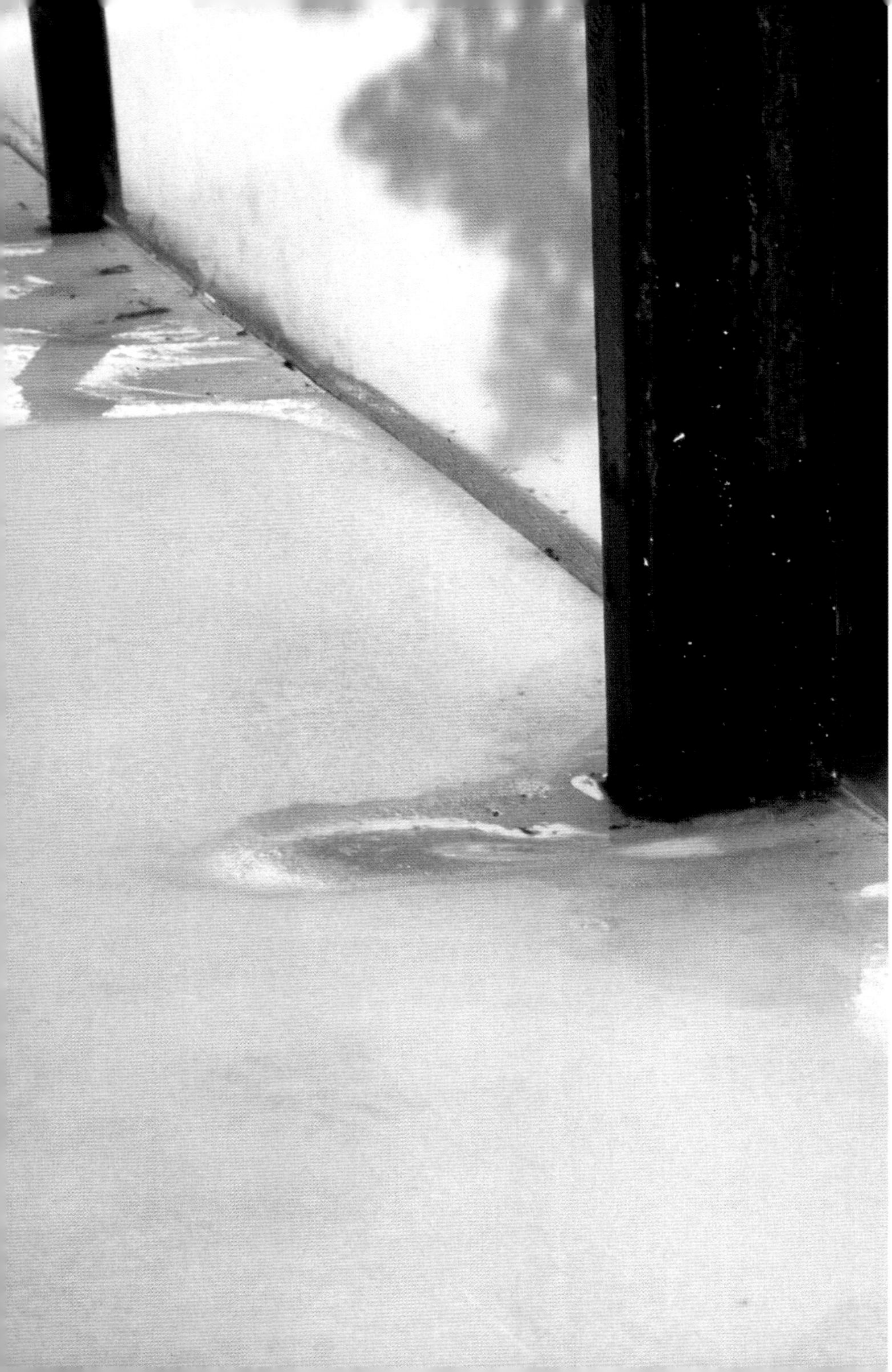

1	**Spiral tower**, 2000	ø 4 m, height 12,63 m; steel, light, color spectrum; Lernacken, Sweden
2	**Spiral tower**, 2000	ø 4 m, height 12,63 m; steel, light, color spectrum; Lernacken, Sweden
3	**5 orientation - lights**, 1999	200 x 70 x 70 cm; light, steel, color filter; installation view: Arte al Arte, San Gimignano, Italy
4	**Spiral tower**, 2000	ø 4 m, height 12,63 m; steel, light, color spectrum; Lernacken, Sweden
5	**5 orientation - lights**, 1999	200 x 70 x 70 cm; light, steel, color filter; installation view: Arte al Arte, San Gimignano, Italy
6	**Green river**, 2000,	Green color, water; realization: Stockholm, Sweden
7	**Green river**, 2000	Green color, water; realization: Stockholm, Sweden
8	**Your natural denudation inverted**, 1999	15 x 25 m; steam, water, basin, scaffolding, trees; installation view: Carnegie International Pittsburgh, Pittsburgh, USA
9	**Your natural denudation inverted**, 1999	15 x 25 m; steam, water, basin, scaffolding, trees; installation view: Carnegie International Pittsburgh, Pittsburgh, USA
10	**Your natural denudation inverted**, 1999	15 x 25 m; steam, water, basin, scaffolding, trees; installation view: Carnegie International Pittsburgh, Pittsburgh, USA
11	**The very large ice-floor**, 1998	Size varies with installation; water, ice-machine, basin; installation view: Sao Paolo Biennale, Sao Paolo, Brazil
12	**The very large ice-floor**, 1998, detail	Size varies with installation; water, ice-machine, basin; installation view: Sao Paolo Biennale, Sao Paolo, Brazil

Elizabeth Grosz

The Future of Space: Toward an Architecture of Invention

Thinking

What can philosophy bring to architectural discourse and its practice (the practices of design, cost analysis, siting, building)? And what can architecture bring to philosophical discourse and its practices (reasoning, arguing, formulating problematics, framing questions)? What are some pertinent points of overlap or mutual investments that may implicate each in the other in mutually productive ways? Perhaps more impertinently, what are the blindspots within the self-understanding of each? And how can each be used by the other, not just to affirm itself and receive external approval but also to question and thus to expand itself, to become otherwise, without assuming any privilege or primacy of the one over the other and without assuming that the relation between them must be one of direct utility or translation? One very small strand draws these two disciplines together, an idea of newness or virtuality, latency or becoming, which may be highlighted and productively developed within both disciplines through the help, the overlap, and the difference that each offers the other. This idea of the virtual, a concept prevalent, if undeveloped, in philosophy (with different effects) that may force them to change quite fundamental assumptions they make about space, time, movement, futurity, and becoming.

Architecture has tended to conceive of itself as an art, a science, or a mechanics for the manipulation of space, indeed probably the largest, most systematic and most powerful mode for spatial organization and modification. Space itself, the very stuff of architectural reflection and production, requires and entails a mode of time, timeliness, or duration. Indeed, space must always involve at least two times, or perhaps two kinds of time: the time of the emergence of space as such, a time before time and space, a temporalization / spatialization that precedes and renders the organization or emergence of space as such and time as such and thus emerges before any scientific understanding of a space-time continuum.[1]

Derrida, for example, claims that the insertion of an interval that refuses self-identity and self-presence to any thing, any existent, constitutes *difference*. This interval, neither clearly space nor time but a kind of leakage between the two, the passage of the one into the other, propels any being beyond itself, in space and in time. Neither space nor time can exist as such "before" this interval, which expands being into a world in order that it be paradoxically both itself and other to itself:

An interval must separate the present from what it is not in order for the present to be itself but this interval that constitutes it as present must, by the same token, divides the present in and of itself, thereby also dividing, along with the present, everything that is thought on the basis of the present, that is, in our metaphysical language, every being, and singular substance or the subject. In constituting itself, in dividing itself dynamically, this interval is what might be called *spacing*, the becoming-space of time or the becoming-time of space (*temporization*). And it is this constitution of the present, as an "originary" and irreducibly nonsimple... synthesis of marks, or traces of retentions and protentions... that I propose to call archi-writing, archi-trace, or *difference*. Which (is) (simultaneously) spacing (and) temporization.[2]

The time and space of architecture, and for that matter, of philosophy, can rarely afford to consider this primordial differential, the movement, the shimmering of the differing of a time and space not yet configured, enumerated, mastered, or occu-

1. Such a continuum – the space-time of contemporary science – always derives from a more primordial understanding of time and space: this was Henri Bergson's critique of Albert Einstein. It is not clear to me, however, that access to this more primordial space and time is provided, as Bergson suggested, by experience.

2. Jacques Derrida, "Difference," in *Margins of Philospby*, trans. Alan Bass, University of Chicago Press, Chicago, 1982, p. 13.

pied. This time before time, the time of the interval, the time of nontime, enables space to emerge as such and is that to which space is ineluctably driven, the "fate" of space.

There is a second kind of time, the time of history, of historicity, the time of reflection, the time of knowledge – a time to which we are accustomed in the history of architecture and of philosophy, in the very idea of history, of orderly progression, of the segmentation or continuity of time and space. Architecture has tended to face time and temporality through the questions posed by history and through its response to the ravages of that history, its orientation toward monumentality. Architecture has thought time, with notable exceptions, through history rather than through duration, as that to be preserved, as that which somehow or provisionally overcomes time by transcending or freezing it.

I am more interested here in the relevance of this earlier sense of time, which I will represent through the concept of the virtual and virtuality, a concept that requires not only a time *before* time but also a time *after* time, a time bound up not only with the past and with history and with historicity but also, perhaps primarily, with futurity, thus providing a mode of resistance to the privilege of the present and the stranglehold that the present and its correlatives, identity and intentions, maintain on space and matter. The times before and after time are the loci of emergence, of unfolding, of eruption, the space-times of the new, the unthought, the virtuality of a past that has not exhausted itself in activity and a future that cannot be exhausted or anticipated by the present. This past, which layers and resonates the present, refuses to allow the present the stability of the given or the inevitable. It is the past that enables duration as a mode of continuity as well as heterogeneity. Both Derrida and Deleuze, in very different ways, indicate this central role of difference as a vector in the modalization of space.

In articulating a notion of virtuality linked to futurity, to becoming and to differentiation, I want to explicate what I understand as a particularly underrepresented philosophical mode, which it may share with architecture, what might be called a "logic of invention" as opposed to an Aristotelian logic of identity, reflection, reason, self-containment. A logic of invention has yet to be invented: only such a logic can mediate between the reflective categories of philosophical thought and the pragmatic requirements of any empirical project, here the architectural project. It is a linkage that invents new philosophies and new architectures. Instead of the self-containment of the syllogism (in which conclusions are logically entailed in validly constituted premises), a logic of invention is necessarily expansive, ramifying and expedient, producing not premises so much as techniques, not conclusions so much as solutions, not arguments so much as effects. Such a logic can never be regulative (distinguishing valid from invalid arguments) but is always descriptive (do this, then this, then this).

Philosophy, according to Deleuze, is both a mode of solving problems and a mode of thinking or theorizing multiplicities. Architecture, too, is bound up with problem solving and with multiplicities, though the multiplicities with which it deals are not simply conceptual or simply material. Philosophy is not, for Deleuze, a mode of mastering the real, framing its rules, understanding its principles; rather, it is what deals with the coagulation, the alignments between the actual and the virtual, the ways in which the actual feeds off and grows in distinction from the virtual and, conversely, the ways in which the virtual continually enriches and diminishes the actual by forcing it to diverge from itself, to always tend toward and to be absorbed by virtuality. Architecture, like philosophy (and for that matter, biology and physics), is perpetually verging on, irresistibly drawn to its own virtualities, to the ever-increasing loops of uncertainty and immanence that its own practices engage and produce. The future of each discipline requires that each open itself up to a reconsideration of the virtual and the promise it holds for newness, otherness, divergence from what currently prevails.

What does the notion of the virtual mean? Here I only have the time (or is it the space!) to deal with one conception in any detail, Deleuze's reading of Bergson, and Bergson's understanding of the virtual and the return of the virtual image to the actual. Deleuze claims that Bergson is one of the great thinkers of becoming, of duration, multiplicity, and virtuality. Bergson developed this notion of duration in opposition to his understanding of space and spatiality. This understanding of duration and the unhinging of temporality that it performs are of at least indirect relevance to the arts or sciences of space, which may, through a logic of invention, derail and transform space and spatiality in analogous ways.

Space is understood, according to Deleuze (who followed Bergson at least up to a point on this) as a multiplicity that brings together the key characteristics of externality, simultaneity, contiguity or juxtaposition, differences of degree, and quantitative differentiations. Space is discontinuous, infinitely divisible, static, and always actual. Space in short is the milieu of things, matter, identities, substances, entities that are real, comparable, and calculable. It is the natural home of science, of the actual, where there are differentiations of degree but not of kind:

"Space, by definition, is outside us...space appears to us to subsist even when we leave it undivided, we know that it can wait and that a new effort of our imagination may decompose it when we choose. As, moreover, it never ceases to be space, it always implies juxtaposition, and, consequently, possible division. Abstract space is, indeed, at bottom, nothing but the mental diagram of infinite divisibility."[3]

Duration, by contrast, is a multiplicity of succession, heterogeneity, differences in kind, and qualitative differentiations. It is continuous and virtual. It is divisible, of course, but it is transformed through the act of division – indeed much of Bergson's work explores the implications of dividing time, among the more serious of which is the freezing of all motion into discrete momentary units. Duration is perfectly capable of subsisting without division, which is always imposed on it from the outside. Duration is not, through its continuity, homogeneous, smooth, or linear: rather, it is a mode of "hesitation," bifurcation, unfolding, or emergence.

If space and time are represented as discrete phenomena, as separate, indeed opposed, in their various qualities and attributes, then not only are these primordial processes of temporization that induce space ignored, but the primitive processes of spatialization through which the notion of duration and temporality exists also fail to emerge. Bergson himself acknowledged this, though only rarely, when he qualified and refined his understanding of space. It is not that space in itself must be or can only be the space of quantification; rather, it is a certain mode of doing science, particularly science under the determinist, predictive Laplacian model, that effects the mathematization and ordering of space and makes this seem to be the very nature of space itself. In a certain sense, Bergson acknowledged the becoming one of the other, the relation of direct inversion between them, when he conceptualized space as the contraction of time, and time as the expansion or dilation of space.

Space is mired in misconceptions and assumptions, habits and unreflective gestures that convert and transform it. Architecture, the art or science of spatial manipulation, must be as implicated in this as any other discipline or practice. According

3. Henri Bergson, *Matter and Memory*, trans. N. M. Paul and W. S. Palmer, Zone Books, New York, 1988, p. 206.

to Bergson, a certain habit of thought inverts the relations between space and objects, when in fact space itself is produced *through* matter, extension, and movement:

> Concrete extensity, that is to say, the diversity of sensible qualities, is not within space; rather it is space that we thrust into extensity. Space is not a ground on which real motion is posited; rather it is real motion that deposits space beneath itself. But our imagination, which is preoccupied above all by the convenience of expression and the exigencies of material life, prefers to invert the natural order of the terms...Therefore, it comes to see movement as only a variation of distance, space being thus supposed to precede motion. Then, in a space which is homogeneous and infinitely divisible, we draw, in imagination, a trajectory and fix positions: afterwards, applying the movement to the trajectory, we see it divisible like the line we have drawn, and equally denuded of quality.[4]

Space in itself, space outside these ruses of the imagination, is not static, fixed, infinitely expandable, infinitely divisible, concrete, extended, continuous, and homogenous, though perhaps we must think of it in these terms in order to continue our everyday lives (and the architect is perhaps more invested in this understanding of space than anyone else). Space, like time, is emergence and eruption, oriented not to the ordered, the controlled, the static but to the event, to movement or action. If we "shut up motion in space," as Bergson suggested, then we shut up space in quantification, without ever being able to think space in terms of quality, of difference and discontinuity. We do not think of space but can at best allow ourselves to utter "places" in a gesture of localization. Space seems to resist this kind of pluralization: it asserts itself as continuous, singular and infinite. Space presents itself as ready-made, as given in its constancy, fixed in its form: it is then a mode of the capture of both space and time when time is understood as the fourth dimension of space common in post-Einsteinian ontology.

It is relevant that Bergson called for a space, spaces, sensitive to the motion and actions that unfold in them. Rather than seeing motion in its scientific terms as distance or space over time, Bergson indicated, though did not develop, a different understanding, where space emerges through specific motions and specific spaces, where motion unfolds and actualizes space.

Space, in effect, is matter or extension, but the "Schema" of matter, that is, the representation of the limit where the movement of expansion would come to an end as the external

4. Ibid., p. 217.

envelope of all possible extensions. In this sense, it is not matter, it is not extensity, that is in space, but the very opposite. And if we think the matter has a thousand ways of becoming expanded or extended, we must also say that there are all kinds of distinct extensities, all related, but still qualified, and which will finish by intermingling only in our own schema of space.[5]

This kind of space could no longer be considered static, infinitely extended, smooth, regular, amenable to gridding, to coordinates, to geometric division, the kind of space one can leave behind and return to intact, independent of what has occurred there. In opening up space to time, space becomes amenable to transformation and refiguring; it becomes particular, individualized. It is not clear that we need to return, as Bergson suggested, to the space of immediate, lived experience. For one thing, our lived experience at the end of the millennium involves spaces that were quite literally unimaginable in Bergson's time and moreover, the immediacy of experience is itself not unmediated by the social modes of inhabitation of space. For another, it is not clear that immediate experience is any more the point of proliferation of virtualities and intensities than, say, the most intensely artificial and manufactured movements and spaces.

In a rare moment, Bergson contemplated the possibility of thinking space otherwise, understanding it in terms other than as the binary opposite of duration. Space too could be conceived, instead of being the pure medium of actuality, as the field for the play of virtualities:

In regard to concrete extension, continuous, diversified, and at the same time organized, we do not see why it should be bound up with the morphous and inert space which subtends it – a space which we divide indefinitely, out of which we carve figures arbitrarily, and in which movement itself...can only appear as a multiplicity of instantaneous positions, since nothing there can ensure the coherence of past with present. It might then be possible, in a certain measure, to transcend space without stepping out from extensity; and here we should really have a return to the immediate, since we do indeed perceive extensity, whereas space is merely conceived – being a kind of mental diagram.[6]

Bergson suggested that we can reinvent, or rather return to a conception of space that does not so much underlie or subtend matter, functioning as the indifferent coordinates of the placement of matter, as function as an effect of matter and

5. Gilles Deleuze, *Bergsonism*, trans. Hugh Tomlinson and Barbara Habberjam, Zone Books, New York, 1988, p. 87.

6. Bergson, *Matter and Memory*, op.cit., p. 187.

movement. It is not an existing, God-given space, the Cartesian space of numerical division, but an unfolding space, defined, as time is, by the arc of movement and thus a space open to becoming, by which I mean, becoming other than itself, other than what it has been.

I try to get back to the bottom of this common hypothesis (shared by philosophical realism and idealism) ... we find that it consists in attributing to homogeneous space a disinterested office: space is supposed either merely to uphold material reality or to have the function, still purely speculative, of furnishing sensations with means of coordinating themselves. So the obscurity of realism, like that of idealism, comes from the fact that, in both of them, our conscious perception and the conditions of our conscious perception are assumed to point to pure knowledge, not to action. But now suppose that this homogeneous space is not logically anterior, but posterior to material things and to the pure knowledge which we can have of them; suppose that extensity is prior to space; suppose that homogeneous space concerns our action and only our action, being like an infinitely fine network which we stretch beneath material continuity in order to render ourselves masters of it, to decompose it according to the plan of our activities and our needs. Then, not only our hypothesis has the advantage of bringing us into harmony with science, which shows us each thing exercising an influence on all the others and, consequently, occupying, in a certain sense, the whole of the extended...[7]

The same attributions of becoming that Bergson accorded to duration can now be seen to accompany spatiality: just as the whole of the past contracts, in various degrees, in each moment of the present, that is, just as the present is laden with virtualities that extend it beyond itself – the ballast of the virtual past being enough to propel an unpredicted future out of an uncontained and endlessly ramifying present – so, too, the whole of space, spatiality, contracts into the specificity of location, and the occupation of any space contains the virtual whole of spatiality, which is to say, the infinite possibilities of my action on and being acted on by matter in space and time. To remember any moment is to throw oneself into the past, to seek events where they took place – in time, in the past; to experience any other space is to throw oneself into spatiality, to become spatialized with all of space. To remember (to place oneself in the past), to relocate (to cast oneself elsewhere), is to occupy the whole of time and the whole of space, even admit-

7. Ibid., p. 231.

ting that duration and location are always specific, always defined by movement and action. It is to refuse to conceptualize space as a medium, as a container, a passive receptacle whose form is given by its content, and instead to see it as a moment of becoming, of opening up and proliferation, a passage from one space to another, a space of change, which changes with time.

Instead of a return to the prescientific immediacy that Bergson suggested as a remedy for the containment that science places on space, I would suggest a different approach to the reenervation of space through duration, the restoration of becoming both space and time. If time is neither linear and successive nor cyclical and recurrent but indeterminate, unfolding, serial, multiplying, complex, and heterogeneous, then space, too, must be reconfigured not as neutral, nor as singular and homogeneous but as opening up to other spaces, not regulating processes and events so much as accompanying them. We do not, as Bergson claimed, need to *experience* or live such a space (or time): this does not seem possible or necessary. We need more adequately intellectual, but above all pragmatic models by which to understand and actively seek the maximal paths of proliferation for virtual time becoming virtual space. These models are not simply modes of complacency that enable us to live our lives as before, now with a justification and a rationale; rather, these models may help us to understand, see, think, build differently, according to other logics of invention and experimentation.

Perceiving

If we want to understand how the virtual may enrich conceptions of space and thus of the architectural project, it may be necessary to make a brief detour through the role that the virtual plays in duration and especially in inserting the past into the present as its state of virtuality. This may in turn provide some of the key concepts or terms by which to think spatiality in terms of virtuality.

Bergson wants to define perception and memory, our modes of access to the present and the past, in operational or pragmatic terms: the present is that which acts, while the past can be understood as that which no longer acts or whose actions are at best virtual.[8] Perception must be linked to nascent or dawning action, action-in-potential. Perception is actual insofar as it is active and thus relates primarily to an impending future. By contrast, instead of memory being re-

8. Ibid., p. 68.

garded as a faded perception, a perception that has receded into the past, as is commonplace, it must be regarded as ideational, inactive, virtual. "The past is only idea, the present is ideo-motor."[9] A present perception and a past recollection are not simply different in degree (one a faded, diminished version of the other) but different in kind. Perception is that which propels us toward the real, toward space, objects, matter, the future, while memory is that which impels us toward consciousness, the past, and duration.[10] If perception impels us toward action and thus toward objects, then, to that extent, objects reflect my body's possible actions upon them.

The present is that which acts and lives, that which functions to anticipate an immediate future in action. The present is a form of impending action. The past is that which no longer acts, although in a sense it lives a shadowy and fleeting existence. It still is. It is real. The past remains accessible in the form of recollections, either as motor mechanisms in the form of habit-memory, or, more correctly, in the form of image-memories. The memories are the condition of perception in the same way that the past, for Bergson, is a condition of the present. Where the past in itself is powerless, if it can link up to a present perception, it has a chance to be mobilized in the course of another perception's impulse to action. In this sense, the present is not purely in itself, self-contained; it straddles both past and present, requiring the past as its precondition, oriented as it is toward the immediate future. Our perception is a measure of our virtual action upon things. The present, as that which is oriented toward both perception and action, is the threshold of their interaction and thus the site of duration. The present consists in the consciousness I have of my body. Memory, the past, has no special link with or proximity to my body. Most significant for the purposes of this argument is that as the present functions in the domain of the actual, the past functions as virtual.

The past cannot be identified with the memory images which serve to represent or make it actual for or useful to us; rather, it is the seed which can actualize itself in a memory. Memory is the present's mode of access to the past. The past is preserved in time. While the memory image, one of the past's images or elements, can be selected according to present interests. Just as perception leads me toward objects where they are, outside of myself and in space, and just as I perceive affection (which Deleuze would refer to as intensity) where it arises, in my body,[11] so, too, I recall or remember only by placing myself

9. Ibid.

10. See figure 5, Bergson, *Matter of Memory*, op.cit., p. 162.

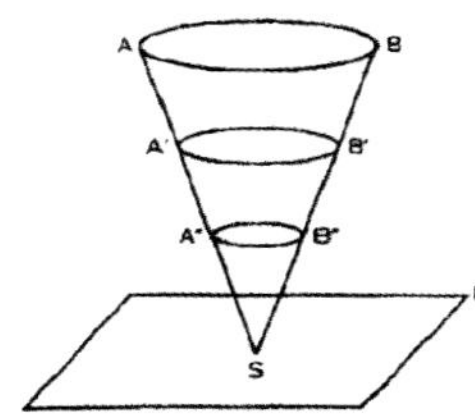

11. Ibid., p. 57.

in the realm of the past where memory subsides or subsists. Memory, the past, is thus, paradoxically, not *in us* just as perception is not *in us*. Perception takes place outside ourselves, takes us to where objects are (in space); memory takes us to where the past is (in duration). In Deleuze's reading, Bergson goes so far as to say that the only subjectivity in life is time and that life participates in this subjectivity to the extent that it is submerged in duration.[12]

Bergson seems to problematize a whole series of assumptions regarding our conceptions of the present and the past. We tend to believe that when the present is somehow exhausted or depleted of its current force it somehow slips into the past where it is stored in the form of memories. It is then replaced by another present. Against this presumption, Bergson suggests that a new present could never replace the old one if the latter did not pass while it is still present. In place of the more usual claim of the succession of the past by the present, this leads to his postulate of the *simultaneity* of past and present. The past is contemporaneous with the present it has been. They exist, they "occur" at the same time. The past could never exist if it did not coexist with the present of which it is the past:

> The past and the present do not denote two successive moments, but two elements which coexist: One is the present, which does not cease to pass, and the other is the past, which does not cease to be but through which all presents pass...The past does not follow the present, but on the contrary, is presupposed by it as the pure condition without which it would not pass. In other words, each present goes back to itself as past.[13]

Bergson argues that the past would be altogether inaccessible to us if we can gain access to it only through the present and its passing. The only access we have to the past is through a leap into virtuality, through a move into the past itself, through seeing that the past is outside us and that we are in it rather than it in us. The past exists, but it is in a state of latency or virtuality. We must place ourselves in it if we are to have recollections, memory images. This we do in two movements or phases. First, we place ourselves in the past in general (which can only occur through a certain detachment from the immediacy of the present) and then we place ourselves in a particular region of the past. Bergson conceives of the past in terms of a series of planes or segments, each one representing the whole of the past in a more or less contracted form. We move from

12. This is already an indication of the strangely postmodernist, indeed, surprisingly posthuman character of Bergson's writing, even those characterized as the most committed to humanism. Indeed, this seems to attract Deleuze's bastardized, anal reading of Bergson: Bergson's own wayward, quiet peculiarity and complexity relative to the simplified characterizations generally used now to discount his work: Bergson is not one of those philosophers who ascribes a properly human wisdom and equilibrium to philosophy. To open us up to the inhuman and the superhuman (*durations* which are inferior or superior to our own), to go beyond the human condition: This is the meaning of philosophy, in so far as our condition condemns us to live among badly analyzed composites, and to be badly analyzed composites our-selves. (Deleuze, *Bergsonism*, op.cit., p. 28.)

13. Ibid., p. 59.

one set of memories to another through a leap into a virtual time. We must jump into the milieu of the past in general in order to access any particular memories. The present can be understood as an infinitely contracted moment of the past, the point where the past intersects most directly with the body. It is for this reason that the present is able to pass.

Each segment has its own features although each contains within itself the whole of the past. Memories drawn from various strata may be clustered around idiosyncratic points, "shining points of memory," as Bergson describes them, which are multiplied to the extent that memory is dilated.[14] Depending on the recollection we are seeking, we must jump in at a particular segment; in order to move on to another we must make another leap: "We have to jump, if the recollection sought for gives no response and does not realize itself in a recollection-image."[15] For Deleuze, this provides a model for Bergson's understanding of our relations to other systems of images as well (and hence Bergson's suitability to Deleuze's analysis of cinema).

It is only through a similar structure that we can detach ourselves from the present to understand linguistic utterances or make conceptual linkages. The structure of the time-image also contains that of the language-image and the thought-image. It is only by throwing ourselves into language as a whole, into the domain of sense in general, that we can understand any utterance, and it is only by leaping into a realm of ideas that we can understand problems.[16] In all three cases, this leap involves landing in different concentrations of the past, language or thought, which nonetheless contain the whole within them to different degrees.

Along with the simultaneity or coexistence of each moment of the present with the entirety of the past, there are other implications in Bergson's paradoxical account. Each moment carries a virtual past with it: each present must, as it were, pass through the whole of the past. This is what is meant by the past in general. The past does not come after the present has ceased to be nor does the present become or somehow move into the past. Rather, it is the past which is the condition of the present; it is only through a preexistence that the present can come to be. Bergson does not want to deny that succession takes place – of course, one present (and past) replaces another; but such real or actual succession can only take place because of a virtual coexistence of the past and the present, the virtual coexistence of all of the past at each moment of

14. Bergson, *Matter and Memory*, op.cit., p. 171.

15. Deleuze, *Bergsonism*, op.cit., p. 99.

16. Deleuze argues that "this time-image extends naturally into a language-image, and a thought-image. What the past is to time, sense is to language and idea to thought. Sense as past of language is the form of its pre-existence, that which we place ourselves in at once in order to understand images of sentences, to distinguish the images of words and even phonemes that we hear. It is therefore organized in coexisting circles, sheets or regions, between which we choose according to actual auditory signs which are grasped in a confused way. Similarly, we place ourselves initially in the idea; we jump into one of its circles in order to form images which correspond to the actual quest." (Ibid., pp. 99-100.)

the present – and at each level or segment of the past. This means that there must be a relation of repetition between each segment whereby each segment or degree of contraction or dilation is a virtual repetition of the others, not identical, certainly, but a version. The degrees of contraction or dilation which differentiate segments constitute modes of repetition in difference.

In Deleuze's reading, Bergson systematically developed a series of paradoxes regarding the past and present that run counter to a more common, everyday understanding:

(1) we place ourselves at once, in a leap, in the ontological element of the past (paradox of the leap); (2) there is a difference in kind between the present and the past (paradox of being); (3) the past does not follow the present that it has been, but coexists with it (paradox of coexistence); (4) what coexists with each present is the whole of the past, integrally, on various levels of contraction and relaxation (*détente*) (paradox of psychic repetition).

These Bergsonian paradoxes, which are only paradoxical if duration is represented on the model of space, are all, Deleuze claimed, a critique of more ordinary theories of memory, whose propositions state that:

(1) we can reconstitute the past with the present; (2) we pass gradually from the one to the other; (3) that they are distinguished by a before and an after; and (4) that the work of the mind is carried out by the addition of elements (rather than by changes of level, genuine jumps, the reworking of systems).[17]

It seems clear that a series of analogous unhingings of the self-containment and fixity of spatiality can also be developed, though Bergson himself refrained from doing so. Duration contains as part of its conceptual content the ideas of (1) unevenness, heterogeneity, states of contraction and expansion, such that time exists in a state of detained elaboration, or in a state of compressed schematism; (2) difference, specificity, and multiplicity: each movement has its own duration, each event its own unfolding. These durations, though, are never simply isolated or self-contained but always both intersect with other durations (the duration of my actions may interact with the durations of the objects and materials with which I work) and participate in a kind of mega-duration, a world duration which renders them in a web or weave of comparable and interlocked durations and becomings; (3) simultaneity, the coexistence of the past in the present, the anticipation of the

17. Ibid., pp. 61-62.

present as the actualization of the past (in other words, the coexistence of two kinds of time, one frozen and virtual, the other dynamic and actual). These two kinds of duration are irreducible in their difference: the past is contemporaneous with the present it has been; and (4) succession, the complication of the past, present, and future. Each is necessarily involved in the function of the others, not by way of determinism (which in fact annuls the existence of the future and enables the effectivity of the past only) but through the divergence of the present from the past, and the future from the present, the interlocking of the past and the future (both virtual, both productive without emerging as such through the present) without the mediation of the present.

The question now remains: Do these rather strange and paradoxical formulations regarding duration have any spatial counterparts? Can the ways in which we conceive of, indeed live, space be subjected to a similar unhinging, a similar destabilization of presence and habitual self-evidence? To return to my earlier question: What would virtual space be like? What does such a conception entail? How can it be thought? (My questions.) How can it be built, lived, practiced? (Your question.)

I spoke earlier about the need for a logic of invention. Instead of requiring logical certainty, the guarantee of universal validity, the capacity to provide rules of procedure independent of the particularities of space and time, such a logic would instead require ingenuity, experimentation, novelty, specification, and particularity as its key ingredients. It would not seek to be certain but rather to incite, to induce, to proliferate. Rather than direct itself to questions of consistency, coherence, and regularity, such a logic would focus on an intuition of uniqueness, the facing of each situation according to its specific exigencies, the openness to failure as much as to innovation. I am not proposing that we replace Aristotelian logic with such a logic of invention; only that we acknowledge that each may work and be relevant in its particular spheres. Such a "logic of invention" has always governed architecture. The question is: What are the best terms by which to articulate this logic? How, in other words, to extract its *own* theory from its architectural practices rather than simply import or impose a theoretical frame from the outside? This is to inquire about architecture's own (theoretical) latencies, its virtualities.

I can offer only a more general understanding of virtuality, what it implies for rethinking of virtuality and what it implies for rethinking or perhaps reinventing space. I have two thoughts: one regarding the rethinking of space in terms of becoming and duration; the other regarding what the virtual can offer to architectural theory and practice.

To look, then, at some possibilities for the reconceptualization of space in terms of its openness to its own processes of differentiation and divergence. It seems possible that many – or at least some – of the qualities that Bergson attributed to duration may also be relevant to a considered spatiality, especially given that the time-space of primordial experience links space, before mathematization, to the movement of duration. It may be that many of the attributes particular to duration have some spatial equivalent. For example, if duration exists in states of contraction and expansion, in degrees of uneven intensity, either elaborated in increasing detail or functioning simply as "shining points" of intensity, then perhaps space, too, needs not be construed as even, homogeneous, continuous, infinitely the same. Perhaps space also has loci of intensity, of compression or elasticity, perhaps it needs no longer be considered a medium. Perhaps it can be considered lumpy, intensified, localized, or regionalized. I am not talking here simply of locale or landscape but also of the fundamental or ontological space that underlies a specific region. Nor am I simply confirming the insights of an Einsteinian space-time, in which there is still a relation of smooth, mathematical alignments between the expansion of time and the contraction of space. The very configurations of space itself may be heterogeneous, just as the movements or configurations of duration vary. Perhaps, in other words, there is a *materiality* to space itself, rather than materiality residing with only its contents.

This implies that space itself, if it is heterogeneous, is multiple, differential, specific. There are specific locations, places, regions that have their own modes of extensity: like intensity, the extensive always radiates from a point, given spatially as "here," the spatial present. The spatial present defines its own region but this regionality both intersects with the regionality of other heres and, like world duration, links to a large space, a world space or even a universal space, which in no way qualifies or marginalizes the concrete differences between different spaces. Cosmological spaces are not the master of overarching space within which places, regions are located in a mode of neutralization; cosmological space could itself be regarded as patchwork and uneven.

If two types of time coexist, one virtual (the past) and the other actual (the present) and their coexistence is necessary for the functioning of either, then perhaps there is a spatial correlation for this unhinging of temporal continuity through Bergson's paradoxical idea of the temporal simultaneity of present and past. Obviously spatial relations happily admit relations of simultaneity: space is that which enables simultaneous or coextensive relation. Perhaps it would be more intriguing to consider spatiality in terms of the coexistence of multiple relations of *succession*, space as a layering of spaces within themselves, spaces enfolded in others, spaces that can function as the virtualities of the present, the "here." Here a notion of virtual space will be of crucial relevance. If past, present, and future are always entwined with each other and make each other possible only through their divergences and bifurcations, then perhaps there is a way to consider spatiality in terms of relations of nearness and farness, relations of proximity and entwinement, the interimplications of the very near and the very far, rather than of numerals of geometry.

This returns us once again to the vexing question of the virtual and its particular spatial resonances. One cannot of course directly specify what a virtual is, for insofar as it is, insofar as it exists, it exists as actual. In the process of actualization, the virtual annuls itself as much in order to reemerge as an actual that thereby produces its own virtualities. At best one can specify what it may produce, what effects or differences it may generate. We need to remind ourselves for a moment how Deleuze distinguished between the virtual and the possible. He claimed that the possible is the correlative or counterpart of the real. There are two distinctive connections between the possible and the real: the real both resembles the possible and is a limitation of the possible. The possible, or at least one of them, is a preformed real: the real is simply the coming into material form if this nonmaterial is possible. The real is a mode of conformity with the possible, its plan or blueprint. Or equally, the possible is simply the retrospectively conceived past of the real. By contrast, the virtual is counterposed with the actual rather than the real (indeed the virtual has a reality without any actuality). The actual in no way resembles the virtual nor does it limit or select from the virtual. It is linked to the virtual through "difference or divergence and ...creation."[18]

It is difference that is primary in the process of actualization – the difference between the virtual from which we begin and the actuals at which we arrive, and also the difference between the complementary lines according to which actual-

18. Ibid., p. 97.

ization takes place. In short, the characteristic of virtuality is to exist in such a way that it is actualized by being differentiated and is forced to differentiate itself.[19]

This means that the virtual *requires* the actual to diverge, to differentiate itself, to proceed by way of division and disruption, forging modes of actualization that will transform this virtual into others unforeseen by or uncontained within it. In other words, virtuality functions evolutionarily: it functions through the production of novelties that remain unforeseen by, yet somehow generated through the virtual materials ("genes" or seeds). The virtual is the realm of productivity, of functioning other than its plan or blueprint, functioning in excess of design and intention. This is the spark of the new that the virtual has over the possible: it is the capacity for generating innovation through an unpredicted leap that the virtual brings to the actual, the capacity of the actual to be more than itself, to become other than the way it has always functioned. It is differentiation, which, while propelled by a tendency or virtuality, can only actualize itself through its encounters with matter, with things, with movements and processes, and thus with obstacles, through which it produces itself as always other than its virtuality, always new, singular, and unique.[20]

How then can space function in ways other than the ways in which it has always functioned? What are the possibilities of inhabiting otherwise? Of being extended otherwise? Of living relations of nearness and farness differently? Architects are no doubt more able to reflect on and produce with these questions than I am.

19. Ibid.

20. Constantin Boundas states this well: "Virtualities generate disjunctions as they begin to actualize the tendencies which were contained in the original unity and compossibility: Differentiation does not happen between one actual term and another actual term in a homogeneously unilinear series, but rather between a virtual term and the heterogeneous terms which actualize it along the lines of flight of several ramified series." Constantin V. Boundas, "Bergson-Deleuze: An Ontology of the Virtual," in *Deleuze: A Critical Reader*, ed. Paul Patton, Blackwell, Oxford, 1997, pp. 81–106.

Mika Hannula

Tidal Waves and Dissidents

I do not know about you, but I like bridges. I would not go so far as to claim that I love bridges, but yes, I do have a strong feel and feeling for bridges. They don't necessarily have to be huge grand constructions. Basically, any old arch-like structure leading from A to B and back again will do: I really like them. Watching, walking on, being with them.

However, there is this certain bridge that I am very fond of. A one in a million thing. A peculiar, powerful bridge, as an image and reality. It does not so much take you from some significant place to another. It simply connects one fairly unimportant and unpopulated island to another similar island, located in the north of northern Europe. In Lofoten. What is actually more interesting, causing much more of a buzz, is what you see from the bridge. And that is the very point of bridges. Two things: illusion of a deeper inter-connection, and a view from somewhere – towards something. A chance to connect.

This time, it certainly is something else, something special. It is a place, as the broad tales tell us, from where the two writers Jules Verne and Edgar Allan Poe got their inspiration. Presumably they watched the incredibly strong currents freaking out in the middle of the vast water masses. Neither Verne nor Poe have what we have: a bird's view, at least a semi-version of it. The bridge provides us with the distance, and the safeness. We can imagine, but not too much – at least not about nature and its potential to destroy. This ability is no longer with us. It proves that knowledge is painful, it rips you off cruelly.

What the famous writers, and any person walking or driving over the river saw was something which in layman's language is labelled as maelstrom. In more scientific language, it is called vortex or eddies, which are both slightly different variations of frontal water tornadoes. To give a professional characterization of them, let me quote Professor Thomas A. Mc Climans, working at the University of Trondheim: "A tidal jet is formed when the tide pushes water masses through a narrow strait or over a shallow sill. Along the edges (fronts) of these jets, we find frontal tornadoes (maelstrom, eddies or vortices). The jets can extend down to the sill depth, expanding to even greater depths farther into the basin. The frontal eddies can lift water from even deeper levels to be mixed in the surface layer."

Thus, it is no wonder that in common use, or what the Germans have nicely labeled as the *Volksmund,* these water phenomenas are normally described as maelstroms, which translates to what they seemingly are, and more importantly, what we want to see in them: bad, malicious currents.

The maxim "you see what you want to see" is actually a very telling and accurate starting point for the image of the maelstrom. In the days of Verne and Poe, the fascination and fear were based on the struggle and conflict between man and nature. A source of superb drama, indeed. It was the time of great inventions and discoveries. Jumping to the beginning of the twenty-first century, the battle between man and nature has found other symbolic forms. Terribly, horrifyingly vibrating water currents no longer cut the ice or roll the dice. The threat they pose is no longer credible. What we need is a much bigger spectacle than a natural phenomena, which, in the end, looks, albeit scary for fishermen and their friends, like water flowing out of your bathtub.

The emphasis is on what it looks like, not what it is, or might be. We have landed at the politics of representation, which has, even if the images are taken from nature, extremely little to do with "real" nature. It has to do with what we dispose and reflect upon as phenomena found in nature. A phenomenon such as a maelstrom.

Therefore it is rather funny that a couple of summers ago, to take a really close and careful look at what a maelstrom is and does, the place to be would not have been that bridge I have mentioned. The right context would have been a provincial art gallery in which Olafur Eliasson staged his vortex-installation. The work was situated in the front room of a relatively small building. As a part of the work, the ground was covered with small rough stones, like the ones used to pave the road with asphalt.

In the middle of the room Eliasson constructed a tall, see-through water tube in which we saw strong currents going from the bottom to the top. It was a whirlwind, a highly captivating event. A vibrating spiral with some strange, unaccountable spirit. Something for the eye to keep on watching and watching. It did cast an evident spell. It was hard not to stare and keep staring at the constantly altering formations of immensely fast water masses moving on up. It was a maelstrom, but definitely not a malicious one. It was an invitation, an openly flirtatious act of fooling the viewer into a game in which no one could say where it would end. It was even safer than looking down from the bridge, but it was closer, much closer in physical terms.

So what did I see, both at the bridge and at the art gallery? Besides the actual events, which I have tried to describe as briefly as possible, how do I relate to them and with what do I relate them?

The shortest answer is so dull that it really hurts. Again and again. However, there is no way I can deny it. For me it was about globalism – nothing more, nothing less. Of course, during the experience, I was only preoccupied with the beauty and pleasure of those events I was witnessing. And with the mighty question of whether finally after five torturous days the hotel cook would find the lost salt bag and pour some of it onto the poor grilled fish. The theme of globalization came later, ridiculously later. But it is, for me, a tight and important connection. Watching, and not being able to move on those strong currents flowing, so elegantly but still with brutal force, I am reminded of my own relationship to the vast changes of the last ten years. The great historical changes which left an indelible mark on our civilization.

Hold on. Obviously I am aware how pathetic this sounds, but that is not my fault. I am talking about globalism as the umbrella of a concept that serves here to refer to the economic, cultural, political, and psychological effects of the regulated, nation-state controlled societies being turned into the playing-field of highly unregulated, foot-loose market capitalism in which multinational corporations hold the central keys and the cards. And now, to be absolutely certain and to avoid the trap of false expectations, I am not going to rant against those nasty multinationals making and killing millions, nor am I going to whine nostalgically about the demise of the poor old nation-state and its ugly nationalism.

No, as a member of the selfish 1990s generation, I am going to talk about me, and, if very lucky, providing we have time and energy, hopefully about you. The symbolism of the maelstrom is just too evident and too fitting to let it past. It begs to be used and abused. If I were a painter, and more precisely an expressionist painter fond of poignant symbolism, I would produce a huge series of variations of these turbulent water currents – and then label them as "Consequences of Globalism, part 33 etc." And I know that my days in poverty would be over soon. Do you hear the lovely sound of the cashiers till singing like a bird on barracuda powder?

But let's get serious. Hand on heart, or in your neighbor's pockets, how do you feel? How do you feel when during the last decades a great deal of the parameters and paradigms, those taken for granted beliefs and customs you have learned to love and hate, have disappeared, or at least lost a hell of a lot of their previous argumentative strength and credibility? Now, tell me, how do you feel? Again, I am not really interested in the obvious cases of people who have lost their jobs because manual labour is no longer needed. Unfortunately, I am also not interested in older people having difficulties coping with change. Of course they do have huge problems, and I have sympathy with them. However, there is no use pretending otherwise: what I am interested in is how your average person, which is always a fabrication, deals with the changes. You know, the ones who are, on average, rather okay. Like this writer, or you, as a reader.

I would argue that most of us are just baffled. Confused, maybe angry, but mainly just lost. We can easily admit it. We do not know what is going on. Rise and fall of stock markets? No matter how much you try to figure it out, it does not make sense. Sometimes you get a knock on the door, insisting that it is all a terrifying practical joke. As if they have changed all the covers on purpose. What looks like a guide to free-market business is actually an ABC text book of Stalinism. And that is why, in the name of plurality, they produce totality. Think about the scale of this conspiracy – and the perspiration to realize it. Weird, right?

But returning to the market mechanisms. You have to believe in it, and you have to act before the others. It is not based on rational behaviour, if you do not count the practical fact that when money starts to go around, those with a lot of it generally end up getting even more of it. And vice versa. This does not mean that a rich person cannot lose, but it means that capital has a tendency to accumulate, and to concentrate.

The growth of inequalities is incredibly scary. Examples can be found between rich and poor nations. The overall debt of third world countries in 1970 is said to have been about 90 million dollars, which amounts to 15 percent of their gross incomes. Moving to 1998, the whole amount is 2000 million, and the percentage is 37: a fact upon which the Jubilee 2000 organization bases its effort to remit whole or parts of this type of debt (Väyrynen 2001, 152). If we look at another extreme case, the relationship between the income of American top executives and the wages of the average production worker, the numbers are very telling. In the mid-1960s the ratio was 39 to 1, but in 1997 the CEO/worker ratio had grown to 254 to 1 (Faux & Mishel 2001, 95).

At the same time, most of us realize that there is hardly any turning back. Cold war corruption and the dirty underwear of the illusion of clear cut all-encompassing answers are gone. Not long, but gone – nonetheless. We do not want to go back to the ugly nationalism of nation-states, and we do not want to close the borders for the exchange of cultural products and information. But still it hurts to know that the world does not make sense, and that your role in it is next to nothing. Sometimes not even enough to be worth mentioning. And that there is no level of white lies to deny this. Empowerment sucks – and it sucks you, and me. Down, down, down. Us, us silly, petty believers.

Now how does that make you feel? Lousy, stupid or angry? Or should we throw them all in the same basket and wrap it up? The closest I get is the word I used previously: confused. I am confused, because I do not like what I see, but I have no idea what do to – and against whom?

I mean, of course reading papers, even a couple of books on the theme, I know the basic anti-globalism strategies, starting from the above mentioned Jubilee 2000 and reaching to the attack-organizations rallying for the establishment of a so-called Tobin-tax. And I know about the protests against, you name it, all the big multinational clothing companies, products on which I sit and those on which I run. And so do you. And I do know about the funny ironic and sympathetic efforts of certain individuals who have been beating the system by its own rules, living on falsified welfare coupons or cashing in on the promises of returning products you have not been satisfied with. And yes, somehow it just does not add up. I watch – and that is all.

Thus, in plain text. The strong, bad maelstrom is the general phenomenon of global capitalism, and you and I are the ones watching it from the bridge, or on the shore, or in a gallery – it makes a difference. However, it does not follow that how I feel is reminiscent of an individual getting thrown into the wild, dangerous maelstroms – the currents of the daily effects of global capitalism. It is, and this is my only saving grace, a little more complicated.

For me, in the end, it is about my possibilities to have an effect. To have an effect outside the domain of anti-consumer campaigns. To be for, or to be against. As a matter of fact, in the case of global foot-loose capitalism, it is not so much about being against, but wanting to limit and regulate its reign and one-sidedness. I want more, more diversity, more available choices, more of the richness of being that I know exists. I want the whole lot of it: peace, love, and harmony. Freedom. Yes, freedom and basic human rights. And this is exactly how I personally feel about the maelstrom. In other words, the name of the game is: how close to the enemy can you go? You are always both inside and outside – a beautiful and tragic case, a permanent struggle with double consciousness. But can you sleep with it, play with it, and even gain knowledge and capital from it?

Well, I do not know. I do not know what the role of a constructive and critical, but still open-minded and positive dissident is. Is there any role at all, or is it just a yesterday's model which is out of air and pow pow pow power? All I know is that I do not just want to stand back and watch. I want to get involved, I want to participate. I want to be with, be responsible. I want. Yes, I do. But can I do it?

To quote Professor McClimans again, I asked his opinion of why these water currents are interesting and he answered: "They are interesting for humanity because they affect navigation, mixing (dilution) of water masses and fishing conditions. Very often it is possible to see gulls and whales in these regions."

And I just hope. I wonder if there might be the slightest hint, the sweet smell of a promise of a possibility in those words of the vortex-specialist for me to be able to build bridges in relation to myself and to the big bad G? Perhaps what I am striving for is also an illusion. The illusion of a heterogeneous, tolerant community of bird and vortex watchers all standing at the same bridge – but not at the same time.

References:

Jeff Faux and Larry Mishel "Inequality and the Global Economy," in *On the Edge. Living with Global Capitalism,* edited by Ill Hutton and Anthony Giddens, Vintage, 2001.
Raimo Väyrynen: "Globalisaationkritiikki ja kansalaisliikkeet (Criticism of Globalism and NGO's) in *Gaudeamus,* 2001.

The author is grateful for the help of Professor Thomas A. McClimans, Trondheim University, Norway.

Frederikke Hansen

If You Think You Have a Psychic Parrot, Click Here. Comments on the Internet by way of browsing <http://www.sheldrake.org>

Richard Barbrook, subscriber to net-critique mailing list Nettime, states in his text *The High-Tech Gift Economy* that those of us who engage in sharing information on the Internet are a kind of present day situationists. We are the true anarcho-communists. The Internet is, as Barbrook has it, a topos for co-existence freed from the regulations of state and market. Hence anarchist and communist.

The net, however, is far from altruistic. The distribution of information in the net is based on a "you get more than you give"-principle. This is what keeps the whole thing going. "Even selfish reasons encourage people to become anarcho-communists within cyberspace," Barbrook tells us. "By adding their own presence, every user contributes to the collective knowledge accessible to those already online. In return, each individual has potential access to all the information made available by others within the net. Everyone takes far more out of the net than they can ever give away as an individual."[1]

1. Richard Barbrook, "The High-Tech Gift Economy," in *README! filtered by NETTIME*, Autonomedia, 1999, p. 134.

Renegade Cambridge biologist Rupert Sheldrake is a prime example of someone making use of the internet in this way. He has in part taken his research out of the lab and into the public space of the world wide web. On "Sheldrake Online," experiments, test results, discourse, and marketing are only a mouse-click apart.

The research Sheldrake carries out is based on his theory of morphic resonance. Morphic units – every "self-organizing" thing from atoms to animals, people, societies, and cultural formations to galaxies, is surrounded by morphic fields special to that particular unit. Like gravitational and electromagnetic fields, morphic fields are regions of physical influence.

By way of illustration: Within and around a school of fish, or a flock of birds for that matter, there is a morphic field which organizes its structure. When all fish in the school, or birds in the flock, move in perfect unison, then they do so as a resonance from all the schools, or flocks, that have moved in unison before them. The behavior has become habitual and trans-historical. "In general, morphic units closely resemble themselves in the past and are subject to self-resonance from their own past states." So Rupert Sheldrake.

It sounds like mumbojumbo. I find this kind of mumbojumbo entertaining and so I enjoy browsing "Sheldrake Online." First thing one encounters is the biologist's new title: *Dogs that Know When Their Owners are Coming Home*. The title being somewhat lame, compared with prior ones like *Seven Experiments that Could Change the World. A Do-It-Yourself Guide to Revolutionary Science,* it does not refer to dogs with healthy sensory organs and normal dog intelligence, but to supernatural powers in animals.

Sheldrake can explain pigeons homing, dogs waiting in excitement for their owners from the instant they think "okay, time to go home" and other supernatural phenomenon with the morphing field theory.

Several times I encounter the sentence: "Do you have a 'psychic' parrot? If you think so, please click here!" I don't, but I click anyway. I am then told what to look out for in my feathered friend detecting its potential psychic powers. I am also given the possibility to get in touch with Sheldrake himself in case I do have a paranormal-like parrot.

Being a scientist, Sheldrake of course carries out numerous experiments and collects lots of data. Here the Internet really comes in handy. He set up the homepage in 1995 when doing experiments with people who know when they are being stared at. In an inexpensive and efficient way, Sheldrake reaches thousands of pet owners and lay scientists, whose statements are collected in a data bank for later processing. In fact, the latest research project on psychic parrots is designed in cooperation with a parrot owner turned scientist, and monitored by her.

I go back to the navigator box and let my little cursor hand glide over the menu. I glance through a biography impressingly larded with academic distinctions from well-reputed institutes (all discretely highlighted and clickable) and then browse the online shop where books and tapes are on sale – via Amazon, needless to say. I skip "Email Rupert." Being on first name terms with Sheldrake bothers me.

The tone in the Internet is easy and free – a hybrid between advertising and modern educational discourses. It is personal and straight-forward.

"Since our earliest days, we have been guided by a passionate commitment to honesty, integrity, and respect for people. We believe in the promotion of trust, openness, teamwork, and professionalism." This oily charm oozes out of the homepage of no other company than Shell, here introducing "Our values." Next thing you know, Shell is confiding in you: "But in the last few years we have had to tackle some particularly difficult issues, and we realize we have not always taken enough care to show how they were resolved in line with our core values." Nobody's perfect!

Thanks to the Internet, though, it is now possible to make up for the previous carelessness. According to Eveline Lubbers, http://www.shell.com receives over 1,100 emails a month. "A full-time staff member answers all these mails personally and within forty-eight hours; there is no such thing as a standard reply."[2]

The level of outspokenness on the Shell website is astonishing. Given the environmental and political calamities the company has inflicted on the world, one would expect them to keep a low profile on these issues. Far from it!

Simon May, Shell's shrewd webmaster, knows that the threat of pressure groups engaging corporate power by exploiting the newest telecommunication tools at the same time offers great opportunity. Visiting the oil major's web page even the most tenacious environmentalist is lurked into feeling sympathy for Shell. After all, they have links to competitors, critics and progressive social organizations. There are even fora where you can discuss Shell uncensored. So, how can you still doubt their good intentions?

2. Eveline Lubbers, "The Brent Spar Syndrome," in *README!* filtered by *NETTIME*, Autonomedia, 1999, p. 283.

I do not mean to suggest that Shell and Sheldrake are fellow conspirators. Sheldrake's only crime is to have substituted a holistic world view for a canonized mechanistic one. However, the two controversial enterprises share a common space with certain styles and modi operandi. Shell and their homepage came to my mind not without reason. Both instrumentalize the controversies they have provoked. What better way to do it than showing the complex web of critical discourse that one is but a part of? In a gesture of transparency the context is summarized through links and "controversies sites."

The Internet might be a public space of non-hierarchical structures, or one of distributed power, as Saskia Sassen would put it. But, as she reminds us, the web is only a part of electronic space. "Electronic space has emerged not simply as a means for transmitting information, but as a major new theater for the accumulation and the operation of global capital."[3]

If I am to believe Sheldrake, then our behavior is handed down to us by morphic resonance from past generations. It is fair to say that we are the first real generation of the Internet. So, is there no resonance to be picked up for the generation X? No guide-lines? Is it really an anarchist field of potlatch economy, as Barbrook suggests, or is it rather a space for contestation between civil and corporate society, as Sassen has it?

Sheldrake is certainly not of much help here. He cannot explain innovation, just repetition: "Is it inspired from above? Welling up from below? Picked up from the air? What? Creativity is a mystery wherever you encounter it [...]. We know creativity happens. And then what happens is a kind of Darwinian natural selection. Not every good idea survives. Only the successful ones get repeated. By natural selection and then through repetition they become probable, more habitual."[4]

I was just starting to like him. Hearing Sheldrake telling funny anecdotes about super powerful pets and deconstructing canonical science with great British wit on the "sound clips" site somehow put him in a new and better light. But, I am disappointed now. And I really don't like the "natural selection" stuff. It makes me think of free market neo-liberalism and homo-cyber-eugenics.

So, I close down the browser and decide to take a break from the world wide web. I think I have taken far more out of the net than I can digest as an individual.

3. Saskia Sassen, "Private and Public Cyberspace," in *README!* filtered by *NETTIME,* Autonomedia, 1999, p. 100.

4. http://www.hootenanny.com/hoot/3/sheldrake.html

István Hargittai,
Magdolna Hargittai

Symmetry Within and Without

Introduction

Olafur Eliasson's art under the title "Surroundings Surrounded" is dedicated, according to the artist, to human perception, physical laws, and the phenomena of nature. These goals unmistakably carry a unifying character and as such, the concept of symmetry is closely related to them. If properly utilized, symmetry facilitates seeing and noticing, structuring, and bridging. Mankind has been concerned with symmetry since ancient times. Perhaps its notion first arose when noticing one's own reflection in water. Apart from the geometrical kind of symmetry, this concept extends to harmony and proportion and its applicability only depends on the degree of abstraction we are willing to extend it to. From the primitive notion of reflection at the earliest of times, the concept of symmetry has evolved into a most sophisticated tool of learning about nature. Suffice it to mention that several of the most important scientific discoveries in the twentieth century were related to

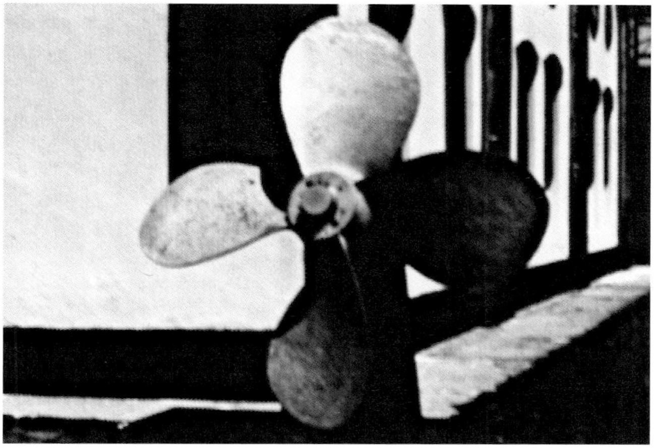

Fig. 1
Propeller in front of the Budapest Foundry Museum

this concept. The examples include the discovery of the violation of parity, the discovery of antiparticles, the discovery of the double helix structure of the substance of heredity, deoxyribonucleic acid, and the realization that the two components of chiral drugs may have vastly different physiological effects. Symmetry is one of the few technical terms that is meaningful for layperson without changing its content. It also has tremendous bridging capabilities between the arts and sciences. Only a few aspects of the symmetry concept will be discussed here. We refer the reader to some of our other writings for additional considerations.[1]

Relaxing the definition

Rigorous symmetry answers any question by yes or no. However, symmetry should not be considered rigorously. The vague notion of approximate symmetry, which has no place in geometrical symmetry, has the greatest utility in both everyday applications and scientific models. Beyond that, symmetry breaking is on a par in significance with unbroken symmetry, or is even more important, in many domains of our inquiry, such as the origin of life and the description of the universe. Uncomplicated symmetries dominate in what we directly experience around us. Freeman Dyson remarked to one of us recently[2] that it "was a big surprise that the whole universe seems to be full of broken symmetries. This turns out to be very powerful so that even if there was no symmetry, you pretend that there is."

1. I. Hargittai, M. Hargittai, *Symmetry: A Unifying Concept*, Shelter Publications, Bolinas, California, 1994, second printing, 1996; I. Hargittai, M. Hargittai, *Symmetry through the Eyes of a Chemist*, second edition, Plenum, New York, 1995; M. Hargittai, I. Hargittai, *Upptäck Symmetri!* Natur och Kultur, Stockholm, 1998.

2. M. Hargittai, Conversation with Freeman Dyson, Princeton, April 2000, unpublished records.

Fig. 2
Railway logo: Austrian

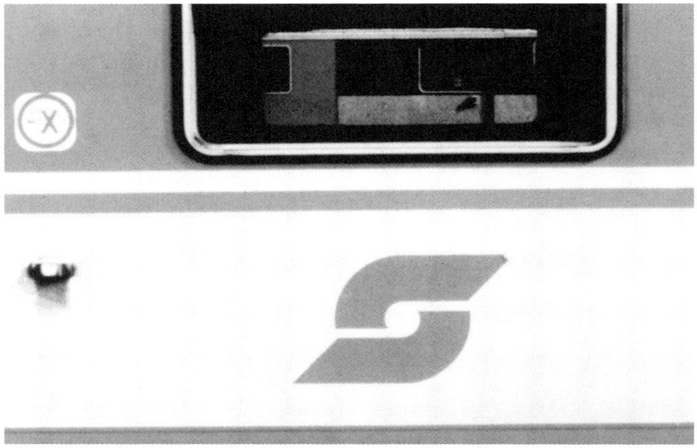

Fig. 3
Railway logo: Dutch

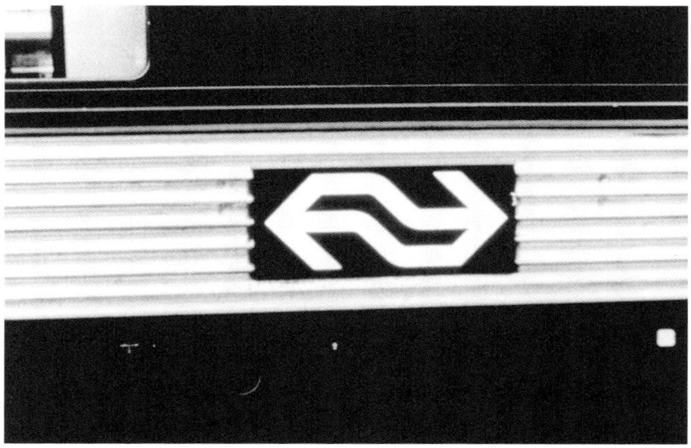

The Greek meaning of symmetry is "the same measure." The Russian crystallographer E. S. Fedorov gave these definitions to symmetry: "Symmetry is the property of geometrical figures to repeat their parts." And: "Symmetry is the property of geometrical figures coinciding with their original position when in different positions."[3] The geometer H. S. M. Coxeter's definition is "When we say that a figure is 'symmetrical' we mean that there is a congruent transformation which leaves it unchanged as a whole, merely permuting its component elements."[4] The mathematician Herman Weyl's relaxed definition is: "A thing is symmetrical if there is something that you can do to it so that after you have finished doing it, it looks the

3. A. V. Shubnikov, *Symmetry and Antisymmetry of Finite Figures* (in Russian), Izv. Akad. Nauk USSR, Moscow, 1951.

4. H. S. M. Coxeter, *Regular Polytopes*, third edition, Dover Publications, New York, 1973.

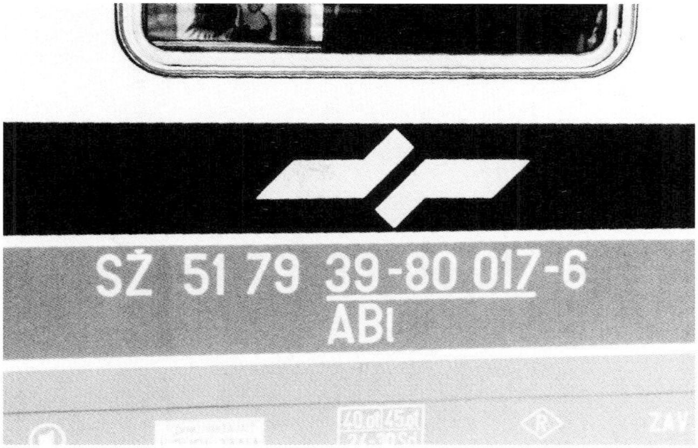

Fig. 4
Railway logo: Slovenian

same as it did before."[5] Our suggestion for a loose definition is "A pattern is symmetrical if there is a simple rule to generate it."[6] This definition is meant to further expand the scope of symmetry. It conveniently includes the fractal dimensions.

Definitions are useful to have but refining them without limit may be counterproductive. We may end up with a complicated, precise definition that is also useless. This is the same when we have a model which stresses certain features and ignores others. As long as we unambiguously define the scope of its applicability, the model will be useful. When we try to supply it with all sorts of amendments, it will eventually become a theory, and in the extreme it will lose any utility in its usage. This observation about models is relevant for the discussion of symmetry because the recognition of symmetry often facilitates the emergence of models.

Perception

In our man-made environment we are exposed to design, often rich in symmetries. In addition to the aesthetic appeal, the symmetries often have a functional message, however subliminally it may be communicated. The ability of this functionality comes from the utility of various symmetries. Consider, for example, the rotating part of some machinery. A propeller has rotational symmetry only and no reflection plane. This is important because a reflection plane stops the motion perpendicular to it. Of course, the propeller would not stop even if it had symmetry planes in whose intersection the axis of rotation is found, but it works more efficiently if it only has rotational

5. Quoted by Richard Feynman in *The Character of Physical Law*, The MIT Press, Cambridge, Mass., 1965, p. 84.

6. I. Hargittai, M. Hargittai, *In Our Own Image: Personal Symmetry in Discovery*, Kluwer Academic/Plenum Publishers, New York, 2000, p. 3.

Fig. 5
Railway logo: British

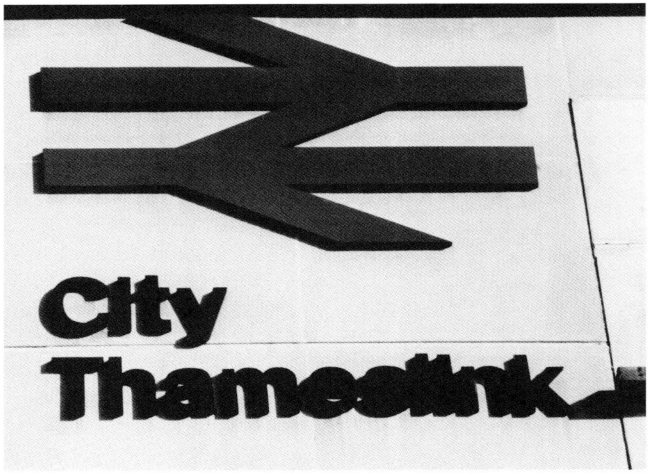

Fig. 6
Railway logo: Spanish

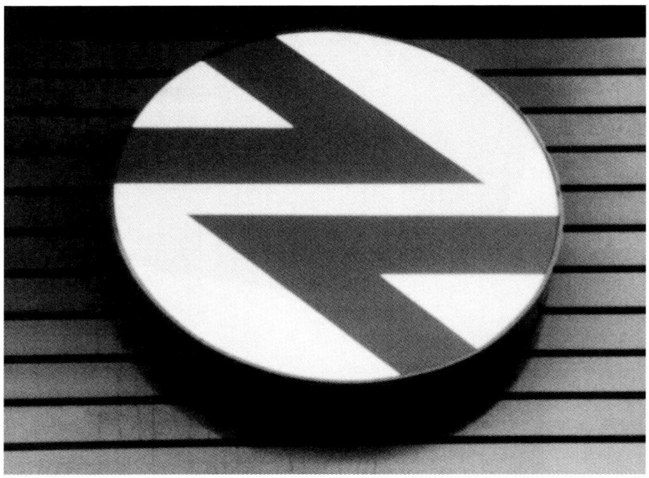

symmetry. The same is true in our perception of patterns possessing or lacking a reflection plane perpendicular to motion.

Consider logo designs.[7] They are meant to be aesthetically pleasing and convey the message of the company they represent. Logos that represent companies connected with motion, which may be transportation or turning money around, express their companies better if they have rotational symmetry only and no reflection planes. The logos do not rotate phys-

7. I. Hargittai, M. Hargittai, *In Our Own Image: Personal Symmetry in Discovery*, op.cit., pp. 17-20.

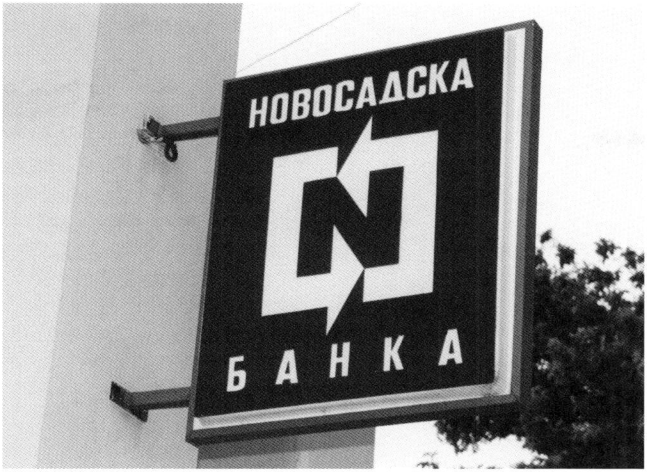

Fig. 7
Bank logo: Twofold
(Novy Sad Bank, Yugoslavia)

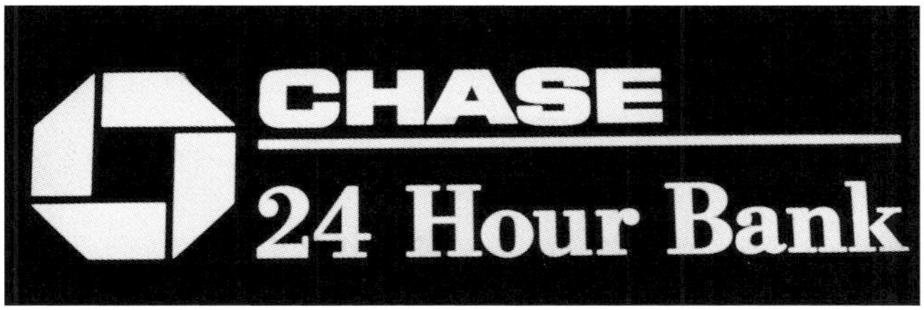

Fig. 8
Bank logo: Fourfold
(Chase)

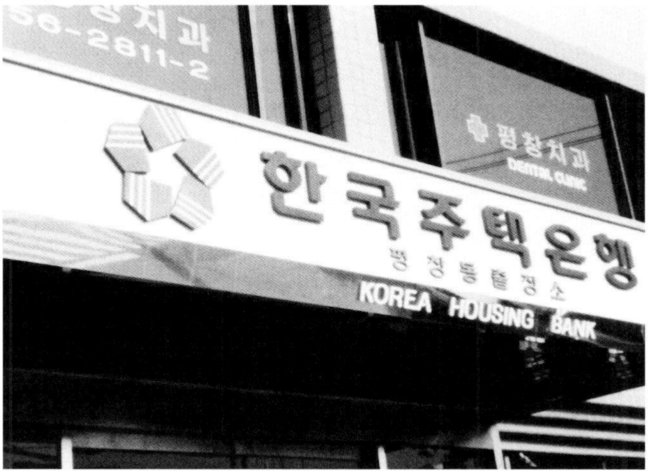

Fig. 9
Bank logo: Fivefold
(Korean Housing Bank)

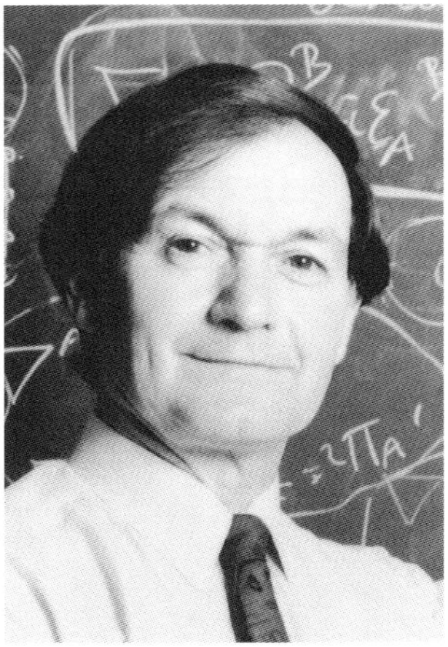
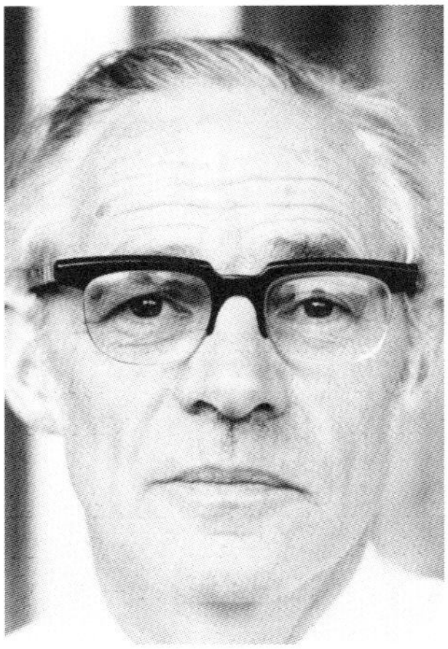
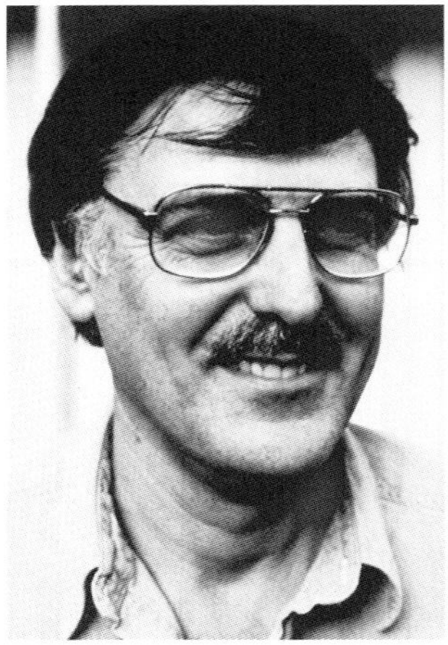

Figs. 10, 11, 12,
(left to right) Roger Penrose,
Alan Mackay, Budapest, 1982
Dan Shechtman, Haifa, 1992

ically, but they induce the feeling of such motion, and here is where perception is decisive. Railway companies often employ logos of twofold rotational symmetry, implying the motion in two opposite directions, taking us there and returning us. Bank operations are less restrictive than railway lines and, while rotational symmetry alone is their best expression, it need not be restricted to twofold rotation, they vary accordingly. Recycling is another kind of human activity that is very suitable to describe by rotational symmetry alone. This does not imply that a company with a logo of the wrong symmetry would perform inadequately; it only suggests that the proper choice of symmetry may be beneficial in correctly projecting the activities of the company.

Two-dimensional patterns can have the same kind of functionality as logo designs. The presence of reflection planes induces the feeling of stopping motion perpendicular to the plane. Decorations of rooms and halls of serious business would benefit from the presence of symmetry planes in the patterns of wall decorations. Dancing halls are better off with only rotational symmetry in their decorations. The design of advertisements is yet another area in which symmetry considerations are important. The relationship between lacking symmetry planes and motion needs emphasis in our discussion because symmetry is more often than not associated with the presence of symmetry planes. However, other symmetry elements, such as rotations and translations are also proper expressions of various symmetries.

Landscaping and the design of our urban environment are full of symmetry considerations, whether consciously or subconsciously. The traditional French garden, for example, puts emphasis on reflection and the traditional English garden deemphasizes it. Symmetry is often associated with regularity, which then leads to the mistaken notion that apparent irregularity means no symmetry. Once we accept the definition that a pattern is considered symmetrical if a simple rule is used for generating it, the apparent irregularity can no longer be equated with the lack of symmetry. Turning this argument around, it suffices to remember Herman Weyl's[8] teaching, in accordance with the ancient masters, that symmetry is also harmony and proportion. The Japanese garden radiates harmony and proportion yet it is "irregular" and one is not supposed to notice the efforts invested in making it look casual.

Internal and external

It is possible to cut as beautiful a shape from a piece of glass as from a piece of diamond, but their properties will not be the same. The strength of diamond comes from its internal structure, from the fact that all carbon atoms build it in a most regular way, making it into an infinite three-dimensional network of tetrahedral arrangement. The preeminence of internal structure needs emphasis because in common considerations crystals are thought to be the quintessential expressions of symmetry in nature due to their external shapes. Crystals have a regular and periodic internal structure, while amorphous bodies are not regular and are not periodic either. For a long time, regular but aperiodic structures were not only not observed, they were considered to be principally impossible. It had become regular textbook material that fivefold symmetry was impossible in solids, and icosahedral symmetry was forbidden by the rules of classical crystallography. For centuries, excellent minds, including Johannes Kepler and Albrecht Dürer, have tried to employ regular pentagons for covering the extended surface with a pattern of repetitive fivefold symmetry without gaps and overlaps.[9] In the early 1970s, finally, Roger Penrose came up with such a pattern. Alan Mackay extended this pattern into the third dimension. At this point Mackay saw no reason why such structures should not be possible to observe. He suspected that such structures were around in nature but scientists were not on the lookout for them due to their preconception of considering them impossible. Independent of Mackay's suggestion and warning, Dan

8. H. Weyl, *Symmetry*, Princeton University Press, Princeton, New Jersey, 1952.

9. For an extensive discussion of the quasicrystal discovery, see, e.g., I. Hargittai, M. Hargittai, *In Our Own Image: Personal Symmetry in Discovery*, op.cit., pp. 144-179.

Fig. 13
Quasicrystals in a quenched Al/Mn sample, by Ágnes Csanády, Budapest, and Hans-Ude Nissen, Zurich

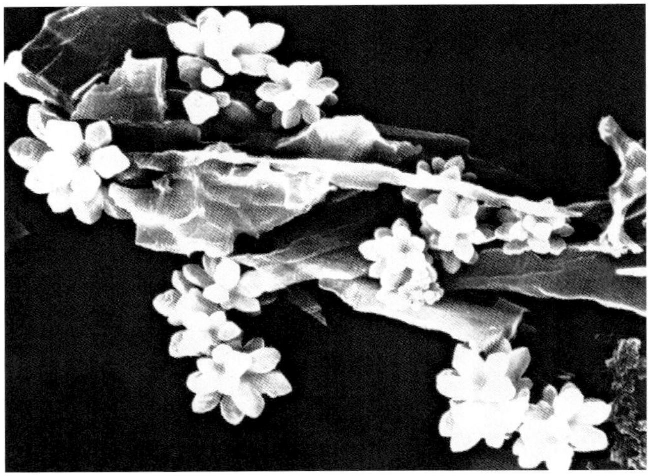

Shechtman did observe solid structures of icosahedral symmetry that proved to be regular and aperiodic. It is a philosophical question whether his observation should be considered a great discovery or whether it had such a great value of novelty because science had put itself into the confinements of classical crystallography. In any case, Shechtman's experiment caused a paradigm change in solid state science and related fields. Today, regular but aperiodic structures are considered to belong to crystals although the original name of quasicrystals prevails for them.

The novel structures of quasicrystals have served as inspiration to many artists, consciously or unconsciously.[10] In this case the artists can be said to create based on nature. The opposite happened to some extent in case of the discovery of the fullerenes. When their discoverers were looking for a structure to interpret some experimental observations, they remembered the pavilion of the United States at the 1967 Montreal Expo, which was designed by Buckminster Fuller. Its sphere-like construction consisted of regular hexagons with a few pentagons inserted among them. The experimental observation was that the high-temperature evaporation of graphite produced all-carbon molecules. Those consisting of sixty carbon atoms showed a conspicuous abundance. This high abundance suggested high stability and high symmetry. In hindsight, the discoverers appeared slow in recognizing the truncated icosahedral shape of this highly stable molecule

10. I. Hargittai, "Quasicrystal Sculpture in Bad Ragaz," in *Math. Intell.*, 1992, 14(3), pp. 58-59.

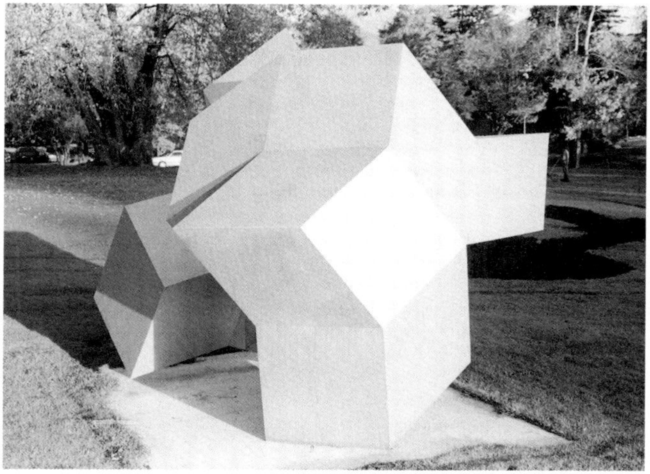

Fig. 14
"Quasicrystal" sculpture
in Bad Ragaz, Switzerland

although the whole discovery lasted but a few days. Invoking Buckminster Fuller's name into this molecular feat, there was a most fortunate synergy between design science and chemistry in which the connection was symmetry. Observing the new substance, the third modification of carbon, beside diamond and graphite, was one thing, producing it was another. Although the problem of synthesizing it has not been solved, it has become an academic question because there are plenty of fullerene molecules in such common substance as soot. Its external appearance reveals nothing about the beautiful shapes of the stable C_{60} molecules. In mathematics and design it has been known that any number of regular hexagons, except one, can be closed in a sphere-like structure, provided that twelve regular pentagons are involved in it. This kind of construction, having icosahedral symmetry, or at least some of its elements, has been utilized from children's climbers to huge domes.

Packing and complementarity

M. C. Escher's periodic drawings provide a model of densest packing. They have been used extensively to demonstrate symmetry properties of patterns in two dimensions. Densest packing is achieved, in most cases, through complementarity in the arrangement of the building elements. The symmetry operations generating these patterns seldom include the symmetry plane. For an arbitrary shape, however, application of the symmetry plane would exclude densest packing by leaving consid-

Fig. 15
Buckminster Fuller

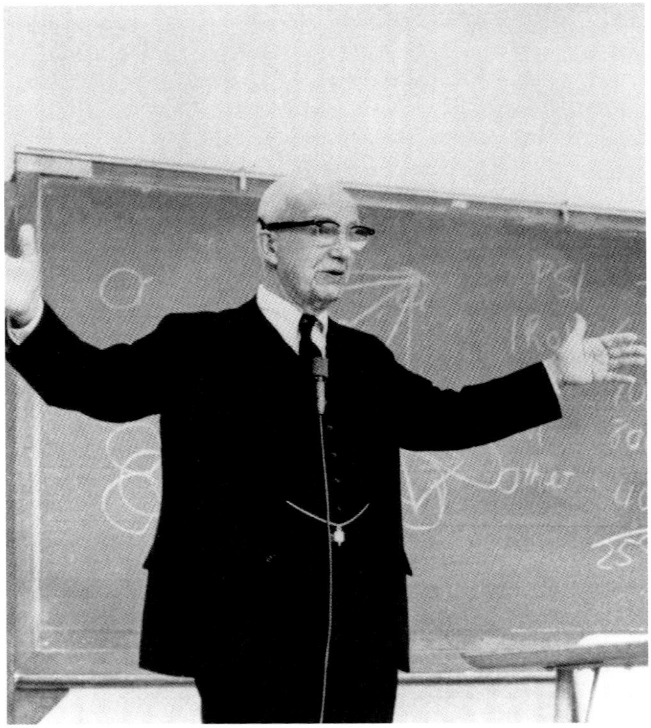

Fig. 16
The Montreal Geodesic Dome,
1995

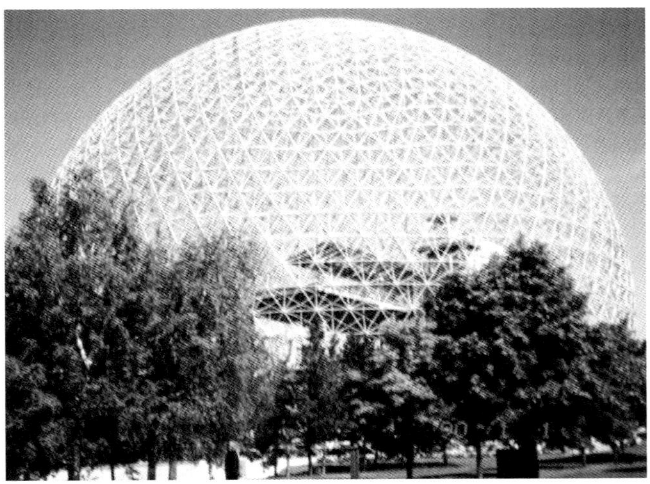

erable chunks of the surface uncovered. Densest packing means the maximal utilization of the available space, be it a surface or a three-dimensional volume.

The empirical observation that "nature abhors a vacuum" has been stated repeatedly since Galileo, but has seldom been scrutinized. The goal in finding the best arrangements of the building elements in nature is not necessarily governed by such a principle. Rather, there is an underlying principle at a deeper level that the arrangements sought should provide the greatest stability, that is, the lowest overall energy. This happens when the amount of possible interactions is maximized between the building elements, provided that they are of attractive nature. If this is the case, the amount of interactions is maximized when the interacting surface areas are maximized. It is this maximum amount of interaction, which is provided by a complementary arrangement of two pieces of the same arbitrary shape rather than by employing a reflection plane. There is complementarity in densest packing in that cavities of one object are filled with the protrusions of the other. Lucretius proclaimed the fundamental principle of best packing arrangements two thousand years ago when he came to the principle of complementarity. Lucretius stated in his *De rerum natura*:

"Things whose fabrics show opposites that match,
one concave where the other is convex,
and *vice versa*, will form the closest union."[11]

Molecular crystals provide numerous examples of densest packing in nature. The great Russian crystallographer, Aleksandr I. Kitaigorodskii[12] predicted that three-dimensional space groups of lower symmetry are much more frequent than those of higher symmetry among crystal structures. This was a prediction at a time when few crystal structures had been determined experimentally.

Kitaigorodskii found that the packing of molecules is spatially complementary. In order to achieve densest packing, the molecules of arbitrary shape complement each other in the best arrangement. Thus molecules having a shape with activity and protrusion will not use the available space efficiently if they turn to each other in such a way that the cavity of one molecule matches the cavity of the other. This would be the case if they were related by reflection. On the contrary, the best arrangement is when the protrusion of one molecule fits the cavity of the other molecule, and so on. This is yet another

11. Lucretius, *The Nature of Things, De rerum natura*, trans. F. O. Copley, W.W. Norton & Co., New York, first edition, 1977. This quoted passage is from Book VI, lines 1084-1086.

12. A.I. Kitaigorodskii, *Molekulyarnie Kristalli*, Nauka, Moscow, 1971, trans. *Molecular Crystals and Molecules*, Academic Press, New York, 1973.

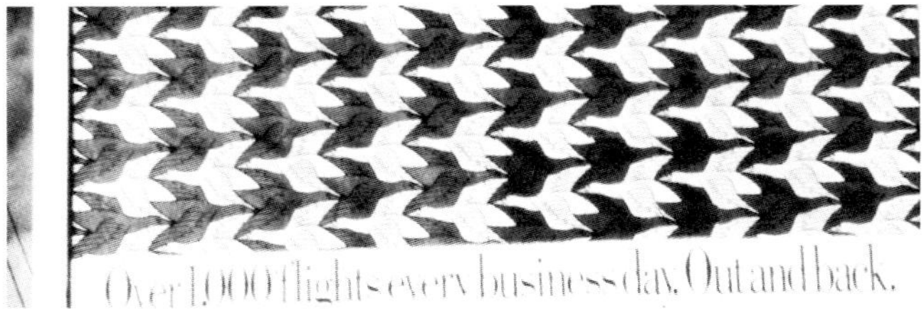

Fig. 17
Escher-like pattern in an airline advertisement near O'Hare Airport, Chicago, Illinois

expression of the principle of complementarity appearing in so many ways in science because it does so in nature.

The principle of complementary arrangement is a seminal concept also in molecular biology. The question first came up in connection with the process of biological molecular synthesis, leading to replicas of molecules present in the cell. Pauling and Delbrück[13] suggested precedence for interaction between complementary parts, instead of the importance of interaction between identical parts. They argued that the intermolecular interactions of van der Waals attraction and repulsion, electrostatic interactions, hydrogen-bond formation, etc. give stability to a system of two molecules with complementary structures in juxtaposition, rather than two molecules with identical structures. Accordingly, they argued that complementariness should be given primary consideration in discussing intermolecular interactions.

The eventual discovery of the mechanism of the function of deoxyribonucleic acid (DNA) through the double helix is the best known illustration of complementarity in molecular biology.

Above, we have repeatedly mentioned the importance of lacking a symmetry plane in many situations. However, this does not mean that preference should be assigned to asymmetry. Repetition is also symmetry and Nature operates with a rather limited number of recurring patterns giving us the hope to learn more and more about it. As the most frequent crystal structures, Escher's periodic drawings are full of rotational symmetry, inversion, and glide reflection, along with translation.

Another facet of the less-symmetry question is that in the rigorous geometrical sense, the symmetry question can be answered by yes or no responses only. Such an approach, however, would greatly limit the utility of the application of symmetry. The relaxation of this rigor can be done in two ways. One is to relax the geometrical criteria of accepting something

13. L. Pauling, M. Delbrück, "The Nature of the Intermolecular Forces Operative in Biological Processes," *Science Vol. 92*, 1940, pp. 77-79.

14. This section is based on personal meetings and discussions with the late Khudu Mamedov by I. H. in addition to Refs. 15 and 16.

15. Kh. S. Mamedov, I. R. Amiraslanov, G. N. Nadzhafov, A. A. Murasaliev, *Memory of Ornaments*, Azerneshr., Baku, 1981 (in Azerbaidani).

16. Kh. S. Mamedov, "Crystallographic patterns," in I. Hargittai, ed., *Symmetry: Unifying Human Understanding*, Pergamon Press, New York, 1986, pp. 511-529.

as beeing symmetrical in spite of imperfections. The other is the consideration of gradual changes in the amount of symmetry. The former needs little explanation: a cube retains its cubic symmetry, though not in the rigorous geometrical sense, even when one of its corners is chopped. For the latter, consider the transformation of a crystal of perfect order to the gaseous state of perfect disorder. The two extreme cases have the highest symmetry and a series of intermediate symmetries in between (in this we suppose that the gaseous sample has ideal isotropy). On the other hand, some would consider the ideal crystal to be a beautiful demonstration of symmetry breaking.

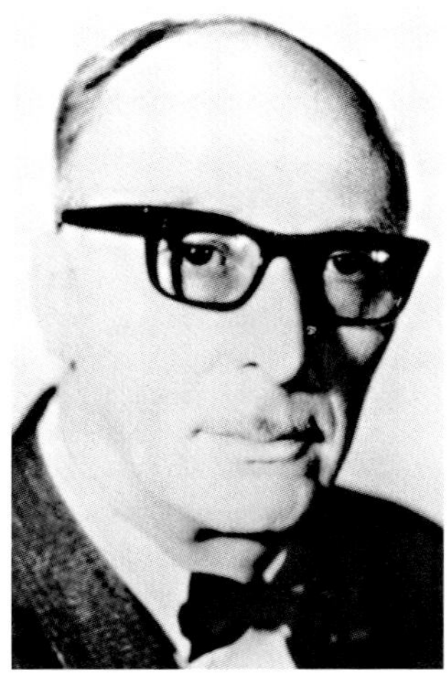

Fig. 18
Aleksandr Kitaigorodskii

Crystals and culture

We would like to devote the concluding part of this essay to Khudu Mamedov (1927-1988), the Azerbaijani crystallographer who considered his mission something not very far from Olafur Eliasson's message.[14] In 1981, Mamedov and three of his associates published a booklet, modest in outlook but rich in content, *Memory of Ornaments*.[15] Mamedov's thoughts are accessible in a chapter of the book.[16] Mamedov was an internationally known crystallographer whose parents had been nomads up to World War II. In his youth he observed that the homemade things with which the nomadic people surrounded themselves were stuffed with geometric patterns, whereas outside the tent nature was full of curved lines and forms. Life in the city was different. Mamedov called the relationship "inversy" and constructed the following simple scheme:

Townsfolk: geometric surroundings / natural art
Nomads: natural surroundings / geometric art

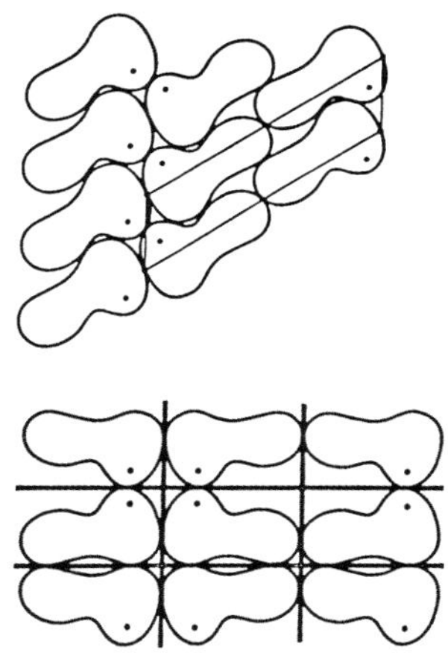

Fig. 19
Packing patterns in two dimensions by Aleksandr Kitaigorodskii. One with twofold rotation only and the other with reflections (the former providing a better utilization of available space than the latter).

Thus, the surroundings and the aesthetic creations complement each other in his scheme. The nomads did not need to carry the "portrait" of an oak with them because they could view the oaks every day and hour. The townsfolk's inclination to depict nature in their arts was seen to be a kind of nostalgia.

During his student years, Mamedov was busy with mastering geology and related sciences. In crystallography, their first basic task was the determination of the symmetry of wooden polyhedra. They found it boring. The students did not understand the origin of the symmetries they had to discover and identify. Once, however, they overcame their difficulties, they started noticing the symmetry elements everywhere. It sufficed

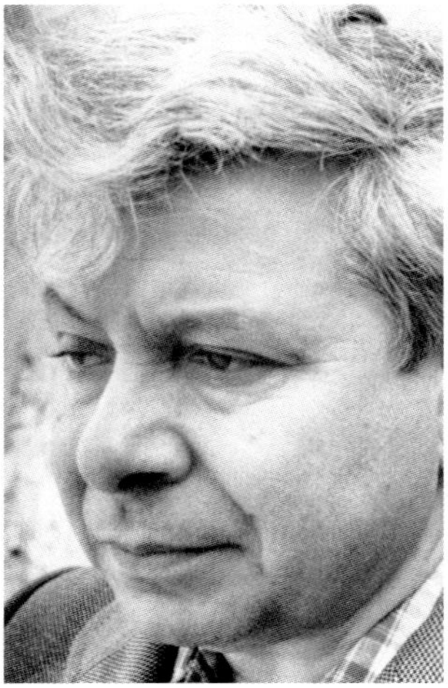

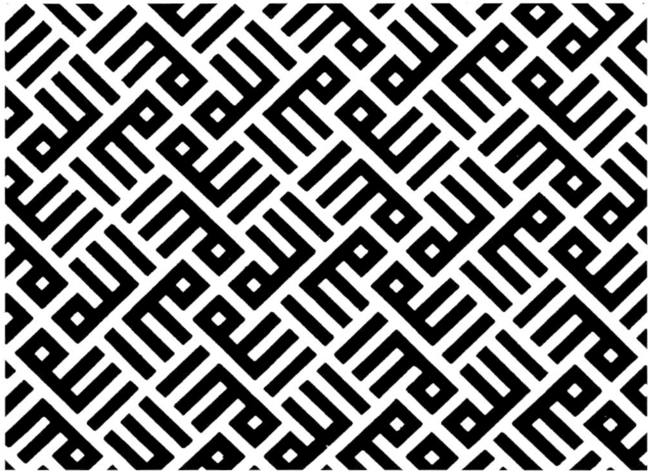

Fig. 20
Khudu Mamedov, Baku, 1982

Fig. 21
Pattern on the wall of the Badra Mausoleum from 1322

to consider carpet patterns in order to find examples of all necessary symmetry elements and demonstrate their functions. They also marveled that there existed non-symmetrical things, possibly with a deeply hidden symmetry. Mamedov was especially interested in crystallographic patterns and their appearance in a historical/cultural context. He liked to use the term "crystallographic" in a broad sense to signify a mode of pattern organization in which the foundation is the tight packing of the constructing elements. There is an endless repetition of the equivalent design element and an activity of the background.

Mamedov's first discovery of a crystallographic pattern outside the world of crystals was on the Badra mausoleum from 1322. The cylindrical surface of the mausoleum is covered with a pattern whose repeating element is the word "Allah" written in Arabic characters. Its two-dimensional pattern was easy to recogize as belonging to the P4 group, which involves fourfold rotation only. Although the original artist probably was not aware of the classification of his pattern, Mamedov thought that such a mode of creating patterns could not exist without antecedents. Mamedov stressed that his "discoveries had been described by art historians, but they had ignored the organizational peculiarities of these patterns." He and his associates created many periodic patterns and in doing so he strengthened the connection between the tradition-rich past and the more enlightened times of modern life.

Henrik Plenge Jakobsen

Diary of Plasma

Day one
My research program is doing reasonably well. Today I finally got the new basic tool materials from Laroche for the new combinations for the linkage between dxx and ppt. I still wonder why they never asked me if I had permission to have these tools. They're probably too busy at the moment. Later I gave the database at the university a call and it seems that Dr. Edwin Goldfire is progressing well, together with his staff and his students. I snapped some good information on their internal net and I'm pleased that they don't know that I'm still around. Today I really have a reason to be optimistic, at least about my program. Later I gave my thoughts and myself a walk. Nothing surprised me.

Purple sky. Need an input of something new. Void. I could cut off genitals and stuff them into the throat of a slimy teacher or politician. Let things happen and pay no attention to them.

Like today when I saw this car crash, no hard feeling, about that, just indifference. The sky is something to be scared of, not the crushed bones of a spine inside a human body.

Think I'm attracted to gravity.

Before bed I stared with fascination at my new tools. All those opportunities. All those virtual successes and failures. Despite my talent for recombinations, and my knowledge of possible mistakes one can make in calculation, I don't feel 100 percent secure about the outcome of the following days. But perhaps there is a way to fuck up gravity – at least in my mind.

Day two
During breakfast I heard the new 45 from Moby. They aren't that splendid any more, at least I didn't find any inspiration in the tune. But coffee was good. Worked immediately afterwards. The urinereactor will soon be ready, so it should soon be able to spin. Don't have enough sterilised material and medium. I need to acquire some more. My laboratory is slightly under-equipped; therefore everything is slower than it normally should be. The memory which attacked me during the sterilisation process produced a sensation resulting in the feeling of a spider moving inside my back. Don't feel like reciting this damned event right now, wished it would never come up to the surface again.

Day three
I had a dream last night. The whole scenery for this dream was not unlike the schema in day six of this diary. I'm afraid of such dreams. The dark spots are terrifying quarks or toxic proteins, which attempt to destabilize my cerebellum. At the moment I dream in schemas. It's an exhausting process since schema's aren't what they appear to signify; therefore I'm forced to decode the signals these modules are transmitting to me. My research is now more concentrated. I wish only to have grey dreams. For a while it has been a thought which has preoccupied me: grey uniform substances which fill up my entire conscience. But I doubt if it's possible to reach the deadpan dreams. Later, at four in the morning I woke up, astonished and sweaty, and was deeper down in the schema, in a dimension underneath the first one. It was no longer proteins or aggressive hadrons but cracked patterns of coagulated cells of blood and sperm. It was like I had captured a conversation

down there – in between a spectre and a posthuman-like-cyborg-thing:

"No more gravity. No more fluctuation of liquids," Spectre said, "to me you seems so motherfucking outdated and stupid, to my group of elements you is like somebody who just arrived from the middle-ages."

"We posthumans don't appreciate the absent of liquids if it means that you doesn't understand the structure of hadrons," Posthuman said.

"Uhhh," Spectre said, "I know everything about hard-ons."

Posthuman didn't take notice of the stupidity of the spectre: "Actually we talked about exterminating all you spectres."

"You'll never succeed in doing it, nor in all your ideas about revolving all existing technologies. I have been here for 3.78 time, you for 0.05 time. And certainly you will exterminate yourself before you disrupt me and my friends."

"Roooar."

I don't know if I or the posthuman had the last word. I got up, took a shower, and then went to the laboratory.

Day four

I had an odd feeling when I woke up the day father died. Without knowing anything I asked my mother if I could stay at home instead of going to school. I don't remember if she agreed or not, but anyway I stayed home. They phoned from the enzyme unit at the factory and said something was wrong, an accident or something, but what they said wasn't straight forward. It was my older sister who arrived in a cab all the way from the capital, one hundred kilometres away from our town, to pronounce the message. I had the same odd feeling this morning; something is wrong with the intention of the whole thing, with the purpose of my ideas, my projects, and my life.

Day five

A horror flashback came to me this afternoon. I was about five or six. As we often did, we used an abandoned basement in the block next to mine as a playground. The basement was mainly cement corridors surrounded by cells made of wooden planks. It had a save switch, and when one turned it on the light only remained for a minute or so. When the basement was dark everybody was full of a profound sensation of fear and insecurity. Some day the enemy number one of the neighbourhood entered the basement without our knowledge. He was a completely fucked up teenager with deeply alcoholic parents. He was always trying to figure out some trick to scare us, for example, by chasing us or beating up kids who were several years younger than himself. At the same time we were his only friends, or rather kids he had contact with. Teenagers of his age only laughed when they spotted this fellow. We knew that his social relations were about zero, but it didn't reduce or alleviate our fear. This guy hunted us into a small room at the most remote spot from the entrance of the basement locked us in and slammed the door behind us, laughing outside like a monster. We couldn't get out and we were scared to death. It felt like an eternity before one of us managed to figure out how to escape through a window situated above our heads. A year or two after this event, when he was about 16, he raped, strangled, and buried a 6 year old girl in a park nearby. That was my first experience of a murderer.

My head is spinning. At sunset I danced around with myself to this tune thinking of stealth bombers. It felt good dancing just before I recaptured my studies. Hard and interesting experimentation until four in the morning.

Day six

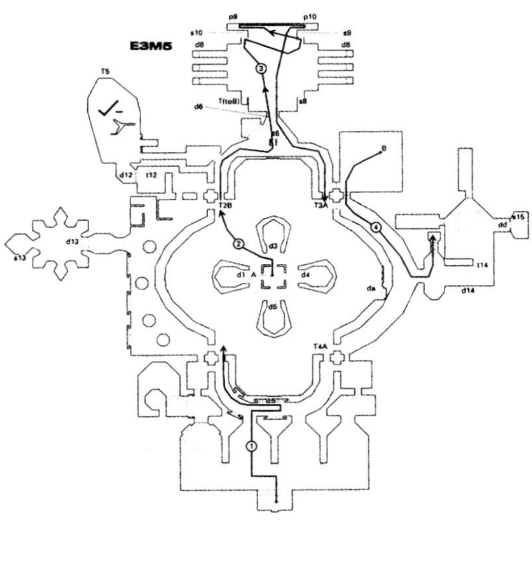

Day seven
I masturbate quite often and I really like it. I was 9 years old when I masturbated for the first time. I would really like to learn some new masturbation-techniques so that I could prolong the orgasm. I would also like to develop methods that could be used during intercourse so that I could fuck and fuck anally for several hours without stopping. Often I think and feel that I don't fuck enough, but I'm satisfied with the frequency of my masturbation. I like girls, and I like men, but my sexual experience is relatively modest concerning men. Actually I have never fucked a guy, and I have never been fucked by one, but I've been close. Sometimes I think that there is too little sex and too many atoms, and too much nothing in our life. If I had the power to do it, I would declare everybody suppressing the orgasm pulverized.

There was a backfire in my urinereactor today; some chemical accelerator accident that I hadn't previewed. A lot of smoke escaped from burning polyvinylchlorid tubes. While writing this I'm still coughing because of all the reeking black smoke I inhaled.

Day eight
Nothing is left – that's what I dreamt. What's left? "Nothing" a girl told me in this dream. What's a dream? Just a hallucination, a construction of my brain – nothing real – just nothing. Let's be serious: there is nothing that can justify the important role and influence dreams have on our conscience. Somebody said that we dream to forget, and she or he may be right, but I'm afraid that it may not be true. This backfire was such a shock to me! I found the cause of what happened. I was the idiot; I induced too many proteins in the soup and the temperature was slightly too elevated. Shit, I used most of today to clear up my own mess.

Many know the sensation of having a totally fucked up mind. Sometimes because things are going wrong, either regarding one's possibilities, the conflicts that one is a part of, or because one is filled up with impressions and inputs that simply can't be obtained normally in the brain because they seem too far out. The speed of input in this world especially drives me crazy. For quite some time I have been thinking about how I could express my perception of this world in which we live in; what kind of image could be representative of the feelings that this perception generates? An image that's more a reaction towards this perception would be to destroy it. For me, destruction has been very constructive, and I think for many people that it's an action which in one way or another has a meaning. Then again there are perhaps other alternatives to destruction. When there was a belief in common goals, there was also a lust to create alternatives; but then all kinds of sociality and solidarity have been blown away. In order to elaborate an alternative space, that now means to elaborate an isolated space – a space only for one or a few individuals. Forget about any scale bigger than micro. Anyway there should be a possibility to elaborate some kind of space or field where one could be able to have an area of construction for ones own life. Don't know... At least a poor illusion or image.

A neutron star is a collapsed star of extremely high density composed almost entirely of neutrons. Pulsars are generally thought to be collapsed rotating neutron stars.

Day nine

Sometimes I have a sensation of only semi-respiration; not because of pollution or cigarettes, just not enough space in psychological and physical terms.

I really doubt those superstring guys – too pretentious. They seem like a gang of oddballs, like all scientists by the way. They suggest that there are ten dimensions: four being perceptible to reality, the six others wrapped into these four. The whole idea of unification underneath the whole thing makes me sick. Why do we always need a simple and aesthetic formula to describe the different forms of matters. Things don't appear simple to me or the people that I have known. Simplicity looks more like a hallucination.

Day ten

Today hanging on the phone chatting with a friend it suddenly dawned on me that we are soon to reach the year 2000. I was reminded because some sport event that will continue into the next millennium was announced on the radio. I told my friend who agreed that the idea is weird.

1. "Neutron; Particle électriquement neutre, constituant, avec les les protons, les noyaux des atomes. – Le neutron diffère du électron par son absence de charge; à l'etat libre, il est d'ailleurs instable et se transforme en un proton et un électron.

Employée à l'irradiation des atomes, il les rend fréquemment radio-actifs. Il peut déterminer la fission de l'uranium et du plutonium."

2. "Neutron-bomb: a small thermonuclear warhead for battlefield use, that would release large numbers of neutrons intended to disable or kill enemy soldiers without destroying buildings, vehicles etc."

Everybody knows fear; it's a feeling which expresses something that makes us anxious. One can fear for the future especially, but also for the past, or fear for the present. A word like neutron is a word which can implicate fear, in terms of the n-bomb, or in relation to the nuclear implants which deal with the danger of poisoning to death what surrounds them. Many times I have thought about this invisible enemy and its threatening perspectives. Fear is in most cases related to power; someone has the power and use it to create fear while others fear that they will loose their power. Fear, power, and neutrons are even directly related in the case of nuclear power implants. A government or a company use the fear to create energy and irresolvable waste problems and material for producing A- & B- & N- bombs. This is the fear that the world has known in the last 50 years, the big common fear that everybody has in the back of their mind.

Marianne Krogh Jensen

Mapping Virtual Materiality

Introduction

Many people still find the concept of "the virtual" a highly abstract one, in part because it implies total intangibility, and in part because it is most often associated with computers and cyberspace. Yet, an understanding of the virtual must not be limited to cyberspace or to what is not real, for even if the concept refers to things that have not yet been realized, these things are nevertheless potential realities. They *exist*, closely linked to our own physical presence – but they have merely not been actualized.

Imagine yourself standing completely still, facing your surroundings as if you were facing a two-dimensional, static picture. Imagine too that time does not exist. Standing thus, one could say that the eyes – or, more broadly, the senses – register and document reality. If you were to add to this your own movements, those of your surroundings, your experiences and time, it would hardly be possible to continue speaking of pure registering. Now it is a question of projections in both directions, outwards and inwards. One could say that there is always a kind of radius around us that contains our perceptions, desires, experiences, attempts at manipulation, and acts of submission – in short, our personal cultivation, which both forms our surroundings and is always being formed by them. I would like to refer to this personal cultivation as "the virtual," with an emphasis on the idea that it can also become something highly material.

All that is needed to perceive these virtual materialities is that we become accustomed to the notion that space can be conceived of in many other ways than those that have dominated our thinking for so long that they now seem self-evident. After all, these are only some of many possible conceptions found within our radius of cultivation. Let us examine a few other perspectives as are formulated in various contexts, focussing on five among many possible alternatives.

Time as quality – intuition as method

It is no coincidence that references to the French philosopher Henri Bergson can often be found today among art critics, architecture critics, philosophers, and so on, as the way in which Bergson defined concepts such as space, time, and intuition had been badly neglected in the spatial theories of his own day. Although Bergson was highly influential in certain circles, he has frequently been excluded from "official" histories of modernism, since he attempted, among other things, to break with the canonical conception of time as the fourth dimension of space – a conception advocated with reference to the theory of relativity by thinkers such as Giedion.

Bergson felt that in striving to categorize motion, modern science ended up emphasizing the *constancy* of motion. By contrast, Bergson wished to emphasis the fluctuation of phenomena as conditioned by the nature of time – not as a mechanical and homogeneous medium that could be divided like the swing of a pendulum into successive moments, but as an internal, heterogeneous course without any succession and without being related to anything numerical.[1]

Bergson points out that in dealing with qualitatively different phenomena, we often treat them as if the differences between them were merely quantitative, a tendency that can be seen in our frequent use of words such as "more," "larger," and "smaller" when we attempt to describe conditions that actu-

1. See Henri Bergson, *Det umiddelbare i bevidstheden. En studie over det umiddelbart givne i de sjælelige virksomheder og tilstande*, Stjernebøgerens kulturbibliotek, Vintens Forlag, Copenhagen, 1980 (1917), and G. Deleuze, *Bergsonism*, Zone Books, New York, 1991.

ally differ in essence. For example, if we were to shine a lantern onto a white wall and then increase the brightness of the lantern, we would doubtlessly describe the effect as a change in the level of brightness – not as a change in the color of the wall. Bergson explains that our tendency to describe such phenomena in this way is an example of representative perception or "acquired perception," since we attribute the effect of the change to its cause. Once again, the concept of numbers appears, requiring perception of a multitude of uniform parts.

Another displacement that is closely linked to the numerical and the quantitative involves the relationship between time and space. Bergson points out that when we quantify time or divide it into a number of segments that make up a whole – i.e. "objectify" it in a phenomenological sense – we are actually attempting to *spatialize* it, as space becomes the material or medium into which our consciousness places what is in reality an indivisible fluctuation. In this way, we convert time into space, so to speak, a gesture that is also exemplified in notions of historical time and the time required to become aware of an experience. Intervals of time only exist for us and that is due to the inter-permeation of our states of consciousness, Bergson argues. Only space can be found outside of this. Because of this, Bergson continues, space can only exist at a single given time, for when we speak of direction, extent, and motion, we have separated the parts from each other and then collated the positions they occupy. What we call "before" and "after" exists simultaneously, side by side. A movement, for example, consists of two separate elements: the space that is traversed and the act of traversing it. The first element is a homogeneous quantity, while the second only exists in our consciousness and is a quality. Yet we confuse these phenomena, Bergson argues, for when we claim to be measuring a movement, this has nothing to do with the course of time, but concerns space and the ability to divide it into simultaneities *ad infinitum*. This point is linked to one of Bergson's sharpest criticisms of Einstein's conception of time, as Einstein's notion of the plurality of time, with time varying from one system to the next, must, according to Bergson, be defined by a reading of several clocks that are mutually independent and external to the body.

It is pointed out, however, that a constant spatialization of phenomena is in a way unavoidable, as it constitutes a part of the very act of reflection. Bergson also points out that this spatialization is a part of a natural process of socialization, as it allows us to refer to the same objects and phenomena, to make use of the same terms and so on. Thus, Bergson sees two realities that differ in terms of their basic nature. One is heterogeneous and defined by perceptual qualities, while the other is homogeneous and conceived of as space. Problems arise when we confuse the two out of habit. When we do this, we transfer the objective status of the external world to the inner world – with the result that the external world becomes the authority in accordance with which the inner world is judged. We allow the external authority to rule and forget that we have, in a way, created it as something external. Forgetting this can be understood as a form of non-freedom, since it can result in a tendency to uniformity and stereotyping. Space does not impart order on the world and it is not constant and static. It is elastic and emergent, and it features different levels of intensity. Our movements do not take place in space, but are actualized and unfold by virtue of our movement itself, by virtue of the material. This constitutes a serious blow to the common Kantian notion of the existence of space being independent of its content, of space as a neutral container.

It is illusory to understand time as a line along which the imagination can move, since duration, as the inner course of time is called, does not progress through time but is time itself. Duration cannot be divided without undergoing a qualitative transformation. It is an unmediated given phenomenon, and can in its discontinuous and layered multiplicity only be conceived of via intuition. Bergson describes this process as a mutual permeation of qualitative changes: they are blended together, permeate each other in organic links, and have no fixed outline. Finally, as a virtual multiplicity, duration is of necessity only a single time, defined by its occurrence within the inner world of the individual subject.

Bergson questions a number of common assumptions regarding our way of conceiving the present and past; perception and memory. He argues that the past occurs simultaneously with the present that was. They appear as analogous. He even goes so far to argue that the past is a condition with respect to the present. In this same way, memory is a condition for perception, since every act of perception blends in with and is permeated by what the body and consciousness remember. A central point in this connection is that the indispensable nature of memory is not to be bemoaned, but acknowledged, so as to avoid confusing perception and recognition, i.e. believing that we experience the world via our senses when we actually experience it via language and images alone. This allows us to avoid reducing differences in kind to differences in degree, as Bergson would have put it.

Finally, it is worth noting that Bergson distinguishes between the actual and the virtual, a distinction that has influenced the later work of Deleuze. The actual is endowed with a potentially "objective" presence, while the virtual corresponds to the subjective and to duration, since its reality lies outside any actuality. These arguments can be used to counter the notion of reality as something ready-made, as a predictable possibility. For if time is something more than merely the fourth dimension of space – if it is a kind of temporizing or unfolding – then chance can be inserted where once there had only been probability.

Lightness

In the 1990s, the American art historian John Rajchman introduced a new interpretation of and context for the concept of "lightness."[2]

Rajchman argues that lightness should not be understood in the modernist sense of a movement away from heavy materials, and a rather literal focus on immateriality and transparency. The notion of lightness in modernism continues to signal an optical, geometric puritanism that can only be defined via binary opposites – the natural and the artificial, the representational and the abstract, etc. – and is a fundamentally static notion. Yet, lightness should not be understood solely in terms of the postmodernist interpretations of recent decades, which viewed the rise of a technological global village and post-industrial capitalism as an elimination of all links to place or region, Rajchman continues. It should instead be compared to matter, which works through materials and textures and belongs to haptical, rather than optical, space. Instead of the force of gravity, which forms the basis for a homogeneous and centered space, Rajchman (along with Deleuze) argues for a "smooth" space featuring a lightness that can manifest itself with a great deal of sensitivity regarding the many ways of being-in-the-world, as well as an understanding of the interwoven nature of these – which can result in a new awareness of the freedom of movement.

In this way, Rajchman attempts to break with the strong tradition within Western (Hegelian) thinking of complementarity with respect to concepts such as symmetry, proportion

2. See John Rajchman, *Constructions*, The MIT Press, Cambridge, Mass.,1998, from which the following quotes by Rajchman have been taken.

and harmony, and he explicitly takes a distance to the Husserlian notion that "the ground anchors us." "It centers us. It orients us in a perspectival view of distances. It links oculo and motor into a single unified kinesthetic field with receding horizons, which permits us to place things in a coordinate space, re-identify objects, and say what's up and what's down." Yet, geometric form is only one possibility among many, if we choose instead to view the "center" as being everywhere, and must therefore seek out a different kind of movement – which Rajchman describes as a never-ending state of eternal shifting across surfaces – then the Earth will once again seem light.

Rajchman has both praise and blame for the electronic or post-industrial technologies that numerous scholars in recent decades (such as Virilio) have described as having dematerializing consequences; the abstraction and multidimensionalizing of the given lead to a "fictionalization" of reality, signs simulate forms. Rajchman points out, however, that this has also given "lightness" a bad reputation as being superficial and non-authentic, which has in turn paved the way for a critical-phenomenological bias in favor of gravity and materiality. On this matter, he feels (once again following Deleuze) that it must be possible to choose a third way that, although dependent on the other two, *avoids* distinguishing between materiality and virtuality, and that can form the context for a mode of existence that creates and re-creates together with others within an unlimited field.

For Rajchman, the whole purpose of advocating lightness is to show that once we allow ourselves to view the world as not assembled, as incongruent and made up of many different divergent paths, it then becomes possible to move out of the familiar system of representation and think instead in terms of still unactualized realities – in terms of virtualities – and thus be able to perceive the multifaceted and unpredictable potential of all things, and to see other (hi)stories in our own (hi)stories. Finally, Rajchman's thinking also has consequences for his conception of the subject, since it is now movements and connecting links that constitute our bodies and existences, which have no inherent qualities themselves, but rather a multitude of different competencies. In the same way that demographic patterns today are replacing the old narratives of continuous and homogeneous origins with a notion of multiple, overlapping fields, the subject now appears as both malleable and indeterminate – its identity is something that is attributed to it – which

Rajchman views as the basis for a new experience of lightness and freedom of movement.

Diagram

Rajchman is also among the writers who have been emphasizing diagrammatic practice as a design strategy that can incorporate the notion of the virtual.[3] Many architects and scholars today have adopted Foucault's and Deleuze's idea of the diagram as an "abstract machine" with the power to break up the classical representational system.[4]

Foucault criticizes phenomenology for its notion of intentionality, and because he sees an incompatibility between what he calls the articulable and the visible, i.e. between content and expression. The truth is inseparable from the procedure by which it is established, as Deleuze concludes. In this connection, Foucault has of course explored the notion of power as a diagrammatic strategy that generates both social space and human individuals. All intentionality, Foucault argues, collapses in the rift that opens up between seeing and speaking; we do not see what we speak of, and we do not speak of what we see, as Magritte, among others, has so often pointed out.

Within this system-critical field of understanding, both Foucault and Deleuze emphasize the notion of the "archivist" as a concept that can characterize the way in which we manœuvre about in our surroundings, which cannot assume any true form, but is instead a collection of relationships between forces. The archivist works not only vertically and horizontally, but also in diagonal dimensions, cutting across all levels and links; the archivist can explore a collection or series of points and at the same time discover that some of the points diverge and therefore must be redistributed within a new space and a new time. Deleuze is well-known for his notions of rhizomes and a thousand plateaus.

Deleuze and Foucault maintain that this sort of "diagonal dimension" can be activated with the help of the diagram. As an "abstract machine," the diagram does not distinguish between notions such as content and expression and different discourses – it is intersocial and in a state of constant evolution. Its purpose is not to represent any existing world, but in a state of continuous mutation to produce a new kind of reality. To underscore the difference between the redundant and the creative, Deleuze repeatedly distinguishes between a "realization of the possible" and an "actualization of the virtual." The realization of the possible involves representation, while the

3. See, for example, John Rajchman, "A New Pragmatism," in Cynthia C. Davidson, ed., *Anyhow*, Anyone Corporation, New York, The MIT Press, Cambridge, Mass., pp. 212-217.

4. See Gilles Deleuze, *Foucault, diagrams*, The Athlone Press, London, 1988.

actualization of the virtual introduces something changeable, which – even if it is real – has not yet been. This is precisely why the diagram must not be used as a metaphor or reference, but as a generator. At issue, then, is a conception of time in which the past, or the archive, precedes and creates the present – not the reverse, in which the present becomes the past. Deleuze refers to this as diagrammatic time.

Extended now

The phenomenologist Edmund Husserl has attempted to describe time as a continuous flow, along somewhat the same lines as Bergson, but divided into an absolute, constituent temporal flow and an immanent, constituted temporality. These two aspects are inseparable, in that the absolute flow – which does not exist in time, but is time – enables us to be aware of the temporal phases of objects.[5]

Husserl asks how it is possible to experience an object as constant, a question he answers by introducing the notion of an "extended present" that, in addition to the present moment, includes what he refers to as "retention" and "protention," i.e. a form of (non-temporalized) memory and expectation. An experience includes not only what occurs at the present moment; the experience of duration is dependent on a tripartite structure of temporal awareness that, according to Husserl, is the very point of intersection for consciousness, and is the flow itself. This tripartite structure is, in principle, never-ending, as it has no "duration" itself. One of Husserl's main points in this connection is that retention and protention are not given indirectly, but as something original: objects are actually presented in this form of memory and expectation – they are not represented. They are perceived by intuition in their givenness as past and future.

Husserl does point out, however, that experiences do not only occur in the form of presentative awareness, but also contain other traces of consciousness via continual representations; when we experience an earlier section of consciousness, it is indeed a question of a mediation, i.e. of a representation, but it is also an act that is experienced. It is not only a picture that "appears," but also the person's entire understanding of what is now experienced again in a new context. In this way, consciousness becomes a type of nested structure, in which one trace is contained within another, and all layers are interlinked. This type of mental construction is also quite useful in connection with a number of other related problems. For example,

5. For a detailed study, see Daniel Birnbaum, "The Hospitality of Presence. Problems of Otherness in Husserl's Phenomenology," *Stockholm Studies in Philosophy 20*, Almquist & Wiksell International, Stockholm, 1998.

one could choose to view the current discussion of synaesthesia as an attempt to gather together what the rationalistic thinking of modernism had separated, so that instead of thinking in terms of five separate senses, each with its own characteristics and stimuli, perception can now be analyzed as a cohesive, multifaceted whole.

What is interesting about Husserl's concept of time with respect to a contemporary perspective on the problem of representation is not only that he describes perception as a kind of "extension" of the present moment, with retention, protention, and representations (memory, the imagination, etc.) all required in order to be able to "objectivize." It is also his insistence that we only accept phenomena as they present themselves to the consciousness or as they are given – that we let the past present itself as the past, for example. If we only allowed the past to appear as a mental image, we would tend to forget that it is past – and we would not discover the related displacement between the body and consciousness.

Networks

Finally, Bruno Latour should be mentioned in this context, as he is one of only a few thinkers who have attempted to formulate a theory describing some of the mechanisms involved in matters such as multiplicities, intensities, diagonal dimensions, diagrammatic praxis, and so on.[6] Latour calls this a theory of agent networks and explains that it is aimed at registering and explaining effects without involving any accompanying ontologies, topologies or politics. The theory operates on a semiotic basis by studying the mechanisms underlying the generation of meaning, but it also exceeds the limits of semiotics without losing its collection of tools, i.e. the ability to define elements such as contexts, senders, receivers, and boundaries.

If one imagines the world to be polycentric rather than anthropocentric, it can be difficult to accept the traditional division between the acting subject and the passive object. Latour chooses instead to conclude that both artefacts and people participate as equal, collaborative agents in what he describes as a general condition for creativity; it is not only that objects are formed by subjects, but subjects are also formed by objects, and the moment of creativity arises only by recognizing this heterogeneity and diffusion and by carefully intertwining weak bands, as Latour expresses it. Chaos consti-

6. See his *Om aktør-netværksteori. Nogle få afklaringer og mere end nogle få forviklinger*, *Philosophia*, årg. 25, 3-4, Copenhagen, pp. 47-64.

tutes the starting-point for this kind of perspective, and a certain order can only be established in provisional network constructions, in which many smaller agents establish temporary links that, via their complexity, create a certain stability, in the sense of inertia. One cannot step outside a network to find explanatory causes, but can only extend the network further.

Latour defines a network as a "system of exchange" between people and their surroundings, in which provisional situations can be stabilized for brief moments, only to be dissolved again in a process of continual transformation leading to new provisional situations. This also eliminates all hope of any higher ideal condition, and of the future as a universally identifiable concept. Latour defines the "agent" within agent network theory in terms of semiotics as something that acts or receives activity from others. It is not that there is a network and an agent who creates the network, but rather an agent whose definition of the world outlines, traces, delineates, describes, and inscribes a course that is called a network; a network is not a thing, but the registered movements of a thing.

The notion of networks renders traditional concepts of mapping our surroundings inadequate, which is why Latour also believes that we must redefine many of the spatial metaphors we normally use in our attempts to describe society, nature, etc. A network has no negative form, no shadow, which has consequences for the relationship between foreground and background. A network is neither a social nor a "real" space, but only links, which also means that geographical concepts such as "near" and "far" cannot be used. Another misleading concept is that of scale, as one network is never any larger than another, only more or less dense, and multidimensional as well. Finally, the inside-outside dichotomy does not work in this connection either, as it presumes the existence of a boundary that separates the internal from the external. Networks are pure boundary.

In the final analysis, this also has clear consequences for the conception of the subject, since agents cannot be understood as fixed entities, but as streams under constant influence. This does not necessarily imply a loss, even if some readers might interpret it that way. One can choose to view it as involving a certain element of freedom, as the topography, types, and numbers of links are not sketched out or inscribed by any "external" factors, but are left entirely to the agent. The network unfolds in its relationships, so that any attempt to explain a network also constitutes a network; there is no clear line between things and representations, as the observer is located on the same level as all other frames of reference. For this reason, it is not a form of metalanguage either – only interpretations, translations and appendices. In this way, agent network theory is not a theory of discovered networks, but the activity of discovering networks. That is why the actual encounter between collaborative agents and actants – and the resulting transformation – is so essential to a definition of the individual: questions regarding identity, characteristics and closed discursive spaces are forced to yield to questions relating to what is moving and how this movement can be registered. This allows a new understanding of cultural production as a creative process – especially with regard to architecture. Technology and nature, for example, are not passive instruments for the artistic creator. It is rather a question of an encounter between the human subject and the technological or "natural" subject constituting a creative process, in which the architect makes the first choice or differentiation.

As a conceptual model, one of the effects of semiotics has been to reveal the once unproblematic relationship between form and content as conventional and opaque. Agent network theory not only acknowledges this but encourages it, and explores the compact and layered complexity of relationships – as well as the necessary mediating movement – as a basic condition. For this reason, it also makes sense to include new media and information technology as collaborating agents. This is of course what is implied by Manuel Gausa's concept of "informational space-time," which he describes as an informal and mutable system of interlinked and interactive points of meaning that have found a new dimensional vector in the horrifically large but indispensable mass of information available to people today.[7] One might add that in this sort of landscape, we have no choice but to "diagrammatize information," as John Rajchman expresses it.

I would argue that in the writing of Bergson and in that of later thinkers such as Deleuze, Rajchman, and Latour, reality appears as something that is constructed by events, collected in our consciousness, thereby contributing to opening up our experience of space and time to diversity and multiplicity.

As such, the virtual has a great deal to do with our physical conditions, and thus takes on an emphatic materiality. The virtual is potential reality. It is the next move.

7. See Manuel Gausa, "Dynamic time – (in)formal order: (un)disciplined trajectories," in Manuel Gausa (ed.), *Spirals*, *Quaderns*, Barcelona, 1999, pp. 6-11.

Rem Koolhaas

The Generic City

1. Introduction

1.1 Is the contemporary city like the contemporary airport – "all the same"? Is it possible to theorize this convergence? And if so, to what ultimate configuration is it aspiring? Convergence is possible only at the price of shedding identity. That is usually seen as a loss. But at the scale at which it occurs, it must mean something. What are the disadvantages of identity, and conversely, what are the advantages of blankness? What if this seemingly accidental – and usually regretted – homogenization were an intentional process, a conscious movement away from difference toward similarity? What if we are witnessing a global liberation movement: "down with character!" What is left after identity is stripped? The Generic?

1.2 To the extent that identity is derived from physical substance, from the historical, from context, from the real, we somehow cannot imagine that anything contemporary – made by us – contributes to it. But the fact that human growth is exponential implies that the past will at some point become too "small" to be inhabited and shared by those alive. We ourselves exhaust it. To the extent that history finds its deposit in architecture, present human quantities will inevitably burst and deplete previous substance. Identity conceived as this form of sharing the past is a losing proposition: not only is there – in a stable model of continuous population expansion – proportionally less and less to share, but history also has an invidious half-life – as it is more abused, it becomes less significant – to the point where its diminishing handouts become insulting. This thinning is exacerbated by the constantly increasing mass of tourists, an avalanche that, in a perpetual quest for "character," grinds successful identities down to meaningless dust.

1.3 Identity is like a mousetrap in which more and more mice have to share the original bait, and which, on closer inspection, may have been empty for centuries. The stronger identity, the more it imprisons, the more it resists expansion, interpretation, renewal, contradiction. Identity becomes like a lighthouse – fixed, overdetermined: it can change its position or the pattern it emits only at the cost of destabilizing navigation. (Paris can only become more Parisian – it is already on its way to becoming hyper-Paris, a polished caricature. There are exceptions: London – its only identity is a lack of clear identity – is perpetually becoming even less London, more open, less static.)

1.4 Identity centralizes; it insists on an essence, a point. Its tragedy is given in simple geometric terms. As the sphere of influence expands, the area characterized by the center becomes larger and larger, hopelessly diluting both the strength and the authority of the core; inevitably the distance between center and circumference increases to the breaking point. In this perspective, the recent, belated discovery of the periphery as a zone of potential value – a kind of pre-historical condition that might finally be worthy of architectural attention – is only a disguised insistence on the priority of and dependency on the center: without center, no periphery; the interest of the first presumably compensates for the emptiness of the latter. Conceptually orphaned, the condition of the periphery is made worse by the fact that its mother is still alive, stealing the show, emphasizing its offspring's inadequacies. The last vibes emanating from the exhausted center preclude the reading of the periphery as a critical mass. Not only is the center by definition too small to perform its assigned obligations, it is also no longer the real center but an overblown mirage on its way to implosion; yet its illusory presence denies the rest of the city its legitimacy. (Manhattan denigrates as "bridge-and-tunnel people" those who need infrastructural support to enter the city, and makes them pay for it.) The persistence of the present concentric obsession makes us all bridge-and-tunnel people, second-class citizens in our own civilization, disenfranchised by the dumb coincidence of our collective exile from the center.

1.5 In our concentric programming (the author spent part of his youth in Amsterdam, city of ultimate centrality) the insistence on the center as the core of value and meaning, font of all significance, is doubly destructive – not only is the ever-increasing volume of dependencies an ultimately intolerable strain, it also means that the center has to be constantly maintained, i.e. modernized. As "the most important place," it paradoxically has to be, at the same time, the most old and the most new, the most fixed and the most dynamic; it undergoes the most intense and constant adaptation, which is then compromised and complicated by the fact that it has to be an unacknowledged transformation, invisible to the naked eye. (The city of Zurich has found the most radical, expensive solution in reverting to a kind of reverse archaeology: layer after layer of new modernities – shopping centers, parking, banks, vaults, laboratories – are constructed underneath the center. The center no longer expands outward or skyward, but inward toward the center of the earth itself.) From the grafting of more or less discreet traffic arteries, bypasses, underground tunnels, the construction of ever more tangentiales, to the routine transformation of housing into offices, warehouses into lofts, abandoned churches into nightclubs, from the serial bankruptcies and subsequent reopenings of specific units in more and more expensive shopping precincts to the relentless conversion of utilitarian space into "public" space, pedestrianization, the creation of new parks, planting, bridging, exposing, the systematic restoring of historic mediocrity, all authenticity is relentlessly evacuated.

1.6 The Generic City is the city liberated from the captivity of center, from the straitjacket of identity. The Generic City breaks with this destructive cycle of dependency: it is nothing but a reflection of present need and present ability. It is the city without history. It is big enough for everybody. It is easy. It does not need maintenance. If it gets too small it just expands. If it gets old it just self-destructs and renews. It is equally exciting – or unexciting – everywhere. It is "superficial" – like a

Hollywood studio lot, it can produce a new identity every Monday morning.

2. Statistics

2.1 The Generic City has grown dramatically over the past few decades. Not only has its size increased, its numbers have too. In the early 1970s it was inhabited by an average of 2.5 million official (and +/- 500,000 unofficial) residents; now it hovers around the 15 million mark.

2.2 Did the Generic City start in America? Is it so profoundly unoriginal that it can only be imported? In any case, the Generic City now also exists in Asia, Europe, Australia, Africa. The definitive move away from the countryside, from agriculture, to the city is not a move to the city as we knew it: it is a move to the Generic City, the city so pervasive that it has come to the country.

2.3 Some continents, like Asia, aspire to the Generic City, others are ashamed by it. Because it tends toward the tropical – converging around the equator – a large proportion of Generic Cities is Asian – seemingly a contradiction in terms: the over-familiar inhabited by the inscrutable. One day it will be absolutely exotic again, this discarded product of Western civilization, through the resemanticization that its very dissemination brings in its wake...

2.4 Sometimes an old, singular city, like Barcelona, by oversimplifying its identity, turns Generic. It becomes transparent, like a logo. The reverse never happens... at least not yet.

3. General

3.1 The Generic City is what is left after large sections of urban life crossed over to cyberspace. It is a place of weak and distended sensations, few and far between emotions, discreet and mysterious like a large space lit by a bed lamp. Compared to the classical city, the Generic City is sedated, usually perceived from a sedentary position. Instead of concentration – simultaneous presence – in the Generic City individual "moments" are spaced far apart to create a trance of almost unnoticeable aesthetic experiences: the color variations in the fluorescent lighting of an office building just before sunset, the subtleties of the slightly different whites of an illuminated sign at night. Like Japanese food, the sen – they may simply be ignored. (There's a choice.) This pervasive lack of urgency and insistence acts like a potent drug, it induces a hallucination of the normal.

3.2 In a drastic reversal of what is supposedly the major characteristic of the city – "business" – the dominant sensation of the Generic City is an eerie calm: the calmer it is, the more it approximates the pure state. The Generic City addresses the "evils" that were ascribed to the traditional city before our love for it became unconditional. The serenity of the Generic City is achieved by the evacuation of the public realm, as in an emergency fire drill. The urban plane now only accommodates necessary movement, fundamentally the car; highways are a superior version of boulevards and plazas, taking more and more space; their design, seemingly aiming for automotive efficiency, is in fact surprisingly sensual, a utilitarian pretense entering the domain of smooth space. What is new about this locomotive public realm is that it cannot be measured in dimensions. The same (let's say ten-mile) stretch yields a vast number of utterly different experiences: it can last five minutes or forty; it can be shared with almost nobody, or with the entire population; it can yield the absolute pleasure of pure, unadulterated speed – at which point the sensation of the Generic City may even become intense or at least acquire density – or utterly claustrophobic moments of stoppage – at which point the tinness of the Generic City is at its most noticeable.

3.3 The Generic City is fractal, an endless repetition of the same simple structural module; it is possible to reconstruct it from its smallest entity, a desktop computer, maybe even a diskette.

3.4 Golf courses are all that is left of otherness.

3.5 The Generic City has easy phone numbers, not the resistant ten-figure frontal-lobe crunchers of the traditional city but smoother versions, their middle numbers identical, for instance.

3.6 Its main attraction is its anomie.

4. Airport

4.1 Once manifestations of ultimate neutrality, airports now are among the most singular, characteristic elements of the Generic City, its strongest vehicle of differentiation. They have to be, being all the average person tends to experience of a particular city. Like a drastic perfume demonstration, photomurals, vegetation, local costumes give a first concentrated blast of the local identity (sometimes it is also the last). Far away, comfortable, exotic, polar, regional, Eastern, rustic, new, even "undiscovered:" those are the emotional registers invoked. Thus conceptually charged, airports become emblematic signs imprinted on the global collective unconscious in savage manipulations of their nonaviatic attractors – tax-free shopping, spectacular spatial qualities, the frequency and reliability of their connections to other airports. In terms of its iconography/performance, the airport is a concentrate of both the hyper-local and hyper-global – hyper-global in the sense you can get goods there that are not even available in the city, hyper-local in the sense you can get things there that you get nowhere else.

4.2 The tendency in airport gestalt is toward ever-greater autonomy: sometimes they're even practically unrelated to a specific Generic City. Becoming bigger and bigger, equipped with more and more facilities unconnected to travel, they are on the way to replacing the city. The in-transit condition is becoming universal. Together, airports contain populations of millions – plus the largest daily workforce. In the completeness of their facilities, they are like quarters of the Generic City, sometimes even its reason for being (its center?), with the added attraction of being hermetic systems from which there is no escape – except to another airport.

4.3 The date/age of the Generic City can be reconstructed from a close reading of its airport's geometry. Hexagonal plan (in unique cases penta- or heptagonal): 1960s. Orthogonal plan and section: 1970s. Collage City: 1980s. A single curved section, endlessly extruded in a linear plan: probably 1990s (Its structure branching out like an oak tree: Germany).

4.4 Airports come in two sizes: too big and too small. Yet their size has no influence on their performance. This suggests that the most intriguing aspect of all infrastructures is their essential elasticity. Calculated for the exact number of – passengers per year – they are invaded by the countless and survive, stretched toward ultimate indeterminacy.

5. Population

5.1 The Generic City is seriously multiracial, on average 8% black, 12% white, 27% Hispanic, 37% Chinese/Asian, 6% indeterminate, 10% other. Not only multiracial, also multicultural. That's why it comes as no surprise to see temples between the slabs, dragons on the main boulevards, Buddhas in the CBD (central business district).

5.2 The Generic City is always founded by people on the move, poised to move on. This explains the insubstantiality of their foundations. Like the flakes that are suddenly formed in a clear liquid by joining two chemical substances, eventually to accumulate in an uncertain heap on the bottom, the collusion or confluence of two migrations – Cuban emigrés going north and Jewish retirees going south, for instance, both ultimately on their way someplace else – establishes, out of the blue, a settlement. A Generic City is born.

6. Urbanism

6.1 The great originality of the Generic City is simply to abandon what doesn't work – what has outlived its use – to break up the blacktop of idealism with the jackhammers of realism and to accept whatever grows in its place. In that sense, the Generic City accommodates both the primordial and the futuristic – in fact, only these two. The Generic City is all that remains of what used to be the city. The Generic City is the post-city being prepared on the site of the ex-city.

6.2 The Generic City is held together, not by an overdemanding public realm – progressively debased in a surprisingly long sequence in which the Roman Forum is to the Greek agora what the shopping mall is to the high street – but by the residual. In the original model of the moderns, the residual was merely green, its controlled neatness a moralistic assertion of good intentions, discouraging association, use. In the Generic City, because the crust of its civilization is so thin, and through its immanent tropicality, the vegetal is transformed into Edenic Residue, the main carrier of its identity: a hybrid of politics and landscape. At the same time refuge of the illegal, the uncontrollable, and subject of endless manipulation, it represents a simultaneous triumph of the manicured and the primeval. Its immoral lushness compensates for the Generic City's other poverties. Supremely inorganic, the organic is the Generic City's strongest myth.

6.3 The street is dead. That discovery has coincided with frantic attempts at its resuscitation. Public art is everywhere – as if two deaths make a life. Pedestrianization – intended to preserve – merely channels the flow of those doomed to destroy the object of their intended reverence with their feet.

6.4 The Generic City is on its way from horizontality to verticality. The skyscraper looks as if it will be the final, definitive typology. It has swallowed everything else. It can exist anywhere: in a rice field, or downtown – it makes no difference anymore. The towers no longer stand together; they are spaced so that they don't interact. Density in isolation is the ideal.

6.5 Housing is not a problem. It has either been completely solved or totally left to chance; in the first case it is legal, in the second "illegal;" in the first case, towers or, usually, slabs (at the most, 15 meters deep), in the second (in perfect complementarity) a crust of improvised hovels. One solution consumes the sky, the other the ground. It is strange that those with the least money inhabit the most expensive commodity – earth; those who pay, what is free – air. In either case, housing proves to be surprisingly accommodating – not only does the population double every so many years, but also, with the loosening grip of the various religions, the average number of occupants per unit halves – through divorce and other family-dividing phenomena – with the same frequency that the city's population doubles; as its numbers swell, the Generic City's density is perpetually on the decrease.

6.6 All Generic Cities issue from the tabula rasa; if there was nothing, now they are there; if there was something, they have replaced it. They must, otherwise they would be historic.

6.7 The Generic Cityscape is usually an amalgam of overly ordered sections – dating from near the beginning of its development, when "the power" was still undiluted – and increasingly free arrangements everywhere else.

6.8 The Generic City is the apotheosis of the multiple-choice concept: all boxes crossed, an anthology of all the options. Usually the Generic City has been "planned," not in the usual sense of some bureaucratic organization controlling its development, but as if various echoes, spores, tropes, seeds fell on the ground randomly as in nature, took hold – exploiting the natural fertility of the terrain – and now form an ensemble: an arbitrary gene pool that sometimes produces amazing results.

6.9 The writing of the city may be indecipherable, flawed, but that does not mean that there is no writing; it may simply be that we developed a new illiteracy, a new blindness. Patient detection reveals the themes, particles, strands that can be isolated from the seeming murkiness of this Wagnerian ur-soup: notes left on a blackboard by a visiting genius 50 years ago, stenciled UN reports disintegrating in their Manhattan glass silo, discoveries by former colonial thinkers with a keen eye for the climate, unpredictable ricochets of design education gathering strength as a global laundering process.

6.10 The best definition of the aesthetic of the Generic City is "free style." How to describe it? Imagine an open space, a clearing in the forest, a leveled city. There are three elements: roads, buildings, and nature; they coexist in flexible relationships, seemingly without reason, in spectacular organizational diversity. Any one of the three may dominate: sometimes the "road" is lost – to be found meandering on an incomprehensible detour; sometimes you see no building, only nature; then, equally unpredictably, you are surrounded only by building. In certain frightening spots, all three are simultaneously absent. On these "sites" (actually, what is the opposite of a site? They are like holes bored through the concept of city) public art emerges like the Loch Ness Monster, equal parts figurative and abstract, usually self-cleaning.

6.11 Specific cities still seriously debate the mistakes of architects – for instance, their proposals to create raised pedestrian networks with tentacles leading from one block to the next as a solution to congestion – but the Generic City simply enjoys the benefits of their inventions: decks, bridges, tunnels, motorways – a huge proliferation of the paraphernalia of connection – frequently draped with ferns and flowers as if to ward off original sin, creating a vegetal congestion more severe than a 1950s science-fiction movie.

6.12 The roads are only for cars. People (pedestrians) are led on rides (as in an amusement park), on "promenades" that lift them off the ground, then subject them to a catalog of exaggerated conditions – wind, heat, steepness, cold, interior, exterior, smells, fumes – in a sequence that is a grotesque caricature of life in the historic city.

6.13 There is horizontality in the Generic City, but it is on the way out. It consists either of history that is not yet erased or of Tudor-like enclaves that multiply around the center as newly minted emblems of preservation.

6.14 Ironically, though itself new, the Generic City is encircled by a constellation of New Towns: New Towns are like year-rings. Somehow, New Towns age very quickly, the way a five-year-old child develops wrinkles and arthritis through the disease called progeria.

6.15 The Generic City presents the final death of planning. Why? Not because it is not planned – in fact, huge complementary universes of bureaucrats and developers funnel unimaginable flows of energy and money into its completion; for the same money, its plains can be fertilized by diamonds, its mud fields paved in gold bricks... But its most dangerous and most exhilarating discovery is that planning makes no difference whatsoever. Buildings may be placed well (a tower near a metro station) or badly (whole centers miles away from any road). They flourish/perish unpredictably. Networks become overstretched, age, rot, become obsolescent; populations double, triple, quadruple, suddenly disappear. The surface of the city explodes, the economy accelerates, slows down, bursts, collapses. Like ancient mothers that still nourish titanic embryos, whole cities are built on colonial infrastructures of which the oppressors took the blueprints back home. Nobody knows where, how, since when the sewers run, the exact location of the telephone lines, what the reason was for the position of the center, where monumental axes end. All it proves is that there are infinite hidden margins, colossal reservoirs of slack, a perpetual, organic process of adjustment, standards, behavior; expectations change with the biological intelligence of the most alert animal. In this apotheosis of multiple choice it will never be possible again to reconstruct cause and effect. They work – that is all.

6.16 The Generic City's aspiration toward tropicality automatically implies the rejection of any lingering reference to the city as fortress, as citadel; it is open and accommodating like a mangrove forest.

7. Politics

7.1 The Generic City has a (sometimes distant) relationship with a more or less authoritarian regime – local or national. Usually the cronies of the "leader" – whoever that was – decided to develop a piece of "downtown" or the periphery, or even to start a new city in the middle of nowhere, and so triggered the boom that put the city on the map.

7.2 Very often, the regime has evolved to a surprising degree of invisibility, as if, through its very permissiveness, the Generic City resists the dictatorial.

8. Sociology

8.1 It is very surprising that the triumph of the Generic City has not coincided with the triumph of sociology – a discipline whose "field" has been extended by the Generic City beyond its wildest imagination. The Generic City is sociology, happening. Each Generic City is a petri dish – or an infinitely patient blackboard on which almost any hypothesis can be "proven" and then erased, never again to reverberate in the minds of its authors or its audience.

8.2 Clearly, there is a proliferation of communities – a sociological zapping – that resists a single overriding interpretation. The Generic City is loosening every structure that made anything coalesce in the past.

8.3 While infinitely patient, the Generic City is also persistently resistant to speculation: it proves that sociology may be the worst system to capture sociology in the making. It outwits each established critique. It contributes huge amounts of evidence for and – in even more impressive quantities – against each hypothesis. In A, tower blocks lead to suicide, in B, to happiness ever after. In C they are seen as a first stepping stone toward emancipation (presumably under some kind of invisible "duress," however), in D simply as passé. Constructed in unimaginable numbers in K, they are being exploded in L. Creativity is inexplicably high in E, nonexistent in F. G is a seamless ethnic mosaic, H perpetually at the mercy of separatism, if not on the verge of civil war. Model Y will never last because of its tampering with family structure, but Z flourishes – a word no academic would ever apply to any activity in the Generic City – because of it. Religion is eroded in V, surviving in W, transmuted in X.

8.4 Strangely, nobody has thought that, cumulatively, the endless contradictions of these interpretations prove the richness of the Generic City; that is the one hypothesis that has been eliminated in advance.

9. Quarters

9.1 There is always a quarter called Lipservice, where a minimum of the past is preserved: usually it has an old train/tramway or double-decker bus driving through it, ringing ominous bells – domesticated versions of the Flying Dutchman's phantom vessel. Its phone booths are either red and transplanted from London, or equipped with small Chinese roofs. Lipservice – also called Afterthought, Waterfront, Too Late, 42nd Street, simply the Village, or even Underground – is an elaborate mythic operation: it celebrates the past as only the recently conceived can. It is a machine.

9.2 The Generic City had a past, once. In its drive for prominence, large sections of it somehow disappeared, first unlamented – the past apparently was surprisingly unsanitary, even dangerous – then, without warning, relief turned into regret. Certain prophets – long white hair, gray socks, sandals – had always been warning that the past was necessary – a resource. Slowly, the destruction machine grinds to a halt; some random hovels on the laundered Euclidean plane are saved, restored to a splendor they never had...

9.3 In spite of its absence, history is the major preoccupation, even industry, of the Generic City. On the liberated grounds, around the restored hovels, still more hotels are constructed to receive additional tourists in direct proportion to the erasure of the past. Its disappearance has no influence on their numbers, or maybe it is just a last-minute rush. Tourism is now independent of destination…

9.4 Instead of specific memories, the associations the Generic City mobilizes are general memories, memories of memories: if not all memories at the same time, then at least an abstract, token memory, a déjà vu that never ends, generic memory.

9.5 In spite of its modest physical presence (Lipservice is never more than three stories high: homage to/revenge of Jane Jacobs?) it condenses the entire past in a single complex. History returns not as farce here, but as service: costumed merchants (funny hats, bare midriffs, veils) voluntarily enact the conditions (slavery, tyranny, disease, poverty, colony) – that their nation once went to war to abolish. Like a replicating virus, worldwide, the colonial seems the only inexhaustible source of the authentic.

9.6 42nd Street: ostensibly the places where the past is preserved, they are actually the places where the past has changed the most, is the most distant – as if seen through the wrong end of a telescope – or even completely eliminated.

9.7 Only the memory of former excess is strong enough to charge the bland. As if they try to warm themselves at the heat of an extinguished volcano, the most popular sites (with tourists, and in the Generic City that includes everyone) are the ones once most intensely associated with sex and misconduct. Innocents invade the former haunts of pimps, prostitutes, hustlers, transvestites, and to a lesser degree, artists. Paradoxically, at the same moment that the information highway is about to deliver pornography by the truckload to their living rooms, it is as if the experience of walking on these warmed-over embers of transgression and sin makes them feel special, alive. In an age that does not generate new aura, the value of established aura skyrockets. Is walking on these ashes the nearest they will get to guilt? Existentialism diluted to the intensity of a Perrier?

9.8 Each Generic City has a waterfront, not necessarily with water – it can also be with desert, for instance – but at least an edge where it meets another condition, as if a position of near escape is the best guarantee for its enjoyment. Here tourists congregate in droves around a cluster of stalls. Hordes of "hawkers" try to sell them the "unique" aspects of the city.

The unique parts of all Generic Cities together have created a universal souvenir, scientific cross between Eiffel Tower, Sacre Cœur, and Statue of Liberty: a tall building (usually between 200 and 300 meters) drowned in a small ball of water with snow or, if close to the equator, gold flakes; diaries with pockmarked leather covers; hippie sandals – even if real hippies are quickly repatriated. Tourists fondle these – nobody has ever witnessed a sale – and then sit down in exotic eateries that line the waterfront: they run the full gamut of food today: spicy: first and ultimately maybe most reliable indication of being elsewhere; patty: beef or synthetic; raw: atavistic practice that will be very popular in the third millennium.

9.9 Shrimp is the ultimate appetizer. Through the simplification of the food chain – and the vicissitudes of preparation – they taste like English muffins, i.e. nothingness.

10. Program

10.1 Offices are still there, in ever greater numbers, in fact. People say they are no longer necessary. In five to ten years we will all work at home. But then we will need bigger homes, big enough to use for meetings. Offices will have to be converted to homes.

10.2 The only activity is shopping. But why not consider shopping as temporary, provisional? It awaits better times. It is our own fault – we didn't think of anything better to do. The same spaces inundated with other programs – libraries, baths, universities – would be terrific; we would be awed by their grandeur.

10.3 Hotels are becoming the generic accommodation of the Generic City, its most common building block. That used to be the office – which at least implied a coming and a going, assumed the presence of other important accommodations elsewhere. Hotels are now containers that, in the expansion and completeness of their facilities, make almost all other buildings redundant. Even doubling as shopping malls, they are the closest we have to urban existence, twenty-first-century style.

10.4 The hotel now implies imprisonment, voluntary house arrest; there is no competing place left to go; you come and stay. Cumulatively, it describes a city of ten million all locked in their rooms, a kind of reverse animation – density imploded.

11. Architecture

11.1 Close your eyes and imagine an explosion of beige. At its epicenter splashes the color of vaginal folds (unaroused), metallic-matte aubergine, khakitobacco, dusty pumpkin; all cars on their way to bridal whiteness...

11.2 There are interesting and boring buildings in the Generic City, as in all cities. Both trace their ancestry back to Mies van der Rohe: the first category to his irregular Friedrichstadt tower (1921), the second to the boxes he conceived not long afterward. This sequence is important: obviously, after initial experimentation, Mies made up his mind once and for all against interest, for boredom. At best, his later buildings capture the spirit of the earlier work – sublimated, repressed? – as a more or less noticeable absence, but he never proposed "interesting" projects as possible buildings again. The Generic City proves him wrong: its more daring architects have taken up the challenge Mies abandoned, to the point where it is now hard to find a box. Ironically, this exuberant homage to the interesting Mies shows that "the" Mies was wrong.

11.3 The architecture of the Generic City is by definition beautiful. Built at incredible speed, and conceived at even more incredible pace, there is an average of 27 aborted versions for every realized – but that is not quite the term – structure. They are prepared in the l0,000 architectural offices nobody has ever heard of, each vibrant with fresh inspiration. Presumably more modest than their well-known colleagues, these offices are bonded by a collective awareness that something is wrong with architecture that can only be rectified through their efforts. The power of numbers gives them a splendid, shining arrogance. They are the ones who design without any hesitation. They assemble, from l,00l sources, with savage precision, more riches than any genius ever could. On average, their education has cost 30,000 dollars, excluding travel and housing. 23% have been laundered at American Ivy League universities, where they have been exposed – admittedly for very short periods – to the well-paid elite of the other, "official" profession. It follows that a combined total investment of 300 billion dollars ($300,000,000,000) worth of architectural education ($30,000 [average cost] l00 [average number of workers per office] x l00.000 [number of worldwide offices]) is working in and producing Generic Cities at any moment.

11.4 Buildings that are complex in form depend on the curtain-wall industry, on ever more effective adhesives and sealants that turn each building into a mixture of straitjacket and oxygen tent. The use of silicone – "we are stretching the facade as far as it will go" – has flattened all facades, glued glass to stone to steel to concrete in a space-age impurity. These connections give the appearance of intellectual rigor through the liberal application of a transparent spermy compound that keeps everything together by intention rather than design – a triumph of glue over the integrity of materials. Like everything else in the Generic City, its architecture is the resistant made malleable, an epidemic of yielding no longer through the application of principle but through the systematic application of the unprincipled.

11.5 Because the Generic City is largely Asian, its architecture is generally air-conditioned; this is where the paradox of the recent paradigm shift – the city no longer represents maximum development but borderline underdevelopment – becomes acute: the brutal means by which universal conditioning is achieved mimic inside the building the climatic conditions that once "happened" outside – sudden storms, mini-tornadoes, freezing spells in the cafeteria, heat waves, even mist; a provincialism of the mechanical, deserted by gray matter in pursuit of the electronic. Incompetence or imagination?

11.6 The irony is that in this way the Generic City is at its most subversive, its most ideological; it elevates mediocrity to a higher level; it is like Kurt Schwitter's Merzbau at the scale of the city: the Generic City is a Merzcity.

11.7 The angle of the facades is the only reliable index of architectural genius: 3 points for sloping backward, 12 points for sloping forward, 2 point penalty for setbacks (too nostalgic).

11.8 The apparently solid substance of the Generic City is misleading. Fifty-one percent of its volume consists of atrium. The atrium is a diabolical device in its ability to substantiate the insubstantial. Its Roman name is an eternal guarantor of architectural class – its historic origins make the theme inexhaustible. It accommodates the cave-dweller in its relentless provision of metropolitan comfort.

11.9 The atrium is void space: voids are the essential building block of the Generic City. Paradoxically, its hollowness insures its very physicality, the pumping up of the volume the only pretext for its physical manifestation. The more complete and repetitive its interiors, the less their essential repetition is noticed.

11.10 The style of choice is postmodern, and will always remain so. Postmodernism is the only movement that has succeeded in connecting the practice of architecture with the practice of panic. Postmodernism is not a doctrine based on a highly civilized reading of architectural history but a method, a mutation in professional architecture that produces results fast enough to keep pace with the Generic City's development. Instead of consciousness, as its original inventors may have hoped, it creates a new unconscious. It is modernization's little helper. Anyone can do it – a skyscraper based on the Chinese pagoda and/or a Tuscan hill town.

11.11 All resistance to postmodernism is anti-democratic. It creates a "stealth" wrapping around architecture that makes it irresistible, like a Christmas present from a charity.

11.12 Is there a connection between the predominance of mirror in the Generic City – is it to celebrate nothingness through its multiplication or a desperate effort to capture essences on their way to evaporation? – and the "gifts" that, for centuries, were supposed to be the most popular, efficient present for savages?

11.13 Maxim Gorky speaks in relation to Coney Island of "varied boredom." He clearly intends the term as an oxymoron. Variety cannot be boring. Boredom cannot be varied. But the infinite variety of the Generic City comes close, at least, to making variety normal: banalized, in a reversal of expectation, it is repetition that has become unusual, therefore, potentially, daring, exhilarating. But that is for the twenty-first century.

12. Geography

12.1 The Generic City is in a warmer than usual climate; it is on its way to the south – toward the equator – away from the mess that the north made of the second millennium. It is a concept in a state of migration. Its ultimate destiny is to be tropical – better climate, more beautiful people. It is inhabited by those who do not like it elsewhere.

12.2 In the Generic City, people are not only more beautiful than their peers, they are also reputed to be more even-tempered, less anxious about work, less hostile, more pleasant – proof, in other words, that there is a connection between architecture and behavior, that the city can make better people through as yet unidentified methods.

12.3 One of the most potent characteristics of the Generic City is the stability of its weather – no seasons, outlook sunny – yet all forecasts are presented in terms of imminent change and future deterioration: clouds in Karachi. From the ethical and the religious, the issue of doom has shifted to the inescapable domain of the meteorological. Bad weather is about the only anxiety that hovers over the Generic City.

13. Identity

13.1 There is a calculated (?) redundancy in the iconography that the Generic City adopts. If it is water-facing, then water-based symbols are distributed over its entire territory. If it is a port, then ships and cranes will appear far inland. (However, showing the containers themselves would make no sense: you can't particularize the generic through the Generic.) If it is Asian, then "delicate" (sensual, inscrutable) women appear in elastic poses, suggesting (religious, sexual) submission everywhere. If it has a mountain, each brochure, menu, ticket, billboard will insist on the hill, as if nothing less than a seamless tautology will convince. Its identity is like a mantra.

14. History

14.1 Regret about history's absence is a tiresome reflex. It exposes an unspoken consensus that history's presence is desirable. But who says that is the case? A city is a plane inhabited in the most efficient way by people and processes, and in most cases, the presence of history only drags down its performance...

14.2 History present obstructs the pure exploitation of its theoretical value as absence.

14.3 Throughout the history of humankind – to start a paragraph the American way – cities have grown through a process of consolidation. Changes are made on the spot. Things are improved. Cultures flourish, decay, revive, disappear, are sacked, invaded, humiliated, raped, triumph, are reborn, have golden ages, fall suddenly silent – all on the same site. That is why archaeology is a profession of digging; it exposes layer after layer of civilization (i.e. city). The Generic City, like a sketch which is never elaborated, is not improved but abandoned. The idea of layering, intensification, completion are alien to it: it has no layers. Its next layer takes place somewhere else, either next door – that can be the size of a country – or even elsewhere altogether. The archaeologue (=archaeology with more interpretation) of the twentieth century needs unlimited plane tickets, not a shovel.

14.4 In exporting/ejecting its improvements, the Generic City perpetuates its own amnesia (its only link with eternity?). Its archaeology will therefore be the evidence of its progressive forgetting, the documentation of its evaporation. Its genius will be empty-handed – not an emperor without clothes but an archaeologist without finds, or a site even.

15. Infrastructure

15.1 Infrastructures, which were mutually reinforcing and totalizing, are becoming more and more competitive and local; they no longer pretend to create functioning wholes but now spin off functional entities. Instead of network and organism, the new infrastructure creates enclave and impasse: no longer the grand récit but the parasitic swerve. (The city of Bangkok has approved plans for three competing airborne metro systems to get from A to B – may the strongest one win.)

15.2 Infrastructure is no longer a more or less delayed response to a more or less urgent need but a strategic weapon, a prediction: Harbor X is not enlarged to serve a hinterland of frantic consumers but to kill/reduce the chances that harbor Y will survive the twenty-first century. On a single island, southern metropolis Z, still in its infancy, is "given" a new subway system to make established metropolis W in the north look clumsy, congested, and ancient. Life in V is smoothed to make life in U eventually unbearable.

16. Culture

16.1 Only the redundant counts.

16.2 In each time zone, there are at least three performances of Cats. The world is surrounded by a Saturn's ring of meowing.

16.3 The city used to be the great sexual hunting ground. The Generic City is like a dating agency: it efficiently matches supply and demand. Orgasm instead of agony: there is progress. The most obscene possibilities are announced in the cleanest typography; Helvetica has become pornographic.

17. End

17.1 Imagine a Hollywood movie about the Bible. A city somewhere in the Holy Land. Market scene: from left and right extras cloaked in colorful rags, furs, silken robes walk into the frame yelling, gesticulating, rolling their eyes, starting fights, laughing, scratching their beards, hairpieces dripping with glue, thronging toward the center of the image waving sticks, fists, overturning stalls, trampling animals ... People shout. Selling wares? Proclaiming futures? Invoking Gods? Purses are snatched, criminals pursued (or is it helped?) by the crowds. Priests pray for calm. Children run amok in an undergrowth of legs and robes. Animals bark. Statues topple. Women shriek – threatened? Ecstatic? The churning mass becomes oceanic. Waves break. Now switch off the sound –

silence, a welcome relief – and reverse the film. The now mute but still visibly agitated men and women stumble backward; the viewer no longer registers only humans but begins to note spaces between them. The center empties, the last shadows evacuate the rectangle of the picture frame, probably complaining, but fortunately we don't hear them. Silence is now reinforced by emptiness: the image shows empty stalls, some debris that was trampled underfoot. Relief… it's over. That is the story of the city. The city is no longer. We can leave the theater now…

Manuel de Landa

Meshworks, Hierarchies, and Interfaces

The world of interface design is undergoing dramatic changes that promise to rival those brought about by the use of the point-and-click graphical interfaces popularized by the Macintosh in the early 1980s. The new concepts and metaphors that are aiming to replace the familiar desktop metaphor all revolve around the notion of semiautonomous, semi-intelligent software agents. To be sure, different researchers and commercial companies have divergent conceptions of what these agents should be capable of, and how they should interact with computer users. But whether one aims to give these software creatures the ability to learn about the user's habits, as in the noncommercial research performed at MIT autonomous agents group, or to endow them with the ability to perform transactions in the user's name, as in the commercial products pioneered by General Magic, the basic thrust seems to be in the direction of giving software programs more autonomy in their decision-making capabilities.

For a philosopher there are several interesting issues involved in this new interface paradigm. The first one has to do with the history of the software infrastructure that has made this proliferation of agents possible. From the point of view of the conceptual history of software, the creation of worlds populated by semiautonomous virtual creatures, as well as the more familiar world of mice, windows, and pulldown menus, has been made possible by certain advances in programming language design. Specifically, programming languages needed to be transformed from their historically rigid hierarchies to the more flexible and decentralized structures that they have gradually adopted as they have become more "object-oriented." One useful way to picture this transformation is as a migration of control from a master program (which contains the general task to be performed) to the software modules that perform all of the individual tasks. Indeed, to grasp just what is at stake in this dispersal of control, I find it useful to view this change as a part of a larger migration of control from the human body first to the hardware of the machine, then to the software, then to the data, and finally to the world outside the machine.

The first part of this migration, when control of machine-aided processes moved from the human body to hardware, may be said to have taken place in the eighteenth century when a series of inventors and builders of automata created the elements that later came together in the loom invented by Joseph Marie Jacquard, a machine that automated some of the tasks involved in weaving patterns in textiles. The Jacquard loom used a primitive form of software in which holes punched into cards were coded to some of the operations in the creation of patterned designs.[1] This software, however, contained only data and not control structures. In other words, all that was coded in the punched cards was the patterns to be weaved and not any directions to alter the reading of the cards or the performance of the operations, such as the lifting of the warp threads. The machine's hardware component "read" the cards and translated the data into the motion in which control of the process resided. Textile workers at the time were fully aware that they had lost some control to Jacquard's loom, and, on several occasions, they manifested their outrage by destroying the machines.

Though the idea of coding data into punched cards spread slowly during the 1800s, by the beginning of the twentieth century it had found its way into computing machinery, first in the tabulators used by Herman Hollerith to process the 1890

1. A. P. Usher, "The Textile Industry, 1750-1830," in *Technology in Western Civilization, vol. 1*, eds. M. Kranzberg and C. W. Pursell, Oxford University Press, New York, 1967, p. 243.

United States census, then into other tabulators and calculators. In all these cases control remained in the machine's hardware. Even the first modern computer, the imaginary computer created by Alan Turing in the 1930s, still kept control in the hardware, the scanning head of the Turing machine: the tape that his fictional machine scanned held nothing but data. But this abstract computer already had the seed of the next step, since, as Turing himself understood, the actions of the scanning head could themselves be represented by a table of behavior, and the table itself could be coded into the tape. Although people may not have realized it at the time, the coding of both numbers and operations in side by side digits on tape was the beginning of computer software as we know it.[2] In the 1950s, Turing created the notion of a subroutine, that is, the notion that the tasks that a computer must perform could be embodied in separate subprograms all controlled by a master program residing on tape. With this, the migration of control from hardware to software became fully realized, and from then on computer hardware became an abstract mesh of logical gates, its operations fully controlled by software.

The next step in this migration took place when control of a given computational process moved from the software to the very data that the software operates on. For as long as computer languages such as Fortran or Pascal dominated the computer industry, control remained hierarchically embedded in the software. A master program would surrender control to a subroutine whenever that subtask needed to be performed, and the subroutine could itself then pass control to an even more basic subroutine. But the moment the specific task was completed, control would revert back up the hierarchy until it reached the master program again. Although this arrangement remained satisfactory for many years – and indeed many computer programs are still written that way – more flexible schemes were needed for some specific, and at the time, esoteric applications of computers, mostly in the field of artificial intelligence.

Trying to build a robot using a hierarchy of subroutines meant that researchers had to completely foresee all the tasks that a robot would need to do and then centralize all decision-making into a master program. But this, of course, would strongly limit the responsiveness of the robot to events occurring in its surroundings, particularly if those events diverged from the predictions made by the programmers. One solution to this was to decentralize control. The basic tasks that a robot

2. A. Hodges, *Alan Turing: The Enigma*, Simon & Schuster, New York, 1983, ch. 2.

had to perform were still coded into programs, but unlike subroutines these programs were not commanded into action by a master program. Instead, these programs were given some autonomy and the ability to scan the database on their own. Whenever they found a specific pattern in the data, they would perform whatever task they were supposed to do. In a very real sense, it was now the data itself that controlled the process. And, more importantly, if the database was connected to the outside world via sensors so that patterns of data reflected events outside the robot, then the world itself was controlling the computational process, and it was this that gave the robot a degree of responsiveness to its surroundings.

Thus, machines went from being hardware-driven to being software-driven, data-driven, and finally event-driven. The typical Macintosh computer is indeed an event-driven machine even if the class of real-world events that it is responsive to is very limited, including only events happening to the mouse (such as position changes and clickings) as well as to other input devices. But regardless of the narrow class of events that personal computers are responsive to, it is in these events that much of the control of the processes now resides. Hence, behind the innovative use of windows, icons, menus, and the other familiar elements of graphical interfaces, there is a deep conceptual shift in the location of control embodied in object-oriented languages. Even the new interface designs based on semiautonomous agents were made possible by this decentralization of control. Indeed, simplifying a little, we may say that the new worlds of agents, whether those that inhabit computer screens or, more generally, those that inhabit any kind of virtual environment (such as those used in artificial life), have been the result of pushing the trend away from software command hierarchies ever further.

The distinction between centralized and decentralized control of given processes has come to occupy center stage in many different contemporary philosophies. Economist and artificial intelligence guru Herbert Simon views bureaucracies and markets as the human institutions that best embody these two conceptions of control.[3] Hierarchical institutions are the easiest ones to analyze, since much of what happens within a bureaucracy is planned by someone of higher rank, and the hierarchy as a whole has goals and behaves in ways that are consistent with those goals. Markets, on the other hand, are tricky. Indeed, the term "market" needs to be used with care because it has been greatly abused over the last century by

3. H. Simon, *The Sciences of the Artificial*, The MIT Press, Cambridge, Mass., 1994, p. 43.

theorists on both the left and the right. As Simon remarks, the term does not refer to the world of corporations, whether monopolies or oligopolies, since in these commercial institutions, decision-making is highly centralized and prices are set by command.

Indeed the sense of the term can be limited even more to refer exclusively to those gatherings of people at a predefined place in town, and not to a dispersed set of consumers catered to by a system of middlemen (as when one speaks of the "market" for personal computers). The reason for this is that, as historian Fernand Braudel has made clear, it is only in markets in this true sense that we have any idea of what the dynamics of price formation are. In other words, it is only in peasant and small town markets that decentralized decision-making leads to prices setting themselves up in a way that we can understand. In any other type of market, economists simply assume that supply and demand connect to each other in a functional way, but they do not give us any specific dynamics through which this connection is effected.[4] Moreover, unlike the idealized version of markets guided by an "invisible hand" to achieve an optimal allocation of resources, real markets are not in any sense optimal. Indeed, like most decentralized, self-organized structures, they are not hierarchical, they have no goals, and they grow and develop mostly by drift.[5]

Herbert Simon's distinction between command hierarchies and markets may turn out to be a special case of a more general dichotomy. In the view of philosophers Gilles Deleuze and

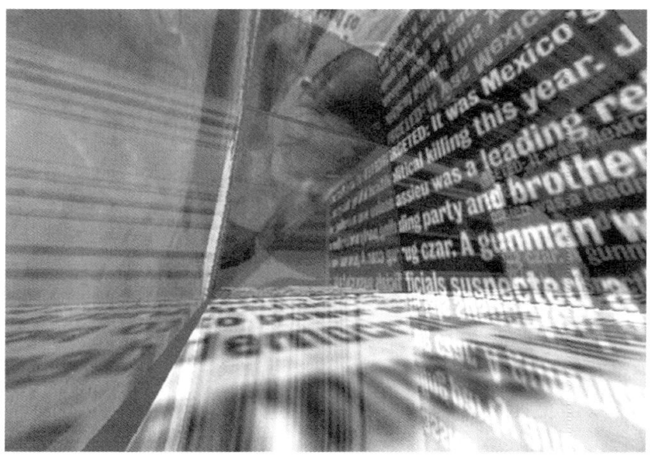

Fig. 1
ENIAC Computer Photograph courtesy University of Pennsylvania, School of Engineering and Applied Science

4. F. Braudel, *The Weels of Commerce*, Harper & Row, New York, 1986, ch. 1.

5. H. R. Maturana and F. J. Varela, *The Tree of Knowledge: The Biological Roots of Human Understanding*, Shambhala, Boston, 1992, pp. 47, 115.

Félix Guattari, more abstract classes, which they call strata and self-consistent aggregates (or trees and rhizomes), are defined not so much by the locus of control as by the nature of elements that are connected together. Strata are composed of homogenous elements, whereas self-consistent aggregates articulate heterogeneous elements.[6] For example, a military hierarchy sorts people into internally homogenous ranks before joining them together through a chain of command. Markets, on the other hand, allow for a set of heterogeneous needs and offers to be articulated through the price mechanism without reducing diversity. In biology, species are an example of strata, particularly if selection pressures have operated unobstructed for long periods of time, allowing the homogenization of the species' gene pool.

On the other hand, ecosystems are examples of self-consistent aggregates, since they link together into complex food webs a wide variety of animals and plants, without reducing their heterogeneity. I have developed this theory in more detail elsewhere, but for our purposes here let's simply keep the idea that besides centralization and decentralization of control, what defines these two types of structure is the homogeneity or heterogeneity of their composing elements.

As both Simon and Deleuze and Guattari emphasize, the dichotomy between bureaucracies and markets, between hierarchies and meshworks, should be understood in purely relative terms. In the first place, in reality it is hard to find pure cases of these two structures: even the most goal-oriented organization will still show some drift in its growth and development, and most markets, even in small towns, contain some hierarchical elements, even if this is just a local wholesaler who manipulates prices by dumping (or withdrawing) large amounts of a product on (or from) the market. Moreover, hierarchies give rise to meshworks and meshworks to hierarchies. Thus, when several bureaucracies coexist (governmental, academic, ecclesiastic) in the absence of a superhierarchy to coordinate their interactions, the whole set of institutions will tend to form a meshwork of hierarchies, articulated mostly through local and temporary links. Similarly, as local markets grow in size, as in those gigantic fairs that have taken place periodically since the Middle Ages, they give rise to commercial hierarchies, with a money market on top, a luxury goods market beneath and, after several layers, a grain market at the bottom. A real society, then, is made of complex and changing mixtures of these two types of structure, and only

6. G. Deleuze and F. Guattari, *A Thousand Plateaus*, University of Minnesota Press, Minneapolis, 1987, p. 335.

in a few cases will it be easy to decide to what type a given institution belongs.

A similar point may be made about the worlds inhabited by software agents. The Internet, to take the clearest example first, is a meshwork that grew mostly by drift. No one planned either the extent or the direction of its development, and indeed, no one is in charge of it even today. The Internet, or rather its predecessor, the Arpanet, acquired its decentralized structure because of the needs of the U.S. military for a command and communications infrastructure that would be capable of surviving a nuclear attack. As analysts from the Rand Corporation made clear, only if the routing of the messages was performed without the need for a central computer, could bottlenecks and delays be avoided, and, more importantly, could the meshwork put itself back together once a portion of it had been vaporized in a nuclear attack. But on the Internet only the decision-making behind routing is of the meshwork type. Decision-making regarding its two main resources, computer (or CPU) time and memory, is still hierarchical.

Schemes to decentralize these aspects do exist, as in Drexler's Agoric Systems, where the messages that flow through the meshwork have become autonomous agents capable of trading among themselves both memory and CPU time.[7] The creation by General Magic of its Teletext operating system, and of agents able to perform transactions on behalf of users, is one of the first real-life steps in the direction of a true decentralization of resources. But in the meanwhile, the Internet will remain a hybrid of meshwork and hierarchy components, and the imminent entry of large corporations into the network business may in fact increase the number of command components in its mix.

These ideas are today being hotly debated in the field of interface design. The general consensus is that interfaces must become more intelligent to be able to guide users in the tapping of computer resources; both the informational wealth of the Internet and ever more elaborate software applications. But if the debaters agree that interfaces must become smarter, and even that this intelligence will be embodied in agents, they disagree on how the agents should acquire their new capabilities. The debate pits two different traditions of artificial intelligence (AI) against each other: symbolic AI, in which hierarchical components predominate, against behavioral AI, where the meshwork elements are dominant. Basically, while in the former discipline one attempts to endow machines with intelli-

7. M. S. Miller and K. E. Drexler, "Markets and Computation: Agoric Open Systems," in *The Ecology of Comptation*, ed. B. Hubermann, Amsterdam, North Holland, 1988.

gence by depositing a homogenous set of rules and symbols into a robot's brain, in the latter one attempts to achieve intelligent behaviour from the interactions of a few simple task-specific modules in the robot's head and the heterogeneous affordances of its environment. Thus, to build a robot that walks around a room, the first approach would give the robot a map of the room together with the ability to reason about possible walking scenarios in that model of the room. The second approach, on the other hand, endows the robot with a much simpler set of abilities, embodied in modules that perform simple tasks – such as collision-avoidance – and walking-around-the-room behavior emerges from the interactions of these modules and the obstacles and openings that the real room affords the robot as it moves.[8]

Translated to the case of interface agents, for example a personal assistant in charge of helping a user understand the complexities of a particular software application, a symbolic AI program would attempt to create a model of the application as well as a model of the working environment, including a model of an idealized user, and then make these models available in the form of rules or other symbols to the agent. Behavioral AI, on the other hand, gives the agent only the ability to detect patterns of behavior in the actual user, and to interact with the user in different ways so as to learn not only from his or her actual behavior, but also from feedback that the user gives it. For example, the agent in question would be constantly looking over the user's shoulder, keeping track of whatever regular or repetitive patterns it observes. It would then attempt to establish statistical correlations between pairs of actions that tend to occur together. At some point the agent would suggest to the user the possibility of automating these actions; that is, that whenever the first occurs, the second should be automatically performed. Whether the user accepts or refuses, this gives feedback to the agent. The agent may also solicit feedback directly, and the user may teach the agent by giving some hypothetical examples.[9]

In terms of the location of control, there is very little difference between the agents, and in this sense the two approaches are equally decentralized. The rules that symbolic AI would put in the agent's head, most likely derived from interviews of users and programmers by a "knowledge engineer," are independent software objects. Indeed, in one of the most widely used programming languages in this kind of approach (called a "production system") the individual rules have even more of a

8. P. Maes, "Behavior-Based Artificial Intelligence," in J.-A. Meyer, H. L. Roitblat, and S. Wilson, *From Animals to Animats,* vol. 2, The MIT Press, Cambridge, Mass., 1993, pp. 459-465.

9. P. Maes and R. Kozierok, "Learning Interface Agents," in *Proceedings of AAAI '93 Conference*, AAAI Press, Seattle, 1993, pp. 459-465.

meshwork structure than many object-oriented systems that still cling to a hierarchy of objects. But in terms of the overall human-machine system, the approach of symbolic AI is much more hierarchical. In particular, by assuming the existence of an ideal user, with homogenous and unchanging habits, and of a workplace where all users are similar, agents created by this approach are not only less adaptive and more commanding, but they themselves promote homogeneity in their environment. The second class of agents, on the other hand, are not only sensitive to heterogeneities, since they adapt to individual users and change as the habits of their users change, but they promote heterogeneity in the work place by not subordinating every user to the demands of an idealized model.

One drawback to the approach of behavioral AI is that, given that the agent has very little knowledge at the beginning of a relationship with a user, it will be of little assistance until it learns about his or her habits. Also, since the agent can only learn about situations that have occurred in the past, it will be of little help when the user encounters new problems. One possible solution, is to increase the amount of meshwork in the mix and allow agents from different users to interact with each other in a decentralized way.[10] Thus, when a new agent begins a relation with a user, it can consult with other agents and speed up the learning process, assuming that is, that what other agents have learned is applicable to the new user. This, of course, will depend on the existence of some homogeneity of habits, but at least it does not assume a completely homogenous situation from the outset, an assumption that in turn promotes further uniformity. Moreover, endowing agents with a static model of the users makes them unable to cope with novel situations. This is also a problem in the behavioral AI approach, but in this model agents may aid one another in coping with novelty. Knowledge gained in one part of the workplace can be shared, and new knowledge may be generated out of the interactions among agents. In effect, a dynamic model of the workplace would be constantly generated and improved by the collective of agents in a decentralized way, instead of each one being a replica of each other, and operating on the basis of a static, centrally created, model.

The degree of hierarchical and homogenizing components in a given interface is a question that affects more than just events taking place on the computer's screen. In particular, the very structure of the workplace and the relative status of humans and machines are at stake. Western societies have

10. Y. Lashari, M. Metral, and P. Maes, "Collaborative Interface Agents," in *Proceedings of 12th National Conference on AI*, AAAI Press, Seattle, 1994, pp. 444-449.

undergone at least two centuries of homogenization, of which the most visible elements are the assembly-line and related mass production techniques whose overall thrust has been to let machines discipline and control humans. In this circumstance, the arrival of the personal computer was a welcome antidote to the development of increasingly more centralized computer machinery, such as systems of numerical control in factories. But this is hardly a victory. After two hundred years of constant homogenization, working skills have been homogenized via routinization and Taylorization, building materials have been given constant properties, the gene pools of our domestic species homogenized through breeding, and our languages made uniform through standardization.

The solution to this is not simply to begin adding meshwork components to the mix. Indeed, one must resist the temptation to make hierarchies into villains and meshworks into heroes. This is because they are constantly turning into one another, because in real life we find only mixtures and hybrids, and the properties of these cannot be established through theory alone but demand concrete experimentation. Certain standardizations – say, of electric outlet designs or of data-structures traveling through the Internet – may actually turn out to promote heterogenization, in terms of the appliances that may be designed around the standard outlet, or of the services that a common data structure may make possible. On the other hand, the mere presence of increased heterogeneity is no guarantee that a better state for society has been achieved. After all, the territory occupied by former Yugoslavia is more heterogeneous now than it was ten years ago, but the lack of uniformity at one level simply hides an increase of homogeneity at the level of the warring ethnic communities. But even if we managed to promote not only heterogeneity, but diversity articulated into a meshwork, that still would not be a perfect solution. After all, meshworks grow by drift and they may drift to places where we do not want to go. The goal-directedness of hierarchies is the kind of property that we may desire to keep at least for certain institutions. Hence, demonizing centralization and glorifying decentralization as the solution to all our problems would be wrong. An open and experimental attitude toward the question of different hybrids and mixtures is what the complexity of reality itself seems to call for. To paraphrase Deleuze and Guattari, never believe that a meshwork will suffice to save us.[11]

11. G. Deleuze and F. Guattari, *A Thousand Plateaus, 500*. Their remark is framed in terms of "smooth spaces" but it may be argued that this is just another term for meshworks.

Lars Bang Larsen

The Urban Plan and Kanonklubben's Garden

In his essay "An Esthetics of Disappointment" from 1966, Robert Smithson criticizes the blind continuation of the "art habit." This compulsion to continue business as usual, according to Smithson, a longing for the fullness of traditional aesthetics, is a desperate nostalgia for purity, and other "rare types of stupidity" which manifest themselves in the art world, "which is no world." He concludes: "A sweet nihilism is everywhere. Immobility and inertia are what many of the most gifted artists prefer. Vacant at the center, dull at the edge, a few artists are on the true path of stultification. Muddle-headed logic is taking the place of clear-headed illogic, much to nobody's surprise."[1]

Smithson's disenchantment with the art world was probably part of his motivation for attempting to break with the architectural confines of the gallery space and establish the dialectic of site and non-site as an artistic dynamic in "Earth Art" or "Land Art." "What is needed," he wrote in 1967, "is

1. In: Robert Smithson, *The Collected Writings*, ed. Jack Flam, The University of California Press, Berkeley and Los Angeles 1996, pp. 334-335.

an aesthetic method that brings together anthropology and linguistics in terms of "buildings." This would put an end to "art history" as sole criterion. Art at the present is confined by a dated notion, namely "art as a criticism of earlier art." Now, this essay may in a sense fall into the trap of the traditional confines of "art history."[2] This, however, is somewhat ironic, because what I will try to do here is to discuss a more than 30 year old Danish activist art project in the perspective of the art historical configuration Land Art, with Robert Smithson as this movement's arguably most salient figure. The fact that this contextualization takes place in the context of Olafur's catalogue should naturally also be considered. The sign of a great deal of today's art is that it craves as reference points, those types of "perforated" aesthetics with an emphatically public dimension. A welcome deconstruction of traditional "art history," of course, but one that in turn needs to allow for its own genuine perforation by other codes and economies than those of the art industry, which – still afraid to disappoint – so easily lend themselves to attitudes of closure. So this is an attempt to expand the local story of a garden which was established in 1969 from within the language of art, with the ambition to confront the limits of this language.

On November 26, 1968, a group of students from the department-schools of painting, mural and sculpture at the Royal Danish Art Academy in Copenhagen decided to form their own department within the Academy. Ole Sporring, Mogens Nørgård, Lene Adler Petersen, Susanne Hartig, Alfred Friis, Niels N. Pedersen, Per Ehrenberg, Søren Keil, Jørgen Holbæk, Lise Kragh, Birgit Diemer, Emma L. Nielsen, Carsten Nash, and Finn Thybo Andersen wished to create an alternative to the Academy's existing schools. Their charter stated – in a showdown with academism and the myth of the genius – and as an argument for work modes where art, politics and everyday life are allowed to interact:

Where the existing schools are based on individual production of "works" in silence and concentration in closed departments, where the students are often placed in discordance with their own wishes, we wish to create a department that is open for all, that is founded on a community of interest, and where the main stress will be on group activity.

We wish to engage in an art form which to a higher degree is determined by situations, to constitute a frame so flexible as to allow as many activities as possible to emanate from

2. Ibid., p. 59.

the group, to create a domicile at the Academy for ideas and debate.

For the time being we conceive of the work form organized thus:

Group meeting three times a week where active groups present a report, new activities are decided upon and if desired realized, and tasks are distributed. Apart from that, groups working on tasks hold meetings on their own.

Pupils from the existing schools who will participate in the new department, wish to continue to be able to utilize the original schools.

We request that the Academy acknowledge our department on the same footing as the other departments, that it apportions us a space with access to a telephone, as well as representation.

Moreover, we would like to remind you that the department is open for all – including professors and teachers!

This was the charter of what later that year would take the name of Kanonklubben, "The Canon Club" so dubbed after the collective acquisition of a Super 8 Canon camera, which would serve as the co-ordinating eye and registrar of the activities of the loosely knit association. During its existence from fall 1968 till spring 1970, when the group was torn apart by internal strife, Kanonklubben accomplished two major projects, other than general Super 8 activity, namely, the garden project at Amager in Copenhagen and the feminist exhibition festival Damebilleder ("Ladies' Images"); one of the first manifestations of feminist art in Europe.

By spring 1970, the municipality of Copenhagen, under the Social Democratic mayor Urban Hansen, finished the construction of Peder Lykke Centeret at Amager. A typical late 1960s housing solution in concrete modules. "Urban Planen" to this day consists of a day treatment center, an old people's home and special dwellings. Architect Ole Haslund, in autumn 1969, asked Professor Dan Steerup-Hansen at the Royal Danish Art Academy to have his pupils participate in a painting exhibition for the institution's inauguration. At the time, the home's garden was under construction – the architect's average flower basins and flagstones-in-patterns thing – and Kanonklubben's members became gripped by the idea of taking over the construction of the garden; a 1600 square metre courtyard, surrounded on all sides by the three story high building. Kanonklubben managed to overrule the architects in charge with a new proposal where experiences from environmental studies would be used as a collaborative starting point for Kanonklubben's membership of students of architecture and art painting. For the planning and building of the garden, Kanonklubben was further supplemented by squatters and artists' colleagues, and consisted for this event – apart from most of its founding members – of Henrik Andersen, Marie Bille, Kirsten Dufour, Bodil Salskov Iversen, Per Johnson, Kirsten Justesen, Oluf Lehnsted, Ingvar Lønsted, Ulrik Neuhaus, Jytte Rex, Birgitte Skjold-Jensen, Sten Bille, and Helle Zacho. In a political appeal, Kanonklubben managed to make the construction workers working on Urban Planen refrain from their piece-rates, and contribute their work force to the rough trade part of the construction (though in the nick of time a grant of DKK 25,000 came in from the Carlsberg Foundation as financial support for wages for everybody involved). A few Kanonklubben members volunteered to work in Copenhagen senior citizen homes in order to research what kind of facilities would accommodate the future residents' aesthetic demands.

"Then a rare – and therefore doubly positive – collaboration developed," reports *Alt for Damerne* - a housewifely Danish equivalent to *Cosmopolitan* – in an exuberant photo feature of the garden from August 1973. "The residents met with young students from the Academy's Garden Department [sic]. And they talked – about birds whistling and the splashing of water, about pavilions in the shade and the urge to watch the flowers grow. In short – about well being and lushness in the garden. The result (...) also shows how the exercise facilities demanded by the care assistants have been incorporated in the most charming manner. It goes uphill by the small lake as well as at the rockery. Good, when you need to learn how to get those legs going again! And there are the silent spots where you can take a rest and listen to and watch the birds. Out of consideration for the wheelchairs, all the pathways are asphalt coated, and the flower beds are usually placed so high as to be within reach for those residents in wheelchairs who wish to sow."

Apart from the taller trees and the bed of roses in the northeast corner – which died at some point but will be replaced presently – the garden still stands today as it did in 1970. However, also Kirsten Dufour's birdbath in concrete and embellished with broken pottery found during digging in the garden and executed in collaboration with residents, is just a melancholic reflection of its former splendor. The garden, still used by residents from all Urban Planen for barbecues and gatherings, is a hilly and bushy landscape, an elementarily inviting site in the midst of an otherwise regulated environment. Even at the time of writing – cold and snowy March – it is obvious how trees and bushes have been chosen to perform a constant botanical variety throughout the year.

The garden was developed in the course of March and April 1970 in the style of a national romantic garden. The pavilion, the rambling roses, the duck's island in the pond, the orchard etc. were a tribute to the elements of the traditional allotment gardens which were razed to the ground during autumn 1969 to clear space for the Urban Plan. It speaks directly to the project's conceptual impulse that Kanonklubben documented the buildings of the allotment gardens before they were removed, as a soon-to-be erased vision of the new garden. Entropy as a determined part of the process of urbanization, rather than as an event in a geological perspective.

Allotment gardens was working class culture's Northern European response to industrialization's pernicious effects on the urban fabric. However modestly sized, the allotment gardens allowed the working class family access to a piece of land which they could cultivate and hence escape the densely populated city centres – even if only in a limited physical and geographical sense. If the garden originally embodied the desire to represent nature in the urban context; and if the allotment garden represents the meeting of nature, urbanity and industrialization, then Kanonklubben's intervention on the two sites on Amager describes the desire to project the image of the traditional Danish garden onto the supposedly unsusceptible, or hostile context of the Urban Plan.

The whole construction process from autumn to spring was recorded by Kanonklubben's Super 8 camera. The soundless color footage establishes a narrative reminiscent of Land Art's dialectic of boundlessness and containment, as displaced to the local problems of a new urbanity. The footage shows how Kanonklubben's members roam about and empty the doomed allotment gardens of their plants (which would be stored away for the wintertime, to be used in the spring), while their kids trash the already decrepit sheds. This wasn't a question about the transferal of material between site and non-site; both sites were, in terms of institutional logic, sites or "the outside world." In this sense the garden project can be viewed as an activist radicalization of Land Art: it didn't refer to a non-site or "abstract container," as Smithson dubbed the gallery space, but was established between the co-ordinates of two everyday spaces with everyday functions. Today, it is difficult to imagine the same artistic dialectic resonate dramatically between site and non-site as it did with Smithson, because the "raw reality" of the site has been in the catalogue of artistic materials for quite a while now, and because objectivity and disinterestedness are hardly projected onto the gallery space to the same degree as implied in Smithson's dichotomy.

The garden project was invested with the rhetoric and gusto of political pathos – in the words of Kirsten Justesen's handwritten working paper, the "Garden Manifesto:" "To elevate a piece of land exhausted by Urban Hansen and covered by his garden architect (the city head gardener) to an organism (society) with optimal functions. Through active physical work to demonstrate an alternative to social work and thereby disclose the established power structure's insufficiency in its most fundamental functions, as well as clarifying a fundamental vision for the social workers' experience retrieval." Through Kanonklubben's collaborative work, the garden at Peder Lykke Centret was initiated as site; not through artistic initiation in the Duchampian sense or direct institutional demand, but through a dialogical form of collaboration, demonstrating that practice and patronage aren't separate activities. This is a thirty year old – and still standing – instance of what through the 1990s has been erupting as inter-disciplinarity and social sculpture in the context of exhibition making, realized as a challenge to the conventional categories of authorship and art work. Kanonklubben's garden is a weird example of the wedding of avant-garde art practice and the popular conception of what aesthetic enjoyment implicates. Here, the collectivist left wing politics of the counter-cultural revolution met the (petty) bourgeois fantasy of the Danish country garden.

The garden project was the expression of the desire to frame, analyze, and restructure a particular location, an artistic inquiry expanded to include the viewer's, or user's, social and physical location. Not unlike the culinary communion of Gordon Matta-Clark's restaurant *Food*, which he started in 1971 together with a group of fellow artists and food enthusiasts, with which he hoped to "complete still another phase of social development and resolve the malaise du siècle;" and Matta-Clarks notion of anarchitecture, not least, in its understanding of undeveloped places and metaphoric voids as alternatives to what is normally considered architecture. The garden project was an employment of artistic resources without the ego charge of signature, realized as a gesture towards the people who would be using it.

"Flowers have no power," Herbert Marcuse dryly remarked in 1967, "other than the power of the men and women who let them grow and protect them." Which may turn out to be no insignificant power form. But still – however nice a spot it turned out to be for the residents – on the level of artistic influence, one can't help to think that the garden project didn't really detonate. However resolved, it was as an isolated function it never became a discussion or a reference point for the artists of that generation, or for future ones. Obviously, Kanonklubben never established the site/non-site dialectic in an institutional or linguistic sense. The group employed the syntax of the sites involved not as a visual language of different modules, but rather as material for a political sculpture set to function in a limited, concrete situation. Smithson, on the other hand, insisted on the linguistic nature of his landscape interventions, on the abstract dramas of non-specificity, crystalline time, and a dialectics of entropic change. Still, it could be argued that Smithson's in every sense groundbreaking work has more in common with the garden project than merely the "aesthetic potential of the boring." (To Smithson the "boring," as a discrete step in the development of the whole site, was "...pavements, holes, trenches, mounds, heaps, paths, ditches, roads, terraces, etc)." But at the end of the day it remains that Kanonklubben on a crucial level let down their own project by focusing the economy of its artistic aspect on the garden's functionality for the bodies that would occupy it. Kanonklubben interpreted reality as a superstructure, and confronted it that way. Physical and traditional sculptural awareness persisted in the garden project, but no linguistic awareness. It can be argued that Kanonklubben's response to the matrix of the Urban Plan was just as rationalistic as the Urban Plan itself, in that Kanonklubben didn't articulate the activist project beyond the politically illustrative and physically functional – that is, beyond the purely exemplary. Even though the garden can be said to have such potential, by dint of its multilayered aesthetics and ramified provenience.

The garden project employed a relativist understanding of the art institution to discuss its location in culture. A location which is neither wholly modern nor postmodern, but – performatively, at least – fuses the idealism of modernity with the radical dialectics of post-modernity. By spring 1970, Kanonklubben had split up into new fractions and groups with more political slants. Some took up squatting, and the rest drifted towards the production and painter's collective Østen er rød (The East is Red), the ragpicker group Tøj til Afrika (Clothes for Africa), and feminist art groups. But for a short while, it seemed that art, everyday life and politics held each other in a productive balance that could have been further developed as a discussion of the foundations of art, and societal agency in general. Maybe what the "failure" of the garden project can help us question, above all, is our desire for art as a category, and for art history as a resource for conveying authority to events in life.

Dennis Oppenheim gets the last word, an appropriately Utopian critique of the art system he delivered at the "Earth" symposium at White Museum, Cornell University, 1969:

"I don't know if any of the artists here are after pure breakdown of some feeble limits. I don't think that is their impetus. But I would like someday to see an art so closely knit with a societal framework that there is no concern with viewing, no concern with recognizing, no concern with making posters, but an art that is inside our head and inside our total system so that it will be out of the caves of the Manhattan lofts and spread across a vaster area."[3]

3. Ibid., p. 182.

Thank you to Finn Thybo Andersen, Kirsten Dufour, and Kirsten Justesen.

Henri Lefebvre

The Production of Space
(Extracts)

The Monument

For millennia, monumentality took in all the following aspects of *spatiality*: the perceived, the conceived, and the lived; representations of space and representational spaces; the spaces proper to each faculty, from the sense of smell to speech; the gestural and the symbolic. Monumental space offered each member of a society an image of that membership, an image of his or her social visage. It thus constituted a collective mirror more faithful than any personal one. Such a "recognition effect" has far greater impact than the "mirror effect" of the psychoanalysts. Of this social space, which embraced all the above-mentioned aspects while still according each its proper place, everyone partook, and partook fully – albeit, naturally, under the conditions of a generally accepted Power and a generally accepted Wisdom. The monument thus effected a "consensus," and this in the strongest sense of the term, rendering it practical and concrete. The element of repression in it and the element of exaltation could scarcely be disentangled; or perhaps it would be more accurate to say that the repressive element was metamorphosed into exaltation. The codifying approach of semiology, which seeks to classify representations, impressions and evocations (as terms in the code of knowledge, the code of personal feelings, the symbolic code, or the hermeneutic code),[1] is quite unable to cover all facets of the monumental. Indeed, it does not even come close, for it is the residual, the irreducible – whatever cannot be classified or codified according to categories devised subsequent to production – which is, here as always, the most precious and the most essential, the diamond at the bottom of the melting-pot. The use of the cathedral's monumental space necessarily entails its supplying answers to all the questions that assail anyone who crosses the threshold. For visitors are bound to become aware of their own footsteps, and listen to the noises, the singing; they must breathe the incense-laden air, and plunge into a particular world, that of sin and redemption; they will partake of an ideology; they will contemplate and decipher the symbols around them; and they will thus, on the basis of their own bodies, experience a total being in a total space. Small wonder that from time immemorial conquerors and revolutionaries eager to destroy a society should so often have sought to do so by burning or razing that society's monuments. Sometimes, it is true, they contrive to redirect them to their own advantage. Here too, use goes further and deeper than the codes of exchange.

The most beautiful monuments are imposing in their durability. A cyclopean wall achieves monumental beauty because it seems eternal, because it seems to have escaped time. Monumentality transcends death, and hence also what is sometimes called the "death instinct." As both appearance and reality, this transcendence embeds itself in the monument as its irreducible foundation; the lineaments of atemporality overwhelm anxiety, even – and indeed above all – in funerary monuments. A *ne plus ultra* of art – form so thoroughly denying meaning that death itself is submerged. The Empress' Tomb in the Taj Mahal bathes in an atmosphere of gracefulness, whiteness and floral motifs. Every bit as much as a poem or a tragedy, a monument transmutes the fear of the passage of time, and anxiety about death, into splendor.

Monumental "durability" is unable, however, to achieve a complete illusion. To put it in what pass for modern terms, its credibility is never total. It replaces a brutal reality with a

1. Roland Barthes, *S/Z*, Seuil, Paris, 1970, pp. 25 ff. (English translation by Richard Miller, *S/Z*, Hill & Wang, New York, 1974, pp. 18 ff).

materially realized appearance; reality is changed into appearance. What, after all, is the durable aside from the will to endure? Monumental imperishability bears the stamp of the will to power. Only will, in its more elaborated forms – the wish for mastery, the will to will – can overcome, or believe it can overcome, death. Knowledge itself fails here, shrinking from the abyss. Only through the monument, through the intervention of the architect as demiurge, can the space of death be negated, transfigured into a living space which is an extension of the body; this is a transformation, however, which serves what religion, (political) power and knowledge have in common.

In order to define monumental space properly,[2] semiological categorization (codifying) and symbolic explanations must be restrained. But "restrained" should not be taken to mean refused or rejected. I am not saying that the monument is not the outcome of a signifying practice, or of a particular way of proposing a meaning, but merely that it can be reduced neither to a language or discourse nor to the categories and concepts developed for the study of language. A spatial work (monument or architectural project) attains a complexity fundamentally different from the complexity of a text, whether prose or poetry. As I pointed out earlier, what we are concerned with here is not texts but texture. We already know that a texture is made up of a usually rather large space covered by networks or webs; monuments constitute the strong points, nexuses or anchors of such webs. The actions of social practice are expressible but not explicable through discourse: they are, precisely, *acted* – and not read. A monumental work, like a musical one, does not have a "signified" (or "signifieds"); rather, it has a *horizon of meaning:* a specific or indefinite multiplicity of meanings, a shifting hierarchy in which now one, now another meaning comes momentarily to the fore, by means of – and for the sake of – a particular action. The social and political operation of a monumental work traverses the various "systems" and "subsystems," or codes and subcodes, which constitute and found the society concerned. But it also surpasses such codes and subcodes, and implies a "supercoding," in that it tends towards the all-embracing presence of the totality. To the degree that there are traces of violence and death, negativity and aggressiveness in social practice, the monumental work erases them and replaces them with a tranquil power and certitude which can encompass violence and terror. Thus the mortal "moment" (or component) of the sign is temporarily abol-

2. Clearly we are not concerned here with architectural space understood as the preserve of a particular profession within the established social division of labor.

ished in monumental space. In and through the work in space, social practice transcends the limitations by which other "signifying practices," and hence the other arts, including those texts known as "literary," are bound; in this way a consensus, a profound agreement, is achieved. A Greek theatre presupposes tragedy and comedy, and by extension, the presence of the city's people and their allegiance to their heroes and gods. In theatrical space, music, choruses, masks, tiering – all such elements converge with language and actors. A spatial action overcomes conflicts, at least momentarily, even though it does not resolve them; it opens a way from everyday concerns to collective joy.

Turmoil is inevitable once a monument loses its prestige, or can only retain it by means of admitted oppression and repression. When the subject – a city or a people – suffers dispersal, the *building* and its functions come into their own; by the same token *housing* comes to prevail over *residence* within that city or amidst that people. The building has its roots in warehouses, barracks, depots, and rental housing. Buildings have functions, forms, and structures, but they do not integrate the formal, functional, and structural "moments" of social practice. And, in as much as sites, forms and functions are no longer focused and appropriated by monuments, the city's contexture or fabric – its streets, its underground levels, its frontiers – unravel, and generate not concord but violence. Indeed space as a whole becomes prone to sudden eruptions of violence.

The balance of forces between monuments and buildings has shifted. Buildings are to monuments as everyday life is to festival, products to works, lived experience to the merely perceived, concrete to stone, and so on. What we are seeing here is a new dialectical process, but one just as vast as its predecessors. How could the contradiction between building and monument be overcome and surpassed? How might that tendency be accelerated which has destroyed monumentality but which could well reinstitute it, within the sphere of buildings itself, by restoring the old unity at a higher level? So long as no such dialectical transcendence occurs, we can only expect the stagnation of crude interactions and intermixtures between "moments" in short, a continuing spatial chaos. Under this dispensation, buildings, and dwelling-places have been dressed up in monumental signs: first their facades, and later their interiors. The homes of the moneyed classes have undergone a superficial "socialization" with the introduction of reception areas, bars, nooks, and furniture (divans, for instance) which bespeak some kind of erotic life. Pale echoes, in short, of the aristocratic palace or town house. The town, meanwhile, now effectively blown apart, has been "privatized" no less superficially – thanks to urban "decor" and "design," and the development of fake environments. Instead, then, of a dialectical process with three stages which resolves a contradiction and "creatively" transcends a conflictual situation, we have a stagnant opposition whose poles at first confront one another "face to face," then relapse into muddle and confusion.

There is still a good deal to be said about the notion of the monument. It is especially worth emphasizing what a monument is *not*, because this will help avoid a number of misconceptions. Monuments should not be looked upon as collections of symbols (even though every monument embodies symbols – sometimes archaic and incomprehensible ones), nor as chains of signs (even though every monumental whole is made up of signs). A monument is neither an object nor an aggregation of diverse objects, even though its "objectality," its position as a social object, is recalled at every moment, perhaps by the brutality of the materials or masses involved, perhaps, on the contrary, by their gentle qualities. It is neither a sculpture, nor a figure, nor simply the result of material procedures. The indispensable opposition between inside and outside, as indicated by thresholds, doors, and frames, though often underestimated, simply does not suffice when it comes to defining monumental space. Such a space is determined by what may take place there, and consequently by what may not take place there (prescribed/proscribed, scene/obscene). What appears empty may turn out to be full – as is the case with sanctuaries, or with the "ships" or naves of cathedrals. Alternatively, full space may be inverted over an almost heterotopic void at the same location (for instance, vaults, cupolas). The Taj Mahal, for instance, makes much play with the fullness of swelling curves suspended in a dramatic emptiness. Acoustic, gestural, and ritual movements, elements grouped into vast ceremonial unities, breaches opening onto limitless perspectives, chains of meanings – all are organized into a monumental whole.

The affective level – which is to say, the level of the body, bound to symmetries and rhythms – is transformed into a "property" of monumental space, into symbols which are generally intrinsic parts of a politico-religious whole, into co-ordinated symbols. The component elements of such wholes are disposed according to a strict order for the purposes of the use of space: some at a first level, the level of affective, bodily, lived experience, the level of the spoken word; some at a second level, that of the perceived, of socio-political signification; and some at a third level, the level of the conceived, where the dissemination of the written word and of knowledge welds the members of society into a "consensus," and in doing so confers upon them the status of "subjects." Monumental space permits a continual back-and-forth between the private speech of ordinary conversations and the public speech of discourses, lectures, sermons, rallying-cries, and all theatrical forms of utterance.

Inasmuch as the poet through a poem gives voice to a way of living (loving, feeling, thinking, taking pleasure, or suffering), the experience of monumental space may be said to have some similarity to entering and sojourning in the poetic world. It is more easily understood, however, when compared with texts written for the theatre, which are composed of dialogues, rather than with poetry or other literary texts, which are monologues.

Monumental qualities are not solely plastic, not to be apprehended solely through looking. Monuments are also liable to possess acoustic properties, and when they do not this detracts from their monumentality. Silence itself, in a place of worship, has its music. In cloister or cathedral, space is measured by the ear: the sounds, voices and singing reverberate in an interplay analogous to that between the most basic sounds and tones; analogous also to the interplay set up when a reading voice breathes new life into a written text. Architectural volumes ensure a correlation between the rhythms that they entertain (gaits, ritual gestures, processions, parades, etc.) and their musical resonance. It is in this way, and at this level, in the *non-visible*, that bodies find one another. Should there be no echo to provide a reflection or acoustic mirror of presence, it falls to an object to supply this mediation between the inert and the living: bells tinkling at the slightest breeze, the play of fountains and running water, perhaps birds and caged animals.

Two "primary processes," as described by certain psychoanalysts and linguists, might reasonably be expected to operate in monumental space: (1) displacement, implying metonymy, the shift from part to whole, and continuity; and (2) condensation, involving substitution, metaphor and similarity. And, to a degree, this is so. Social space, the space of social practice, the space of the social relations of production and of work and non-work (relations which are to a greater or lesser extent codified) – this space is indeed condensed in monumental space. The notion of "social condenser," as proposed by Russian architects in the 1920s, has a more general application. The "properties" of a spatial texture are focused upon a single point: sanctuary, throne, seat, presidential chair, or the like. Thus each monumental space becomes the metaphorical and quasimetaphysical underpinning of a society, this by virtue of a play of substitutions in which the religious and political realms symbolically (and ceremonially) exchange attributes – the attributes of power; in this way the authority of the sacred and the sacred aspect of authority are transferred back and forth, mutually reinforcing one another in the process. The horizontal chain of sites in space is thus replaced by vertical superimposition, by a hierarchy, which follows its own route to the locus of power, whence it will determine the disposition of the sites in question. Any object – a vase, a chair, a garment – may be extracted from everyday practice and suffer a displacement which will transform it by transferring it into monumental space: the vase will become holy, the garment ceremonial, the chair the seat of authority. The famous bar which, according to the followers of Saussure, separates signifier from signified and desire from its object, is in fact transportable hither and thither at the whim of society, as a means of separating the sacred from the profane and of repressing those gestures which are not prescribed by monumental space – in short, as a means of banishing the obscene.

All of which has still not explained very much, for what we have said applies for all "monumentality" and does not address the question of what particular power is in place. The obscene is a general category of social practice, and not of signifying processes as such: exclusion from the scene is pronounced silently by space itself.

The space of architects

Cases are legion where the empirical approach to a given process refuses to carry its description to a conceptual level where a dialectical (conflictual) dynamic is likely to emerge. For example, countries in the throes of rapid development blithely destroy historic spaces – houses, palaces, military, or civil structures. If advantage or profit is to be found in it, then the old is swept away. Later, however, perhaps towards the end of the period of accelerated growth, these same countries are liable to discover how such spaces may be pressed into the service of cultural consumption, of "culture itself," and of the tourism and the leisure industries with their almost limitless prospects. When this happens, everything that they had so merrily demolished during the belle époque is reconstituted at great expense. Where destruction has not been complete, "renovation" becomes the order of the day, or imitation, or replication, or neo-this or neo-that. In any case, what had been annihilated in the earlier frenzy of growth now becomes an object of adoration. And former objects of utility now pass for rare and precious works of art.

Let us for a moment consider the space of architecture and of architects, without attaching undue importance to what is said about this space. It is easy to imagine that the architect has before him a slice or piece of space cut from larger wholes, that he takes this portion of space as a "given" and works on it according to his tastes, technical skills, ideas and preferences. In short, he receives his assignment and deals with it in complete freedom.

That is not what actually happens, however. The section of space assigned to the architect – perhaps by "developers," perhaps by government agencies – is affected by calculations that he may have some intimation of but with which he is certainly not well acquainted. This space has nothing innocent about it: it answers to particular tactics and strategies; it is, quite simply, the space of the dominant mode of production, and hence the space of capitalism, governed by the bourgeoisie. It consists of "lots" and is organized in a repressive manner as a function of the important features of the locality.

As for the eye of the architect, it is no more innocent than the lot he is given to build on or the blank sheet of paper on which he makes his first sketch. His "subjective" space is freighted with all-too-objective meanings. It is a visual space, a space reduced to blueprints, to mere images – to that "world of the image" which is the enemy of the imagination. These reductions are accentuated and justified by the rule of linear perspective. Such sterilizing tendencies were denounced long ago by Gromort, who demonstrated how they served to fetishize the facade – a volume made up of planes and lent spurious depth by means of decorative motifs.[3] The tendency to make reductions of this kind – reductions to parcels, to images, to facades that are made to be seen and to be seen from (thus reinforcing "pure" visual space) – is a tendency that degrades space. The facade (to see and to be seen) was always a measure of social standing and prestige. A prison with a

3. Cf. Georges Gromort, *Architécture et sculpture en France,* a volume in: *Histoire générale de l' art française de la Revolution à nos jours,* Librairie de France, Paris, 1923-1925.

facade – which was also the prison of the family became the epitome and modular form of bourgeoisified space.

It may thus be said of architectural discourse that it too often imitates or caricatures the discourse of power, and that it suffers from the delusion that "objective" knowledge of "reality" can be attained by means of graphic representations. This discourse no longer has any frame of reference or horizon. It only too easily becomes – as in the case of Le Corbusier – a moral discourse on straight lines, on right angles and straightness in general, combining a figurative appeal to nature (water, air, sunshine) with the worst kind of abstraction (plane geometry, modules, etc.).

Within the spatial practice of modern society, the architect ensconces himself in his own space. He has a *representation of this space,* one which is bound to graphic elements – to sheets of paper, plans, elevations, sections, perspective views of facades, modules, and so on. This *conceived* space is thought by those who make use of it to be *true,* despite the fact – or perhaps because of the fact – that it is geometrical: because it is a medium for objects, an object itself, and a locus of the objectification of plans. Its distant ancestor is the linear perspective developed as early as the Renaissance: a fixed observer, an immobile perceptual field, a stable visual world. The chief criterion of the architectural plan, which is "unconsciously" determined by this perceptual field, is whether or not it is realizable: the plan is projected onto the field of architectural thought, there to be accepted or rejected. A vast number of representations (some would call them "ideological" representations, but why bother with a term now so devalued by misuse?) take this route; any plan, to merit consideration, must be quantifiable, profitable, communicable, and "realistic." Set aside or downplayed from the outset are all questions relating to what is too close or too distant, relating to the surroundings or "environment," and relating to the relationship between private and public. On the other hand, subdivisions (lots) and specializations (functional localizations) are quite admissible to this practically defined sphere. Much more than this, in fact: though the sphere in question seems passive with respect to operations of this kind, its very passive acceptance of them ensures their operational impact. The division of labor, the division of needs and the division of objects (things), all localized, all pushed to the point of maximum separation of functions, people and things, are perfectly at home in this spatial field, no matter that it appears to be neutral and objective, no matter that it is apparently the repository of knowledge, *sans peur et sans reproche.*

Let us now turn our attention to the space of those who are referred to by means of such clumsy and pejorative labels as "users" and "inhabitants." No well-defined terms with clear connotations have been found to designate these groups. Their marginalization by spatial practice thus extends even to language. The word "user" *(usager),* for example, has something vague – and vaguely suspect – about it. "User of what?" one tends to wonder. Clothes and cars are used (and wear out), just as houses are. But what is use value when set alongside exchange and its corollaries? As for "inhabitants," the word designates everyone – and no one. The fact is that the most basic demands of "users" (suggesting "underprivileged") and "inhabitants" (suggesting "marginal") find *expression* only with great difficulty, whereas the *signs* of their situation are constantly increasing and often stare us in the face.

The user's space is *lived* – not represented (or conceived). When compared with the abstract space of the experts (architects, urbanists, planners), the space of the everyday activities of users is a concrete one, which is to say, subjective. As a space of "subjects" rather than of calculations, as a representational space, it has an origin, and that origin is childhood, with its hardships, its achievements and its lacks. Lived space bears the stamp of the conflict between an inevitable, if long and difficult, maturation process and a failure to mature that leaves particular original resources and reserves untouched. It is in this space that the "private" realm asserts itself, albeit more or less vigorously, and always in a conflictual way, against the public one.

It is possible, nevertheless, if only in a mediational or transitional way, to form a mental picture of a primacy of concrete spaces of semi-public, semi-private spaces, of meeting-places, pathways and passageways. This would mean the diversification of space, while the (relative) importance attached to functional distinctions would disappear. Appropriated places would be *fixed, semi-fixed, movable or vacant.* We should not forget that among the contradictions here a not unimportant part is played by the contradiction between the ephemeral and the stable (or, to use Heidegger's philosophical terminology, between Dwelling and Wandering). Although work – including a portion of household production (food preparation, etc.) – demands a fixed location, this is not true of sleep, nor of play, and in this respect the West might do well to take lessons from the East, with its great open spaces, and its low and easily movable furniture.

In the West the reign of the facade over space is certainly not over. The furniture, which is almost as heavy as the buildings themselves, continues to have facades; mirrored wardrobes, sideboards and chests still face out onto the sphere of private life, and so help dominate it. Any mobilization of "private" life would be accompanied by a restoration of the body, and the contradictions of space would have to be brought out into the open. Inasmuch as the resulting space would be inhabited by *subjects,* it might legitimately be deemed "situational" or "relational" – but these definitions or determinants would refer to sociological content rather than to any intrinsic properties of space as such.

The restoration of the body means, first and foremost, the restoration of the sensory-sensual – of speech, of the voice, of smell, of hearing. In short, of the non-visual. And of the sexual – though not in the sense of sex considered in isolation, but rather in the sense of a sexual energy directed towards a specific discharge and flowing according to specific rhythms.

But these are no more than suggestions, or pointers.

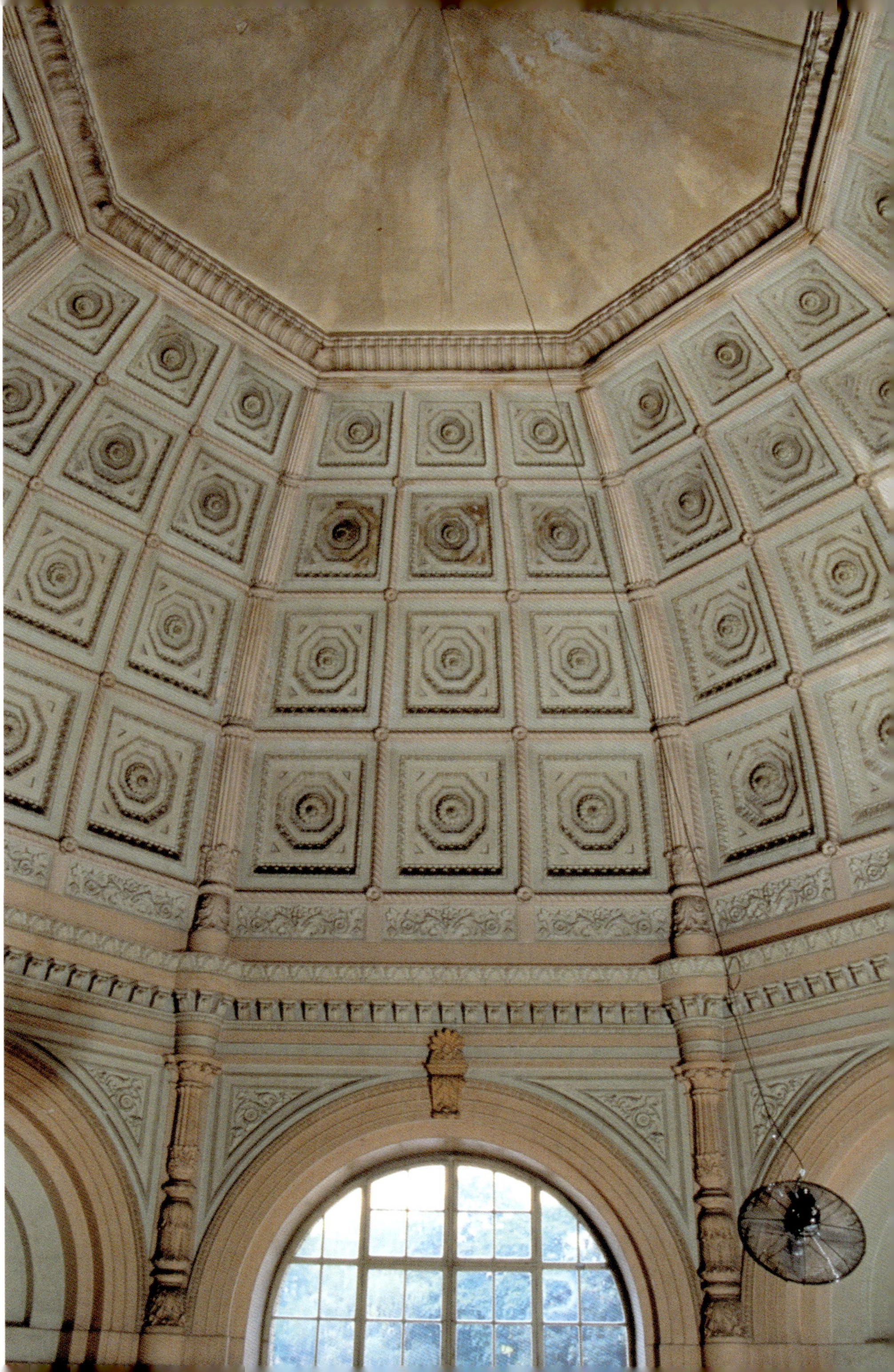

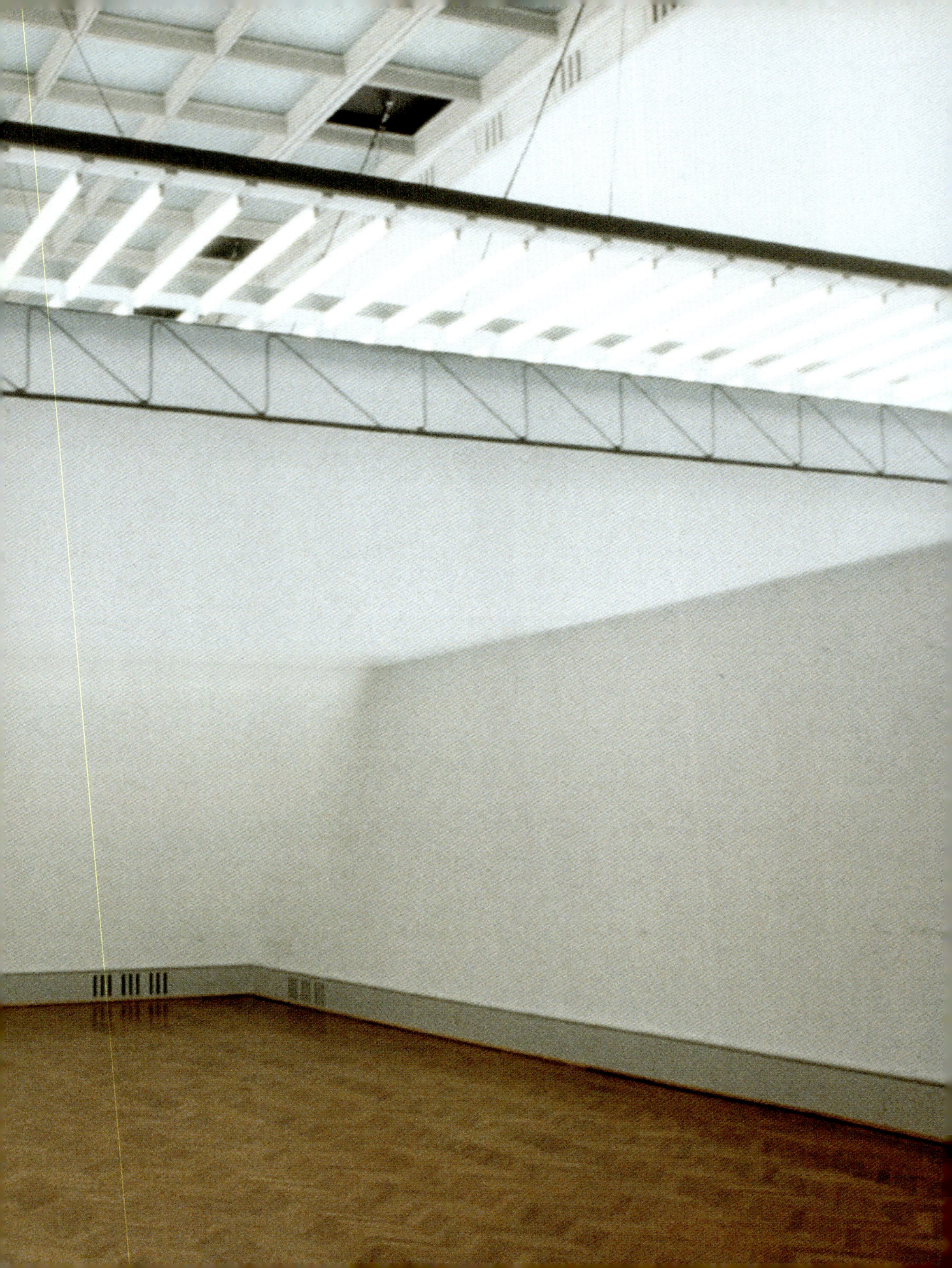

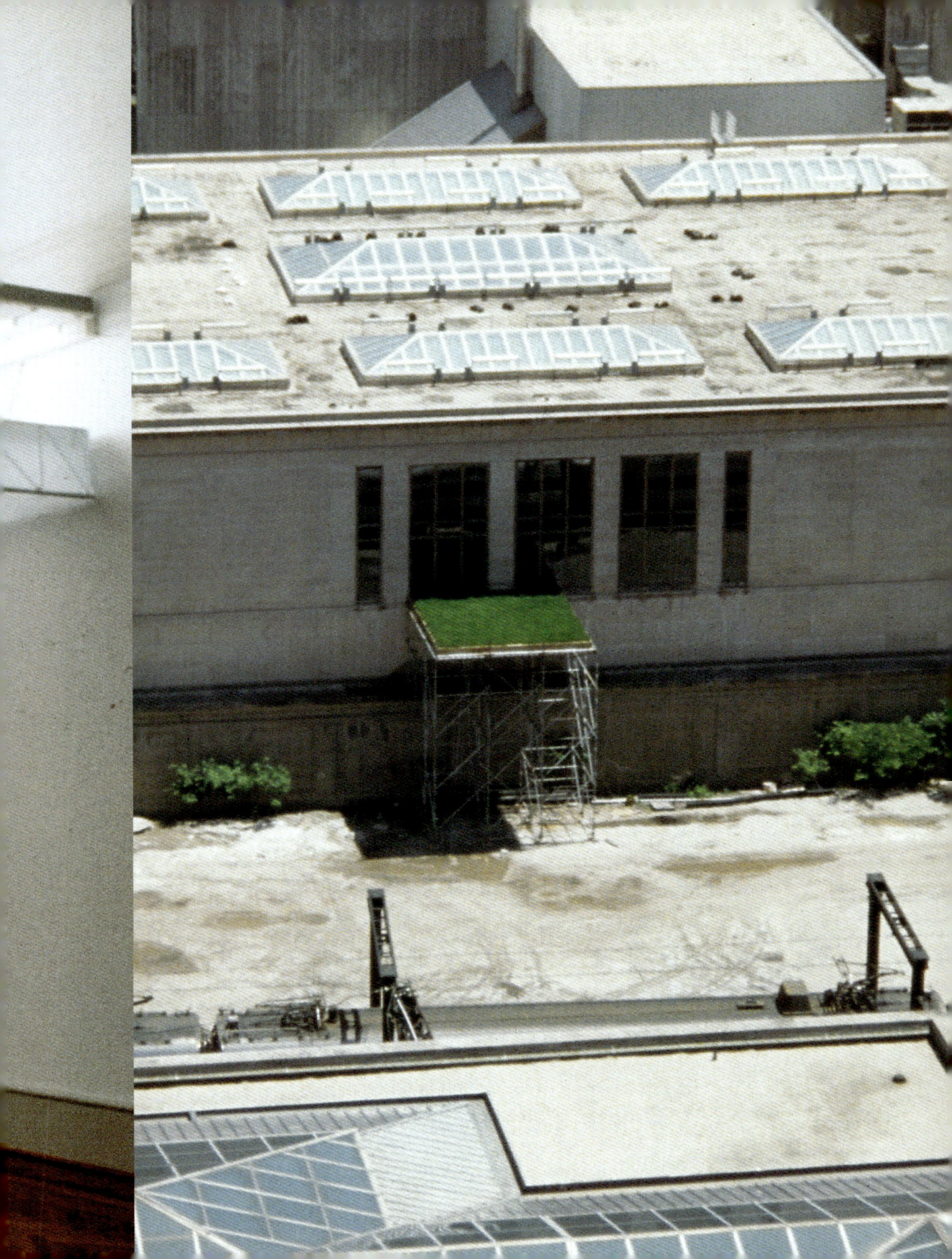

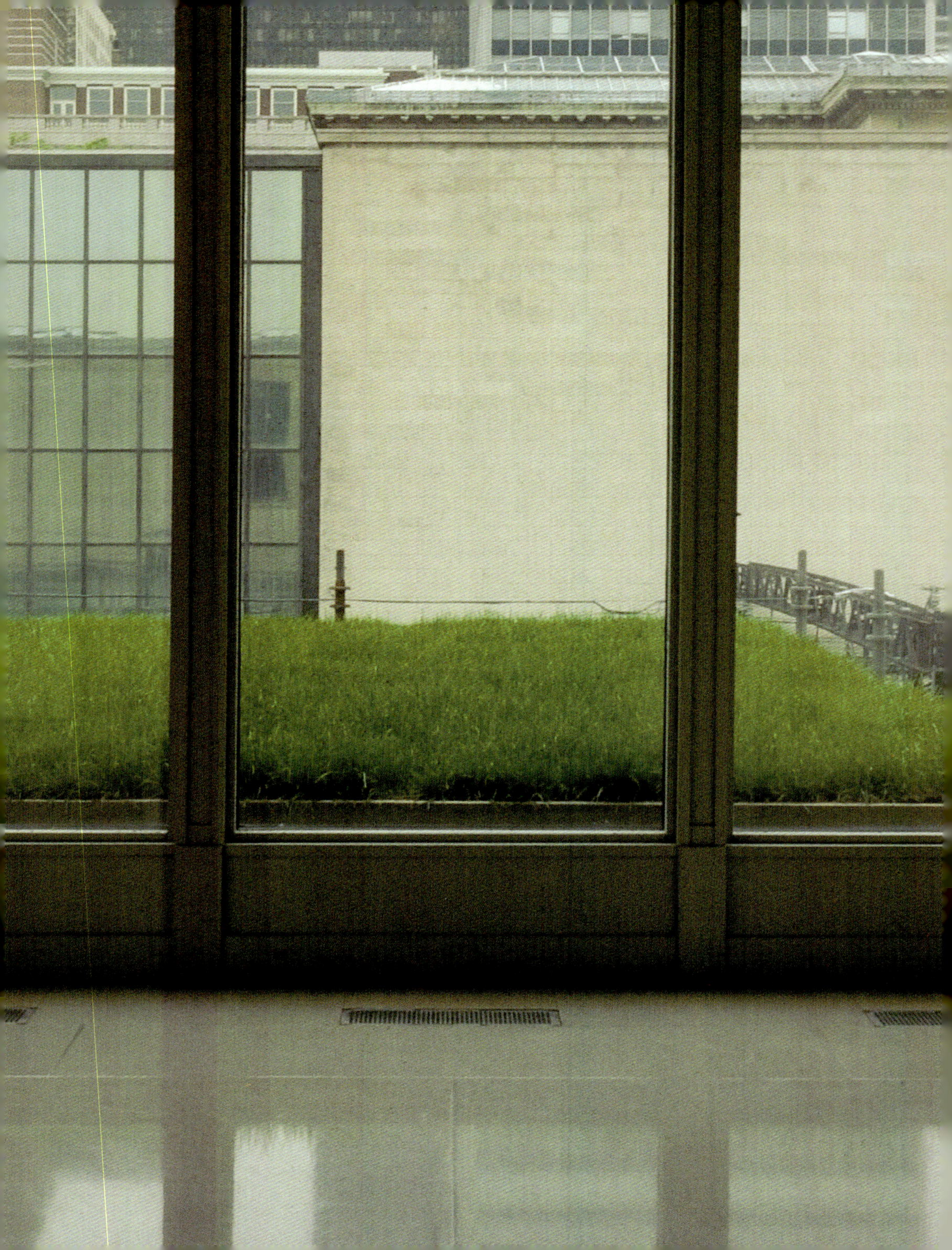

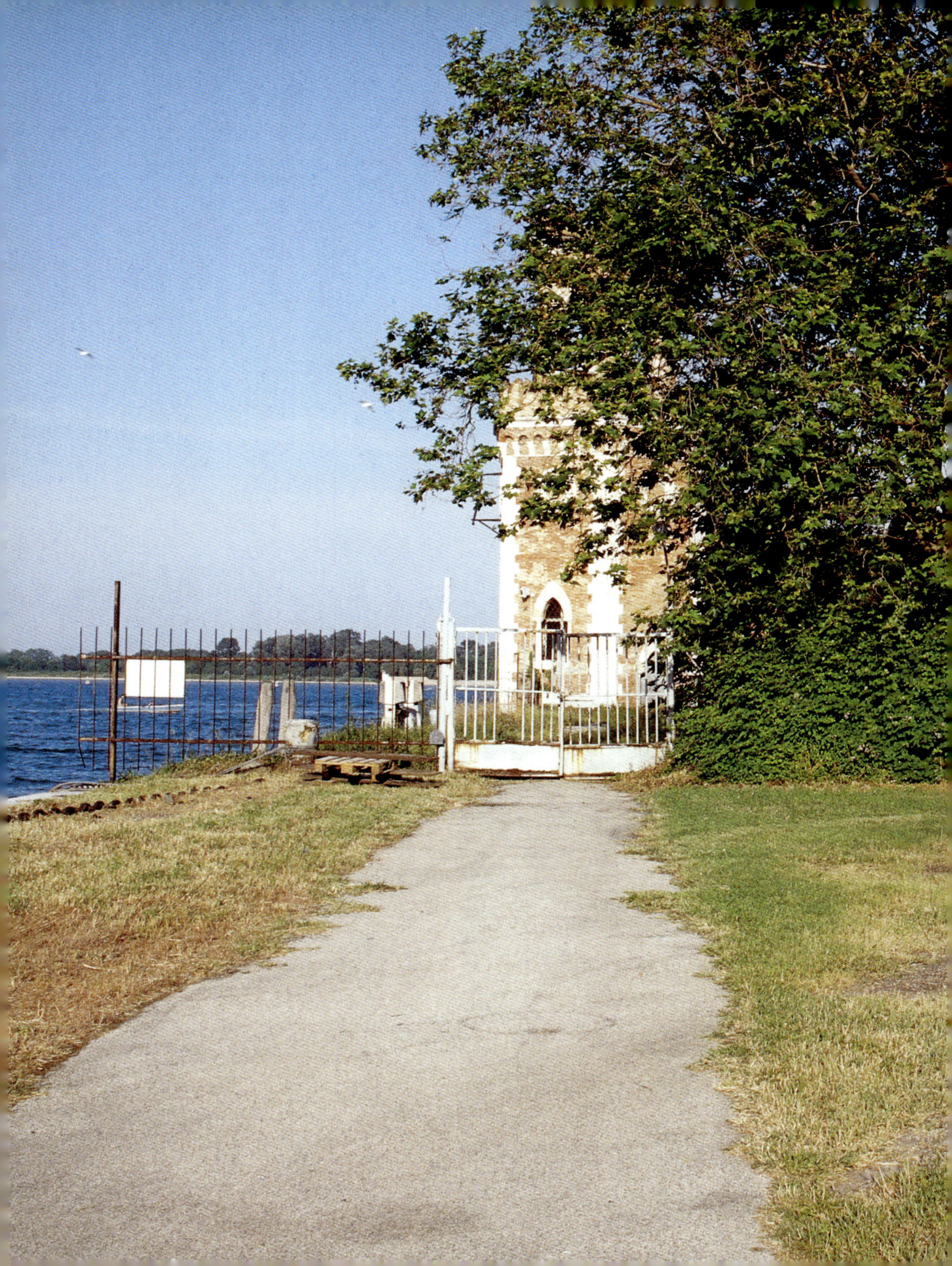

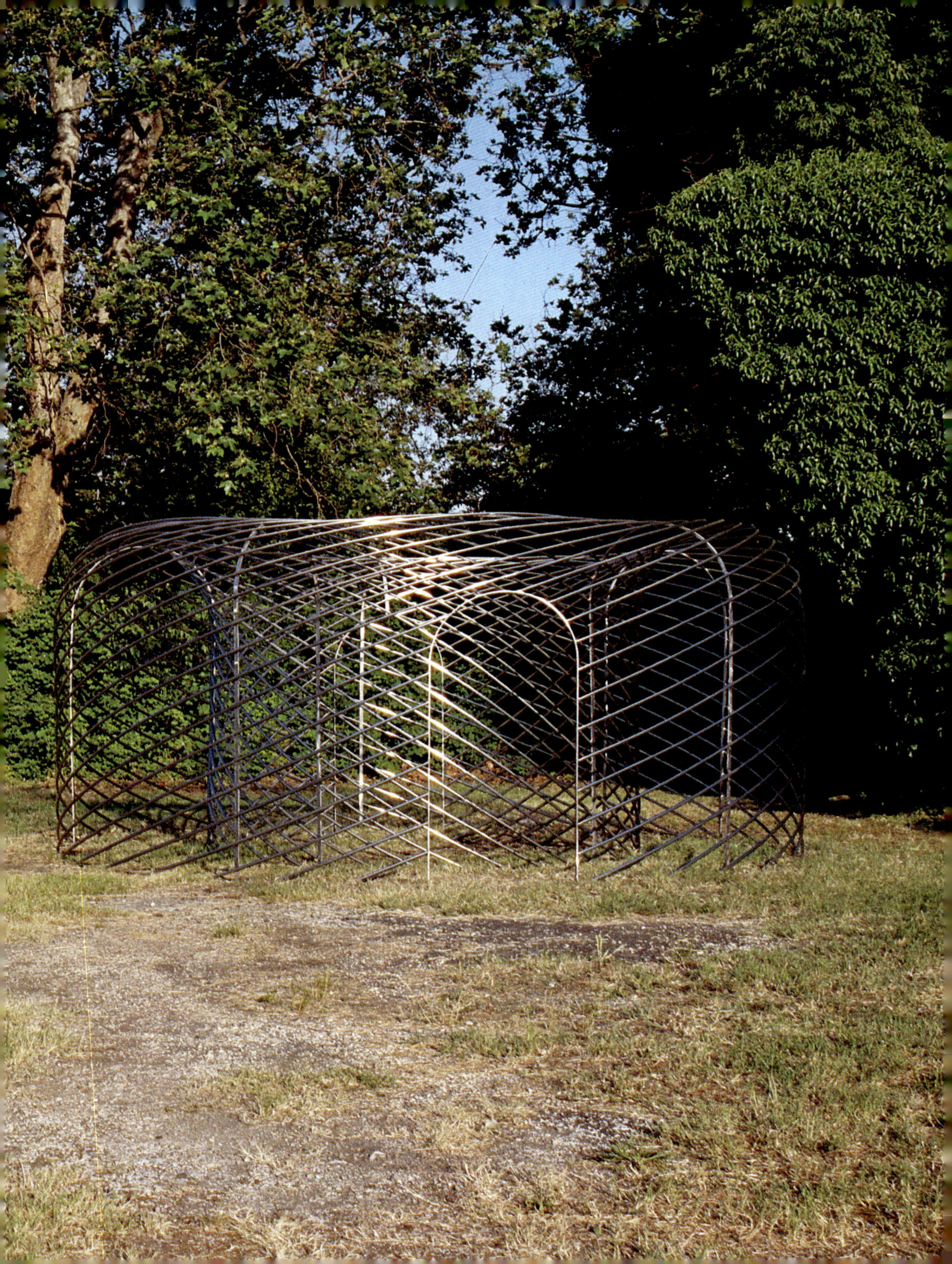

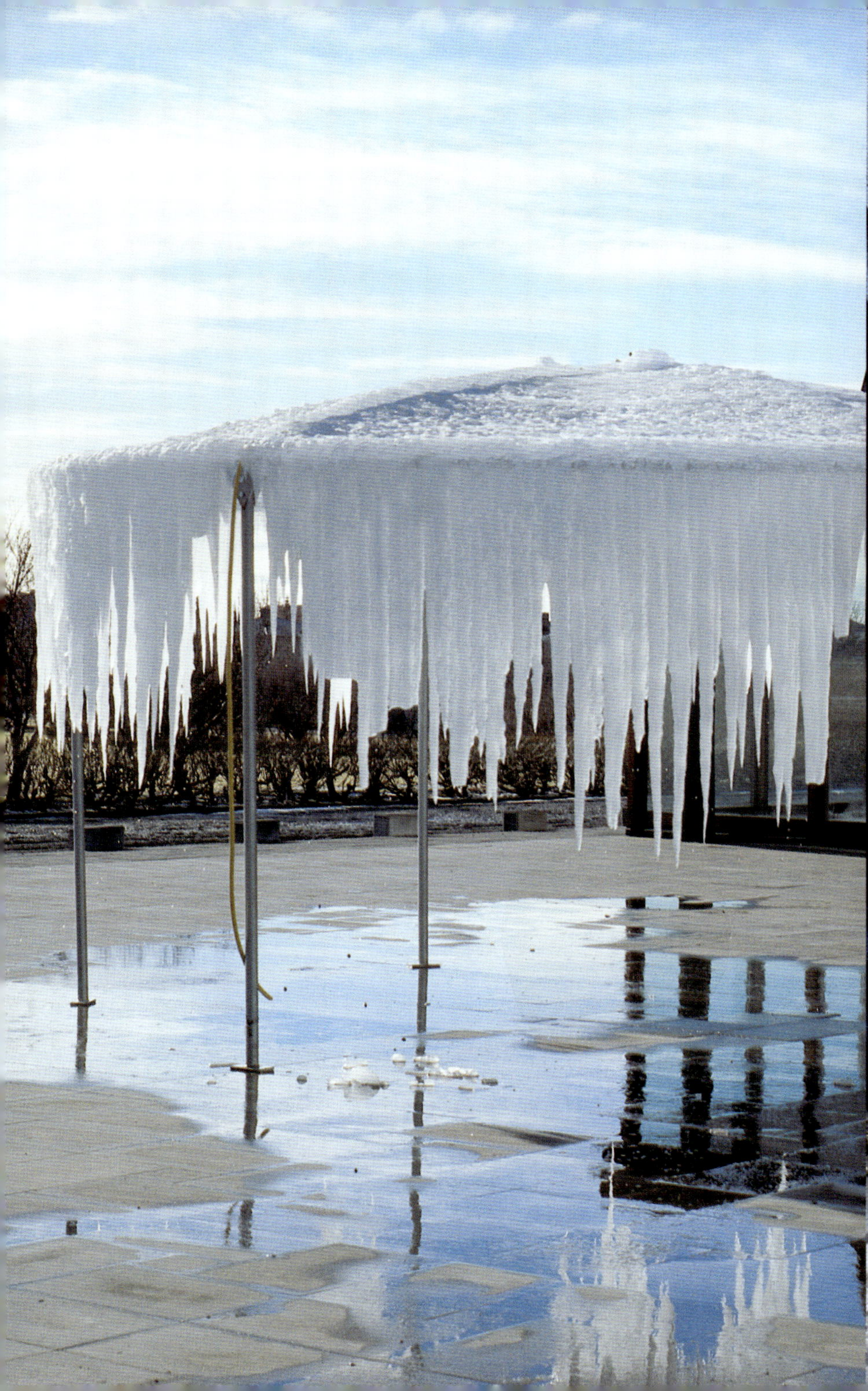

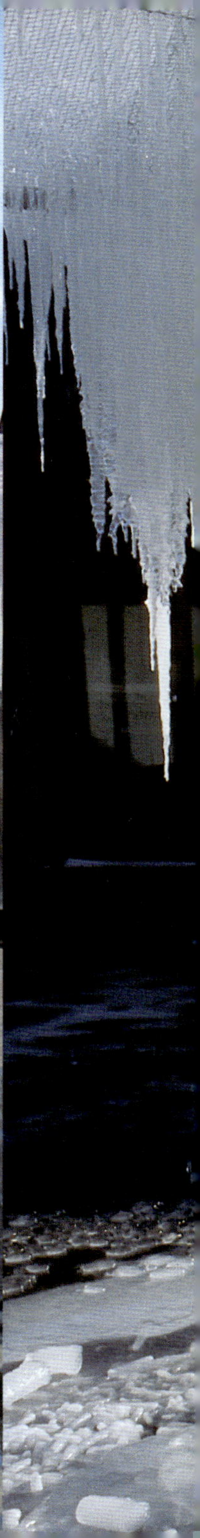

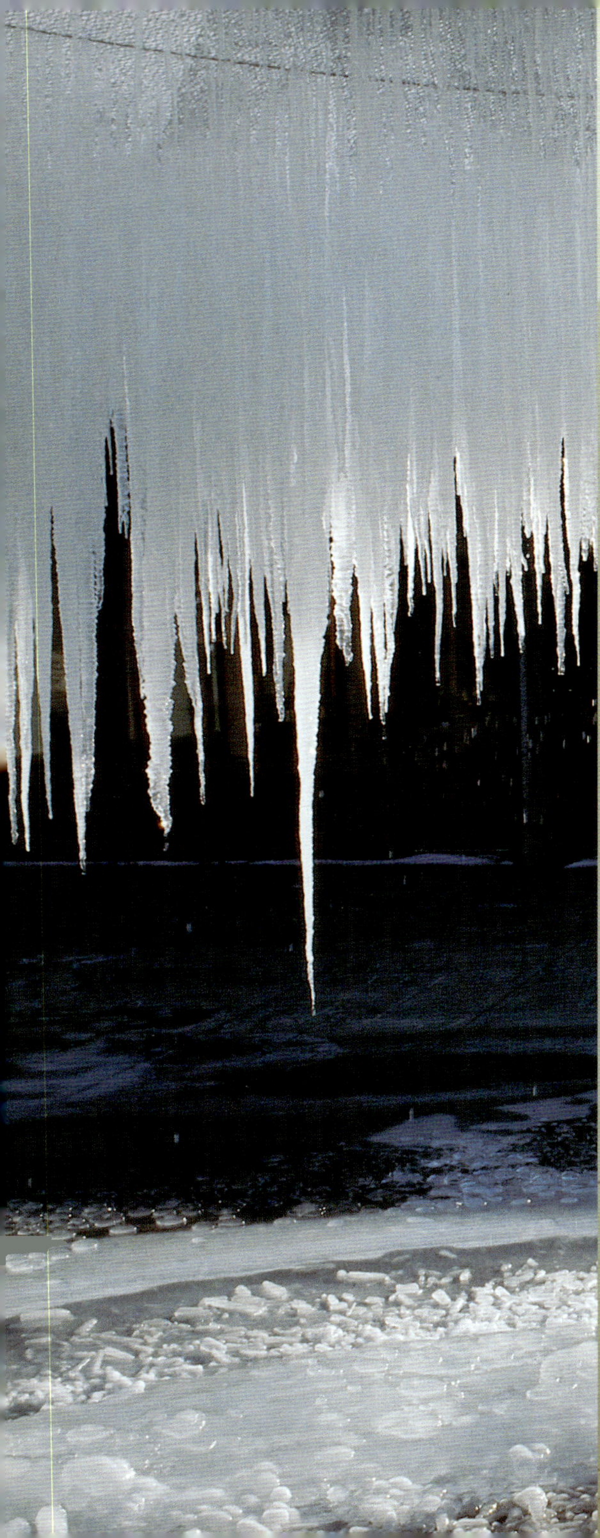
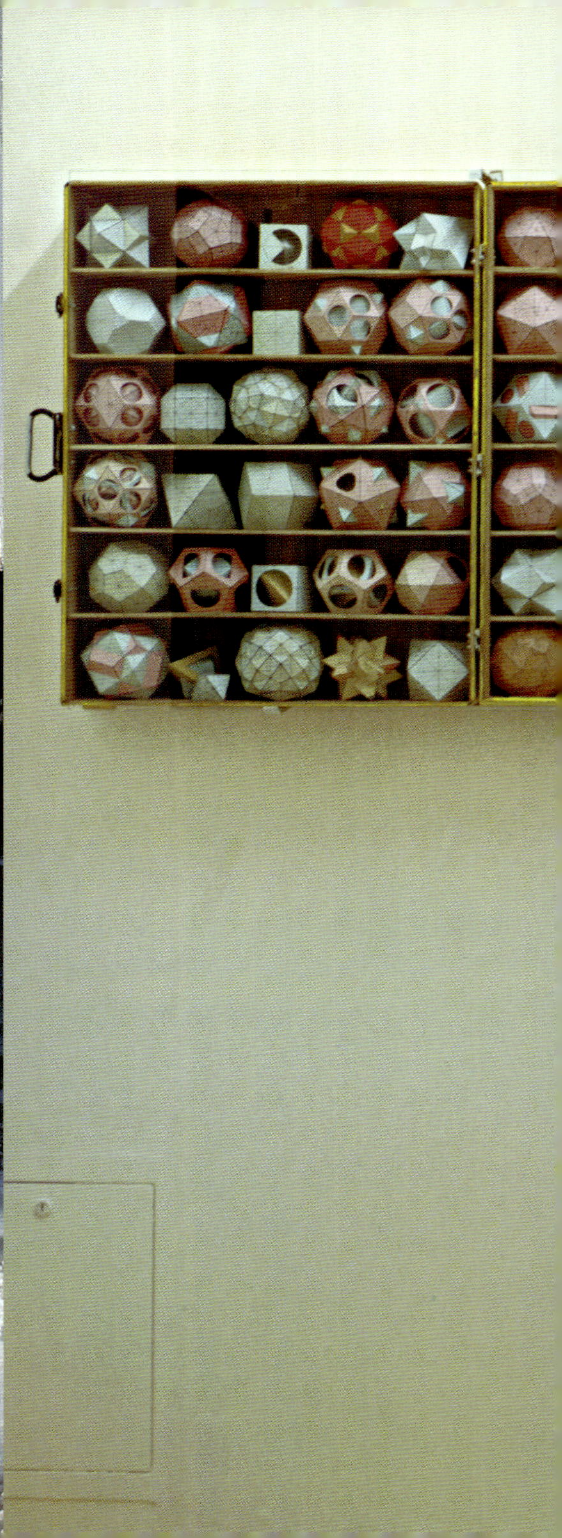

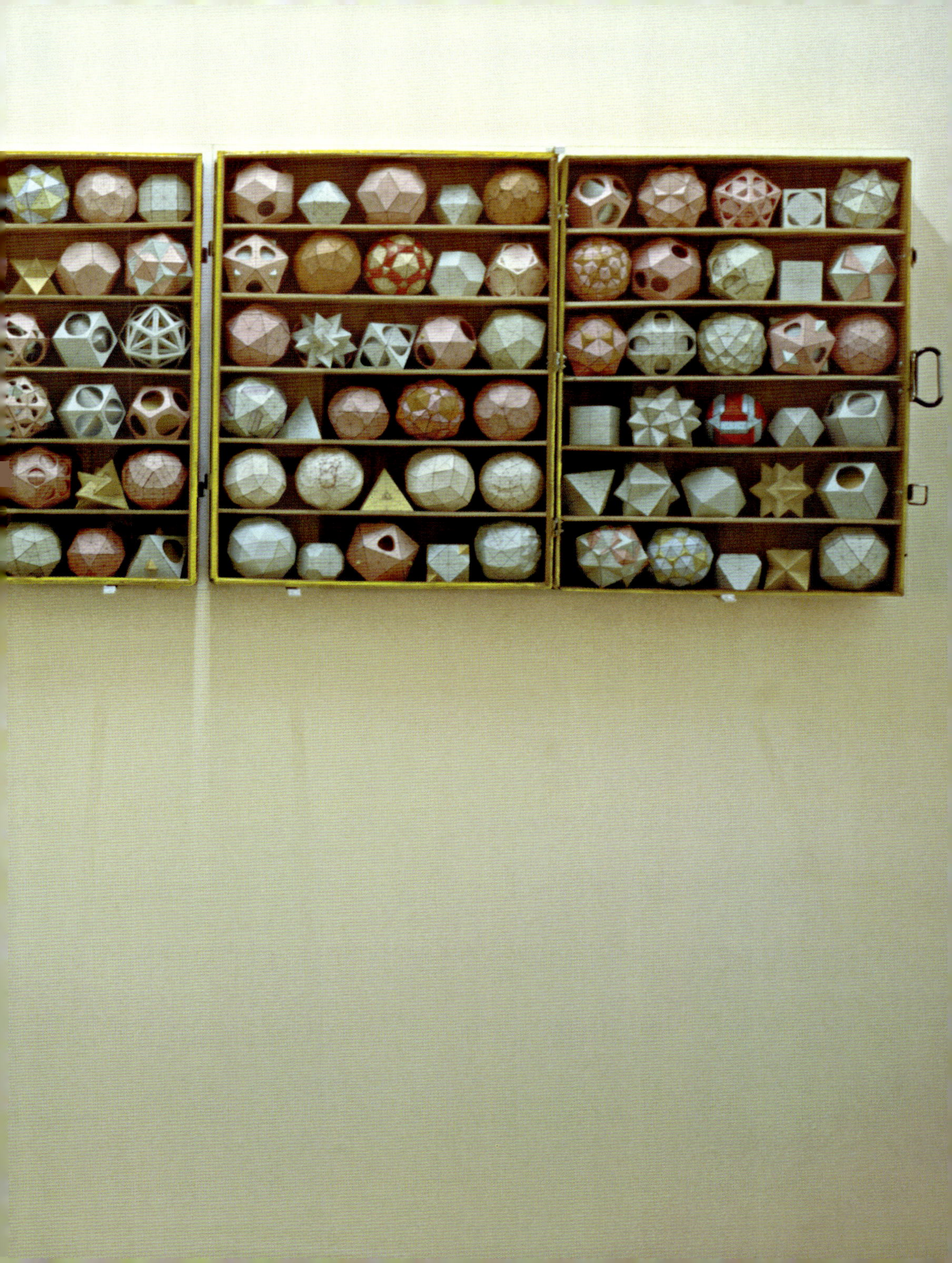

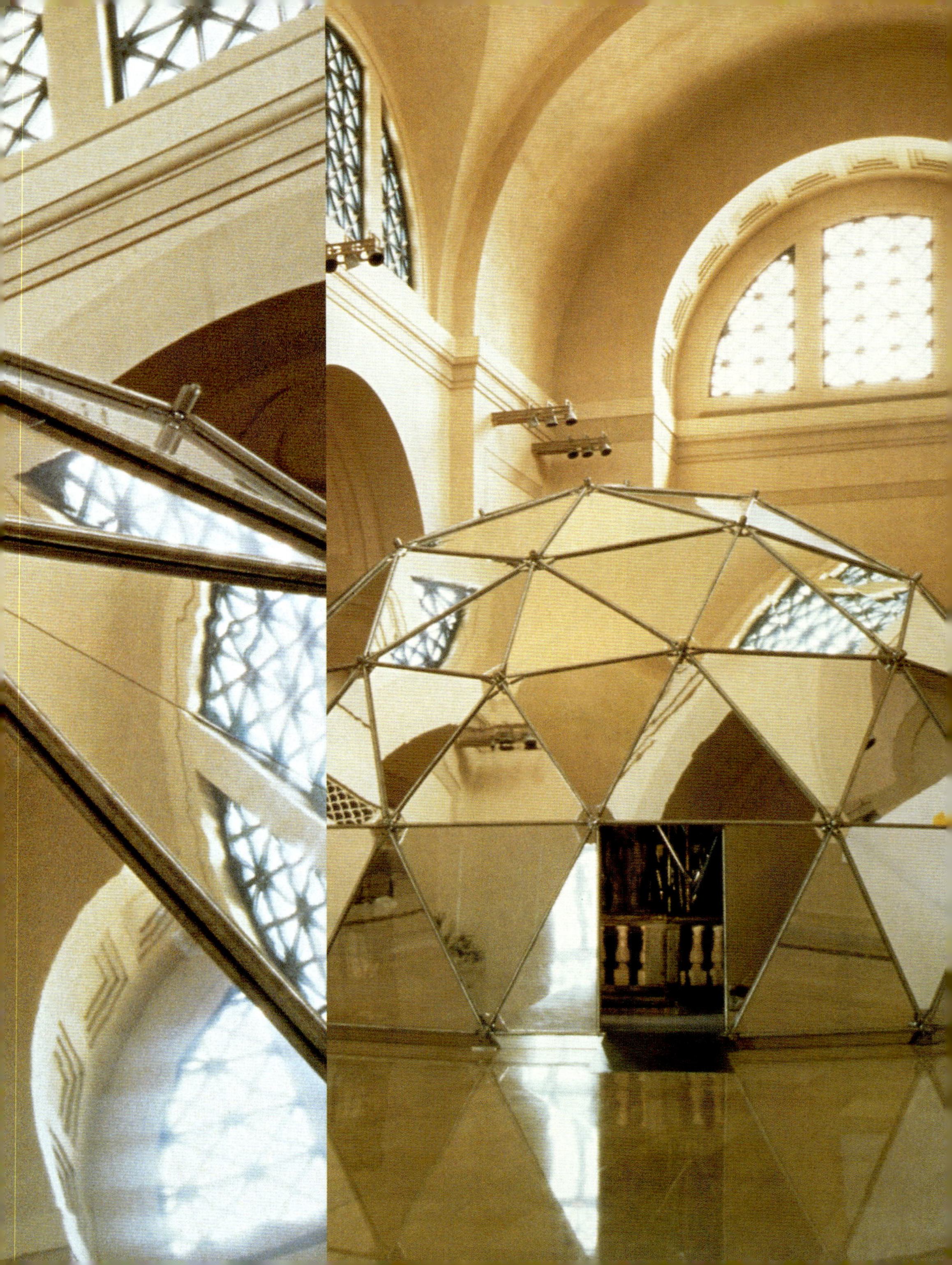

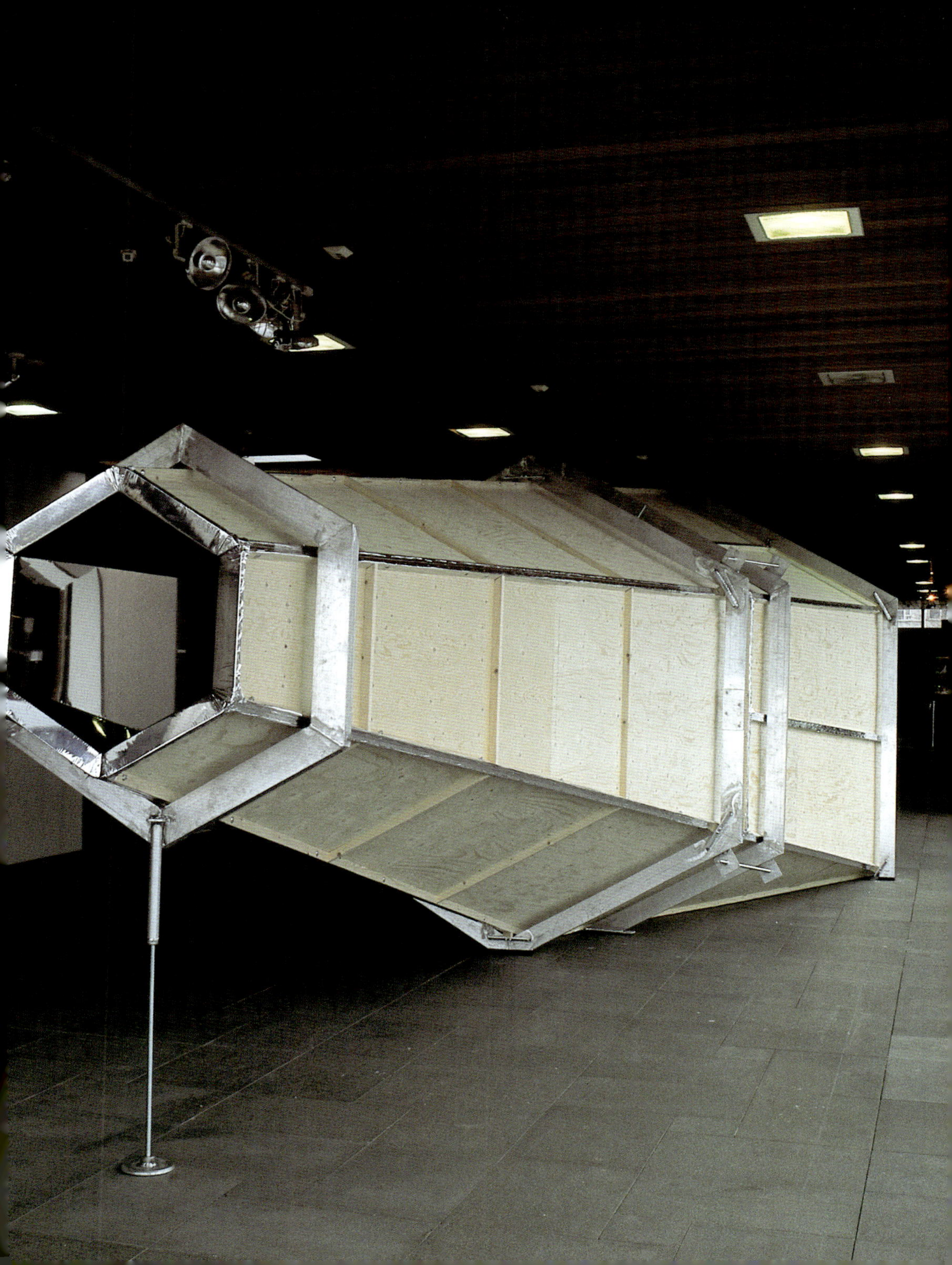

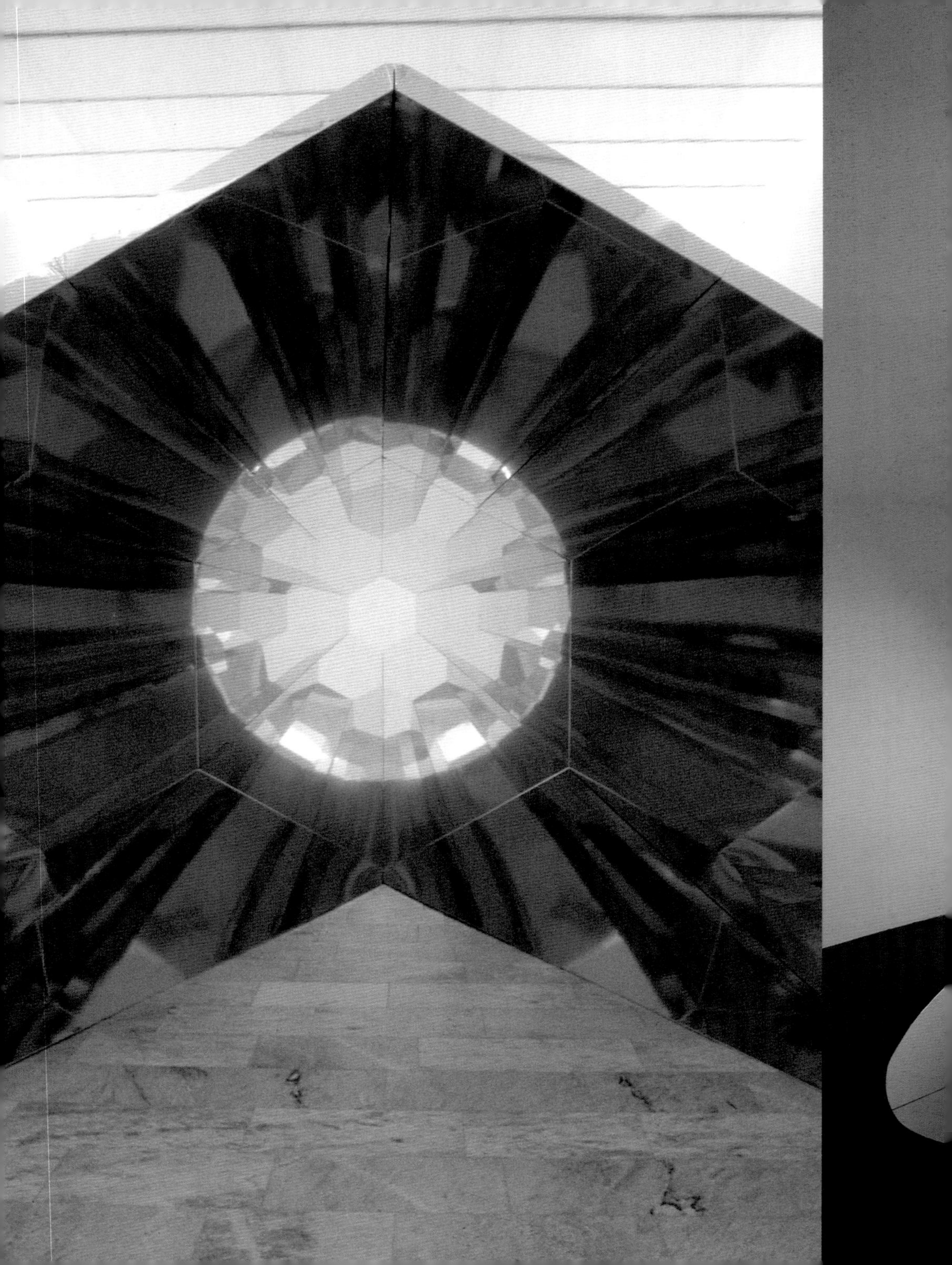

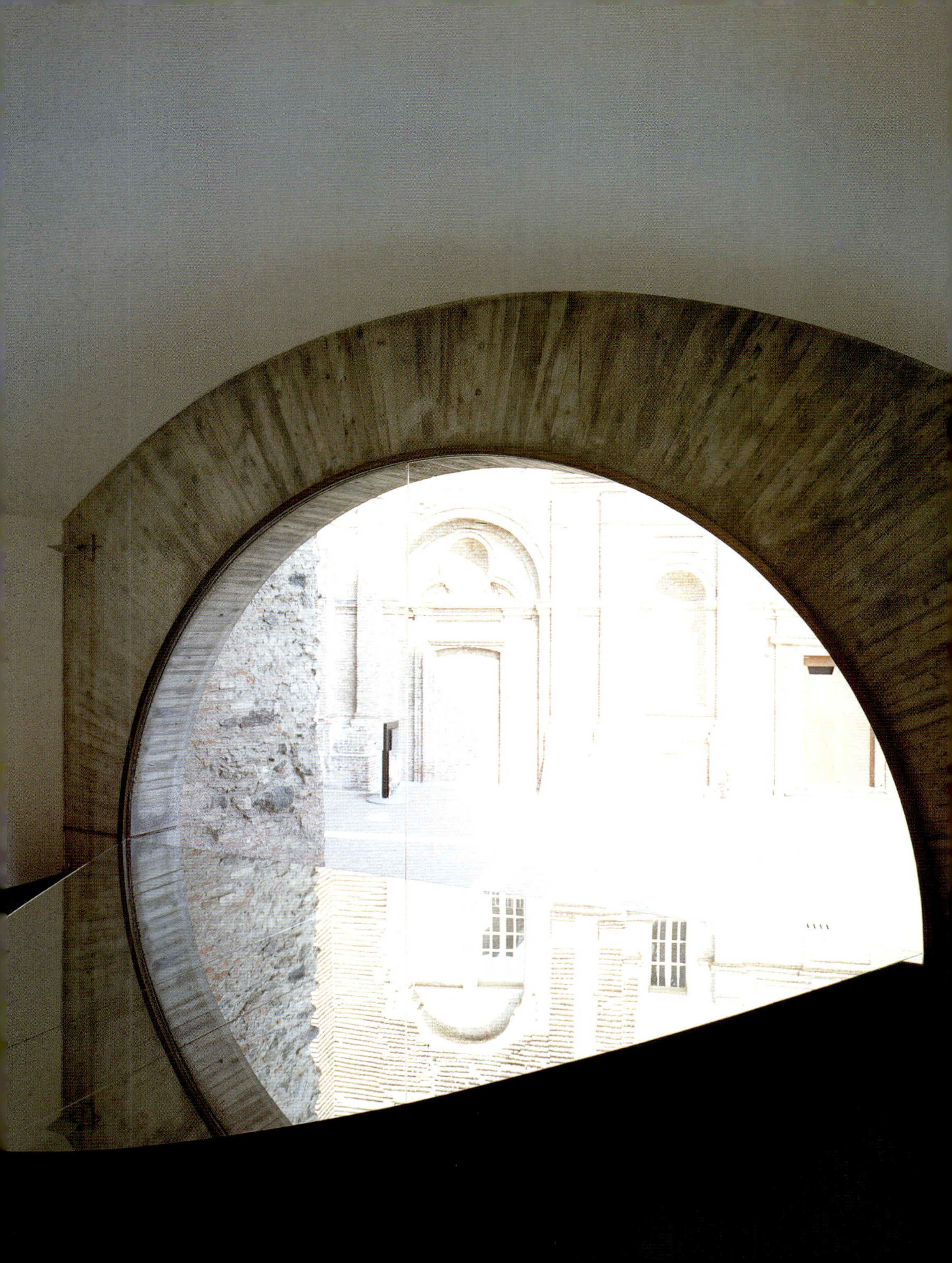

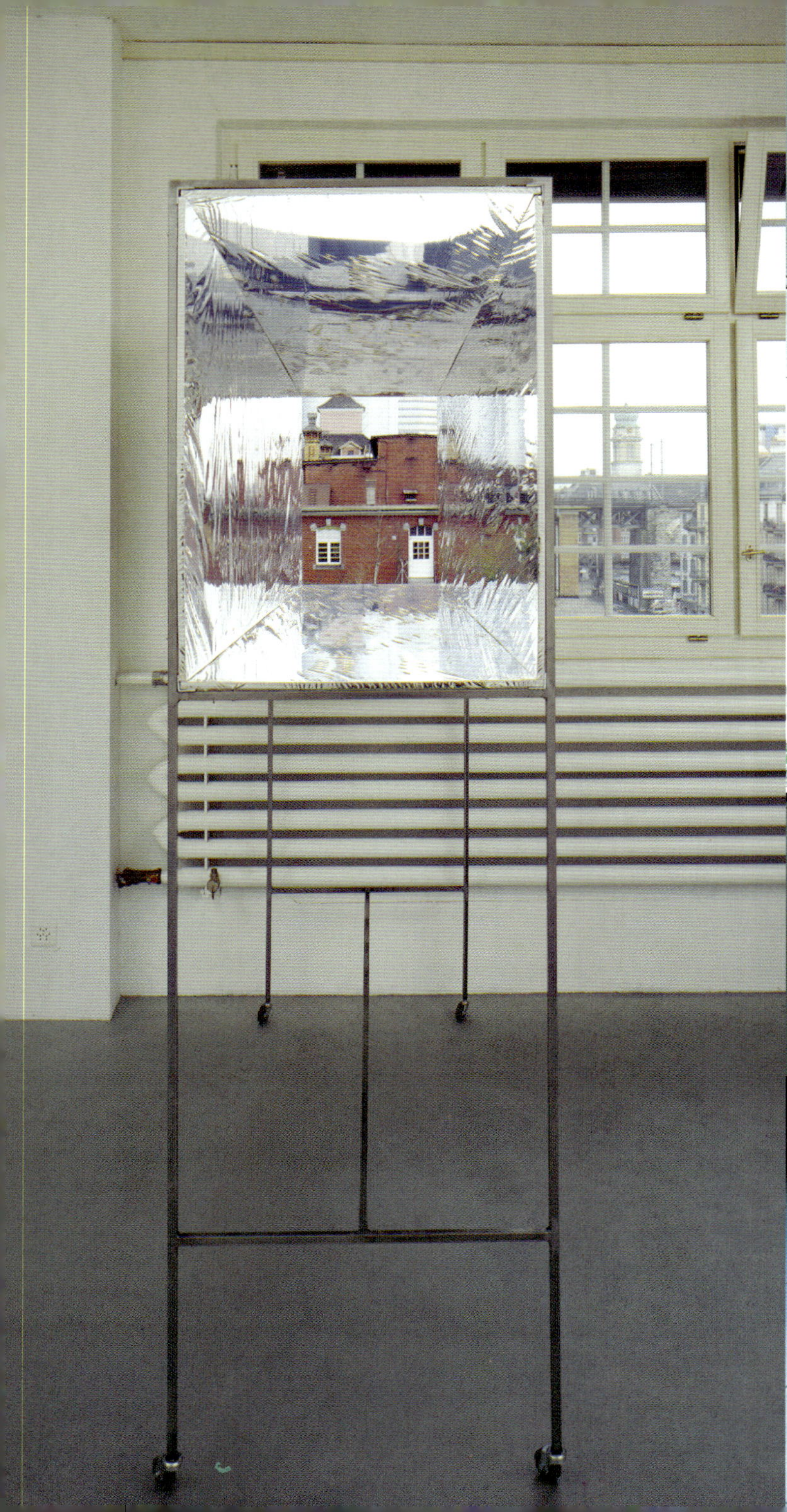
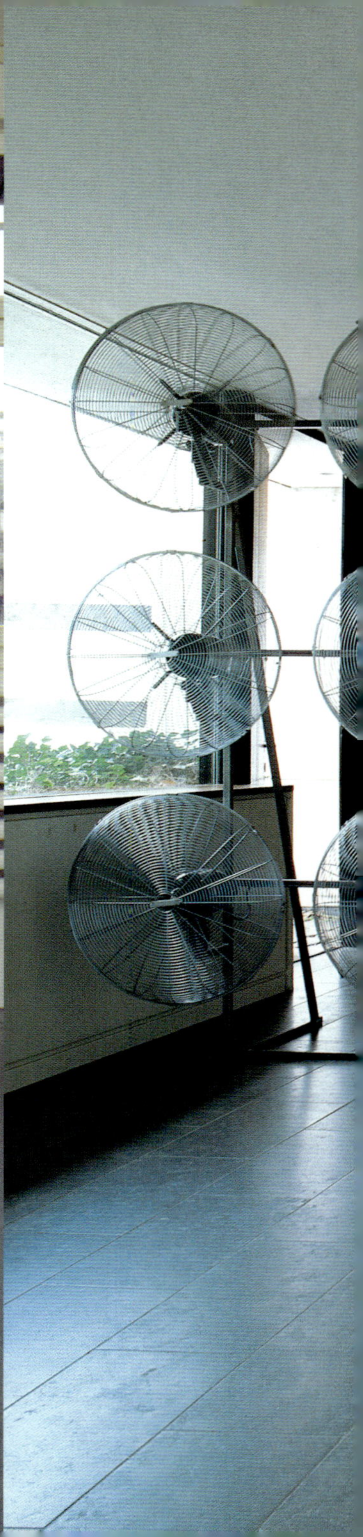

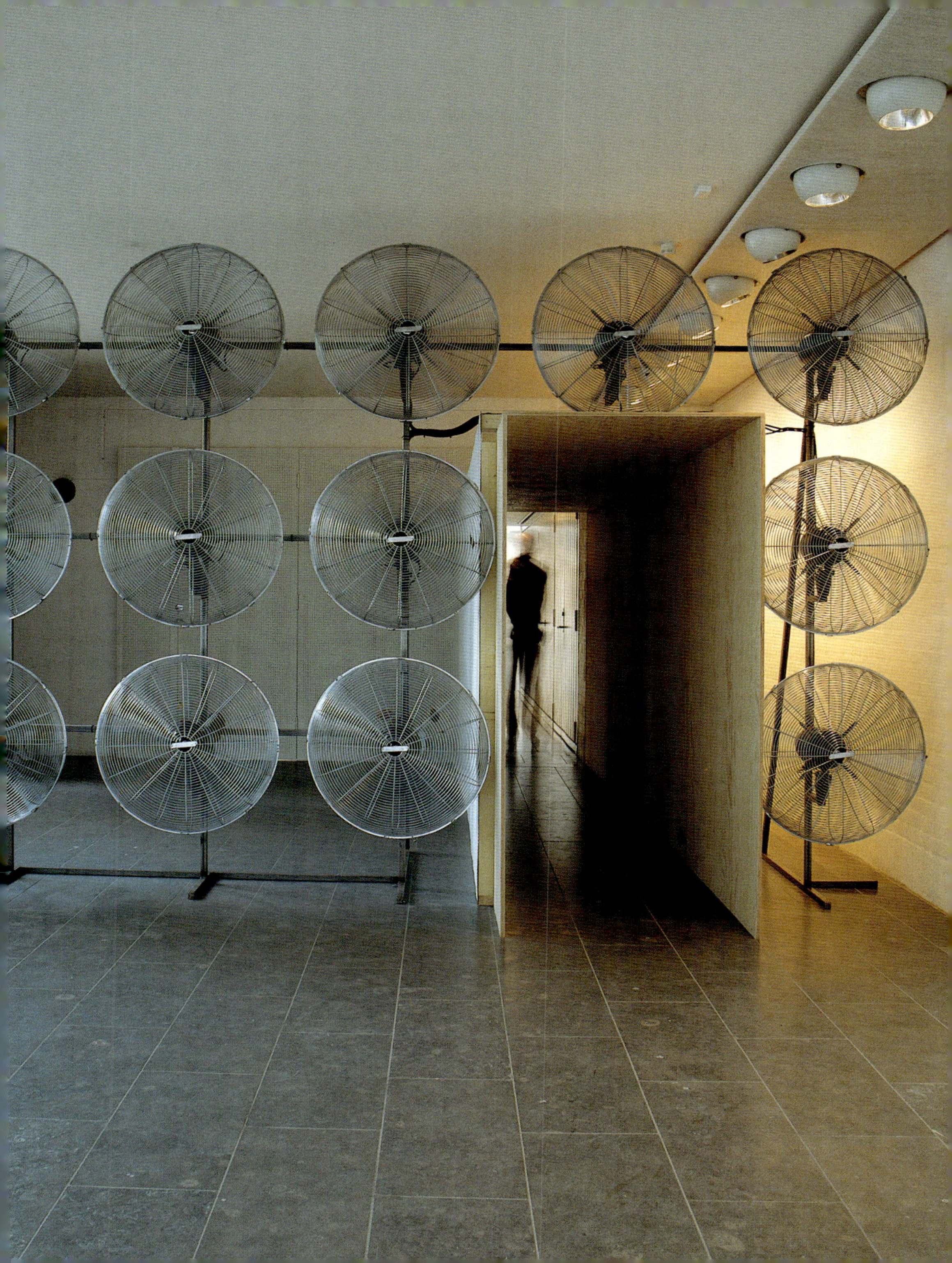

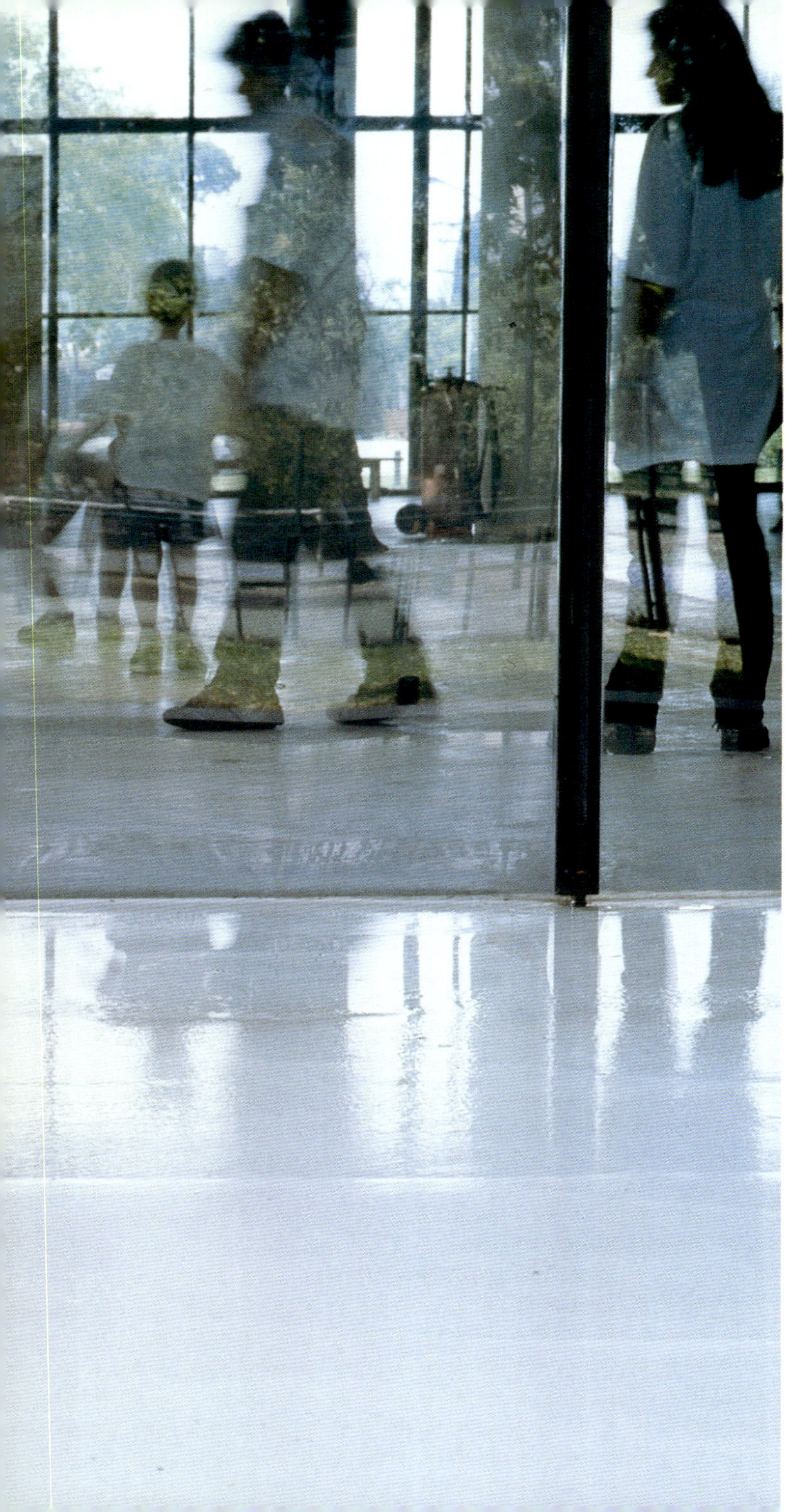

1 **Untitled**, 1998	Size varies with installation; ventilator, wire; installation view: Berlin Biennale, Berlin, Germany
2 **Your intuitive sky**, 2000	Size varies with installation; metalbox, foil, neon tubes, light sensor; installation view: The Art Institute of Chicago, Chicago, USA
3 **Succession**, 2000	Size varies with installation; grass, soil, scaffolding; installation view: The Art Institute of Chicago, Chicago, USA
4 **Succession**, 2000	Size varies with installation; grass, soil, scaffolding; installation view: The Art Institute of Chicago, Chicago, USA
5 **Spiral pavilion**, 1999	ø 6m, height 2,6 m; steel; installation view: Venice Biennale, Venice, Italy
6 **Ice pavilion**, 1998	ø 3 m, height 2,5 m; steel, water, sprinkler; installation view: Kjarvalstadir Museum, Reykjavík, Iceland
7 **Ice pavilion**, 1998, detail	ø 3 m, height 2,5 m; steel, water, sprinkler; installation view: Kjarvalstadir Museum, Reykjavík, Iceland
8 **Various models by Einar Thorsteinn**, 2000	Various sizes; paper; installation view: Neue Galerie am Landesmuseum Joanneum, Graz, Austria
9 **Wonderland Dome**, 2000, detail	ø 10,5 m, height 6,5 m; mirror, steel; installation view: The St. Louis Art Museum, St. Louis, USA
10 **Wonderland Dome**, 2000	ø 10,5 m, height 6,5 m ; mirror, steel; installation view: The St. Louis Art Museum, St. Louis, USA
11 **Your compound view**, 1998	8,1 x 2,7 x 3,2 m; mirror, wood, steel; Collection Kjarvalstadir, Iceland
12 **Your compound view**, 1998, detail	8,1 x 2,7 x 3,2 m; mirror, wood, steel
13 **Your circumspection disclosed**, 1999	Size varies with installation; window, mirror; installation view: Castello di Rivoli, Torino, Italy
14 **Fensterkaleidoskop**, 1998	Size varies with installation; kaleidoscope through window on rack; installation view: Galerie Peter Kilchmann, Zurich, Switzerland
15 **Your windless arrangement**, 1997	Size varies with installation; 20 ventilators; installation view: Louisiana Museum of Modern Art, Humlebæk, Denmark
16 **The very large ice-floor**, 1998	Size varies with installation; water, ice-machine, basin; installation view: Sao Paolo Biennale, Sao Paolo, Brazil

Günter Leising

Light and Order

The nature of light

Light is an electromagnetic wave of transverse character and its propagation velocity of 300,000 km per second is the highest propagation velocity possible in nature. But light is at the same time also a stream of quasi-particles, which are named photons. These statements have to be analyzed in terms of the meaning of their denominations.

Light has a color and this color is quantified by a parameter called wavelength. The red light of a laser pointer has a wavelength in the range between 0.6 to 0.7 micrometers (1000 micrometers = 1 millimeter). The sensitivity of the human eye has its maximum around 0.55 micrometers, this is green light (similar to the color used in traffic lights).

In the early days of physics people believed that light behaves like a beam of matter and a number of experiments like light reflection on a mirror supported this explanation. The light reflected from a mirror or glass surface has the same angle relative to the mirror surface as the incoming light – this is one of the basics of geometric optics. This experiment can be easily performed with a laser pointer directed at a reflecting surface and by observing the reflected beam on a sheet of paper or on a wall. (By the way this experiment is the base of the detection principle of a modern atomic force microscope, which is capable of analyzing the topography of a surface of matter with atomic resolution.)

But this "corpuscle theory" of light could not explain most of the other effects related to light, such as the refraction of light, the diffraction of light and the effects which are observed when light is scattered by particles or matter.

The characteristic parameters of light, i.e. the electromagnetic wave, are the following:

The light intensity, which is given by the number of photons or the amplitude of the electromagnetic wave (precisely, the amplitude squared) and the direction of its propagation. The length of the electromagnetic wave, which is an essential parameter is determined by the light generation process. The electromagnetic wave emitted from a light bulb contains only quite short wavepackets (in the order of a few millimeters' length) due to the statistical nature of its creation process. A laser can generate light waves of hundreds of kilometers' length.

And most importantly, light as an electromagnetic wave possesses a polarization direction, which is basically the plane in which the electromagnetic wave oscillates. This polarization direction of the light wave is essential for the effects where light interacts with light and with matter and can be analyzed with a polarizer.

People have always been fascinated by light and have tried to examine its nature and study its effects. The interaction of light with the surface of matter is the key element of how we "see" artwork i.e. paintings and how this visual impression is the input for a much more complex sensing process of a more general nature. Generating light, treating light, managing light, manipulating light, and most importantly of all, storing light, are the driving forces for scientists and artists (and of course many other disciplines).

The burgher of Schilda performed a key experiment, which was not at all understood by the majority of people concerning its significance and implications. The "Schildbürger" fabricated boxes with a lid, went out into the harsh sunlight, opened the lids and let the intense sunlight flood the volume of the boxes. After a while they closed the lids quickly and with the belief that they have captured the sunlight in the boxes they ran inside to illuminate their rooms with the "stored" sunlight. And as one might guess, this did not work.

But.

We are not allowed to blame the "Schildbürger" for the basic idea for this type of experiment. Criticism can only be raised at the fact that they did not thoroughly think about how to perform such an experiment and ignored planning the experimental conditions based on the properties of light.

Light is very difficult to store!

Imagine a "wild" thing like a photon traveling 300,000 km per second.

Lets do a mental-experiment: Imagine a tiny rubber ball "flying" around at the velocity of light in your living room like an inflated balloon, which escaped before you could close its opening. It will hit the walls of your living room every 0,00000001 seconds or, better, 100 million times every second. With each contact with a rough or disordered surface of matter, the light beam loses a small part of its energy and after some hits the light beam has dissipated its entire energy into matter. This dissipated energy is not lost but it leads to a warming of the matter.

If one could manage to create a surface with exactly 100% reflectivity, it would be possible to store a light beam forever in a box made up of such surfaces. In reality it appears to be very difficult to fabricate surfaces with exactly 100% reflectivity. We will see in the section Matter, that perfect order of matter, which would be required for such a surface will only be realizable in a dynamical manner. There are already experimental results, where colleagues succeeded in storing light for a small, limited time period.

Light and Impression

Light is a subjective impression of living organisms, which are equipped with light sensors ("eyes"). In human beings these natural sensors or detectors are constructed in such a manner that they are able to adapt to strongly varying light levels from extremely bright light to very low light levels in the "dark." At moderate and high light levels (daylight) these sensors are capable of detecting nuances of light level differences and coloration differences.

At low (dawn) and very low (night) light levels the detection system eye is forced to detect any light wave or photon, which is captured by the eye lense. Therefore at low light levels the eye shall only see "gray light" levels, because the sensing system eye is ignoring its color differentiating power in favor of enhancing its detectability.

In contrast to other living creatures like bees, the human eye is not able to "see" the polarization of light. Bees, due to their need for a sophisticated navigation system to fulfill their duties of targeting flowers and collecting honey during daylight, are equipped with an eye system that allows detection of the polarization nature of light captured by the eye. The reason for this special equipment is straightforward. The navigation strategy of bees is based on the position of the sun and if the sky is clear there is no problem in deriving the flying direction relative to the sun's position. If the sky is covered with clouds the light reaching the earth's surface is scattered by the water particles (droplets) in the clouds. For a human being, it is therefore not possible to locate the position of the sun from the earth's surface due to the fact that this scattering effect in the clouds provides a more or less homogeneous illumination of the earth's surface. But there is information about the sun's position in this light coming to the earth. As explained before, light is a transverse electromagnetic wave and as such it possesses a propagation plane of the wave, which determines the direction of polarization. In any light scattering effect, the polarization of the light waves plays an important role. Therefore the sunlight scattered by the clouds contains the information of the sun, position in its polarization.

Light and Matter

The generation of light is connected with matter in a general sense.

There is no light generation without matter.

We adhere strictly to the generic meaning of light generation, so effects like light conversion (as in the case of luminescence, where high energy, i.e. blue light, excites a molecule, which emits light of lower energy, i.e. another color. This effect is used in highlighter inks).

The generation of light is connected with particles, atoms, molecules in any state (gas, liquid, solid, plasma). We would need a large chapter to cover all the possible processes of light generation. Therefore we limit ourselves in this context to a few processes, which are then also used in the following discussion. The easiest process of light generation is based on

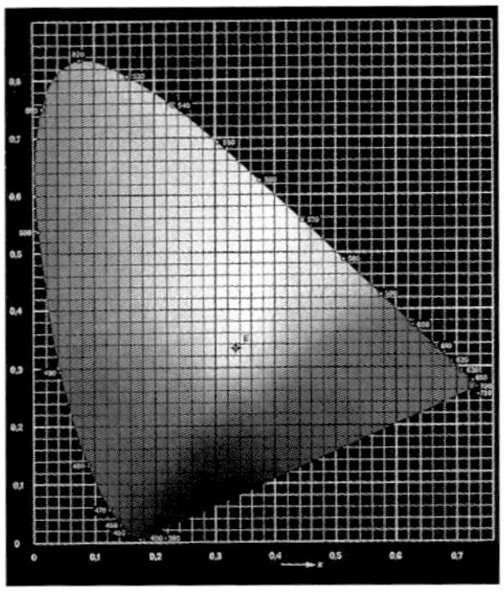

Fig. 1
CIE color table to quantify colors by coordinates.

heat. When a filament in a light bulb is heated to high temperatures by an electric current passing through it, light of different wavelengths (colors) is generated at the same time, giving the impression of white light (if the filament temperature is sufficiently high). The color temperature (from warm red governed light to harsh blue dominated light) of the generated light is controlled by the temperature of the filament.

Light can be measured and categorized by two coordinates (x,y) due to its color composition (see fig. 1). The quality of light can also be measured and categorized by a technique called spectroscopy. A spectrometer measures the intensity (or better, the number of photons) for each wavelength of the spectral range of interest.

The continuous multi-wavelength emission of the light bulb is generated by individual light emitters located in the filament material. Each photon coming out of the bulb has its own and individual history of creation. They do not care for each other, neither in their stages of creation nor on their propagation path during their lifetime – unless they are forced to interact and this will be discussed in the next section.

Light and Order

A laser (light amplification by stimulated emission of radiation) is an example of a light source where order in matter and order in sequence lead to a light source which emits light of high quality. The laser light is characterized by a few facts, which lead us back to the beginning where we characterized light by its basic parameters: wavelength, intensity, direction and polarization. A laser is constructed to emit all its generated photons with one exactly defined wavelength and therefore one can achieve very high laserlight intensities. The laser emits its photons into one defined direction (this is the reason why laser light emission is used in pointers; by pointing at something; a word, a phrase, a text segment, or an object, this entity is isolated from its surrounding, it is segregated from the uniformity of the crowd it belongs to). Last but not least, the light coming out of a laser (pointer) is completely defined concerning its polarization (in a good laser the emitted light is polarized in only one plane).

Now let us come back to the fact that order in matter and order in sequence leads to the creation of laser light. First of all, only a selected number of materials (particles, atoms, molecules) are constructed in a way that they will allow the buildup of an ordered system for lasoring. Let us take the ruby laser (which was the system with which the first solid state laser was fabricated) as our example. Ruby is a material which exhibits a deep red coloration. This coloration is due to a specific color center in the material. The base material for ruby is Al_2O_3, aluminium oxide also known as sapphire. The aluminium oxide contains traces of Chromium atoms, which form the centers responsible for the color. If a ruby rod is illuminated by white light, it shows a red luminescent emission (around 0.7 micrometers wavelength) due to these color centers. Each color center is contributing red photons to the emission process individually. So, at which time a color center is excited and in which moment a color center is emitting a photon, are completely free processes and of individual, i.e. statistical, nature. Although the emitted light gives the impression of one (red) color, the individual photons have different (red) wavelengths showing a quite broad wavelength distribution. The red photons are emitted in all possible directions, there is no restriction at all and the polarization of the emitted light is completely random.

Let us now realize a ruby laser. A 10 centimeter rod of an artificial ruby crystal is fabricated and its end faces are polished to high optical quality. This ruby rod is placed in the center of a coiled flash lamp (see fig. 2). The essence of stimulated emission is the following: With the flash light pulse, the excitation of the color centers happens at the same time. Now imagine a high density of excited color centers in the ruby crystal waiting

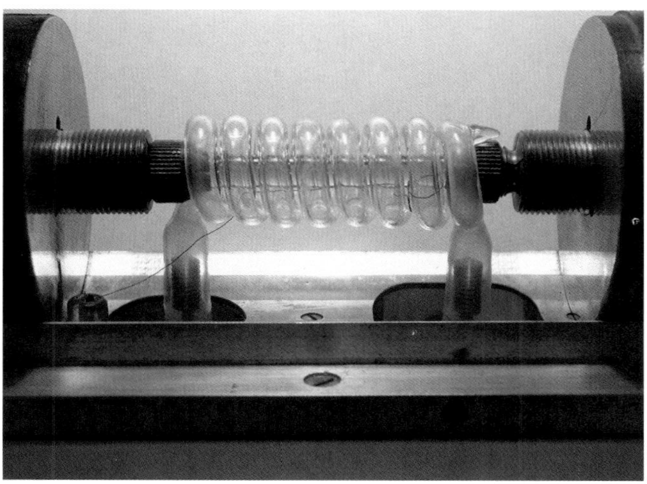

Fig. 2
Original Ruby Laser

to emit light. If one of the centers start with the light emission, this light beam propagates in the ruby rod and is reflected back by the polished end faces of the rod. This light beam is stimulating (kicking) the other excited color centers to start their emission and consequently a multiplication (avalanche) effect is set off and a laser pulse of high intensity is emitted from the end of the ruby rod. This sequential order is the key issue for the laser function and the more precisely this sequence is realized, the higher the quality of the laser light produced.

A similar effect of light and order is observed in matter (we will discuss a photonic crystal as an example), where the electromagnetic wave is forced to interact with itself due to a defined and periodic order of matter.

Imagine a powder of aluminium oxide, in its pure form (sapphire). It is a highly transparent, very stable material and its color would be white (like powdered sugar) if inspected under the white light of, e.g. a halogen lamp.

Let us now assume that all the grains of the powder are small spheres of exactly the same diameter of 0.5 micrometers: there would be no change in its appearance; it would still be a white powder. Now we produce a dispersion of the powder, by pouring the powder into water, stirring thoroughly and then we place the dispersion on a quiet, vibration-free place. The spheres now start to drift slowly to the bottom (sedimentation). If this happens very, very slowly, each sphere takes its place in a dense packing of spheres (which is called hexagonal dense packing). After some time (a few weeks) the sedimented material can be removed and dried. If this material is inspected by white light illumination a strong coloration of the solid material is visible (see fig. 3). We have produced an artificial opal. How does the coloration come along ?

The prerequisites for this color (photonic) effect are the facts that

- the oxide spheres are of exactly the same diameter and
- they order themselves in a very defined periodic manner.

Systems which fulfill these requirements are called photonic crystals.

The presence of entities (spheres) with defined dimensions, i.e. diameter, (in the range of the wavelength of the light used for illumination) and their periodic arrangement forces light to interact with itself in a defined manner. The periodicity of the photonic crystal determines the color of the crystal, whereas the optical properties of the matter determines the saturation of the color effect. The base effect of interaction in photonic

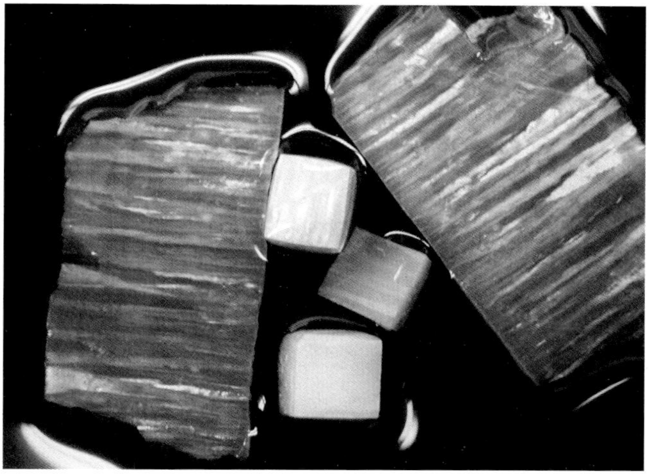

Fig. 3
Artifical Photonic Crystals - Opals (the size of the largest crystal is about 2 cm)

systems is the interference of the light beams with each other. The periodicity of the photonic crystal is the sequence parameter for this interference effect. If this interference is constructive then the light beams interact in such a manner that they add up their intensity after interaction. If this interference is destructive then the light beams interact in such a manner that there is no intensity observed after interaction (providing that the two two light beams in question have the same amplitude).

This light and order relation can also be discussed from a more general point of view, corresponding to effects such as those described in Elias Canetti's *Crowd and Power*. Canetti defined a sort of "mass crystals" and he derived a similar interaction behavior for the relation of the "mass crystal" with the crowd.

Physical properties such as binding energy, compactness, order, and uniformity gain a similar meaning, when one is observing and describing the interaction dynamics of individuals in a disordered and an ordered crowd; whereas the "mass crystal" is a type of permanent seed.

In a "mass crystal" ordered distributed functions exist like in an orchestra.

Their effect and appearance is based on their action, i.e. interaction, with the exterior as a whole.

The existence of the single elements (spheres) outside the crystal is colorless; they are transparent; they are invisible.

Epilogue

The constructive interaction (in phase interference) of light mediated by matter results in the creation of light in a certain area or volume; the destructive interaction (out of phase interference) leaves light-free areas or volumes, which are in darkness.

Black is a color and, due to the nature of color it is based on light.

Darkness is not black.

In areas and volumes of darkness there is no light intensity.

Bruce Mau

12 Strategies. Notes

During the time I spent working in London, my work day was eighteen hours, and I realized that when you devote that much time and effort to mundane projects, they absorb your entire life. It's that simple. So, the first decision I made when the studio was starting up was that, if I was to continue to work eighteen hours a day (which seemed inevitable), the projects had to be stimulating and research-driven.

Our intense kind of research process constantly renews our work and transforms us. The process is unpredictable and the results seldom what we anticipate. The studio's process is not a stylistic system with signature fonts used repeatedly, not a recipe of colors, not a formula for approaching space or shaping form. The process flows in the reverse direction: the projects provoke us to learn about the world, and the research constantly produces different kinds of work that, we have discovered, cannot be arrived at by other means. It may be a difficult thing to grasp for people at the other end of the process, but the work arises as a methodological consequence – not from streaming projects through some stylistic posture.

In order to work and to live this way you need time. The obstacle is that the economy of design work is not set up to operate with a research process as a central component. The businesses that designers customarily have as clients seldom, if ever, plan for adequate design time when scheduling their projects. The serious designer must learn to become a time thief. Publishers, for instance, refuse even to hear about paying a designer to accompany the author on his or her artistic or intellectual travels in order to become intimately familiar with what is going on inside a book. The result is that to develop a responsive and considered research process one has to proceed by hook and by crook. One way or the other, you will travel with the author, but you may well find yourself traveling in economy. Optimize. That is what the whole research process is about. When I say research, I mean going out into the world and grappling with the forces directly shaping our working context. That's what "getting engaged" is all about. It's about trying to make sense of how the environment in which we work is being rapidly transformed, and what the implications of that are for our practice.

Twelve strategies

This essay is a reflection on design methodology and the context in which it is currently evolving. It is an attempt to discover what it takes to produce a new work today, an attempt to articulate some of the creative, spiritual, and intellectual processes that one must mobilize in order to live this way. It is an interrogation of states of mind – of enthusiasm, suspicion, and nerve, of brutal sophistication and of the naïve megalomania necessary to create what others have called postindustrial culture. But it is also a meditation on how one might sustain nervous connection to a hypercharged global image machine without simply reproducing the most horrific and destructive aspects of the social and economic milieu.

What we wish to do here is to take stock of some of the ways in which our studio reacts to contemporary culture. Our goal is to approach design as more than a set of formal solutions. We have tried to develop a new stance for the designer, one that confronts demands both from the world of business and from the world of culture.

This text is organized around twelve of the many conceptual strategies employed by our studio. These strategies are openings; we are not driven by them, but use them interchangeably as relays or expediencies – in other words, as tools. What distinguishes these strategies from others is that they are provisional rather than self-contained ends.

We do not imagine the production of form to be the end-point of design. We look for something more difficult and tenuous: to engage as directly as possible the environment within which design occurs. Adopting provisional strategies, then, is a technique for providing the designer with a space within which to work, one outside of the relentless demand for form or novelty. At certain moments it is the search for freedom.

Traditionally, the designer begins work only after content has been shaped. The designer determines how something is said, but has no influence over what is being said. We are interested in expanding and extending the role of the designer to include the substance of the message itself. The content – what is being said – is the trigger for form. Our goal is to produce an environment of collaboration for the development and integration of content and form.

We are living through a transformation that is altering all our forms of exchange: our biological capacity to reproduce; the ways and means by which we interact with one another; the definition of work and the workplace; the forms, and the forms of circulation, of our cultural products; and finally, the urban milieu in which all of these things are integrated. In the last two decades we have witnessed a revolution in our capacity to invent and manipulate images. The digital age has inflicted insecurities, crisis, drama, and conflict on every discipline that relies on the image for its modus operandi. Indeed, it has left almost no field intact. Even the newspaper, once a text-based medium, now seems a flimsy remnant of its former self, inundated by the image, desperately striving to be like television.

With our new-found manipulative capacities we have rushed blindly toward the ideal, removing, retouching, and perfecting every flaw and wrinkle. A recent cover of Mirabella magazine displays a supermodel whose image is a montage composed entirely of fragments. Our craving for perfection has sentenced women and men by the thousands to the gym, to the surgeon, and occasionally even to their deaths in an effort to align their own image with a thin digital strip of perfection. Montage is now deliriously self-inflicted.

The capacity to alter and reproduce images is being extended to natural and manufactured objects, with all of the attendant dilemmas and paradoxes that capacity involves. Devices to generate and replicate complex new objects may soon be as widely distributed and accessible as personal computers. These information-management tools already travel the globe freely, emerging wherever possible or necessary, creating a supranational web of technique. Taken together, changes like these are fundamentally redefining the context of global images within which local cultures must distinguish and sustain themselves.

It is this new cultural environment that makes adopting a critical stance so difficult. The promiscuity of the image, and our unprecedented abilities to create, modify, and disperse images, increase in subtlety and force daily. We speak of the ability of images to "target" specific audiences, and the precision and force of such "targeting" (the techniques by which images may be used to produce definite ends) are alarming. It is as if the communications environment has itself become toxic.

Paradoxically, these same conditions provide a window of opportunity. As tools proliferate horizontally, opportunities and expertise realign vertically. Every software application that can be loaded onto a computer increases our capacity to produce within the envelope defined by the software parameters. In our studio, for instance, we have the capacity to create typefaces, manipulate images, design books, produce websites, generate cinema, record and manipulate audio, and create three-dimensional objects – all in a digital realm – and then circulate those objects and products in the world. Our ability to extend our reach is increasing, and, more important, so is our capacity to combine and hybridize our work.

If the computer becomes for images the equivalent of a typewriter for text, "authors" on a computer may use graphic vocabularies the way they once used text. As software and image production technology become smarter and cheaper, we may begin to approach the capacity for invention that has only ever been the province of literature. Instead of signaling the end of the book, the computer triggers its reinvention as a radicalizing visual medium. We view these changes as a chance to depart from the Fordist politics of form-giving that accompanied design practice when the production of images required resources that only larger, bureaucratic interests could muster. In response to the imposed division of labor between form-giving and content-making, we propose a long-overdue reunification.

Our insistence on playing a collaborative editorial role as part of the design process has been fundamental in shaping the direction of our practice and in leading us toward the development of content. Our studio seeks an increasingly active role in the projects we undertake, not merely to service the demands of the client, but rather to collaborate in insuring the seamless realization of an innovative cultural product.

This allows us to develop something new: a laboratory environment where the holistic project of design can be pursued. We believe that the most effective and ambitious practice involves the creation of new cultural artifacts. In pursuit of this, one cannot rely on any one formula or point of view. The technique of transgression, long a favorite of the avant-garde, has lost power as a critical strategy in an environment where every transgression is instantly trumped and appropriated as a media and marketing strategy. The objective is not to develop form per se, but culture: to engage in design as a critical stance. The new approach promises to end boundaries, borders and artificial limits, and to shatter the brutal confinement of creative lives stuck within the structures of an imposed professionalism.

This is a diagram of the typical trajectory of a book project. It shows the wandering of the author as he or she interprets the world, gathering and eventually synthesizing information. Once compressed, the content is relayed to what the Dutch would call a form-giver, the one who designs the final product.

Compare the amplitude. The amplitude is our ability to freely engage and interpret the world directly, to move away from what is already known, and to explore.

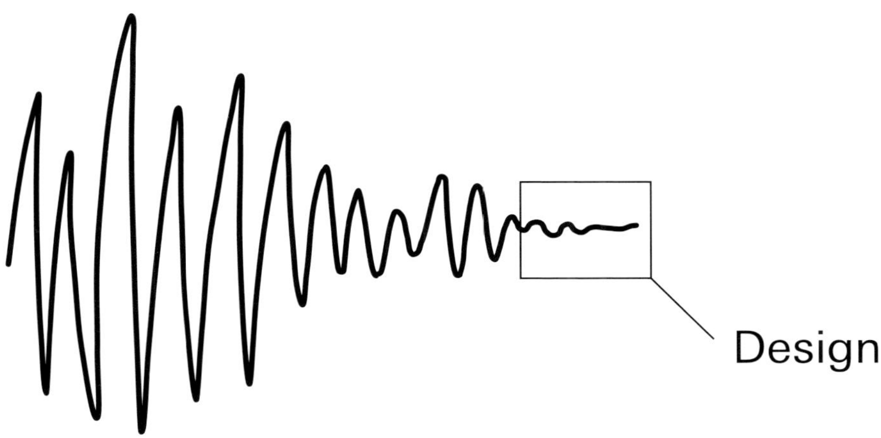

This is a diagram of a new approach, where the creation of content and form are in dialogue from start to finish. When design practice is enlarged and superimposed on the creation of content, the designer takes part in the same processes of wandering and refinement as the author does.

While the pathways followed by designer and author occasionally diverge, it is the separation and tension between them that generates ideas and qualities that could be produced in no other way.

The new approach replaces division of labor with synthesis, clients and commissions with collaborators and partners, executing tasks with negotiating terrain, maximum output with maximum feedback, and form applied to content with form and content evolving and enriching each other simultaneously. We replace resource extraction with investment, efficiency with depth, speed with growth, and professional classification with integration.

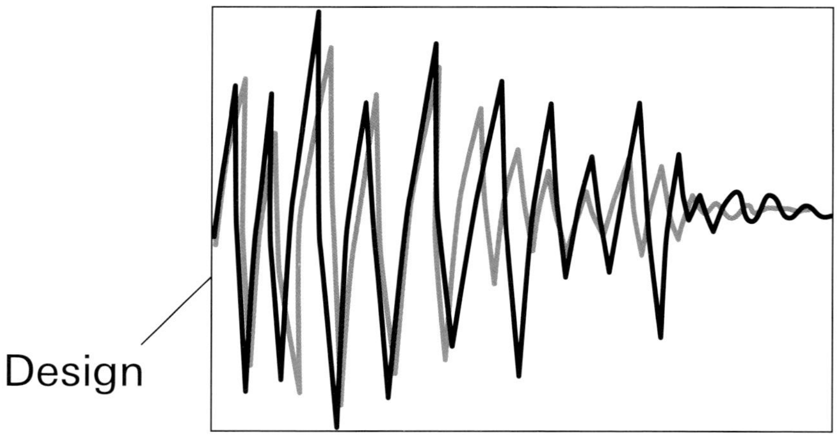

We are not sure whether this new way of working means the end of design, or whether it means that designers become authors, or authors become designers, or all three. We are convinced that this approach is rich with potential and capable of producing results not otherwise possible.

Our approach to design practice arises from a deep contradiction. We attempt to excavate a space of freedom from the corrosiveness of form, all the while accepting that our product itself is form. It is a contradiction that we accept and work with. We explore form as a particular momentary stability within a condition of continuous, evolving instability. In the end, the objective is to design new objects that possess clarity and complexity within an environment within which to work and live.

Anders Michelsen

The Artificial Environment: Smart Design Design Semantics and Designer-Intelligence

1. The artificial environment: introduction

During the 1980s an interdisciplinary group of scientists and technicians developed one of today's most momentous design projects, the *Biosphere II* in Arizona. Seen from the outside, the big greenhouse-like construction barely reflects its radical content. It resembles today's trivial high tech architecture and may even recall Chrystal Palace from the first world exhibition of 1851. But in the domes, halls, arches, extensions, and corridors one finds an advanced 'copy' of the Earth's biosphere, an artificially made environment for organic life, which the organization behind the project believes can be used in the plans to make other planets in the solar system habitable for humans through "terraforming." The Biosphere II Project consists of two "culture biomes," agriculture and city, while nature appears as five "nature biomes," rain forest, savanna, desert, marsh, and ocean. A longterm plan with gradual testing of every imaginable problem, from humidity over marshlands, to selections of small singing birds, brought the system to the point of an ecological balance at the beginning of the 1990s. There is no denying the fact that this balance is artificially made, even though the construction must comply with the laws of nature with painful precision. The system thus demands extensive technical plants, is monitored by computers, and is so sensitive that even short passages of clouded weather (outside) release increased emission of greenhouse gasses in Biosphere II. Nevertheless, an enduring ecological balance was successfully maintained in the system from 1991 to 1993, when eight human test-inhabitants survived in almost complete systemic enclosure.

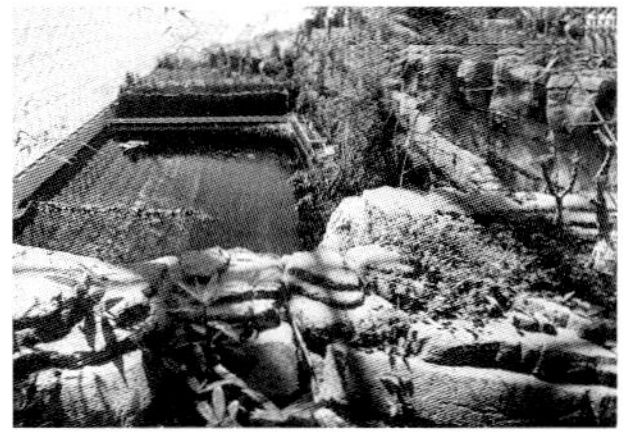

Fig. 1
Biosphere II: Coral reef with its own wave generator.

Although Biosphere II was a pilot project in the early 1990s, and by then, there were many visions to terraform other planets in the solar system, this project points primarily to a new design complexity on Earth. Artefacts such as Biosphere II indicate a new realm of design, which takes the various aspects of nature-culture models, e.g. the functional idiom of industrial modernity, to a new threshold. It is obvious that this construction is neither nature, but nor is it culture in the traditional sense of the inherited dichotomy: it relates these poles in new ways. It aims at displaying the entire complexity of nature in one strike, but at the same time it is a helplessly constructed artefact, situated as a monstrous vessel in the perplexed context.

Despite its artificiality, the nature of Biosphere II is not merely a culturally or socially produced hallmark of the huge agencies of modern technoscience, design, and production: it is constructed on a *second level*, or more precisely, in *second order*. What appears in its "inner" world is not the object- or system-definition which defines the heritage of modern design, like a car, a skyscraper, a spaceship or an agroindustrial complex. It is an entity with an extraordinary complexity: a paradoxical object which is obviously capable of a range of self-organized, albeit highly guided adaptive options and potentials.

What comes to mind is the term Gilbert Simondon employed, when he defined the "mode of existence" (mode d'existence) of the computer in the late 1950s as a technological "ensemble," based on this particular object's historic capability for a "margin of indeterminacy" which made it qualitatively different from the object-definition as "element" of the early mechanical and encyclopedic age, or the object-definition as "individual" in the mature industrial age of the late nineteenth century.[1] The technological ensemble is responsive and

1. Gilbert Simondon, *Du mode d'existence des objets techniques*, Aubier, Paris, 1989 (1958).

adaptive, it displays a degree of freedom, or to be precise, gradations of adaptive independence within contexts of use and users (Simondon discusses this in terms of homeostasis and information). In short, Biosphere II is a pertinent example of what has come to be known in recent decades as *smart design* (or more poetically with a somewhat different meaning, what Edgar Morin called a "poetic" technology in the 1970s.)[2]

Since the first outlines of cybernetics, research into automata etc. after World War II, ideas of how the computer may 'give life' to a technologically - provoked second - order existence has proliferated, not least as a new way of bridging the gap between the realm of the organic and mechanic, these "badly posed questions" as Norbert Wiener wrote in 1948. Smart design may be seen as one concrete offspring of this heritage, which in the last decade has served to underpin visions of objects and systems which radically decenter the human; what we may call a "cyborgological" design-thought, a "full range of intimate organic-machinic relations," "... posthumane creatures equal to but different than humans..."[3]

Nevertheless, it is important to remember that for all its internal vitality, the explicit aim of the Biosphere II is to demonstrate artificial closure (e.g. in an extraterrestial context). In its intentional artificiality, the project is not really aimed at rephrasing what Wiener saw as badly posed questions. It may be poietic, but it is neither an example of the automaton which set the scene in Wiener's days, nor an example of the various issues of self-organization and autopoiesis etc. which has influenced subsequent discussions. It may have the character of a realized automaton, a huge robot if one likes, but this is not really important. Its character of technological ensemble and its peculiar artificiality create a distance from the heritage of cybernetics, systems theory, etc.: Biosphere II is an example of what the Italian design theorist Ezio Manzini has defined as "an artificial environment" in need of "a new ecology."[4]

Insofar as Biosphere II is smart, it is also made. Or to put it differently, smart design is still *design,* no matter how smart. In a sense, Biosphere II is an entity constructed by means of 'reverse' observation, i.e. an entity which can be defined simply by the observation of an explicit artificial procedure. However, it is more correct to say that it is observed and constructed in *simultaneous* but not *similar* manners. Or to put it differently, the second order construction of Biosphere II may be observable from a second order perspective, but its 'sedimented' char-

2. Edgar Morin, *La méthode. I. La Nature de la Nature*, Éditions du Seuil, Paris, 1977.

3. Chris Hables Gray, Heidi J. Figueroa-Sarriera & Steven Mentor (eds.), *The Cyborg Handbook*, Routledge, New York/London, 1995, p. 3.

4. Ezio Manzini, *Artefacts. Vers une Nouvelle écologie de l'environment artficiel.* Les Essais, Centre Georges Pompidou, Paris, 1991.

acter as *de facto* artificiality, as fait accompli, circumscribes a new contingency.

Manzini argues, significantly, for the existence of a *schism* between the creation of the artificial *and* the lack of insight into the distinctive character of the artificial. "To man the artificial is a completely natural activity,"[5] he writes, but the resulting artificiality, nonetheless appears as "an unknown artificial world that we must examine, to discover its qualities and laws."[6] In the following I will use this idea to explore aspects of smart design. I will proceed by way of two "indicators" of the artificial environment: *design semantics* and *designer-intelligence* (due to lack of space I will leave out other aspects of smart design [e.g chemistry and nanotechnology]):

(a) *Design semantics as indicator: the end of the mechanical era:* A discussion of the attempt of the 1980s and 1990s design semantics to establish a new concept for the changing design object in an extended understanding of context.

(b) *Designer-intelligence as indicator: information technology:* A brief outline of how designer-intelligence in contemporary design of information technology can be seen as an indicator of smart design within an artificial environment.

2. Design semantics as indicator: the end of the mechanical era. In the article "The End of the Mechanical Age,"[7] Ezio Manzini argues, that a closer consideration will show the development to have shaken the foundation of theory and praxis of modern design, "...materials, components, and manufacturing processes have emerged that are of a profoundly different nature from those of the beginning of the century."[8] The "new world" as outlined by pioneers such as Hannes Meyer in Bauhaus in the mid-1920s as a linear movement against "the victory of conscious humanity over amorphous nature,"[9] has been replaced by a complexification of design, which may be considered according to the paradigms of complexity, rather than the singular object-reflections of the design theory of the mechanical era.

This is featured in the theory of so-called product semantics or design semantics of the 1980s and 1990s. In the article "On the Essential Contexts of Artefacts or on the Proposition that 'Design is making sense of Things'" from 1989,[10] one of the key texts of design semantics, Klaus Krippendorff writes that "product semantics" is "a study of the symbolic qualities of man-made forms in the cognitive and social context of their

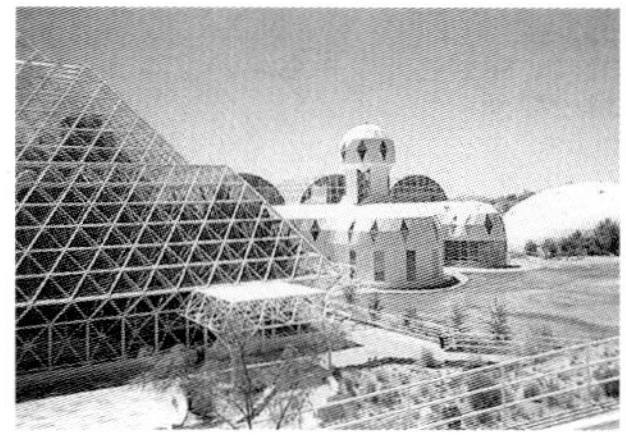

Fig. 2
Biosphere II, Arizona, USA

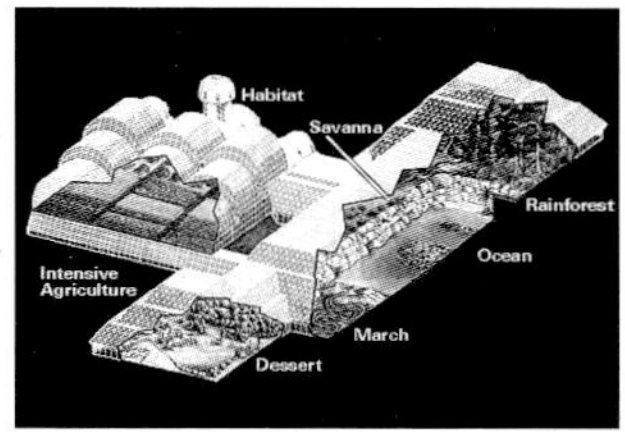

Fig. 3
Map of Biosphere II

5. Ibid., p. 44.

6. Ibid., p. 52.

7. Ezio Manzini: "The End of the Mechanical Age," in Carlo Pirovano (ed.), *History of Industrial Design 1919-1990. The Dominion of Design*, Electa, Milano, 1991.

8. Ibid., p. 34 ff.

9. Ibid.

10. Klaus Krippendorff, "On the Essential Contexts of Artefacts or on the Proposition that 'Design is making sense of Things,'" in Victor Margolin and Richard Buchanan (eds.), *The Idea of Design. A Design Issues Reader*, The MIT Press, Cambridge, Mass., 1995.

use and the application of the knowledge gained to objects of industrial design."[11] Thus, product semantics is not styling, a design program, or a design movement, as known from the history of modern design. It directs itself towards the significance that artefacts have for the user in a broader sense, toward "... how technical objects are symbolically embedded in the fabric of society, and what contributions they thereby make to the autopoiesis of culture."[12] "What something is (the totality of what it means) to someone corresponds to the sum total of its imaginable contexts," according to Krippendorff[13] and this must be studied by watching relations between user instances and contexts.[14] Krippendorff presents four levels of contextuality, descending from the general to the specific:

1. In the broadest sense "an ecological context" "...in which populations of artefacts are seen interacting with one another and contributing to the autopoesis (self-production) of technology and culture" is theorized.

2. A "context of genesis" is theorized by examining the procedures through which designers, producers, distributors, etc. participate in creating and consuming artefacts and contribute to "the technical organization of culture and material entropy."[15]

3. A context of "sociolinguistics" is dealt with by analyzing peoples' communication with each other and with artefacts, thereby co-constructing "...realities of which objects become constitutive parts."[16]

4. Finally, the theory turns towards an "operational context" which contemplates users' direct interaction with artefacts.[17]

Krippendorff's outline may be used to reason the *plausibility* in a study of the artificial environment:

The basic operational context defines the immediate complexity of the object. Artefacts take part in manual, visual, haptical, and perceptual feedback, which through a repertoire of potential conditions presents a built-in logic: "sets of variable or semantic dimensions," defined in relation to the operational context, dimensions such as: "identities; qualities; orientations; locations; affordance states; dispositions, and logic; motivations; and redundancies."[18]

11. Ibid., p. 157.

12. Ibid.

13. Ibid., p. 159.

14. Ibid., p. 160.

15. Ibid., p. 162.

16. Ibid.

17. Ibid., p. 163.

18. Ibid., p. 162 ff.

This complexity is translated into a sociolinguistic context, where artefacts play specific roles in human communication and "support linguistically mediated social practices," which Krippendorff defines through four sociolinguistic usage forms:[19] (a) As expression of the user's identity. (b) As a sign of social differentiation and integration. (c) As content in communicative connections. (d) As material support of social relations.

Krippendorff continues with an outline of a generative context: "Artefacts are not only instrumental to users (operational context) and constitutive of social realities (sociolinguistic context) ...they are also created, produced, marketed, consumed, retired, or recycled, and experiences with them inform a subsequent generation of artefacts."[20] It is an "...ongoing process of technological autopoiesis," which manifests itself *qua* artefacts. This process has neither a natural goal nor a natural final state. It feeds itself and has itself as goal. In the end it is only limited by the problem of material entropy and increasing pollution.[21]

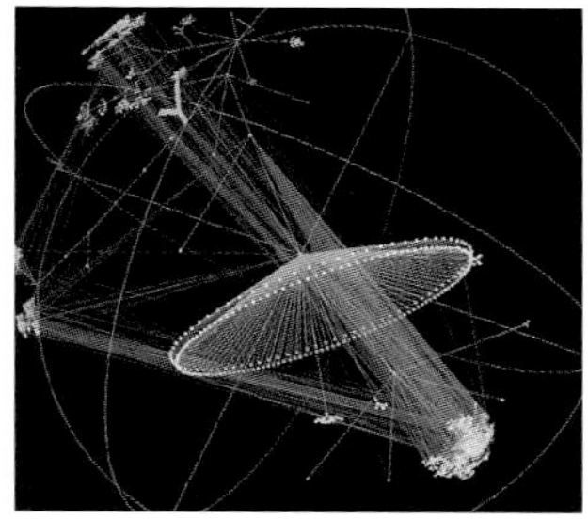

Fig. 4
3D Hyperbolic Graph of Internet Topology

Inspired by Jacob von Uexküll's biology, Krippendorff defines an ecological context in the end.[22] Artefacts may be considered populations, which through interaction with one another and people constitute specific environments from a "local" viewpoint, for which reason the artificial environment in its entirety can not appear as a transparent world, but must be described as the emergent result of interactions. Interactions may thus have different characters, Krippendorff believes. They may be competitive, symbiotic, parasitical, etc., but in the consequent processes a larger ecological cohesion is formed, expressing a balance between different impulses which the ecological context will try to uphold.[23] He writes (following Kenneth Boulding):

"...there are many species of artefacts, perhaps even more than biological species now existing. Items described in an unabridged Sears catalog are probably more numerous than biological species listed in a high school text on biology, and this catalog is far from being representative of the products available worldwide. Species of artefacts also cover greater ranges than do biological species. They range wider in size: skyscrapers are larger than elephants, artificial molecules are smaller than amoebas. They range wider in complexity: computer chips have more memory than lower animals, not to speak of stock markets that even humans cannot comprehend, and they can function much longer than any living organism, as museums can testify. Human beings can be considered arte-

19. Ibid., p. 170.

20. Ibid., p. 173.

21. Ibid.

22. Ibid., p. 179 ff.

23. Ibid.

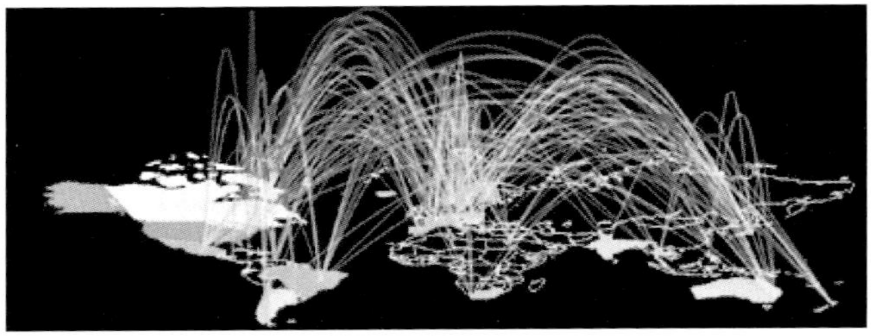

Fig. 5
Arc map displaying a 3D network structure.

facts to the extent they are social beings, speak a common language, assume social roles, conform to behavioral conventions, and are, in these respects, replaceable. Organizations are artefacts as well, created by humans, interacting with one another in particular environments containing various resources, markets, stake holders, and regulatory agencies. The implications for product semantics of placing artefacts in ecological contexts are enormous..."[24]

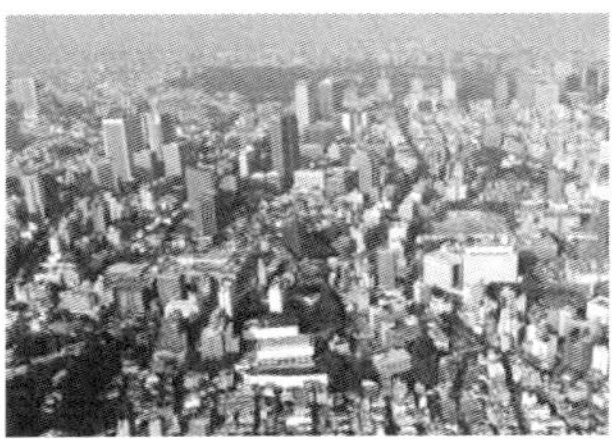

Fig. 6
Tokyo, Japan, 1993

3. Designer-intelligence as indicator: information technology
In Los Alamos National Laboratory in the USA, scientists have developed an epochal computer simulation of the traffic in real life Albuquerque, New Mexico,[25] which indicates the developmental directions and potentials in relations between technology and contemporary design. The simulation is called *Transims* and, for the first time ever, has simulated the entire traffic in a city with 200,000 households and 400,000 road users, who use 30,000 roads every day. A rush hour sequence may take the shape of a three-dimensional, multicolored overview of the city's road system on a computer screen, which visualizes development and intensity of the traffic: At 6 a.m. most roads are white, most road users are still in bed. At 8 a.m. the rush hour is in full swing and highways and other central roads are a menacing orange or completely red. At 9 a.m. many roads have turned into mighty orange, red and purple, while local roads have taken on a strong green color, traffic is reaching its peak. Among other things, Transims has made it possible to make environmental predictions for large traffic systems and calculate traffic reactions to new infrastructures such as bridges, traffic lights and bypasses. Every second a new version of the simulation is being computed, integrating detailed data such as tire pressure and emission for singular vehicles, traffic flow on designated roads, reactions to traffic jams, road accidents and other random events.

24. Ibid., p. 180.

25. Cf. John L. Casti: *Would-be Worlds*, John Wiley & Sons Inc., New York, 1997, p. 131 ff, p. 135 ff.

Historically a model like Transims draws on the longstanding research opened by Wiener and others after World War II, including what I have characterized as a cyborgological design-thought. However, as design one may regard Transims as a prime example of a distinctive *designer-intelligence,* which demonstrates a specific range of partly self-organized, partly guided, adaptive options. On the one hand, the model is an example of a technological system that can develop complex patterns. On the other hand, the model takes part in the issue of the artificial environment. Or, to put it differently, for all its complexity the model is modelled.

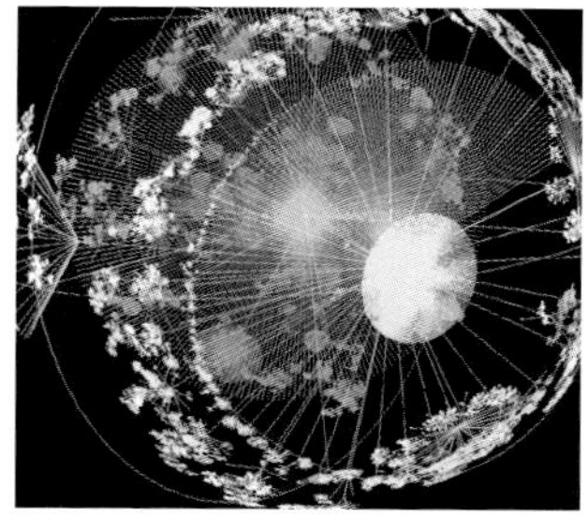

Fig. 7
3D Hyperbolic Graph of Internet Topology

Transims and Biosphere II may be seen as configurations of designer-intelligence, which for heuristical means may be placed at each 'end' of an artificial environment, which ranges *from* the 'virtuality' of real time computer modelling *to* the material real time 'simulation' of Biosphere II. The phenomenon of designer-intelligence is thus more than an important growth potential in contemporary design, it is also an indicator of more general aspects of an artificial environment, which may be specified tentatively as *three modalities of designer-intelligence:*

1. *Object intelligence* based on a *gradual but not defining* incorporation of intelligence, i.e. adaptive functions (e.g. memory) in the design object. One may find object intelligence in many varieties, from micro wave ovens to advanced systems such as Transims, i.e. information processing systems linked to various 'platforms' (e.g., from micro controllers to wireless Internet access), and hardware and software transducer technologies, that connect computer systems with people and other parts of the physical world, backed by sensor- and effector mechanisms, etc. Nevertheless, these systems will most often need substantial interaction with an external user in order to function. Significant aspects of the Biosphere II relate to such systems, because the construction demands constant external monitoring and control, which, conversely, may serve to indicate how object intelligence, already in todays form, affects inherited ideas of form, space, and objectivity in the direction of artificially made environments.

2. *Intelligent objects* and structures that "mime" significant aspects of incorporations (organic); that is *a defining but*

gradual appliance of designer-intelligence in the design object. Intelligent objects can be automata, e.g. robots, but they can also be "knowbots" or software agents. The most advanced versions of intelligent objects today are often found in military contexts, such as the robot plane DarkStar, capable of completely independent stealthy surveillance for long mission periods is based on on-board computer control and satellite navigation. M. V. Gandhi and B. S. Thompson predict[26] that intelligent objects, to a great extent, will be defined through "miming," "mimesis," or biomimesis, "biomimethics" of organic life, "... exhibiting nervous systems, brains, and muscular capabilities," including organic features such as "self-repare, self-diagnosis, self-multiplication, and self-degradation."[27]

3. *Distributed intelligence* as developed through the coupling of object intelligence and intelligent objects, e.g. via wired and wireless, "ubiquitive" packet switching in computer networks. Here the network may be seen as an intelligent connector (applying computer based routers, protocols, etc.) between various forms of designer-intelligence, accessing different functions and objects in miscellaneous artificially made environments within computer systems or outside.

One may thus consider designer-intelligence as an indicator of the extent, the tendency, and the character of the issues which Manzini terms an "artificial environment," or to phrase it conversely, the idea of the artificial environment is hardly conceivable without designer-intelligence. The concept of designer-intelligence may, at the same time, be elaborated by the "turn" from object towards contextual complexity discussed by Krippendorff above:

1. In an operational context, one can easily argue for increased contextual complexity when considering the forms of intelligence discussed above, which, so to speak, fund the artificial environment with a plethora of "variable and semantic dimensions" in the operational context.

2. In a sociolinguistic context, one can trace a similar increase in complexity, for instance by means of broad band facilities in computer-mediated communication based on distributed intelligence, as indicated today on the Internet or in the advanced C3I military networks.

26. M. V. Ghandi and B. S. Thompson, *Smart Materials and Structures*, Chapman & Hall, 1992, p. ix, p. 58 ff.

27. Ibid., p. ix.

3. In a generative context, one may imagine new relations between autopoietic self-organization and allopoietic construction, as already seen in postindustrial networks.

4. Perhaps the sketch makes most sense in the ecological context, where it may serve to indicate, expand, and put in perspective Krippendorff's idea of populations of artefacts.

4. End: scale-extrapolation, imagination, and autonomy

Designer-intelligence points not only to the immense relevance of Manzini's idea of the artificial environment as a complex novelty. It is not difficult to see how the various modalities of designer-intelligence may radicalize the schismatic character of the artificial environment, by introducing the problem of a scale-extrapolation of the relations between the design object and, in particular, the human user-context:

1. In the direction of a still more radical miniaturizing, which means that design will increasingly 'operationalize' spheres that are immediately inaccessible to the corporeal-phenomenological scale of the human being and which must consequently be operationalized through 'translations' such as user-interfaces.

2. In the direction of macro-physical expansion, e.g. in interstellar constructions and the telematics of the Internet, where the human body seems to be on the verge of the possible, as seen in the acute problems of information overload in networked 'ubiquitousity' or physiological problems on long stays in extra terrestial space.

3. "Incorporatively," or by way of "incorporation"[28] in the concrete form of a gradual change of the users 'body' through protheses, implants, informational systems, body nets, etc. that change it "from within," not only through direct impact but also through an ever more constructed environment for its corporeal existence.

With this, the question of the relation between the user instance and an artificial environment is posed with a particular radicality. Seen from the viewpoint of the modern design tradition, in particularly the human scale, 'the human factor', "our own body which is in the world as the heart is in the organism,"[29] as Maurice Merleau-Ponty wrote in 1945 (shortly

28. Cf. the extensive definition given by Jonathan Crary and Sanford Kwinter in Crary and Kwinter, eds., *Incorporations. Zone 6*, Urzone Inc., New York, 1992.

29. Maurice Merleau-Ponty, *Phenomenology of Perception*, Routledge and Kegan Paul Ltd., London, 1986 (1945/1962), p. 203.

before the momentous break-through of systems theory, computer science, and biology) will be forced to assimilate this scale-extrapolation (even if this takes the concrete shape of an alliance based on mutual adaption, as George Canguilhem believed, and which has been at the center of debates on cyberspace, etc.).[30] The various contemporary visions of new technologies, from nanotechnology to weather modification (not to mention biotechnology) presents real and important trajectories and 'topographies' within an artificial environment.

Nevertheless, it is far too early, or all together wrong, to draw the radical posthuman ontological consequences which informs cyborgological design-thought (with its various social-constructivist and poststructuralist offspring). One example: the evidence of new conflict potentials, e.g. problems of "structural irrelevance" of large parts of the human world[31] in the invigorated global (Western) capitalism of the 1990s shows that for all its complexity, the 'spread' of the artificial environment cannot escape the conflicts of global enclosure. Even if the solution to this may be an affirmation of a new inequality, radicalized in visions and metaphors of extraterrestial escape (by figures as different as Jean François Lyotard and Hans Moravec), this escapism cannot escape the fact that the artificial environment is a highly hybrid conjecture.

One fundamental issue seems to me to be how the self-constitution of the human as imaginary social-historical collective (Cornelius Castoriadis)[32] will react to the pressure from a cyborgological design-thought which imagines phenomena such as smart design to be a reason to doubt the 'co-extensive' preconditions of technology and science in human beings, society, and history. Not least among the scientific and cultural elite of today, one sees a dangerous tendency to neglect this question through a wholly unreflected *imagination* of technology and science (e.g. by neglecting the importance of social and individual imagination for concepts like self-organization, artificiality, poiesis, complexity, etc.). However, exactly this element of the artificial may take the 'surrounded surroundings' of smart design right back into the tensions of the current era. Or to put it in a rather different manner: if it is correct that the artificial environment is schismatic, *in this sense hybrid and imagined*, smart design cannot liberate the prospects of second order technology from the ghost of autonomy.

30. Georges Canguilhem, *La connaissance de la vie*, Librairie Philosophique J. Vrin, Paris, 1992.

31. Cf. Ankie Hoogvelt, *Globalisation and the Postcolonial World. The New Political Economy of Development*, Macmillan Press Ltd., Houndmills and London, 1997.

32. Cornelius Castoriadis, *L'Institution imaginaire de la société*, Éditions du Seuil, Paris,1975; David Ames Curtis (ed.), *Cornelius Castoriadis, World in Fragments. Writings on Politics, Society, Psychoanalysis, and the Imagination*, Stanford University Press, Stanford, 1997.

Ove Nathan

The Quest for the Great Symmetry

Our ideas about nature and celestial space have always been stamped by the notion about symmetry and balance. However, there is a conspicuous lack of balance in the universe between matter and antimatter. The symmetry here is not immediately obvious if it is there at all.

Throughout the course of time, notions about symmetry have been woven into the very fabric of people's picture of physical nature. In the time of Aristotle, in ancient Greece, it was supposed that the Earth was situated in the center of a system of several, revolving celestial spherical shells.

Inside of this symmetrical system of diaphanous crystal spheres, the sun, the moon and the planets were each bound to their own respective spherical fields. And the most outlying, spherically shaped field was a crystal sphere with all of the fixed stars. The symmetry and the harmony were perfect in this Aristotelian world-view. Unfortunately, the scheme couldn't hold water. Although the system was ingeniously built up with many coupled spherical shells, it just could not serve to explain astronomic data gathered in later times. And today, Aristotle's crystal spheres amount to nothing more than an historical curiosity.

In direct contrast to the ancient world view, Newton's system of the world was based on meticulously made observations and mathematical considerations. But here, unfortunately, the symmetry of the orbs fell by the wayside. The ancients' beautiful circular movements were superseded by elliptical planetary orbits which were faintly deformed, at that, since the movement of each and every one of the planets is slightly disturbed by that of the others. But even though the perfect, ancient symmetry was dropped with the advent of Newtonian mechanics, the notion of fundamental and beautiful symmetries managed to live on in natural science. In the twentieth century's quantum mechanics, the notion of symmetry has, as a matter of fact, experienced a Renaissance. All of our own epoch's theoretical formulations concerning elementary particles, quarks and leptons – or whatever these particles may be called – are connected to conceptions about abstract symmetries, which are woven into the very fabric of the laws of nature and into the description of particles.

One of these fundamental particle symmetries is the symmetry between a particle and the appurtenant antiparticle. For every elementary particle, there is a corresponding antiparticle, which has the very same mass as the particle but has the opposite sign for some of the particle's quantum numbers. Accordingly, the particle and the antiparticle have opposite signs (i.e. positive and negative) when it comes to their electrical charge. The electron's antiparticle goes by the name "positron." This positron behaves in many ways as though it were a positively charged electron. Were an electron and a positron to be brought into the near vicinity of one another, their aggregate mass could be converted to energy, in the form of electromagnetic radiation.

This process, where matter and antimatter are transformed into radiation, is denoted as "annihilation." Conversely, electromagnetic radiation of a sufficiently high energy can be transformed into mass and engender a particle-antiparticle pair.

But – as far as mankind can see out into the universe, we are faced with a striking imbalance, a conspicuous flaw in the symmetry. Judging by what we can see, stars, nebulae, planets, asteroids, comets, cosmic rays – and whatever else we may find out there in space – all consist of ordinary substance. Nowhere is there to be found any direct testimony to the existence of antimatter, with the exception of a number of solitary secondarily generated antiparticles found inside cosmic radiation.

It must be pointed out, however, that it is not all that easy to differentiate between matter and antimatter out in space. This is because the photon, that is to say the light particle, is its own antiparticle. If we were to receive light from an antistar consisting entirely of antiparticles, the light would accordingly be altogether identical with that which we receive from an ordinary star of the same type. But if there actually were regions in outer space with considerable accumulations of antimatter, there would be a high probability that this antimatter would – at some point in time – come into contact with matter, with annihilation as the direct outcome. And yet, the astronomers have not been able to detect the corresponding annihilation-radiation anywhere.

The universe's conspicuous asymmetry between matter and antimatter is still lacking for a satisfactory explanation. Astrophysicists and physical cosmologists of the present day describe the composition of the universe with their point of origin in the so-called Big Bang phenomenon.

The Big Bang lies somewhere supposedly 13 to 15 billion years back in time and marks the beginning of physical time. The spatial extension of the universe at that time was infinitesimally small (the "head of a pin") and the temperature was tremendously high. After the Big Bang, what began were spatial expansion and a process of cooling down, both of which have extended to the present day. But already a few minutes after the Big Bang, atomic nuclei of hydrogen and helium were formed. These nuclei serve as the point of origin for the much later formation of the substance that we ourselves consist of and which surrounds us. The fundamental processes in the incipient phases of the universe are conjectured to have been symmetrical in matter and antimatter. These fundamental processes create particle-antiparticle pairs, or annihilate them, without making a distinction between matter and antimatter.

But at some point in time or another, sometime between the beginning of time and that moment when electrically neutral atomic substance was formed, there must have been an imbalance between matter and antimatter.

Perhaps this imbalance arose only a microsecond after the Big Bang, and maybe the imbalance was of the order of magnitude of one part in a billion, in favor of matter. When this tiny surplus of particles was first established, all the antiparticles would then have been susceptible to becoming annihilated by particles, and the result would be a universe whose substance consists of the particle surplus. This surplus might accordingly amount to not more than one-billionth part of the original quantity of particles, but it would be ample for creating the universe we know today.

We still cannot indicate a precise mechanism that accounts for the formation of this ever so slight imbalance between particles and antiparticles. But there are hypothetical suppositions. Perhaps the key to the phenomenon can be found in certain ruptures in symmetry that turn up in the decay-processes of certain particles of the so-called meson-type, those that physicists call K-mesons and B-mesons.

New experiments with B-mesons are being planned. When the results of these tests are made available some day, we might then be able to take one step closer to the understanding of the universe's striking imbalance.

Even if we cannot find antimatter in the universe, we can certainly study many properties of antiparticles in the laboratory. Today, the positron is one of nuclear physics' old and scrupulously investigated acquaintances. Another well-known antiparticle is the antiproton. Since the proton (the nuclear particle of the hydrogen atom) has a positive electrical charge, the antiproton is accordingly negatively charged. But the antiproton's mass is precisely the same as that of the proton.

Today, antiprotons are fabricated industrially. A number of the larger particle-physics laboratories are capable of producing focused beams of rapidly moving antiprotons, which can then be utilized as projectiles in the experiments. The list of known antiparticles is considerably longer, but the positron and the antiproton are the two entities that have been investigated most extensively.

Metaphorically speaking, atoms are built up of three kinds of Lego-blocks: electrons, neutrons, and protons. In order to create an electrically neutral atom, there have to be just as many electrons as there are protons. The hydrogen atom is the simplest of all atoms. Here, there are no neutrons and only one proton and one electron.

Throughout the course of the twentieth century, theoretical and experimental physicists have been working to determine the quantum structure and the pattern of radiation emanating from the hydrogen atom with the utmost degree of exactitude. Today, the hydrogen atom can be said to be a standard laboratory for testing out the advanced discipline of theoretical physics known as relativistic quantum electrodynamics.

The mirror image of a hydrogen atom is an antihydrogen atom, where a positively charged positron is circling around a negatively charged antiproton. Together, these two antiparticles then come to establish an electrically neutral system.

The symmetry in the laws of nature is organized in such a way that precise predictions about the electromagnetic behavior of the antihydrogen atom can be posited on the basis of the known properties of the hydrogen atom.

In all its simplicity, the gist of the prediction is that the pattern of radiation from an antihydrogen atom will be identical, in every minute detail, with the radiation pattern emanating from a hydrogen atom.

What is less clear is the question about the free fall of the antihydrogen atom in the earth's gravitational field. Will antimatter fall with the same rate of acceleration as matter? In other words, is the gravitational-mass attraction between matter and antimatter the same as it is between one form of matter and another? No one can really say with complete certainty.

As it appears, there are good reasons for subjecting an antihydrogen atom to closer inspection. That ought to be a simple enough task, since positrons and antiprotons can be produced in ample quantities. But unfortunately, it is awfully difficult to produce even one single antihydrogen atom, not to mention a whole lot of them. And it requires a great degree of skill to contain the fragile product for a sufficient period of time, long enough to execute precision measurements of the radiation spectrum.

The problem here is that antiprotons have to be created with impact processes in laboratories, by the means of which energy is transformed into mass.

Processes of this kind involve such tremendous forces that the resulting antiprotons are endowed with tremendous energies and they are moving with velocities that approach the speed of light. However, in the ordinary hydrogen atom, the electron and the proton move around in a slow waltz time, with much lower velocities. The same thing ought to be the case in the antihydrogen atom.

Therefore, we will have to be able to subdue the antiprotons' rapid flight down to a steady crawl and to subsequently conjoin the slow-moving antiproton created in such a way with an equally slow-moving positron in a lasting marriage.

This requires a skill that calls for nothing less than the utmost in modern experimental technique, especially because one single antiatom, or even two, can serve merely for purposes of demonstration.

There must be a sufficiently large number of antiatoms in order to make a spectroscopic precision experiment. And the antiatoms will have to be contained securely for a sufficient period of time in the laboratory, preferably for weeks or months.

But the antiatom is a fragile entity, when we consider that matter and antimatter can annihilate immediately upon their encounter. The antimatter must consequently be held in absolutely strict isolation from matter inside the walls of the container, and accordingly, the demand for a superfine vacuum becomes extreme. The first and up until now only successful attempt to fabricate antihydrogen was carried out in 1996, inside the joint-European research center, CERN. In CERN's particle accelerator, it is possible to produce a beam of extremely high-energy antiprotons.

With a number of different contraptions, it is possible to decelerate the antiprotons to some degree and to pack them into a so-called magnetic storage ring, where the antiprotons can be "stored" as a focused beam. Inside the storage ring, it is then possible to arrange a "meeting" between antiprotons and neutral atoms, and this meeting can lead to the production of pairs of electrons and positrons.

If, then, a positron and an antiproton eventually come to move around with approximately the same velocity, it is entirely possible that they can contract a marriage, with the result that an atom of antihydrogen is spawned. In 1996, a total of nine atoms of antihydrogen were successfully detected.

Not all that many, but nonetheless an encouraging result, taking into consideration that this was the very first certain demonstration whatsoever of the existence of antihydrogen.

When such great exertions are made for fabricating antihydrogen, this is being done – as has been mentioned previously –

with the aim of testing out a fundamental symmetry in nature, a symmetry that the physicists denote as CPT.

Here, 'C' stands for electrical charge, 'P' for parity, which has something to do with reflection, and 'T' for time. If we begin with a physical matter system, for example a hydrogen atom, we can find our way to the corresponding antisystem by simultaneously shifting the sign of the electrical charge, carrying out a special spatial mirroring and letting time run backwards.

And the supposition is that all fundamental processes of nature in the system will remain unaffected, when this CPT operation is carried out. What is especially anticipated as well is that all of the radiation processes in antihydrogen will elapse precisely as they do in hydrogen.

On the other hand, we cannot know beforehand how an atom of antihydrogen will fall within the earth's gravitational field. Possibly, the gravitational force between matter and antimatter will be the same as it is between matter and matter, but it cannot be excluded that an essential difference may come to reveal itself. This last question represents a special challenge to both theoretical and experimental physicists. Here science has yet another fundamental question toward which to address itself as we cross the threshold of a new century.

Jeff Noon

Pollen

(…) The road was a carpet of soft blooms that my wheels crawled through. The traffic lights at Oxford and Whitworth were entangled by vines. It was difficult to see the lights change, red to yellow to green; everything was green stems, red and yellow flowers. It didn't matter; mine was one of the few cars left on the street. The fever was taking its time with me. All I could think about was Jewel, back in the flat, suffering. I had even bought him a Gumbo YaYa pollen mask. I had smeared Sneeza Freeza on his nostrils. I had lined his room with Gumbo YaYa's Very Own Protective Seal. All for nothing; my child was dying. I knew this now. The fever had made a flourishing desert out of my city. It was a Mancunian paradise that nobody wanted, not even the dogs, who had finally run for cover from the pollen. Maybe they were just building up to a big showdown, conserving their resources. Friday morning. Here and there a few streetcops were wandering, robos in the main, but totally masked, up to the eyeballs. No one was safe.

The cops weren't there to stop crime any more, they were more like protectors, keeping people off the streets, away from the pollen. Above the doors of the Palace of Vurt Theatre, a laser-sign pulsed out the following message: HIS MAJESTY'S HEALTH WARNING: THE POLLEN COUNT IS RISING. SNIFFING FLOWERS IS DEADLY. All along Oxford Street columbines, japonicas, mimosas and a thousand other varieties of flowers were growing from the cracks in the pavement, dragging at my wheels. Sixty five per cent of the population were now suffering from severe hayfever. The number of known fatalities was now well into double figures, not including the initial murders. The towers of Manchester were being suffocated by flora. It was a jungle that I had to drive through. So many people dead, and still no clear cop-path to an answer. No leads to the flower girl called Persephone. Chief Kracker had put out an all-points bulletin on my "miscreant behaviour" and cops city-wide were on the lookout for my traces. I had, of course, vanished myself from the station, whereabouts unknown, since yesterday's debacle with Clegg and Belinda. I was AWOL and stunted in the case, even whilst the city was growing crazy from the seeds. The pollen count had risen alarmingly in the last few hours, 1200 and growing stronger, almost as though the flowers were growing impatient. Bad times on planet Earth. The city was weeping. If Manchester went under the spell of flowers, then the whole world could suffer likewise, all the cities following, one by one. The Authorities had put blocks on the four gates in order to stop the Vaz truckers spreading the fever. Maybe it was too late. The People were blaming the cops for the danger, led on by that Gumbo YaYa's pirate voice.

I passed a street sign on the Rochdale Road that read *Welcome to Namchester*. Ahead of me the seven towers of Nam stood in silence, stark against the heated sun. Ten years ago this area had been desolated by the High-rise Wars, now the towers were home to the well-done and the well-to-do. Zero greeted me at the gates to Fortress One, which was a moist block of cement enwrapped with flowers. Zero led me up to his rooms, his face covered by the latest "entirely newly improved" pollen mask. The wound in his shoulder had been sealed by robo-Skinner. His flat was richly appointed in all the human comforts, no hint of the Dog World. A young man was sitting on the pumped-up sofa-bed holding an armoured specimen box like it was a live rat with bad blood. He was a pure-hearted loner. His Shadow was wreathed by weakness. Zero

Introduced him as Jay Ligule, from the Manchester University Botany Department. Ligule had brought evidence with him, some micro-feathers.

The Alexandra Park incident had finished Zero with Kracker. Zero Clegg was a lone dog now, slipping the noose. I could feel his spirit running wild through his Shadow. He was free from the vanished master.

From now on we would be riding unofficially.

Jay Ligule was waving the micro feather at me, like I should be able to taste those things. I told him that feathers meant nothing to me. But Zero had worked out the scenario. He'd "borrowed" a feather-translator from the cop station. Ligule had transposed the info onto antique video. "This is the little culprit," Ligule said, as a moving display came up on the screen. "Amaranthus Caudatus. Or at least, some kind of variant. A tropical plant, usually blooms in high summer, and then only in the South of England."

"The South, you say?" Zero hated the South.

"Yes. Amaranthus ... it comes from a Greek word. Meaning an imaginary plant, one that never fades. Commonly known as Love-lies-bleeding."

"I reckon I've cracked this case, Smokey," Zero said. "I reckon we're looking for a mad botanist with a poetic streak. I reckon we catch this bugger, shove him in Strangeways Feather? What do you say?"

Strangeways Feather was where they put prisoners in those days, storing their bodies in racks whilst their dreams drifted through tiny cells in the Vurt. It was cheap and nasty, but it worked.

Jay Ligule looked up from the video screen. "Take a look.

... tiny life swimming there ... pieces of stuff ... minuscule monsters ... fronds were twitching ... knots of blackness here and there ... moments of recognition, drifting into mystery ...

You see the darker spots?" Ligule said. "These are the human element." "Human?" I asked.

"Basically what we have got here is a new kind of hybrid. Human and plant. Those dark spots you saw were human genes lodged inside plant cells. We have never seen anything like this before. Kirkpatrick was shocked by it."

"Kirkpatrick?"

"Glasgow University. She's the leader of the field in plant reproduction."

"She wouldn't be a mad botanist, by any chance?" asked Zero. "Maybe with a poetic streak?"

"She called this specimen a monster. We have a serious problem here, she said. Humans and flowers are having sex."

Zero sneezed.

"Hayfever is caused by sex," Ligule continued. "You know that? It is the outcome of flowers trying to love one another. And failing. The fever is the outcome of bad plant sex."

"Kinky," Zero said. "You want to explain?"

"Of course I do," Ligule began. "Pollen is produced by the anther of a flower, the male organ. From there it is carried by the wind or by insects, until it reaches the stigma of another plant. Or even the same plant. The stigma is the female organ. The stigma is moist and covered in fine hairs. It clutches at the pollen, making it feel at home, so that it can release its proteins. These proteins dig their way into the stigma, searching for the egg inside. This is the way of love for flowers. Sometimes a human comes in between."

Zero: "This causes hayfever?"

"The pollen lodges in the human's nostrils. It finds a moist and hairy place there, and thinks this is the stigma. This is where I must bury myself. The grain releases its proteins, causing a breach in the nasal cavity. Of course the human body registers this as an attack and therefore activates its immune system. We try to expel the invader, through our nose and our eyes, with snot or tears. Hayfever is a defence mechanism."

"You're saying that humans and plants are having sex?" Zero asked, making a sneeze from behind his latest mask. "Jesus! You pay a week's salary for these things ... doesn't do anything."

Ligule joined him in the sneeze and then continued. "The body is no longer rejecting the pollen grain. It is treating it like a lover. The immune system is trying to fight this impulse, but the reproductive system is fighting against it. And winning. The body is accepting the plant sperm. Kirkpatrick has examined some of the corpses. The pollen has made its way down to the womb. It is fusing with the human egg, as though it were a plant egg. Kirkpatrick reckons it to be the next step."

"What step would that be?"

I asked. "The next phase of evolution, given that the country as a whole is increasingly drawn to interbreeding."

"Jesus-Fever!" Zero was breathing deeply through his mask, making a sound like a victim. I could only feel for him, but at the same time Ligule's theories were appealing.

"Has Kirkpatrick any idea where these grains are coming from?" I asked.

"We think it goes back to Fecundity 10," Ligule said. "We think that Casanova has stepped into the plant kingdom."

"What are you telling us?" Zero asked.

"Floraphilia, Kirkpatrick is calling it."

"She means by that?" Zero again.

"We are saying that somebody has fucked a flower, and this hayfever is the baby of that union."

"Dog-Christ!" wheezed Zero.

"We must burn all the bodies," Ligule added. "As a precaution. They mustn't be buried."

"Why's that?" I asked.

"It would be like burying a seed." (...)

Hans Ulrich Obrist

Interview with Ralph Erskine, Stockholm, summer 2000

Hans Ulrich Obrist:
My first question was about your moving to Sweden before you studied in England. Something which I found interesting when reading your biography and texts about your work, is your dialogue with Gordon Cullen and his drawings. I was wondering if you could tell me about your beginning in England and your friendship with Gordon.

Ralph Erskine:
Well, it wasn't really a close friendship. We just studied at the same time but he studied the year before me in the Regent Street Polytechnic. He was already a very good architect at that time.

But how was your beginning in architecture? When did you decide to become an architect? Was there any triggering momentum?

I wanted either to work in open air or else do something with drawing. Since they told me that there were too many architects, I chose surveying, speaking of open-air, but of course it wasn't. It was mostly mathematics, in which I am not gifted. But fortunately I was studying at the Regent Street Polytechnic, where they trained builders, architects, and surveyors. I saw what the architects were doing and I thought: this is what I want to do so I changed my direction.

Did you have any heroes or influences at the beginning, architects whose work you looked at particularly?

Well, you know the usual architects that were popular at that time, like Frank Lloyd Wright, Le Corbusier or Aalto. I had certain influences from all these architects.

And then at the age of 25 you decided to leave England to move to Sweden. There is a big difference between voluntary and involuntary exile.

Well, you know when we started, most of the advances in new architecture were from Sweden. I also heard that there was a good prospect, of getting work here. So I decided to come to Sweden because at that time, you could get work. When I saw the Swedish architecture I liked it very much and found the attitude very sympathetic.

Were you also attracted by the very particular Swedish modernity?

Yes, that was the main reason for coming here. Sweden was the only country building modern architecture in any great amount. The ideas came from central Europe, but the Swedes were changing their society, making their social revolution, and they thought the modern architecture suited them very well, especially after the Stockholm exhibition in 1930.

With Asplund's presence.

That's right. In England, very little modern architecture was being built and not much in other countries either, not Denmark, not Norway, not America. Sweden was in ahead in practicing modern architecture. That's why I came.

This leads me to another question which actually has to do with the issue of utopia, because many of the architects of your generation whom I have interviewed for this series of interviews talk a lot about the unrealized project and the ideas that have remained utopian to most other countries. So, was it the idea that in Sweden this utopia was actually built not as a utopia but as a concrete reality?

You know at that time they were building a lot in Sweden, and I first got a job doing a small house and that led bit by bit to other work, so finally I opened my little office. At first, I was working entirely alone, I had a little office, and I started getting commissions. And then one thing led to the other, so fortunately, I had quite a lot of work in my time which have been built.

What percentage of your ideas would you say have been built?

I don't know. I can't tell you that. I have never counted. But quite a lot. Quite a lot indeed.

It is extremely impressive looking at this Academy Editions book how many have actually been realized.

Yes, a lot has been realized. I have been very fortunate there. Of course, it was as you quite rightly mentioned, because of my coming to Sweden.

Another question in relation to this is "the other modernity." Alvar Aalto defined Finland according to a different kind of modernity, and Asplund defined Sweden as a very local modernity. So I was wondering if you could tell me a little bit about your view on this.

The modern movement was very abstract, but in Sweden, it was less so. People rightly say that Asplund's and Aalto's architecture was less abstract, much warmer, much friendlier, much better fitted into nature and the township. This was special and I liked it very much. That has influenced me a lot and I tried to do the same thing.

And what about Markelius?

He certainly influenced me as well. When I came here, there were quite a lot of different architects: Sven Markelius, Paul

Hedqvist. Architects were practicing modern architecture and some of them were doing it very well.

And as a young architect moving to Sweden, did you meet them?

Some of them, but not all of them. I met Asplund and Markelius. Aalto I've met, but I've never had much contact with him.

You've said that you had very early commissions. Your first commission was a country cottage, which was built for an inventor, a rather unusual client. Could you tell me about this?

I got this job through another architect actually, and they wanted the building to be built in log-cabin look, so they sent me out to Dala to check with the people who had built them. It was partly through this builder from Dala that I got going, because I built a house, which is kind of a mixture between English and Swedish attitudes. A little bit personal for this inventor. The man who built it liked it very much as well, and he was doing quite a lot of small country cottages for people for their free time. He asked me to design for him, which I did. That was what started me going and actually led me into contact with other people and many other things. This man put me in contact with an organization (Friluftsfrämjandet) which is encouraging fresh-air-life and skiing. I did their building south of Stockholm which is still there: It's called Lida friluftsgård. That also helped me to get going. It attracted attention. There was also a woman who had a book called *Home in Sweden*, and she illustrated some of my ideas and that also helped. So, these were the kinds of things which got me going as an architect.

Another question is about your office, how it started. You mentioned that in the beginning you were alone, and then you worked with collaborators. There is a famous story about you buying a boat; the Verona, *in 1955.*

I had an office house just above where this house is, actually. It got too small for me, so I wanted a larger one. I thought I'd rent an option in town, but I found it very expensive, so I started thinking of having an office on a boat. I advertised in England and so got this boat *Verona*, which I sailed over here. That was very nice indeed, because already we'd been moving to the country during the summers. Summer is short here, so you try to do everything to enjoy it.

So in the summer the studio moved according to the weather?

That's right. That was very nice indeed.

One thing, which is very beautiful, is your relation to your theoretical work about climate. Your idea that a building can adjust to the climate or the building goes to the climate.

That's right. That's why I bought this boat.

Did you also follow your clients with your boat? The idea that you sometimes went with the boat and the office could move to a job.

No, clients sometimes came to us in the country, but not so often. That was one of the advantages; we were left in peace to get our work done out there on the islands.

But once you moved your office, not your boat, when you had one in England.

I didn't have an office in England at all except when I had a large job in Newcastle/Byker.

You started an office in physiology and moved your office very far to the construction site.

That's right. I had contact with the people who were going to move in, because a lot of people were already living there. Part of the scheme was to give them better houses. That was one of the reasons for opening the office in the area.

My next question, still related to your early work in Sweden, is about the immaculate indigenous architecture of Sweden and of your work.

Influences were much more from people like Aalto, Markelius, and Asplund. Not so much from the old architecture.

In terms of the location you're discussing, there is the issue of climate and your architectural town drawings which began in the 1950. I was wondering if you could summarize the forty years following this period?

I still have the same attitude, you know. This house I built in 1963 illustrates my ideas such as protection against the hard climate. The roof is separate, that's a technical thing, so the heat from the building doesn't melt the snow on the roof, which then would run down as water into the gutter and freeze there. This technique you can find in many countries which have a cold climate: Switzerland, Finland, Japan. Once you recluse the building, you have a free development, which can be carried out in a semi-tropical climate with windows of different sizes and locations so that you are placed in contact with your surroundings. I've also given my buildings the character of local housing in a modern way, like using plaster and black metal roots. I have used modern materials and a modern setting.

You've also mentioned in your writings about the Medieval wall city. How far would this idea of the Medieval city go?

I find the Medieval city much more sympathetic than most modern cities and much more than ancient cities which were usually designed according to the idea of the access going to the most important person – the lord or the main church or whatever. The Medieval city gives this rather mixed structure intimacy with casual meeting places, which I like very much. Other people always enjoy these Medieval townships. Such places encourage spontaneous life, also spontaneous building in contact with the life that goes on in such situations as people move together to exchange ideas and goods and everything.

I read in Neuroscience *that there is an increasing interest in the city from neurologists. The brain and the city. There was an interesting text by a German neurologist Wolf Singer who compares the structure of the city to the brain. There are issues, which are related to your visionary text about the arctic city, in terms of self-organization. How do you see this connection to the brain, biology and to the notion of self-organization of the city?*

I work in a pragmatic way. What I observe in myself and what I observe in other people. There are of course, a lot of physical and social reasons for architecture and city structures. Most people spend their life in modern cities, which I find in many ways a bit inimical to spontaneous life.

So for you it is more an observation from life than a dialogue with scientists?

Definitely. It's very much based on how people actually behave. Again, it's a rather pragmatic attitude, very typical for Sweden which was one of the reasons why I felt very much at home here. Not so theoretical.

Most important has been the dialogue with people?

Partly a direct dialogue and partly observing what people do. As a psychologist once pointed out for me "You can learn much more or you can learn a hell of a lot from what people do." Sometimes, when they talk, they say things because they feel they should, but when they act you can interpret. If you can interpret the act, it is all very true to what their feelings are.

Your architecture reflects a dialogue with different people. Can you also describe it as interdisciplinary? How would you see this notion of the interdisciplinary?

Obviously, architecture is interdisciplinary, and technical. It involves feelings and experiences. That is one of the joys of architecture, because you are moving and thinking different roles.

Do you have a dialogue with artists, filmmakers, or other participants when you're working?

Yes, to a certain degree, but it's also a discussion with ordinary people. I like to talk to the people who are going to live in the building I'm designing.

I'd like to ask you another question in relation to the arctic city. You use the term "to make virtue into necessity." I find it very interesting in the Nordic countries and in Switzerland, they have a high degree of innovative architecture calling out to this extreme condition. Do you think it pushes toward inventions?

If you're open to this and find these experiences positive, then it does push you into inventions. A case I would like to stress is a hotel I did in the mountains. First, I designed a glass building.

I thought, how fantastic to do a large glass building up in the climate of the mountains in Sweden. Then of course, I didn't actually talk to the client about my idea, because I realized that they wouldn't approve of this and it would be far too expensive. Then I did the opposite thing. When I thought about it, the glass building didn't really show the architect as clever. It showed that the engineers were building all the stupid ideas the architects had. Instead I built it into the ground and let the snow collect up against it to help protect it. The clients liked this very much, and it was built in Borga. This innovation came because of the dialogue that *I could have had* with the client. I could think of how they would react to the different ideas I came up with.

Did you get any response from this building?

Very much indeed. Then I gave it very strong colors because I had observed that the climate in the winter had rather little color with the snow and the landscape. Other influences were the Lapp's bright-coloured clothing.

You mention in this text of the architectural city that it also has to be another form of intensity. This climate-driven intensity is made into a virtue basically by having more intensive exchange. You say that these arctic cities have somehow to be better than the cities in the south. Can you explain how you imagine them to be better?

I mentioned that they'd be rather protected, rather enclosed against the climate. I have done sketches of such places. I tried to build these in Canada, but only a part of them were built. Obviously in the arctic situation, you're often placing your city in a natural environment. You chose to place it where it would take advantage of the climate: a south slope for example for protection from the wind. And you would have a long building, which would protect from the unpleasant northern or eastern winds. Only this would give you a certain feeling of intimate contact. They are built for people in a rather special situation. When I was working on Svappavara, my idea was placed in the township so you could see the traffic on the road. In a normal situation you try to avoid the traffic, because you have too much of traffic. In the arctic or in the sub-arctic or more desert situations it is the opposite: too little life. You try to get in contact with any human life which is going on in the situation.

So traffic becomes a virtue?

Not inside the town, but outside the town it does become a virtue.

A last question about the city. Which city is the one you like most?

The most traditional answer I could give you is that I like Mediterranean cities in Europe. But, I also like Stockholm very much indeed. It is a beautiful city. When I came here, it was a provincial city, but now it is international and lively. A lot has changed since I came here, mostly for the better, in some ways for the worse. It loses some of its identity because of this internationalization.

And then talking about your social housing. My first question is about the influence of England and the influence of Sweden. How far did you procure British neighborhood planning and how much did these ideas change you, being in Sweden and having a social vision of Sweden?

Of course, the social vision of Sweden was very important. It was one I already had certain allegiances with from my family background and from my school in England. You mentioned the English ideas brought up many other things in the new towns. These ideas also influenced me, but were not completely developed in England. But, linked with the Swedish social attitude, I think they became positive factors for me.

How was your contact when you were in Stockholm, with the theoretical ideas of the social vision? Did you meet any of the protagonists or was it just by daily life?

Daily life. Most people, but also specialists, were very sympathetic to the whole of this development. Otherwise, they could not have done it. It was not a very class society then, so I met people from all the different classes in Sweden and in Stockholm. The discussion with them always influenced me.

How would you define participation?

It's a matter of discussion with people and getting in contact with them, preferably with those who are going to live in the area. If you can't do that, you can select a group of people who would presumably have the same kind of ideas as those who would later move into the area. I have done that as well. Discussing with them, showing them sketches and models. They understand models better than they do drawings. I like to get their reactions and adjust the project to fit their attitudes: either what they express in words or what they express in actual actions. It is a matter of democracy. People should have the right to be involved in the buildings they are going to use and live in.

Do you have any particularly memorable examples from your many experiences with social housing projects?

Yes, especially in Newcastle in Byker, where we moved in to the area. We made such good contact with the people that it became a bit of a problem. We had better contact with them than the politicians had. The politicians didn't like this so much and we had to be very careful to keep their allegiance.

That's what happened to Lucien Kroll in Belgium. The contact with the students became better than with the politicians, so the university fired him.

That's right. But they didn't fire me. I think they liked what I was doing and that was the main thing. I did a plan for two thousand dwellings. For most of these dwellings, I actually designed the buildings as well. I got on very well with the housing officers.

What about your experiences in Sweden. Did you find the participation different?

It is different because Swedes are not as spontaneous as the English or other Europeans. It worked here as well because they were receptive to the idea. That kind of philosophy fit with their attitudes.

Are there any particularly memorable moments in Sweden, when you felt the participation was really reaching the point where you were satisfied?

Yes, especially the work that I've done north of Stockholm, in a region called Gästrikland, in Storvik. I also had a bit of contact when I did the group of houses for the forest workers.

Sometimes you get ideas you wouldn't have had by other methods. Especially if you don't only meet with intellectual people but participate in meeting people with all kinds of attitudes. That can be very positive.

You call this "information exchange" in an earlier text. Can you say it's bilateral?

It is very much so. Obviously, you have to have the attitude that this is positive. If you're that kind of person who gets irritated with people who don't think the same way as you do, then of course participation won't work. I was more disappointed that people didn't give me more surprises than they did. It was much nicer when they came with an idea which was unexpected. There is a general rule, which I've discovered: less sophisticated people are better at this than intellectual people. The intellectual people usually know what they want to achieve and they can argue. The less intellectual people feel what they want. They don't argue about it. They just tell you in a more spontaneous way which gives a much better result.

How did you create this atmosphere of getting people involved? Sometimes people could call your office, and it was almost like a hotline.

The best example was in Newcastle where we moved the office into the area. In that case people who wanted to move into the new buildings were already living there. In other cases, I arranged frequent meetings with them. It even went well with the Eskimos in Canada who didn't speak English well or when I did a project in Helsingfors in Finland. They didn't speak Swedish or English. Sometimes things worked in that type of situation because then you read more in the way they were behaving. Having the models with the Eskimos, you could more or less know what they were talking about by what they were pointing at. They talked about themselves, their life, the hunting, the fishing and how they were getting the animals they had killed. When I was working in Stockholm with the University library, I also had contact with the people there. These people were professors. I always quote the case when there was another man with me, a furniture designer. That time there was a lot of discussion about open landscape offices. He wanted to do this kind of landscape office. Being an intellectual, one of the professors said: "You said that we were going to come to an information, but you are trying to indoctrinate us. Instead of talking about a landscape office and a cell office, the common terms used are "large-room office" or a "small-room office." The intellectual was reacting in a totally different way. It wasn't so much contact. It became a conflict. I can get around that because I've never enjoyed conflicts much. I usually get people to collaborate with me.

The idea is then that it is going to be a big collaboratorium?

As time goes on, you learn more and more and find that you're not getting so many surprises; you know what's going to happen. I feel it is a certain advantage for me, but it is a much bigger advantage to the people who are going to move in. They learn about architecture, and what they can or can't do with their buildings, which becomes very important for them. From a kind of collaborative dialogue situation, you almost become a teacher.

Have there been moments where you had to say no to the ideas people came up with?

If they wanted the wrong thing, you always had to be honest and say so. Then you had to decide afterwards whether you were going to do what they wanted and change your mind. Or whether you were going to insist on doing what you felt you should have done. That is a difficult situation, but negotiation is also a part of democracy. People's involvement with the buildings they are going to live and work in should be a basic democratic right.

Another question about this participation. A particularly interesting case was in the township Resolute Bay, in the Northwest Territory in Canada, where you also triggered these very public dialogues with Eskimos. Could you tell me a little more about this?

I've already mentioned using models, and these were white. But, that didn't matter because their landscape town was white most of the year with snow. It became a kind of a learning situation. Once or twice I came a bit late and they told me I shouldn't do that. Then another time they came late because of some hunting, and they wanted to slaughter the animals and I said: you shouldn't be late either. Since a lot of them could not speak English or French, I had to get them to discuss the project and the model, and I had to try to understand when they talked and when they pointed at it. There was the question of where we would put the town center. I had to fly 300 km to get there. I had some people from the local government with me and I realized that the discussion was not working. What actually was happening, was that the people from the south were talking about the school and that it should be near to the center. That way the parents, who had no schooling, could see what the children were doing and what they were involved in. When this discussion had been going on a bit, I realized that it was going wrong. What was actually happening was that when the Eskimos were talking about the center, they meant the middle of the town. When the people from the south were talking about the center, they meant the shopping center. Finally, I put the school in the middle of the township. In that way, people at home could keep an eye on the kids, the school and what was happening there. And for the Eskimos, this was the right choice.

And you insisted on their behalf?

Yes.

One thing concerning the self-organization aspect deals with what the German neuroscientist Wolf Singer writes in his text about the brain and the city: "We should stop designing whole cities like Brasilia because there are these locally interactive service." Do you agree?

Yes, I agree. I think you always consider having a kind of a master plan for the main lines of the town, but you shouldn't design the whole town. That should definitely have a considerable element of growth. It is pretentious to design a whole town. I've already told you about the Medieval town, and one advantage is that you can see that there has been a township which has grown. It is different from the designed towns, the Renaissance towns which arise and so forth. I much prefer the Medieval town because I think it fits with people in a democratic society much better. In an authoritarian society, the Renaissance town can be very good. You have to have a basic philosophy.

Something which I have observed in your writings and also in your interviews is that you have provocative and contradictory references to biological or organic issues. At the same time you also deny that these are purely organic (materials).

I feel that you are between the organic architecture and the rationalist architecture. Can you tell me a little bit about this in-between space?

Just by using the expressions "organic" or "rationalist" architecture you are taking a very definitive position about the character of the building or the township. I think it's wrong when it already tends to be a bit dogmatic. I prefer to be more spontaneous and find experiences, which lead me to the final solution. This house is based on my own life experiences. When I designed the house, there were four children in it. There is a door up there, and they could come and go as they liked. I always said that it was a psychological door because the door was there. They didn't need to be watched; we didn't want to watch them; we didn't need to steer them. The psychological door was very successful. This is the kind of thing you learn with time.

So it is the idea of not freezing, to keep it fluid?

That's right. People should have the possibility of choice in their buildings and in their township. A characteristic of the Medieval town is that it is formed by a multitude of individual choices.

Another question about participation is related to the project in the village near Arlanda Airport. Could you tell me a little bit about this. There was another element involving not only the relationship of urbanism and architecture to the community, but also the relationship between the different urbanisms.

It was rather well-organized for participation, and we were working with different groups. They were also influenced by the architects involved. The politicians wanted to build the township near the railway. I thought that it should be built in a very beautiful location, towards the lake, which most people in this country enjoy. I did a sketch. I thought it was very nice, but it was not approved by the politicians. I was in-between the different architects. We had very good discussions with them. Then we had group meetings with the different people we chose. Since no one we knew was going to move into the town, we selected a representative group. We worked with our group, and then sometimes we got all the groups together and had discussions with them. It was rather well-organized but it gave no result.

Were there any discussions between you and Alexander?

Yes. I remember he was trying to work on his language, which I thought was very interesting. When I was showing him around Vällingby, one of the new suburbs here, he asked me who was living here. I answered: all sorts of people. What do you mean, from different classes and backgrounds? Yes, I said, which was one of the Swedish attitudes they wanted to achieve. Well, that's not good, he said. Why not, I asked. He thought it was much better that people should have the opportunity of living together with similar people. It was an idea I took up and thought it was probably a good thing, but the group shouldn't be too big and it shouldn't be exclusive. The group should have contact with other groups, which influenced me a lot. I thought Alexander was an interesting fellow.

My next question is related to the notion of participation and also to your whole idea about dwellings and social housing. In the relation to Byker but also other projects, you used metaphors related to "having a walk" or "having a stroll." What did you mean by these metaphors?

I'm not quite sure what you are talking about, but I said if I had been doing some models I would take a walk through the project.

It is not only about designing social housing but also the in-between space, the landscape. Somehow, this is something, which seems to be missing in recent architecture.

Yes, you are quite right. This was a very important side of it. Byker was a good situation for this, because the people who lived there were very communicative with one another. Most in a positive way but also in a less positive way. I tended to emphasize the experiences they could have, the advantage or disadvantage they could have from the different ways of forming the township.

Did it also mean designing the walkways and the in-between spaces?

Yes, this certainly influenced me when I was designing the town. But the times have changed. I think I prefer more intimate townships and walkways with experiences similar to those you get in the Medieval township. The trouble is that nowadays there is much more vandalism than when I planned. In a town like that it is more difficult to keep an eye on what people are doing.

So the intimate side becomes difficult in reality?

Yes, it can have disadvantages.

Do you have solutions for this dilemma?

No. I don't see any solution. It is a problem and I don't have an answer to that other than considering the alternatives.

Actually: if you look at the chronology of your works in the 1980s, office buildings become much more important: the Arc in London, the Lilla Bommen in Gothenburg.

That's what I meant when I told you about the Eskimo township where the centre is moving to the shopping centers and away from the town square.

How did you include office buildings and create a community of social space?

With ideas similar to those of a township like the Arc in London. It has a meeting place, a square where you can keep in contact with other people. And there are more anonymous places where you can get out of contact, which is also important. I always felt that with the Arc, I was working very much the same way as I would work with a township.

So for you it is not different? It is very similar and the country becomes a building?

Well, that is being a bit extreme, isn't it?

Yes. Now a question about shopping centers: the Luleå-Shopping Center. It seemed to be a very exciting, visionary project in 1954, 1956 – the first time you designed a shopping mall. Could you tell me about your ideas with this project?

Partly I had observed shopping centers in Canada at that time and they were open air. The climate was very unpleasant in the winter, and that led me to support and suggest that we should have an indoor center but being indoors, I again tried to give the similar experience that you have in a town. There were the more intimate places, and the more public places and that is definitely so in the Luleå shopping center. It's all changed now. But buildings like that change, as the years go by. But, in the beginning it was very much like a town inside a building.

So it's almost like in a Russian Matruschka where you have the doll within the doll and the town within the town. A town always hides another town.

Yes, a little bit. That's right.

I wanted to ask you about your unrealized projects, because it's a question I always ask in interviews; it's the only question which pops up in every interview. Is there a favorite unrealized project that you really would like to build or which you regret that hasn't yet been built?

I did the scheme for a little town in the north of Sweden, Svappavara it is called. The buildings were built without any relationship to each other, so it was a big failure actually. That wasn't the vision of what it should have been. They built the buildings without contact to one another.

And your idea was that all were piled.

No, well I think there's a perspective of a township in here. (looking at some drawings) That's the screen building here. That was built to protect against the wind and it worked very well in Byker, but in Svappavara it just left quite a wound. It protects nothing, and that's rather stupid. It was built around this idea with the protecting wall and little groups of buildings inside, protected by this outer wall. The outer wall was to the north and the east where you have the bad weather, and it helps protect against the wind and reflects light back into the township on the south side. Then these little south-side townships, there where several of them, in suitable places here there was a south slope, which is the best situation. And they also could have a little terrace house to give further protection. It all involved protecting against what was unfriendly in this environment. Looking towards the south and the road out there you could see the traffic – the connection with the rest of the world. But, none of that got built – just odd buildings and that's a big failure. It would have been as nice as Byker is but it didn't get built in the north. When I got to the north, I thought that they were going to be experimental but they weren't. They were into technical things but they weren't into cultural things. The opposite. What they wanted was an imitation of bits of Stockholm, and then I realized that if I wanted to build that township in the north, I should build it somewhere else first, so they could see what I was talking about. They are so isolated, but they want to "belong" and in a way, by imitating what the cities are doing, they feel that it helps them to belong. But it doesn't actually work well.

So, it is a post-colonial idea of being colonized by Stockholm?

Well, that also turned up. There was this kind of conflict situation that they couldn't solve. They wanted to belong, but they wanted to imitate. The Finns were imitating Helsingfors, the Swedes were imitating Stockholm, and the Norwegians were imitating Oslo. They kept on talking about having contact with one another in the northern region but it never really worked. I thought that if I could build this little township in Sweden as a model, preferably near Stockholm, then it would be easier to build it in the north, afterwards. That was a surprise for me. In a place called Tibro I built a scheme which had some of these characteristics in it, but they wanted to imitate Stockholm in the north, not Tibro. Another scheme was Resolute Bay in Canada that I would have liked to do properly. They moved the airport to another township here there was a new mine being opened, so Resolute died.

One question is about exhibitions. One of the exhibitions you designed was a temporary one you did in 1980 in Kungsträdgården. You said it was influenced by the celebration of the Stockholm exhibition in 1930 with Asplund.

That was what we wanted to achieve. We thought it was going to be a sensation. Actually, I think that the buildings I did were very nice indeed and very suitable. But, the exhibition was done by amateurs, and unfortunately it didn't have the impact at all that was expected. The Stockholm exhibition in 1930 was professionally done. And we are back into participation.

This was taking participation too far. If you take it so far that people should design their own houses, the result is usually not good. I like it when they do a sketch because it gives me ideas and it initiates a dialogue. In 1980, exhibitors did the exhibition themselves and it wasn't good at all.

And what were your intentions with the design?

I hoped I would design the building, and I had done this in a positive way, amongst the trees in Kungsträdgården. I thought the exhibition was to be professional. One bit was extremely well-done in the enclosed building for a multiprojection. The rest was an open exhibit by different enthusiasts. The enthusiasm was there but it didn't say anything at all, and was not effective.

Did you design other exhibitions?

No, I think that was the only time.

My next question is more anecdotal. You mentioned the office on the move but another element which is on the move is one in which your drawings often include a balloon. Can you tell me about its meaning?

It has no meaning whatsoever. It was just that I was doing a competition one time and at that time people would draw very modern airplanes so I reacted and I drew a balloon. I've taken the balloon as a kind of a personal signature for the drawings I've done myself. That is the only thing it means and it is not an important thing at all.

It is like in the Hitchcock movies with objects, which are like floating signifiers. It is your Mcguffin.

There were certain painters who drew butterflies or whatever in all the paintings they did. Some had this kind of visual signature and that's what it is.

You drew this for the first time in a competition?

Yes, in a competition I was doing with a friend of mine who lives here. It was for a school in a town called Linköping.

Another question is about the future. What would be your advice to young architecture students for the future? How do you see the situation now?

The situation now is not very happy, not for me anyway, perhaps because I'm old. I think it is far too much influenced by the media. A lot of buildings nowadays are designed not so much for the people who are going to use them, but more to be photographed and taken into the media. They become, so to speak, advertising for the client and for the architect, and the result is that they are sensational buildings which rather destroy the feeling of the community. If you look at the old town here, obviously all the buildings are different from one another but they all express the common need of getting together. Nowadays, everybody has to advertise. You don't need to go and visit buildings, but you buy books and photographs and so on. For example, London city is very much destroyed by these extraordinary buildings. It seems to me to be opposite, even the artistic opposite of what you should be doing in building a township. A township is arising because people are moving to a connection point. They want to exchange goods, ideas, and experiences and this is the common need. This common need should be the first one expressed which means that the township should have some sort of common identity. The old town here has illustrated this very well, and there, even the modern buildings have something of the character of the older buildings without being an imitation. No, I don't think the situation is very happy for architecture now. I don't know if my analysis is right. They have been very conscious of this common need in the center of Stockholm. It has been regulated since the seventeenth or eighteenth century, regarding the heights, the volumes and even the materials and colors. It still hangs together because an architect doing a new building in the center will try to observe the common characteristic of the town. In new towns, in this country as well, it is the opposite. There are buildings totally different from one another. I think it is a shame. I believe the matter of context is very important. Certain architects have ignored the context. But, I think the context is to be given a lot of respect. So, what I usually say to young people is that architecture is the art of useful things. Buildings should be useful. Function, which includes the experience of it, is a very important side of architecture.

You founded the Erskine foundation with the money you won from the World Prize in 1984. There you emphasize particularly the issue of a humanistic and an ecological approach. Can you tell me something about this?

The humanism is very definitive. Buildings are for human beings, and human beings are going to use them or experience them. Some people experience buildings by walking around in the town seeing only the outside of the building. This is also a kind of participation in the experience of the town.

We've come to a wonderful ending, but I was curious to know a little bit more about your foundation.

I was given a very large prize, so I created a foundation for the Ruth and Ralph Erskine fund. There is a medal I've designed for the Erskine foundation; naturally it is not a gold medal but a wooden medal which illustrates the human being, the family and the building. It is given as a prize to a building, which is functional and for underprivileged people. Most prizes nowadays are given to rather exotic buildings, designed for big firms or rich people. Mine, however, is meant to be for underprivileged people in any community, anywhere in the world. It is for a functional, economical and beautiful building.

One thing I forgot to ask you before. It was when you talked about the arctic city. I wanted to ask you because you were invited by the Group X. What is your contact with them?

I kept contact with de Carlo and I went to his meetings in Italy as Peter Smithson did, whom I usually looked up when I went to London. It was really those two I kept contact with from this Team 10. I always thought Team 10 was a bit of a mixed phenomenon for good and evil.

But you were always independent from all these movements and groups?

Yes, that is largely true.

Robert Osserman

Encompassing the Earth

What god soever this division wrought, and every part to due proportion brought; first, lest the earth unequal should appear, he turned it round, in figure of a sphere.

Ovid, Metamorphoses, *first decade A.D.*
Translation by George Sandys, 1626

One of the enduring myths of the Western world is that in order to gain support for his expeditions, Christopher Columbus had to first overcome a pervasive belief that the earth was flat rather than round and that by attempting to sail west to Asia he would risk sailing off the edge of the earth. The myth undoubtedly stems in part from a compression of the historical past, conflating the early Middle Ages, when a belief in a flat earth was indeed widespread in Europe, with the late Middle Ages – centuries later – by which time Europe had caught up with, and partially surpassed, the state of knowledge of ancient Greece and medieval Islam.

Ptolemy – astronomer, geographer, and mathematician – lived in Alexandria over a thousand years before Columbus, during the height of the Roman Empire. During the second century A.D., he worked to consolidate and extend the scientific accomplishments of the previous centuries. Among his achievements was the completion of two works that were considered by Islamic scholars and Renaissance Europeans to provide the definitive descriptions of the heavens and the earth. The first book came to be known by the Latinized version of its part Arabic, part Greek title, *Almagest*, meaning "the greatest." The *Almagest* became for astronomy what Euclid's *Elements* was for geometry: the definitive treatise on the subject for over a thousand years.

In the same way, Ptolemy's *Geography* became the standard reference on that subject, to which all others deferred. Although one would expect the subjects of geometry, "measuring the earth," and geography, "describing the earth," to be indissolubly linked, their early histories were quite distinct. Geographical information was both scanty and unreliable, and maps were not meant to be interpreted too literally. Eratosthenes is credited with being one of the first to introduce mathematical methods into mapmaking. His methods were refined by Hipparchus, one of the great astronomers of antiquity, and also the first, to our knowledge, to develop trigonometry: the systematic study of relations between angles and side lengths in a triangle. Ptolemy made use of previous methods and discoveries, fully utilizing geometry in the service of geography. He wrote:

In Geography one must contemplate the extent of the entire earth, as well as its shape, and its position under the heavens, in order that one may rightly state what are the peculiarities and proportions of the part with which one is dealing... It is the great and exquisite accomplishment of mathematics to show all these things to human intelligence...

After the fall of Rome, mapmaking in Europe reverted to its earlier, more fanciful state, based on beliefs and hearsay, rather than on facts and science. It was not until the thirteenth century that Ptolemy's *Geography* once more became available, but at that time in the original Greek, a language that was not widely known. Another two hundred years passed before it was translated into Latin; the first printed version dates from 1472. Columbus himself owned a copy printed in 1479.

The spherical shape of the earth is accepted as established fact in Ptolemy's *Geography.* Several subsequent books written between 1200 and 1500 continued the discussion of the shape of the earth; the title alone of one of the most notable of them provides clear evidence of how educated people in the fifteenth century viewed the world. It was called simply *The Sphere.* The book's author was known as Sacrobosco, a Latinized version of the name of an Englishman, John of Holywood, who wrote a number of books in the early part of the thirteenth century. Probably no other textbook in history has been as successful as Sacrobosco's – it remained in print and was still in use five hundred years after it was written. (If one were to count Euclid's *Elements* as a textbook, it would undoubtedly own the record for longevity, but it was written in quite a different spirit and certainly was not intended as a text.)

What Sacrobosco did in his book was to adapt key passages from the *Almagest* of Ptolemy, add some newer material, and omit a number of technicalities, to arrive at a more accessible description of the workings of the universe, as best understood at the time. As the title indicated, the "sphere" was the key to everything. The earth was a sphere lying inside the great sphere of the fixed stars, while the sun, moon, and planets were attached to intermediate spheres. The evidence that the earth was round and not flat was taken straight from Ptolemy:

If the earth were flat from east to west, the stars would rise as soon for westerners as for orientals, which is false. Also, if the earth were flat from north to south and vice versa, the stars which were always visible to anyone would continue to be so wherever he went, which is false. But it seems flat to human sight because it is so extensive.

The Sphere includes a variant of Eratosthenes' estimate of the circumference of the earth and a calculation of the earth's diameter, using the value 22/7 for π.

How influential was Sacrobosco's book? One of the requirements to attain the degree of the Licentiate in Paris in 1366 was interpreted by the faculty to mean that one must attend a series of lectures on *The Sphere* and one other book. *The Sphere* was one of the requirements for the A.B. degree in Vienna in 1389, as it was at Oxford in 1409, and at Erfurt in Germany in 1422. At least two other major universities at the time, Prague and Bologna, included *The Sphere* as required reading in their curriculum.

By Columbus' day the view that the earth was spherical was clearly neither idiosyncratic nor controversial. Ironically, one of the arguments that apparently *was* used against Columbus by the advisers to the Spanish court *depended* on the assumption that the earth was spherical (combined with an understandable confusion about the workings of gravity). The argument advanced was that as one traveled farther and farther from home, one would be sailing downhill at a steeper and steeper angle. Eventually, one risked reaching a point where the uphill sail back home would be impossible, even with the strongest of winds.

It is hard today to appreciate the degree to which the earth and its oceans appeared immense and forbidding – the vast scale, the terrible dangers that explorers like Columbus were aware of, compounded with the even greater fears of the unknown. And all was magnified by rumors and tales enhanced in the telling. One extensive undertaking of the time – exploring the western coast of Africa – lasted almost an entire century. The exploration of the African coast by the Portuguese involved experts in navigation, cartographers, nautical instrument makers, and shipbuilders. During this period, generations of sailors, navigators, and captains saw firsthand during their voyages the changes in climate, the unfamiliar positions of the sun and the stars, and the appearance of whole new constellations, all brought about by the curvature of the earth.

The real issue for Columbus and his contemporaries was not the shape of the earth, but its size; and on that question there was indeed room for controversy. During the five hundred years or so between Aristotle and Ptolemy there had been a number of estimates of the size of the earth. Eratosthenes' estimate was among those closest to the truth (although perhaps overestimating the correct value by about 10 percent, depending on how the units of measurement then used are interpreted today). Ptolemy chose for his *Geography* an estimate that was as much as 20 percent too low. Since by the fifteenth century Ptolemy was regarded as the authority on the earth's geography, the value he gave for the circumference of the earth – about 20,000 miles – was widely accepted. For Columbus, Ptolemy's estimate had the additional appeal of bolstering the explorer's case for the feasibility of sailing west to the Orient. (On an earlier trip to Africa, Columbus made measurements of his own that tended to confirm the figure given by Ptolemy.) In addition to underestimating the size of the earth, Ptolemy vastly overestimated the size of Asia. The resulting map depicted an earth whose expanse of ocean between the western tip of Europe and the eastern tip of Asia was well within the range of provisions that ships of the day could carry.

In 1484, King John II of Portugal appointed a team of experts, called the Junta dos Matemáticos, to review proposals for maritime exploration and to advise on their feasibility. The members of the Junta not only were well versed in all the scholarly work on geography and navigation, but also had at their disposal the reports from the many earlier Portuguese voyages of exploration. It was undoubtedly their opinion – fully borne out by subsequent events – that Columbus was overly optimistic in his estimate of the distance to Asia.

After being rebuffed by Portugal, Columbus took his case to Spain, where – despite many delays – he finally received royal backing for his expedition.

Columbus was wrong not only in his estimate of the distance to the Orient but also in the assumption that there would be no land on his route between Europe and Asia. Since he was wrong on the first count – the distance was in fact far greater than his provisions could possibly have lasted – had he been right on the second and had a vast ocean to traverse, he would almost certainly have perished. To his very good fortune, he was wrong on both counts, and in this case two wrongs made a triumphant "right," with all the attendant fame and glory.

Columbus' voyages literally changed the map of the world. Before those voyages, European mapmakers often depicted the world as a large circle or oval with Europe, Asia, and Africa inside, surrounded by ocean. Columbus would have rightly interpreted the left-hand border as depicting the same line on the earth as the right. In other words, sailing off the left-hand edge of the map would have resulted in sailing onto the right-hand edge of the map, just as, five hundred years later, video-game aficionados became accustomed to seeing images vanish from the left-hand edge of their screen and reappear on the right.

With Western civilization's discovery of the Americas, it became more convenient to picture the world in the form of two hemispheres – Eastern and Western – each depicted in a circle of its own. Sailing out of one circle on such a map is tantamount to sailing into the other one. From the Eurocentric viewpoint of those making the maps, the Western Hemisphere became the "New World" and their own hemisphere, the "Old World."

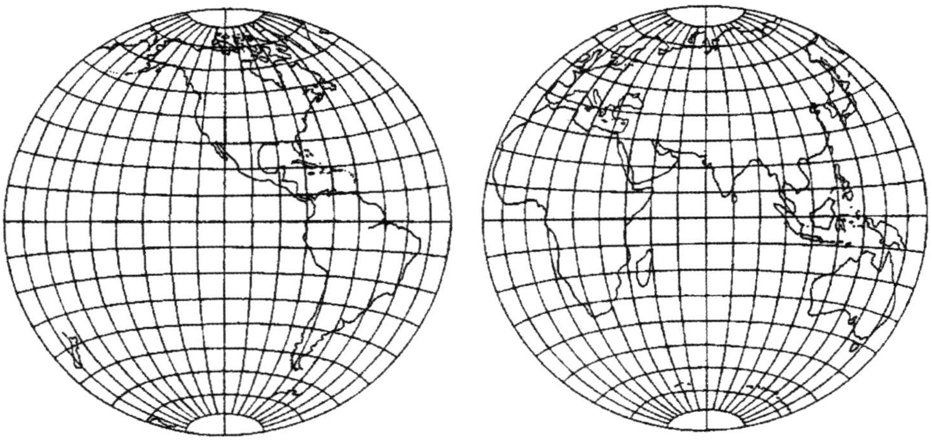

Fig. 1
The Western and Eastern Hemispheres

The depiction of the earth in the form of two hemispheres has become so commonplace that some of its subtler points may be overlooked. First, the division into Eastern and Western hemispheres is purely arbitrary – the earth can be divided in half for mapmaking purposes in any number of ways. A more natural division is into Northern and Southern hemispheres. In fact, any great circle on the earth could be used to divide the earth into two equal halves, each of which is depicted as the inside of a circle. In the case of the Northern and Southern hemispheres, their common boundary is the equator. Every point on the surface of the earth is either above the equator, below the equator, or on the equator. All points that lie above the equator are depicted on such a map as points inside one circle, while all points below the equator are depicted by points inside the other. A location on the earth lying right on the equator is depicted twice on the map – on each of the circles depicting the outer edges of the two hemispheres. For example, the point near the west coast of Africa where the Portuguese first crossed the equator appears on the outer edge of the Northern Hemisphere and on the outer edge of the Southern Hemisphere.

One of the less desirable features of the two-hemisphere map is that certain points that are close together on earth – say just above and just below the equator – may not be close at all on the map. It is, however, a drawback that cannot be overcome. One can prove, using a modern branch of mathematics known as *topology*, that *any* map of the surface of the entire earth must have the same weakness; one cannot concoct a way

Fig. 2
The Northern and Southern Hemispheres

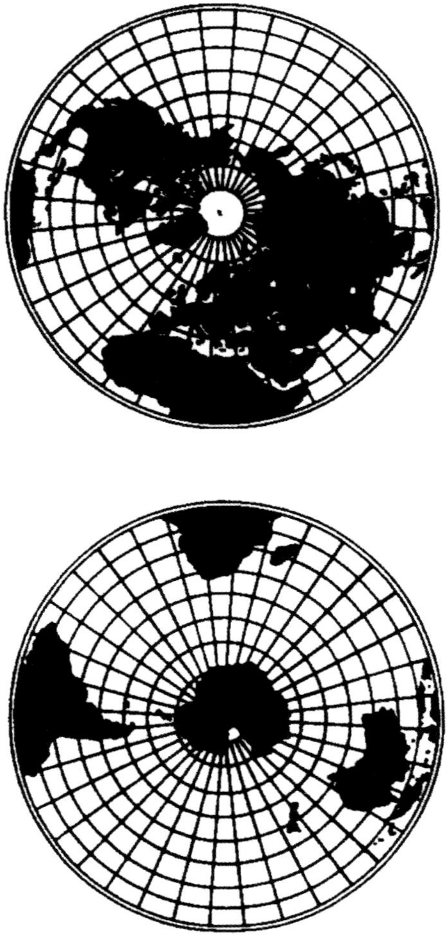

of depicting the whole earth on a sheet of paper so that nearby points on the earth will always be close to each other on the map.

This weakness, however, is more of a mild inconvenience than a serious problem to map readers and navigators. A more critical question is how one depicts the geographical features inside each hemisphere so that distances and directions can be reliably read off the map. Early maps were notoriously inaccurate. The incomplete and unreliable data upon which the maps were based were only part of the problem. More fundamental was the question of how to transfer measurements of latitude and longitude on the surface of the earth to corresponding locations on the map without producing vast distortions. For purposes of navigation it was particularly important to have a map on which one could rely. There are two features that navigators especially prize. First, that all routes due north from any point on the map be depicted by the direction "straight up." Second, that all compass directions be correctly depicted on the map relative to the northerly direction, so that a river flowing east-west would be horizontal on the map, and a road going northeast should be depicted at a 45° angle – halfway between horizontal and vertical.

Any map that has those two properties we will call a *navigator's map*. Such maps automatically have certain additional properties: parallels of latitude are depicted as horizontal lines, and the map has a fixed scale along each parallel of latitude – in other words, three points equally spaced along the same latitude appear equally spaced on the map. Most importantly, if one wants to sail from Lisbon to a particular point on the coast of North America, then setting a fixed compass direction indicated by the direction of the straight line between the corresponding points on the map provides a route to the precise destination.

The first actual map designed on these principles was drawn in 1569 by the Flemish cartographer Gerhard Kremer, whose last name means "merchant" and who went by its Latin equivalent: Mercator.

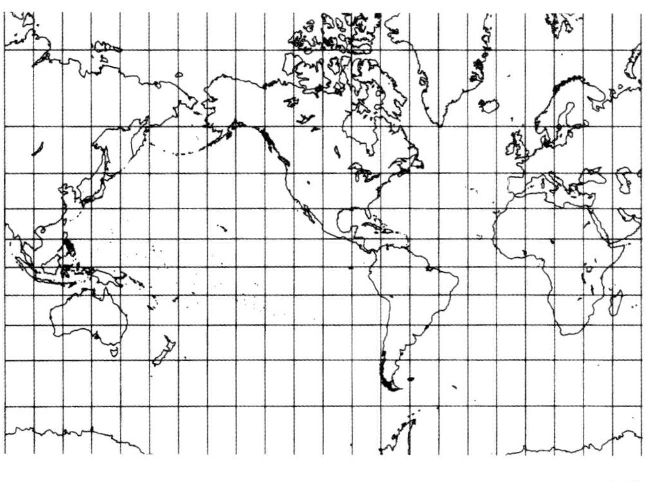

Fig. 3
A Mercator projection

Nowadays, the name Mercator is all but synonymous with this particular map. In his own time, however, Mercator's fame was not restricted to mapmaking. He was well known and enormously successful in the long tradition of master craftsmen in Renaissance Italy whose scientific instruments were equally prized as works of art and were collected by the Medici. In 1541, Mercator made a globe for Charles V, the Holy Roman Emperor, who then commissioned a set of surveyor's instruments. The combination of beauty and accuracy brought Mercator many commissions and considerable wealth and fame. But his primary passion appears to have been mapmaking; he spent many years working on a definitive edition of Ptolemy's *Geography*, and he was universally recognized as Europe's premier cartographer.

All of that meant little to posterity, which focused on the single map drawn by Mercator in 1569, of which a sole exemplar survives. Mercator has also been the victim of a quirk of language that has led to a widespread misconception about how his map is designed. The word "projection" is interpreted by cartographers in a much broader sense than in common usage or in mathematical terminology, where the expression conjures up the image of a small transparent globe, with all the desired geographic features drawn on its surface, and a cylinder wrapped around it, touching the sphere along the equator. A light placed at the center of the sphere will "project" the sphere onto the cylinder – that is to say, it will cast shadows of each continent onto the cylinder, and each meridian will pro-

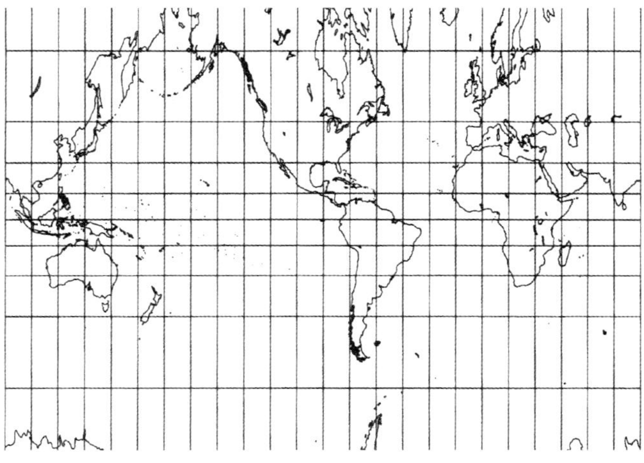

Fig. 4
A cylindrical projection. The distortion of the map toward the poleis is far greater for the cylindrical projection than for Mercator's map.

ject onto a vertical line. When the cylinder is cut along one of those lines and unrolled onto a plane, the result will look very much like Mercator's famous map, with many of the same features: meridians will be vertical lines, parallels of latitude will be projected as horizontal lines, and there will be equal scaling along each fixed latitude. Nevertheless, it is not a true Mercator map: all compass directions other than north-south and east-west will be wrong.

Mercator's map is not based on any such simple projection or geometric construction. Mercator explained the principles on which the map was drawn as follows:

In making this representation of the world we have had to employ a new proportion and a new arrangement of the meridian with reference to the parallels ... we have progressively increased the degrees of latitude towards each pole in proportion to the lengthening of the parallels with reference to the equator.

In other words, in order to have the angles come out right, Mercator stretched the map in the vertical direction (which is what he means by "increasing the degrees of latitude toward each pole"), and the amount of vertical stretching is the same as the amount of horizontal stretching. But the amount of horizontal stretching along any parallel of latitude is simply equal to the ratio of the length of the equator to the length of the given parallel, since the equator and all the parallels of latitude appear as horizontal lines of fixed length: the width of the map. With these general guidelines and using as much art as science, Mercator produced his map. It was not until century's end that Edward Wright gave an explicit formula for the amount of stretching at any given latitude, and used it to compile a table of small increments of latitude and the corresponding locations on Mercator's map. Wright's tables allowed anyone to construct the map (without having to master the principles on which it was based). However, Wright's tables still provided only an approximation of a true Mercator map. That was the best that one could hope for, since the exact equations for Mercator's map require the use of logarithms, which had not yet been invented at the time. It was not until 1668, just ninety-nine years after Mercator conceived the idea for his map, that mathematicians succeeded in applying the newly invented subject of integral calculus to obtain the exact equations for Mercator's map. With those equations in hand, anybody – or, in modern times, any computer – can produce a Mercator map drawn to whatever degree of accuracy is desired.

The biggest drawback of Mercator's map was its progressive distortion from the equator toward the poles. A pair of points on a pair of vertical (or longitudinal) lines on the map remain a fixed distance apart, while the corresponding points on the actual surface of the earth get closer and closer together as they approach the pole. As a result, a region lying far to the north or south will appear much larger on the map than the same-size region located near the equator.

Ideally, one would like to have a map with the desirable features of Mercator's map but without the distortion. However, it is a geometrical fact (whose complete proof had to wait several hundred years) that the two properties of a navigator's map – a vertical north and directions relative to north depicted correctly – determine the map completely (up to the overall scale): it must be Mercator's map. Our choice is either to sacrifice one (or both) of the desirable properties or else to accept the distortion.

The problem is not limited to maps attempting to depict the entire earth. It arises with every map of a city, region, or country. Such maps typically provide an arrow that indicates the direction "north" for all points on the map, and a fixed scale, such as "an inch to a mile," meaning that the distance between any two points on the map, measured in inches, converts to the actual distance between the corresponding points on the earth, measured in miles. But it is impossible for any map to have both a fixed direction for north for all points on the map and a fixed scale. Such a map would automatically have to depict compass directions correctly, and thus would have to be Mercator's map; but it could not then have a fixed scale, since the scale on Mercator's map is different on different horizontal lines. The reason that a city or county map can *claim* a fixed scale and a fixed direction for north is that the variation of scale on a Mercator projection for a relatively small region (at least away from the poles) is small enough to be negligible.

Since a fixed scale on a map is incompatible with a fixed direction for north, one could ask if it is possible to produce a map of the earth with a fixed scale by allowing the northerly direction to vary from point to point, as it does in the usual depictions of the earth in two hemispheres. In other words, is there any map at all that has no distortions? Despite centuries

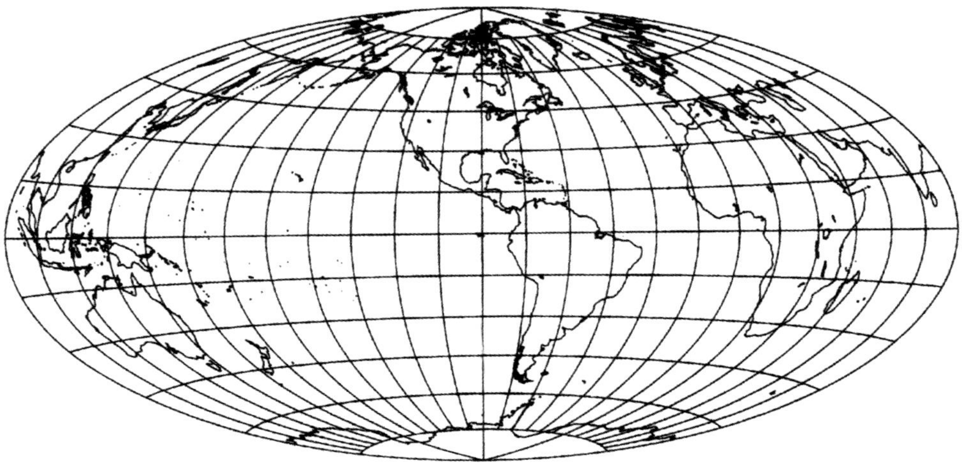

Fig. 5
A Hammer projection. One of many attemps by cartographers to find new and better ways to depict the earth's surface. This one dates from 1892 and has been widely adopted.

of efforts leading to ingenious partial solutions to the problem, cartographers were continually frustrated; it was as if they were dealing with an unsightly tube of toothpaste – squeezing it at one place would always result in a bulge somewhere else. The problem was finally resolved in the mid-eighteenth century by the leading mathematician of the time, Leonhard Euler.

Euler's mathematical interests ranged from the purest theoretical investigations to the most practical applied problems. Intrigued by the mapmakers' difficulties, he proved conclusively that what they had been trying to accomplish was in fact impossible. There is no map of any portion of the earth's surface which, translated onto a flat sheet of paper, has a fixed scale. Every map, in fact, is a compromise.

As Euler's theorem shows, there can never be a perfect map. The challenge to cartographers is to devise new ways of mapping the earth that either minimize the overall distortion or else are particularly well adapted to a certain purpose. They responded with literally hundreds of different maps, of which several dozen are in common use. For example, during the twentieth century, as ocean crossings were gradually replaced by air travel, the "navigator-type" maps became less relevant. Oddly enough, a much more useful map for navigating by air is one that had been invented long before Mercator's map. It was introduced by al-Biruni sometime around the year 1000, and is called an *azimuthal equidistant projection* by cartographers and an *exponential map* by mathematicians. A better

Fig. 6
An egocentric map based at San Francisco. The map shows at a glance that the direct route from San Francisco to Riyadh in Saudi Arabia goes directly over Moscow and Baghdad. (It also shows that Rio de Janeiro is farther from San Francisco than Buenos Aires and only a little closer than Hong Kong). Since the antipodal point to San Francisco lies in the Indian Ocean, off the coast of Madagascar, the whole outer ring of the map corresponds to a small piece of the Indian Ocean surrounding the antipodal point, and Madagascar is stretched out on the map to roughly the same length as North America.

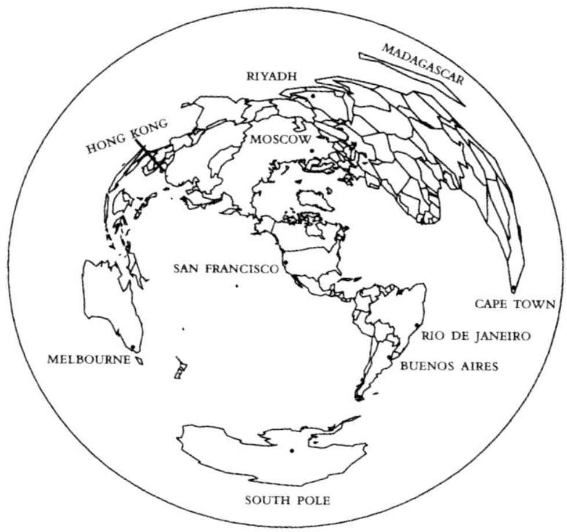

name for it would be an *egocentric map*. Choosing one's hometown or other favorite location as the focus, one can draw such a map with that place at the center, surrounded by the rest of the world. Distances from the center to any other point on earth are drawn to scale, and directions around the central point are correctly indicated. These two properties, together with the given scale, determine the entire map. The main features of such a map are that it represents the region around the central point quite accurately, and it provides a quick way to determine the distance from the central location to any other point on earth: just measure the distance on the map and multiply it by the scale factor. Furthermore, the straight line on the map joining the center to any other point shows instantly which cities, countries, and other landmarks one will pass over if one flies the direct route from the central location to the second point.

As Euler's theorem tells us, these attractive features of an egocentric map relative to its central point must necessarily be paid for by distortions elsewhere on the globe. And in fact, the further away from the center that one looks, the more the map is distorted. The reason is that each circle around the center of the map corresponds to a circle of points on the globe at a given distance from the central location. As those distances approach half the circumference of the earth, the circle on the map gets larger, since it is further from the central point, while the corresponding circle on the globe contracts down toward the antipodal point: the point on the earth exactly halfway around from the central location. The distortion is most extreme at the antipodal point, which is not represented by a single point on the map, but is stretched out to an entire circle – the outer boundary of the map. In fact, starting at any point on earth and heading off in any direction always leads to the antipodal point after going a fixed distance: halfway around the globe.

Little did al-Biruni suspect that his new map of the world would someday – many centuries later – prove singularly useful for future modes of navigation. Even less could he have foreseen that his map would someday provide a particularly appropriate way to view and understand the entire universe. The best route to that understanding is not the direct one, however, and we shall have to make several side excursions along the way to explore the key notion of "curvature" before arriving at our destination.

Fig. 7
How to construct an egocentric map based on your hometown: Place a globe of the earth on a large sheet of paper with your hometown's location on the globe touching the paper. To find the precise point of the map corresponding to any position on earth, stretch a string along the globe from the point of the globe touching the paper (your hometown) to the desired position on the globe, and then stretch the string along the line of the paper directly below where it was on the globe.

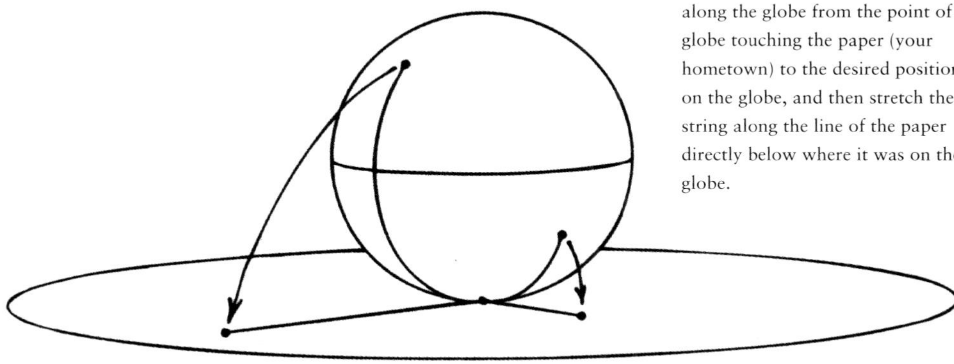

Franz Pichler

Victor Schauberger and the Turbulence of Water

Introduction

In the little village of Klaus, where Victor Schauberger had worked as a forest ranger for several years, the official exhibition of the governement of Upper Austria in 1997, *Land of Hammer* presented a little sub-exhibition with the title *Water is Force*. This exhibition gained strong support by the display of original exhibits from Victor Schauberger's historical water research, such as the "energy engine" (Heimkraftwerk = home power generator) and the hyperbolic cone. These objects are owned by the family Schauberger (PKS, Lauffen/Bad Ischl) and were kindly loaned for the exhibition. Apart from the written concept of the exhibition, no other document was prepared. This paper should be considered as a late contribution to this exhibition. The goal is to present some ideas which could form a basis for further research on the open questions concerning the "forces of water."

By suggestion of the publisher of this book, the phenomena related to turbulence should be investigated and presented.

Turbulence might indeed be the solution of the secret of water as considered by Victor Schauberger. In the first part we report on some biographical facts on Victor Schauberger and continue by sketching a systems theoretical approach to investigate the "levitation of water" (water has memory). Our writing does not claim to give a contribution to the current state of water research. We purposely rely on an ad hoc style which we consider an example of scientific oriented "brainwriting."

Victor Schauberger and the force of water

Landslides and creeks which turn to wild waters within minutes cause death, damage roads and agricultural land and leave behind victims.

On the other hand, such "forces of water" enable transport circuits and contribute in a useful way to civilization. Guided by a track, floating water was utilised for centuries to bring timber from the mountain areas down to the bottom of the valleys. In some areas of the alps, the remains of constructions of such wooden transport circuits can still be seen.

Down the river Steyr in Upper Austria, the floating of timber was of practical interest over a long period of time and contributed to the economy of the region. Today, mountain roads and trucks have replaced the old transport chains for floating timber.

Victor Schauberger (1885-1958), former forest ranger in the duties of the forest property headquarter of the German family of Schaumburg-Lippe in the village of Steyrling, is the inventor of unusual technical constructions of timber floating systems. However, his inventions have also found practical applications.

Numerous related patents and installations provide proof of his inventiveness and of his success in putting it to practical use. The best example may be the huge and complex timber floating system in Neuberg/Mürz in Styria of the year 1928. The movie *Tragendes Wasser* (water as carrier) from the year 1935 shows lumberjacks during their work of floating timber with this installation. In addition to the stream-lined construction of the wooden timber channels – to avoid friction of the floating timber from water turbulence – a novelty of the system was that at certain distances, "old," used water was replaced by "fresh," cool water. By this method, as Victor Schauberger discovered, the transverse strength of the floating water in terms of carrying timber, reaches a maximum. Such studies and achieved results brought Victor Schauberger to the idea of "implosion" (as opposed to "explosion"): By twisting ("Einwirbeln") of a stream of water through a complex system of tubes (the hyperbolic cone of the PKS being an apparatus for demonstration of that effect, compare with fig. 1) the direction of energetic forces should become channeled. In other words, the chaoticaly distributed forces as they exist in turbulent water should become (as result of a laminar stream of water) directed and able to drive a common turbine. The "Energy Engine" (Heimkraftwerk) of the year 1952, which still exists as a prototype in the museum of the PKS in Bad Ischl, presents an example for a possible engineering construction to realize the application of an "implosion-engine" in the sense of Victor Schauberger.

In addition to Victor Schauberger's ideas on energy uses of the "forces of water," he was also interested in investigating natural water as a substance important for human life. He considered water coming directly from the springs in the mountains of the Alps to be of the best quality. In 1932 he had already begun doing experiments to improve the water quality and to produce mineral water by technological means. The hydromechanical methods which he applied, could – in a certain sense – be interpreted as being inverse to the idea of an implosion. In principle, his approach was as follows:

To get an "improvement" in the quality, natural water is brought mechanically from a state of equilibrium to a state of turbulence and the subsequent steady state represents water in a different structural order with a new (improved) quality. Today many products – and people believe in it – float the market. However, only a few relate this function to the original ideas of Victor Schauberger. The "Martin Wasserwirbler" (see the article by Jens Fischer cited in the references) and the "Levitiation Engines" of Hacheney (Friedrich Hacheney 1994) seem to follow these ideas.

In the summer of 1958, Victor Schauberger was invited (together with his son, Dipl. Ing. Walter Schauberger) to visit the USA, present his inventions, and contribute as an expert to practical applications based on his numerous patents. The time-consuming negotiations with his American partners ended without success and Victor Schauberger and his son returned to Europe. Victor Schauberger died in Linz on September 25, 1958 a few days after his return from the USA.

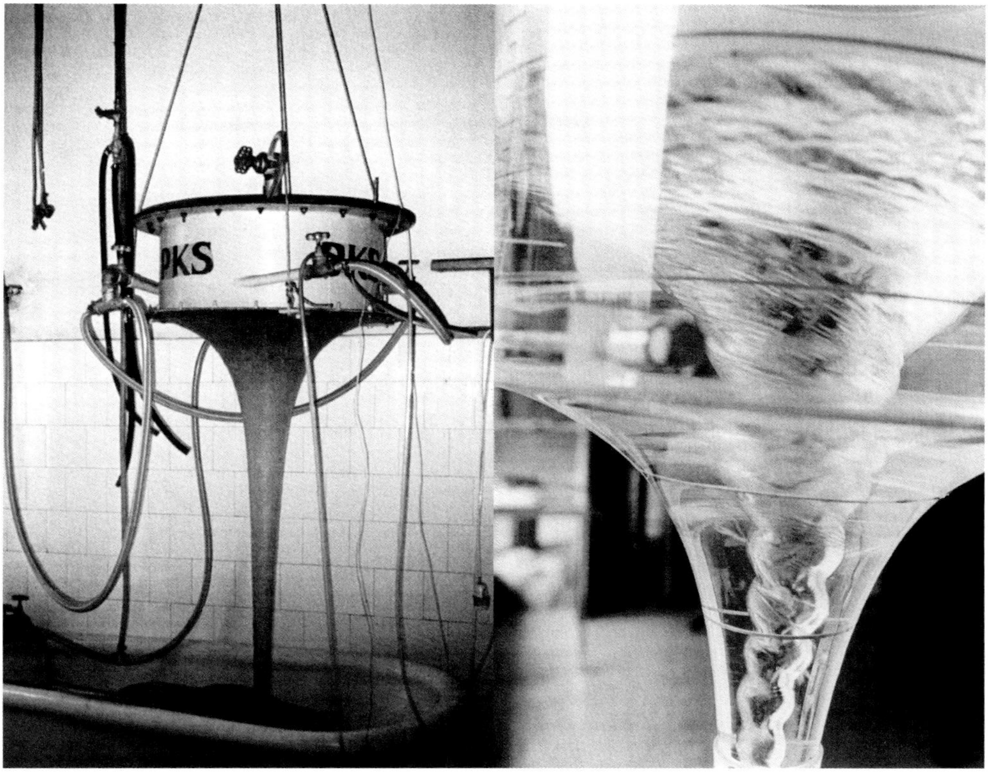

a) b)

Fig. 1
a) Hyperbolic Cone
b) Waterspout made by running water in the hyperbolic cone

Water-multi-level model

Natural water, that is chemically purified water (aqua destillata) together with other embedded substances (gases, metals, minerals, acids, etc.) has, as is known, an extremely complex structure. Depending on the problems stated above, in order to model natural water, different disciplines have to be consulted and have to contribute to the modelling task. The integration of the different domain-oriented models (to get a single multidisciplinary model) can be established by the usage of the concept of a multi-level model, where each level (in systems theory called "stratum") models natural water at a certain kind or degree of abstraction. For the purpose of this paper we want to assume a four-level model as shown in fig. 2.

Fig. 2
Four-level model of natural water

chem/phys macromodel	Level A
↓	↑
hydrodynamic model	Level B
↓	↑
cluster-dynamics model	Level C
↓	↑
molecular-dynamics model	Level D

Level A gives a description of natural water in the usual form of chemical and physical properties such as molecular constitution (H_2O), dissolved substances, pH value, temperature, volume, weight and others.

Level B models natural water from the hydromechanic point of view. For any unit of volume of natural water, the geometrical position and a gradient to define a vector dynamic is given (e.g. by a partial differential equation of Navier-Stokes types). Associated constants (like the Reynold number R) describe hydrodynamical properties of the global state of natural water on that level.

Level C is the level for the modeling of natural water which attracts our utmost attention in this paper. The model on this level should reflect the cluster structure of the molecules. The clustering (if it ever exists) should, by hypothesis, provide special qualities of natural water for human consumption or technological use. In the later part of this paper we will address this problem in more detail.

Level D should represent natural water as a dynamic system which models the dynamics on a molecular level. The forces which are assumed at this level can be divided into external forces (kinetic forces applied to molecules via the environment of the water tank together with the influence of its specific geometrical form) and internal forces (electro-static forces, magnetic forces, electro-dynamic forces, Van der Waal's forces and others possible forces). A local generative model for the molecular dynamics must be formulated by means of such forces. State machines in the form of specific Petri-nets or cellular automata (Wolfram 1986) could be appropriate systems theoretical concepts for that modeling task.

"Levitation" of water: systems theoretical interpretation

We see the problem of "levitation" (a term used by Hackeney 1994) as the problem of controling natural water by external forces to a dynamic state such that the associated model at level C (molecule-cluster dynamic model) shows stable clusters of molecules in its states.

As a mechanism for the creation of clusters, we take as an hypothesis the results of chaos-theory which tries to explain biological evolution by the phenomena of (mathematical) morphogenesis (René Thom, 1972). The states of the "C-model," which should show a cluster structure, we assume to be associated to strange attractors (in the sense of Ruelle-Takens' 1971 definition, compare with Bergé, Pomeau and Vidal, 1984) in the molecular level dynamics. For the appearance of strange attractors, a certain nonlinearity of the state equation of the D-model is necessary. In chaos-theory, nonlinear maps and equations (such as the Hénon-map, the horseshoe-map, the baker-transform, the Lorenz-equations, the Roessler-equations, and others) show the mathematical mechanism in the generation of strange attractors.

In our case of natural water, a specific molecular model has to be constructed for that purpose. It is not known to the author whether such a model already exists today. The assumption that strange attractors should be the systems theoretical means to "lift" the molecular dynamical model of level D to the cluster-dynamical model of level C is in line with a current scientific approach to explaining turbulence (in a hydromechanical model of level B) by strange attractors.

The "lifting" of models by means of strange attractors is known in biology as a construction of a "morphological field" (e.g. Rupert Sheldrake, *The Presence of the Past,* Times Book, New York, 1988).

Our principal proposition for further research for explaining the "levitation" of water is to base the investigation of the "levitation of water" in analogy to the "morphological fields" in biology on the concept of strange attractors of chaotic processes.

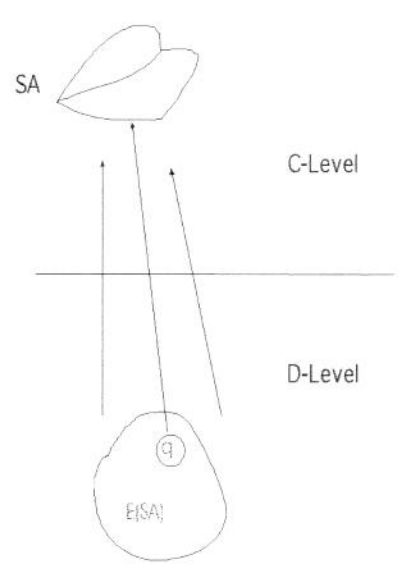

Fig. 3
Assignment of a state q of a D-model to related strange attractor SA in a C-model. E (SA) is the basin of the attractor SA.

Topological characterization of the clustering process

In the following we will try to establish a basis to characterize some set-theoretical features of a strange attractor SA(q) which is related to a state q of the molecular model on D-level. We assume that a tank B is filled with natural water NW in which additional to H_2O molecules of the substances $S_1, S_2, \ldots, S_n$ are contained their quantities card S_1, card $S_2, \ldots$, card S_n.

All molecules of NW which are not contained in S are assumed to be H_2O molecules.

For each molecule s_i from S_i we denote with $U(s_i)$ the (finite) set of molecules of the different possible substances which are "close" to S_i.

We now want to characterize each molecule $s_i \in S_i$ ($i = 1,2,\ldots,n$) by the distribution (in quantity) of the different possible substances in $U(s_i)$ ("surroundings") and by their distribution in further possible neighborhoods which enclose $U(s_i)$ ("surroundings surrounded").

By card $U(s_i)(s_j)$ we denote the number of molecules $s_j \in S_j$ which are contained in $U(s_i)$. Therefore, the function card $U(s_i)(.): S \rightarrow \{0,1,2,\ldots\}$ describes the distribution of the different substances in the "closest" neighborhood for each molecule of S.

To give an example: card $U(s_i)(s_j) = 1$ for $i=j$ and card $U(s_i)(s_j)=0$ for $i \neq j$ shows, that only molecules H_2O of pure water are "closely" surrounding S_i.

We extend the concept of neighborhoods of S_i by the incremental addition of substances to be considered as neighbors of S_i.

By $U^2(s_i)$ we mean $U^2(s) := \bigcup_{s' \in U(s)} U(s')$. $U^2(s)$ consists of U(s) together with all neighbourhoods U(s') for the molecules s' which are in U(s). $U^2(s)$ is called the neighborhood of second order of s. In general, by iteration we get the neighbourhood $U^k(s)$ of k'th order of s by $U^k(s) := \bigcup_{s' \in U^{k-1}(s)} U(s')$.

By $U^0(s_i)$ we denote the "trivial" neighborhood $U^0(s_i) := \{s_i\}$. To introduce the distribution (in quantity) of the different substances which surround a molecule s_i in the neighborhood of k'th order, we introduce, in analogy to the case k=1, the function card $U^k(s_i)(.): S \rightarrow \{0,1,2,\ldots\}$.

We now have reached the point where we are able to characterize the neighborhood of a molecule s_i from the tank B by the list $\underline{U}(s_i) = (U^0(s_i), U^1(s_i), \ldots, U^2(s_i)), \ldots)$ of "surroundings" of different order and, to characterize s_i in a quantitative manner, by the list card $\underline{U}(s_i)(.) = ($card $U^0(s_i)(.)$, card $U^1(s_i)(.), U2(s_i)(.), \ldots)$ of distributions of different order.

Our goal is, by means of such set-theoretical arguments concerning the neighborhood of a molecule s_i, to get the necessary conditions for the characterization of the local molecular dynamics.

Let us now assume that for any molecule s_i the influence by forces does not extend beyond the order m of its neighborhoods. Then the lists $\underline{U}(s_i)$ and card $\underline{U}(s_i)(.)$ become finite vectors $\underline{U}(s_i)=(U^0(s_i), U^1(s_i),\ldots,U^{m-1}(s_i))$ and card $\underline{U}(s_i)(.)=$ (card $U^0(s_i)(.)$, card $U^1(s_i)(.),\ldots$, card $U^{m-1}(s_i)(.)$), respectively. By transposition of card $\underline{U}(s_i)(.)$ we get the $m \times n$ matrix $M(s_i)$:=card $\underline{U}(s_i)^T$ with $M(s_i)(k,j)$ = card $U^k(s_i)(s_j)$ for $k=0,1,2,\ldots,m-1$ und $j= 1,2,\ldots,n$.

The matrix $M(s_i)$ gives for s_i a convenient representation for the quantitative distribution of the different substances in the relevant neighborhoods of s_i.

To reach a local dynamic description for a model of NW at level C (being some kind of a homomorphic image of the molecular dynamic model of level D) we use $M(s_i)$ as the state related to s_i. A local state transition which takes $M(s_i)$ at time t to a new state $M'(s_i)$ at time t+1 can be described by a function δ with $M'(s_i)= \delta(M(s_i),a)$. The parameter a can be seen as an input which controls the local state transition over time. With the concept of the state $M(s_i)$, the input a and the local state transition function δ, all related to s_i we have all components to define the time-invariant state machine $SM(s_i)$.

$SM(s_i)$ represents the local dynamics for s_i at level C. Since the possible numbers of different configurations of the matrix $M(s_i)$ is finite, we conclude that $SM(s_i)$ is a finite state machine. With the assumption that there are N molecules in S (card S=N) we are in the position to define the "overall" state machine SM by the finite list SM = $(SM(s_i))s_i\in S$ of length N. With SM we have reached the goal of our paper here: to construct a generative model for the description of the cluster-dynamics at level C of the four-level model of natural water.

SM shows for any molecule s_i (S how stepwise under an input sequence $(a_0,a_1,\ldots,a_{n-1})$ the number of substances in the different neighborhoods $U^k(s_i)$ $(k=0,1,\ldots,m-1)$ is changed. However, the validity of SM to contribute to problem solving is limited only to a quantitative analysis regarding substances from S. For other types of investigations (for example for an analysis of the neighborhoods $U^k(s_i)$, to discover their geometric nature or for investigations of the kind of neighborhoods $U^k(H_2O)$ of H_2O molecules) similar state machines could be constructed.

Our example, however, is well suited to demonstrate the principal concept which we propose for the construction of models at level C which can be related to molecular models of level D to serve for the investigation of the role of strange attractors for "water structuring" ("levitation" of water).

Considerations concerning the molecular dynamics

A molecular dynamics model MD is given if for any molecule m (NW, a related trajectory (orbit) can be determined which for any instant $t \in [t_0, t_1]$ determines the related location $(x,y,z) \in \mathbf{R}^3$ of the molecule. A physical measurement of trajectories of this kind currently seems impossible. However, also the determination of equations for the molecular level which describe the influence of forces to a single molecule m of NW and which allow the derivation of related trajectories can generally be considered a difficult task. The fields of biophysics and microbiology investigate similar kinds of models and the results derived in those fields could be of great help.

Our hypothesis, as we pointed out earlier, presumes that the molecular dynamical model MD at level D becomes chaotic under certain conditions, (caused by external forces together with a certain geometric form of the tank B) and the trajectories turn into strange attractors of MD. The types of strange attractors (structure, geometry, Hausdorff-dimension, and other characterizations) can be assumed to depend greatly on the applied forces and on properties of the natural water NW in B. By the existence of strange attractors, we can try to construct a homomorphic ("dynamorphic" according to the definition of Michael Arbib) image as a model for the assumed cluster-dynamics at level C. In the case of the state machine SM as a possible model at level C, the state assignment from MD to SM can be defined (for substances s_i located at (x,y,z,t)) by $s_i \rightarrow M(s_i)$. Strange attractors SA in MD correspond to related steady states $M^*(s_i)$ in SM.

$M^*(s_i)$ is not a "true" picture of a strange attractor but can only be considered a projection in the sense of a Poincaré-map of chaos-theory. We already mentioned above that additional to states of the kind $M(s_i)$ (which mathematically are integer-valued matrices) other state definitions for the neighborhood systems are possible (e.g. state definitions which represent a geometrical structure of the neighborhoods). For a scientific approach (to find relevant concepts for the definition of states for the C-level model) we suggest performing simulation studies with the model MD at molecular level D and investigate by it the existence and the kind of associated strange attractors.

Conclusion and outlook

This paper followed a goal based on the pioneering investigations of Victor Schauberger: to establish for natural water a general systems theoretical approach for the construction of a model, which may explain the properties of "water has memory" or "water contains information" (as they are assumed in some popular writings). Peter Weibel suggested basing such models on the phenomenon of "turbulence." The current scientifically "deep" explanation of turbulence is established by chaos-theory using the concept of strange attractors. This fact gave the direction for our "brain writing." As a result, we constructed for the level of cluster dynamics, the state machine SM to describe by its steady states $M^*(s_i)$, Poincaré-cuts of possible strange attractors of a dynamical system MD at the molecular level. We mentioned that our approach allows, in a similar way, the construction of other kinds of state machines for level C such that their steady states may "detect" specific features of a strange attractor of MD.

Another similar task would be to construct state machines for level C such that their steady states reflect properties which are caused by the existing hydrogen bonds of the H_2O molecules and result in clusters of different geometrical forms. All such investigations would, however, need the validation of the models through simulation studies.

The author is grateful to Kurt Schilcher (nanolythics, Feldkirchen, Upper Austria), Gerald Lasslberger (BIOS, Linz) and especially to Jörg Schauberger (PKS, Lauffen/Bad Ischl, Upper Austria) for the effective and fast provision of relevant literature on "water research."

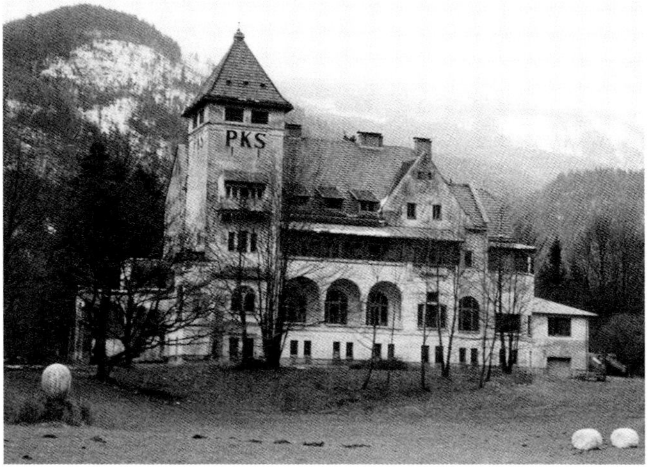

Fig. 4
PKS-Villa in Lauffen/Bad Ischl
(PKS= Pythagoras-Kepler-Schule)

Remark:
After finishing this paper I got hold of the Ivan Engler (ed.), *Wasser-Polaritätsphänomen, Informationsträger, Lebens-Heilmittel,* 1999. This book contains valuable material for further work, especially the article by H. Klima, *Wasserstrukturen in dissipativen Systemen* and by G. Resch and V. Gutmann, *Wissenschaftliche Grundlagen des Wassers als Informationsträger.*

References

S. Lattacher, *V. Schauberger,* Ennsthaler Verlag, A-4402 Steyr, 1999.

O. Alexanderson, *Lebendes Wasser,* Ennsthaler Verlag, A-4402 Steyr, vol. 8, 1998.

R. Thom, *Structural Stability and Morphogenesis,* W. A. Benjamin, Inc., Reading, Mass., 1975.

P. Bergé, Y. Pomeau, C. Vidal, *Order within Chaos, Towards a deterministic approach to turbulence,* John Wiley & Sons, New York, 1984.

J. L. Casti, *Complexification,* Harper Collins Publishers, New York, 1994.

S. Wolfram, *Theory and Applications of Cellular Automata,* World Scientific, Singapore, 1986.

F. Hacheney, *Levitiertes Wasser in Forschung und Anwendung,* Dingfelder Verlag, second edition, 1994.

I. Engler, *Wasser - Polaritätsphänomen, Informationsträger, Lebens-Heilmittel,* Deutscher Spurbuchverlag, new edition, 1999.

J. Fischer, *Experimente mit Leitungswasser – Die Geschichte des Original Martin Wasserwirbler,* Selbstverlag Jens Fischer, Am Hinteren Feld 13, D-29683 Fallingbostel.

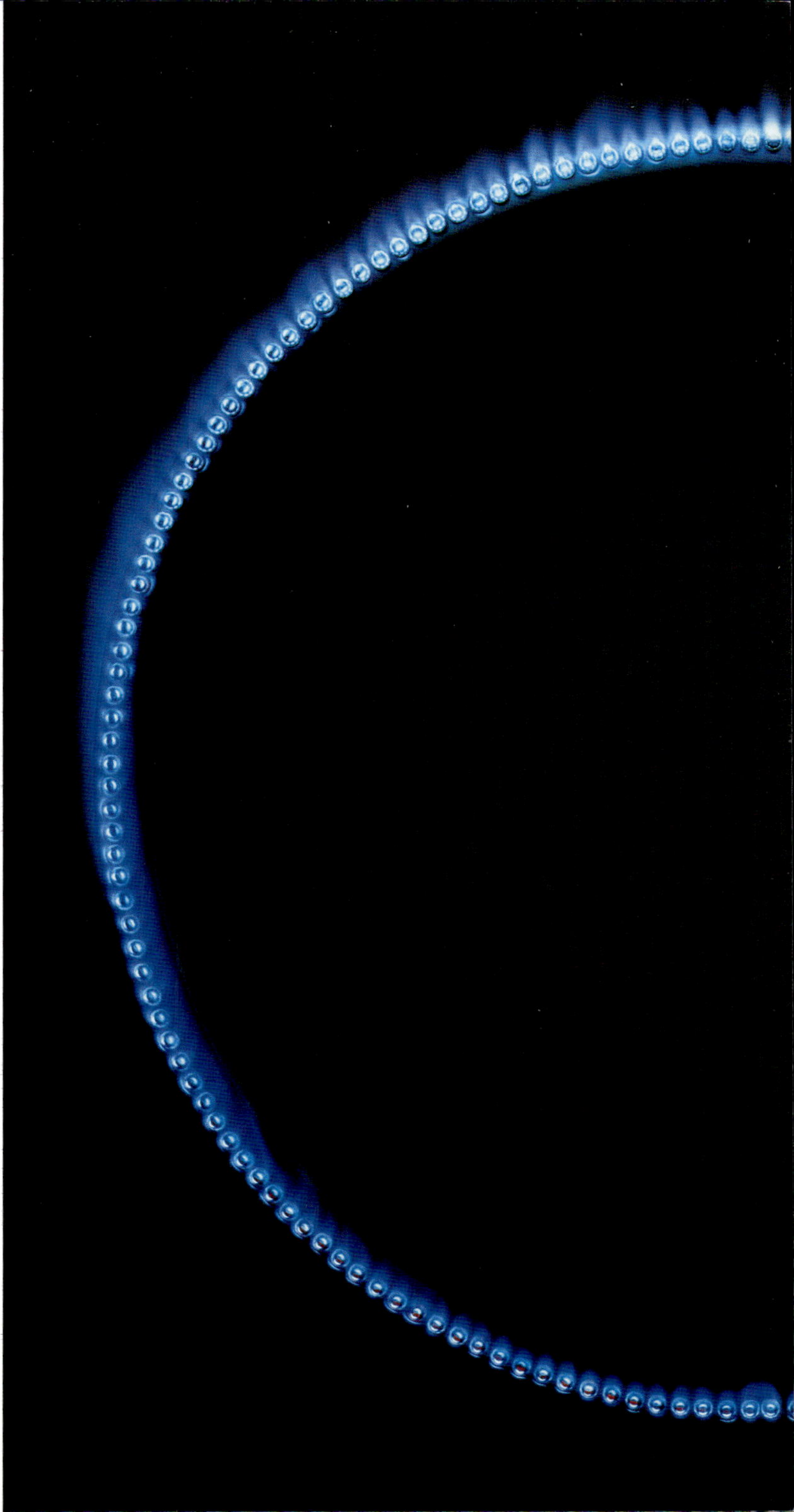

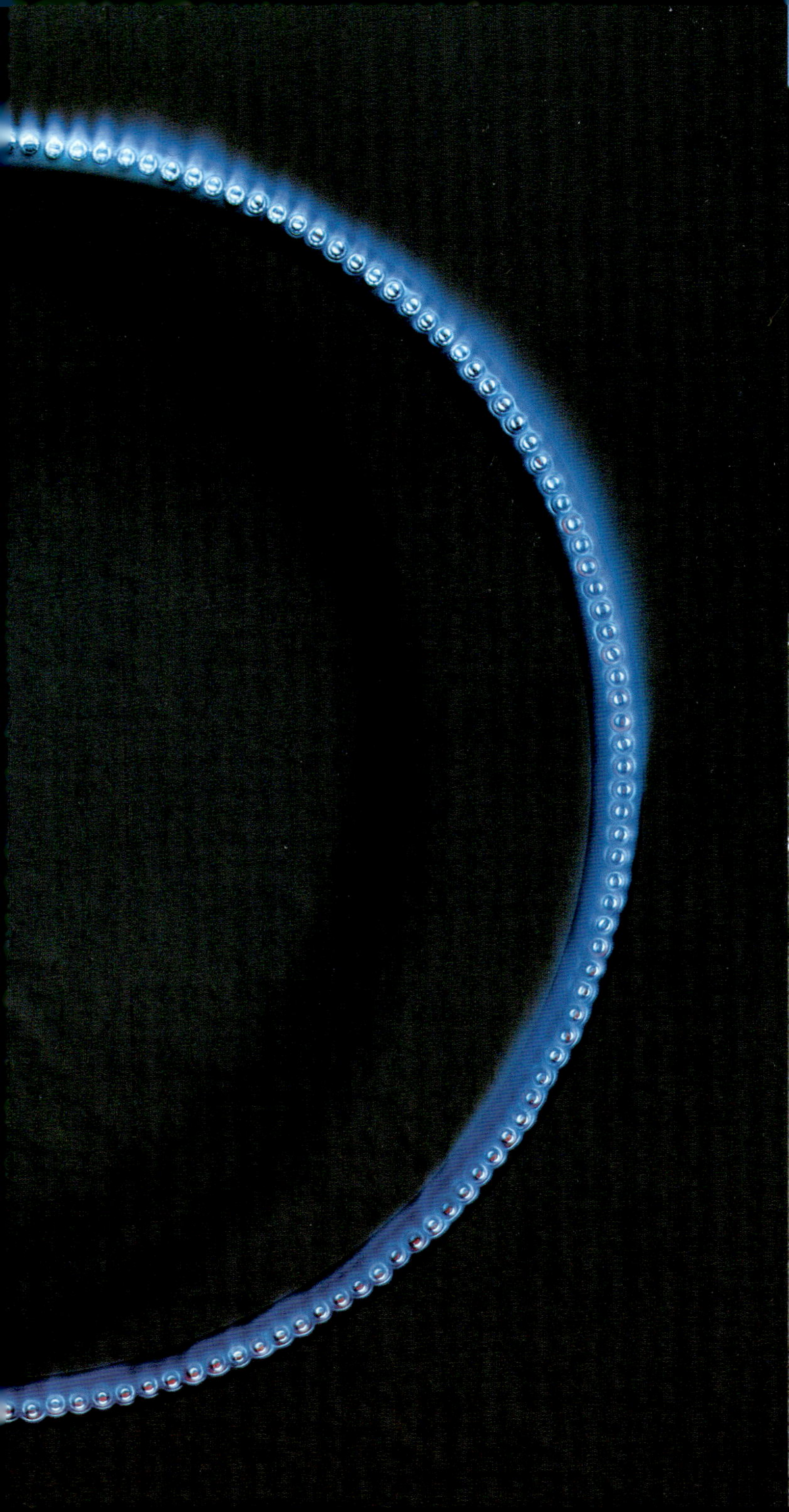

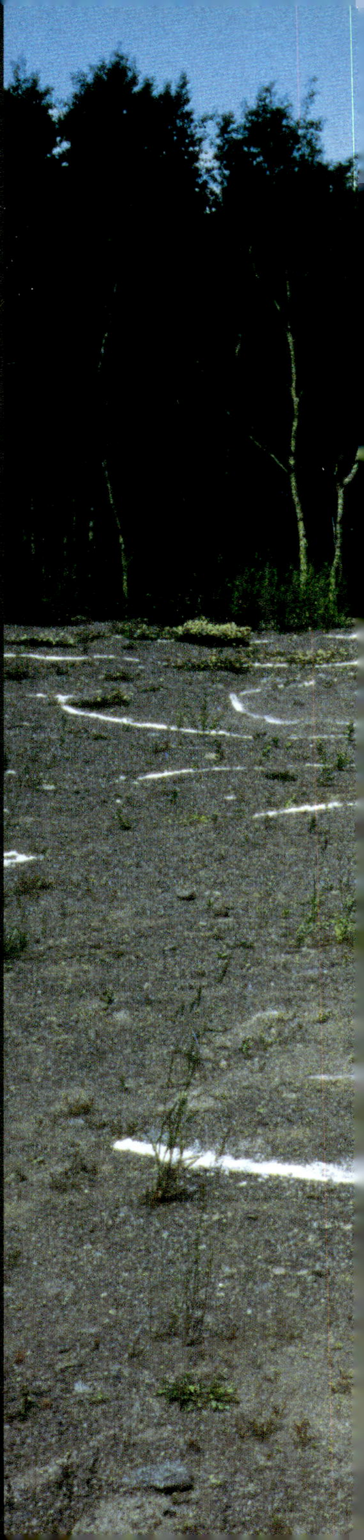

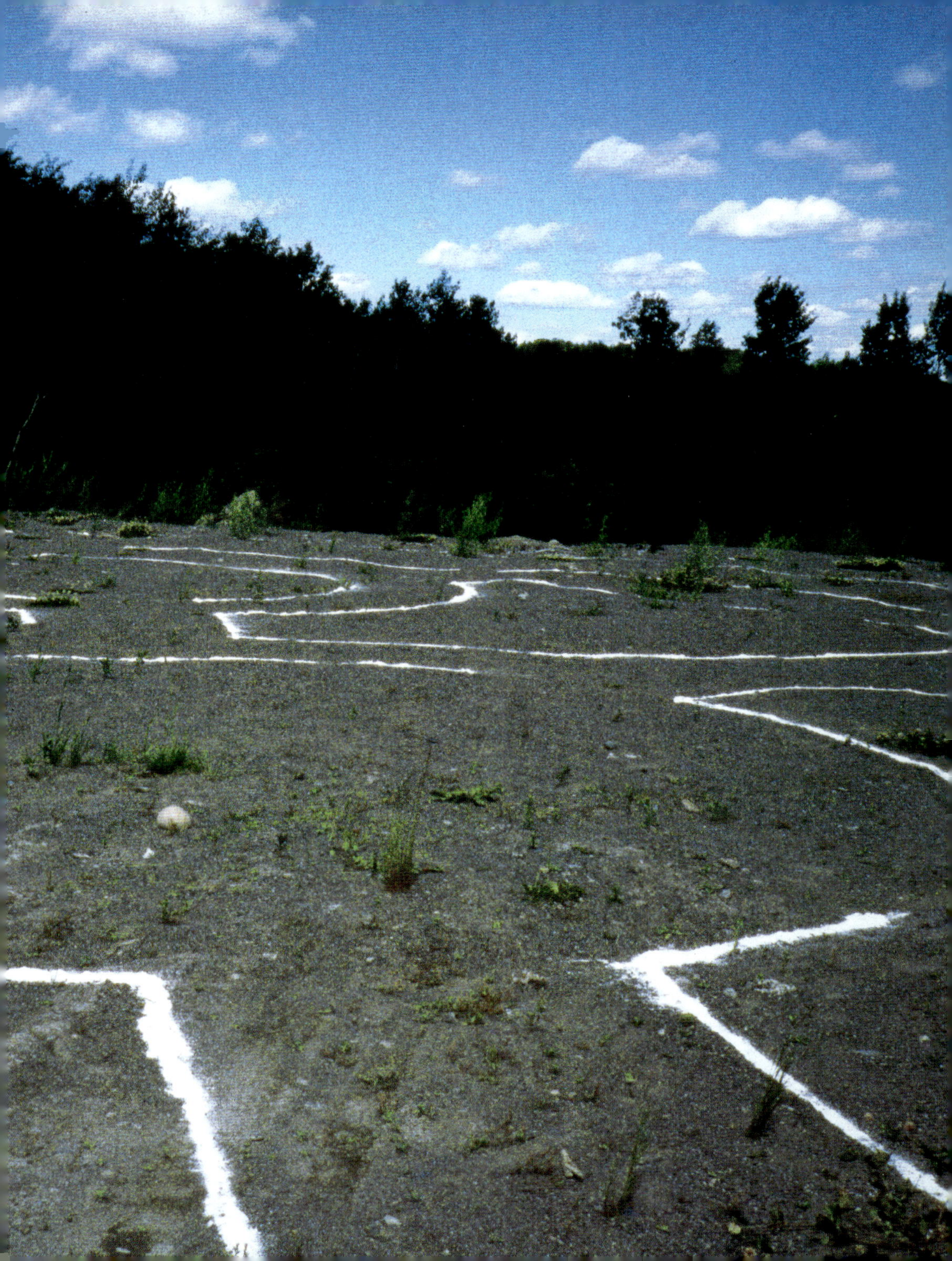

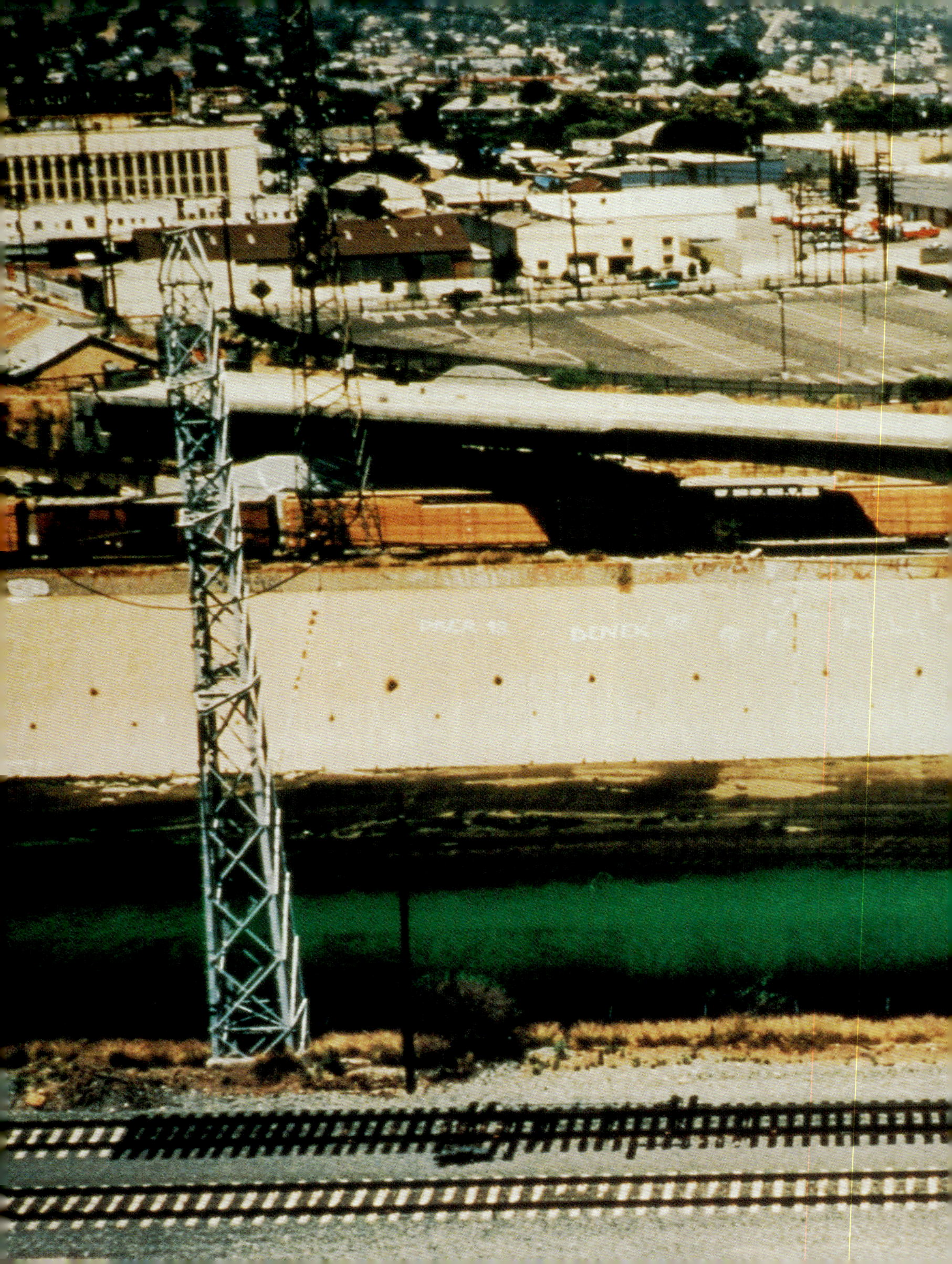

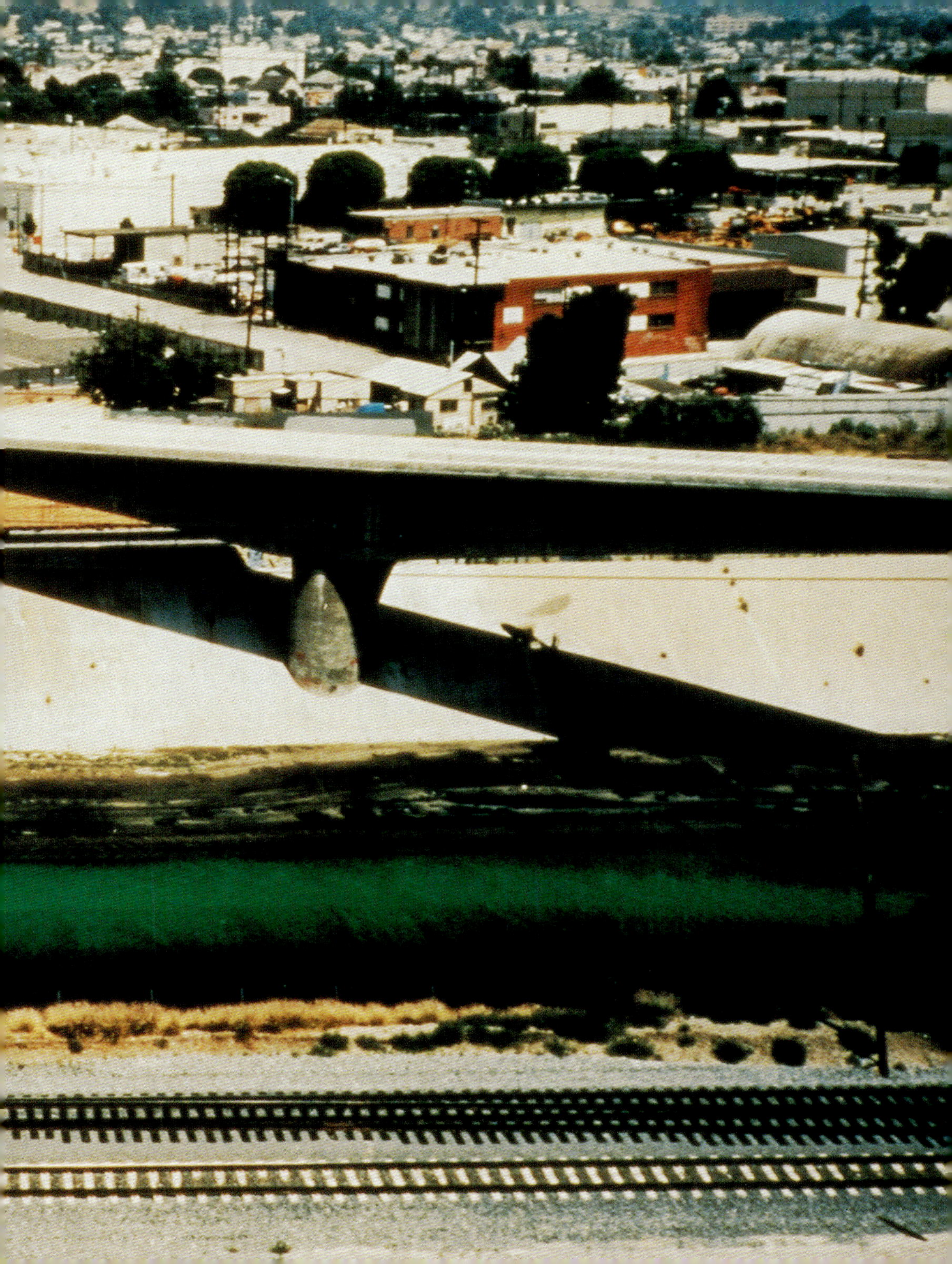

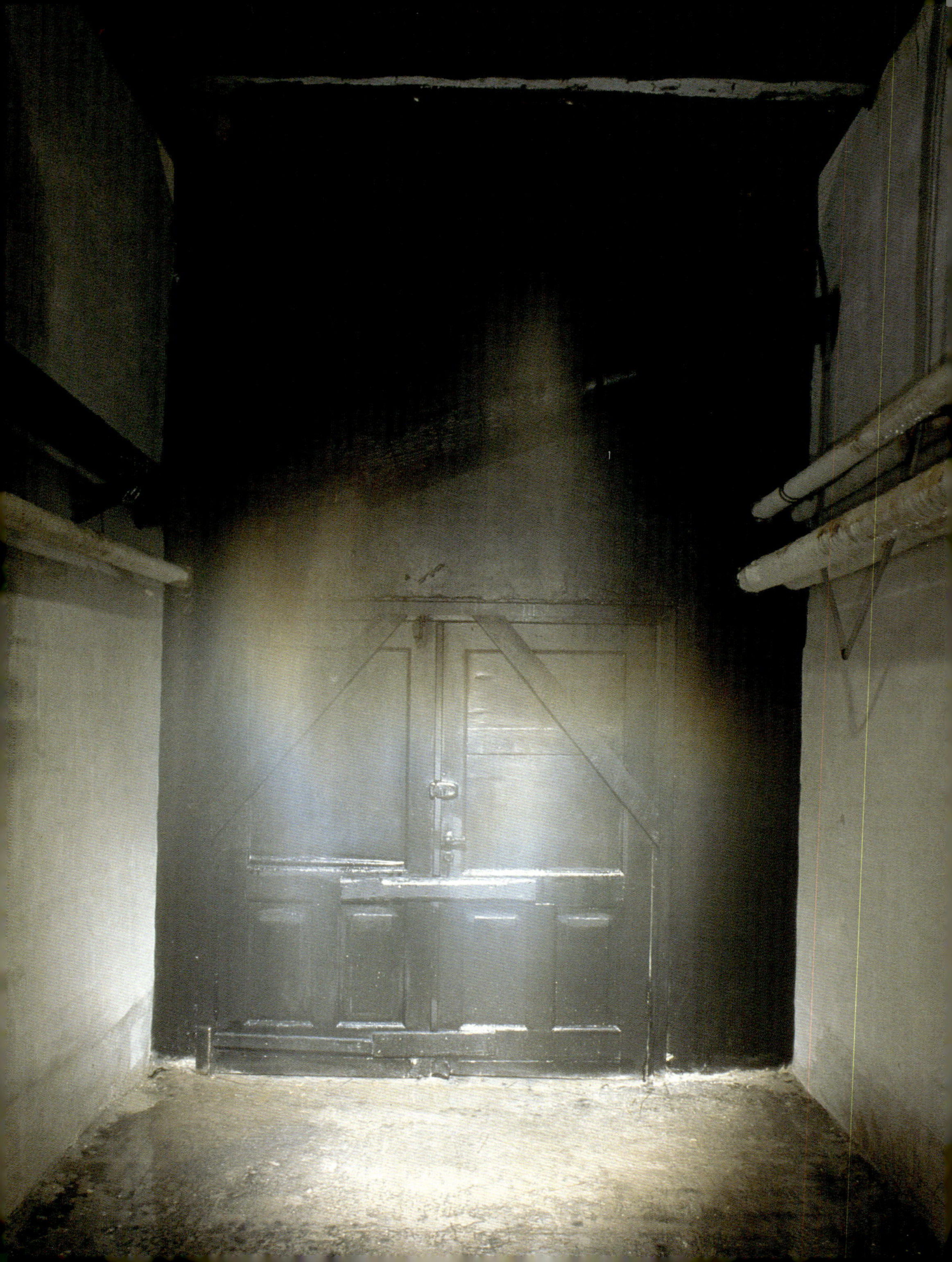

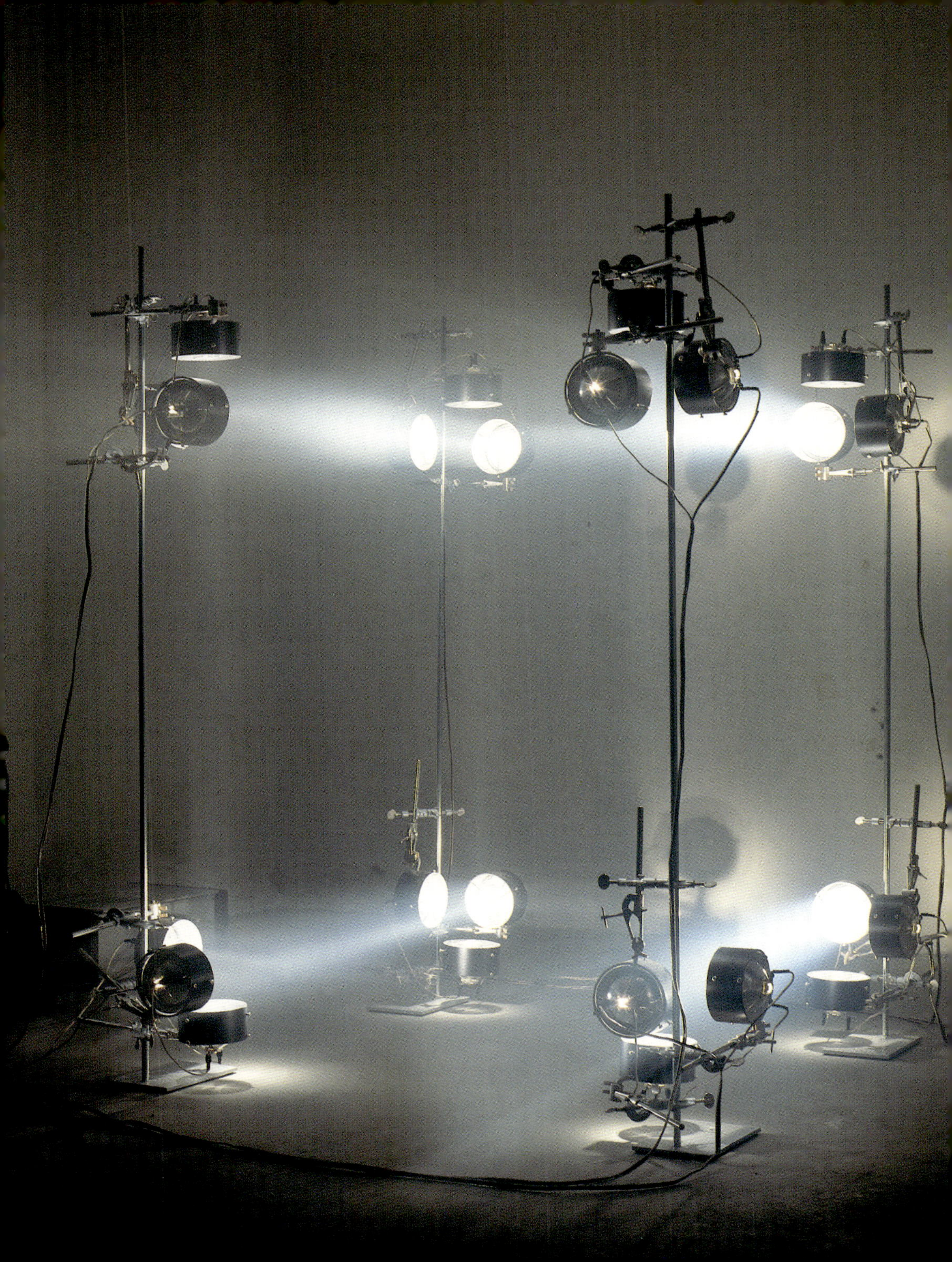

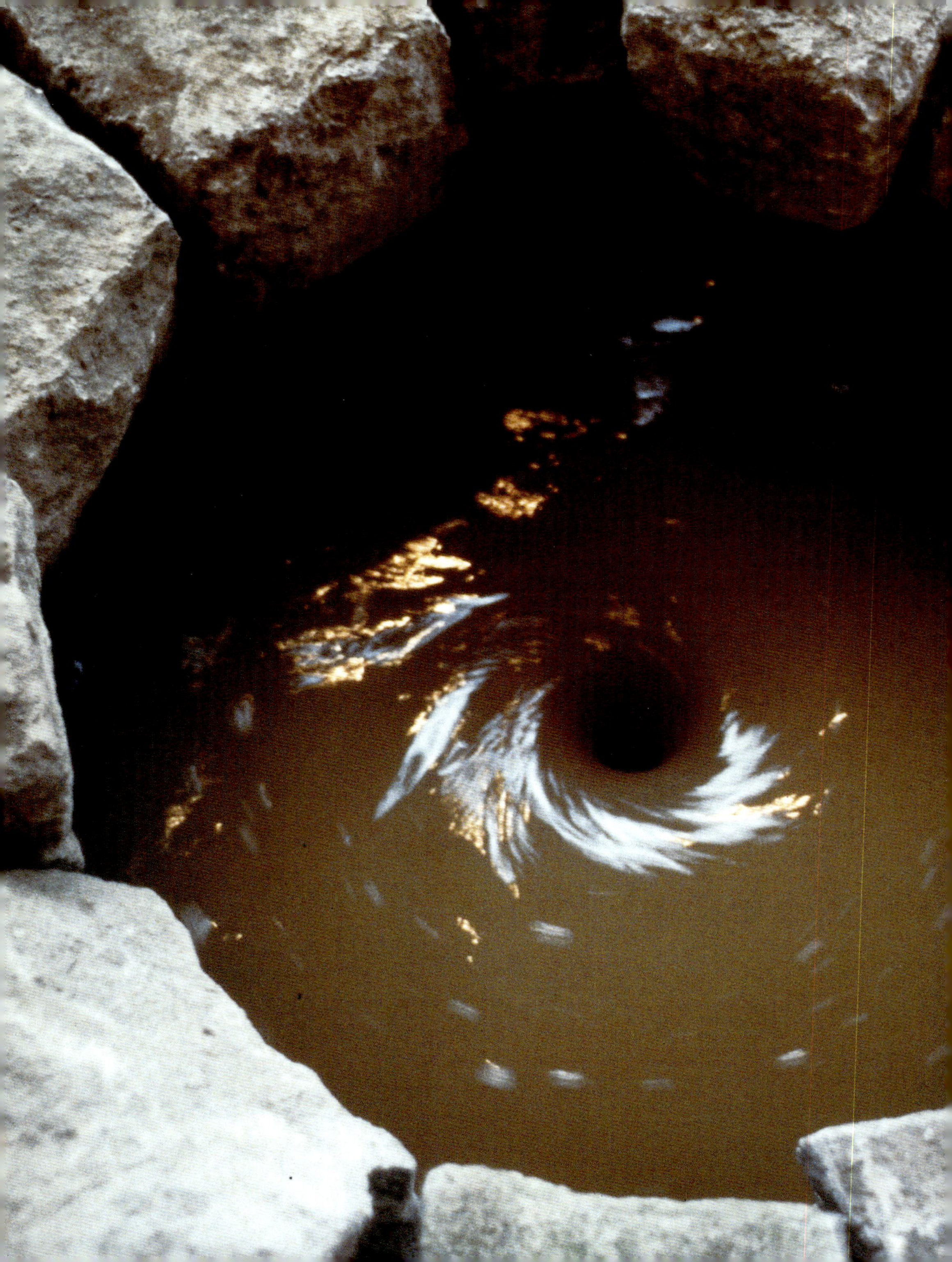

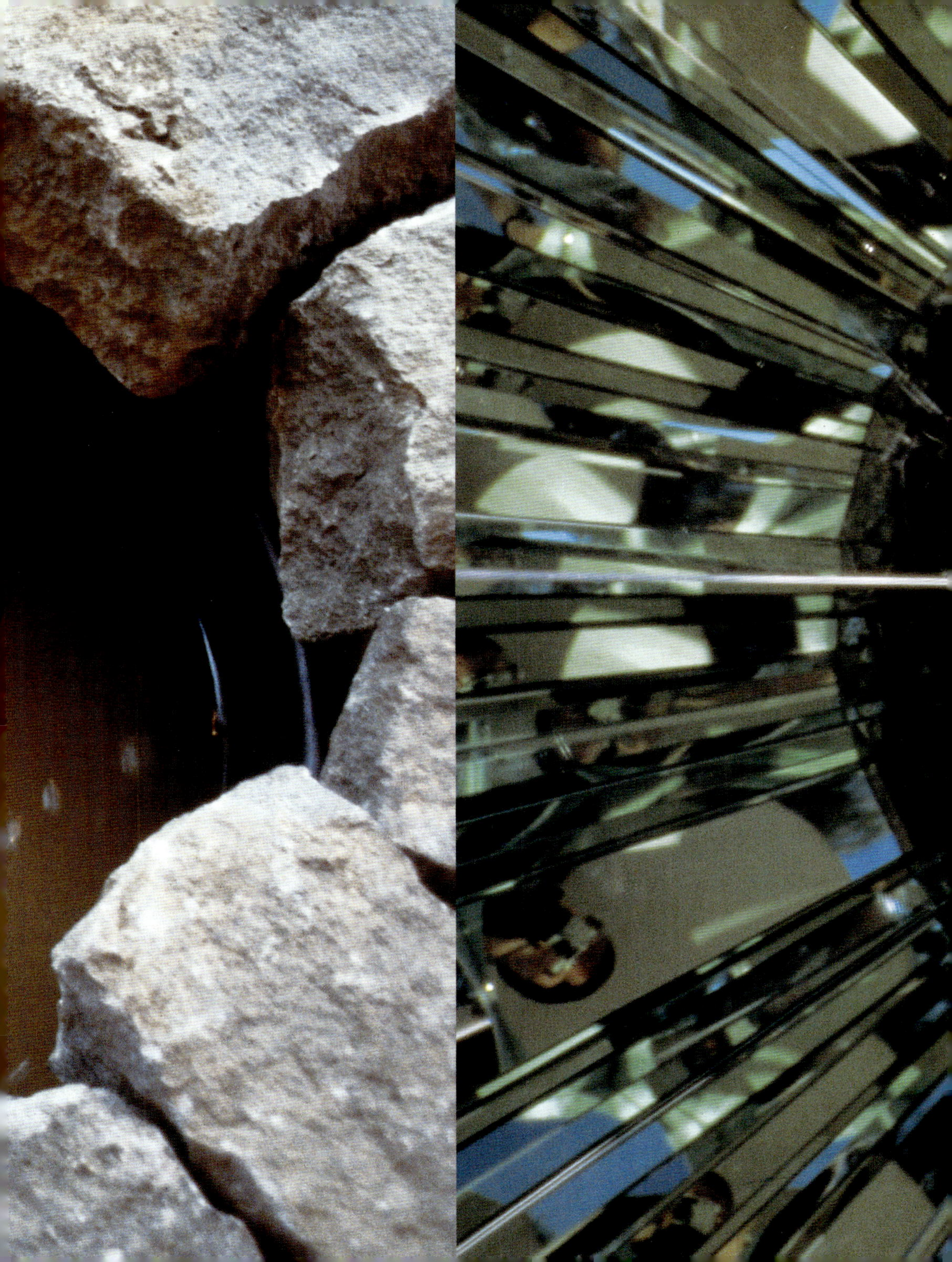

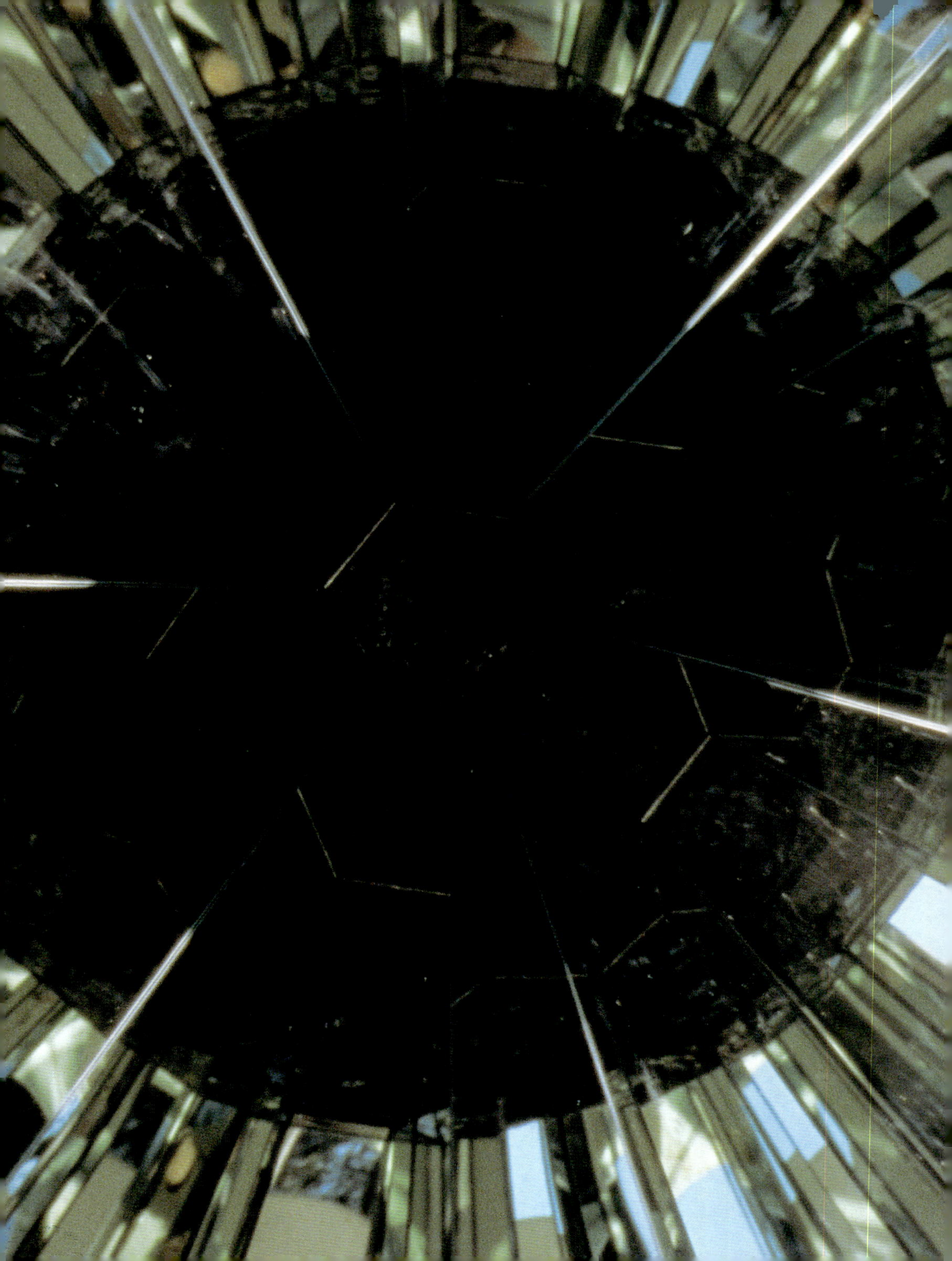

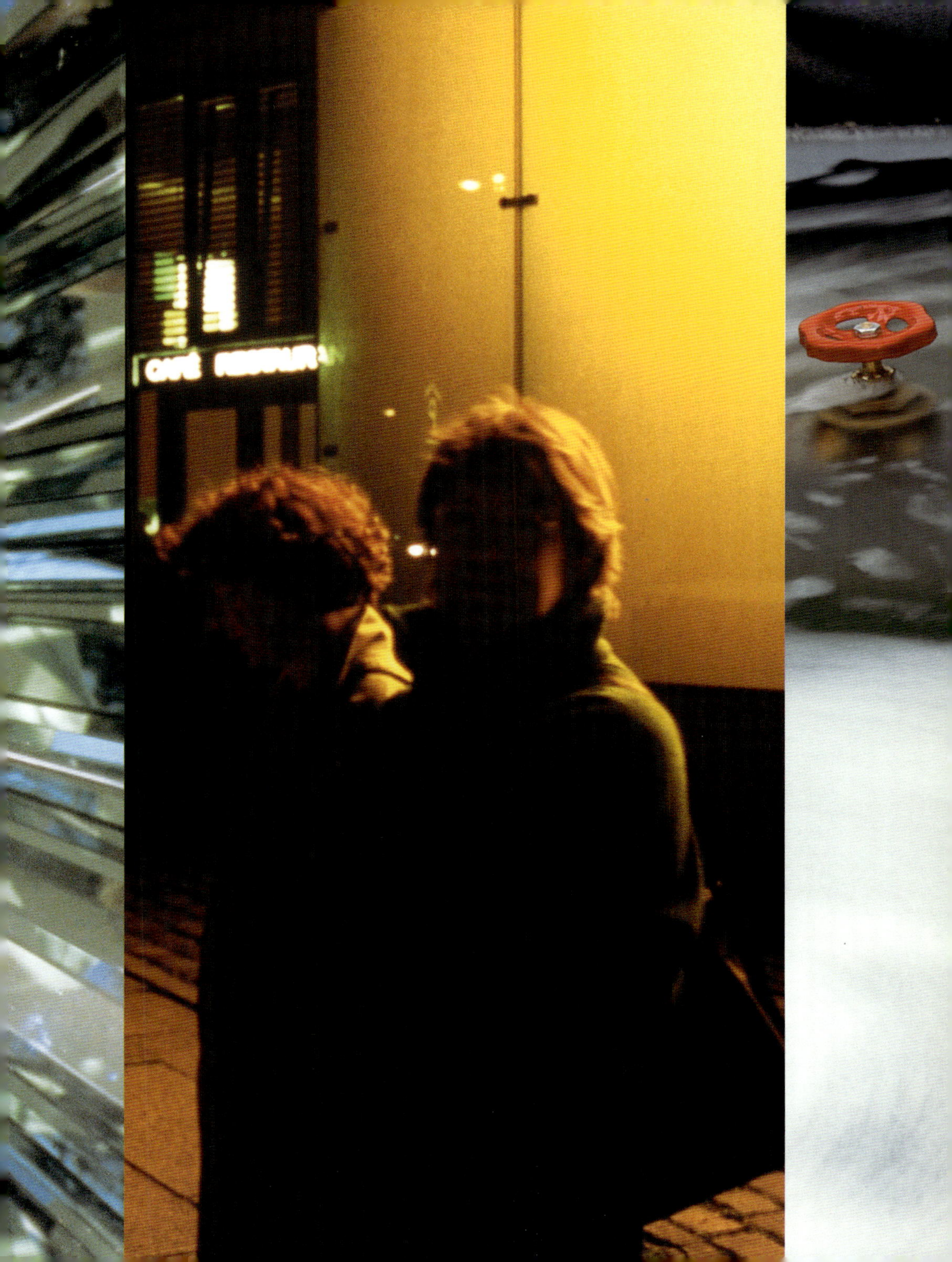
CAFÉ

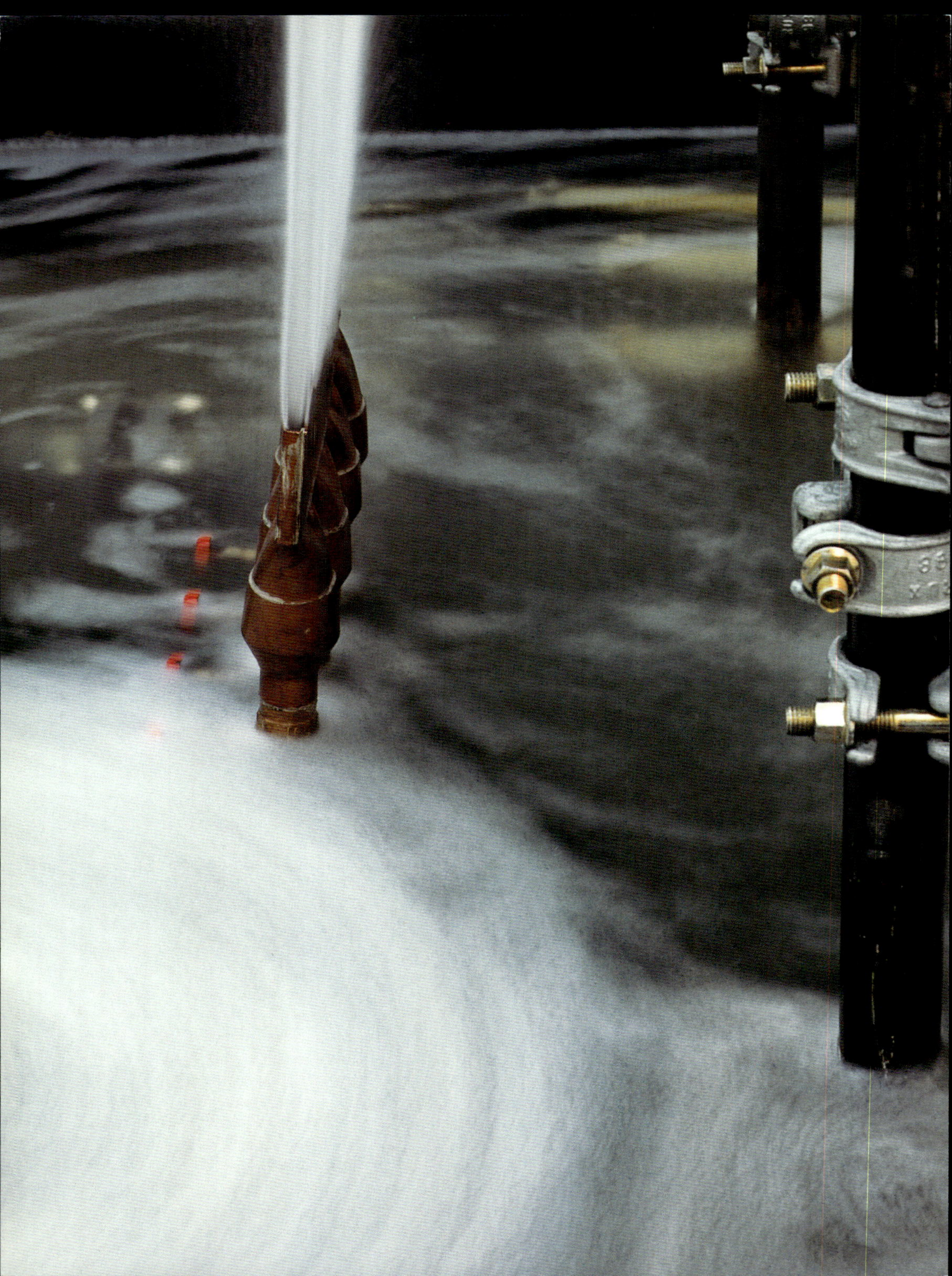

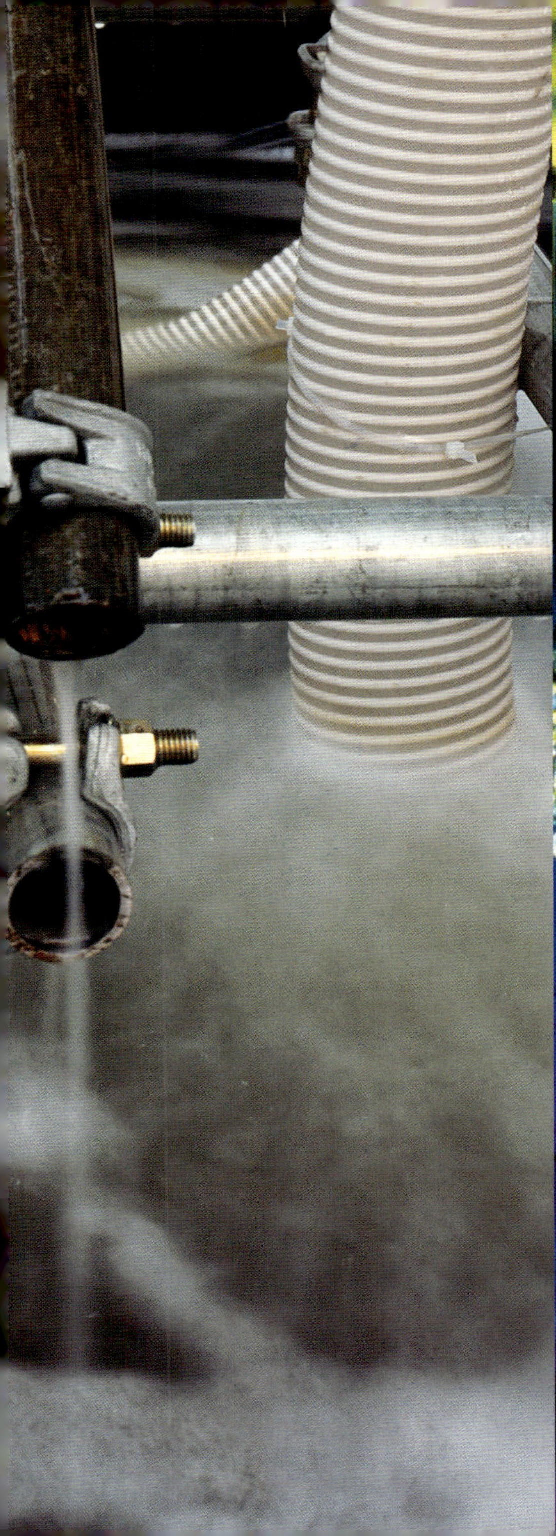
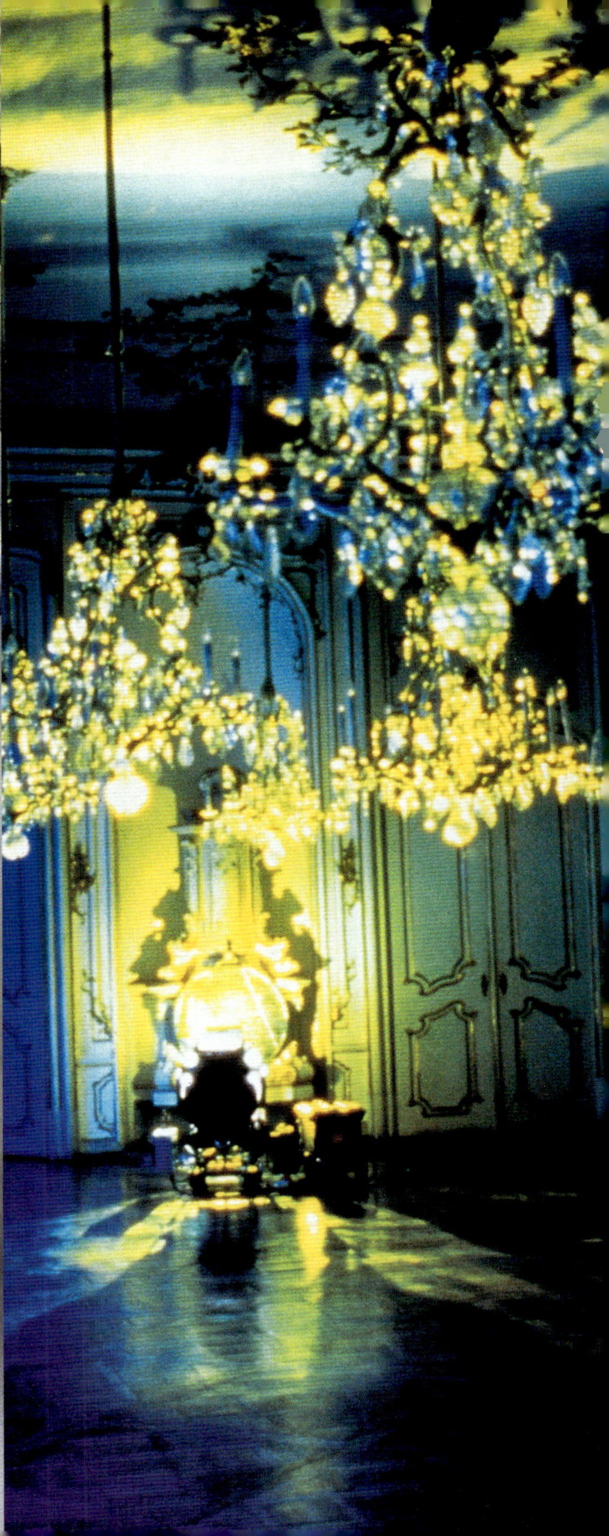

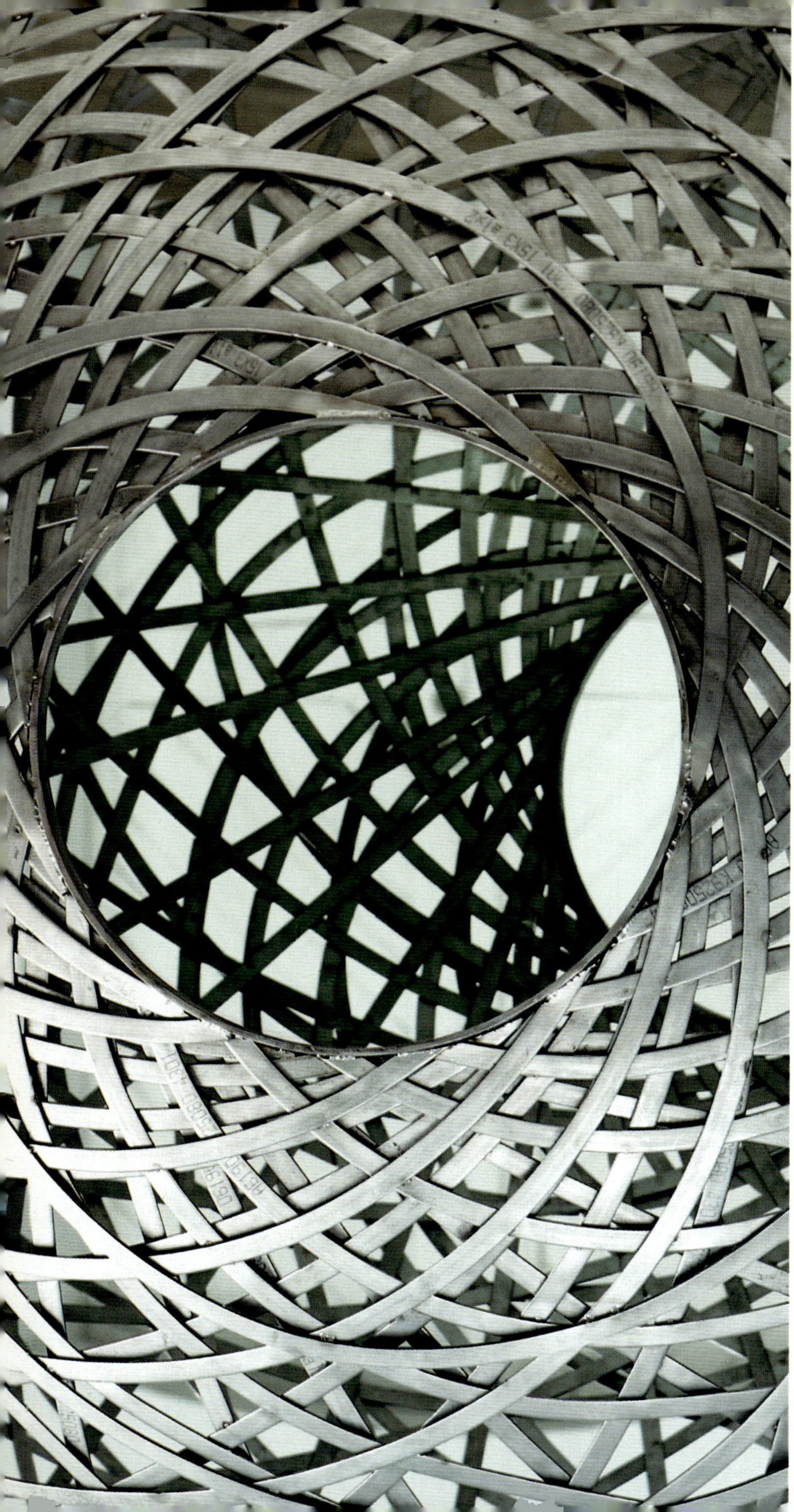

1	**No nights in summer, no days in winter**, 1994	Diameter 0,6 m; fire ring, gas, metal, hose
2	**Proposal for a park**, 1997	Size varies with installation; white chalklines on ground; installation view: 3e Symposium en arts visuels de l´Abitibi-Témiscamingue, Quebec, Canada
3	**Tell me about your miraculous invention**, 1996, detail	Size varies with installation; installation view: Galleri Andreas Brändström, Stockholm, Sweden
4	**Untitled**, 1994	Installation view: Lukas & Hoffmann, Art Cologne, Cologne, Germany
5	**Green river**, 1998	Green colour, water; realization: Los Angeles, USA
6	**Beauty**, 1993	Water, lens, spotlight; installation view: "Black Box," Copenhagen, Denmark
7	**1m³ light**, 1999	1 x 1 x 1 m; light, spotlight, fog machine
8	**Well from the parallel garden**, 1998, detail	Stone well with water typhoon inside
9	**Well for Villa Medici**, 1998, detail	Villa Medici, Rome, Italy
10	**Thoka**, 1995, detail	Size varies with installation; light, fog-machines, yellow filter, timer; installation view: Kunstverein Hamburg, Hamburg, Germany
11	**Yet untitled**, 1998, detail	Scaffolding, water, pump, plastic, wood, hoses
12	**Die organische und kristalline Beschreibung**, 1996	Size varies with installation; lightprojector, wave-effect-machine, yellow and blue filters, convex mirror; installation view: Neue Galerie am Landesmuseum Joanneum, Graz, Austria
13	**Fivefold eye**, 2000	Diameter 150 x 75 cm; stainless steel, mirror

John Pløger

Architecture's Ethical Ambivalence – Aesthe-Ethic Urbanism

Introduction

Urbanism is most often conceptualized either as "the art of building cities," or the control and steering of city development and transformation. Seen politically, the practice of urbanism develops within a juxtaposition of urban policy and design of cities (regulations, the power of politico-economical forces, urban visions, etc.). Planners most often consider urbanism to be a more or less pragmatic enterprise, following the "principles" of building cities (a material-functional matter), or as a necessary response to demands by political or economic forces. Of course, if possible, supplemented by architectural visions.

Needless to say, there has been a lot of criticism of such positions. Henri Lefebvre[1] claimed that every urban plan is a concealed program for everyday life, and Richard Sennett claims that urbanism, as a *spatial orchestrating* of human lives and

1. Henri Lefevbre, *The Production of Space*, Blackwell, Oxford, 1997.

behavior, is about social control and the fear of disorder.[2] This perspective can be radicalized that urban planning – at least in modern times – is about getting a significant relationship between *form and norms*,[3] which in fact reveals a planning ideology claiming to be able "to design the social by spatial means."[4] Architecture is, however, about much more than aesthetics, more than "form follows function;" it's also – and, following the arguments above, may be foremost – about "function following form." Urban planning and building urban environments are a matter of producing significant socio-spatial fields of action.

Contemporary urban planning represents a return of the aesthetic to planning,[5] but within this perspective most studies of urban planning ignore one rather important aspect, namely the ethic as an underlying discourse what we normally only discuss as aesthetic planning. The epistemology of the aesthe-ethic belongs first and foremost to aesthetic philosophy and to some extent to a philosophy of humanity. Within the scope of this article I cannot trace this heritage in detail;[6] what I want to outline is, how late modern urbanism relies on a specific philosophical "logic" or significant process, namely the idea of saying that the aesthetic is *directorial*[7] towards the ethic.[8]

One reason why urban planning and architectural theory neglect the influence of the aesthe-ethic relationship and its philosophical discourse is closely related to architectural theories' common ambivalence towards what could be termed the spatialized ethic, or the ethical effect of surroundings.

The ethical ambivalence within architecture

Ethics is the abstract, philosophical reflection on the founding principles of morals, on manners and customs, how care is shown in the Other's face, normative and moral principles for sociality and proximity with others.[9] If it is not controversial to say that architects have an ambivalent relationship towards the ethic, it is still very rare that they articulate or reflect this problem within the discourse itself. The ambivalence – as will be discussed – concerns several problematics: (1) The problem of (spatial) representation and re-presentation, and more specifically the fact that "translation is the common feature in all forms of life..."[10] Architectural theory and practice are ambivalent towards the question of how architecture assumes meaning. Is it mimetic, situated, by memory or tradition, by

2. Richard Sennett, *The Conscience of the Eye. The Design and Social Life of Cities*, London, Faber & Faber, 1991.

3. Paul Rabinow, *French Modern. Norms and Forms of the Social Environments*, University of Chicago Press, Chicago, 1989.

4. Niels Albertsen, "Byen, det sociale og retorikken" (The City, the Social, and Rhetoric), in C. Lykke Christensen & C. Thau (eds.), *Omgang med tingene*, Århus Universitetsforlag, 1993, Århus, pp. 181-203.

5. Michael Sorkin, (ed.), *Variations on a Theme Park. The New American City and the End of Public Space*, The Moonday Press, New York, 1992; Sharon Zukin, *The Cultures of Cities*, Blackwell, Oxford, 1995; M. Christine Boyer, "Urban Form and Urban Representation," in Dennis Crow, *Philosophical Streets*, Maisonneuve Press, Washington, 1991, pp. 93-113.

6. A lot of influential aesthetically and ethically oriented philosophers have to be left out. For example, Martin Heidegger, who in fact considered the relationship explicitly, and he never became "ethical" in a pure sense of the word. To him ethics was a matter of being and not about moral, and ethics. Other philosophers who can be read within an aesthe-ethic perspective are E. Burke and T. W. Adorno. Christian Norberg-Schulz, a Norwegian

the realm of the ontological, or by language? (2) Architectural theory also seems ambivalent towards how its spatial practice is related to the hegemonic ethics of society, or is seen as a work of art in itself, and thereby how architecture is or is not part of society's ethical signification processes.

Architectural theory and practice could meet these ambivalences self-critically by putting forward the question: Is it possible to delegate ethics to the material structures of the city? The question seems important because it is rather common – as will be illustrated – to work with the assumption, the possibility of producing a significant effect between architecture experienced as beautiful, or surroundings and the "good life." Architecture has meaning and intention. Ethical presuppositions and a priories are in fact rather common to the discipline and its hegemonic discourses, and architecture has, for instance, been seen as society's tool to improve equality and freedom.[11] The architectural point of departure may at first be described as believing that "the sensed sensitivity (towards architecture and surroundings) is the presupposition for the possibility to relate ethically towards our surroundings."[12] More precisely, it is the real life sensing of aesthetics that constitutes the social premise for ethical awareness and considerations.

Architectural discourse has first and foremost been "the discourse of form" and "style," and the influence of phenomenology in particular caused architectural theory to consider practice, body, sensing, and perceiving, sense of place, the spirit of place, rather than the social in itself. Today there seems to be a greater focus on the social and cultural, at least from a philosophical perspective.[13] Social theory is still rare within the discourse. The philosopher Karsten Harris is one of the few who stresses the ethical function of architecture, saying:

Architecture has an ethical function in that it calls us out of the everyday, recalls us to values presiding over our lives as members of a society; it beckons us toward a better life, a bit closer to the ideal.[14]

Harris thinks of ethics as something like *ethos,* that is, "character, nature of disposition," and the way human beings "exist in the world: their way of dwelling."[15] If architecture should have ethical effects, and effect on the ethos, it should, so to

architect – to whom I will return later on – heavily influenced by Heidegger, approaches the aesthe-ethic by tradition and use of place. Here ethics is left to ontology, and this perspective ignores, among other things, the reflexive and societal aspects of the relationship.

7. The German word would be "anweisen," and "directorial" here means something like "pointing at" through e.g. analogy, metaphors, or/and metonyms.

8. First and foremost, this should be discussed departing from Kant, but his aesthetic philosophy is supposed to be well-known to the readers. However, see my discussion on the subject in Pløger, "The Aesthe-Ethic Turn in Planning – Late Modern Urbanism," in *Space & Culture "Anti-Methods,"* No. 6, 2000, pp. 84-96.

9. Niels Gunder Hansen, *Etik i 90'erne* (The Ethics of the 90's), Gyldendal, Copenhagen, 1991.

10. Zygmunt Bauman, *In Search of Politics,* Polity Press, Cambridge, 1999, p. 201.

11. Finn Werne, *Arkitekturens ismer* (The -ism of Architecture), ARKVS, Stockholm, 1998, p. 135.

12. Claus Bech Danielsen, *Økologien tager form. Byøkologi, æstetik og arkitektur* (Ecology takes form. Urban Ecology, Aesthetics and Architecture), Chr. Ejlers Forlag, Copenhagen, 1998, p. 56 .

speak, "recall" (by evoking a memory) the hegemonic values of society, and the intersubjective preferred ethical values (for "a better life") among citizens and different social groups in society. Architecture by definition intends to express society's cultural values, or communicate a taken for granted (or universal reasonable) ethical and normative scheme of signification through form and style, and through tradition and memory. In other words, architecture requires the pre-existence of an ethical community and an adequate understanding of the meaningful relation between form and value.

Aesthetics and ethics – an uncomfortable relation

While still recognizing the ambivalence of the ethical question within architectural theory, suggesting that the history of urbanism – as zoning, grid-planning, design of houses, and public space, the functionalist dictum that form follows function, and crime preventative planning – implies a relationship between aesthetics and ethics, at least historically, should still be rather non-controversial. A rather obvious example is the architecture of the Third Reich, which entails the aestheticization of ethics through its monumental architecture.

But as Wolfgang Welsch says, "traditionally the aesthetic was considered dangerous; it was thought that ethical barriers must be imposed on it."[16] The founder of the modern conceptualization of aesthetics, Baumgarten, underscores the seventeenth century society's desire to master *the sensuous,* the aestheticized feeling, because "the senses ought to be the slave of reason."[17] Perceiving should not be an autonomous act separated from sensation in so far as sensation is too immediate and unreliable, compared to the distanced "cool" act of perceiving. Baumgarten himself wanted to improve the position of "the sensuous cognitive faculty," and according to Welsch, he develops the idea that there is no cognition without aesthetics.[18] This leads him to the conclusion, that "true knowledge would henceforward have to be aesthetico-logical knowledge," and the goal should be to make aesthetics "assist us towards the desired mastery over the senses."[19] The aesthetic should have authority over ethics.

Immanuel Kant developed Baumgarten's perspective and argued that the beautiful is a symbol of what is morally good. To Kant, the visibly and perceptibly beautiful is an expression of the morally good, because it symbolizes goodness, purity,

13. Neil Leach, *Rethinking Architecture. A Reader in Cultural Theory,* Routledge, London, 1998, p. 13.

14. Karsten Harris, *The Ethical Function of Architecture,* The MIT Press, Cambridge, Mass., 1998, p. 291.

15. Harris, op.cit. 13, p. 4.

16. Wolfgang Welsch, *Undoing Aesthetics,* Sage Publication, London, 1996, p. 60.

17. Ibid. p. 47.

18. The concept of the aesthetic is, as so many other concepts, characterized by semiotic ambiguity and it refers among other things to the sensuous, the sensible as well as beauty, nature, and knowledge. One can trace the concept back to the Greek form aisthesis, which refers to the sensible. The sensible here contains a bifiguration between the sensible in its "cognitive" and its "emotional meaning," which corresponds to a bifiguration between perception and sensation (see Welsch op.cit., p. 9).

19. See Welsch op.cit, pp. 41, 63.

strength, and order. It's possible to say that, according to Kant "the beautiful is a symbol of the ethically good [Sittlichkeit],"[20] and the beautiful thereby works both as a symbol of morality and as an aid to virtue.[21] Consequently, "for Kant, the core to aesthetic experiences is human beings' possibility of recognizing themselves as moral and free beings (Kant in fact seldom spoke about ethics)."[22]

This aesthetic philosophy rests on an aesthe-ethic relationship made by *analogies,* because it argues that the aesthetic is directorial towards the ethic. The aesthetic experience should give people a feeling of an analogy to a "good life," norms and morals. In other words, people's aesthetic experiences and judgements should direct them towards the thought of the possibility of realizing common ethical standards, an intuitive feeling and experience of the analogy between the sensed beautiful and the ethically reasonable.

If this point provokes architects and planners, New Urbanism is a good way of illustrating the case.

New Urbanism and ethical planning

New Urbanism[23] is a contemporary architectural movement which seems to be having considerable influence in the U.S. and in parts of Europe through the Prince of Wales' movement, *A Vision of Europe.*[24] This movement sees itself as a critique of late modernism and its architectural expressions. Modern architecture is criticized for preferring gigantism and inhuman functionalism (think of the endless suburban block-buildings). As a necessary counter-critique, New Urbanism says that human beings must again be the measure of planning, and there is a need therefore to return to architecture on a human scale.

This human scale is not primarily a matter of physical scale, New Urbanism allows monumental architecture as well as picturesque village-like environments. It is, rather, a matter of believing that design and aesthetics can restore important aspects of human life. Like the Beautiful City Movement[25] this movement prefers the architecture of classicism for several reasons.

Classicism is a design style that gives dignity to people's homes (especially working class homes).

Classicism demands beauty in design as a way to give dignity to human living.

20. Knud E. Løgstrup, *Kants æstetik* (Kant's Aesthetic), Gyldendal, Copenhagen, 1996, p. 52.

21. Terry Eagelton, *The Ideology of the Aesthetics,* Blackwell, Oxford, 1991, p. 89.

22. Svend E. Larsen, *Naturen er ligeglad. Naturopfattelser i kulturel sammenhæng* (Nature doesn't care), Munksgaard / Rosinante, Copenhagen, 1996, p. 137.

23. This section is taken from Pløger, 2000, op.cit.

24. *A Vision of Europe 1997. Byens fornyelse* (The Renewal of the City), Oslo. Presentation of an exhibition on "New Traditionbased Architecture and Urban Planning," Oslo 7. - 30. April 1997.

25. William H. Wilson, "The Glory, Destruction and Meaning of the City Beautiful Movement," in S. Campbell & S. Fainstein (eds.): *Readings in Planning Theory,* Blackwell, Oxford, 1996, pp. 68-103.

Securing a classicistic comprehensive visual order, and returning to classical forms using traditionally based handcraft will secure historical continuity. Classicism therefore will enhance the sense of belonging to place.

Classicism points to the need to restore respect for traditions, including traditionalist and timeless architecture.[26]

The ideology of New Urbanism, Neo-classicism and Neo-traditionalism (its different disguises) thus complies with much contemporary European planning politics. Throughout Europe there is a strong political commitment to planning policy that favors preservation and restoration of built environments as the main tools for urban regeneration.

In fact, New Urbanism is as much an ethical project as an aesthetic one. The movement tries to argue that design and architecture represent the essential spatial forms of our ethical being, and that classicism is the symbolic materialization and eternal beginning of a good life, because classicism represents the basic ontological means to human life, such as historicism (continuity and permanence), traditionalism (civility and civilisation), and sociality (ethics and belonging to place through the "genius loci").

One of Prince Charles' and New Urbanism's favorite architects, Leon Krier, once said at a public meeting in Oslo[27] that it is necessary to return to "architectural archetypes" and the vernacular, which he defined as "traditionalism to place" in order to restore the (post)modern failures. Furthermore, he argued that this kind of architecture is good because it is pleasant to many people, and therefore important in itself.

The well-known Poundbury village near Dorchester in the United Kingdom is one example of this movement's dream of building the secure idyll of the little village. A group of architects went to Poundbury and they are cited as saying: "We have to get back what we have forgotten about wholeness, beauty, and harmony. We have got an architecture which does not give people dignity."[28] Dignity is said here to be the product of aestheticized surroundings and the formfulness of space.

First of all, these statements show a confused intermixture of abstract space (principles) and social space (values) and favor the mentioned *environmentalism*, which says it's possible to

26. Nan Ellin, "Postmodern Urbanism," in *A Vision of Europe*, Blackwell, Oxford, 1997. *Byens fornyelse* (The Renewal of the City), Oslo, 1996. Presentation of an exhibition on "New Tradition-based Architecture and Urban Planning," Oslo 7 - 30 April 1997.

27. Quotation from personal notes from a public meeting with Leon Krier, Oslo, 14 April 1997.

28. Said by some Oslo-based elite architects in the newspaper *Aftenposten* 18 March 1997. They don't talk about Poundbury also representing the rigid control of construction and the maintenance of the interior, its physical surroundings and facades. A form of control that mimics the Disney Company Celebration Park projects.

design the social by forming space. Secondly, these statements imply that these architects actually think there is a connection between the aesthetic and the ethic, arguing that the design of urban spaces mediates dignity and traditionalism. Other critics see this as a return to conservative cultural archetypes. As one critic says, these movements are saying that if the world is fragmented, and if we are confused by the cultural *Freisetzung*, New Urbanism believes "our physical environment can express our lost ideals."[29]

The aesthe-ethic and social space – a phenomenological argument

The ethics of form, structure and function denote and connote much architectural philosophy, at least because the debate concerning architecture's "sincerity" and "appropriateness" has been mostly moralistic.[30] Let us take the phenomenological philosophy, which in Scandinavian architectural theory is almost synonymous with Christian Norberg-Schulz.[31] Inspired by Heidegger's philosophy of being and dwelling, his concept *Genius Loci* plays a determinant role in architects' ambitions to construct "places of 'permanencies'."[32] In his own words, architecture can "first get its full meaning as part of a place, whose identity endures through all changes."[33]

According to Norberg-Schulz's phenomenology, people have to identify and come to terms with "the spirit of place," its Genius Loci, its abstract and permanent spiritual meaning, if they want to dwell in places qualitatively. A place's Genius Loci is preserved by traditions and identity-securing values immanent in spatial objects or built environments. It is the spatial organization, form, and figure that constitute the identity of space, its Genius Loci. This identity should signify the very essence of being and *Sittlichkeit;* in essence, ethics and virtues. To perceive and recognize the place's Genius Loci, in fact, is an ontological a priori to feel oneself as "a dignified being," and thereby the possibility of feeling like a worthy being. Space that cannot be recognized as a meaningful Genius Loci creates a "loss of place,"[34] makes places non-places. These places are alienating because they are recognizable neither through memory, nor by tradition, nor by representing a timeless significant architectural heritage.[35]

One may say that the concept Genius Loci represents the spatialization of ethics through time (the permanence of forms

29. Karl Otto Ellefsen, "Tilbake til framtida?" in *The "New" Urbanism.* (Back to Future? The "New" Urbanism), *Byggekunst* No. 3/97, 1997, pp. 13-15.

30. Leach op.cit.

31. See C. Norberg-Schulz, *Intentions in Architecture,* Universitetsforlaget, Oslo, 1993.

32. David Harvey, *Justice, Nature & the Geography of Difference,* Blackwell, Oxford, 1996, p. 308.

33. The journal *Akitektnytt* No. 11/1995, p. 207.

34. Christian Norberg-Schulz, *Et faglig testamente* (A Professional Testament), Arkitektur i Norge, Årbok, 1996, Norsk Arkitekturmuseum, Bonytt A/S, Oslo, 1996, pp. 116-124; C. Norberg-Schulz, Stedsbruk (The Use of Place), *Nordisk Arkitekturforskning,* 1994:1, 1994, pp. 7-16.

35. Norberg-Schulz has especially influenced Norwegian guidelines on "how to make a place analysis." These guidelines, together with a new "beauty-paragraph" demanding considerations of beauty on every planning issue, have become the hegemonic discourse of Norwegian aesthetic planning (Norsk Form, *Omgivelser som kultur. Handlingsprogram for estetisk kvalitet i offentlig miljø* (Surroundings as Culture), Kulturdepartementet, Oslo, 1992; Norsk Form, *Forskning for estetisk kvalitet i offentlig rom*

and objects in place, handcraft and a timeless architectural style). By contrast, it seems to the mimetic and nature-given pre-modern architectural theory that the modes of relating to space and place here is not something you can leave to people themselves. You cannot rely only on the sensible self; you have to socialize[36] people aesthetically. On the one hand, phenomenological architects argue that aesthetic judgements are the product of immediate sensing forms and objects in space, but that too is a possible problem, because it can lead to oblivion as well as aesthetic relativism. One must therefore rely on the existence of an aesthetic commonality very much like a Kantian Sensus Communis.

A *Sensus Communis* consists of common "faculties of judgement" which are not based on reflection, but on a common ability to "take notice of."[37] Kant's concept helps architectural philosophy to explain the communicability of aesthetic recognition without grounding it as cognitive and subjectivist, but still expressing reason. As part of a Sensus Communis we will intuitively – without notice – feel what is aesthetically good or bad, pleasant or non-pleasant, because "what brings us together as subjects is not knowledge but an ineffable reciprocity of feeling."[38] A Sensus Communis is a community of feelings, not convictions, language or cognitivism.[39] Aesthetic judgements cannot be reduced to reason as logos, but are a recognition that belongs to a state-of-mind between reason and sense. The effect and influence of the aesthetic therefore cannot be reduced to a matter of individual taste; it is the outcome of "the humanness we share" beyond logos. Aesthetic experiences are exactly the point from where human beings recognize themselves as "moral and free beings,"[40] withholding that moral (ethics) are only available as a possibility.

The aesthetic and social space

The phenomenological and ontological approach to the aesthetic seems ambivalent about the problem of reflection vs. sensing, hermeneutical practice vs. intuitive practice, body vs. mind. For instance, a judgement is a value setting, and then discursive problematics are lined up. So one problem is, what about language and discourse? Another is, what about the social? Is aesthetic quality a property to architecture itself, or is quality first constituted in diverse social processes of reception and cognition?

(Research on Aesthetic Quality in Public Spaces), Norsk Form, Oslo, 1994). The "place-analysis" consists of four subjects of research: the historical development of the place, nature, and landscape, the organization of the built environment, the characteristics of single buildings and other elements. Christian Norberg-Schulz and his writing on "Place and Architecture," published 1982 (Ministry of Environment, *Stedsanalyse – inn-hold og gjennomføring* (Analysis of Place – content and practice), Miljøverndepartementet, Oslo, 1993.

36. The German term *Bildung* may be more appropriate here, because of its connotations with public manners and mannerism.

37. Løgstrup op.cit, p. 34. A difficult concept to translate from Danish to English. In Danish *'vi skønner det'* means that one "knows" intuitively, without necessarily knowing why we understand.

38. Eagleton op.cit., p. 75.

39. The Sensus Communis is above all an ideal norm, based on a transcendental argument (the commonness of aesthetic judgement as necessary to and a precondition for being and experience).

40. Larsen op.cit., p. 135-7.

The architectural theorists discussed seem to take a pragmatic stand on these problems. On the one hand, as shown, they see the aesthetic in a Kantian sense of *the sensible*. And as in Kant, reasonable judgements are believed to be the universal, common goal of every human act; that is cognitivism. Experiencing beautiful objects arouses a human feeling of belonging to a community of reasonable sensors of pleasurable feelings. The architects' and planners' task is to secure this feeling of belonging to common values and norms as the product of sensing and not cognitive or hermeneutical processes.

Inspired by Michel Foucault, one may say this discourse argues for the existence of *spatialized dispositives*. Good form (harmony, recognizable Genius Loci, wholeness) and beautiful surroundings are seen as directorial towards common ethical values. Architects that accept this argue that pleasurable aesthetic experiences and feelings lead to a form of conductive ethics, common ethical norms such as responsibility, caretaking, and intersubjective virtues.

As practitioners, architects and planners are conscious of form and design working as mediators of values and the valuable. The architect's and designer's task is to produce a *correspondence*-experience between the sensed and its social effect. The premise is that the object sensed as beautiful will "evoke resonance" (sympathy, intuitive approval), preferably as "authentic, beautiful, true, etc."[41] It would be hard to ignore that this "logic" relies on an aesthetic-ethical discourse, because clearly the aesthetic is seen through analogies as directorial towards the ethic.[42] The analogical thinking is rather obvious, and it is both grounded on ontology (being) and cognitivism. And in the end, aesthetic planning should have both "cognitive functions as well as ethico-political effects."[43]

This position produces a precarious ambivalence, where architects risk being criticized for believing in a form of spatial determinism ("Beautiful places create nice people.") or an a priori aestheticism ("The aesthetic is the mother of ethics."). Even though most architects recognize this ambivalence, and often favor aestheticism based on ontological arguments (see later) to argue against the critique; the problematic causes a schizoid state of mind, because at the same time architectural theorists know that the appropriation of architectural works of art can never be controlled.

41. Henrik K. Nielsen, *Æstetik, kultur & politik* (Aesthetics, Culture, and Politics), Århus Universittsforlag, Århus, Denmark, 1996, p. 63.

42. If they do not accept the existence of an aesthe-ethic discourse, one must suspect that among the arts, especially architecture, a special sort of Homo Aestheticus, *the aesthete* – the man or women of sensible, sensuous, refined, and discerning taste – is the ideal figure underlying their discourse. Against this critique, one often hears architects arguing that architectural practice is not in itself a matter of aestheticism, because in most cases demands of functionality will inevitably be involved, too, and this prevents a purely aesthetic practice. Nevertheless, architects, aesthetically speaking, will always be in search of the perfect juxtaposition of beauty and art. Partly to awaken a public attention to form and architecture, and partly, through the architectural practice as a work of art, to impress the participants in their own hegemonic discourse.

43. Eagleton op.cit., p. 366.

Architecture and the problem of representation

Genius Loci is of existential importance to dwelling, to psychic well-being, too, and therefore one must always preserve the *essence* of places' and spaces' spirit in new historical and cultural contexts. The place and space must not lose their identity and living traditions, such as handicrafts, traditional architectural style, and traditions, because they all help to preserve the identity of place, and hence its Genius Loci. In other words, Genius Loci represents place's historical anchor to preserve collective identity.

However, everywhere in our social life we are surrounded by and intertwined with representational spaces, and to discuss a socio-spatial relationship requires that one understands *how* representational spaces are *read*.

The presentation of concrete spatiality is always wrapped in the complex and diverse re-presentation of human perception and cognition, without any necessity of direct and determined correspondence between the two. These representations, as semiotic imagery and cognitive mappings, as ideas and ideologies, play a powerful role in shaping the spatiality of social life. There can be no challenge to this humanized, mental space, a spatialized mentalité.[44]

Space may be primordially given, but its organization and meaning are the product of "social translation, transformation, and experience."[45] It is this social translation, by way of experience and discursive practice, which produces space as social space. More precisely, Zygmunt Bauman argues that meaning and significance are the products of three distinct, and yet interwoven social processes; "those of cognitive, aesthetic and moral 'spacings' – and their respective products," which is the relation between the abstract (cognition), the affectual (aesthetic), and the ethically (moral).[46]

People's hermeneutic practice, their social spacing, always produces a re-presentation of a representation, and the significance of events, surroundings and space is a matter of a subject's position and competence in reading space. Architecture and built environments aim to *signalize* significance, but these spatial forms have to be *read* in order to assume *meaning* in peoples' value-schemes, experiences or everyday practices.[47] Architectural significance has to be re-presented,

44. Edward W. Soja, *Postmodern Geographies. The Reassertion of Space in Critical Social Theory,* Verso, London, 1989, p. 121.

45. Ibid. pp. 79-80.

46. Zygmunt Bauman, *Postmodern Ethics*, Blackwell, Oxford, 1993, p. 145.

47. Rob Beauregard, "If Only the City Could Speak: The Politics of Representation," in H. Liggett, D. C. Perry (eds.), *Spatial Practices,* Sage Publication, London, 1996, pp. 59-81.

and this has to be done by analogies to something "known" (metaphorical, memory, experience). Representation's re-presentation concerns the real-and-imagined world,[48] where the "real" world is made up of experiences, social ontology, epistemology, and discursive formations. The significance and meaning of space depend on how they are read, on "the Seeing Eye," but the eye "sees" through discourses in use. Understanding meaning (Sinn verstehen) is strange enough to architectural phenomenology, but a priori to human practice; it's taken as a priori that man only can dwell if he or she "expriences his [or her] existence as meaningful."[49]

Conclusive remarks

Philosophical reflections on space are always needed, because physical space is an abstraction which we, according to Bauman, cannot experience directly. We grasp physical space by processes of social spatialization (cognitive, moral or aesthetic), by reflecting and sensing architecture and built environments, by use of collective mythologies, history, moral, common sense, etc. I have tried to show how at least phenomenological architects and planners – through their neo-Kantianism – whether or not aware of the problematic, argue that aesthetics is both a primary ontological premise to human life and a mediator towards ethics.

The history of philosophy makes clear that talking about an aesthe-ethic relationship is problematic, always developing, so to speak, on a cognitive edge. Within ethics, reason is certain, with aesthetics it is uncertain because it is related to sensation rather than perception.

What I have tried to outline here is that the return of the aesthetic to physical planning underscores the existence and function of an aesthe-ethic "logic" of urbanism, which so far has mostly been neglected in planning discourses. It depends on a supposed aesthetic ontology (the aesthetic as directorial [Anweisung] to the ethic), and a supposed aesthe-ethic dialectic based on the existence of a priori Sensus Communis. Architectural theory is built upon a problematic move, seeing architecture as a form of descriptive ethics through form, style or/and function, that leads to normative meaningfulness. This necessitates both the a priori of an aesthe-ethic relationship and the idea of a spatialized dispositivity.

48. Edward W. Soja, *Thirdspace. Journeys to Los Angeles and Other Real-and-Imagined Places,* Blackwell, Oxford, 1996.

49. Hilde Heynen, *Architecture and Modernity. A Critique,* The MIT Press, Cambridge, Mass., 1999, p. 19.

Furthermore, to say that architecture is significant means linking the spatial and the architectural to the mental and social in terms of the mediating role of words, signs, and hence cognition and production of meaning. What is aesthetically valuable is also historically and culturally conditioned. This problematic may concern the arts as well as architecture.

Andrzej Przywara, Adam Szymczyk

On Melioration and Electrification as Twin Sisters of the Fine Arts

In the years 1845-1849, German engineers built the Great Brda Canal in the Bory Tucholskie region of what is today northern Poland. The aim of the project was, as so often is in our history, to tamper with the designs of nature. Its immediate object was to use the waters of the river Brda to irrigate the Czerskie Leki meadows, a sizeable expanse of potentially fertile land situated between the small town of Czersk and Bar Logi village. The canal is some 30 kilometres long. Near the village of Fojutowo it crosses a brook called Czerska Struga. Unlikely as it may seem, this is a two-level crossing of the two waterways. The canal's water flows six metres above the river surface on an aqueduct, a more than 75-metre long architectural construction of yellow brick and stone.

The Fojutowo aqueduct is today a monument to nineteenth century building skills, as is its half-a-century older peer, the Newcastle swing bridge in northern England, a construction that fundamentally alters our thinking about the shape and operating principles of bridges. Thanks to powerful hydraulic machinery situated in a tower in the middle of the river, the Newcastle bridge can make a horizontal 90-degree swing and position itself along the river's course to make way for ships and barges. When the traffic passes, the bridge again positions itself across the river Tyne, and the archetypal image of a bridge is restored. Recession in England, and the resulting changes in the economy which reduced the importance of Newcastle harbour, have made the bridge an expensive anachronism – the town has several other, more convenient bridges. Similarly, the nineteenth century melioration of Czerskie Laki is from today's viewpoint an engineering fancy, with the Fojutowo aqueduct as its crowning glory. Today, nobody in their right mind would attempt to meliorate the meadows in Bory Tucholskie with a 30-kilometre canal, mainly because there are very few projects of such scale in Polish agriculture these days, and those certainly have nothing to do with soil irrigation, as most of the land was meliorated a hundred years ago.

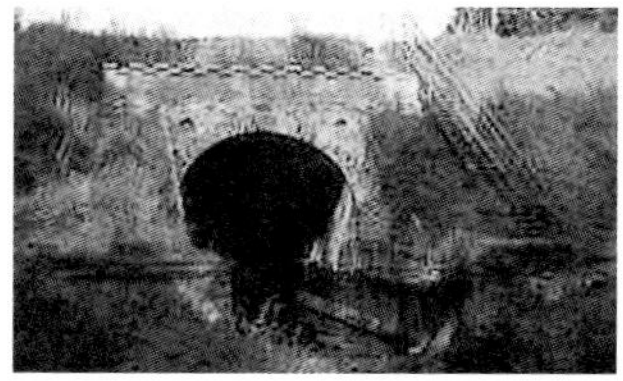

Fig. 1
Aqueduct in Fojutowo.

In any case, the aqueduct is a tourist attraction for a select few – it is not very famous, access is difficult, and it is hardly noted on most maps. A traveller reaching Fojutowo will learn from local folk that the "aqueduct is there, past the village." And the presence of a word so obviously Latin in origin in the Kashubian dialect, which is spoken in the area, lends the whole situation a strange flavor (the word "aqueduct" is probably known and used within a 15-kilometre radius around the structure, but no farther).

After a brief march we reach the aqueduct, which is small, single-spanned, and overgrown with foliage, as if imbedded in the surrounding meadows and nearby woods. Only when standing on the aqueduct and looking down from the level of the canal, do we understand what an extraordinary place we have found ourselves in. Behind us is a canal, and several metres below a brook situated perpendicularly to it. We can go down six metres of metal stairs to reach the Czerska Struga and walk along its course through a 75-metre tunnel, only to walk back up an identical flight of stairs at the other end. This appears to be a magical trick, but it can be explained rationally: we have just crossed a channel over which there is no bridge and kept our feet dry. We have walked beneath it. Apparently, tourism and artistry can still intersect, as in Caspar David Friedrich's times, although the contemporary critique of culture stresses the growing impossibility of individual

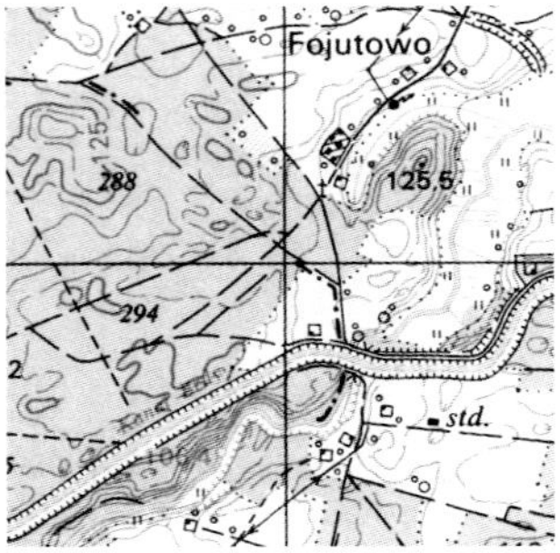

Fig. 2
Crossing of Great Channel of Brda and Czerska Struga River near Fojutowo, detail.

experience (including the experience of art, the difficult striving towards it, and the joy of discovery) in the modern model of uninvolved and simplified locomotion, which has replaced travel.

Our aqueduct is also a symbol of a certain style of thinking that subordinates its means to the goals it defines. This brings to mind a Polish movie from 20 years ago in which a group of engineers and high-rank communist party members *(apparatchiks)* frown over a model of a new urban development: "We'll put this building here," says one *apparatchik* moving a sizeable cardboard apartment block to a new location. "But, comrade, there is a lake there!" one of the engineers observes. "So we'll put the lake ... there!" replies the *apparatchik* and moves the lake. The utopian mentality behind engineering projects in Europe is closely related to the Enlightenment. In Eastern Europe, it dates back at least to the times of Peter the Great. In Andrei Platonov's story "The Epiphan Sluices," an engineer named Bertrand Perry, who, incidentally, comes from Newcastle, pays with his head for a failed attempt to build the Oka-Don canal. Platonov's writings contain the ultimate sublimation and philosophical rationale of actions opposed to the forces of nature and consistent with the quasi-metaphysical mission of the enlightened mind. One of the greatest twentieth century Russian writers, Platonov, was personally involved in the land-improvement projects of the 1920s. Concurrent to his literary activity, he received an excavator from the factory to regulate rivers in the Voronezh guberniya, sat for a (brief) time on the Central Committee of the Agricultural and Forestry Workers' Trade Union, and served as a delegate at hydrology and hydro-technology congresses in Moscow and St. Petersburg. He also took part in study tours for "literary brigades" (to Turkmenistan, among others) and expeditions (to the Caspian Sea and the Kara-Kum desert), whose object was to fuse literary/artistic perception with real human labor undertaken to completely subordinate and transform nature. Land improvement, in spite of its name, is yet another means of realizing human domination over "untamed" nature, an instrument of controlling the element of water (just as electrification is an attempt to impose human laws on the rhythm of night and day). Water flows where the engineer directs it, not where it has always flown. Platonov died in poverty of tuberculosis in 1951, during one of many campaigns against his writing in Soviet Russia. The great water regulation projects, the building of canals by Gulag inmates and the reversing of the course of rivers carried out in the Soviet Union turned out to be tragic mistakes, often referred to in contemporary critiques of utopian aspirations.

The tiny aqueduct in Fojutowo, a product of German engineering ideas of the early industrial age, although basically as revolutionary as the Oka-Don canal, has finally been degraded to the realm of the picturesque and is now perceived as an element in a protected cultural landscape.

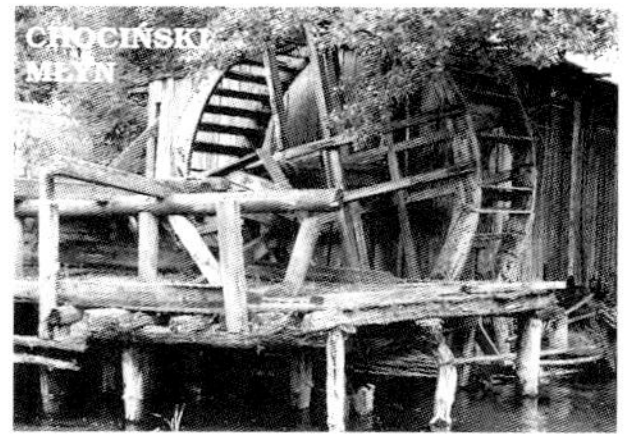

Fig. 3
Water Mill from the second half of the nineteenth century on Chocina River.

Alongside the idea of intersecting the huge expanse of Russia with a system of water canals which would enable man to curb unruly nature, there was also the electrification campaign, described with great passion in a series of Platonov's stories. The description of a bulb being twisted into a socket and miraculously bathing a Russian peasant's *(muzhik's)* shack in light bespeaks faith in the unlimited possibilities created by electrification. Electricity, generated in Platonov's stories by overshot and undershot water wheels on rivers, transformed into a thousand flames to light up the darkness surrounding man in the empty landscapes of Russia and the no less immense darkness of the human soul. Under his family's careful gaze, in the blinking electric light, a peasant reads a book "loudly repeating the syllables of the following word: mo-mo-mo." A network of electric wires entwined all of Russia in accordance with the principle that: "Communism equals the rule of Soviets plus the electrification of the country." The Promethean myth seemed to expand on a cosmic scale. The melancholic distance, the vast expanse of land – a Russian speciality described in a mystical tone by Rilke in a letter to Lou Andreas Salomé – suddenly seemed measurable and possible to control. What poets had always tried to fathom was finally accomplished by engineers erecting electricity poles, like the ones which, in one of Tarkovski's movies, sprout in rows out of a waving wheat field as if symbols of a new religion.

The proletariat's technological thought, freed from constraints, resulted in inventions that perfectly symbolized the aspirations of the new man. Today, in the presence of the incessant glare and the ubiquitous lighting of airports, streets, railway stations, and shop windows, the description of the invention of the sun in Platonov's 1936 story "Vprok" (the word translates into "superfluity") may seem as naively simple as an account of first principles. The story's protagonist arrives at the "Good Beginning" farming collective *(kolkhoz)*. There his attention is drawn to a "wooden watch tower, ten or twelve metres high. A metal device glittered at the top of the tower, a reflector judging by its shape, placed in such a way as to direct the rays of the light's unknown source towards the *kolkhoz*." As it turns out, the source of light is a small water-power plant, located in a granary on a creek bank.

Wires from the granary trailed over the willow brake, over fences, and, branching out on their way to the *kolkhoz*, reached out towards the sun. We also went that way. The wires looked very solid throughout, and the sun itself did not show a single defect. The tin mirror provided me with a particular feeling of satisfaction: the curve of its reflecting surface was so accurately calculated that the whole power of the light was directed towards the *kolkhoz* and its garden crops, wasting nothing on the sides. The source of light was a wooden disc on which a hundred 100-candle half-watt bulbs were mounted, so that the sun's total lighting power equalled ten thousand candles (...). The electric sun, built by a local blacksmith, was supposed to provide a final solution to the problem of night and day:

Operating manual of the Electrosun of the Good Beginning *kolkhoz:*

1. The sun is organized to offset the dark and cloudy shortcomings of the celestial body of the same name.
2. The sun maintains light over the *kolkhoz* between six in the morning and six in the night every day throughout the whole year. In the presence of lasting natural light, the *kolkhoz's* sun is switched off, and switched on again in the lack thereof.
3. The purpose of the *kolkhoz* sun is to radiate light for life, labor and cultural work of the *kolkhoz* workers, for useful livestock and gardens, within the compass of its rays.

The Electrosun, the most desired and touching device that human beings of that time could invent, serving, among other things, to improve the quality of "cultural work," was short-lived due to blown fuses and short-circuited wires, as the electrotechnician narrator is informed by the demobilized Red Army soldier Kondrov. "'Our sun don't shine, understand?!' Kondrov exclaimed bitterly. 'It's gone out... I'll go and start the wheel and the dynamo, and you'll see that our sun don't shine!'" The disappointed *kolkhoz* workers mutter: "All in all, ours is a scientific government, but still the sun don't shine!"

Platonov, a master of cosmogonical construction and deconstruction of the human world, had no illusions: entropy accompanies every invention like a shadow. The fault is in human nature and in the abyss that invariably separates us from reality. Chasing after it is no use:

"After all, man changes more slowly than the world he changes himself. Here lies the tragedy's centre of gravity." Man has nothing to do but contemplate the image of a world diffused as if in a kaleidoscope into thousands of micro-images and micro-worlds. A graphic equivalent of Platonov's destructive demiurgy are Pavel Filonov's paintings, where forms of humans, animals, and worlds disintegrate and merge again in crystal fragments. Things created by an artist's hand bear in themselves their own distorted reflection, they are creations that, at the moment of birth, trigger the process of disintegration.

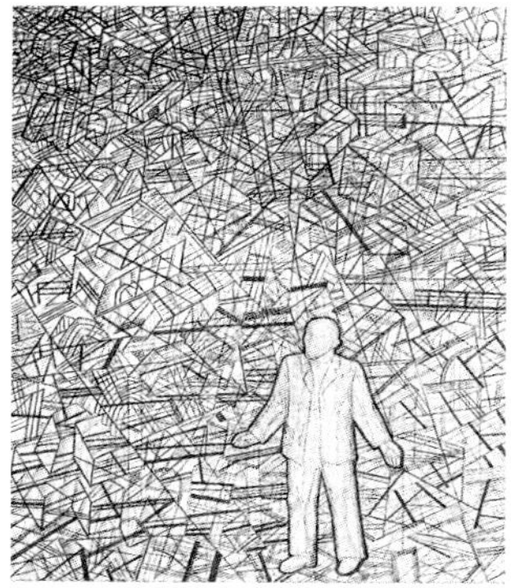

Fig. 4
Pavel Filonov, *Goelro*, 1930.

John Rajchman

The Virtual House

The problem can be put in this way: the virtual house is the one which, through its plan, space, construction, and intelligence, generates the most new connections, the one so arranged or disposed as to permit the greatest power for unforeseen relations. But what is this idea of the virtual as multiple potentials for new connections or unseen relations? A starting point lies in the distinction drawn by the philosopher Gilles Deleuze between the virtual and the possible, or the actualization of the virtual and the realization of the possible. It is part of a larger attempt to understand the notion of potential outside the given identities of form, function, and place, and it leads to the following principle: the world that is best is the most "multiple," the most virtual. The problem of the virtual house may then also be put this way: it is the one that most catches us by surprise in our very manners of thinking and being. Perhaps the strongest modernist works have done this in their own way, but that doesn't mean that the virtual house should look like any of them or repeat their manifestos. In fact, the virtual looks like nothing we already know or can see. The aim of this description is thus not to say what the virtual house should resemble, represent, or symbolize; that, by definition, is not possible. It is rather to try to formulate some questions implicated in the idea of the virtual house.

Concept

The idea of the virtual is quite old. The word comes from virtus, meaning potential or force, and often comes coupled with the actual, meaning that through which the potential or force becomes at once visible and effective. As such, it names one of the oldest problems in philosophy: it was involved in the very ideas of oikos, polis, ethos (home, city, manner of being). Long after Aristotle, Leibniz, and Bergson would take it up again. Deleuze takes up the arrow in turn, launching it in a new direction. To actualize the virtual, he says, is not the same as to realize the possible, and it is crucial not to confuse the two.[1] In a phrase taken from Proust, the virtual is "real without being actual, ideal without being abstract." It thus acquires a power of a peculiar kind calling for a special kind of intelligence.

The actual is then what manifests and effectuates the virtual, but the actual never completely shows or activates all that the virtual implies. Something always remains. For Bergson, for example, the virtual is the force of the past always still with us in the present, yet to be actualized, unfolding in our lives beyond what we are able to recollect or recognize. The virtual lies in those forces or potentials whose origins and outcomes cannot be specified independently of the open and necessarily incomplete series of their actualization. Such is their multiplicity (or complexity) that it can never be reduced to a set of discrete elements or to the different parts of a closed or organic whole. (This is what Bergson called "qualitative" rather than "quantitative" multiplicity.)

The virtual is thus not an abstraction, a generality, or an a priori condition. It doesn't take us from the specific to the generic. It increases possibility in another way: it mobilizes as yet unspecifiable singularities, bringing them together in an indeterminate plan. How are we to conceive of, and therefore deal with, potentials or forces that depart from the possibilities of given forms, structures, or ideas, affecting us in ways that go beyond what we can wholly grasp and working in other ways than through overall organizations or blueprints?

1. See, for example, Gilles Deleuze, *Différence et répétition,* Presses Universitaires de France, Paris, 1968, pp. 269 ff.

The actual and the virtual are thus not logically congruent or commensurable. Actualization is never in the image of the virtual force it effectuates. Unlike the possible, whose realization always leaves us the same, the virtual is something we must always experiment and work with in order to see. It confronts us as a question or problem to which we don't know yet how to respond in advance. We don't know yet how to react to it since it falls under no available description. Deleuze thinks that the "time images" of postwar film are virtual in this sense: they make visible something intolerable for which there existed no preset manner of thinking.

What would it mean for the virtual to be part of the very idea of construction? Let's take Deleuze's Leibnizian account of the baroque house, where the real and the ideal no longer belong to different realms but inhabit the same uncentered perspectival "possible world" – the very world that God has selected as best. Perhaps we today no longer need Leibniz's postulate of compossibility among different perspectives nor, therefore, the baroque idea of a God who has already selected. A neo-Leibnizian definition of the virtual house might then be this: it is the house that holds together the most, and most complicated, "different possible worlds" in the same container, allowing them to exist together along a constructed plane with no need of a preestablished harmony.

Smart houses

Smart machines are different from dynamic or mechanical ones. Unlike the locomotive devices like the airplane or the car that interested Marinetti and Le Corbusier, here information moves instead of the body. Thus these smart machines help create new spaces of body and mind. Their impact on architecture has not yet been resolved. So far we have been presented solely with a kind of programmatic progressivism or futurism difficult to separate from marketing hype and promotion. The problem is usually posed in terms of a virtual space where bits are called upon to do what was formerly done by atoms, creating invisible cities patterned on the real ones that they at once simulate and displace. The virtual house might then mean one of two things: it might mean a house wired for home automation, equipped to sense, serve and protect the body – what Paul Virilio calls the "handicapped body." Bill Gates' house is an extravagant advertisement for this. The problem it raises is that of architecture in smart environments according to a model where the environment is a batch of bits and the architectural unit is the computer or mind that processes them. Or again, the virtual house might mean the house on the screen according to the paradigm in which one talks of virtual libraries, museums, or shopping centers. Apart from the obsolescence of the simulated functions, this raises certain architectural problems: that of images no longer framed by walls or anchored in tectonic space but floating, moving as though pieces of information on a screen; and more generally the problem of a less grounded sense of the body and movement. Instead of a house for an insulated, handicapped body aided by machines that do everything it wants, the virtual house becomes here the house of this less grounded condition of image and body, as though it were a house for an unreal, disembodied mind linked to all others in a virtual realm.

But are these the only possibilities for architectural thought or intervention in the "age of smart machines?" Do there not exist other, less comforting, less automatic potentials not patterned on simulation and interactivity that the sense of the virtual developed here might bring out?

The virtual house is a special sort of machine with an "artifice" or "intelligence" that is not wholly informational. For the virtual is not another unreal realm that only doubles or "simulates" the nature we already know or see. Rather, it supposes something singular, yet to be constructed in the arrangements that determine our nature. To virtualize nature is thus not to double it but, on the contrary, to multiply it, complicate it, release other forms and paths in it. The virtual house might therefore be very smart after all, even delirious, while remaining perfectly real.

Virtual construction

A virtual construction is one that frees forms, figures, and activities from a prior determination or grounding, of the sort they have, for example, in a classical Albertian perspective, allowing them to function or operate in other unanticipated ways; the virtuality of a space is what gives such freedom in form or movement. Thus virtual construction departs from organizations that try to set out all possibilities in advance. It constructs a space whose rules can themselves be altered through what happens in it. But how then can there be such a thing as a "virtual plan?"

The usual way to increase possibility is to abstract from specificity, thus finding something more generalized. Increasing possibility comes at the price of reducing specificity. The house with the most possibilities might thus seem the one with the least specificities – the empty house, the house of silence or absence, awaiting a revelation that never comes. The virtual house is not like that. Its arrangement or disposition allows for the greatest number of singular points, the most complex connections made from them. If the virtual house is not completely specified by fixed qualities, it is because it is a dynamic space prior to any qualifications – so "smooth" that fixed qualities do not stick to it, are always slipping off it. Its geometry is not drawn from fixed points. The virtual functions by multiplying, by throwing together singular points and seeing what they can do. Thus it inserts chance where there was only probability.

The ruse of the possible is to make it seem that outside the aegis of the specifiable all is illogical, unplannable, ineffable-pure anarchy, disorder, chaos, irrationality. As if the only powers were those of organization, determination; as if there didn't exist potentials of another sort, working according to another kind of plan. One way out of the suffocating sense of too much programmed, instrumentalized possibility has been a theology of the impossible, a mysticism of the unsayable and the invisible. But while voids, erasures, and absences can of course all be used to help virtualize or singularize a specific space, the virtual plan is never obtained simply by emptying a space or via the via negativa. For it is after all a plan, not a primal void. The virtual plan is thus not a general, abstract, or master plan; yet neither is it an empty or deconstructed one, functioning by unbuilding, undoing, or collapse alone. It is free just because it is neither ideal nor impossible. That is why the virtual house is the most intense house, the one to most "affect" in ways that surprise us, obliging us to go beyond what normally seems possible.

Thinking virtual

Architects have thought in terms of utopia and ideological program. They have thought in terms of transgression and formal play. The virtual introduces another style of thought. It has nothing to do with an ideology, a belief in an encompasssing order, real or utopian. It thinks in terms of arrangements of body and soul, irreducible to any such symbolic order, any such law of possibilities. If it is critical, its critique does not consist in saying "no" or transgressing a supposed order or paternity. It says "no" only to affirm new possibilities through a virtual construction that says "yes" as well as "and."

We already know the principle of this style of thought: the more connections, more singular points connected, the greater the "virtuality" of the resulting arrangement. Already with Leibniz the "best world" is not the perfect world but the one with the greatest virtuality; such is his baroque way of approaching a principle of selection and belief no longer based in divine judgment or in a Judgment Day. For while he still supposes a division of the world into saved and damned, he holds that the damned damn themselves by failing to develop the virtuality of which they are capable. For a principle of judgment he thus substitutes a principle of "virtuality" in our manners of being, a jurisprudence of the singular. Freed from Leibniz's lingering baroque salvationism, such is the principle of selection of the virtual house: the one that keeps our possibilities, our hopes from salvationism, and our impossibilities, our despair from resignation.

These are some senses in which the virtual house may be said to be the house that in its plan, space, construction, and intelligence gives the greatest number of "new connections." But of course there is a problem. It has yet to be designed.

Otto E. Rössler, Peter Weibel

Endophysics or Our Rainbow World

Abstract
It is said that at the end of a rainbow there is a pot of gold. Where that end is, however poses a problem, since it is different for every observer. The rainbow is actually a distorted virtual image of the sun. Nevertheless, it looks like a real object. Could it be that similar distortions apply to other "real" objects?

Is the so-called objective reality only the endo side of an exo world? Time and again, the history of cultural production has provided evidence that man senses the possibility of the world as being only the endo side of an exo world.

Endophysics is a science that explores what a system looks like when the observer is part of that system.

The world interpreted as observer-relative and as interface is the doctrine of endophysics. The world changes as our measuring chains, our interfaces, change. The boundaries of the world are the boundaries of our interface.

The world is made of rubber, only we do not notice this because we, too, are made of rubber.

An old question

To what extent does objective reality depend on the observer? Since the invention of perspective in the Renaissance, and the invention of group theory (Helmholtz-Lie-groups) in the nineteenth century, we know that the appearance of the world depends on the observer's location in it. Accordingly, computer programs of the "virtual reality" type generate a "lawfully non-invariant" (that is, covariant) representation out of an absolute (invariant) one that is present in the computer memory. Even though the lawful distortion of perspective vision is tantalizing, it leaves our secure sense of an existing "objective" reality undisturbed.

The rainbow challenges this security. Virtual reality programs containing rainbows have not so far been developed. The transformation rules are different from those for other objects. This has to do with the fact that a rainbow is a rather special kind of object: it is a distorted virtual image of the sun. Thus, if the observer is travelling, so is the rainbow. If the observer artificially increases the distance between the eyes by the use of mirrors (which can be mimicked in a virtual reality simulation by changing the size of the internal observer's representation), the rainbow consistently keeps an infinite distance, despite the fact that it is overlaid over much closer objects. While no one doubts that a pot of gold is waiting at the end of the rainbow, it is somewhat difficult to simultaneously stay and watch and sneak towards the right place to find the pot.

Thus, the properties of certain objects (in the present case: their location) depend on properties of the observer (like the latter's location and pupil shape) in a way which goes beyond the similar distortions of 3-D Helmholtzian perspective or 4-D Minkowskian projection. Could it be that the principle illustrated by the rainbow is of a broader significance?

The interface between observer and rest

An observer, who is part of the world, cannot see that world from an objective vantage point. The homogeneous matrix algorithm of the virtual reality flight simulators (cf. Newman, Sproull, 1979) shows how nontrivial a task is to generate the right interface. The observer, far from being intimidated by the rich and changing structure of the sequentially applying perspectives, actually needs this kind of packaging in order to extract the correct, invariant representation from it. "The intimacy of a head near one's own is like the lights and doorway of a house" (Rodney, 1991). In principle, there are many more parameters to try out than those of observer location and size: Observer motion immediately comes to mind. Both "visual flow" phenomena and relativistic distortions are hereby generated and can indeed be reproduced through simulation (Sutherland, 1966, 1970). Next, take recurrent movements by the observer, like a shaking of the head: the effect on the interface can be dramatic, especially if the shaking is fast. Indeed, such conditions can do irreparable damage to the goal of finding an invariant representation.

Historically, the interface problem was first seen by Boscovich (1755), who asked what happens when both the observer and the surrounding world shrink concomitantly, along with all the forces involved. Obviously, the same impressions would be generated within the mind. The interface would remain unaffected. Similarly, if the shaking of the observer's head is accompanied by a shaking of the rest of the world, nothing is happening for the observer. Therefore, time-dependent features of the interface deserve a closer examination.

The interface generated by Brownian motion of the observer

Brownian motion or "Archimedean motion" is interesting because of the energy and momentum conservation involved. Any observer who is built out of particles that are in random thermal motion stands in an interesting dynamical relationship with the rest of the world.

Archimedes first saw that the joint "center of gravity" can never be moved. How, therefore, does the rest of the world appear to such an observer? It only makes sense to ask this question today, since the necessary, simultaneous simulation of many particles is a fairly recent option (Alder and Wainwright, 1957).

Every external object will be found to be performing a Brownian motion relative to the observer. The strength of this motion will be dependent on the object's mass: the smaller the mass, the larger the apparent thermal agitation. This is because the center of gravity of the observer and the external object are linked by a relative Brownian motion. A very small mass object, therefore, can never be observed accurately by a thermally trembling observer. The thermal noise of the observer will always "infest" the object in such a way that it is the latter which appears to be thermally agitated by the temperature of the observer, even if the object's actual motional temperature is zero.

The effect is the same as if the observer himself or herself was a Brownian particle. How does the world look to a particle in Brownian motion? The virtual reality paradigm, in principle can be used to find an answer.

A Quaker's world

Finding the necessary peace of mind to find an answer in the right way is not easy. Numerically, the task is also very demanding. What is needed is to design a whole reversible micro-world in a computer? The "eye" inside (that is, the internal macroscopic observer) is to be built out of the same micro-constituents as the rest. The special thermal (momentum-conserving) relationship between that "eye" and a particular micro-object, valid in the computer universe, can then be looked at by a human macro-observer outside that world (if he wears the right kind of goggles). It will be rewarding to implement this task, say, in the year 2010, but even today it is already possible to glimpse some of the unusual rainbow phenomena that will emanate from this contraption.

False uncertainty

An irreducible uncertainty is a first implication. The chaos in the observer translates into chaos outside the observer. Apart from the unit thermal noise energy inside the observer (E), which is equal to one half the Boltzmann constant times the temperature of the observer, we have a second intrinsic constant, namely a typical duration (T). This characteristic time interval is related to the mean collision interval inside the observer: after this time interval has passed, the microdynamics inside the observer change course relative to the external object. A precise calculation of T for classical billiard systems is an open problem (Rössler, 1991 a). The mean shaking period T needs further clarification from a conceptual point of view as well. If the observer were alone in the universe with the object, the center of gravity of the observer and that of the object would not perform a Brownian motion relative to each other. However, as soon as any third object (for example, a mediating particle) is coupled with the observer, it is only toward this combined set that the external object remains in a state of constant motion. Indeed, the multi-particle observer now generally reverses course, every unit time interval T, relative to the external object.

The resulting "relative diffusion" between external object and observer is governed by the product of E and T, divided by the object's mass (M). This result holds true when the external object is "directly" (that is, without a measuring chain) coupled with the observer (Rössler, 1987). Unexpectedly, the more general case of "indirect" coupling (via a measuring chain) is still governed by the same law, since the measuring chain is unable to undo the objectively existing mutual relationship between observer and object.

The resulting "uncertainty" mimics quantum mechanics. This is because the presence of a diffusion law of the same qualitative type as described above (an action – like E times T – divided by the object's mass) is sufficient to generate the Schrödinger equation (Fényes, 1952; Nelson, 1966).

False certainty

We still need to know what happens when the observer forces a micro-object into a certain definite observational state. For example, the measurement situation may be chosen such that the microobject must reveal its position in a yes-or-no decision. The problem at hand is analogous to the problem of the formation of an "eigenstate" in quantum mechanics. Such a restricting type of measurement can certainly also be performed in our simulated world.

A new phenomenon arises here. While the previous finding (uncertainty) did not yet qualify as a rainbow phenomenon in the strict sense, since mere blurring does not bring in a new phenomenological quality, a new quality emerges in the present case. It is the quality of a well-defined localization in position space (or momentum space, respectively) appearing for the observer, which is at variance with the correct location. For if the observed location of the object were identical with the correct location, the relative Brownian motion of the observer would, in effect, have been eliminated, even though this cannot happen. The apparent location of the object, valid in the interface, is therefore different from the objectively applying location. This prediction can be verified in the proposed simulation of the interface. Since everything that happens in the simulation is known explicitly, it is possible to compare the content of the interface with what really happens to the particle in question. This comparison is, of course, a privilege confined to the external operator, since the internal observer is stuck with the interface.

The yes-or-no decision which appears on the interface depends on the internal dynamics of the observer as much as those of the object. According to Nelson's (1966) stochastic mechanics, that is, diffusion theory, the probability of a certain occurring decision depends on the square of the amplitude of the diffusion-generated Schrödinger equation. The confirmation of the diffusion-theoretical result can be expected, once the first simulation of the interface becomes available. However, there is a "complication" to be expected in that case, which is absent in the standard formalism of stochastic mechanics. In the latter, the occurring decisions ("eigenstates") are assumed to be permanent. Here, the distortion of the objective world is such that the recorded state, as it appears in the interface, depends on the momentary state of motion of all particles inside the observer. In other words, the interface is a momentary state of affairs. All measurements, no matter how long the measuring chain is in terms of space and time, are determined by the momentarily valid relationship between the internal dynamics of the observer and the dynamics of the rest of the world.

An external super-observer who watches the momentary interface as a function of time, will therefore record a "superposition" (that is, a temporal integration) over all the momentarily valid "quantum decisions." The momentarily valid "eigenworlds," while mutually different, all fall within the probability distribution prescribed by the wave function of stochastic mechanics.

In quantum mechanics, a similar problem is known as "the measurement problem." For example, in the language of Everett's (1957) "relative state" formulation, the different "eigenworlds" that apply at every moment are said to be "shielded" from each other. A version of Everett's formalism exists (due to Bell, 1981) in which the different "eigenworlds" are assumed to exist, not simultaneously as in the usual Everett picture, but sequentially – each confined to a very small time window. Bell only wanted to show the mathematical equivalence of this view with the standard, multiple-worlds interpretation. Both interpretations of quantum mechanics are usually considered rather outlandish. Here, the second interpretation again arises unexpectedly in a quite different context.

Bell's insight that the observer would "not notice" being in a different quantum world from one moment to the next (since worlds by definition are complete, that is, contain no trace of another world) applies here as well. It follows that the "integration" which an outside observer of the simulated interface experiences is an artefact.

If the outside human observer were a part of the same interface, unable to escape from it through the use of an outside memory, the phenomenon of integration would disappear and a single consistent "eigenworld" would apply at every moment, complete with its own recorded past and anticipated future. Thus, the job of a demiurge – to notice the implications that his own actions (laws and initial conditions) generate for the inhabitants – is surprisingly difficult.

A new type of rainbow

The distortion of an objective world as mirrored in an interface can thus go unexpectedly far. The notion "rainbow world" applies to each distorted representation no matter how short-lived. In the one world, for example, Schrödinger's cat is alive and well, while in the other, the same "hellish contraption" (Schrödinger, 1935) has taken another course. Moreover, that same branching may have taken place some time ago, so that the one outcome would have produced a cat that is playful and frisky right now, while the other entails a cat that has been subjected to organic decomposition for quite a while. It appears very hard to reconcile both rainbow worlds with one and the same exo reality.

Equally hard to accept is the claim that these two different internal refractions of the same objective reality alternate at a rapid pace in an unnoticeable way. Accordingly this "rainbow movie" (one time slice after the other) contains many consistent "sub-movies" of which a different one is in charge at every moment.

The counter-intuitive notion of a rainbow movie needs further scrutiny. One of its features, however, is, unexpectedly, very close to everyday experience. It is the fact that each moment has its own world (eigenworld). In quantum mechanics, the same 1:1 relationship was noted by Deutsch (1986). Here, the same result arises in a completely transparent context (provided all difficulties have been mastered). The inhabitants of a reversible universe are strangely glued to a single moment in time. They call it their world, "as it is real now." While the mutual incompatibility of the different "now worlds" lacks a representation in the interface as mentioned, the interface still gives away the fact that a single instant in time is privileged over all others because it "defines a world."

The latter prediction – existence of a "now world" for internal inhabitants – is, when transplanted back to our own world, at variance with traditional science, which lacks the notion of a privileged now.

The paradigm of virtual reality has made the topic of the "interface" scientifically acceptable (cf. *Ars electronica,* 1986; Weibel, 1990; Diebner et al., 2001). The momentary position of the camera distorts the world in a way which makes it fully palpable as an invariant new reality. Generating such an interface is not easy and requires a lot of computer processing power. Experimenting with this interface is presently an important technological and conceptual challenge. How, for example, does a rainbow look inside when it is "reduced" by a cat's vertical pupil rather than a round one? How about a cat's pupil that is many meters long, either vertically or horizontally?

A second novel question refers to temporally changing realities, if the changes occur in both the position of the "eye" and that of the external object in a correlated fashion. Such changes will obviously not show up in the interface (since the "Boscovich difference" is zero; Rössler, 1991 b). Third, there is a very special interface generated between a microscopically described reversible observer and the rest of the same microscopically simulated world. Phenomena only known from the counter-intuitive realm of quantum mechanics suddenly arise as implications of a situation that is, conceptually, completely transparent. At the same time, "nowness-bound rainbow worlds" become a topic for scientific discussion.

Thus, "playing with cameras" can be a rewarding pastime. Diverse phenomena known from everyday experience can be retrieved. At the same time, a new type of suspicion regarding our own world arises: maybe, our own world is a rainbow world, too?

Once such a suspicion has taken hold, the next logical step is to call for new diagnostic tools that can be used in our own world to demonstrate the existence of the new predicament and to explore and perhaps manipulate it. However, the decisive step is getting suspicious in the first place. The present suspicion, which goes back to Kant and Boscovich, and before them to Anaximander, has now found a new medium for its study.

To conclude, the concept of the rainbow has been re-examined from the vantage point of virtual reality simulations.

A rather unusual type of virtual reality is needed for such a simulation. Eventually, reversible simulated worlds will be useful for a further understanding of the human/world interface (a proposal which at first sight is confined to the study of an ice skater who cannot get rid of whole-body angular momentum, or of an Archimedean system of interacting balls and springs like in a model of a molecule). The first detailed report about the properties of such a "conservative virtual reality" will come in about ten years time. Presently, only "informed guesses" are possible. In this way, it is possible to arrive at a new "hopeful suspicion": the VR paradigm may reveal more about our own world than the ordinary course of science has prepared us to believe. For example, the walls of the prison of the now become palpable. Further distortions of the invariant (exo) reality may exist which can likewise be unmasked by the new Hermetian paradigm of computer-generated worlds.

References:

B. Alder, T. E. Wainwright, "Phase transitions for a hardsphere system," in *Journal of Chemical Physics 27,* 1957, p. 1208.

Philosophien der neuen Technologie, Ars Electronica 1988, Merve, Berlin, 1986.

J. S. Bell, "Quantum mechanics for cosmologists," in C. J. Isham, R. Penrose, D. Sciama, eds., Clarendon Press, Oxford, 1981, pp. 611-637.

R. J. Boscovich, "De spatio et tempore, ut a nobis cognoscuntur (On space and time, as they are recognized by us)," in J. M. Child, ed. R. J. Boscovich, *Theory of Natural Philosophy,* Latin-English Edition, Open Court, Chicago, 1992, pp. 404-409. Reprint of the English translation: The MIT Press, Cambridge, Mass., 1966, pp. 203-205. English re-translation in Rössler (1991b). Compare also Fischer (1991).

D. Deutsch, "Three connections between Everett's interpretation and experiment," in R. Penrose, C. J. Isham, eds., *Quantum Concepts in Space and Time,* Clarendon Press, Oxford, 1986, pp. 215-225.

H. H. Diebner, T. Druckery, P. Weibel, *Sciences of the Interface,* Genista Verlag, Tübingen, Germany, 2001.

H. Everett, III, "Relative state formulation of quantum mechanics," in *Review of modern Physics,* 29, 1957, pp. 454-462.

I. Fényes, "A probability-theoretical foundation and interpretation of quantum mechanics," (publ. in German) in *Zeitschrift für Physik,* 132, 1952, pp. 81-106.

R. Fischer, "A neurobiological re-interpretation and verifica-

tion of Boscovich covariance, postulated in 1758," in *Cybernetica,* 34, 1991, pp. 95-101.
E. Nelson, "Derivation of the Schrödinger equation from Newtonian mechanics," in *Physics Review,* 150, 1966, pp. 1079-1085.
W. N. Newman, R. F. Sproull, *Principles of Interactive Computer Graphics,* 2nd ed., McGraw-Hill, New York, 1991.
T. Rodney, *The Runaway Soul,* Farrar, Straus and Giroux, New York, 1979.
O. E. Rössler, "Endophysics," in J. L.Casti, A. Karlquist, eds., *Real Brains, Artificial Minds,* North Holland, New York, 1987, pp. 25-46.
O. E. Rössler, "Four open problems in four dimensions," in G. Baier, M. Klein, eds., *A Chaotic Hierarchy,* World Scientific, Singapore, 1991a, pp. 365-369.
O. E. Rössler, "Boscovich covariance," in J. L. Casti, A. Karlquist, eds. *Beyond Belief: Randomness, Prediction and Explanation in Science,* CRC Press, Boca Raton, 1991b, pp. 69-87.
Endophysics, The World as an Interface, World Scientific Publishing Co., Singapore, New Jersey, London, Hong Kong, 1998.
P. Weibel, "The two levels of reality, exo and endo," in Y. Shikata, ed., *Art Lab 1st Symposium, The Current Condition and the Future of Digital Art,* Canon, Tokyo, 1991, p. 16.
E. Schrödinger, "The present situation in quantum mechanics," (publ. in German) in *Naturwissenschaften,* 23, 1935, pp. 807-812, 823-828, 844-849. English translation: *Proceedings of the American Philosophical Society,* 124, 1980, pp. 323-338.
I. E. Sutherland, "Computer inputs and outputs," in *Scientific American,* 1966, September issue; "Computer displays," *Scientific American,* 1970, June issue.
P. Weibel, "Virtual worlds: The emperor's new bodies," in G. Hattinger, M. Russel, C. Schöpf, P. Weibel, eds., in *Ars Electronica 1990, vol. 2,* Veritas Verlag Linz, Linz, Austria, 1990, pp. 9-38.
P. Weibel, B. O'Kane, "Das tangile Bild – Endoapproach to electronics," in M. Waffender, ed., in *Cyberspace,* Rowohlt, Reinbek near Hamburg, Germany , 1991, p. 154.

Gerhard Roth

Can One Meaningfully Speak of a World Independent of Consciousness?

(...) A current objection to constructivism runs: it is true that most of constructivism's epistemological arguments are justified, even if they are neither new nor original. But with respect to the rejection of the knowability of a world independent of consciousness, that is going too far, that is *too radical.*[1] Philosophers were and are divided in their opinions about the existence and the knowability of reality. *Ontological* realists proceed from the assumption that there is a reality, and *cognitive* realists assume in addition that it is, with regard to experience, at least partially accessible. According to Kant, we can be simultaneously an ontological realist and an epistemological idealist. One believes then in the existence of a world independent of consciousness, but maintains it is unavailable for experience. The Scottish philosopher and epistemologist David Hume considered the idea of the existence of a world independent of consciousness neither provable nor disprovable, whereas Berkeley, as an objective idealist, considered this idea super-

1. R. Nüse, M. Groeben, B. Freitag, and N. Schreier, *Über die Erfindung/en des Radikalen Konstruktivismus,* Deutscher Studienverlag, Weinheim, 1991.

fluous and even dismissible. I won't go into his reasons here.

But does it make any sense at all to assume the existence of a world independent of consciousness if I, at the same time, can experience nothing of it? One might seek a basis in the *logical* necessity of such a supposition. If, as in the preceding chapter, I proceed from the assumption that reality is produced through the corporeal brain, then it follows logically that there must be an entity which is not a part of reality. The whole array of operations – the function of perception (for which the senses are necessary) what they do, how the brain functions – all of this naturally is meaningless if I do not at the same time assume that there is a reality in which a brain exists and to which I can relate these statements.

Now this seems to be a paradox. First I claim that reality is completely unknowable, and now I'm saying one could relate these suppositions within reality to it. Yet, I contend that my standpoint is not contradictory. Although in epistemological terms reality is completely inaccessible, I have to assume its existence, first of all, in order not to run into elementary contradictions, and secondly, no one can forbid me from having thoughts about the character of reality, namely, with the goal of being able to explain better the phenomena *in my reality*. It is only that I may not claim any objective validity, rather, I underscore the *practical* value of my theory. This is the case with many conceptions of models in the natural sciences. Thus, physicists do not believe that atoms are built exactly the way Bohr's model of the atom says they are. Yet, many things in chemistry and physics are possible to be explained along those lines.

Beyond this, it is indeed extraordinarily difficult to address in a meaningful way the character of reality. First of all, we can ask: where does reality exist? If we say it exists "outside" or "beyond" reality, then we are making spatial statements which only have meaning within my reality. Reality (*Realität*) does not exist outside or beyond reality (*Wirklichkeit*), and one cannot see it through "holes" in reality. I cannot even ascertain the limits of reality.

Many philosophers have attempted to establish the essence of reality by deriving everything from the appearances (*Erscheinungen*) of reality, which obviously only has validity within our experiential world. Such an "epistemological reduction of phenomena" begins with our making clear to ourselves that things in a world independent of consciousness have no colors, that there are no melodies there, no aroma of roses, nothing hard nor soft. All these things, we ascertain, are the ingredients of our brain. Nonetheless, one could object, these constructs refer back to *real* actions or effects, for example, to a certain wave length of light or to superimpositions or sequences of sound waves of a certain frequency. Someone versed in physiology of the senses and the brain would counter that these relations are precisely *not* unequivocal. We can perceive a red under many wave lengths or even as a red imitation of a green impulse. There is actually nothing there at all that would unequivocally correspond physically to the sensation of "red." In the case of what our memory "adds" to the immediate sense-data to establish a complete perception, there are not even the "effects" of sensible impulses yet.

Similarly, the size and the shape of things do not correspond to reality. A shape that appears to us as perfectly round is nothing other than a round (and actually not even perfectly round) image available to the retina or the so-called primary retinotopic map in V1/A17. Nothing is reproduced there; rather, nerve cells are firing. The perfectly round circle is perfectly round on the basis of our foreknowledge.

We can extend this reduction to the concepts of space and time, and we will ascertain that they too lose all meaning if we separate them from our reality. Real space is – as we have heard – neither "real" three-dimensional Euclidian space nor relativistic, but rather a conception in our reality (*Wirklichkeit*); and statements such as "over," "behind," and "in" have no meaning outside our reality. The same holds for time. Is reality then completely without properties?

"Stop!" – a lot of people will say now. Of course there are properties of reality, namely all those which physics has determined as the foundation for all of natural science. It is not for nothing that many cognitive philosophers and psychologists call reality the "physical world." This science says expressly that light, even if it has no colors, does have certain different wave lengths, that space is not three-dimensional Euclidean, but rather, in relativistic fashion, four-dimensional (with time being a kind of fourth dimension); it says that what we consider to be "solid matter" is "in reality" closer to empty space, with a few molecules and atoms; and so forth. It establishes standards that are independent of every observer and are valid in all parts of our cosmos. The world described by physics has to be identical with objective reality!

This conception of the objective character of the propositions in physics is indeed widespread, but not pertinent. All the concepts of physics are produced in the human mind, and they rest on human conceptions and conventions, which have been laboriously established over centuries or even millennia. They presuppose other concepts from which they have been derived, or they are presuppositions (*Setzungen*) that cannot be further explained (or only in circular fashion), such as the concepts of "mass," "power," or "energy." Physics makes use of the language of mathematics, which is itself not without presuppositions, but rather relies on (un-derivable) axioms.

It also has to be asked *which* sort of physics is supposed to reflect reality. There is no such thing as *the one* physics, but rather numerous domains of physical phenomena, which in part exist independently of one another, such as electrodynamics and mechanics, or are partly in contradictory relation to each other, like micro- and macro-physics. Does quantum physics reflect reality better than the physics of solid bodies or the theory of relativity? If one wanted – as many do – to consider quantum physics as the foundational representation of reality, one would encounter great difficulties with the question of whether or not electrons or quarks "really" exist. The question as to the reality of such phenomena beyond the physical experiment is not an object for physics and it is certainly not meaningful to pose it if one has to assume, as a quantum physicist, that the properties of the examined phenomena are only engendered in the course of measurement in the first place.

The same holds for the laws of nature. Laws of nature are verified with the help of experiments, in which sometimes complicated apparatuses for measurement are engaged, each of which only operates under very circumscribed conditions and which presuppose *special* theories. Outside of these presuppositions there are no laws of nature. Physics is, like every natural science, a *description of the phenomena in reality*, which is tied to the conditions of this reality and thus constitutes a part of it. Physics might be the best, most critical or most general description of the phenomena in reality, but it does not surpass reality.

Every reflection about objective reality, whether scientific or not, is finally tied to the conditions of human thinking, speaking, and action, and must be verified therein. The constructs of our brain, therefore, are not arbitrary. (…)

Jaime Salazar

MVRDV, VPRO

Although it may not appear so, this book is based on a story more than on an architecture. The story of an architecture made for a producer of messages, a number of television and radio studios. An architecture which already has an informational goal per se; that is, for understanding and seeking, in reality itself, the generative bases of architectural form. A curious coincidence. The architects with the greatest experimental ambition in the architecture of the information era are commissioned to create the new headquarters of a media company whose rationale is also the unbiased exploration of reality. Therein lies the basis of the story. And so this book sets out to consider architecture, once again, as the terrain of a more general argument about reality, and not merely the fact of producing buildings. A single "science of creating architecture" does not exist, one that might be delimited or defined, just as the method through which it is manifested cannot be delimited. In this book, the book in itself, television, radio or architecture are not different media, but rather different messages springing from a single global medium of information. Thus, the story this book tells is the particular story of various "generators of information" – VPRO – which, linking up with various "generators of space" – MVRDV – produce the result featured in these pages.

The epoch in which we live has increasingly adopted the motive power of information, to the point of converting this into the raw material, of sorts, of contemporary reality. We depend to such an extent on ways of handling information, whatever these may be, that no current procedure can now be understood without their presence. They have completely transformed our culture, our values and attitudes towards the world. The idea behind this book is that we take on board the idea that *in our times, handling of information is becoming a basic code for acquiring knowledge about reality.*

This handling of information is, for all intents and purposes, transforming our way of understanding and applying any production processes. And architecture, of course, is one of these processes.

We know that the computer era has now taken over once and for all.

The era of mechanization is passing away, but for all that, only rarely do we assimilate, in concrete terms, the absolute transformation this entails. Assimilating phenomena that still don't have a fixed structure to be assimilated is confusing. We find ourselves caught in a moment in which we have a clear notion of something being different, yet we persist in trying to understand this according to concepts that don't, on the whole, apply. In order to respond to certain things, we'd do better to pose the right questions first.

Considering that architecture is to a large degree computerizable is not a mere formal or stylistic change. In fact it is not even a change. It is a global transformation of the medium, one which generates a different way of understanding processes. It is neither good nor bad. It is simply unstoppable. It is implanted in us, even though it is still difficult at times to assimilate it. *It is a process of "secondary abstraction" – a computer abstraction on top, of modern abstraction – which defines, a different architecture,* as modern abstraction was also due to a transformation – an unstoppable one – of the method by which classical architecture was still being produced. To consider this transformation does not in the least imply, as could be argued, defending the definitive dehumanization of architecture, the overall delineation of procedures, the final dissolution of the artistic meaning implicit in architecture. Not at all. The opposite, in fact.

The computer abstraction of architecture transforms our way of understanding the production process, but also the very meaning of architecture as a productive activity in relation to reality.

Architecture as interface

If there is something the entire debate around architecture might agree on today, it is the enormous complexity of the phenomena of reality in which all material production must move. Reality is complex. In order, therefore, to operate within it, is it still possible to approach reality from a single author's intervention? Is it still possible to put forward architectures that respond to reality from a personal angle, even when such an angle touches on the artistic and the technical? And, should the personal angle not be enough, would that mean the end of architecture as the production of an individual author?

Our conception of architecture is along the lines of a basically hierarchical activity; that is, one which depends on a series of linear decisions of cause and effect. The architect conceives his design by drawing on a certain amount of information, elaborates a project which other parties subsequently realize in the actual building. From that moment on, the author's abstract scheme, his design, enters into contact with reality and acts within it. But let us imagine, instead, another possibility. We will suppose that we can conceive or address architecture not only as that linear set of activities, extending from the design to the final utilization of the building, but as a more complex, non-linear network of people, materials, information and energy which result in the constructed building. A network that is not approachable from our usual linear view of phenomena alone, but from a more complex relationship of effects, self-organized in part, impossible to be decided consciously, which would lead to a more ample and sincere view of the present-day production of architecture.

But not only the present-day. If we stop to think about the history of architecture we have learnt, we will come up with a long list of names and works, but this will be more problematic so with anything extending beyond that linear, hierarchical vision, and that of the individual author, which we associate with a particular architectural œuvre. Nevertheless, we know that in many cases there are other factors which are equally as important as the author's intervention, even though it is that alone which might have endured. The rapport with the client, a fixed location, the involvement of other material agencies, etc. Although it may not seem so, the history of architecture is by no means merely the sum of authors and their works.

While the debate about ideas on the design of architecture has become ever more complex over the years, that complexity has not been adequately applied to the actual processes of production and to the relationship between the architect and reality. Reality is highly complex and it is important to elaborate increasingly complex models for translating these phenomena into given forms. Meanwhile, the architect's activity continues to be an author's activity – vertical, categorical, and totally hierarchical – one that tends to impose these models on reality through designs.

Let us introduce, then, that new variable into the discussion. We will contend that the computerization of the world brings us the data necessary to make this possible. The production of architecture is no longer a material production solely determined by the human factor, but is partly developed according to dynamics which extend beyond the absolute control of the people who conceive buildings.

The development of new models of reality and the potential capacity for calculating material procedures, have introduced this new and different quality. The architect is no longer the unique author, the sole master of the form.

This does not imply, however, the absolute negation of the architect as author, but only a transformation of status. Architecture is the material production of objects, and such production – like any other – must be considered as a complex interaction of flows of information, matter, and energy, over and above the mere linear sum of the parts – human, material or categorial – which comprise it.

Endophysics, a recent branch of physics, introduces the idea that our perception of reality is a question of interfaces. The interface as a model, or as a perception, of reality. Objective reality does not exist, since our relative position within reality annuls any absolute relationship to it. Endophysics relativizes our relationship to the world by considering that the external position of an observer is only possible in the shape of a model and is never within reality itself. According to Gödel's[1]

1. Douglas R. Hofstadter, *Gödel, Escher, Bach: An eternal golden braid,* Basic Books, New York, 1979.

theorem of indefinition, it is only from outside a complex universe that it is possible to give a complete description of it. Applied to architecture, this endophysical idea forces us to the conclusion that our view of reality is a question of interfaces.

"The world changes in relation to our interfaces with it. The limits of the world are the limits of our interface. We do not interact with the reality of the world, we do so with its interface" (Peter Weibel).[2]

And so we will consider architecture as an interface, and therefore the transformation of reality as a transformation of the architectural interface. We will posit, then, an alternative view of the history of architecture as an interface with the world. We can describe many historical phenomena in a different way; in relation to information and to interaction, for example. Or architecture's transformation from classical grammar to modern abstraction, for instance.

In classical architecture the interaction of the architect was practically nil and that of the user non-existent. The architect made use of a series of aesthetic invariants, which he applied by following equally invariant grammars. Let's say that the author's rare variations on that system are those which have actually subsisted until our own times as decisive moments in the history of classical architecture. That is, the architectural interface was a barely interactive and highly hierarchical method.

When the transformation of the medium takes place through abstraction, the architectural interface gains in interactivity, both for the architect and for the user. The architect acquires a lot of autonomy in his activity – his activity is much more interactive with the medium – because form ceases to ultimately depend on a rigid formal or aesthetic syntax. And the user equally gains, too, in his capacity for interaction. Not as much as the architect, but now his perception, the perception the user has of a building, becomes an important factor of the architecture. The user interacts with modern architecture through his perception of the object, his changing vision of the object. Relative to this vision of architecture as interface, the next step is in the increase of interaction, not on the part of the architect who has already acquired complete autonomy within modern architecture – but on the part of factors external to the author, like the data of reality itself or the increased interactivity of potential users. That is, *in the interface of any architec-*

2. Peter Weibel, "Over and Beyond the Limits of Reality," Lecture held at the *Ars Electronica 92* Symposium, Linz, Austria.

ture coming after modernity the interaction of other factors external to the architect increases.

Information

But in what way? How can the interaction of other factors external to the architect increase? We come back once more to the comparison between the modern and the postmodern idea. One of the basic characteristics of the change lies in the perception of speed. According to Paul Virilio, classical modern society is founded on a physically perceptible mechanical speed, such as fascinated the Futurists at the beginning of the twentieth century. In architecture, the entire production of architectonic objects until far into the century – even today – is still based on this perception of time and space. The object is created a priori by the architect as a message impermeable, for all intents and purposes, to the interaction of the perceiver, if this is not simply through his perception: a passive activity. Considering architecture as the former interface, the user's interaction – albeit fundamental – is practically nil.

Postmodern speed, on the other hand, is absolute. It is the speed of information, the speed of light. In what way can the perception or the interaction of the architectonic message change in an environment of instantaneous speed? Obviously this does not entail an acceleration in the perception of architecture to unimaginable speeds, but a change in the nature of the interface of the architecture. If the interactivity between architect and user was practically nil before, the tendency would now be towards an evergrowing increase in the interactivity of both. The outcome of absolute speed is simultaneous space and time.

In the simultaneity of space and time, information becomes the relational medium between both parties, by means of which interactivity increases. That is, in a postmodern design process the architect and the user "interact" through information, and this capacity for interaction is greater each time.

"The aesthetics of interactivity are based on action much more than on visual perception" (Dick Rijken).[3]

This transformational and generic notion of the potential of information society and of the interactive dimension is nothing new. From the founders of cybernetics, such as Norbert Wiener,[4] to the inspired thinking of Marshall McLuhan, many voices have warned of the dangers that the technological

3. Dick Rijken, in conversation with B. Lootsma, *Media and Architecture*, VPRO and Berlage Institute, Amsterdam, 1998.

4. Norbert Wiener (1894-1964), one of the founders of cybernetics or "the science of control and communication in the animal and the machine," a science based on information theory and feedback, and how animals and machines manage to "do" things.

implementation and the ever-increasing, unstoppable development of global information may involve. Certain philosophical positions exist today that argue against the definitive and basic destructiveness provoked by the era of information, of the interaction or the final implanting of an absolute and trans-ideological, reality on the world. In *The Perfect Crime,* for example, Jean Baudrillard[5] makes no bones about the final conclusion of this tendency towards electronic, computer, or virtual dissolution. For Baudrillard, the world has already committed the crime of exterminating illusion. Magic has disappeared, because the entire history of humanity up to now has been the history of the progressive "unmasking," extermination and crime of the illusion through a simulation effect, which is precisely a gigantic enterprise of disillusion to the advantage of an absolutely real world.

"We live in the illusion that the real is what is most lacking, when the opposite is the case: reality has reached its extreme. By dint of technical prowess, we have attained such a degree of reality and objectivity that we can even speak of an excess of reality, leaving us much more anxious and disconcerted than the lack of reality, which we were at least able to compensate for with utopia and the imaginary, while for the excess of reality there is no compensation or alternative."

"Modernity as a whole has had the advent of this real world as its goal, the freeing of men and of real energies, focused on the objective transformation of the world, and extending beyond all the illusions whose critical analysis nourished philosophy and praxis. Today the world is more real than we imagined. An inversion of real and rational data has been produced by their own fulfilment."

"With virtual reality and its consequences, we have gone over to technique as the ultimate phenomenon. Beyond this there is no reversibility, no traces, not even nostalgia for an earlier world. The hypothesis is that of irreversible disappearance, within the purest logic of the species. That of an absolutely real world in which we would have succumbed to the temptation of leaving no traces."

For Paul Virilio,[6] in *The Information Bomb,* the danger is not in information per se, but in interactivity and its dimension as global cybernetic feedback in real, instantaneous time.

5. Jean Baudrillard, *Le crime parfait,* Galilee, Paris, 1995.

6. Paul Virilio, *La bomba informática.*

"Interactivity is to information what radioactivity is to energy: a colossal force."

"Today's politicians don't understand technique, techno-scientific potential and globalization. The real power is held by the market's feudal barons: the Gateses, Murdochs and Soroses."

The computerization of procedures and the interaction implicit in them cannot, for all that, be rejected out of hand. The computerization of the world is neither good nor bad. It simply is. Utopian messages or regressing to anachronistic positions serve for nothing in an era in which ideas are slower moving than reality itself. In his essay "Fresh Conservatism," Roemer van Toorn[7] describes the general situation for a whole generation – of contemporary art and culture as it flails about between mere uncritical acceptance and the transcendence of today's hyper-real, alienating state of affairs. According to Van Toorn, the danger inherent in such a tightrope situation is that its apparently uninhibited, novel and innovatory attitude towards reality only masks the destructive potential of the forces Virilio describes. Therein lies the risk. There is no earlier formula on which to base oneself. The only possible innovative action, for all that, is to accept and assimilate the situation, not reject it. *And this by rediscovering the artistic dimension – a different dimension – the authentic dimension of postmodern architecture in the computer era, of a trans-aesthetic architecture,* of which the MVRDV scheme for VPRO is an implicit example. A dimension that can lead to curious effects, once the information on a building like the VPRO building has become diffused in the global information sphere. For example, what Van Toorn says about the building has great similarity to the plot of the first story appearing in the final part of the book.

"The insatiable communicator, like some contemporary globetrotter moving from one spectacle to another with his sensory feelers constantly alert, can find peace here."

Is Van Toorn referring in his commentary to Benito Navalon Molina, perhaps?[8]

In-form-ation

The main consequence of architecture as the interface of computerized reality is that there is a direct relationship between information and form.

In the postmodern project, or that of secondary computer abstraction, information "takes on" a shape, and this discov-

7. Roemer van Toorn, "Fresh Conservatism." Essay based on two conferences – at the Berlage Institute and the seminar *Poldergeist of the Cooper Union* – published in *Quaderns 219* "(Re)activa."

8. Compare with the story by Rafael Reig, "Preventive custology," in Jaime Salazar, *mvrdv at vpro*, ACTAR, Barcelona, 1998, p. 282.

ery is the most fascinating achievement of the architectural scheme implemented by MVRDV.

Unlike modern abstraction, which tends to disengage the form of any concrete syntactic meaning, postmodern secondary abstraction adopts the data of reality and transforms them into buildable matter. Architecture, then, is no longer a "knowing game of pure, light-filled volumes," but an "effective recycling of real data into buildable matter." Let's consider that possibility of converting information into matter. The idea is barely thirty years old. Our current reality is still in a hybrid state – up to a point it is still more mechanical than computerized – but there's nothing to suggest that the electronic computerization of the world might not increase to the point of taking the place of the mechanization which has typified the century that's drawing to a close.

There exists an infinite number of procedures which can serve as an example of that current hybrid condition. Let's consider, for instance, one example of physical transformation that is directly dependent on information: urban mobility. An application which may make architects think of the physical application certain computerized procedures can have on reality. When architects or town planners consider mobility, they do so by immediately thinking of some kind of physical support – a medium, in short – that renders such mobility possible. In support terms, the physical supports of a visible infrastructure would be considered along with roads, but also the invisible, and equally physical, infrastructures of the communication networks that are similarly responsible for transforming post industrial urban mobility.

That is a fact, no doubt about it. But it is also a fact that *our contemporary hybrid situation – one that is more ecologico-informational than mechanical – introduces new variables which combine with that physical idea* – visible or invisible – to make any investigation – and not just as physical action alone – of mobility more interesting.

Faced with the problems caused by saturation, consumerism, and environmental degradation, an alternative form of property develops. With car-sharing – or multiple ownership – the energy, economic and spatial expenditure of many cars with many individual owners is converted into less cars, plus the computer-generated information necessary for having access to them at any one moment. Unlike renting, a monthly subscription allows the co-owner to have access to a car in a series of fixed city locations at any moment of the year. Each shared car thus replaces five or ten individual cars.

A mass of combustion engines is converted into less engines, and into information. As for urban mobility, massive combustion gradually gives way to less combustion, backed up by electronics. What is now happening with the actual automobile engine is also happening with mobility as a social or urban factor. *The transformation of means from the "purely solid" to the "computerized" is obvious, even though it's difficult at times for us to understand this.* This transformation is important in that it enables us to entertain the possibility of understanding the design and production processes of architects as something non-linear.

A few years ago, Manuel de Landa[9] speculated on the possibility of using self-organizing logics for current traffic systems which wouldn't depend on vertical structures of centralized decision-making.

"The real application of artificial intelligence depends on an interaction with non-linear dynamics. This means that invisible computerization needs to be applied for the support and for the development of self-organizing networks of human production" (Manuel de Landa).

The authentically transformative dimension of MVRDV's "computer" approach to the design of architecture lies there. MVRDV designs with a *logic according to which complex reality is broken down into simple, quantifiable data which can be readily re-elaborated into buildable matter.* The design process, then, isn't rooted in voluntary modern abstraction, but in a computer – "binary" – abstraction of reality. The curious and fascinating thing about such a procedure, as Stan Allen[10] has pointed out, is that despite the apparently impersonal automation of the procedure, the result is not in the least automatic. Despite having "decodified complex reality into bits of LEGO" and having recombined it anew, there is no echo in the edified building of this process. In MVRDV's own commentaries, they wisely speak of contents, phenomena, never of the technical or procedural support which makes these possible. For example, in the case of VPRO the main challenge consisted in freshly "reproducing", in a new floorplan design, the whole social, environmental, ideological and operational content characteristic of VPRO, without complicating the result with architectonic "background noise." The infrastructural or

9. Manuel de Landa, "Homes: meshwork or hierarchy;" essay presented during the second edition of the symposium *Doors of perception.*

10. Stan Allen, "Artificial ecologies;" article on the work of MDRDV published in *El Croquis 86.*

technical support of the building is hidden as much as possible, in such a way that the architecture built provides a mainly "transparent" setting for VPRO's implicit content. Once again, the message is the medium.

There is a growing tendency for *postmodern design procedures to become more generic and to gradually detach themselves from their respective technical surroundings,* since the importance of the material means by which this is generated becomes ever more relative. VPRO is also an architectural hybrid, designed "by computer," but executed according to as-yet non-computerized procedures. Nevertheless, the media of construction – of the material production of the architecture – are being progressively computerized and added to the common fund of information on which the architect increasingly bases his work.

Haacke
It all began with a cube

Let's go back thirty-five years in time. To New York, and the summer of 1965. Hans Haacke, a former student of the Werkakademie in Kassel, has recently settled in the United States. Before that, he has spent two years in Paris. After collaborating on the Documenta in Kassel and forming part of the "Zero" group, he has met the most outstanding representatives of abstraction in early 1960s Paris. Yves Klein, among others. In Paris he has become completely convinced that the attempts of artists like Klein to renew the mystical dimension of abstract art are heroic but useless in relation to the reality in which he lives.

Haacke ends up rejecting, once and for all, the production of conventional artworks, works fixed by the artist's irrefutable subjectivity and presented in a gallery for the public's delectation. He begins to conceive the idea of elaborating systems, rather than works, which are open temporal processes. Systems in which time, energy and space assume complex, self-generating forms which do not begin functioning before being shown to the public. He dubs these "Realzeitsysteme," or "real-time systems."

He calls his first system "Condensation Cube." It is a static cube of plexiglass which he partially fills with water. With the difference of temperature between inside and outside, the walls of the transparent cube start to cover over with tiny droplets caused by the condensation of the water. "The condensation process continues," he writes, "and the cube's appearance slowly changes, without ever repeating itself. Its condition is similar to that of a living organism which reacts flexibly towards its environment. The image of the condensation cannot be predicted with any certainty; depending on statistical changes, it varies. I like that freedom." Haacke is increasingly taken with cybernetics as a model for understanding complex structures of behavior. Growing out of the military-scientific developments of the Cold War, this new science is devoted to studying information and assessing its use in artificial machines. "Condensation Cube" is the first of Haacke's "real time" physical systems. He will continue experimenting in this area until the end of the 1970s. "Wave" (1965), "Blue Sail" (1965), and "Circulation" (1969) are still physical systems of water or air. "Ant Coop" (1969) and "Chickens Hatching" (1969) are already animal systems. He writes about the aim of the systems:

"*...to create something which gives in to the environment, which reacts, changes, is unstable...*
...to create something indeterminate, which is always perceived differently, with a form that is not accurately predictable...
... to create something that cannot 'function' without the help of the environment...
... to create something that responds to light and to changes of temperature, is sensitive to air currents, with a functioning that depends on the forces of gravity...
... to create something that the 'spectator' can manipulate, can bring to life through his actions...
... to create something that evolves in time and allows the 'spectator' to experience time...
... to articulate something Natural ..."

Haacke gradually supplants his laboratory-style "real-time systems" – first physical, then natural and animal – with social and economic human systems. He first creates a series of installation-surveys called "Polls," and in 1971 invents a "real-time social system," called "Shapolsky et al. Manhattan Real Estate Holdings, as of 1 May 1971." This consists of an exhaustive study, using property registration data, of the speculative practices of a number of companies developing a Manhattan neighborhood. The situation criticized there drew attention to the fraudulent activities of the Shapolsky development group and their effects on the urban form of the Lower East Side.

This exhibition was intended for the Guggenheim Museum, but was mysteriously withdrawn six weeks before its opening.[11]

Hans Haacke's "real-time systems" are, then, a first stab at making formal use of information. Haacke helps us grasp the potential of understanding information as the possible raw material of form, but also of understanding that *beyond its apparent transparency, the use of data throws up readings that are much more polemical than what actual artistic practice appears to show. Once again, the meanings derived from the merely apparent mechanical use of information go way beyond the activity itself, and right there is where the trans-artistic idea of Haacke' s art, or the architecture of mvrdv, lies in wait.*

mvrdv

Twenty-six years after Haacke's "real-time social system," Winy Maas, a member of MVRDV, measures the effects of town planning for the masses and calls these "datascapes."[12] This involves carefully observing the social, economic, speculative, and other causes that generate specific changes in urban form.

"These phenomena occur according to apparently disorganized patterns whose almost total chaos possesses hidden logics enabling "densities" to emerge from among the immense and indifferent mass of objects. Such densities are revealed on being sublimated in a set of given circumstances or maximized limitations are assumed in advance. Densities that emerge in the form of the data landscape below them."

MVRDV's architecture has already been analyzed on a number of occasions. In their work, MVRDV openly reject artistic subjectivity and replace it with scientific analysis. Their approach – more analytic than artistic – to the designing of architecture has been considered, in all its forms, as basically an authorial option. Different and more suggestive than others, but authorial all the same. This is true in part, but it is clear that it has in turn opened a door onto a different kind of architectural method. This is not just the work of more architects, but an architecture of a different – partly different – kind to authorial architecture. And with it, a door has also opened onto the possibility of tackling the complexities of the processes of current reality in a non-linear way. For MVRDV, reality is already sufficiently complex in itself, without adding further levels of complexity to it on which to base the purposive activity of

11. This installation was finally presented in the group exhibition *Art without Limit,* Memorial Art Gallery, University of Rochester, NY, March 1972.

12. Winy Maas, "Datascape," text published in *FARMAX*, 010, Rotterdam, 1998.

architecture. If we look at the current debate, what we have before us is a vast panorama of ongoing self-justification.

The basic reasons for planning go: the more complex it is, the better. The rationale behind a work is almost as important as the work itself. In an essay on MVRDV, Stan Allen pinpointed what he considers the fundamental reasons for the creative power of their work. Its force resides precisely in the lack of force their theory has. That is, in the absence of theory. In the automatic irrefutability of their procedures. Instead of going back to the origins of the universe to explain their work – which would amount to demonstrating a classical modern ambition – it suffices for them not to have a theoretical explanation for what they do: for them reality suffices to explain it. Winy Maas is proud of this. Any of the forms "processed" in the seemingly mechanical elaboration of real data is equal in complexity to the forms created personally by any of the architects who make up the current "star system." Despite there being an evident ambition behind this, such an ambition is transformed. The architecture of the information era is based on the dissolution of the architectural message in the actual medium. There is no established aesthetic, or ordained typological process, or a priori determining factor. The only determining factors arise from the specific data of reality. Data such as the physical limitations of the building regulations, the particular characteristics of the future users – many of which can be quantatively analyzed – energy or lighting factors, etc. The design proceeds "from below," starting with the expedient of reality, instead of proceeding "from above;" that is, from the author's interpretive subjectivity. One of the basic decisions of "real-time systems" lies in establishing the boundary of the system, to what point within this it is permissible to intervene. As important as the system per se is the physical boundary within which this system is capable of functioning.

Haacke' s transparent cube defines the terms of the system in the same way that mvrdv's boundaries of maximum occupation define the terms for the development of their "real-time" design for the new VPRO headquarters in Hilversum.

Interaction
The medium and the message

One of the ideas worth re-examining is the object-based conception of architecture. The most obvious and unquestioned idea behind architecture is the fact that the act of architecting is directed towards creating built objects, buildings. Even this book, which sets out to partly question that idea, focuses on a building in order to do this. As mentioned earlier, we understand architecture in terms of objects and thus also in terms of the individuals who created those objects. Despite the fact that such an evaluation or historical vision hardly corresponds to reality, the negating of that idea can still provoke discussions of the most violent kind.

First let us establish a parallel notion, one which may shed light on this somewhat paradoxical affirmation: the notion of the medium and the message. This idea was intuited by Marshall McLuhan,[13] who was led to affirm that "the medium is the message," a sublime paradox which, although restricted to communication, is useful for defining any productive act in our own information era. Through it, generically, McLuhan definitively weakened the distinction between the main focus of attention – the figure, let's say – and the seemingly irrelevant setting – the background – in which a given action unfolds. Message and medium, figure and ground: the one is the other. Translated to architecture, the message – the object, the figure, the building in short – is no longer understood as an object in itself, but rather the medium in which this is generated; that is, reality. One of the characteristics, then, of postmodern architecture is *the progressive dissolution of the architectonic message – the design – in the medium – namely, reality*. The VPRO building may be considered as a form which is not defined by formal invariables, but by real variables. At least such a dimension is what makes it extraordinary, beyond the normal run of things. At least in part, this turns it into something non-artistic, something not submitted to the subjectivity of the artist-architect. And this is true in part. Within the limitations imposed on it by its time, the building for VPRO is not exactly a building. Ideally, we might consider it the transformation, in built matter, of the medium formed by VPRO. That is to say, it wouldn't be a built object in the usual sense, but a process open to the non-linearity of synergies which may arise, over and above the decisions of its authors. In subjecting part of the form of the design to statistical development, the "message" of the building is much closer to the VPRO "medium" that has generated it.

13. The original paradox is by Marshall McLuhan (published in Marshall & Eric McLuhan, *Laws of Media,* 1988), but its translation into parameters related to a specific contemporary architectural sensitivity is by Manuel Gausa. The paradoxes mentioned along the process of the elaboration of the VPRO project are based, above all, in his lucid reflections.

Katya Sander, Ashley Hunt

revolutions per minute

THINGS TO DO:
1) Locate yourself. Look around. Read the walls around you, the spaces you move through, read the messages which move through you; address you.

3) Note the Revolutions: The French, The North/South, The East/West, The Soft, The Flower, The Wall, The Peoples. [Sorry, I was on the other line, can you say that again please?] The French revolution. The streets. The bodies. Citizenship. Democracy. Enlightment. Science. Descartes. Body vs. mind. The fighting. A rupture, a split, a difference. (revolution)

2) Who are the people?

4) Look up the word "concatenate." Then point to the line between democracy and free-market capitalism: differentiate, delineate, un-tangle please;

5) Recognize the desire to resist; imagine thoughts, words, images, tools;

6) Word: Take back the term "popular," distinguish between popular as 'widely appealling' and popular as 'of, for and by "the people."'

7) Recognize that which is articulated or represented as such, but is not Resistance.

8) "Make sure the message gets out there, is understood, and believed;"

9) Escape the "revolution;"

10) Join the revolution;

Look around, read the billboards, watch tv. Find yourself surrounded by words of resistance, situated in a battle, adressed as a warrior, a pirate, a revolutionary. Voices whisper about your mission, and images of faces desire your power to resist, to fight, your anger – and where it can take you; it's potentiality. Locate yourself positioned between fronts, apparently supporting one and fighting the other, but also running on a treadmill in Bally's 24 Hour Fitness Crunch Club, between the mirrors accumulating an army of selves, movements and machines, a boot camp, military training, precision, staying ready in highest alert, always waiting for a final battle. Our discontent, frustration and unrest, our desire to move, to push, to pull and shout aloud is talked of and talked to; narrated into a web of images of revolution to hail us, to capitalize on our resistance... Resist aging, fight the weight of your body; that which you're being t(s)old ties you down, makes you tired, grows ugly, wears out like make-up and a bad shirt; that which positions you in these rooms, this language and this mess which you never asked for in the first place, that which makes you hungry, sad, sick and desiring – contingent: your body. Battleground and enemy in one; the site of what you struggle over as well as the struggle over you. It will eventually betray you, it will age, change, allow diseases and finally die. The body as oppressor. [but it is also what makes you strong, the desire of that body will connect you to me and we will dance in the dark, behind the garage]. Fight for freedom, we're told. "I shop therefore I fly." (Newark International Airport, dutyfree)

B:
[does it again] listen: talk to me, i'm

THE IMAGE
An ad is running on tv. A voiceover is talking about how important it is to "get your message out there," to have it heard by people, to have them understand and believe it. It is for some internet company. The footage is of Martin Luther King speaking. It is his Lincoln Memorial Address, but the Washington Mall in front of him is empty, there is nobody to hear him. Then the internet company arrives, and the Mall becomes full; crowded. His voice is now heard under the voiceover. "I have a dream." It is important to get your message out there, that people get it, understand it and believe in it, the voiceover repeats, over the dream. (time)

A:
now that we know about bodies and minds... well, not what bodies and minds are or how we define bodies and minds, but how they are defined for us, put into language, split us and play against us, around us and throughout us

B:
who, what, wait

A:
body defined

B:
wait, by whom, what body?

A:
as that which can be wounded, stopped, contained, exposed or hidden, usurped, nourished or killed. mind as that which can be coerced, frightened, intimidated, disciplined, co-opted, silenced, misled, tempted. stories around us, everywhere, tell us, invent us: our bodies and minds defined as two, apart, for an instrumental purpose – it renders them caught up in each other...

B:
[does it again]

THE REVOLUTION

A huge b/w billboard leans over the highway. "reVOLVOlution" it says. Nothing else. There is a thin shadow, a profile of a black car, hidden in the dark.

The revo(vo)lution is luring, threatening, almost here, only a syllable away. It surrounds me, hides inside language, even.

A: [continues] ... it short-circuits the two, makes them work against each other, it catches discontent, frustration & restlessness in a loop, and it internalizes oppression(s) into their own actions and beliefs, into the very fiber of their identity and desire. (fascism)

THE RIGHT

Two young women are sitting on the backseat of a luxurious car. Leather seats and champagne. Outside it is night. They are only wearing makeup, high heals, slippers and bras. "The right to be the woman I really am" is written under them. They laugh. It is an ad for some underwear company. "The woman I really am." I have been granted that right. I am still not quite sure by whom. Am I an aggregate of rights?

B:

[stops them] you talk with parentheses. who does all this? language? what language – spoken where, and by whom? i tell you: language won't hurt you, it makes no difference. (believe me)

THE LANGUAGE

"Can I get MTV from kissing?" a billboard asks from the side of a public phonebooth. "When you have MTV it feels as if everybody knows." "3 out of 4 people have MTV and don't know it." "Everyone should know about MTV." The writing is in huge white, informative letters over images of young, ordinary people.

"Language is a virus from outer space" William Borroughs has noted. An invasion, a disease. MTV's co-option of the AIDS-awareness movement not only seeks to align the tv-channel with one of the biggest popular resistance movements in recent times, it also narrates itself as that which should be resisted. It is ironic [I know] and at the expense of AIDS-awareness campaigns – refered to as if they are already history, a revolution told; a past. At the same time MTV takes pleasure (and presumes that we do too) in threatening to take us over, revolutionize our bodies, as if it is a force which we cannot escape but only maybe avoid temporarily. And in being that which leaflets, flyers, teachers, and education seem to warn against. (IwantmyMTV) "Abstinence is the best defence against MTV." Fearful sexuality. Substitute it with its image: The rhythms, the sweating, the skin, the close-ups, the sighing voices, and pumping base, the lush interiors and seductive gazes, the lips, the touching, suggesting, the movements; we become patterns, surfaces, soldiers, animals, machines. Language as intercourse, the body as a sign – a sign in crisis; defected. (desiring)

B:
[one more time, admit it] do it again, show me again, around that/over there

A:
a body in a space. a body positioned. a body as part of a larger social body.... you see, a social body includes both the powerful and the powerless within it, not some inside and simply some out. slaves in a slave society are not outside the social body but are essential to it, they are constitutive of the slave society itself and all of its institutions, laws and beliefs. their resistance is a condition of RESPONSE, their desires and needs buttressed and circumscribed by the mechanisms which guarantee their oppression, including keeping them from recognizing their resistance as RESISTANCE.

B:
[you want to turn it off?] oh you know, i don't know, i don't think it's – isn't it the same in america? and besides, even if i had i wouldn't

THE ENLIGHTMENT
A web company, offering to webbers "free" participation and membership in a "web community," hailing itself as "The Only Truly Democratic Community on the Web;" the only cost being that each page is littered with flickering, blinking advertisement banners. It is a hypercapitalist endeavor, not only because there was "capitalizing" happening, inserting marketing into community space and our social organization, but because the very existence of this community is, in the first place, simply to generate consumers for the advertized clients. The notion of democracy serves more as a familiar trope than

a socio-organizational principle, and the virtual appearance of a community is merely a vehicle for mapping commerce. The image is Delacroix' painting of Mother Courage leading the mobilized downtrodden French in courage and power over the barricades. The caption reads: "The last time the people had this much say in their community, heads rolled."

A:
such a split of body and mind leaves us nonetheless individuals and individuals only, alienated and blind to the larger social body of which we are a part. it is not that we are detached from this social body, but that we do not recognize how we are attached, or for that matter, that we are.

Erik Scheldon

Solar Surrounded

Photo Electro Chemical (PEC) solar cell technology is young and relatively inexperienced compared to the well-known silicon technology. The main principle behind the PEC solar cell is identical with the photosynthesis of plants; the transformation of solar energy and CO_2 into nourishment.

Introduction to the PEC solar cell technology

The history of the PEC technology can be dated back several decades but most important contributions to the technology came in the last eight years.

The ongoing activities at Solar Energy Centre Denmark aim at developing the already known technology of PEC cells and contributing new technology to develop a cell with a higher performance and an improved durability.

The main principle behind the PEC solar cell is identical with the photosynthesis of plants, when they transform solar energy and CO_2 into nourishment. The PEC cell is not to be

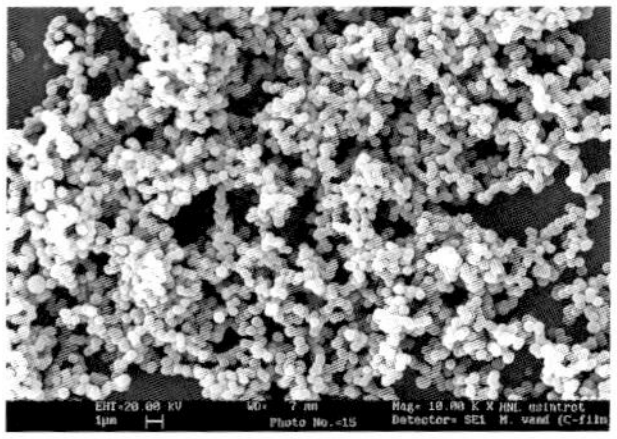

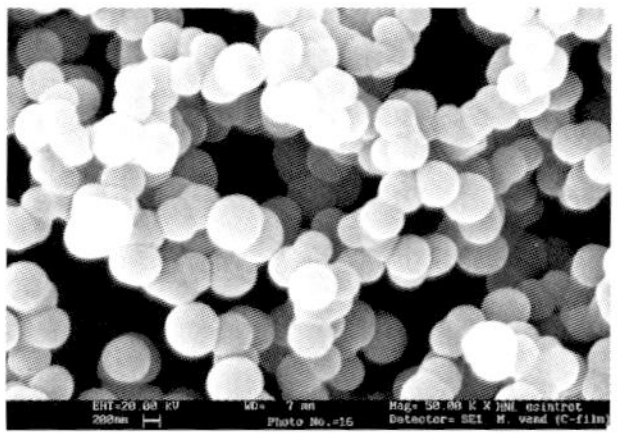

Fig.1 and Fig. 2
Anatase particles

confused with normal photosynthesis due to a decisive difference. The organic photosynthesis takes place in material in constant decomposition and re-establishing under digestion of energy. Whereas the PEC cell has no organic components and it must not be re-established in its lifetime.

Anatase particles

In a PEC cell, solar radiation is absorbed by a special synthetic dye, which can be optimized to catch photons of a certain frequency and wavelength.

The price for the materials in the PEC cell can be reduced considerably compared to the traditional mono- and polycrystalline cells.

The ongoing activities in the Danish Solar Energy Centre aim at developing already known technology of PEC cells and contributing new technology to develop a cell with a higher performance and an improved durability. The objective is to create a cell whose performance is comparable to commercial crystalline products but with a lower production price. The aim is also to concentrate on using technologies available to a larger part of the industry than is the case with the present PV production technology. This is necessary to ensure a larger dissemination of solar cells as more companies have the possibility to start production and through increased competition, contribute to ensuring the development of the cell and reducing the price.

Working principle

In principle, the PEC cell works like an approximation to photosynthesis. When a photon hits the dye, energy is transferred to the dye molecule thus obtaining a higher state of energy corresponding to the band gap of the semiconductor, TiO_2. An electron is thus transferred from the adsorbed dye via the semiconductor to the back contact, SnO_2. TiO_2 is a well-known material, e.g. as a filling agent in paint and toothpaste. TiO_2 can assume different crystalline structures. The porous anatase form is used in PEC cells. The dye is usually a Ruthenium based complex adsorbed onto the semiconductor surface. The dye is regenerated by an I-/I3- electrolyte. The back contact is coated with a catalyst serving as promoter for the reoxidation of the electrolyte. The cycle is completed and the current is generated (see the illustration of working principle below).

Advantages of PEC:

Inexpensive materials
Minimal initial investments
Simple technology
Attractive cost/efficiency ratio
Extremely flexible design
Potentially attractive building element

Schematic illustration of the PEC solar cell:

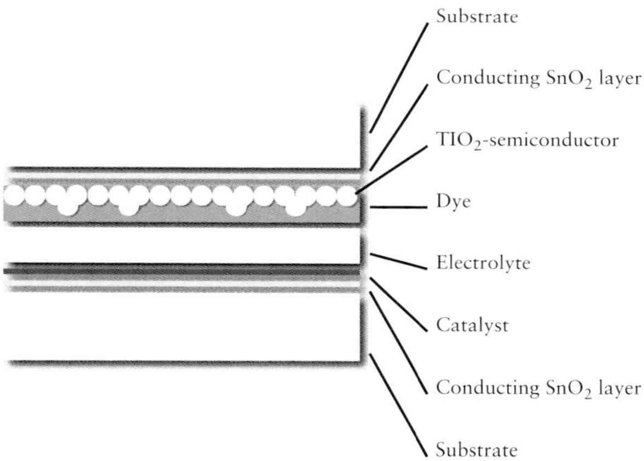

Working principle:

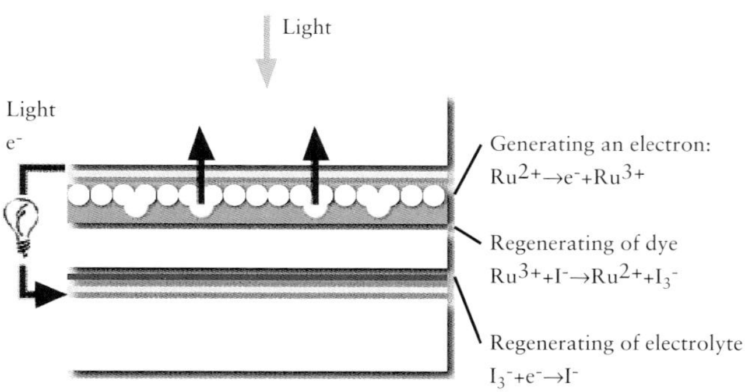

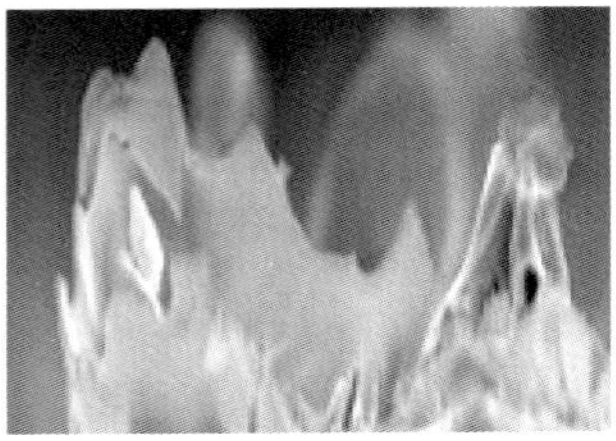

Fig. 3
Anatase film from the side.

Research activities

Key research activities at the Solar Energy Centre concentrate on making the Photo Electrochemical Cell more appealing to industry – in terms of manufacturing – by using well-known techniques.

Sealing: Development of a sealing technique to prevent cell degradation and to demonstrate an acceptable effective lifetime.

Manufacturing techniques: Development of manufacturing processes based on techniques well known to industry and ensuring a competitive manufacturing price of a cell with an acceptable efficiency. Initial manufacturing investments are minor, making the PEC cells attractive for industrial development.

Development of a design providing the cell with architectural merits in building integration compared to conventional solar cells due to the flexible design of the PEC cells:

Due to the construction of the cell as a sandwich of two pieces of glass, luminous intensity and light distribution can be controled. Individual cells or modules can be connected in larger systems where light, diffuse light and shadow effects can be used purposely. Thus, a multifunctional building envelope can be created based on "guiding daylight."

Kurt Schilcher

Water Structuring: Dynamics and Order in Liquid Water

Introduction

There is no doubt that water is one of the most important liquids on earth. It is not only fundamental for our planet's climate in regulating the temperature of the inorganic surface of the earth, it is also fundamental for the existence of life and the evolution of life processes. Of all known liquids, water is probably the most studied and least understood, although a lot of physical properties are accepted as international standards, e.g. its triple point, density, mass, and viscosity (Franks, 1972-1982).

The availability of water and its utilization were also fundamental prerequisites for the development of human civilization. The existence and the outstanding significance of many former cultures, e.g. the famous "very advanced civilizations" in Mesopotamia or in Ancient Egypt, were a direct consequence of the rivers Euphrates, Tigris, and Nile, which provided the people with all essential materials to survive. Human

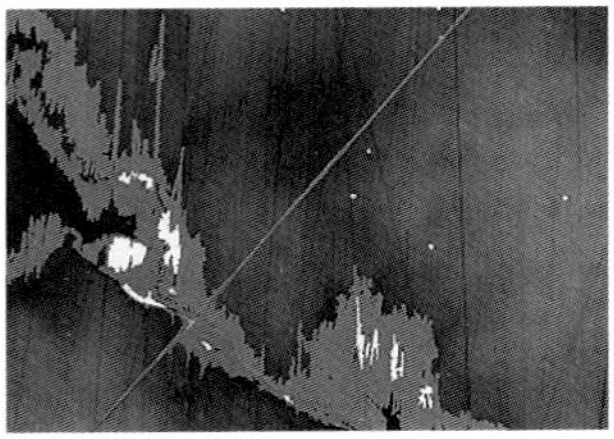

Fig. 1
Harmonices mundi - variatio I
motif: microstructures on polished precious metal – chromate-treated, magnification: 2000 X

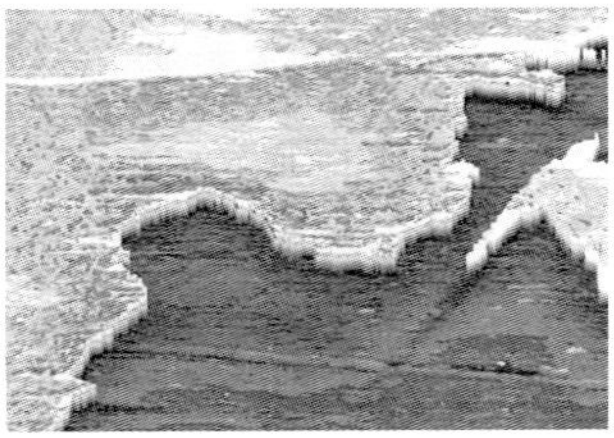

Fig. 2
Shimmering mirrors motif: surface of a chromate-plated steel tube, magnification: approx. 2.700 X

life is closely related to water. Its influence on cultural evolution is undisputed. Water forms the outward appearance of the world. Its effects may be very different; sometimes they are of a destroying nature, sometimes they are life-supporting. Water exerts force. "Water is force." This slogan was the motto of a separate exhibition in Klaus (Upper Austria) devoted to the life and works of Viktor Schauberger on the occasion of the Upper Austrian Landesausstellung 1997. Schauberger was one of the first who recognized that liquid water may be considered as a special 'carrier of information'. The basis of his ideas were the turbulences in liquid water. From a technical point of view, turbulences in water are well described by the laws of hydrodynamics, which explain the dynamic properties of liquid water within a broad range, from simple laminar flow conditions to complex chaotic situations. All dynamic behaviour of liquid water is closely related to water ordering and water structuring. So, for a better understanding of whether turbulences or other external influences have a net effect on the gain or loss of information on liquid water, it is useful to treat this question from a physical point of view. I will start with structure-determining factors and the energies associated with hydrogen bonding. They meet the basic requirements of forming water clusters in liquid water.

Data and facts from physical chemistry

The water molecule consists of one oxygen atom and two hydrogen atoms, each of them separated by 0.099 nm from the centre of mass of the oxygen atom. The three atoms form a bond angle of 104.67° in vapor and 109.47° in ice (Némethy and Scheraga, 1962). The molecule shows a distinct polar charge distribution that can be modeled by four charges located along the four arms of a tetrahedron, where hydrogen bonds actually take place with an intermolecular distance (z1) of 0.276 nm to the adjacent water molecules in ice IH (hexagonal type of crystallization – 'normal ice'). In liquid water z1 varies between 0.285-0.3 nm (Morgan et al., 1938; Némethy and Scheraga, 1962; Rao, 1972). These hydrogen bonds give water the typical and unique properties which are often designated as "anomalies" in literature, such as large cohesive energy or latent heat, high melting point, high boiling point and high heat capacity. Other consequences of hydrogen bonding are the high surface tension and the ability to suspend colloidal particles and biological structures.

The definition of hydrogen bond is rather complex, because it is often based on the actual used operational criterion. Pimentel and McClellan (1960) give a very general description of hydrogen bond. They define hydrogen bond as an interaction between a functional group A-H and an atom or a group of atoms B, when (a) there is evidence of bond formation (association or chelation), and (b) there is evidence that this new bond linking A-H---B involves the hydrogen atom already bonded to A. For the system water and from a more physical standpoint, hydrogen bonds come from the attraction of the slightly positive hydrogen atom of one water molecule by the free electronic doublet of the oxygen atom on a second water molecule. It is a typical dipole-dipole interaction, although other interactions are also involved (delocalization energy, dispersion and exchange repulsion) with resulting bond energies ranging from 3-5 kcal/mole (see table). These energies make

Table:
Energies concerning hydrogen bonding.

Methods	**ΔH (kcal/mole)**	**References**
Statistical analysis	3.57	Némethy and Scheraga (1962)
Near-infrared spectroscopy (experiment)	3.7-4.5	Buijs and Choppin (1963)
Second virial coefficient (experiment)	3.5 (in vapor)	Kell and McLaurin (1969)
Density (experiment and theory)	2.6	Grjotheim and Krogh-Moe (1954)
Raman spectroscopy (experiment)	2.8	Walrafen (1966)
Atomic force microscopy (experiment)	2.82	Schilcher (1997)

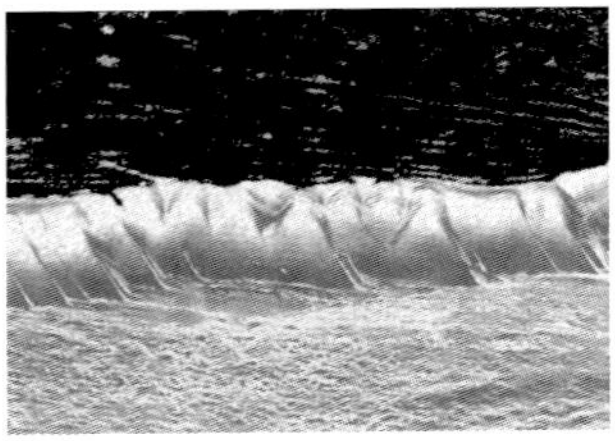

Fig. 3
The sea of the scales, motif: microstructures on the surface of a scale of Chromis sp., magnification: approx. 1.300 X

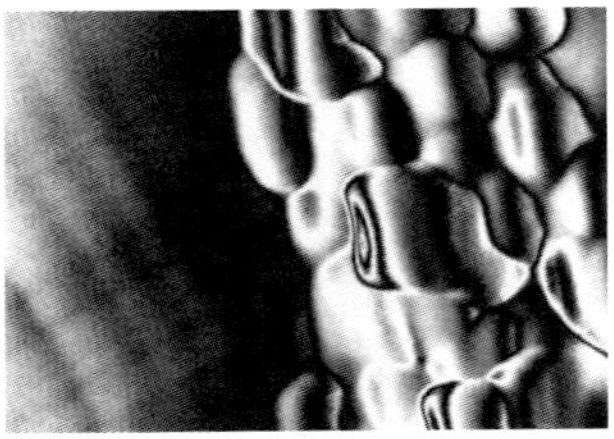

Fig. 4
Borderland, motif: zinc-plated sheet steel – phosphate-treated, magnification: 80.000 X

hydrogen bonds so sensitive to thermal fluctuations and as a consequence so important in biology. From Rayleigh, scattering the typical life time (τ_{HB}) of a hydrogen bond in liquid water was determined to be smaller than 1 ps at a temperature of 25° C (Lüdemann, 1993).

So far, no exact theory of liquid water has appeared, so there are no reliable energy values associated with the breakage of one hydrogen bond in liquid water. Several estimates have been made, all ranging from 3 to 5 kcal/mole for a hydrogen bond (Pimentel and McClellan, 1960), but there is much confusion, because they all refer to different processes. Another problem is the difficulty in deducing thermodynamic parameters like Gibbs free energy (ΔG) or entropy (ΔS) from experiments and calculations. Till today, ΔS values have not been experimentally amenable for the transition: non-hydrogen-bonded water to hydrogen-bonded water. Only modified enthalpy values (ΔH) or energy values (E_H) that do not account for the order of the system are measured directly (see table) and thus, an exact analysis of all thermodynamic parameters cannot be performed.

New very promising approaches came from high-resolution microscopy. Force mode measurements with a scanning force microscope (SFM) (Binnig et al., 1986) in liquid water demonstrated that water can be ordered between surfaces, thus giving rise to the release of the smallest water clusters into the bulk solution. The corresponding gain in chemical potential resulted in a normalized energy value E_H of 2.82 kcal/mole (Schilcher, 1997, see table).

Water ordering

Water shows different behaviour in terms of order and structuring in bulk solution and at a surface. Bulk water ordering as now understood is closely related to the "flickering cluster" concept of Frank and Wen (1957), who postulated the formation of hydrogen bonds in liquid water as a cooperative phenomenon. Several bonds are formed and broken simultaneously, thus producing short-living ($\tau < 10^{-10}$ s) clusters of hydrogen-bonded regions surrounded by non-hydrogen-bonded water monomers. The cluster formation may be interpreted in terms of a resonance scheme with the surrounding unstructured water and other clusters in the bulk solution. The nature of the denser, unstructured component is not well specified. Maybe, it contains monomeric water or clusters of a lower order (Jeffrey and Saenger, 1991).

Water is also ordered on surfaces, especially on oxides, and this form of ordering is called bound or surface water. Bound water is a consequence of strong chemisorption of water molecules induced by hydroxylation of the oxide surface. A first layer of water molecules is stably anchored onto the solid via OH-groups, and this first oriented layer in turn imposes order in the surrounding liquid by intermolecular hydrogen bonding. Polarization effects of the solid surface and the geometry of the lattice may strengthen this ordering process. Onto this primary hydration shell, further structured (hydration) shells physisorb vertically via hydrogen bonds with a characteristic decay length (λ) and a characteristic coefficient (β), which may be interpreted as a measure for the loss of order. This mechanism corresponds to polymerization of surface water. The number of the ordered water layers is very controversial in the literature. Values range from a few layers to more than one thousand layers (Bérubé and de Bruyn, 1968).

The addition of electrolytes to water destroys the order of "flickering clusters" as well as that of physisorbed water layers. This change is accompanied by an increasing entropy of the solution. This disrupting or structure-breaking action relates to the orienting influence exerted by the electrical field on the adjacent water molecules, which will constitute a primary hydration shell of the ion. The competition between this shell and the tetrahedral-coordinating influence of the outer unperturbed water molecules creates a 'thawed region' of thickness d separating the primary hydration shell from the water clusters (Frank and Evans, 1945; Buijs and Choppin, 1963; Bérubé and de Bruyn, 1968). The same mechanism is completely transferable to the structure-breaking action of the physisorbed water columns in the transition region: *surface water* $\Leftrightarrow$ *bulk water,* thus effectively decreasing the number of the physisorbed water layers. At high salt concentrations the physisorbed region will be completely destroyed. Typical structure breaking ions are Na^+, K^+, Cs^+, and Cl^-. In contrast to the structure breaking function of many ions there are some ions which promote structure ordering beyond the first hydration shell. In these cases, which occur with small and highly charged ions (Mg^{2+}, Ca^{2+}), the charge separation in the outer molecules of the first or second hydration shell would favor the accumulation of water molecules via hydrogen bonds, thus promoting cluster growth. The net effect is an increase in the degree of order.

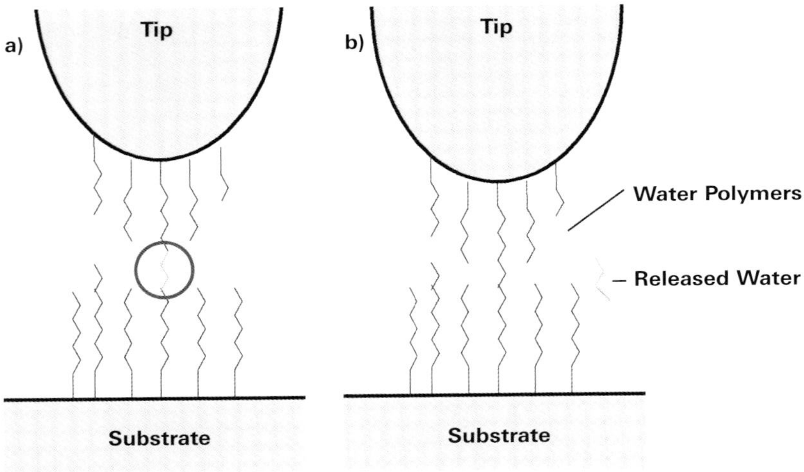

Fig. 5
Atomic force microscopy in force mode operation. The tip-substrate interaction during trace induces surface water release into bulk water.

Two opposing, protruding water polymers (blue) are connected (encircled region). Before connection (a) all water is forced by the surfaces into order, after connection (b) a water trimer (cyan) is released into bulk water, thus resulting in a smallest residual force value F_1.

The SFM works like an "atomic gramophone." A sample is raster-scanned laterally (image mode) or vertically (force mode) by a piezoelectric actuator with subnanometer accuracy under a sharp tip positioned at one end of a cantilever. Forces between the tip and the sample surface cause the cantilever to bend or to deflect. These fine deflections are detected optically and transformed into a map of surface topography with at least atomic resolution. The force mode is a special mode, where the lateral scan defining x and y voltages of the piezo are held constant, and only the z voltage is ramped. As a result of this operation, the piezo moves the sample up (trace) and down (retrace) with constant speed, and the corresponding cantilever deflection is measured, which can be directly transformed into forces using Hooke's law.

Force mode measurements with SFM clearly confirmed the suggestions known from the literature and gave new insight into the molecular mechanism that actually takes place when two surfaces, each of them hydrated with surface water, come into close contact. The following model of structure-forming interaction could be drawn from the data. The geometry of the hydration shells strongly depends on the lattice parameters of the underlying surface. If the lattice constant of the surface is equal to the lattice constant of ice IH, for example, the water will arrange to a compact 3-D crystal. This type of water crystallization takes place on mica (Schilcher, 1997). Silicon cannot structure water to a compact 3-D crystal. Because of its different lattice geometry, it will force water to arrange in flexible, structured water columns of different length on its surface. During approach, when the sample moves to the tip, the opposing water columns that are adsorbed on each surface link to a connective column, thus giving rise to the release of smallest water clusters (trimers) into the bulk solution. The corresponding gain in chemical potential results in an attrative force that can be observed in force mode operation. In the formation of one single connective bond, water is transferred from an ordered state into an unordered state. Thus the observed minimal quantal force value F_1 may be attributed to energy values EH of the amount of released water at the level of hydrogen bonds. The normalized measured EH value was 2.82 kcal/mole, as already mentioned, which was in good accordance with literature data (typically 2.6-4.5 kcal/mole, see table) using the assumption that water is only released in water clusters of three linearly arranged water molecules. The dimension of the cluster size (0.8 nm) closely resembled the observed correlation length of 0.6-1.1 nm of liquid water (van Oss, 1988). There were other evidences for the release of water trimers but they are very sophisticated and would go beyond the scope of this article (for a detailed analysis see Schilcher, 1997).

Force mode also revealed the influence of salts with respect to order degradation. The addition of electrolytes destroyed water ordering effectively, thus reducing the observables to a negligible value.

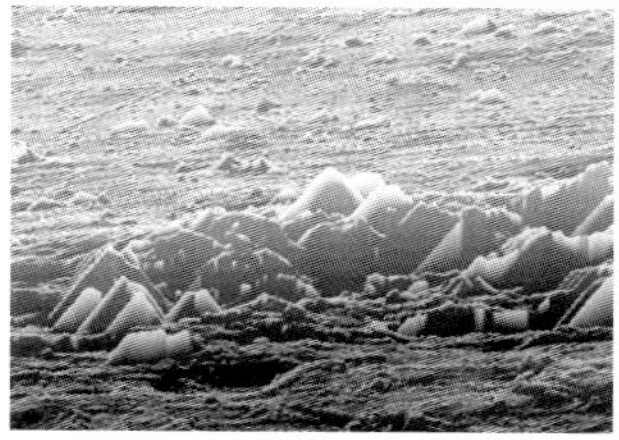

Fig. 6
Like the surface of Mars (April 1st, 2000) ..., motif: microstructures on the surface of a yoghurt beaker, magnification: approx. 2.700 X

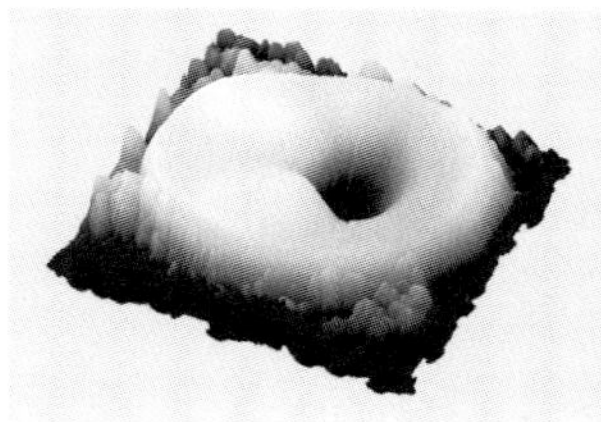

Fig. 7
Sweet dreams of Transsylvania – phantasia no. I ..., motif: human red blood cell (erythrocyte) smeared onto a glass cover slide, magnification: approx. 4.000 X

Summary and conclusion

Water is a very fascinating substance with a lot of remarkable properties, many of them still remaining obscure to today. Numerous people, serious scientists as well as water diviners and "esoteric-trained" people, study this liquid very intensively with different methods, each having different successes. But till today, no one has been able to give a clear and convincing answer about its information-relevant properties. The literature is full of special water types and many strange and curious paths are tread to mark their particular advantages. The border between reality and belief is often a very narrow one.

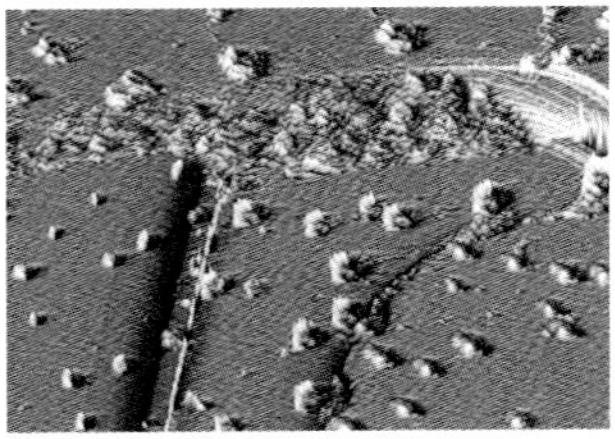

Fig. 8
A spine or graphic variations on a painful theme ..., motif: microstructures on a spine of Diadema sp., magnification: 5.000 X

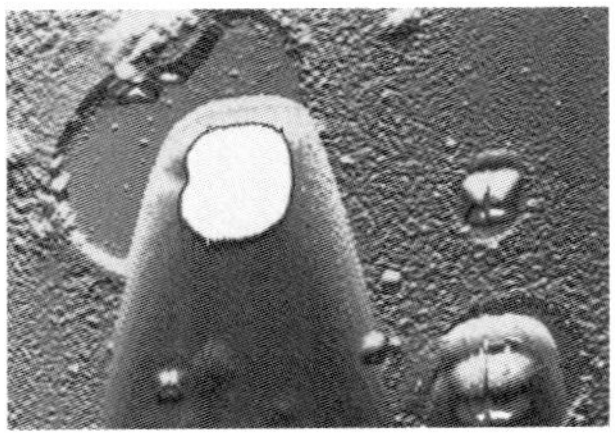

Fig. 9
In the shadow of Persephone ..., motif: microstructures on a polyethylene film, magnification: 2.700 X

The aim of this article is to focus on the inherent "dynamic" nature of liquid water at ambient and steady-state conditions, when it is not agitated – dynamic in terms of a fluctuating "living organism" according to the "flickering clusters" concept of Frank and Evans, and not in terms used in hydrodynamics. Liquid water is not a static liquid, it is a very dynamic entity, continuously forming and reforming water clusters at a timescale of picoseconds. Order and disorder permanently alternate in space and time. Maybe this is the real mystery of water.

Appendix
There is another form of (visual) art that deals with the problem of the reception of reality in a similar way. Its name is mantography and its basis are informations arising from high resolution microscopy. Mantography is a special form of reality art that aims to recognize and realize the inherent character and the substantial properties of the material objects in our world by the creative processing and designing of microscopical images. It tries to give an answer to the following basic questions: Are the models which we are making of our world and its surroundings more real than reality itself? What can we ultimately perceive? The reality itself, or a model of reality, or a model of the model of reality? How far may we rely on scientific research? Do we get caught in a net of scientific wishful thinking?

The name mantography originates from Manto, a daughter of the blind prophet Teiresias (Greek mythology – Theban legendary cycle), who was capable of seeing the "nonvisible" and foretelling it in a visionary manner. Following this mythological model mantography tries to open the "inner eye" for the real things in our world by drawing its secrets from a microscopical point of view and imparting its messages in a similar visionary way. As a source of inspiration, images from scanning probe microscopy (atomic force microscopy, scanning tunneling microscopy) are used which are individually processed by special PC-supported graphical software to obtain their typical mantographic character.

References

Y. G. Bérubé and P. L. de Bruyn, *J. Colloid and Interface Sci.*, 28, 1968, pp. 92-105.

G. Binnig, C. F. Quate and C. Gerber, *Phys. Rev. Lett.*, 56, 1986, pp. 930.

K. Buijs and G. R. Choppin, *J. Chem. Phys.*, 39, 1963, pp. 2035-2041.

K. Buijs and G. R. Choppin, *J. Chem. Phys*,. 39, 1963, pp. 2042-2050.

H. S. Frank and M. J. Evans, *J. Chem. Phys.*, 13, 1945, pp. 507.

H. S. Frank and W.-Y. Wen, *Discussions Faraday Soc.*, 24, 1957, pp. 133-140.

F. Franks (ed.), *Water. A Comprehensive Treatise.*, vol. 1-7, Plenum Press, New York, 1972-1982.

K. Grjotheim and J. Krogh-Moe, *Acta Chem. Scand.*, 8, 1954, pp. 1193-1202

G. A. Jeffrey and W. Saenger, *Hydrogen Bonding in Biological Structures*, Springer Verlag, New York, 1991.

G. S. Kell and G. E. McLaurin, *J. Chem. Phys.*, 51, 1969, pp. 4345-4352.

H.-D. Lüdemann, in: *Water and Biological Macromolecules* (E. Westhof, ed.), *(Topics in Molecular and Structural Biology, Vol. 17)*, Macmillan, 1993, pp. 45-59.

J. Morgan and B. E. Warren, *J. Chem. Phys.*, 6, 1938, pp. 666-673.

G. Némethy and H. A. Scheraga, *J. Chem. Phys.*, 36, 1962, pp. 3382-3400.

G. Némethy and H. A. Scheraga, *J. Chem. Phys.*, 36, 1962, pp. 3401-3417.

G. C. Pimentel and A. L. McClellan, *The Hydrogen Bond*, W. H. Freeman and Company, San Francisco and London, 1960.

C. N. R. Rao, in *Water. A Comprehensive Treatise* (F. Franks, ed.) vol. 1, Plenum Press, New York., 1972, pp. 93-114.

K. Schilcher, *Forces due to surface water measured by force microscopy. Consequences for anchoring biological cells to surfaces,* thesis, Linz, 1997.

C. J. van Oss, M. K. Chaudhury, and R. J. Good, *Chem. Rev.*, 88, 1988, pp. 927-941.

G. E. Walrafen, *J. Chem. Phys.*, 44, 1966, pp. 1546-1558.

Jane Schul

Plants for the Tunnel of Scent Seasons

Spring/early summer

Akebia quinata
Clematis montana 'Elisabeth'
Clematis montana wilsonii
Lonicera japonica
Wisteria sinensis 'Sierra Madre'

Summer

Lathyrus 'Matucana'
Lonicera japonica
Rosa 'Applejack'
Rosa 'Ilse Krohn Superieur'
Rosa 'Lady Hillingdon, climbing'
Rosa 'Mme Alfred Carriere'
Rosa 'Mme Butterfly, climbing'
Rosa 'Mme Isaac Pereire'
Rosa 'Zephirine Drouhin'

Late summer/autumn

Clematis rehderiana
Lonicera japonica
Lonicera x americana
Rosa 'Applejack'
Rosa 'Ilse Krohn Superieur'
Rosa 'Lady Hillingdon, climbing'
Rosa 'Mme Alfred Carriere'
Rosa 'Mme Butterfly, climbing'
Rosa 'Mme Isaac Pereire'
Rosa 'Zephirine Drouhin'

Plants for the Tunnel of Scent
Light and Shadow

Sun

Akebia quinata
Clematis montana 'Elisabeth'
Clematis montana wilsonii
Clematis rehderiana
Lathyrus 'Matucana'
Lonicera japonica
Lonicera x americana
Rosa 'Applejack'
Rosa 'Ilse Krohn Superieur'
Rosa 'Mme Butterfly, climbing'
Rosa 'Mme Isaac Pereire'
Wisteria sinensis 'Sierra Madre'

Half-shade

Akebia quinata, mørkviolet
Clematis montana 'Elisabeth'
Clematis montana wilsonii
Clematis rehderiana
Lathyrus 'Matucana'
Lonicera japonica
Lonicera x americana
Rosa 'Applejack'
Rosa 'Ilse Krohn Superieur'

Rosa 'Lady Hillingdon, climbing'
Rosa 'Mme Alfred Carriere'
Rosa 'Mme Butterfly, climbing'
Rosa 'Mme Isaac Pereire'
Rosa 'Zephirine Drouhin'

Shade

Clematis montana 'Elisabeth'
Clematis montana wilsonii
Clematis rehderiana
Lonicera x americana
Lonicera japonica
Rosa 'Mme Alfred Carriere'
Rosa 'Mme Isaac Pereire'
Rosa 'Zephirine Drouhin'

Suggestion: Planting in the Tunnel of Scent

Inner ring

y	Akebia quinata
h	Clematis montana 'Elisabeth'
t	Clematis montana wilsonii
b, j, r	Clematis rehderiana
d, h, l, p, t, y	Lathyrus 'Matucana'
v, f	Lonicera japonica
d, n	Lonicera x americana
u, g	Rosa 'Applejack'
q, m	Rosa 'Ilse Krohn Superieur'
s, k	Rosa 'Lady Hillingdon, climbing'
a, i	Rosa 'Mme Alfred Carriere'
o	Rosa 'Mme Butterfly, climbing'
e, x	Rosa 'Mme Isaac Pereire'
c	Rosa 'Zephirine Drouhin'
l, p	Wisteria sinensis 'Sierra Madre'

Outer ring

6	Akebia quinata
2, 22	Clematis montana 'Elisabeth'
10, 18	Clematis montana wilsonii

16	Clematis rehderiana
2, 6, 10, 14, 18, 22	Lathyrus odoratus 'Matucana'
4, 12	Lonicera japonica
8, 20	Lonicera x americana
15	Rosa 'Applejack'
13	Rosa 'Ilse Krohn Superieur'
9, 19	Rosa 'Lady Hillingdon, climbing'
1, 5	Rosa 'Mme Alfred Carriere'
11, 17	Rosa 'Mme Butterfly, climbing'
7, 23	Rosa 'Mme Isaac Pereire'
3, 21	Rosa 'Zephirine Drouhin'
14	Wisteria sinensis 'Sierra Madre'

Plants for the center

I	Alyssum montanum
II	Convallaria majalis
III	Daphne cneorum
IV	Daphne blagayana
V	Dianthus gratianopolitanus
VI	Dianthus petraeus
VII	Lavandula angustifolia
VIII	Thymus x citriodorus

'Golden Dwarf'

IX	Thymus pulegioides
X	Viola odorata 'Sulphurea'

Bulbs

XI	Lilium candidum
XII	Narcissus poëticus "Actaea"

Annuals

XIII	Lobularia maritima

Richard Sennett

The Technology of Unity

Sigfried Giedion's classic manifesto *Space, Time and Architecture* is a modern expression of the cult of the object. His manifesto is doubly interesting because it justifies this worship of objects by appealing explicitly to an ideal of natural unity. To be sure, Giedion's Nature is not Thomas Jefferson's. The modern architect believes that we have discovered a principle of unity in Nature wholly unsuspected before Einstein. This principle is the unity of space and time. Giedion's charge to his colleagues is that modern architecture must make use of this modern knowledge of the physical world. Indeed, he believes, modern artists are beginning to do so, while the makers of streets and houses have yet to catch up with Einstein:

Space in modern physics is conceived of as relative to a moving point of reference, not as the absolute and static entity of the baroque system of Newton. And in modern art, for the first time since the Renaissance, a new conception of time leads to a self-conscious enlargement of our ways of perceiving space.[1]

That is, what Einstein calculated, Picasso painted. A cubist portrait may show simultaneously the side and the front of a face. Viewers have the sense of their own point of view simultaneously in two places rather than of the face turning. Rightly or wrongly, Giedion thought that being in two different places simultaneously was what modern physics revealed about Nature. Moreover, Giedion believed modern architecture is a particularly favored modern art because it can use new building materials and technology to make simultaneous time and space palpable in houses and factories.

These are not quite as abstruse assertions as they seem: Take a building like the one Walter Gropius and Adolf Meyer built in Cologne in 1914, the Administrative Office-Building of the Werkbund exhibition. Gropius declared that "the outward forms of the New Architecture differs fundamentally in an organic sense from those of the old," because in this building you are simultaneously inside and outside.[2] In front the entrance is flanked by two spiral staircases sheathed in glass, jutting out from the façade. From the outside, you can see people moving up and down between floors. In the back, the main floor is entirely sheathed in glass, so that everyone is visible inside. You can see through walls, your eyes move inside to outside, outside to inside. The confines of the interior have lost their meaning. Moreover, at street level Gropius and Meyer have used glass in and around the doors so that you can literally look through the building to people entering from the other side. This is wholeness, but of a more radical sort than Jefferson or the younger John Wood conceived. Inner and outer become apparent at once, like the front and side of a cubist portrait.

No big thing reveals itself at a glance. However, here you can find no overall image into which the parts resolve themselves, though everything is so open. Each space seemingly has its own logic; to understand how the stairs feel you have to walk them; the door, so oddly not a barrier, invites you to enter. And this invitation to move makes again a more complicated picture than the open window of the past. Time has appeared in the picture, movement-time. By guiding the inhabitant's movements, this office building seems to tell a story as complex as a modern novel. Gropius, Mies van der Rohe, and Marcel Breuer sought that. They wanted to make spaces

1. Sigfried Giedion, *Space, Time and Architecture*, fifth edition, Harvard University Press, Cambridge, Mass., 1982, p. 436.

2. Walter Gropius, *The New Architecture and the Bauhaus*, trans. P. Morton Shand, The MIT Press, Cambridge, Mass., 1965, p. 20.

that create a special kind of coherence due to the sequence of movement, movement through space binding person to building. All the inventions that opened up the interior of Enlightenment houses like Monticello seem to culminate in these modern structures. Inside and outside, room and room, are unified – a unity we start to experience the moment our bodies begin to move.

Modern architecture has sought to satisfy an Enlightenment craving: to live in a physically unifiable world. Certain architecture of the late Renaissance and early baroque period lay the groundwork for satisfying this craving. The undulating walls of Francesco Borromini's buildings make the eye travel across the wall plane slowly; it is hard to look at a wall plane all at once in a Borromini building, like the church of St. Ivo in Rome (1642-1660). The flexible ground plans of the Turinese architect Guarino Guarini – as in the church of St. Lorenzo, 1668-1687 – created mysterious spaces of great drama and no obvious purpose, to be fathomed only as one moved through them. These structures radically defy the modern minimalist maxim crystallized by the art critic Michael Fried: "at every moment the work itself is wholly manifest."[3]

For Giedion's near contemporary Geoffrey Scott, bodily movement was the secret in defining human scale in the environment, a secret he thought the Renaissance understood and modern planners do not. "We project ourselves into [the spaces in which we stand], fill them ideally with our movement."[4] When the body feels engulfed, because the shape of a street or square or interior has no relation in its immensity to any particular movement within it, then the form is out of scale; if a sidewalk is too narrow for the body to feel at ease in walking, the street is as out of scale as a ceiling that is too low. The Renaissance architect, in Scott's view, struggled with heavy materials and structural constraints to achieve the human scale that the Renaissance painter brought to life on canvas. The modern architect need not.

Yet here, in purely visual terms, is the germ of the idea of an object's integrity. Freedom of movement and of scale through and about the building and the space around it has given the modern architectural structure a life of its own, different from the life of buildings in the past. Coherence in design is now freed of the engineering obstacles imposed upon earlier buildings. The technologies of modern construction (glass walls, steel framing, electric lighting) make this new kind of free movement possible. They remove the old logic of neces-

3. Michael Fried, "Art and Objecthood," 1967, reprinted in Gregory Battcock (ed.), *Minimal Art: A Critical Anthology*, Dutton, New York, 1968, p. 145.

4. Geoffrey Scott, *The Architecture of Humanism: A Study in the History of Taste*, 1914, reprint, W.W. Norton, New York, 1974, pp. 169, 170.

sary distinctions, of interior location of windows and bearing walls, as well as divisions between inside and outside. This makes it possible to build at last the Enlightenment ideal of the open form; in principle, barriers in a building have ceased to be as significant as they were in eras when engineering constraints more tightly dictated form. A building that can be made simply for the sake of its expressive form is a modern ideal of architectural integrity.

An old material has been put to new use in the service of this ideal. This material is glass. The walls in large buildings are now most often built with it in large plates, the plate glass set in steel frames opening up the entire world outside to the person working or living high up in the sky. In 1914, the engineer Paul Scheerbart declared that glass could dissolve the barriers of experience between inside and outside, in terms that would have been recognizable to an educator or a gardener in the 1770s:

We mostly inhabit closed spaces. These form the milieu from which our culture develops (...). If we wish to raise our culture to a higher plane, so must we willy-nilly change our architecture. And this will be possible only when we remove the sense of enclosure from the spaces where we live. And this we will only achieve by introducing Glass Architecture.[5]

This new technology of unity reveals how the architectural form has become socially aloof.

Manufactured glass is at least four thousand years old, but not until the Christian era did people learn to make it transparent; they discovered transparency through experiments in heating and cooling the mixture of soda and lime that is simple glass. Not until 1674 was it known how to alter the properties of glass by changing the very materials of which it could be made. In that year, the British chemist George Ravenscroft replaced the soda lime mixture by a lead alkali one. This glass, which we use still for fine crystal objects, had far greater transparency and strength than soda-and-lime glass, but it was much too expensive for windows. The older glass cost little to make but broke easily when cast in large panes. Toward the end of the eighteenth century, the technology was perfected by reliably producing sheet glass, thanks to the use of cast-iron rollers for smoothing. Windows in all kinds of structures could now be made larger, but in the nineteenth century, truly radical

5. Quoted in Reyner Banham, *The Architecture of the Well-Tempered Environment,* second edition, The University of Chicago Press, Chicago, 1984, p. 126.

glass architecture appeared in two special building forms, the greenhouse and the arcade.

Greenhouses like those Joseph Paxton built for the duke of Devonshire at Chatsworth, which we know only from drawings and photographs, or Kew Gardens, or the Jardin des Plantes, are extraordinary buildings. The dappling play of light and shadow in these enormous glass halls, as clouds pass, as time passes, make space into action. The rooms constantly change their form, just as a stage is transformed through lighting, but here there is no sense of artifice; the sunlight alone does the work. Or rather, there is an artifice that does not register on our senses as a stage set because all the actors here are plants: the nineteenth century greenhouse abolished the distinction between inside and outside in terms of light, while radically controlling this barrier in terms of heat and the penetration of smoke. The plants therefore flourished and the people walking among them experienced the sensations of being outside and inside simultaneously. This organic artifice under glass remains as magical to us as it was to the Victorians.

Moreover, glass created a more obvious drama, a drama of scale. A building sheathed in iron-framed glass radically reduced the cost of building big and also cut the time necessary for construction. Kew Gardens outside London and the Jardin des Plantes in Paris rose in a fraction of the time required to build St. Paul's or Notre-Dame. Glass was the material that overcame men's sense of great space as difficult to enclose. Until quite recently, then, the visual experience of joining inside and outside was a matter either of direct exposure, through an open window, or of looking through an often ripply material cut into small pieces and framed in wood or metal. Fully apprehending the outside form within, yet feeling neither cold nor wind nor moisture, is a modern sensation, a modern sensation of protected openness in very big buildings.

In the nineteenth century it is true, glass was used somewhat tentatively in dwellings for human beings. This ambivalence appeared in the building of arcades. With the prominent exception of the Galerie d'Orléans in the Palais Royal, most of the early nineteenth century arcades are ordinary stone or brick buildings shoved close together, the space between them roofed over by glass, like the Crystal Palace in London, or the Palais de l'Exposition in Paris, were designed as temporary structures. To live entirely exposed to the outside seemed akin to walking around naked, which was not an appealing condition to our Victorian forebears. This was why they used glass less freely than their technology permitted, even in factories or offices. And indeed there is an inherent Victorian logic to the deferred construction of glass buildings until the elevator, the steel skeleton, and in our century air-conditioning, ensured that exposure would take place far above the ground, up in the sky, where no one could see you.

The peculiar physical sensation aroused by plate is complete visibility without exposure of the other senses. It is the physical sensation on which is founded the modern sense of isolation in a building. And, in this, the history of glass is inseparable from the history of lighting. The open gas lamp of the mid-nineteenth century was succeeded by the "Ricket's globes" that enclosed the flame and prevented gas fumes from permeating a room; this made it possible to use sheets of glass as permanent seals in windows, opening only for light. In a model house built in Liverpool in 1872, designed to illustrate an early version of combined central heating and ventilation,

the windows were not openable. Fresh air was fed in from the basement warmed in a furnace, and distributed via a central lobby on each floor and through a perforated cornice into the room. Over each gasolier was an outlet grille that led to a duct.[6]

This model house is a primitive version of the technology that would operate in the skyscraper interior to isolate the interior from the outside, even though everything outside was visible. The combination of visibility and isolation then grew stronger with the development of air-conditioning and the thermal glass wall (in which two panes of sheet glass are held within a mental frame, creating a thermal barrier) a half-century later. Corbusier's Cité de Refuge, constructed in Paris in 1932, brings this combination to fruition: it has a curtain wall facing south of thermal glass, and air circulation like that in the Liverpool house but, as expanded by the French architect Gustave Lyon for the Salle Pleyel in Paris, is a completely sealed structure. (The Cité de Refuge turned out to be a technological disaster because of the stifling heat trapped by the glass, and Corbusier was shortly to face it with a *brise-soleil.*) Despite its thermal problems, the principle of the sealed box of complete visibility has become the environmental model on which glass is today employed in most tall buildings.

The difficulties of the glass box, however, go much deeper than the temperature of the skin. In them we see modern technology used to make coherent structures, as the Enlightenment

6. Witold Rybczynski, *Home. A Short History of an Idea,* Viking, New York, 1986, p. 146.

would have conceived of physical coherence: all the rooms flowing into one another, the building, and its surroundings visually interwoven. Yet, these structures also betray strong powers of isolation; they are "integrated" objects that can be sealed. Though technology has heightened visibility through plate glass, the world made visible through this window has been devalued in its reality. This is true of sensate reality: a man sees from his office window a tree blowing in the wind but cannot hear the wind blowing. It is true of social reality: in Detroit's Renaissance Center, which is a very bad pastiche of a wavy glass tower that Mies van der Rohe conceived for Berlin decades earlier, deals unfold during the day insulated from the wail of police sirens in the streets below, the police beacons glinting and glancing off the wavy glass walls like quick sunrises and sunsets. The barrier of transparency in a plate-glass shop window ensures that an object for sale cannot be touched. The division of the physical senses that began in the Victorian greenhouse, and is so arousing there, has become now more deadening: sight is more routinely insulated from sound, touch, and other human beings.

The combination of visibility and isolation today marks the way buildings relate streets at ground level. Great sheaths of plate glass are routinely used as ground-level walls; there are usually just a few, restricted entrances. Thus, the building is more isolated from the street than older buildings with smaller windows that open, even though there is, to use Giedion's phrase, visual "penetration" between the inside and the outside. On parts of Park Avenue in New York, block after block of unbroken street wall is made of plate glass sheathing banks, office supply showrooms, luxury car dealers, and expensive clothes shops, each ground-level business with a single, policed entrance. One might also experience a similar sense of disconnection if the tightly controlled entrances were set in brick walls, but not in quite the same way: seeing what you cannot hear, touch, or feel increases the sense that what is inside, is inaccessible.

These curious powers of isolation revealed in a visually open, free architecture explain in part how the built environment has become at odds with the social life of the city. One could explain these uses of glass simply in terms of economics or power. For instance, plate glass so deployed is the perfect building material for a neutral city, since it devalues the tactile reality of what one sees. But culture adds to power the problem of legitimation. "Integrity" is a moral category. The form of the object has acquired, as it were, rights against being tampered with. Architecture forms a special case in relation to the ideal of integrity, for it comes into being in ways paintings, sculptures, and poems do not. The making of a piece of urban architecture is a messy process, involving an army of specialist designers and technicians at war with opposing armies of government officials, bankers, and clients. To assert that the buildings which result have the single-minded imprint and pristine integrity which earns them the right not to be touched subsequently is in one way, therefore, ludicrous. But modern architects do assert that right.

An architect of the sublime

The grounds for asserting this right appear most graphically in the work of perhaps the greatest of modern architects. Mies van der Rohe was the architect who did more than anyone else to make plate glass the physical stuff through which our century sees. It was Mies who in 1921 conceived an office building for the Friedrichstrasse in Berlin entirely sheathed in glass, Mies who a year later unveiled a model of a glass tower with walls of billowing curves and folds, thus converting the metaphor of a curtain wall into a literal if ideal vision of curtains of glass rising forty stories into the air. It was Mies who, exiled to Chicago in 1937, began to build these ideal visions of glass in that city where the early skyscrapers with inner glass atriums had already suggested that the transparency of a window might be extended to the transparency of an entire wall, from which it was only a logical next step to an entire tower that might become transparent. It was Mies who built in New York in 1956-1958 the city's greatest glass tower, the Seagram Building on Park Avenue, a work of extraordinary elegance. And of course it is Mies, archon of modernism, who is now accused of fathering a soulless environment of glass towers in which men and women are as cut off from one another as from the outside: Mies, the father of visual solitude.

In one way this could simply mean that Mies in his Berlin days did not imagine that towers manufactured by machines entirely of manmade materials would thicken and reproduce themselves in cities, crowding close together, just as Raymond Hood, the genius presiding over Rockefeller Center, sought to prevent the manufacture of modernity from creating a mountain of metal and glass. Mies usually drew his earlier towers as single structures alone on the horizon, where one saw them freely from all sides.

The glass world imposes solitude upon its inhabitants: if I put the matter thus, I write as though the material dictates the meaning. Instead, glass has to be used in a certain way to arouse a sense of lonely space. The difference appears in the contrast between the glass houses built by Philip Johnson (his own in New Canaan, Connecticut or an earlier glass house in Cambridge, Massachusetts) and the Farnsworth House Mies built after World War II in Plano, Illinois. Johnson's glass house in Cambridge sits directly on the ground, the floor and the ground being virtually at the same grade. The Cambridge house forms one side of a rectangular courtyard, the other three sides are enclosed by a high fence, the court is paved, its edges are planted; the inside of the house achieves a real unity with this protected exterior space. In Johnson's New Canaan house, the trees and shrubs seem as much a part of the décor as the lamps and paintings. In these glass boxes, there is a comfortable feeling of unity with nature; gentlemen of the eighteenth century would feel at home in them.

Yet, in the Farnsworth House of Mies, the space arouses quite different emotions. It is a rectangle of glass walls sheathed in white-painted steel; the box floats on eight steel stilts four feet above the ground; a rectangular terrace, also on stilts, lies along one side of it and slightly lower. There is a functional reason for the stilts, since the land is the floodplain of the nearby Fox River, but form has not followed function here. As the irate first owner was later to complain, there were far more efficient ways to design a flood-proof house. A house on stilts, indeed, proclaims that this is a threatened dwelling; when you look at the Farnsworth House, especially up from the ground as you approach by foot, you sense it. Though the present owners have sought to create an English groundsward around the house, I'm told the ground is usually as soft and squishy on this floodplain as it was the day I visited – beautiful land but uncomfortable. Among other things, there are snakes. The Farnsworth House, with its base at chest level, its terrace at waist level, seems to hover, floating like a spaceship, and you hurry forward to hoist yourself up to this refuge.

The house, however, does not offer sanctuary. The threat of nature that urged you toward it is reinforced once you reach the terrace; there is no refuge for you or for any other living thing here. The use of huge sealed sheets of glass for every exterior vertical surface means you cannot go in where you see safety. Nor is the sight of people within reassuring; they look as if they don't belong there, as if no one belongs inside. Mies achieves this effect in part by the unusual height of the glass walls, in part by the heaviness of the wood pedestal that contains the kitchen and bathrooms, which sits in the center of the glass box. The pedestal is perfectly balanced weight against the wall planes; the furniture precisely and elegantly defined within the interplay of central mass and outer boundaries. But the intrusion of someone dozing in a chair (though it's hard to nap in a Mies Barcelona Chair), someone else reading a magazine while munching potato chips – all these normal signs of domesticity become obscene. Instead, this is a space in which we experience the terror of nature sharpened by a building offering no promise of refuge. It is a modern expression of the sublime.

In principle, the glass panel should be the most "friendly" of building elements, in the sense of most flexible and adaptive to various human needs and design programs. This was the lesson of Paxton's Crystal Palace and the other exhibition halls of its type. Again, nothing in form could seem farther from Mies than Buckminster Fuller's geodesic domes, especially as the domes were articulated by François Dallegret to cover both a building and the area just around it so that inner and outer space become absolutely one. Dallegret's was a reasonable version of Fuller's own dream to cover all of Manhattan with a dome. (In fact, the hemispherical shape creates serious practical problems of air stratification and heating; it is also hard to accommodate the workings of windows and doors to a curved integument.) But Fuller domes betray the same logic as do the glass towers of Mies, as structures in and of and for themselves. Fuller believes that glass might be a "unifying" material in the Enlightenment sense. In practice unity means to him what it meant to Mies: visibility combined with isolation. The domes work best when set by themselves alone in a forest.

Simon Sheikh

Space Fellow Travellers
An Interplanetary and Interpretative Voyage to the Worlds of R. Buckminster Fuller and Sun Ra

In science fiction films such as Stanley Kubrick's famous *2001: A Space Odyssey* (1968), and Douglas Trumbull's lesser known *Silent Running* (1971), we are presented with not only a vision of infinite space (and space travel), but also with the spaceship itself as the central locus of the film, with huge spaceships capable of sustaining life and of containing a whole minuscule world within – the multiple spaces and functions of the spaceship in *2001* and the gardens in *Silent Running*. In the former film, the spaceship is the metaphor for the postindustrial fusion of living and working in one place, for the perfect high-tech unit; and in the latter film, the spaceship is no less than a metaphor for planet Earth itself and its ecological problems after industrialization. Besides the idea of the spaceship as microcosmos, both films also share an ambivalent attitude towards technology and its implementation; its effect on the bodily subject. In *Silent Running*, technology is at once sustaining and destroying Nature (i.e. the known world's last gardens), and in *2001*, technology is at once sustaining and destroying Man.

The notion of the spaceship is also crucial to the visions of architect-scientist-philospher R. Buckminster Fuller (1895-1983) and musician-mystic-politician Sun Ra (1914-1993), who both used the spaceship as a central metaphor, albeit with very different implications and ideals. They represent – obviously – a rational and mystic approach to space (and space technology), but also an open and a hermetic language or discourse. They represent, if you will, two different worlds, two very different spheres. Fuller is, naturally, a well known design-scientist and Sun Ra a perhaps less well known avant-garde jazz musician. But they not only represent scientific research – high culture – and free jazz – low culture, but also white and black America. Different cultures and classes. These differences can be found in their respective visions overall; their concept of space and metaphorical use of the spaceship as a vehicle of communication and production.

Significantly, both figures are children of industrial, Fordian society, and thus both products of modernity. And they represent the two important currents within modern thought and artistic production the rationalist position and the mystic. Enligthenment and darkness. An impulse to clarify the order of things, technological strategies and means of production and an impulse to obscure meanings and create a cryptic, coded system of signification. Whereas R. Buckminster Fuller, in his own words, wanted to provide us with an "operation manual" for planet Earth as a "spaceship," Sun Ra enigmatically stated, that "space" was "the place" to be, and claimed to come from Saturn rather than Earth.

Design science revolution

R. Buckminster Fuller, who often introduced himself as "the world's most interesting failure" was in fact the fifth generation of Fullers to attend Harvard, where he was, however, dismissed twice, finally leaving without a degree to instead pursue a career as an engineer and later, WWI naval officer, before finally joining his Father-in-law's architectural firm. Fuller was later to combine these different skills – academic thinking, mechanics, (military) leadership and discipline, architectural planning and business management – into his work as inventor and philospher, into the R. Buckminster Fuller system, *Synergetics*. The term is a conglomoration of "synergy" and "energetic," refering to both geometry and physics, but also indicating modernist notions of progression, speed, velocity, and movement. "Synergy" implies the combination or cooperation of separate entities to create an effect that is bigger than the sum of its parts, and "energetic" implies the use of forces in motion, and thus the ability of transformation.

These scientific concepts were extended into a system of total and totalizing, geometry-based design, used in Fuller's numerous unit structures labelled "Dymaxion:" Dymaxion Houses, Dymaxion Mobile Dormatories, Dymaxion Bathrooms, Dymaxion Dwelling Machines, Dymaxion Deployment Units and Dymaxion Cars. All of these Dymaxion constructs were based on the same, simple geometric figure of the tetrahedron, a space made out of triangular shapes, something Fuller defined as the minimum system in the universe, and a geometric order that directly corresponded to its molecular structure, thus representing a universal, "natural" technological method. In Fuller's tetrahedon structures, nature, progress, and technology merge into an ultimate, cosmic order, and it enabled him to provide a matrix for all constructions, be they the Dymaxion Houses or the later, large geodesic domes. The combination of tetrahedon shapes became a simple organizing principle applicable to all types of buildings – it was easy to assemble, it could be easily extended into large structures such as domes, and thus easily create any type of space, no matter what its size or function. In this sense, it is of course essentially modernist in its conception of an all-encompassing matrix. Indeed, it could easily be argued that Fuller just takes the ideas of post-Fordian industrialism; efficiency, transformability, accessability, and discipline; and makes them universal values – as if the American dream, post-industrial, progressive suburban white middle class bliss is a universal principle for organizing society through "natural" technology! Which, of course, it is and isn't.

However, Fuller is not just a rationalist in the modernist technocratic sense: he is also very romantic in his utopian merger of scientific design and "natural," "cosmic" order, indeed almost pantheistic. He believed, perhaps very naively, that there was no contradiction between technological order and natural order, but rather that one was – ideally – an extension of the other, as can be read in his best-selling "manifesto" *Operating Manual for Spaceship Earth*. Here, philosophy, ecology, futurism, and science merge, and Fuller comes across as something of modernist Renaissance man (a contradiction-in-terms); Architect, Mathematician, Engineer, Visionary, Humanist, Inventor, Scientist, Teacher, etc. In true modernist fashion, Fuller tried to establish a synthesis (or "synergetics") of thought and practice that could apply to all spheres of life and production, making the world – planet Earth – a perfect vehicle, an operational spaceship.

Alien Nation

Sun Ra's spaceship was an altogether different proposition. It travelled elsewhere and with different travellers. And it travelled on different routes and unknown paths. Sun Ra, who always claimed to be a visitor from outer space, entered our planet in 1914 and left again in 1993, leaving behind a number of artefacts; records, poems, films, and sound-images. In earthly terms, he was born Herman Poole Blount in Birmingham, Alabama. A place that advertised itself as "the magic city," but which was mostly renowned for its thorough segregation and being a stronghold of the KKK, once boasting of having the largest membership in all of the U.S.

Sun Ra literally felt out of place, even within the Afro-American community, and left to travel. In one sense he left for the major jazz centers such as Chicago, New York and Philadelphia, where he would reside with his orchestra over the years, and in another sense for the spaceways; through music and through the construction of his own iconography, his own black mythology. Like so many jazz performers, Sun Ra changed his name, and by doing so he reinvented himself in his own image, as so many Afro-Americans would later do for political reasons (most notably Black Muslims). By ceasing to be Herman Blount, Sun Ra liberated himself from history, from a particular time and place. Instead he became vague about specifics and official American history and created his own lineage and indeed future. Sun Ra tried to write his own, alternative history and engaged in a practice of counter-memory; a black mythology derived from equal parts of theosophy, Egyptology, and science fiction.

His language was not always clear, rather it defied logic and linearity, and came across as strange, intriguing and even downright silly. He not only claimed to be from Saturn, and never to have been born, but also called himself Sun Ra, in effect a double and perhaps schizo-analytic name, Sun and Ra having the same meaning in English and ancient Egyptian, respectively. And he named his independent record label Saturn Records and his orchestra the Arkestra, like a ship, a vehicle for the chosen ones. He ran the Arkestra like a monastery, puritanically and with great discipline, as if the musicians were his crew on board a spaceship. The music they produced was also out of place, and indeed out there. The Arkestra produced free form space music, and its members were always outsiders in the jazz scene, first within the big band area where Ra's compositions were deemed too dissonant and noisy, and later within the free jazz movement which Ra helped create by being an actual big band, and eventually including dancers, space-age costumes, visuals and ritually chanting "space is the place" on stage. It is therefore not surprising that *Sun Ra and his Astro Intergalactic Infinity Arkestra* were to have more influence on such pop groups as the White Panther affliated political punk rock band MC5 and the space-age, black nationalist funksters Parliament-Funkadelic led by George Clinton. Sun Ra's music was supposed to take you "out there," from the deep south into deep space, as indicated in the titles of so many of his compositions; "Interstellar Low Ways," "Interplanetary Music," "We Travel the Spaceways," "Outer Spaceways Incorporated," "Space is the Place," "Journey to Jupiter," "Next Stop Mars," "Rocket Number Nine Take off for the Planet Venus," etc.

Sun Ra felt no sense of belonging within white American's history, and literally described himself as an alien, as coming from outer space. Outer space being, of course, black and unknown. Outer space is only partly mapped, a space into which new, unseen histories and theories can be projected. And with America being white, Sun Ra and his Arkestra did not belong – they belonged more in outer space than in the USA. The Arkestra, its music, its theory and practice, were like a virtual spaceship that could get Sun Ra and his fellow travellers out of here. Out into space.

As such, with Sun Ra and his futurist black myth we are dealing with a concept of the spaceship that is radically different from R. Buckminster Fuller's rationalistic, humanist version of spaceship Earth. Where Fuller's propositions were technological, white, overground and rationalistic, Ra's were metaphorical, black, underground, and mystic. An ideology that is essentialist and transparent, and another that is particular and opaque. Two visions of the spaceship as metaphor for the human condition that still run as currents, ideals, mirrors and unconsciousness in contemporary cultural production, whether we are discussing the aesthetic claim of the specific art object or the discourse of an artistic project as such.

References:
Amiri Baraka, *Eulogies,* Marsilio, New York, 1996.
R. Buckminster Fuller, *Operating Manual for Spaceship Earth,* Southern Illinois University Press, Carbondale, 1969.
Joachim Krause & Claude Lichtenstein (eds.), *Your Private Sky,* Lars Müller Publishers, Zurich, 1999.
Robert W. Marks, *The Dymaxion World of Buckminster Fuller,* Reinhold, New York, 1960.
John F. Szwed, *Space is the Place – The Life and Times of Sun Ra,* Pantheon, New York, 1997.

Michael Speaks

It's Out There…
The Formal Limits of the American Avant-Garde

In an essay published earlier this year, I proposed that a new image of architecture has begun to develop in the Netherlands.[1] This image, I suggested, is one whose Dutchness is fixed neither by national or professional identity, nor by ideology, but instead names a disposition towards the artificial urban milieu that today is the Netherlands but which is fast becoming the rest of the world. In that essay, I went on to suggest that this new urban disposition defines what is fresh and exciting about an emergent generation of Dutch architects, and moreover, that it is what distinguishes them from their North American and European counterparts. Two features of this urban disposition were identified. The first is a de-emphasis on form development and a renewed focus on the analysis and manipulation of material and immaterial processes such as those recognized by the Rotterdam Maaskant Prize jury. They, you might remember, were the jury who broke reality in their nomination of the harbor of Rotterdam as the 1996 recipient

1. See Michael Speaks, "Just There Modernism," in *Nine + One: Ten Young Dutch Architectural Offices*, NAi Publishers, Rotterdam, The Netherlands, 1997, pp. 18 - 26.

of the Maaskant Prize: Rotterdam harbor is a particularly instructive and inspiring example of a "modern" environment, of a space whose organization is not so much dictated by traditional planning and urban design concepts as by the rapid and creative management and steering of trends, movements and forces in the field of transport and communication.[2] The second feature of this new disposition is a post-avant-garde attitude that I called, after Joost Meuwissen of One Architecture in Amsterdam, "just there" modernism. In my essay, I focused especially on the implications of "just there" for the banal. Everyday reality is intensified and made to become something else, something unexpected, something new. "Just there," I tried to suggest, focuses on the limitations and constraints that architecture necessarily transforms into conditions of possibility. "Just there" is thus always connected to what cannot be "just there:" to what shapes what is "just there," and more importantly, what also offers the potential that any architecture must exploit in order to transform what is "just there" into something else... Even if only by a thread, "just there" is always connected to what is "out there."

This was only implicit in my previous essay, but it is what I meant to suggest by focusing on the "urban disposition" of these fresh young Dutch architectural offices, for it is this that allows them to irrigate their architectural intentions with the potential of urban life, to put it in the language of a famous contemporary Dutch architect. In what follows, I want instead to focus on the contemporary American equivalent of these fresh Dutch architects, though, as will become clear, there is no real equivalency among them, for while the Dutch have moved beyond the constraints of avant-gardism, the Americans seemed still fascinated with its possibilities. Rather than focusing on the connection between what is "just there" to what's "out there," however, I want to suggest that in the most advanced registers of contemporary American architecture there is a kind of structural condition that makes impossible any connection between what is "just there" and what is "out there." And that is because what is always "just there" is form. Going from "just there" to what is "out there" one is always stopped at the border; you think you can see beyond it, but what you see is always defined by this border, by form itself.

Despite our collective boredom with ideology, politics, philosophical truth, and other such accounts of those larger realities which exceed the banality of everyday life, we Americans are

2. Cited from the abridged version of the Jury Report, in *Archis 17*, 1996, pp. 8-9.

nonetheless still interested in what's "out there." As the popularity of the television series *X-Files* attests, there is in fact great interest in what's "out there," in what's just beyond our grasp, literally beyond our intellection and capacity to make visible. You will recall that each episode begins with the teaser "the truth is out there." The implication is that to find it we only have to follow the thread that leads from here to there. With its stylized banality, *X-Files* has set the "just there" standard for a new inquiry into the vast array of forces that shape the everyday, and it has done so precisely by connecting the leaden normalcy of town life and petty criminality to paranormal events that make old fashioned conspiracy theory seem small indeed. More importantly, *X-Files'* framing of what's "out there" is consistent with a number of recent attempts to make comprehensible the dark, unfathomable chaos lurking just outside our door. The explosion of theories of postmodernism in the 1980s and complexity theory in the 1990s come to mind, of course, as well as the now ubiquitous globalization discourse. One of the most interesting recent expressions of this desire to make comprehensible what's "out there," however, is the increasing use of ecological models to explain the relationship between complex, dynamical systems and their environments. Take, for example, Noel Boaz's recently published *Eco Homo,* in which he argues for a climatological account of the emergence of the human species; or economist Alain Lipietz's use of political ecology to put forth a new post-left political agenda: or the plethora of new management and scenario planning books such as Arie de Geus's *The Living Company* and James F. Moore's "national bestseller," *The Death of Competition,* on whose dust jacket internet guru Esther Dyson writes: "Moore catches the fundamental shift in business thinking – and behavior – today: the economy is not a mechanism, businesses are not machines. They are co-evolving, unpredictable organisms within a constantly shifting business ecosystem that no one controls." As this blurb suggests, what is especially appealing about ecological models is not only that they seem to offer a flexible means by which to deal with turbulent environments, but they also offer a way to think of seemingly lifeless, static forms such as corporations, economic communities, or political ideologies, as dynamical, living, changeable, life-forms which interact with and alter their environments.

But we are here to discuss that life-form otherwise known as architecture, and so we will. How we do that, however, will depend on whether by architecture we mean a dynamic life-form open to external influences, or a lifeless object on and in which those influences are registered as avant-gardist gestures. It will also depend on what importance we attach to "the new," whether it is the source of difference and new life or the source of sameness and decrepitude. Reporting on what appeared in 1995 to be renewed architectural interest in the ecological, *Assemblage* profiled two designs entered in the Cardiff Bay Opera House Competition, including Greg Lynn's formally inventive entry, based in part on Gregory Bateson's book, *Steps to an Ecology of Mind.*[3] In their editorial comments, *Assemblage* insists that what is not different or new about this project is its formal strangeness, that is, the fact that, as they say, it looks so new. What is new, they rather enigmatically suggest, are the project's "ecological aspects," realized through "process studio techniques tempered by non-automatic generative rules and critiques of the competition brief." They imply that this is connected to Lynn's interest in the problem of the supple, the fluid, and the body, all, in their view, pre-eminently ecological concerns. Commenting on some of Lynn's source materials, they in fact remark that Bateson's book, on which Lynn draws, "is not so much about the science of teratology and the rules for the mutation of form" as a search for "an ecology of ideas" that can help us understand "man's relation to his environment," adding, parenthetically, "an architectural problem if there ever was one." So it comes as something of a surprise when they conclude that "the most amazing, and ultimately most persuasive, thing about these projects is that *nothing has ever looked like this before.*" They go on to qualify this by observing that "nothing looks different unless it is different and, further, it is virtually impossible to set out intentionally to find a new look." Perhaps this is so, perhaps "this look" and the design techniques used to generate it are part of something different, something new, but *Assemblage* is unable to say just what that is. On the contrary, their focus on "the look" and thus on the formal aspects of the relationship between ecology (understood there as one name for a renewed interest in the relationship between complex systems and their environments) and architecture, while not wrong exactly, does obscure what one might have thought were the real "ecological aspects" or implications of Lynn's Cardiff Bay Opera Project. Namely, that if taken seriously, an ecological disposition would require us to think in a new way not only about the "ecological," biomorphic look of Lynn's project, but

3. See "Computer Animisms (Two Designs for the Cardiff Bay Opera House)," in *Assemblage* 26, 1995, pp. 8-37.

also, and more significantly, about the relationship between his practice of architecture (which includes "the look" and the techniques used to generate it) and those larger forces external to architecture, as do, for example Reyner Banham's *Los Angeles: Architecture of Four Ecologies,* in which he describes, among other things, the conditions necessary for the emergence of new architectural life, or Rem Koolhaas's proto-ecologistic (in this larger sense) assertion of "Bigness," that limit beyond which architecture becomes urbanism.

The need to rethink not only architectural forms but the forms of architectural practice becomes even more appropriate when we consider Lynn's accompanying text, "The Renewed Novelty of Symmetry." Here Lynn follows Bateson's model of symmetry breeding a way to introduce novelty into a system, novelty being the ultimate guarantor of continued existence for evolving life-forms. As Lynn points out, one of the fascinating insights offered by Bateson is that the introduction of novelty leads not to disorganization within the system. Surprisingly, lack of external information leads to a less ordered, less coherent system, which means a less adaptable and thus more susceptible system. When external information is introduced into a system, it triggers sets of regulators that prevent default symmetrical arrangements with less organization; this results in more complex, internally coherent organization. The point is that diversity and external influence result in more internally coherent and fluid organizational structures. As Lynn writes in his concluding paragraph:

Symmetry breaking is not a loss but an increase in organization within an open, flexible, and adaptive system. Symmetry breaking from the exact to the anexact is the primary characteristic of supple systems. These, flexible economies index the incorporation of generalized external information through the specific unfolding of polymorphic, dynamic, flexible, and adaptive systems. Symmetry is not a sign of underlying order but an indication of a lack of order due to an absence of interaction with larger external forces and environments. Given this complex conceptualization of endogenous and exogenous forces, deep structure and typology are just what they seem to be: suspect, reductive, empty, and bankrupt. An alternative is an internal system of directed indeterminate growth that is differentiated by general and unpredictable external influences, producing emergent, unforeseen, unpredictable dynamic, and novel organizations.[4]

4. Greg Lynn, "The Renewed Novelty of Symmetry," in *Assemblage 26,* p. 14.

It would seem to require an extraordinary effort to stop at "the look" when the very nature of these models requires that we move beyond "the look" and think about architecture's relationship to its exterior, namely, to the globalized urban world in which it must, as a practice, struggle to survive. Lynn's description of supple systems seems an excellent description of architecture if by that we mean not simply a supple form but a supple form of practice. Indeed it seems an excellent description of a practice such as Lynn's own, which takes in external information, such as the very Batesonian model under discussion, triggering a set of internal regulators which prevent the system from defaulting into a less organized, less adaptable system, inducing instead the emergence of a more complex, adaptable system. But therein lies the problem: if, as *Assemblage* seems to suggest, it is only "the look" that is new, then the only means by which Lynn is able to address the complexity of contemporary urban life is through form. All of the quite remarkable things Lynn attributes to supple systems are thus registered only on the forms themselves. The introduction of external information (Bateson) leads in that case not to a more complex organization, a new practice of architecture able to adapt to this complex world, but only to a defaulted, less organized, system or practice of architecture as form-producer.

Now it would be unfair to criticize Lynn for not taking this kind of metacritical position on his own work; that is, for not pushing the implications of his supple systems analysis past the form, and the design techniques which create them, to include an analysis of his practice of architecture itself. The same cannot be said for *Assemblage,* however, a magazine that stakes its reputation on its hypercriticality and sensitivity to external conditions. And yet, *Assemblage* cannot really be faulted either, for there is a kind of structural condition that prevents them and Greg Lynn from exploiting the real "ecological aspects" of his project. Despite being pulled out into the exterior of architecture by his stated interest in urbanism, and by theoretical models such as those of Bateson, Lynn is more powerfully drawn back into contemporary American architecture's most powerful interiority: form. And strange as it may seem, he is lured there (like *Assemblage*) by his search for the new.

The question of the new has been raised often in the last number of years, especially in the United States, where it always seems to be on the agenda. But more often than not, this interest in the new is a complicated and often contradictory affair. The 1988 MoMA "Deconstructivist Exhibition," for example, gave the world of architecture a new, "avant-garde" style, while its theoretical underpinnings mitigated precisely against style, and against the new. As Mark Wigley, associate curator of the exhibition, wrote in the *Deconstructivist Architecture* catalogue: "Even though it threatens this most fundamental property of architectural objects, deconstructivist architecture does not constitute an avant-garde. It is not a rhetoric of the new. Rather, it exposes the unfamiliar hidden within the traditional. It is the shock of the old."[5] With the arrival of such news, many of those interested in little more than "the new" moved on to other theoretical conceits, such as "the fold" and on to other French theorists. Indeed, in the interim between 1988 and 1994, there was a growing and palpable disappointment with deconstruction, some of which was directed towards Derrida himself when, at the 1992 *Anywhere* conference in Yufuin, Japan, he refused to outline a project for the new, preferring instead to discuss deconstruction in terms of a formal structure he called "faxitecture." What this meant in practical terms was that Derrida did not offer the architects a clear way to convert deconstruction (as the theoretical protocol) into architectural form. Derrida's failure to offer a project of the new in fact became a kind of sour refrain mouthed especially by Jeffrey Kipnis during much of the conference. Though it is impossible to know for sure, one can only imagine that Derrida's refusal (as well as the ascendance of Mark Wigley's more considered reading of Derrida as a Heideggarian) was one of the reasons for Kipnis' turn away from deconstruction and its stated refusal of the new. Kipnis, you will remember, is a self-proclaimed Nietzschean. But, since this was the period in which Kipnis was becoming a designer and not merely a theorist (a larva to butterfly transformation that is virtually irresistible to architectural theorists), there are design implications as well. Writing in his now famous essay "Towards a new Architecture," collected in the *AD Folding in Architecture* publication, Kipnis decried what he called a general cultural disinclination towards the new. "Briefly, it [this retreat from the new] manifests itself as a rationale which holds that the catalogue of possible forms (in every sense of the word institutional, social, political and aesthetic) is virtually complete and well-known."[6] In an attempt to redress this situation, Kipnis offered a new set of design principles, all of which might be said to operate under the rubric of what

5. *Deconstructivist Architecture*, eds. Philip Johnson and Mark Wigley, Museum of Modern Art, New York, 1988, p. 18.

6. See Jeffrey Kipnis, "Towards a New Architecture: Folding in Architecture," in *Architectural Design Profile No. 102*, ed. Greg Lynn, Academy, London, 1993, p. 42.

he called intensive coherence, "a coherence forged out of incongruity." "Intensive coherence," he writes, "implies that the properties of certain monolithic arrangements enable the architecture to enter into multiple and even contradictory relationships."

Like Kipnis, Greg Lynn proposes to address the fluid and complex conditions of late twentieth century urban life by calling for architectural forms that are themselves more fluid and complex. Writing in the same issue of *AD*, Lynn criticizes deconstruction's inability to produce new design techniques which might result in an architecture which is both internally coherent yet open to its exterior conditions. Instead, deconstruction, he suggests, only gives us architectures which are incoherent and which have a conflicted, contradictory relationship with their contexts or exteriors. Deconstruction allows only static collaging of existent or rosterable architectural forms with existent contexts. Lynn wants an architecture, which, like those influenced by deconstruction, is heterogeneous, but he wants one that is also malleable, fluid, and supple. Lynn thus looks outside architecture to the culinary arts, to Gilles Deleuze, René Thom and other sources in order to develop new, folded, pliant design techniques which might result in architectural forms that are themselves pliant and fluid with respect to their external conditions. Lynn has since developed more fluid and more temporally based design techniques, including his impressive animation modelings enabled by Alias software, all of which, to cite his book, seek to produce life-like, "animate form."[7] In essays such as "Form and Field," first given as a lecture at the *Anywise* conference in Seoul, Korea, in 1995, Lynn argues that given the material and immaterial structural changes occurring today, architecture must become more animate – it must move! The classical models of pure, static, essentialized and timeless form and structure, he says, "are no longer adequate to describe the contemporary city and the activities it supports." Lynn thus calls for motion based design techniques, a new attention to "shaping forces," and an anorganic vitalism, all of which are meant to engender a new relationship between a stable (as opposed to static) architecture as a producer of discrete form in productive tension with urbanism understood as a practice of shaping gradients within fields. Lynn argues that using animation videos to conceive the urban context as animate, as in-motion, allows us to understand the relationship between architecture and urbanism in a new way:

7. See Greg Lynn, *Animate Form*, Princeton Architectural Press, Princeton, 1998.

Through history, movement in architecture has involved the arrest of dynamic forces as static forms through mapping. Thus urban fields and movements have been understood as the fixed lineaments upon which forms could be mapped. To work as an architect with urban forces in their nonformalized state it is necessary to design in an environment that is dynamic. Architects need to develop techniques like [D'Arcy] Thompson's model that relate gradient fields of influence with flexible yet discrete forms of organization. This means moving from an architecture based on the equilibrium of Cartesian static space to one designed within dynamic gradient space. Architecture will not literally move, but it must be conceptualized and modeled within an urban field understood as dynamic and characterized by forces rather than forms.[8]

Yes, absolutely, but one would want to ask why does architecture itself not move? Why is architecture itself not animate?

When asked this question by Jeffrey Kipnis at the 1995 *Anywise* conference, Lynn responded as follows:

Kipnis: "Let me hold you accountable to the question, Greg. Because you stay at the level of dynamic animation, we could be fascinated by what we see, but because you do not resolve it as a fixed static object with materials, structure, and construction, at which point we see its real consequences, we're left fetishizing the video rather than really understanding its design consequences. Is this true or not?"

Lynn: "I want to resist answering that question. In other situations in which I have shown material like this, the response has been: 'Well, are you saying architecture has to move in order for this to be an interesting design approach?' I would say no."

Kipnis: "You say no, but you do not show us what happens when you take the motion away."[9]

If the urban context or field is a dynamic play of forces, as Lynn suggests, does this mean that architecture is no more than a static form that arrests those forces? Lynn, in fact, says the opposite: that architecture should no longer be understood as static forms, but as stable forms which dynamically give order to an urban field. This is precisely what we see in his animations: architecture as a dynamic force shaping other dynamic forces. But when it becomes form, the audience asks, when it

8. *Anywise*, ed. Cynthia Davidson, The MIT Press, Cambridge, Mass., 1996, p. 97.

9. Ibid, p. 112.

becomes architecture, does it remain dynamic? Lynn cannot answer: the implication is that when it is being designed it is animate, but not architecture; when it becomes architecture, however, when it becomes a form, it becomes static. Is this because for Lynn, as for Kipnis, and *Assemblage*, architecture is only the object-form at the end of the process? If architecture is stable and not static, as Lynn insists it must be, and if it is temporally inflected, implying movement, why does it not flow like its urban context with which it presumably interacts? Why does the movement stop when it becomes form? Why does his architecture stop moving when it is no longer design technique and becomes architecture? The answer lies with Peter Eisenman.

Lynn's critique of static form in the above cited essay, and typology and deep structure in his Cardiff essay, is an implicit critique of Peter Eisenman, the unofficial dean of the American avant-garde, and Lynn's former employer and mentor. Lynn wants new forms which answer to the new, dynamic, fluid conditions of late twentieth century urban life; he wants animate forms, but, as we have seen, he is only able to offer animate techniques which produce, in the end, forms that seem no more animate than those he sets out to surpass. Now Eisenman, unlike Lynn, is not interested in new forms which might better deal with the new conditions of the late twentieth century, but in dislocative forms, forms which dislocate and call into question what he calls the metaphysics of architecture. It is in fact this activity which defines architecture for Eisenman. The essence of the act of architecture, he says, "is the dislocation of an ever re-constituting metaphysics of architecture." In his essay, "Misreading," collected in *Houses of Cards* (1987), Eisenman writes: "The history of architecture can be seen as the continual rereading, and misreading, of the metaphysics of architecture though successive dislocations, and the subsequent institutionalization of each dislocation, which thereby reconstitutes the metaphysics." (Eisenman's architectural project is consistent with Derrida's philosophical project; both are simultaneously transgressive and conservative of their respective discourses: and both dialogue with those discourses in the very terms given them by the discourse. For Derrida this is the language of Heideggerian metaphysics, and for Eisenman, this is form. I say this only to note, without going into detail, the connection between Eisenman's dislocation and Derrida's deconstruction, both of which differ fundamentally from the project of Gilles Deleuze, whom Lynn often cites.) For Eisenman, the new is not even desirable in itself, and that is because it often conceals beneath its newness the metaphysics of architecture. Eisenman's critique of modern architecture will take precisely this form: while it seemed new and different from the *beaux arts,* modern architecture functionalism is consistent with humanist or anthropocentric architecture dating to the Renaissance. Modern architecture, despite its new, technologically derived forms, still operated within the metaphysics of humanism, and so while new, Modernism was not dislocative. This metaphysics of architecture is arranged around what Eisenman today calls an inferiority, or by any other name an epistemology or ideology. Much of his own work, from the early essays and houses, to his most recent projects, has attempted to destabilize the interiority of functionalist humanism that dominated modernism, and that, in his opinion, persists today in even the most sophisticated architecture should never, as Modernism did, place itself in the service of any exterior discourse, such as politics, or philosophy, but should instead articulate itself as an autonomous practice of form following form. Even when architecture turns to its exterior, as Eisenman did with Chomskian linguistics, psychoanalysis, deconstruction, folding, etc., it must always do so with the aim of dislocating and relocating the interiority of architecture itself, and that interiority for Eisenman is always form. Eisenman thus always carries out his project of dislocating the metaphysics of architecture on the object itself, or rather one should say that the mark of this dislocative project is always registered as form. For Eisenman, the great architectures, the ones with what he calls "presentness," are ones which dislocate by their form a previous form or type, forever transforming that type. He often cites his own Columbus Convention Center in Columbus, Ohio, as an architecture which, while it might be new and interesting, is not dislocative: his Wexner Center, also in Columbus, Ohio, on the other hand, is a form which he argues calls into question the museum type itself, and as such is a dislocative and not simply a new architecture. Ultimately, Eisenman insists that architecture will continue to evolve only by turning inward, by focusing on its interiority, that being for him, in the last instance, form.

Lynn and Eisenman are literally pulling form in opposite directions. Lynn wants new forms which answer to new, exterior conditions, but he neglects the critical question raised by

Eisenman about the interiority of architecture, about, in other words, what architecture is and does. Eisenman calls into question architecture's humanist interiority – architecture, that is, as a practice of housing and making safe. But he does this only in order to establish a new interiority, that of form generation. Eisenman wants to replace the humanist, modernist, form-follows-function interiority. Lynn, on the other hand, wants to move architecture away from this interiority to its exteriority, from static form – typologies, deep structures, etc. – to stable form which interacts with the dynamics of its urban context. But he can do so only from within Eisenmans's interiority of form, by way of form itself. Thus rather than questioning Eisenman's interiority of architecture, rather than questioning the status of architecture as a generator of form (as he does, for example with urbanism which he insists is an animate field of forces) Lynn accepts this interiority and takes form generation as far as it will go. He tries to make form animate, he tries to take form out to meet its urban exteriority, but in the end, he is only able to devise more and more animate techniques to design what are ultimately static forms. But if Lynn were to raise the question that Eisenman does, if he were to question architecture's interiority, he would then be able to move beyond Eisenman's interiority of form to a new consideration of architecture as a new kind of urbanism in-transit, something I have argued is at the center of the work of a number of young Dutch architectural offices.

The real question not only for Lynn, but for this form-driven American avant-garde, is whether they will be able to discover a dislocative architecture that rather than dislocating form or type dislocates the form of architectural practice itself; that, in other words, calls into question the interiority of architecture as a practice of form production, opening it to the kind of expansion that has occurred in the Dutch context where the freshest practices focus on an animate form of practice, not on animate forms. Such a dislocation would necessarily take leave of the discourse of architectural interiority altogether and focus on architecture as a practice of fixity that manipulates or exploits movement in order to induce the production of new urban life. Architecture would then be able to become both a stabilizing *and* an animating force in the metropolis without feeling compelled to make its forms move. As Rem Koolhaas has observed in his distinction between Mies and Rietveld, there are practices which fix in order to open up avenues of freedom, and those that seem to offer an infinity of choice but which give no choice of freedom. Forms that "look like" they are fluid with their urban contexts may in fact interdict, and forms which "look like" they are interdictive may in fact be fluid with their urban contexts. If this were to be recognized, the question would no longer be "what is the essence of architecture," (form, light, image, etc.) but "what can architecture do" when it looks to its exterior, to the globalized metropolis? This is a question that Eisenman, Lynn, Kipnis, *Assemblage,* and indeed the entire American avant-garde seem never to ask, and that is because they are always stopped at the border, stopped by form. Only such a dislocation can guarantee architecture continued life in a world in which it seems to have lost its object, its mission, and its way. Indeed, this is precisely what is at stake in Koolhaas's "Bigness," in which the art of architecture must give way to a reduced, and interconnected set of practices that "depend," as he says: on technologies, engineers, contractors, manufactures, and currency markets. This is also what is at stake in the new practice of urbanism implied in "What Ever Happened to Urbanism?"; an approach and not a professional practice which takes up the problem of shaping the conditions under which new urban life can emerge and proliferate. Of course this is also what is at stake in Sanford Kwinter's "new pastoralism," and Bernard Cache's insistence that architecture is the art of the frame, that it is the framing of the conditions under which life emerges.

Ultimately, architecture will have to develop a dynamism that matches that of the globalized metropolis. In order to do so, it must become, among other things, an animate form of form shaping, a practice of creating forms which themselves may not be animate, but which induce or create the conditions under which new urban life will emerge. The real implications of architectural ecologism, of which the work of Greg Lynn is just one example, will only be understood when we begin to think more clearly about how the practice of architecture can adapt to the turbulent conditions of late twentieth century life, how it can become something different, and yet remain the same, remain architecture. Perhaps the practice of architecture should become everything Lynn says about form and about technique: a pliant system, a blob, a semi-fluid/semi-solid practice, or even a body, as defined by Lynn in a recent text in which he again turns to the exteriority of architecture:

For Margulis, a body is not an ordered whole but a provisional colony of previously discrete free-living entities that fuse together to live as a collective of organs able to reproduce and sustain themselves as a complex. These complexes can then become the organs of higher-order complexes through further linkages, exchanges, parasitisms, and codependencies. Instead of analyzing a body to find its essential structure, the inside resides in the functional and machinic behaviors of all the organs, in their ability to behave as an ensemble with the coherence and stability of a singular organism. The new concept of the organism resembles the definition of an ecosystem, which has no single identity but exhibits self-regulation and persistence nonetheless.[10]

Lynn cites this account of the body as a way to illustrate the new model of the body implied in his wonderful "blob" architectural forms. But what if this model took him and us past those architectural forms, past the border of Eisenman's formalist interiority? If we were to understand architecture itself as a provisional colony of discrete practices, then urbanism might also be redefined as a dynamic body, corpus, or corporation made up of smaller bodies, or "living companies," as Arie de Geus, past head of Scenario Planning at Royal Dutch Shell, says in his book of the same title.[11]

In *The Living Company*, an important new study of corporate life, de Geus develops the thesis that only those companies that learn can make themselves adaptable enough to survive in the turbulent commercial reality that exists today. Unlike "economic companies," which close themselves off to this environment, preferring the guidance of shareholder profits and short term gain, "living companies" are open to their exteriors and are motivated not only by profit but by a desire to survive, to live on as companies. The "living company" is thus defined not by its product, owners, profits, or even corporate ideology, but by its sensitivity to an ever changing, fluid, commercial environment. *The Living Company,* like the account of the body offered above by Greg Lynn, and surprisingly like the body put forward in Gilles Deleuze's wonderful book, *Spinoza: A Practical Philosophy,* is favorably disposed towards its chaotic exterior from which it gathers new information, or as de Geus says, from which it learns. As in Lynn's account of supple systems, this triggers sets of internal regulators which increase the order of the system, and make survival more likely. In de Geus's account, corporate learning occurs by way of scenario planning. Scenario planning attempts to project scenarios of possible futures that the company might find itself living; it does this in order to access and make visible virtual paths of company movement which are constructed from analyzing the

10. Greg Lynn, "From Body to Blob," in *Anybody,* ed. Cynthia Davidson, The MIT Press, Cambridge, Mass., 1996, p. 97.

11. Arie de Geus, *The Living Company: Habits for Survival in a Turbulent Business World,* Harvard Business School Press, Boston, 1997.

turbulent environment itself. Scenario planning is not predicative, however, not employed to reduce disorder, thus making the right path or plan obvious. Instead, scenario planning allows a company to increase order through learning, and as a result to enhance its own flexibility and adaptability to conditions over which it has no control. To return more explicitly to Lynn's Cardiff text, "The Renewed Novelty of Symmetry," the living company breaks symmetry and increases order as a way of enhancing its own survival, while the economic company, in a desperate attempt to find the right or correct plan, refuses to acknowledge its exterior. Now I do not want to push this analogy too far, but de Geus's book *The Living Company* might have something to offer architecture, something other than a new set of design techniques. In short, it might offer architecture "a pass" across the border of form, and thus a ticket to a new life in the new metropolis. Nowhere is the need for such a pass more evident than in architecture's recent turn to ecologism and vitalism. Indeed, one can only hope that architecture will follow the path of the living company, corporation, body, or practice. If, on the other hand, this new vitalism or ecologism, of which Greg Lynn's "animate forms" are but one example, continues to follow the plan of the economic company, closed to what is "out there," then it will profit only those CEOs and corporate board members for whom short term profits made in-form – creation is the primary objective. If this occurs, it will only be a matter of time until Lynn and other members of the American avant-garde assume their places at the board room meeting tables of such companies. Perhaps they have already been seated.

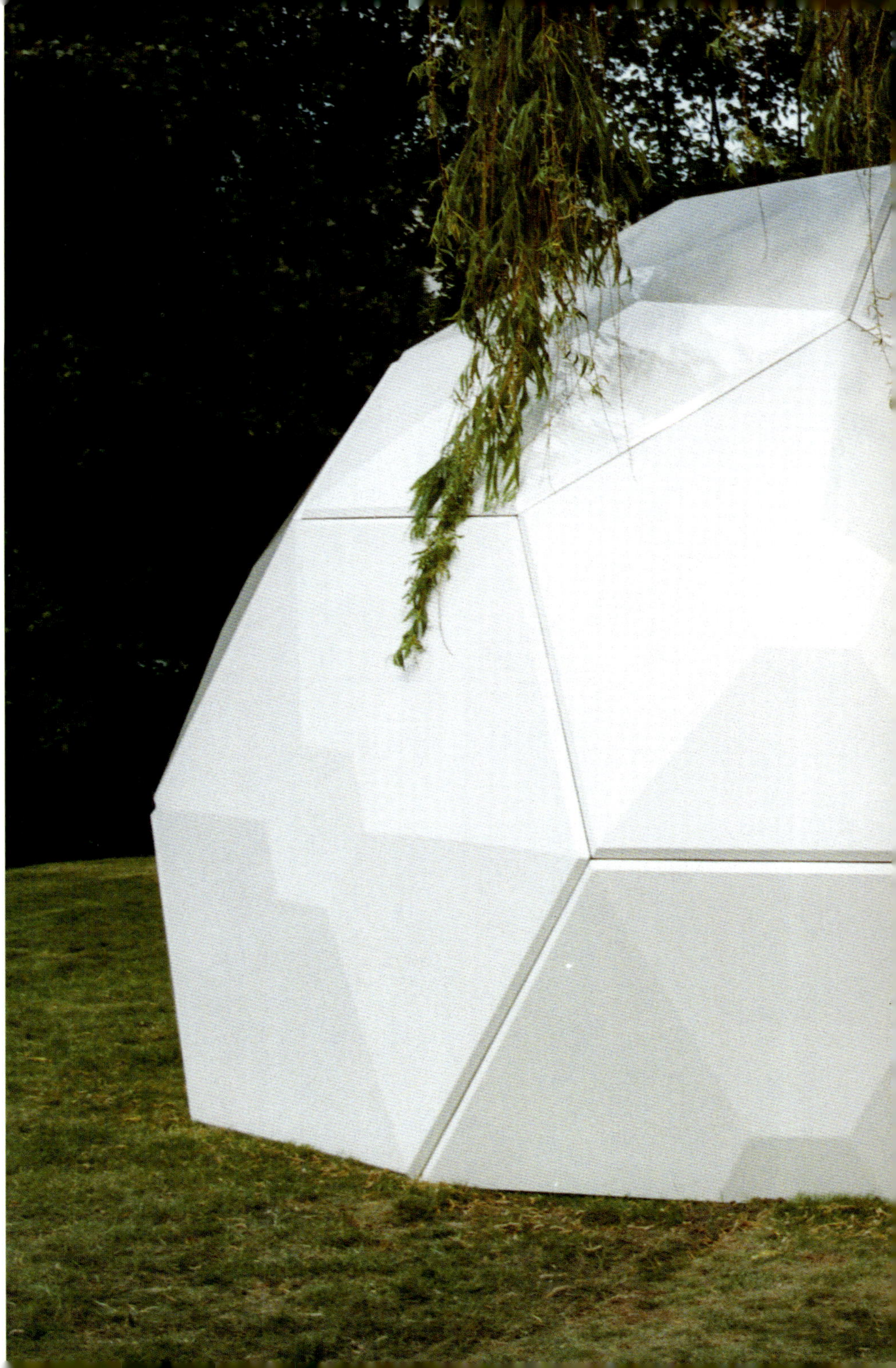

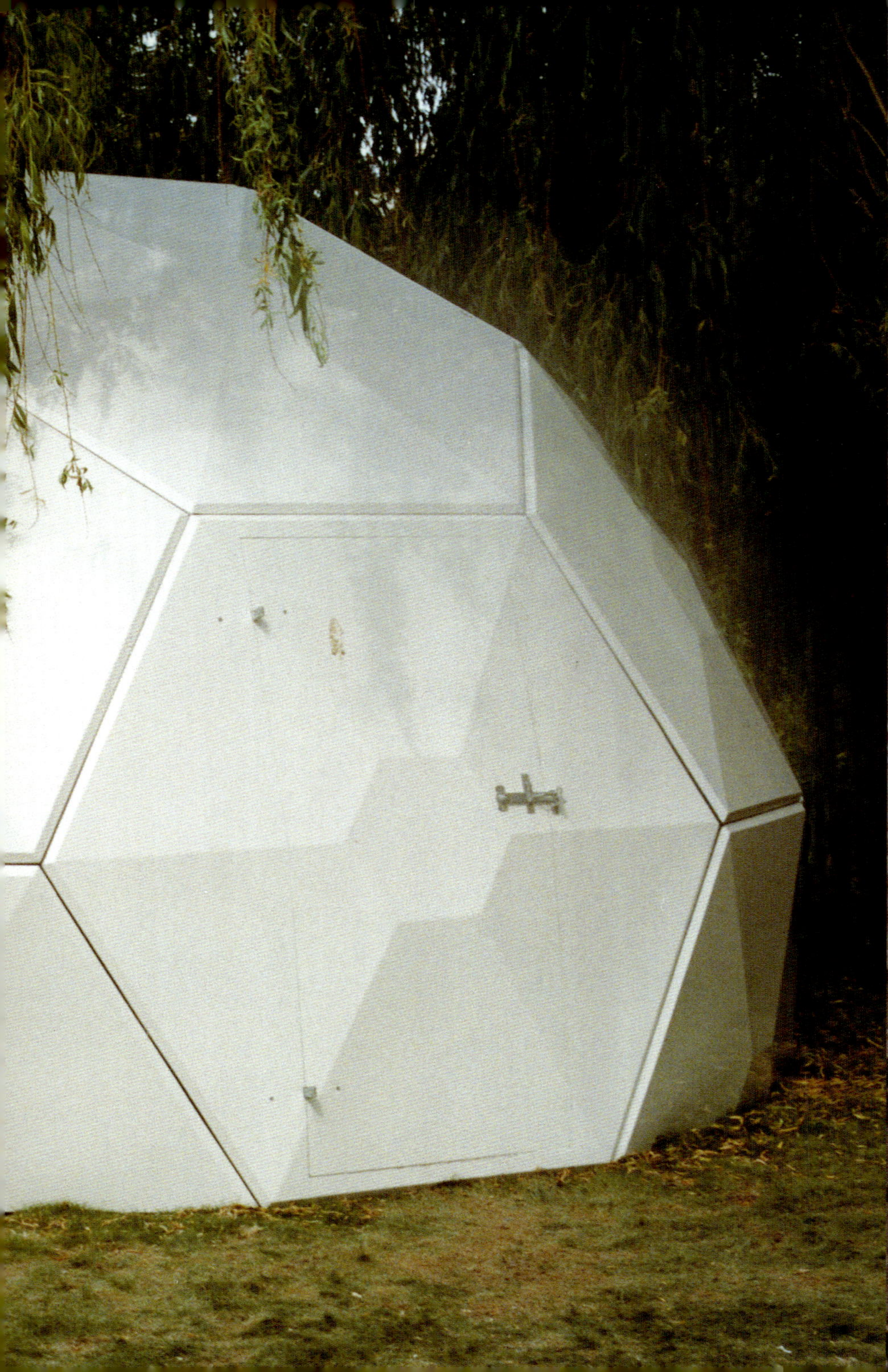
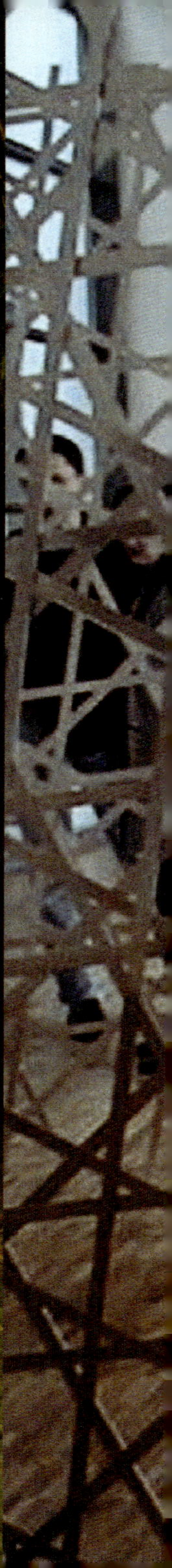

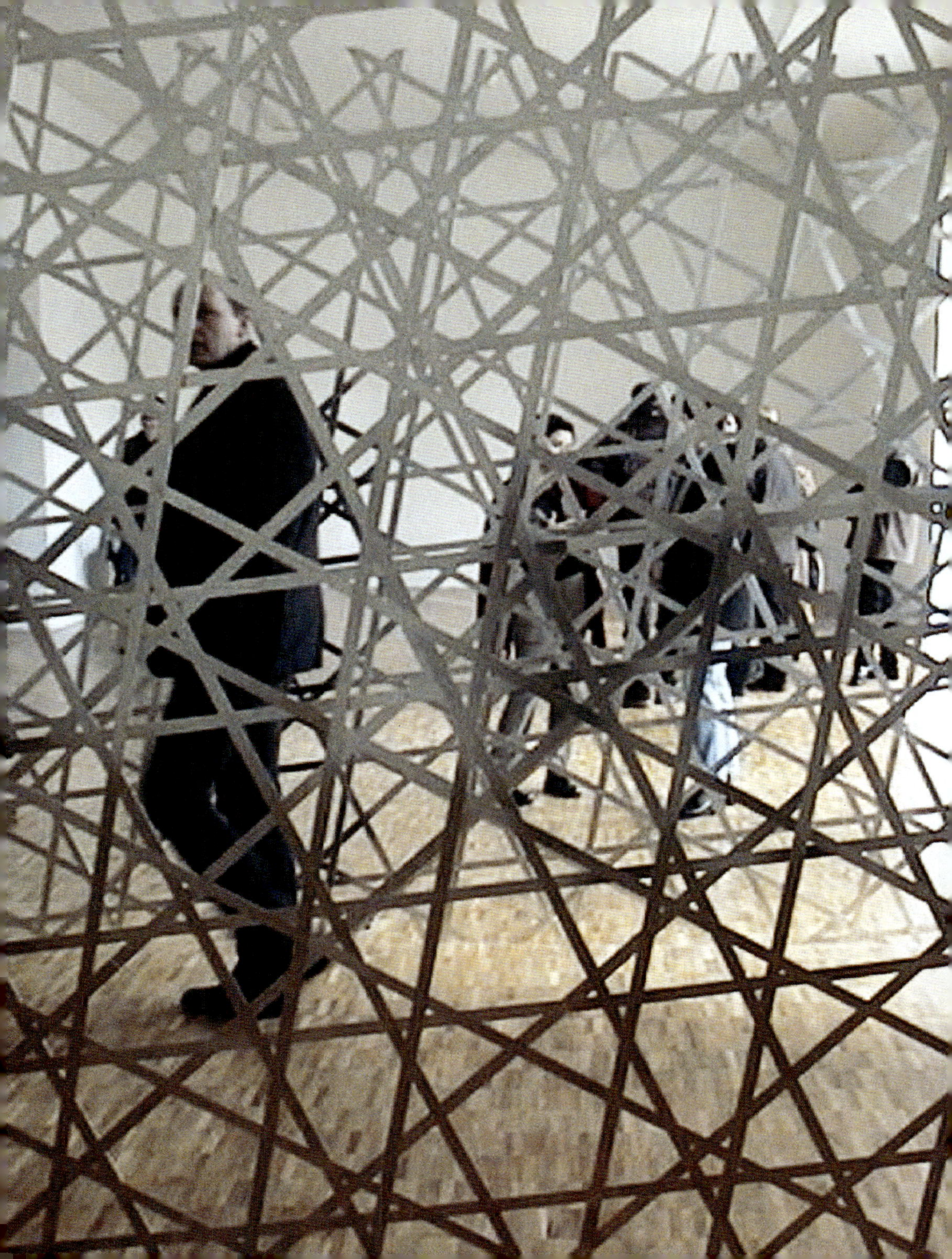

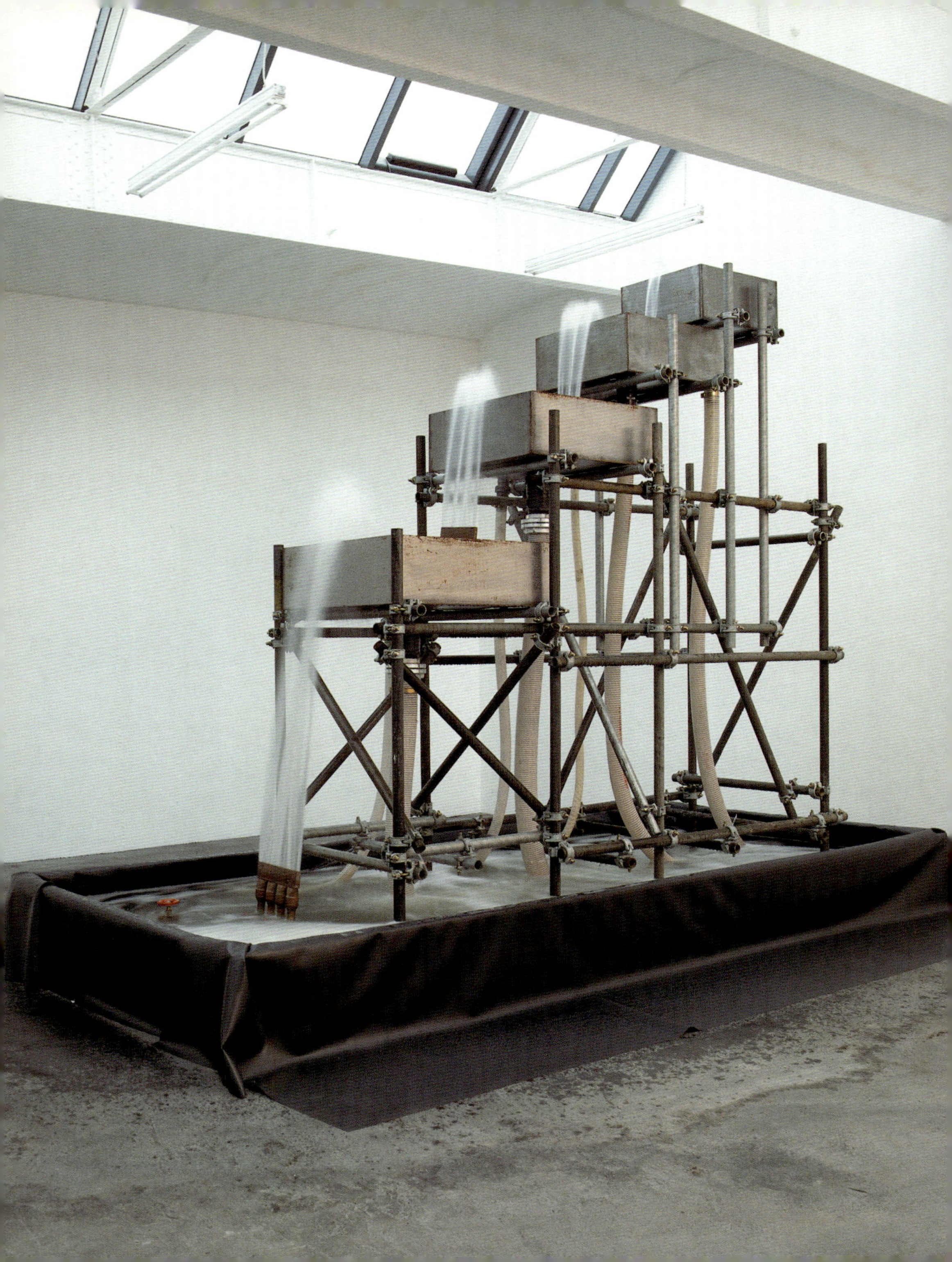

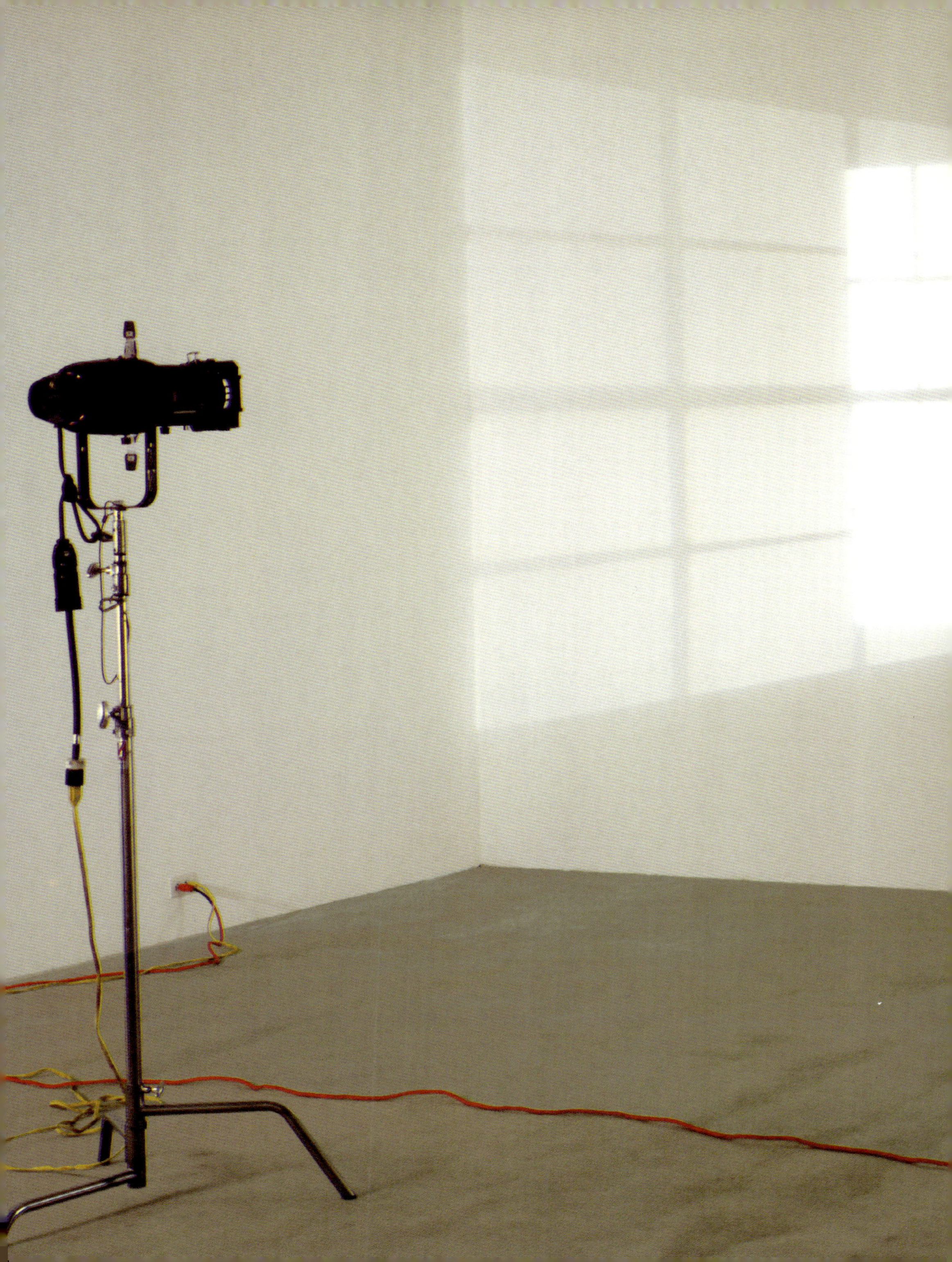

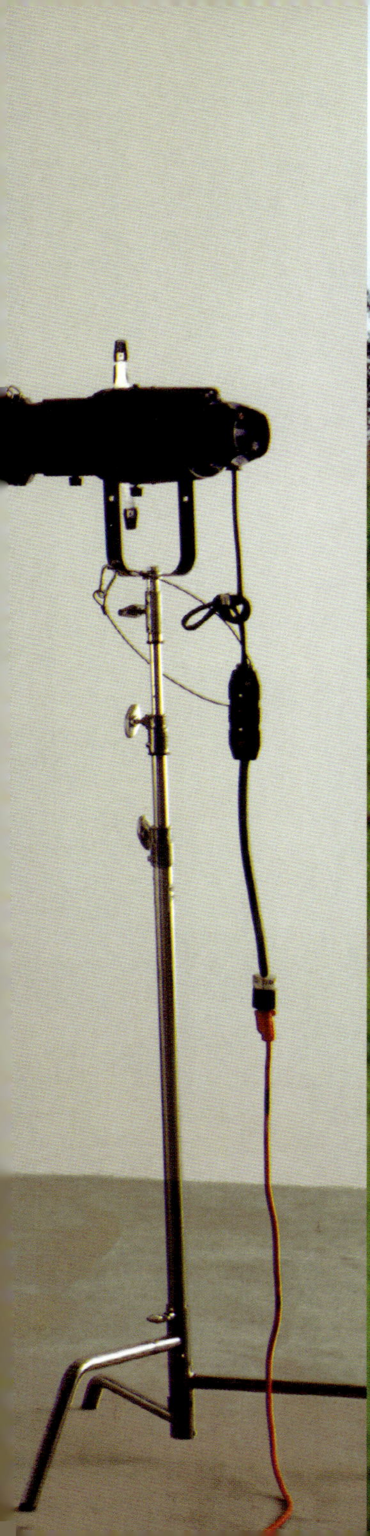
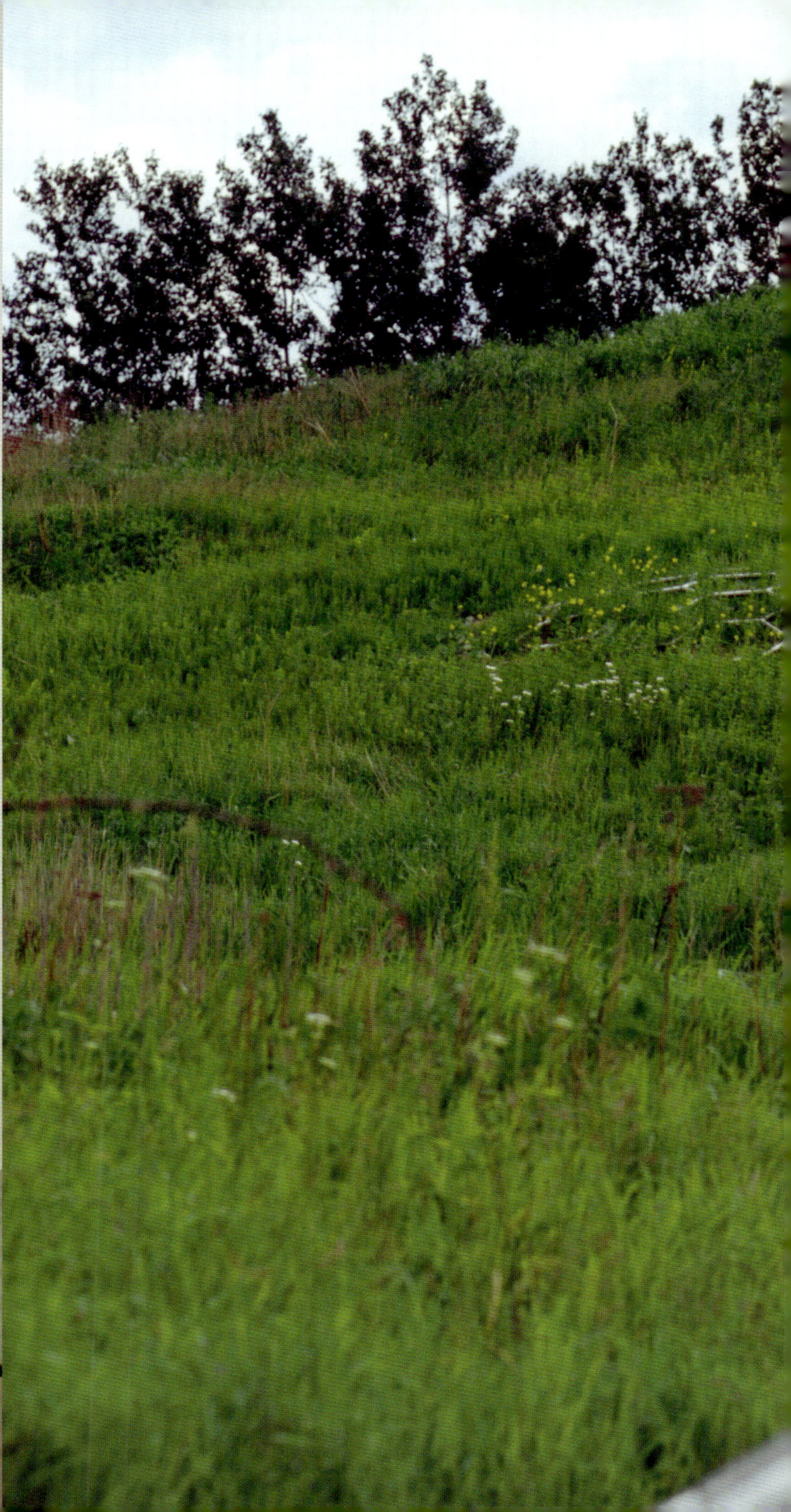

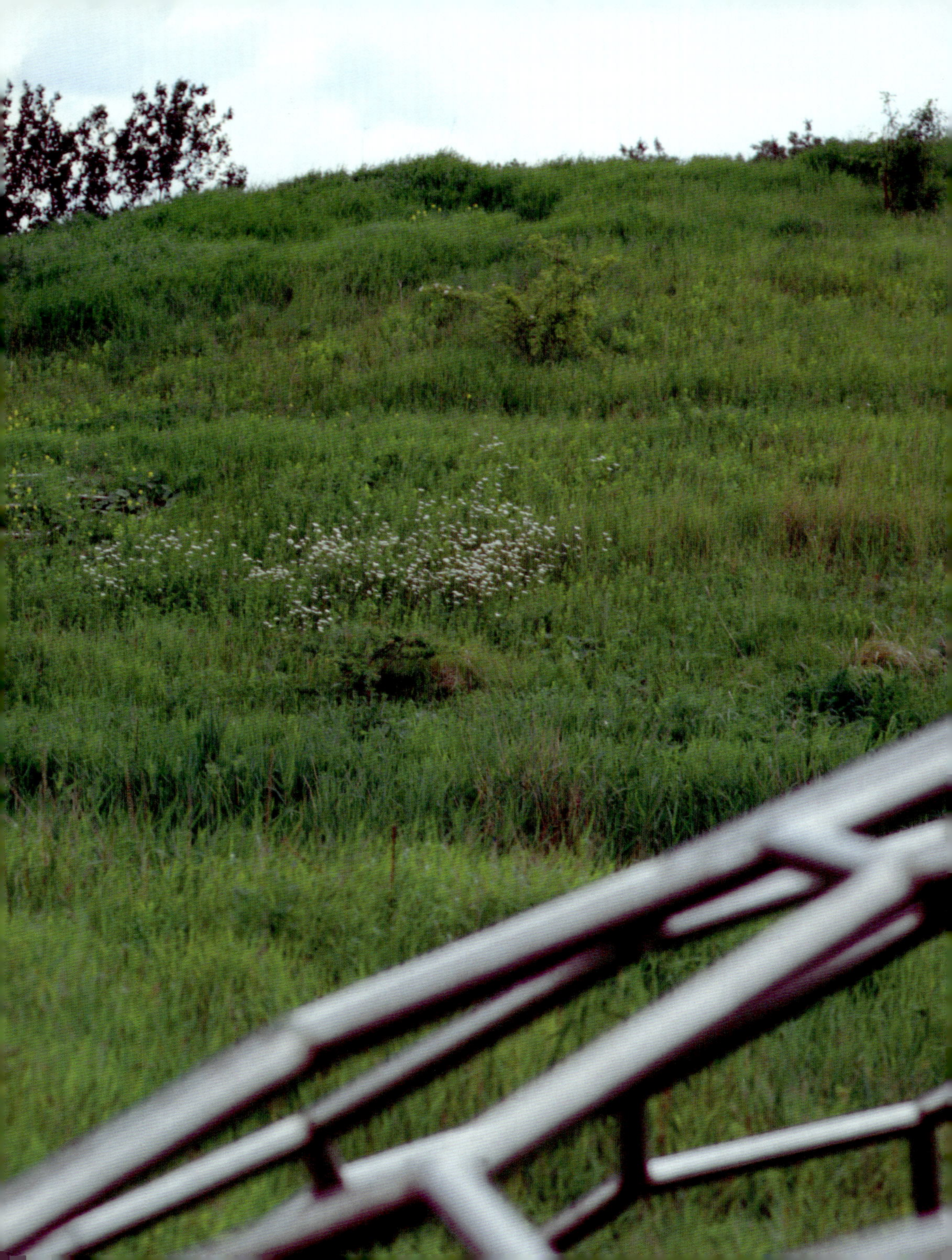

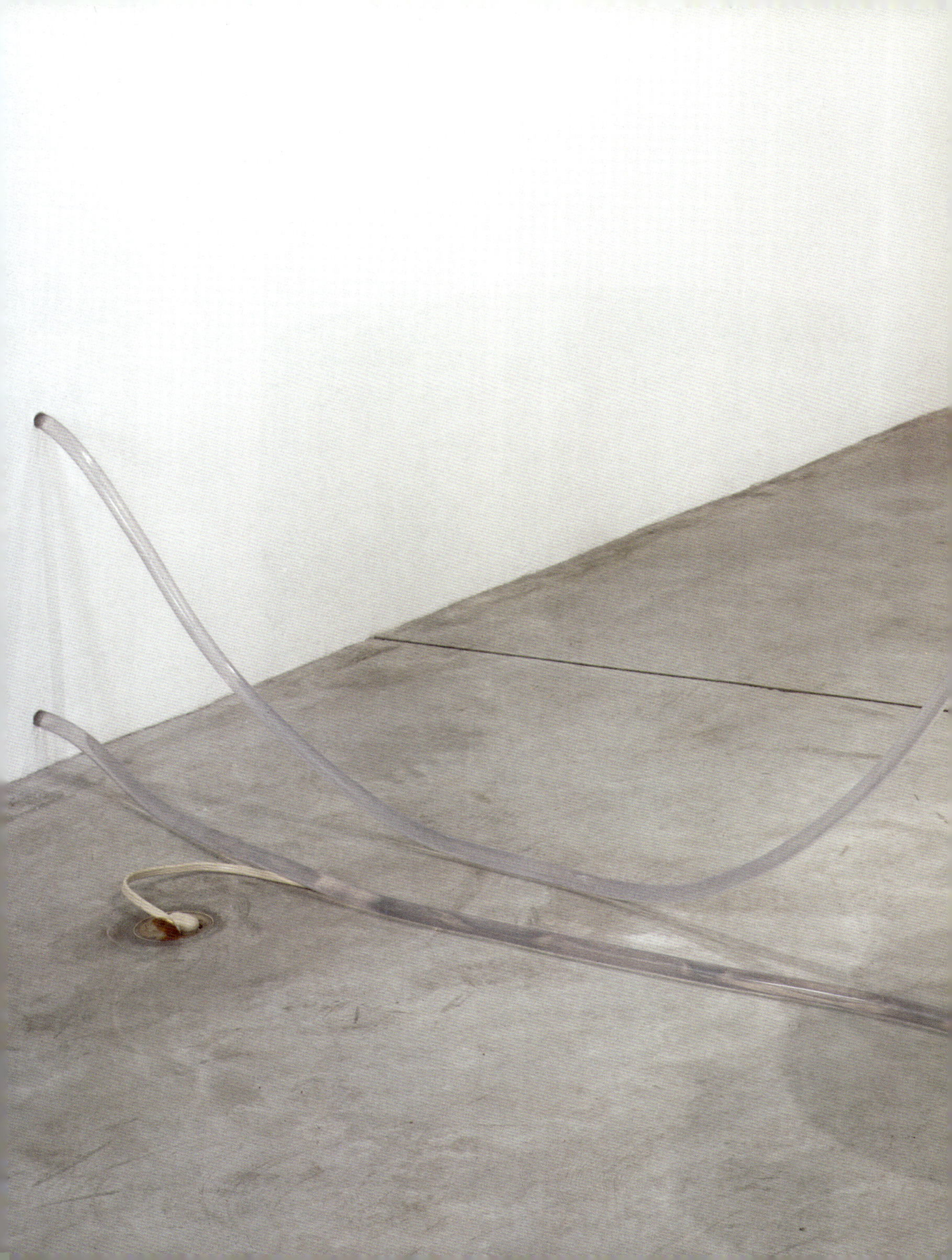

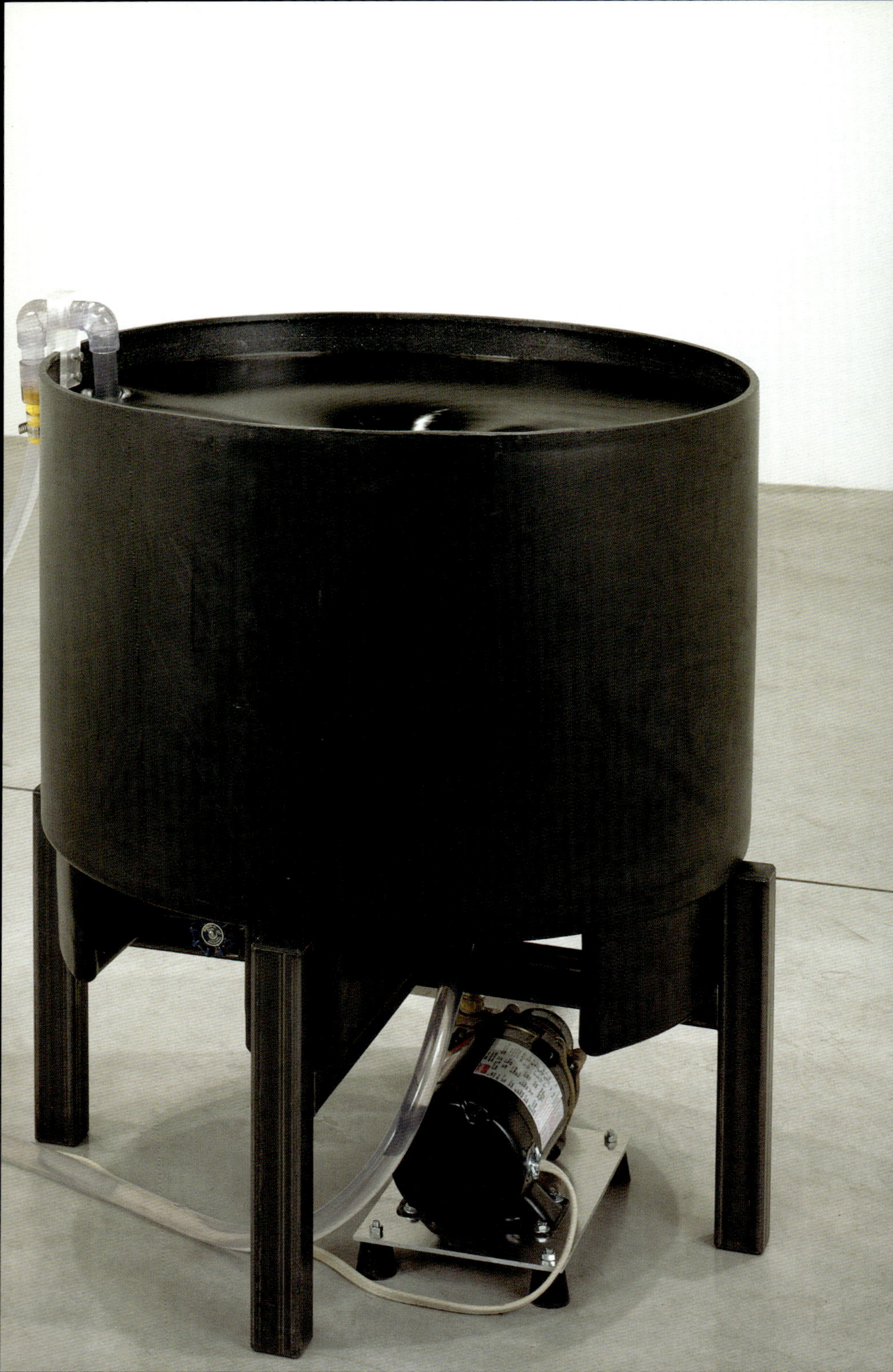
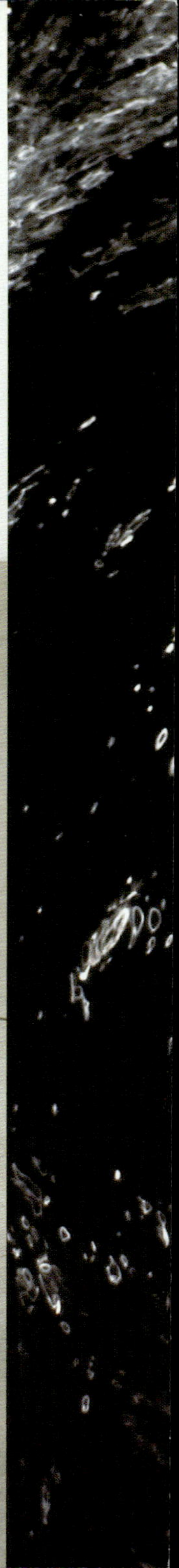

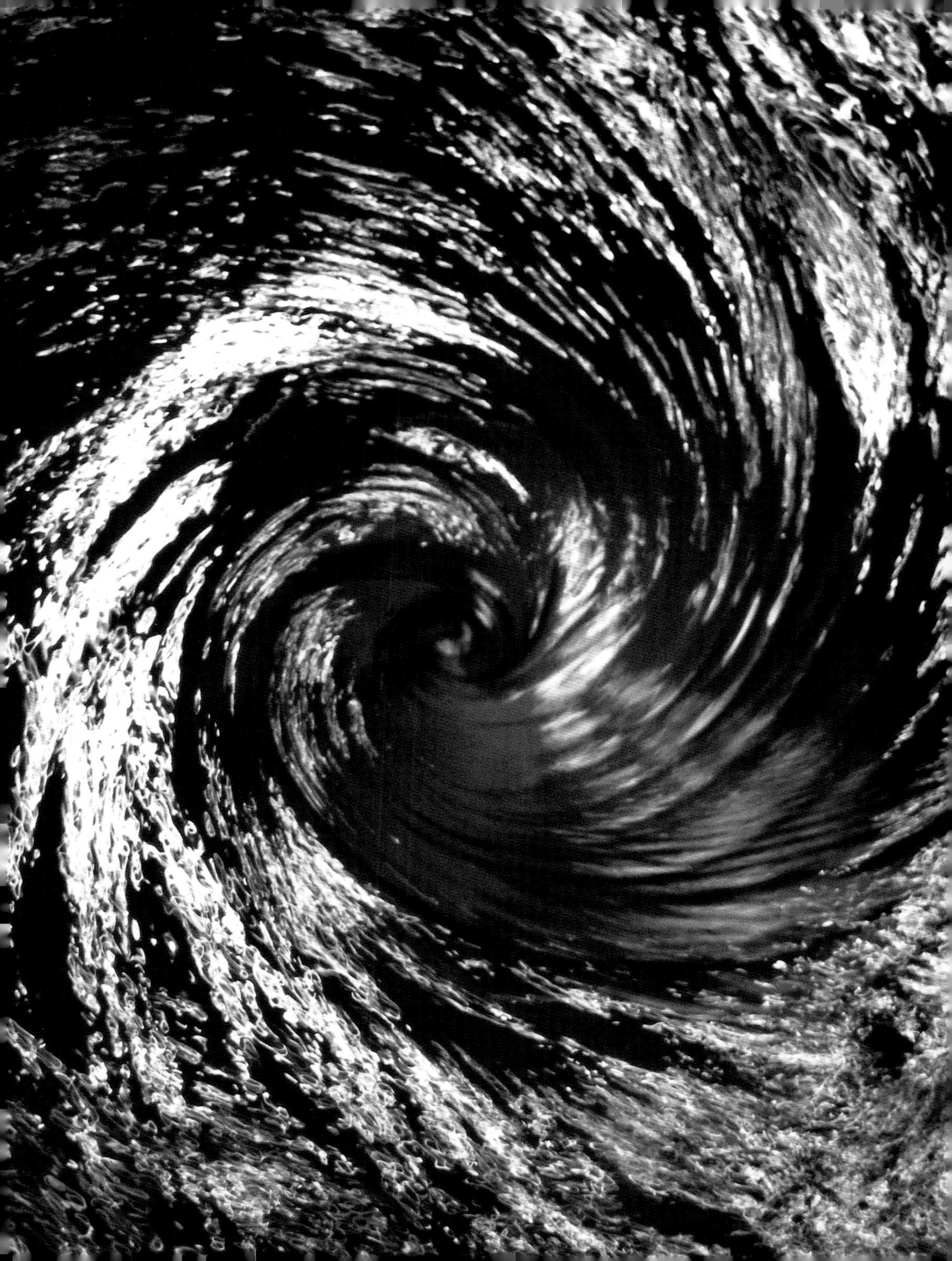

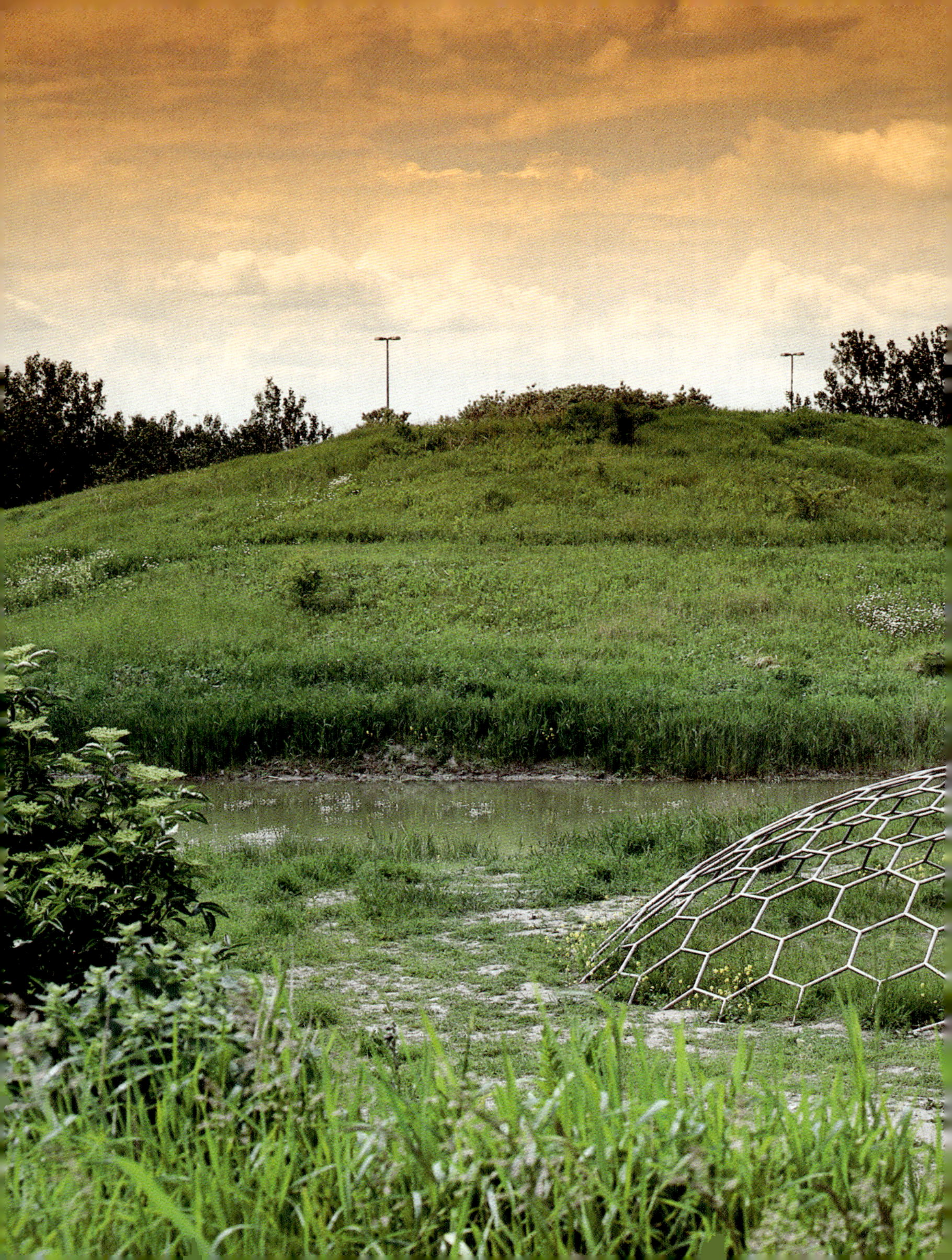

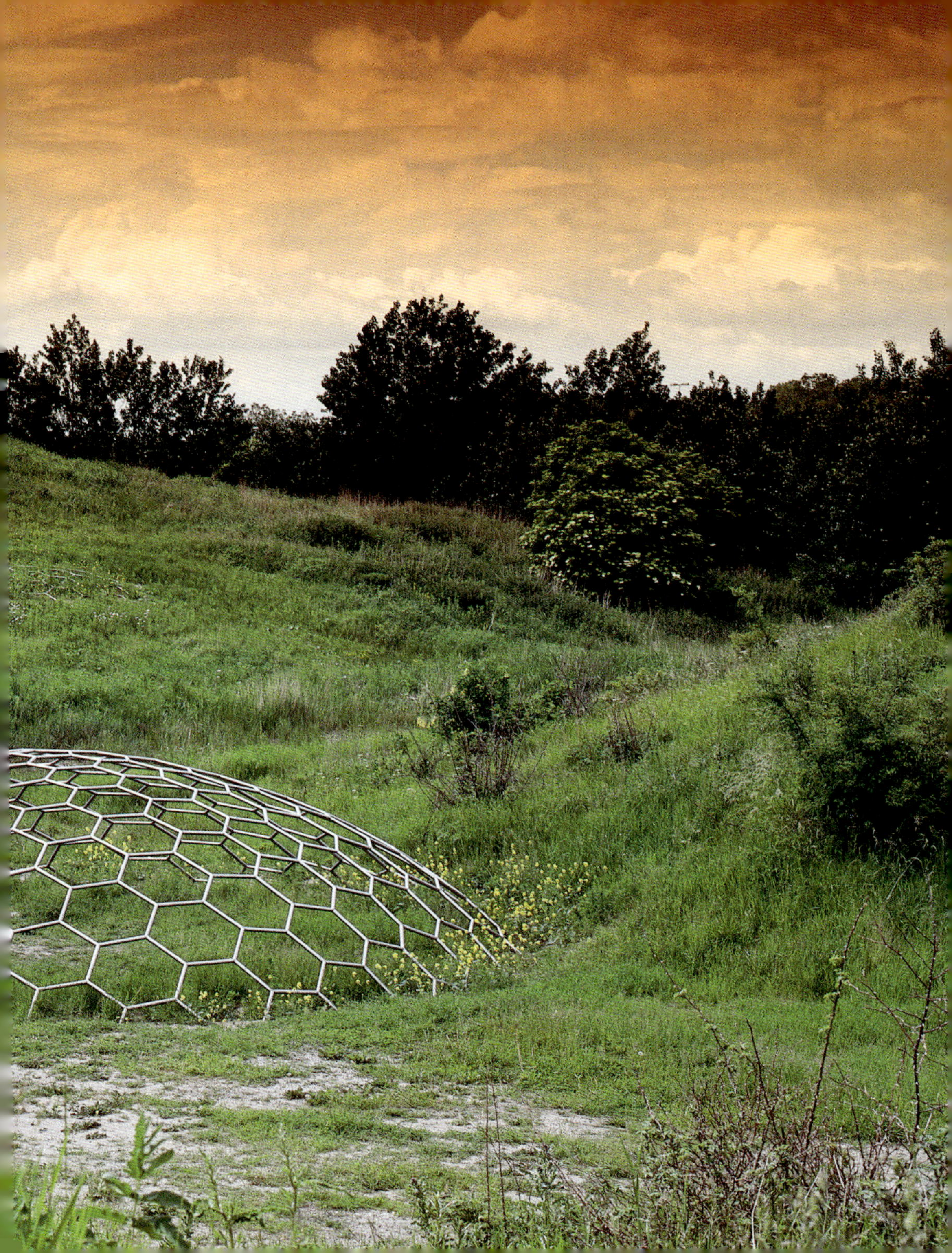

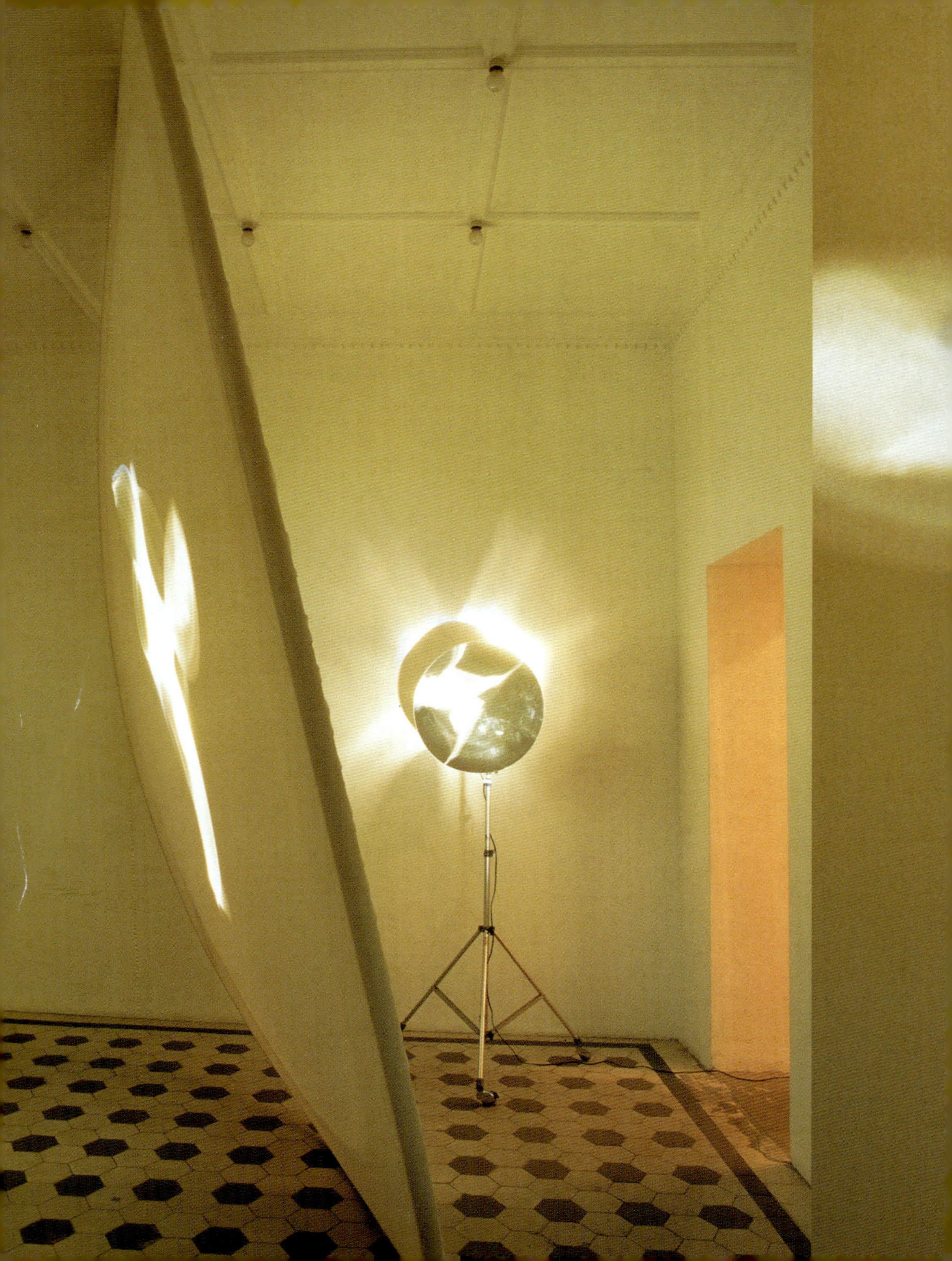

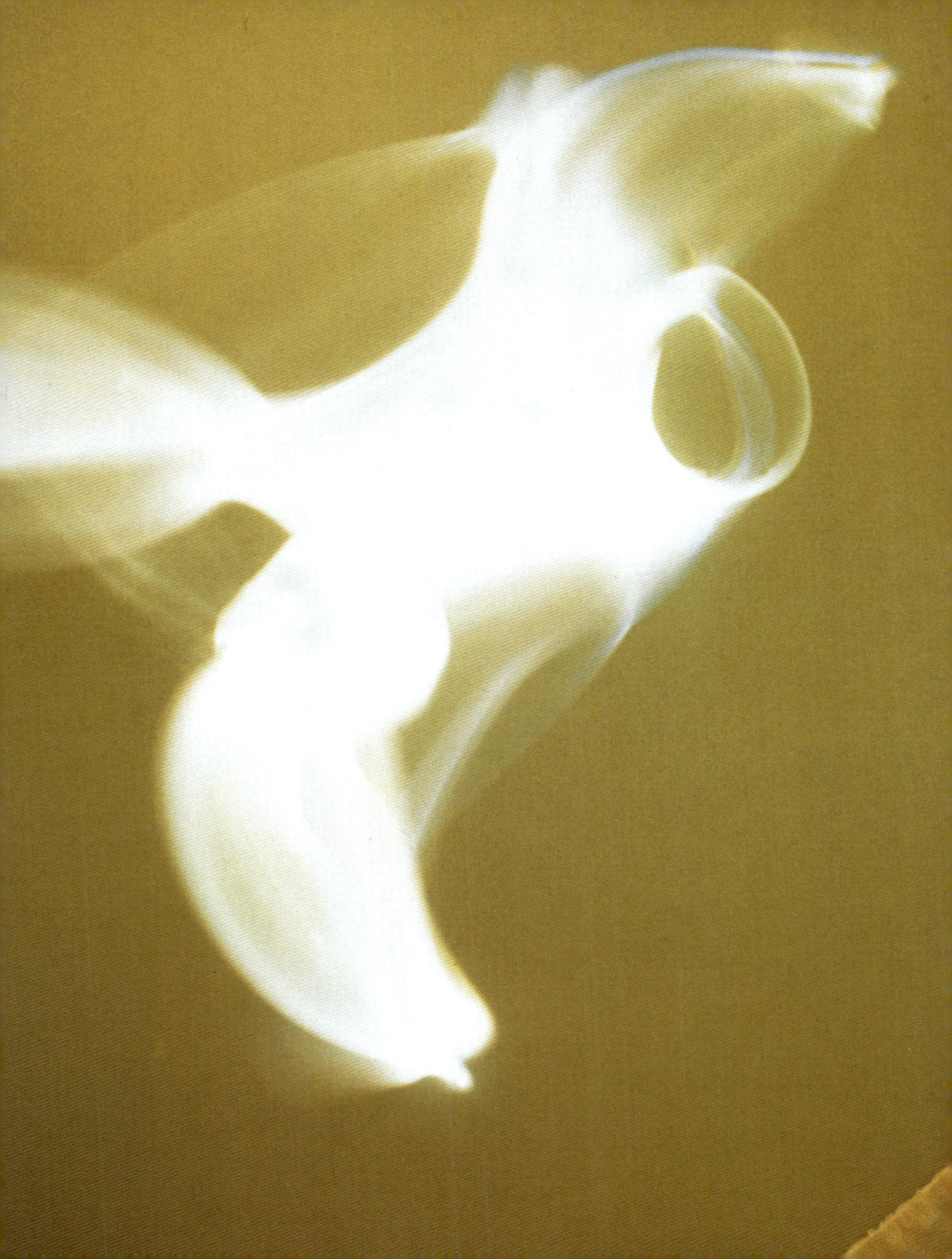

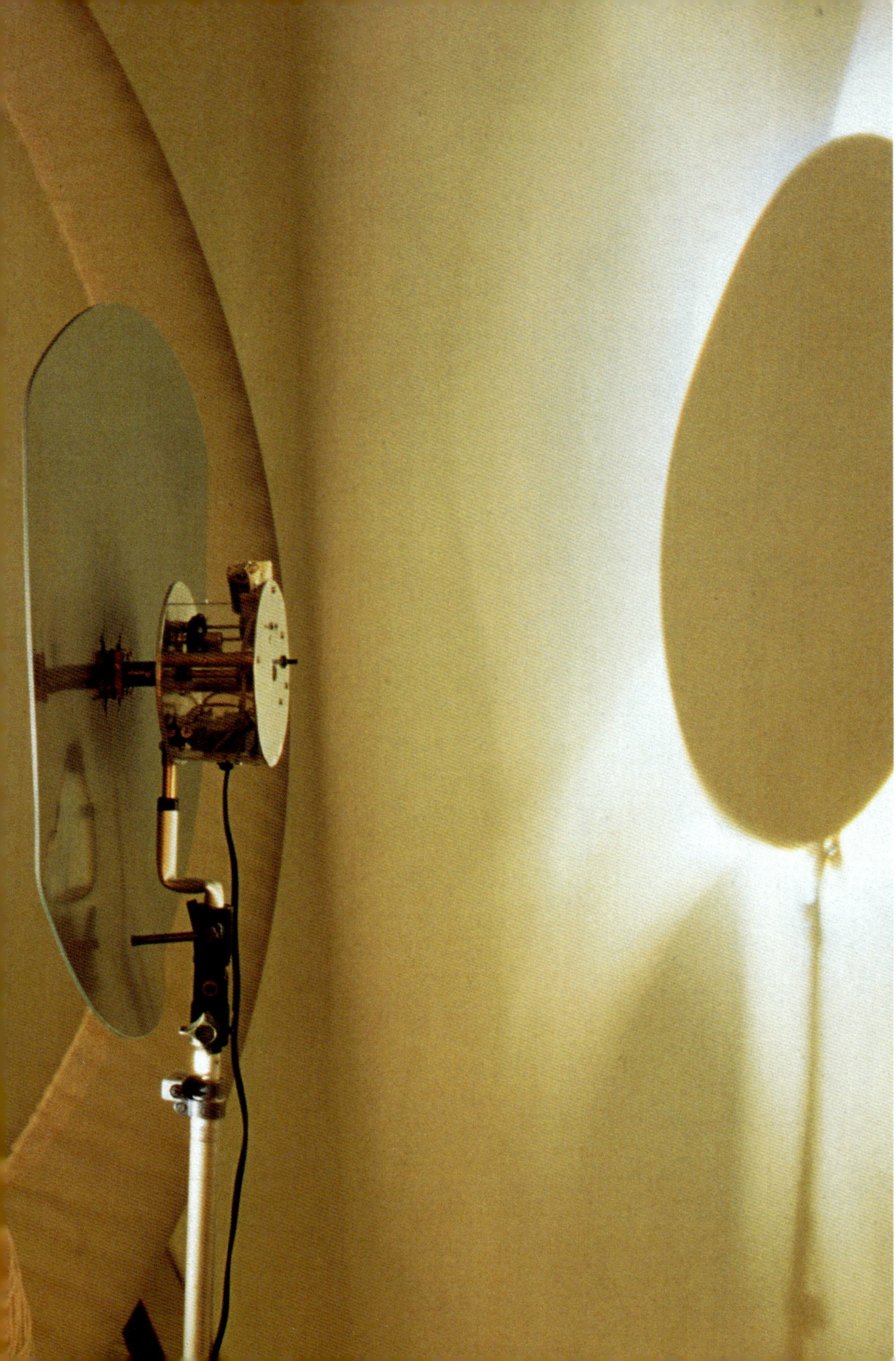

1	**By means of a sudden intuitive realization, show me your perception of presence**, 1996	300 x 510 Ø cm; water, strobe light, water pump, plastic sheets, fiberglass; installation view: Manifesta, Rotterdam, The Netherlands, 1996
2	**Fivefold symmetry walls**, 1998	Size varies with installation; aluminium; installation view: Galerie für zeitgenössische Kunst, Leipzig, Germany
3	**Yet untitled**, 1998	Size varies with installation; scaffolding, water, pump, plastic, wood, hoses; installation view: neugerriemschneider, Berlin, Germany
4	**Double window projection**, 2000	Size varies with installation; two spotlights; installation view: De Paviljoens, Almere, The Netherlands
5	**8900054**, 1998, detail	steel
6	**The inventive velocity**, 1998	100 x 84 x 84 x cm; pump, water, container and hose; Bonakdar Jancou Gallery, New York, USA
7	**The inventive velocity**, 1998, detail	100 x 84 x 84 x cm; pump, water, container and hose; Bonakdar Jancou Gallery, New York, USA
8	**8900054**, 1998	ø 9m, height 2,05m / ø 3,5 m, height 0,26 m, steel; Kopenhagen, Denmark
9	**Eine Beschreibung einer Reflexion, oder aber eine angenehme Übung zu deren Eigenschaften**, 1995	Size varies with installation; light, mirror, projection foil; installation view: neugerriemschneider, Berlin, Germany
10	**Eine Beschreibung einer Reflexion, oder aber eine angenehme Übung zu deren Eigenschaften**, 1995	Size varies with installation; light, mirror, projection foil; installation view: neugerriemschneider, Berlin, Germany

Einar Thorsteinn

A Mathematical Order of Polyhedrons
Fourfold to Fivefold Symmetry Transitions

The forms we usually call polyhedrons are most frequently ordered into three groups: 1) the Platonic solids, 2) the Archimedean solids, and perhaps 3) a group of so-called irregular solids. These three groups are based on the assumption that the regularity of polyhedrons is primarily dependent on the regularity and number of their exterior faces, and that the polyhedrons with few faces can, as solid masses, be cut down to form new polyhedrons as some of their names suggest – for instance Snub Cube or Snub Dodecahedron. This explains why the polyhedrons have been handled as massive forms instead of structures. This assumption gives an incorrect view of the nature of polyhedrons particularly in the field of molecular crystallography. Here we will look at the polyhedrons as grid structures with more or less flexible joints or as molecular-transformable masses.

In this introduction to a thesis for a development pattern for polyhedron formation it is the purpose to show some more sides to their nature. All known polyhedrons can be included in the new order thus found. But they will fit into it only by way of their stage in the development pattern. This new order, when used as an "instrument," will additionally enable one to find a number of new polyhedrons which are regular in the sense that they are formed by a mathematical order. A detailed description of how each polyhedron is structurally and formally based upon the formation of a preceding polyhedral pair, is included here. The necessary exception to this is the Tetrahedron.

We describe and give the name Tango to a new primary transformation which fills the last gap of the structural order of the polyhedrons and with which this new order of the polyhedrons can be logically understood.

A few new polyhedrons formed by this instrument – still nameless – will be described. Most of them have a fivefold symmetry. This presents, therefore, a direct connection to the present research on quasicrystals.

Polyhedral pairs

It is well known that polyhedrons come in pairs: each more or less regular polyhedral structure asks for a corresponding structure which orderly fixes itself to the former. When the two are harmonically combined around a common center, all the corners or vertices of each polyhedron point exactly to the center of all the faces of the other. All their sizes then correspond. When thus fixed, all their edges cut in a 90° angle. We will call this polyhedral combination or geometric compound their "wedding."

A Tetra wedding

When studying all the polyhedrons our eyes naturally stop at the one with the least number of faces, edges and corners: the Tetrahedron (or Tetra for short – the ending "hedron" will be left out of all polyhedral names in this article). The Tetra is unique in many other ways. As its number of faces and corners are equal – or four each time – the Tetra as an exception has itself as a mate: two Tetras form a polyhedral pair. (see fig. 1).

In order to visualize this better, one can enclose a small Tetra inside a larger Tetra in such a way that the first touches the face centers of the other from the inside. We then make the smaller Tetra grow to the same size as the larger. After that all their edges cut at their center points in a 90° angle. This is a Tetra wedding.

A closer look at a Tetra wedding reveals two peculiarities, of interest for the development pattern: 1) The crossed edges of the two Tetras form equilateral squares of which they are the hypotenuses. There are six such hypotenuse crosses, so the structure of the Cube (Hexa) has emerged, exactly enclosing both Tetras. 2) The lines where the two Tetras cut are the geometrically correct edges of a small Octa. The Octa placed inside the Cube only touches the centers of the Cube´s square face at six points with its vertices.

In general terms one can say that between any two points in a polyhedral wedding, new imagined beams automatically connect that then describe a new geometrical structure – or a polyhedron. Such points are, for instance, both the corners – vertices – of the preceding structures and the cutting points of their edges. Its sizes have a harmonic relationship to the preceding or parent structures of that wedding.

For the mathematical order, the Tetra is important in one more way. Its vertices – all eight of them in a Tetra-Star polyhedron or Tetra wedding – have a fixed place in one of the two polyhedrons at all stages of this development pattern. Thus, along with the process eight Tetra-Star vertices automatically connect to eight vertices of one partner of each polyhedral pair. This will be called here the Tetra-Star Fixture.

A Cube-Octa wedding

A Cube and an Octa – thus formed by two Tetras – are the next pair. Their edges also cut each other at their centers in their wedding compound. Seen from the Tetra wedding, however, in order to form this new geometric compound – the small Octa formed inside the Cube must now grow out of the Cube in the length ratio 1:2 and volume ratio 1:8. For practical reasons the smaller size of the Octa will be called its "birth" size and the larger size its wedding size (see fig. 2).

The Cube on the other hand is bound by the Tetra-Star Fixture which controls its size. The same applies to all other polyhedral pairs which are formed in the same way.

A Rhombic Dodeca-Cubocta wedding

In the same type of transformation, the wedding of Cube and Octa creates a new pair of polyhedrons. The 90° crossing edges of the pair form a Rhombic Dodeca and the lines where they cut become the edges of a Cubocta. Again, the latter is inside and touches the face centers of the former with its vertices. In their wedding compound, the edges of Cubocta are cut by the Rhombic Dodeca's at their center but the edges of Rhombic Dodeca on the other hand are cut by the Cubocta in the ratio 1:2 (see fig. 8).

Again, before the wedding is perfect, the Cubocta has to grow in size as the Octa did before: its edge growth ratio is now 3:4 and the volume growth ratio is therefore 27:64 (see fig. 3).

Two-frequency and Cross-Formation

In the last two wedding compounds we have been looking at two respective primary development transformations which produce a new polyhydral pair each time: two new polyhedrons. These simultaneous transformations are: Two-frequency and Cross-Formation.

They can work on any polyhedral pair wedding, forming indefinitely more polyhedrons with less and less degree of regularity. However, at certain intersections in the process a second primary development transformation now appears and regularly works on certain wedding compounds. In this way, a degree more regular polyhedrons are again formed, but now with fivefold symmetry elements, even if they had had fourfold symmetry before. And along with that, the numeric polyhedral values change to the golden ratio numbers that follow any fivefold symmetry. The Rhombic Dodeca / Cubocta wedding compound is one of those intersections.

What triggers this second primary transformation is, among other things, the fact that the preceding transformations (Cross-Formation / Two-Frequency) after two applications in a row, in the process, have built some structurally unstable elements into the polyhedrons in question. An open square in one and fourfold symmetrical corners in the other.

This second transformation makes clear how misleading it is to regard polyhedrons as solids. A solid mass is difficult to change structurally. It is therefore more appropriate to call them grid-structures with flexible joints; their edges being their only boundaries. One can also regard them as a collection of atoms or molecules. Molecular masses may be "glued" together with molecular forces but still have a possibility of an interior movement. Such shape-shifting could still be possible within certain structural rules.

Jitterbug

The well-known half of the second development transformation was given the name Jitterbug by the late R. Buckminster

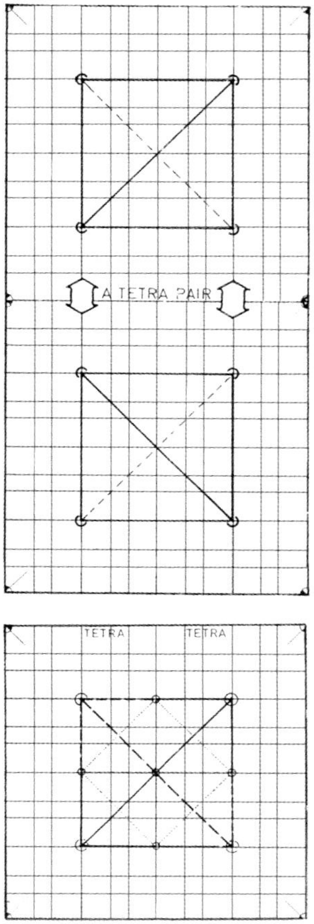
A TETRA PAIR
TETRA
TETRA

Fig. 1

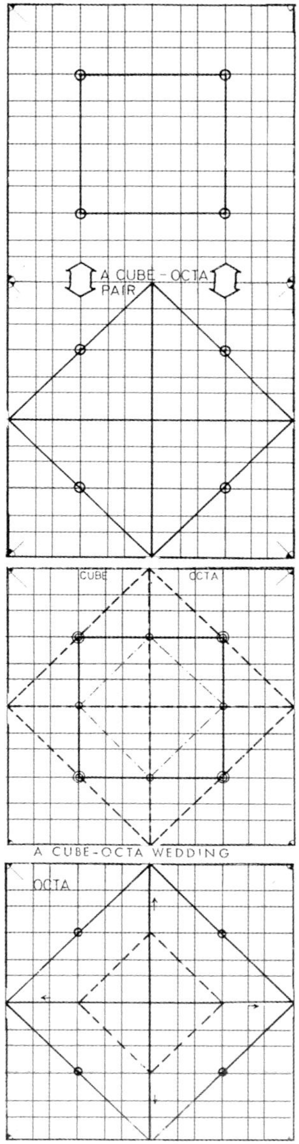
A CUBE - OCTA
PAIR
CUBE
OCTA
A CUBE-OCTA WEDDING
OCTA

Fig. 2

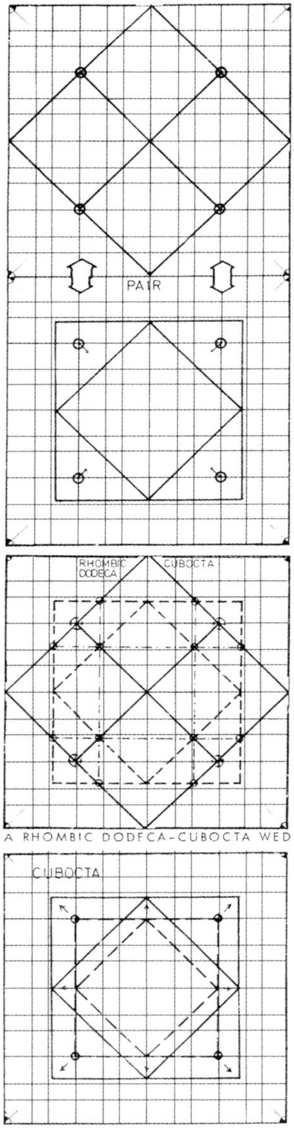
PAIR
RHOMBIC DODECA
CUBOCTA
A RHOMBIC DODECA-CUBOCTA WED
CUBOCTA

Fig. 3

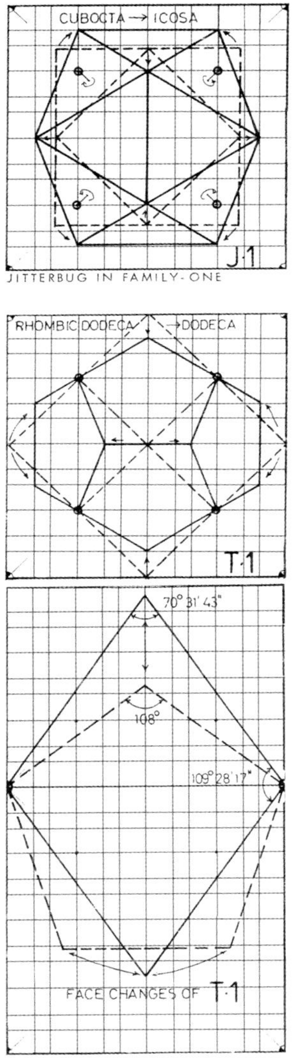
CUBOCTA → ICOSA
J·1
JITTERBUG IN FAMILY-ONE
RHOMBIC DODECA → DODECA
T·1
70° 31' 43"
108°
109° 28' 17"
FACE CHANGES OF T·1

Fig. 4

Fuller. It becomes possible when outside pressure works, for instance, on the structurally unstable Cubocta in a wedding compound with Rhombic Dodeca. Two things then happen: Cubocta's eight stable triangles turn on their central axis, and its six unstable squares take on rhombic shapes and fold the former square diagonally in the middle. It would inevitably fold together to form an Octa if they were not hindered by its partner, the Rhombic Dodeca, which is simultaneously undergoing this transformation. Thus the six square faces stop folding into a rhombus and the stable triangles stop rotating as the distance between its two diagonally opposite former square frame corners is the same as its edge length. This is the edge length of the polyhedron being formed: an Icosa (see fig. 4).

While the transformation occurs, the edges of the polyhedral pair remain locked in a 90° position. The triangles will rotate exactly 20°14'19.3". Instead of twenty-four edges of the Cubocta we now have 24 + 6 = 30 edges of the Icosa. Six new edges have thus been formed. In the same process the eight Cubocta triangles will move slightly inwards as its edge length grows from 0.942809 to 1.000000 (ratio = 1: square root of 9/8).

If one just looks at the reason for the edge growth of Cubocta to Icosa in the Jitterbug transformation, one may fail to understand what is going on. What happens always affects the whole geometric compound. In this case, the whole Rhombic Dodeca / Cubocta wedding. The lengthening of the edge is dimensionally controlled by the Tetra-Star Fixture.

Tango

The other half of the second primary transformation, not found until now or described, is the Tango. Jitterbug and Tango always occur simultaneously. The reason for the name is obvious: Tango has a resonance to the older half of the transformation: Jitterbug. Both of those generally tend to describe the terms of the geometrical movements which occur in the polyhedral shape-shifting. Tango, for instance, turns a Rhombic Dodeca into a Dodeca. The Rhombic Dodeca has eight soft and six sharp corners: the eight soft corners correspond with the Cube and thus are controlled by a Tetra-Star Fixture.

If one first looks at the Tango transformation from the point of view of a Cube, its eight soft corners remain fixed. But the Cube's twelve edges between the fixed points – into which they are in fact emerged – work as the axes of the twelve rhombic Dodecahedron faces on which they now start turning. Due to geometric connections and outside pressure they start transforming.

In this way the rhombic faces – with the hypotenuses ratio 1 to Sq Rt of 2, and the edge length of sin 36° – are transformed into regular pentagonal faces with the edge length of 2 sin 18°. This transformation always occurs in the Cross-Formation to Tango side of the shape-shifting.

The six sharp corners involved however – corresponding to the corners of a wedding size Octa – are drawn inwards at the same time. In that act, this vertex point is drawn into a line. There can be a left or right way for this to happen as four Octa-based faces touch here. Which way the vertex-line is drawn out will depend upon which direction the Cubocta triangles will turn.

As the six new edges being formed grow and are drawn a bit inwards, the four "old" rhombic edges now shorten. The reason for this is that all the geometric faces remain flat throughout the whole process. The movement of the polyhedral pair stops when the fifth edge of a Dodeca thus formed has the same length as the other four (see fig. 4).

The transformation duo Two-Frequency / Cross-Formation doubles the number of edges of each succeeding pair. On the other hand, the Jitterbug / Tango transformation only adds 1/4 more edges to their new formations as one pair transforms into another. It is a proportional growth of 4:5.

A Dodeca-Icosa wedding

Dodeca and Icosa are also a well-known polyhedral pair (See fig. 5). Their edges again cut in the ratio 1:1 pointing to more regularity.

Some edge length and volume ratios

The seven polyhedrons so far mentioned: Tetra, Cube / Octa, Rhombic Dodeca / Cubocta and Dodeca / Icosa thus already decide among themselves the ratios of their edge lengths and the ratios of their volumes: All being controlled by the Tetra-Star Fixture.

These ratio numbers are harmonic with one another. The same goes for a considerable number of other polyhedral pairs when harmonically ordered and bound by the Tetra-Star Fixture.

For practical reasons we now give the edge of the Tetra the length square root of 2 or 1.414214. This gives us the following data for these seven polyhedrons:

(Tetra small)	Edge:	0.471404	Volume:	(0.0123456789)	R:	2
Tetra		1.414214		0.333333		54
Cube		1.000000		1.000000		162
Octa birth		0.707107		0.16666		27
Octa wedding		1.414214		1.33333		216
Cubocta birth		0.707107		0.833333		135
Cubocta wedding		0.942809		1.975308		320
Rhombic Dodeca		0.866025		2.000000		324
Dodeca		0.618033		1.809017		324 x3.618/4
Icosa		1.000000		2.181695		135 x 2.618

In order to gain more understandable volume ratios: on the far right the volumes have been multiplied with the number 162. Of those, the volume of the Cubocta / Rhombic Dodeca pair in the wedding size is of interest: 320/324 equal to 0.987654321. The distinction of the face of the Rhombic Dodeca is the ratio of its hypotenuses which is 1:1.414214. The volumes of Dodeca / Icosa at first seem less harmonic than the others. However, they are both part of a golden ratio relationship as I will explained later on.

A Trapezoidal Icositetra-Rhombicubota wedding

Next we look at two more weddings: the wedding of Cubocta and Rhombic Dodeca is an intersection in the process. It also can form another pair of polyhedrons by the former transformation Two-Frequency / Cross-Formation. The new ones are Trapezoidal Icositetra and Rhombicubocta. In order to form this new geometric compound, again the one formed by Two-Frequency, Rhombicubocta, has to grow from its birth size (see fig. 6).

The Rhombicubocta has two different edge lengths. The shorter edge of its birth is part of its equilateral triangles and the longer is part of its equilateral squares. The edge size ratio is 1:1.414214.

Here, however, we come to a new stage in these first primary transformations: now it is not enough for the polyhedron to grow in order to cut all the edges of its wedding mate: It must also change its two edge lengths with two different growth ratios to fulfill this condition. We find that those growth ratios are 12/7 and 6/7.

The wedding type Rhombicubocta has the opposite specifications: the longer edge is a part of the polyhedrons equilateral triangles and the shorter edge is a part of its equilateral squares.

A second unstable wedding

The last described wedding can also become an unstable one: Jitterbug / Tango can work on it. Jitterbug transforms Rhombicubocta into Snub Cube and Tango transforms Trapezoidal Icositetra into Pentagonal Icositetra (see fig. 7).

The Jitterbug side: the eight stable triangles of Rhombicubocta now rotate 20° 20'15.9" and move slightly inwards. The six equilateral squares also rotate and move inwards but the other twelve oblong squares now transform into 24 equilateral triangles. At the same time the two edge lengths change into one (see fig. 8).

The Tango side: Trapezoidal Icositetra has the same eight fixed points (soft corners) as before with another six sharp corners (corresponding to the corners of an Octa). These fourteen corners function as the fixed ends of twenty-four axes about which the faces of the Trapezoidal Icositetra turn and change.

At each of the twelve corners corresponding to the corners of a wedding size Cubocta, the edges now part into two and move in opposite directions (see fig. 8). The moving parts move slightly inwards and through that, the edge lengths shorten. However, also here the six corners corresponding to the edges of an Octa move slightly inwards. When equilibrium is found, the irregular symmetric rhombuses have transformed into irregular symmetric pentagons with two different edge lengths (see fig. 8). The additionally formed edge is of the shorter type.

This gives us the following data for these four polyhedrons:

Rhombicubocta birth	Edges:	0.471404 0.666666	Volume:	1.679013	R:	272
Rhombicubocta wedding		0.808122 0.571428		2.674441		432x(1+1/7itp)
Trapezoidal Icositetra		0.552770 0.745356		2.66666		432
Pentagonal Icositetra		0.5691216416 0.4008905686		2.2955977		
Snub Cube		0.6755079539		2.4386591		

The edge lengths of Rhombicubocta and Trapezoidal Icositetra are all square roots of some whole parts 1.00000 or 2/9 and 4/9 – 11/36 and 20/36 – and 16/49 – 32/49.

The edges of Rhombicubocta while wedding, are cut in their center points, but the edges of Trapezoidal Icositetra are both cut in the ratio 3/4. The edges of Snub Cube are cut in

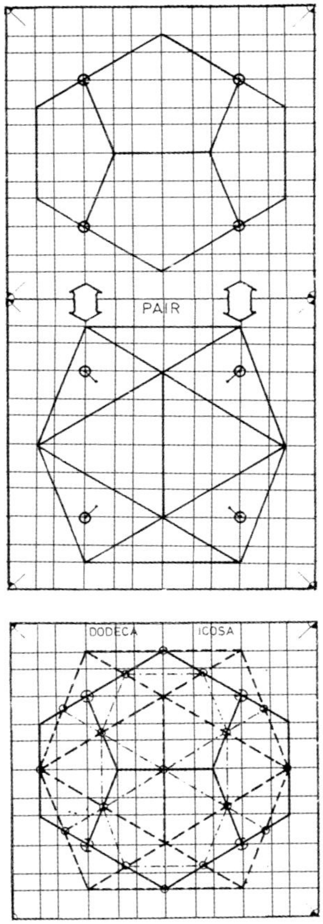
PAIR
DODECA
ICOSA

Fig. 5

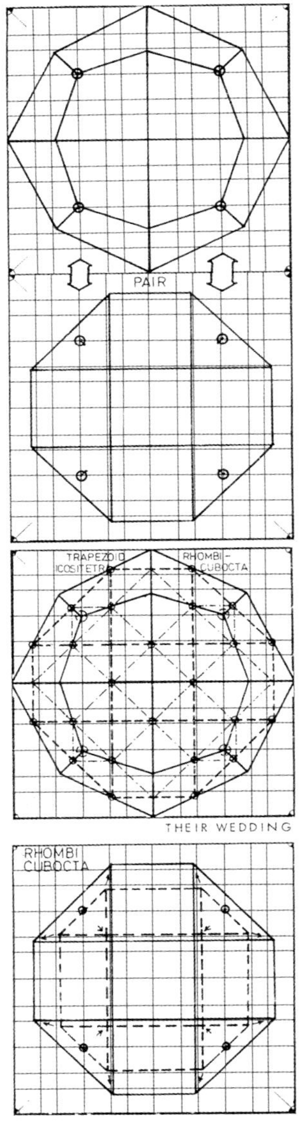
PAIR
TRAPEZOID
ICOSITETRA
RHOMBI-
CUBOCTA
THEIR WEDDING
RHOMBI
CUBOCTA

Fig. 6

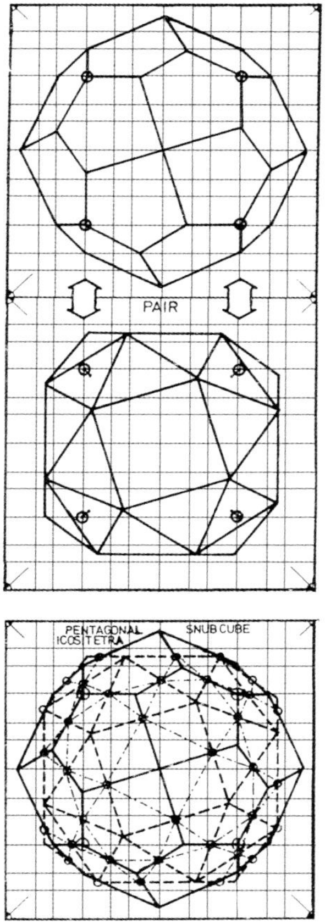
PAIR
PENTAGONAL ICOSITETRA
SNUB CUBE

Fig. 7

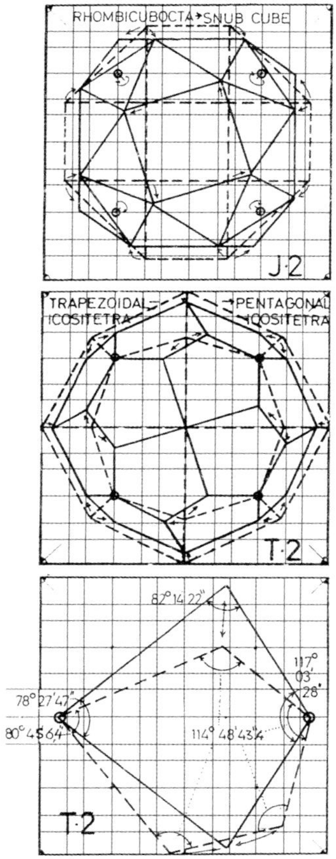
RHOMBICUBOCTA→SNUB CUBE
J·2
TRAPEZOIDAL ICOSITETRA
PENTAGONAL ICOSITETRA
T·2
82°14'22"
117° 03' 28"
78°27'47"
T·2

Fig. 8

their center points but the edges of Pentagonal Icositetra are cut in the ratios 1:1 (shorter) and 1:1.8392867 (longer).

A Rhombic Triaconta-Icosidodeca wedding

Next we look at three more weddings: The Dodeca / Icosa wedding will form a new pair of polyhedrons by Two-Frequency / Cross-Formation transformation. They are Rhombic Triaconta and Icosidodeca. To make their wedding possible, the size of the Icosidodeca has to grow as before (see fig. 9).

The growth ratio is now 3.6180339/4 in length. At this wedding the edges of the Icosidodeca is cut in the ratio 1:1, but the edges of Rhombic Triaconta are cut in the ratio 1:2.6180330 or the golden ratio to the second power.

A Trapezoidial Hexaconta-Rhombicosidodeca wedding

The Rhombic Triaconta / Icosidodeca wedding forms, as before, two new polyhedrons by Cross-Formation / Two-Frequency. They are: Trapezoidal Hexaconta and Rhombicosidodeca. The volume of the one formed by Two-Frequency, Rhombicosidodeca, has to grow from its birth size (see fig. 10). This polyhedron has two different edge lengths. The shorter edge is part of the polyhedrons equilateral triangles and the longer edge is part equilateral pentagons. The edge size ratio is 1:1.6180339. But here again as with Rhombicubocta, these elements must change in two different ratios in order to make the wedding perfect.

We find the growth ratios which are: 1/1.902113 (one to the square root of 3.6180339 and 1/0.7265425 (2.6180339 to the square root of 3.6180339). The wedding type Rhombicosidodeca still has the edge size ratio 1/1.6180339 but now it is again the other way round: the longer edge is part of its equilateral triangles and the shorter edge is part of its equilateral pentagons.

The edges of Rhombicosidodeca are cut in the center points by its mate, but as could be expected, the edges of Trapezoidal Hexaconta are both cut in the ratio:
3.6180339:4.

A third unstable wedding

The last wedding compound described here in full is an unstable one. Jitterbug and Tango work on the pair. Jitterbug transforms Rhombicosidodeca into Snub Dodeca and at the same time Tango transforms Trapezoidal Hexaconta into Pentagonal Hexaconta (see fig. 11).

The Jitterbug side: The twenty triangles of Rhombicosidodeca rotate 19°30'54.15" and move slightly inwards. The twelve regular pentagons also rotate and move inwards and the thirty oblong squares transform into sixty regular triangles. At the same time the two edge lengths change into one (see fig. 12).

The Tango side: As before, Trapezoidal Hexaconta has the eight fixed points (soft corners) plus another twelve fixed points or a total of twenty. Those correspond to the corners of Dodeca. With still another twelve corners corresponding to the corners of Icosa, all thirty-two function as ends of sixty axes about which the faces of Trapezoidal Hexaconta turn and are transformed.

At each of the thirty corners corresponding to the corners of the wedding size of Icosidodeca, the edges now part and move in opposite directions (see fig. 12). The moving parts move inwards and thus the edge lengths shorten. However, the twelve corners corresponding to Icosa also move slightly inward. When equilibrium is found, the irregular symmetric rhombuses have transformed into irregular symmetric pentagons that have two different edge lengths (see fig. 12). The additionally formed edge is of the shorter type.

At their wedding, the edges of Snub Dodeca are cut in their center points but the edges of Pentagonal Hexaconta are cut in the ratios 1:1 (shorter) and 1:2.4997528 (longer).

This gives us the following data for these six polyhedrons: Of those volumes and lengths all are golden ratio related numbers. It is however noticeable that the volume of Rhombic Triaconta does fit into the volume ratio series as 405. The reason for this must be that the number 2.5 which is rational has an opening into the golden-number field! The distinction of the face of the Rhombic Triaconta is the ratio of its hypotenuses, which is 1:1.6180339 or again the golden ratio.

Icosidodeca birth,	Edge:	0.500000	Volume:	1.729440	R:
Icosidodeca wedding		0.552786		2.337046	
Rhombic Triaconta		0.587785		2.500000	405
Rhombicosidodeca birth		0.276393 0.447213		2.231471	
Rhombicosidodeca wedding		0.525731 0.324919		2.755736	
Trapezoidal Hexaconta		0.320603		2.763932	405x4/3.618
Pentagonal Hexaconta		0.417216 0.238429		2.439054	
Snub Dodeca		0.409040		2.574425	

The numbers are not easy to understand at first glance. It is however interesting to note that now two polyhedrons with fivefold elements in their surfaces have undergone another fivefold Jitterbug / Tango transformation with the result that they have gained more regular forms. Still they have a kind of double fivefold symmetry in the surfaces.

We now finish this description of the development pattern but will look closer at the significance of the different sizes and ratios found.

Polyhedrons in a mathematical order

The nine polyhedral weddings or geometric compounds formed by the development pattern include seventeen different polyhedrons. They are either the five Platonic polyhedrons or originate directly from them by the new defined development pattern. Still those polyhedrons are all of three groups mentioned before: Platonic, Archimedean and so-called irregular groups. Five of these are Platonic, six are Archimedean and the other six are so-called irregular. (The seven other Archimedean not yet mentioned here are formed by the secondary transformation Three-Frequency. Both from the Platonic group (five) and then from Cubocta and Icosidodeca which are of the circular-edges group in the second stage of each of their families).

Only seven of these seventeen polyhedrons have twofold and fourfold symmetrical elements. Whereas ten have fivefold symmetrical elements, still there seems to be a direct link between the fourfold and fivefold symmetries in the faces of the 3-D polyhedrons – in view of their formations. And perhaps this link between fourfold and fivefold symmetries may generally connect through volumes and fixed volume transformations.

When considered from this point of view, neither the Platonic nor the Archimedean groups can be logical holistic systems. They are, rather, dependent on pure aesthetic opinions for their formal order. A closer look at the ratios and sizes of all known polyhedrons will show us that they will have to be reconsidered for their judgment of regularity.

Defining the polyhedral families

With the new definition presented here, the seventeen polyhedrons constitute three groups or Families: Family One; Family Two; and Family Five. The first family is the basis for all the others (see fig. 13).

Family One includes all the Platonic polyhedrons and two more that are important. Starting from the Tetra-Star polyhedron compound and ending with the Dodeca / Icosa compound. Family Two starts with the Cube / Octa compound and ends with the Snub Cube / Pentagonal Icositetra compound. In these two first Families only two polyhedral compounds have fivefold symmetry: the last stage in each Family. Finally we have Family Five. It starts with the Dodeca / Icosa compound and ends with the Snub-Dodeca / Pentagon Hexaconta compound. This Family is all of fivefold symmetry.

Right here there is a borderline of knowledge in this same process, beyond which little is known. However, when studied, almost all polyhedrons turn out to be formed of fivefold symmetry. So basically one can claim that fivefold symmetry is the main expression of the regular polyhedrons formed by the development pattern.

Through this instrument many more polyhedrons can see the light of day. And some will be mentioned here briefly.

For each Family, the development pattern has four stages with three intervals between them. The first two stages are covered by one transformation: Cross-Formation / Two-Frequency. This is then followed in the third interval by the second transformation: Jitterbug / Tango. Some geometric compounds necessarily occur in two Families – for each new compound formed can be an originator of a new Family.

The three Families obtain their names from numerical ratios of some number of parallel elements which are included in the polyhedrons of the same developmental stage. As an example, let us look at the Cube, the Rhombic Dodeca, and the Rhombic Triaconta which all have a place in the second developmental stage of each Family. Their edge numbers are 12 - 24 - 60 and the face numbers are 6 - 12 - 30. That gives us the numerical ratios 1 - 2 - 5, or the Family names One - Two - Five.

Any number of Families can be called to light with the same development pattern. However, without the use of the development pattern it is very difficult to define the new structures. Structures once visible seem quite logical. This is perhaps the reason why some of the new polyhedrons shown in fig. 14 and 15 are, or have been, little known until now.

Family Four

There is only space to briefly mention two more Families here: they are Family Four, with originators are Rhombic Dodeca and Cubocta, and Family Ten. The four stages of Family Four show us structures with alternatively 24 - 48 - 96 - 120 edges.

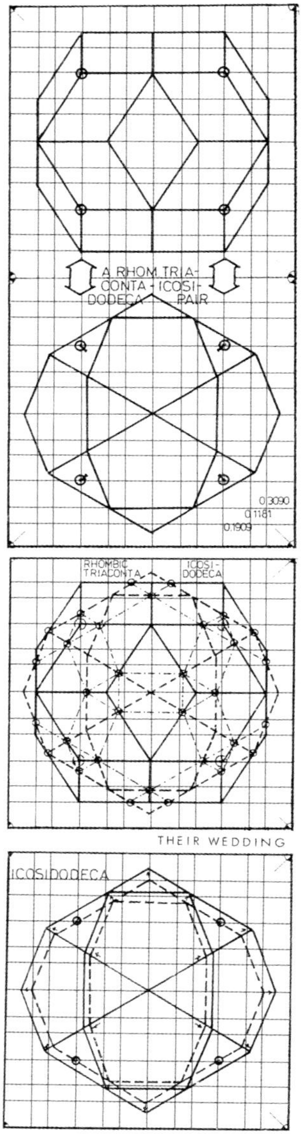
A RHOM TRIA-
CONTA - ICOSI-
DODECA PAIR
0.3090
0.1181
0.1909
RHOMBIC
TRIACONTA
ICOSI-
DODECA
THEIR WEDDING
ICOSIDODECA

Fig. 9

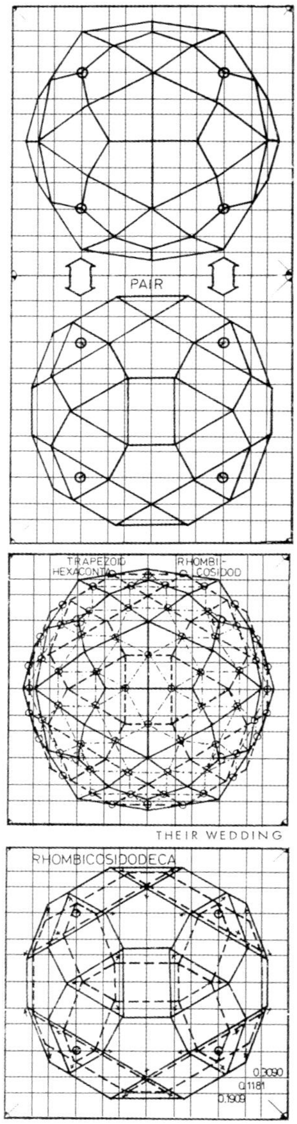
PAIR
TRAPEZOID
HEXACONTA
RHOMBI-
COSIDOD
THEIR WEDDING
RHOMBICOSIDODECA
0.3090
0.1181
0.1909

Fig. 10

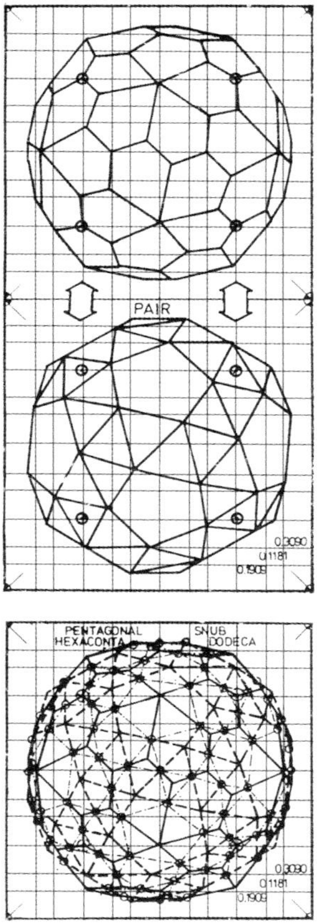
PAIR
0.3090
0.1181
0.1909
PENTAGONAL HEXACONTA
SNUB DODECA
0.3090
0.1181
0.1909

Fig. 11

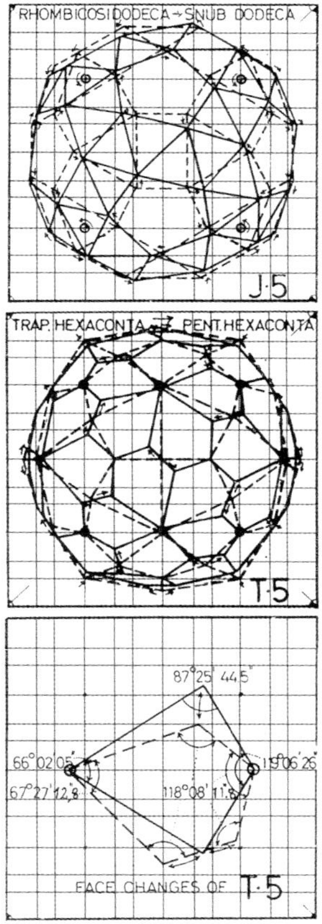
RHOMBICOSIDODECA → SNUB DODECA
J·5
TRAP. HEXACONTA ⇄ PENT. HEXACONTA
T·5
87°25' 44.5"
66°02'05"
67°27'12.8"
118°08' 11.8"
119°06'26"
FACE CHANGES OF T·5

Fig. 12

Of those, we already know the first two geometrical compounds which are also the second and third developmental stages of Family Two. The third stage has a geometric compound that has one Two-Frequency structure with four types of faces:

1. Equilateral squares, a total of 6
2. Squares with the side ratio 1 : 1.2247448, a total of 24
3. Triangles, a total of 8
4. Rhombuses with the hypotenuse ratio 1 : 1.414214, a total of 12

This gives us a total of 50 faces for the new polyhedron.

The mate is a Cross-Formation structure. It has two types of symmetrical rhombuses, twenty-four of each or a total of fourty-eight faces. Here, though, a new irregularity occurs: The eight fixed Tetra vertex points (the distance is sin 60° to the central point of the structure) now have to move outwards in the ratio 1:1.050952 as the overall growth demands it, the reason being more and larger distances to the other vertexes.

We now also have two types of Cross-Formation type structures like before: Birth and Wedding types.

The geometric compound in stage four is one Jitterbug structure with three types of faces:

1. Equilateral squares, a total of 6
2. Triangles, a total of 56
3. Rhombuses as before, a total of 12 faces

This gives us a total of seventy-four faces. Again here after the Jitterbug / Tango transformation – or fourth stage of Family Four – we come back to more regularity than was in the stage before as the eight Tetra vertices now move back to the original distance of sin 60°.

The mate is a Tango structure. It has two types of pentagonal faces – one symmetric the other asymmetric. It has twenty-four of each or a total of fourty-eight faces (see fig. 14).

Family Ten

The originators of Family Ten are Rhombic Triaconta and Icosidodeca. The four stages of Family Ten show us structures with alternatively 60 - 120 - 240 - 300 edges. Of those we already know, the first two geometrical compounds are also the second and third developmental stages of Family Five. The third stage has a geometric compound that has one Two-Frequency structure with four types of faces:

1. Pentagons, a total of 12
2. Squares with the side ratio 1 : 1.17557, a total of 60
3. Triangles, a total of 20
4. Rhombuses with the hypotenuse ratio 1 : 1.6180339, a total of 30

This gives us a total of 122 faces for this new polyhedron. The mate is a Cross-Formation type structure with two types of symmetrical rhombuses – sixty of each or a total of 120 faces. Again the Tetra vertex points move outwards and is now in the ratio 1:1.019847 moving back again to the original distance after the Tango transformation – fourth stage (see fig. 15).

The last pair formed in the transformation process has one Jitterbug structure with three types of faces:

1. Pentagons, a total of 12
2. Triangles, a total of 140
3. Rhombuses as before, a total of 30

Which gives us a total of 182 faces for the new polyhedron.

The mate is a Tango type structure with two types of pentagonal faces. One is symmetric the other asymmetric. It has sixty of each or a total of 120 faces (See fig. 15).

Ratios and regularities

As those familiar with numbers will notice, most of the sizes of the seventeen polyhedral structures that have been explained here have relationships both inside and outside their Families. The edges of their originators in birth sizes give us their Family ratios:

Edges

Family One:	two Tetras	ratio: 1 : 1
Family Two:	Cube and Octa	1 : 1.414214 - (0.707107 : 1)
Family Four:	Rhombic Dodeca-Cubocta	1 : 0.8164966 - l.224744 : 1)
Family Five:	Dodeca and Icosa	1 : 1.6180339 - (0.618033 : 1)
Family Ten:	Rhombic Triac.-Icosid.	1 : 0.850651 - (l.175570 : 1)

Of those ratios, those of Families One, Two and Five are the best known but the other two have certain qualities, too.

Another set of ratios appears three times in the developmental pattern of each Family. We shall call them the Threefold Ratios:

They appear in:

Family-One:	1 : 2	
Family-Two:	3 : 4	
Family-Four:	12 : 7	and 6 : 7
Family-Five:	3.6180339 : 4	
Family-Ten:	2.6180339 : Sq Rt of 3.6180339	and 1 : Sq Rt of 3.6180339

These ratios are found in the following:

1. Edge growth ratios in the second developmental stage – between birth and wedding of the Two-Frequency structures.
2. Edge cutting ratios of the Cross-Formation structure in wedding in the third developmental stage.
3. They (or their mean when two) – are the ratios of volume difference of the Cross-Formation structures in the second and third developmental stages.

One more proof of the regularity of the polyhedral development pattern are the volumes of the polyhedrons. The volume ratio series shown here and the volume growth ratios show us some of it, but there is more to come:

One example is the difference of the volume of a Cross-Formation polyhedron to the volumes of the geometrical compound which has formed it:

Volume of Cube minus Tetra:	1.00000 - 0.333333	= 0.66666
The last two numbers have the ratio	1 : 2	
Volume of Rhombic Dodeca minus Cube:	2.00000 - 1.00000	= 1.00000
The last two numbers have the ratio	1 : 1	
Volume of Rhombic Dodeca minus Octa:	2.00000 - 1.33333	= 0.66666
The last two numbers have the ratio	2 : 1	
Volume of Rhombic Triac.minus Dodeca:	2.50000 - 1.809017	= 0.69098
The last two numbers have the ratio	2.618033 : 1	
Volume of Rhombic Triac. minus Icosa:	2.50000 - 2.1816949	= 0.318305
The last two numbers have the ratio	6.8541 (1.61803394 in 4.power) : 1	
Volume of Trap.Icostet.minus Cubocta:	2.66666 - 1.97530	= 0.691366
The lost two numbers have the ratio	20 : 7	
Volume of Trap.Icostet.minus Rhom.Dodeca:	2.66666 - 2.00000	= 0.66666
The last two numbers have the ratio	21 : 7 - (3 : 1)	

The harmony of ratios

What do all these ratios stand for? This is a question that will take some time to answer. But the answer must be found in the fact that the returning ratios, like the Family ratios can be expressed with only a handful of logical angles. And also that they can be expressed as sine and cosine of logical angles such as one part of the equal division of a full circle like 90°, 72°, 60°, 45°, 36°, 30°, and 18° or angles that are themselves important building elements of the polyhedrons such as 70°31'43" – 54°44'08" – 35°15'51" – 31°43'03" – 58°16'57". To sum up this excursion into the world of geometric structures: the Tetra is the tone C of the structural world. Its size decides the sizes of all other polyhedrons in the development pattern. Doing that reveals that their edge lengths and volumes are related by ratios. The ratios are functions of certain harmonic angles. The key to this understanding is the four stage development pattern described here. This now opens up new possibilities to study infinite numbers of new structures and ratios.

As polyhedral geometry has shown, it is repeated in biologic structures built by nature – and is closely related to crystallography and especially fivefold symmetry quasicrystals. It is the hope of the author that this new order of the structural world of polyhedrons can be used to explain mathematical systems in other sciences.

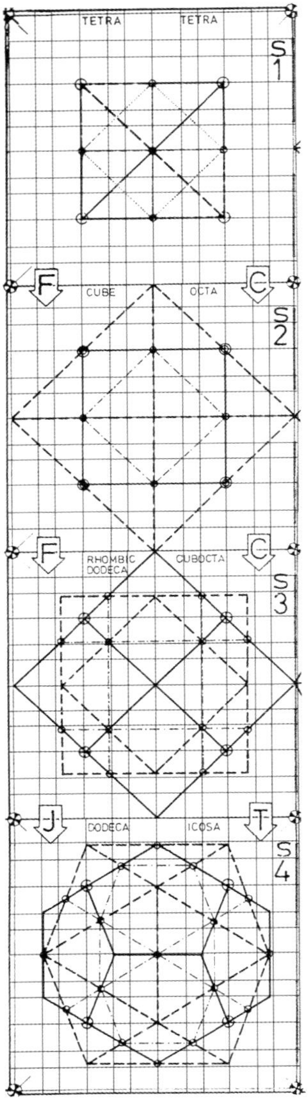

Fig. 13a

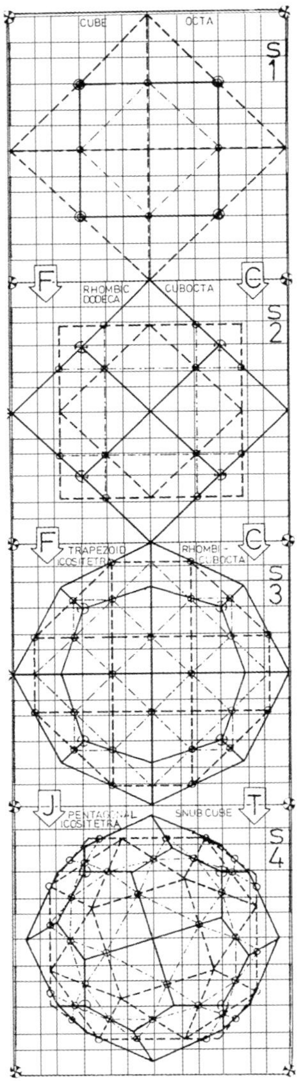

Fig. 13b

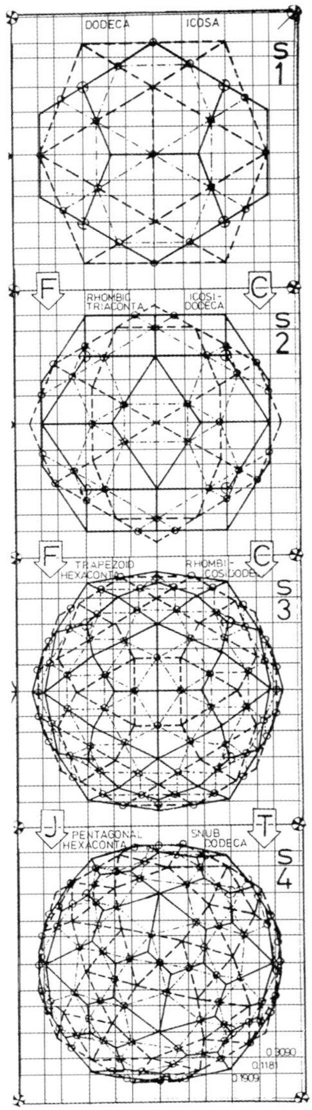

Fig. 13c

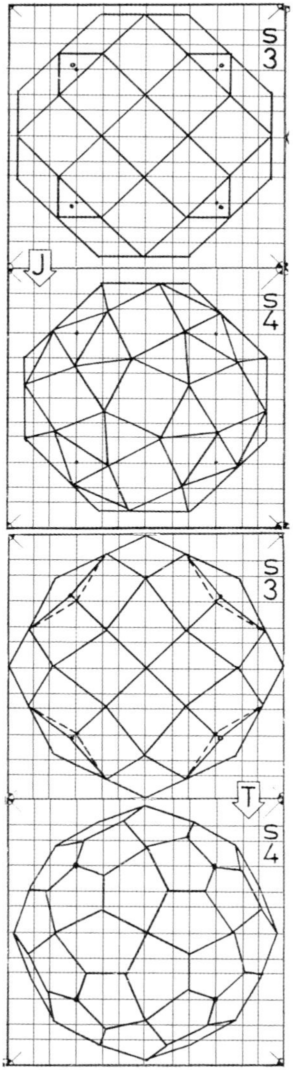

Fig. 14

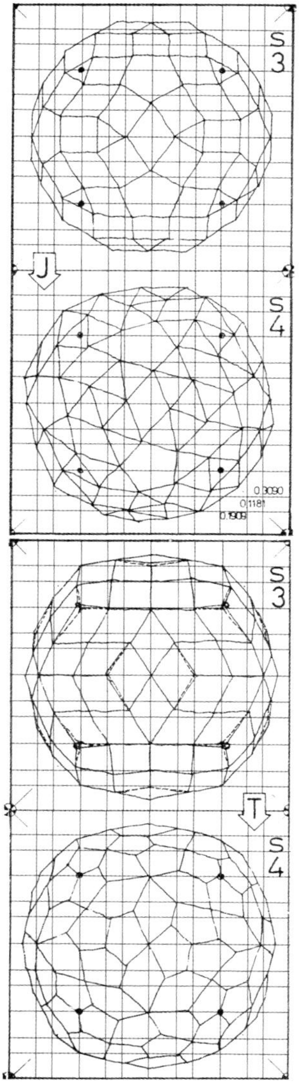

Fig. 15

Anthony Vidler

Any Mores

Misreading the publicity handout, which I received before the detailed programme, and not alerted to the Latin skills of the organizing team, I had thought that this session was about "Anymore *mores*," as opposed to "Anymore mores." Thus I was prepared to speak on the question, perhaps already addressed in previous sessions, as to whether there was "any architecture, anymore." A question that seemed to imply that, indeed, there was a distinct possibility that there was no architecture anymore. But the question "Are there *mores* anymore in architecture?" is of course deeply related to the first, "Is there architecture anymore?" Since the eighteenth century, generations of critics have linked the fundamental characteristics of architecture – structure, style, function, technology, social purpose – to its ethical and moral role.

It is not surprising that the question arises once more in the context of a digitized fin de siècle, which seems to have substituted surface for structure, arbitrary form for function, technological hubris for social values. Calls for a return to the fundamentals of "tectonics," stemming from a deep-rooted sense that the principles of modernism are being undermined, or for a commitment to a "New Urbanism," out of a sense of loss – of community, of place, of neighborhood – in the face of indiscriminate development, are reminiscent of earlier reactions against modernism itself, and before that against the first age of industrialism. Architecture, since its first definition as a profession dedicated to serving the private and public realms of bourgeois life in the Enlightenment, has always cherished its fundamentalists and its revivalists, whether they were Greek, gothic, classic, modern, or postmodern.

The question that arises in the moment before Y2K, however, is of a different order entirely to those relatively confined reactions and responses to industrial production and society. It is whether we should see the advent of universal digitalization as simply one more shift in the modes of production and consumption, to be absorbed or criticized in the same way as glass and iron, steel and electricity; or whether the transformation it proposes is in the process of developing an entirely new world order, demanding new epistemological instruments, and thereby new models for its representation and manipulation.

In architectural and aesthetic terms, we are certainly witnessing a change in the modes of representation that alters, if not entirely replaces, the perspectival frames through which we have been viewing since the Renaissance. The difficulty of representing perspectival space in "virtual reality" crude wire-frame models seems to point to the foreignness of traditional "reality," to the digital world. Perhaps we might frame the difference in terms of the place of the subject in space. Simply put, where perspectival space presumes a viewer's eye, a station point and a vanishing point, digital space knows of no such restriction. Its auto-generated characteristics privilege no vertical or horizontal dimension; its internal and external are subject-neutral. The subject in animation software is rendered as a robotic instrument of three- and four-dimensional exploration and rendering; the spaces it produces are delineated, in principle, for similar nonhuman subjects.

Equally fundamental would be the seamless relations, in digital modeling, between modes of representation and modes of production; this holds not only in the realm of biological and genetic reproduction, but also in the more primitive domain of architecture, where the complicated surfaces and structures developed by animation and morphing programmes can be transposed digitally to the factory floor, thereby completely transforming the notion of mass production and standardization. It is at least ironic that what the arts and crafts nostalgics saw as the fatal separation introduced by industrialization between delineation and manufacture has now, in this way, been overcome by industrialization's next stage.

All of which raises the question of mores once more, but in ways that can no longer resort to "authenticity" of structure or materials, form or style. Where, as Walter Benjamin noted, the first era of industrialization introduced for the first time materials that could be shaped in multiple forms – iron and glass – setting off the call for a rigorous morality of structure and style as a "control" mechanism, so to speak, now, in principle at least, the formal and the material have been themselves subsumed within the digital. Further, the literal disappearance of the human subject in digital space, one, interestingly enough, already anticipated by psychoanalysis and philosophy, provokes a series of questions about the role of this "architecture" in society.

Even as we must look on these changes with a certain optimism – for nostalgic reaction, as has been demonstrated by the fate of all such reactions in the recent past, will have little effect on the inexorable processes at work in the technological sector – and seek to tie them to our own interests, social and aesthetic, it must be admitted that the early results of digital application have demonstrated a number of tendencies that run counter to the verities of modernist morality. First, the ease and speed with which form can be manipulated in animation points to a logic of endless morphological transformation that even an uncritical celebration of process finds hard to arrest: how to determine a stop point, a termination for interminable analysis and generative iteration? Second, the existing software seems to privilege formal transformation of outer surface rather than inner space; as in the imaging of dinosaurs, once patiently built up from skeleton to outer skin, modeling is now worked from the scanning of a three-dimensional solid and its subsequent surface animation, leaving the interior to chance. As Greg Lynn has noted, occupation of such an interior might be compared to inhabiting the Statue of Liberty, possible but not predicted by the form of the outer skin.

Here, all the traditional truisms of modernist ideology – the plan is the generator, the outside skin as transparent to the space of the inside, the structure as exposed – are not simply reversed but denied or blocked. These considerations have impeded any unqualified acceptance of the new media, and certainly call for very different criteria of form and function, to use these somewhat outdated terms, than those of modernism.

But perhaps the overwhelming difficulty of working to formulate a new moral code for the new architecture is the resistance posed by our conceptions of history, to which are bound our beliefs in, or against, progress. For the question of whether architecture is anymore alive has been the continuing problem, not simply of modernity but of historicized modernity: from Hegel and Hugo in the 1830s to the present. Such questions, whether from the left or the right, have taken their place in broader terms in the set of those that posit the "death" of cultural practices and beliefs – the death of God, the end of art, the end of history – questions in a vulgar sense derived from a mechanistic but compelling reading of Hegel and, later, the sense of an ending/beginning that emerged in the fin de siècle. They were given intellectual force by the feeling of radical disenchantment, as Max Weber put it, brought on by rational, systematic, bureaucratic, modern thought, as it rejected all myths, faiths, mysticism, in a second, post-romantic wave of neo-Enlightenment thought.

For Weber, "disenchantment" meant literally "de-mythologized" – no more enchantment, no more fairy tales in favor of rigorous social science and materialist critique. From Weber to Manfredo Tafuri, intellectuals, both liberal and left, have held onto this axiom of reason. Alberto Asor Rosa, as we know, characterized Tafuri as the most absolutely disenchanted of historians. But, while the Weberian/Tafurian model of disenchantment (often masquerading as skepticism and unbelief, if not cynicism) generally wants to hold onto a progressive, demasking, truth-seeking ethic, the term has also served conservatives as an ideology to prove their own negative characterization of the present – no more faith or belief, and thence no more ethics, morals, at least as we have known them in the good past. For conservatives, disenchantment was an indication that a stage of history had been reached that was beyond history; history had for all intents and purposes stopped. The modern epoch was characterized as a *posthistoire* site, where all good things had come to a close. As formulated by interwar and post-World War II thinkers such as Arnold Gehlen and Hendrick de Man (Paul de Man's uncle), the end of history was signaled by the end of movement, of progress, and evolution.

As Hendrik de Man wrote:

The term post-historical seems adequate to describe what happens when an institution or a cultural achievement ceases to be historically active and productive of new qualities, and becomes purely receptive or eclectically imitative. The notion of the post-historical would fit the cultural phase that, following a "fulfillment of sense," has become "devoid of sense." The alternative then is, in biological terms, either death or mutation.

More recently, the Italian philosopher Gianni Vattimo has resurrected the term *post-historical* to, as he puts it, "prove" postmodernism in a book that, in quasi-Nietzschean terms, explores the question of the "end" of history and art. There is a profound immobility in the technological world, which science fiction writers have often portrayed as the reduction of every experience of reality to an experience of images (no one ever really meets anyone else; instead, everyone watches everything on a television screen while alone at home). This same phenomenon can already be sensed in the air-conditioned, muffled silence in which computers work. Here, extrapolating from Vattimo and less concerned with his notion of postmodernity, we might want to imagine at least one possible version of the digital world as post-historical. Something like that flattened out, gray-screened sky above the world of William Gibson's *Neuromancer*. Gibson's cyberpunk "disenchantment" would then be one side of the Weberian coin, one that sees in the absence of faith, myth, and belief, in modernity, the collapse of human values, and that understands the present only in terms of a dystopian nightmare. *Posthistoire* would be, in these terms, a real ending, with hope for little more than, as de Man believed, "death or mutation."

This was the end predicted by de Man's contemporary and fellow believer in *posthistoire* fatalism, Hans Sedlmayr, an art historian whose strictures against modern architecture, outlined in his *Art in Crisis, The Lost Center* (1945), were the result of his hatred of the democratic, socialist, and avant-garde heritage of the French Revolution. For this historian of the baroque, architecture ended with 1789. "The events to which we refer as the French Revolution are only a fractional part, even though they are the part that is most patent to the eye, of that huge inner catastrophe (…) this climax of history (…) our concern is direct and personal and immediate (…) by the light of it we know ourselves." Sedlmayr's method was pseudopsychological, his pathological subjects, buildings, seen as "manifestations, not merely (...) historical facts, but (...) symptoms (help) in forming a diagnosis of the malady that affects our time. (...) This our age is sick" *(Art in Crisis, p. 1)*. Here, Sedlmayr was the self-appointed doctor, a parodic and vulgarized Freud, or perhaps a Reich, offering small comfort to an age already lost: "Just as in psychological disturbances it may help towards the restoring of a lost balance if we assist unconscious thought to rise to the level of consciousness and so bring it under control, so an analogous examination of our age, as reflected in its art, may not only prove of theoretical interest" *(Art in Crisis, p. 2)*.

These etiologies of modernism were advanced between 1939 and 1945, in response to his calculated withdrawal from enthusiastic participation in the National Socialist movement and his shift toward a general sense of nihilism in the face of modern culture. His architectural villain was Claude-Nicolas Ledoux, accused of projecting a house in the form of a sphere – a groundless and rootless form not worthy of the name house and destructive of a humanist architecture, conceived as premised on vertical walls, deep foundations, and principles of beauty ostensibly derived from Vitruvius:

Such a radical new form, for instance, is inherent in the idea of using a sphere as the basic form of an entire house. Most people have treated this notion as nothing more than a bad joke or a very ordinary piece of lunacy, while the more charitable have looked upon it as an experiment with form. The thing is certainly insane enough, but if it were no more than that, we should hardly be justified in wasting much time over it. A nonsensical idea, however, need by no means be wholly without significance (...) such abnormalities reveal specific characteristics.

(...) Thus the sphere when used as the shape of a building is a critical form, which illuminates the deeper and more hidden spiritual strata of an entire age. It is a symptom, a symptom of a profound crisis both in architecture and in the whole life of the human spirit. Here we are beginning to deal with the zone of the unconscious, for the actual meaning of such forms is hidden from their creators (Art in Crisis, p. 4).

Ledoux was the more criminal for Sedlmayr, in having made possible similar substitutions of geometry for architecture in the 1900s, including the reprehensible avant-garde designs of Melnikov, a favorite of Rem Koolhaas, who had the audacity to propose a transparent sphere. Here it is interesting to see Sedlmayr's resistance to modernism as an opposition to its supposed dematerialization of architecture, its "reduction" of architecture to geometry. As he noted, where formerly architecture had been a question of real architectonic elements – walls and other physical elements rooted in foundations – now it was not only uprooted and without foundation, but also its essence was no longer physical but geometrical. Moreover, it was, in the sphere, given over to a nonhuman, non-ground based subject – something like an alien from outer space. Architecture had become its forms of representation, which in turn were ignorant of human subjectivity and physicality – a question that, as we have indicated, is raised in an even more dramatic form today.

The pertinence of Sedlmayr's observations, however, rests not so much on this parallelism but on his reliance on a historical model of change that inevitably led to his conclusion of death and ending. For as a student of Riegl, he had early on incorporated Riegl's historicized optical theories into his own analysis of architectural space. But if Riegl had seen the history of spatiality moving from Egyptian hapticality, through Greek "normal" vision, to Late Roman ambiguity (of figure and ground), Sedlmayr projected these intuitions into the baroque period, which, with Wölfflin, he understood to be the last, great evocation of humanist spirituality, which, in its manipulation of space for religious effect, had nevertheless exhausted all the resources of architecture as traditionally conceived, and thereby literally "blown apart" architectural stability. Piranesi, then Ledoux, and then Le Corbusier were the unhappy results of this explosion, which seemed to mimic the sickness of industrial and mass society as a whole. History here was a motor, an instrument, if not of Spenglerian decline, of humanist collapse, and architecture was to be seen as the (pathological) symptom of such a history.

The opposite pole of the debate saw a happy outcome for historical development – the Hegelian "positive" ending was, of course, the utopia of modernism, a vision of "ineffable space" transcending time at the end of time, a history-less world once and for all constructed for the good society. It was Sedlmayr's contemporary, and in some respects his nemesis, Emil Kaufmann, who represented this pole of architectural interpretation in the Vienna School of the 1920s and 1930s. Indeed, most of Sedlmayr's crucial architectural examples had been literally stolen from the research of this former colleague, co-contributor for a time in the influential Viennese journal *Kunstwissenschaftliche Forschungen*, edited by Otto Pächt.

Kaufmann, the Jewish student of Riegl and Schmarsow, was never to gain entry to the academic establishment in anti-Semitic Vienna, and was forced instead to take up a bank-teller's job until his equally forced emigration to the United States in 1941. Writing, not accidentally after Kaufmann had left for the States, Sedlmayr belatedly acknowledged the source of his own epochal conclusions:

The very beginnings of this work were inspired by the research of Emil Kaufmann on Ledoux, which came to my notice in 1930. I saw at once that Kaufmann had succeeded in making a discovery of the utmost importance towards the understanding of our age, but that at the same time he had not wholly recognized the true significance of his own discovery, and that the phenomena so clearly perceived by him were not correctly evaluated (Art in Crisis, p. 256).

Sedlmayr's cowardice was equaled only by Kaufmann's bravery. In 1933 he published his little book with a large title: *Von Ledoux bis Le Courbusier*. Most commentators have simply remarked on the fact that Le Corbusier, together with other modernists such as Richard Neutra, only appears in the last three pages of the book; only Hubert Damisch has recognized the special valor needed even for a coded defense of modern architecture at this juncture. With epigraphs from Rousseau, Kant, and Montesquieu, Kaufmann's essay was a spirited plea for Enlightenment values on the level of that launched by Ernst Cassirer in his essays on Kant and Rousseau that same year – the year, we should remember, of Hitler's putsch. For Kaufmann, Ledoux's special quality was that he had, in an age of reaction, welded an idea of social justice with a practice of ideal forms, the kind of utopia, Kaufmann stated openly, that characterized the Modern Movement's attempt to join the new society to the new abstract forms. He was also well aware of the fragility of this utopia:

In architecture, just as in politics, the reactionaries were to triumph over the inspired, though not sufficiently realistic modernists. But the temporary victory of the conservatives should not lead us to believe that the achievements of the progressives lacked significance. Having lived in the atmosphere of growing political and social discontent, the revolutionary architects wished to realize, for the common good, the ideals of the time by contriving architectural schemes such as had never existed before. They did their part in the double task of the period: tearing down the old and building the new. Like others who served the same cause, they were not spared the ordeals of their times and were menaced by its fanaticism. In the end, they themselves became disillusioned and reactionary (Three Revolutionary Architects, pp. 434-35).

For Kaufmann, however, as opposed to Sedlmayr, this did not mean a loss of hope – indeed, his last pages evince a utopian faith of his own that it would be in California, under the aegis of Richard Neutra, that these ideals would finally be realized. Eventually, three years before his death, Kaufmann succeeded in reaching the West Coast, and it is perhaps symbolically right that he was to die returning to Los Angeles by train, at the station of Jackson Hole, Wyoming.

In the silent discussion between Sedlmayr and Kaufmann, we are presented once again with all the complexities of "disenchantment." On the one hand, a disenchanted conservative against modernism in all its forms; on the other, a proponent of neo-Kantian disenchantment as a progressive modernist.

It is here that this discourse is deeply connected to the "Are there architectural mores anymore?" question and, it turns out, precisely in the context of the Sedlmayr/Ledoux argument. After all, it was Ledoux who was the first "modern" to include the word "mores" in the title of his treatise, *Architecture Considered in Relation to Art, Mores, and Legislation* (1804). He had chosen this title as a response to a Revolutionary competition, which asked the question, "What does art do to improve the mores of society?" His idea of mores (in French, *moeurs*) was inherited from an Enlightenment sense of progress, of inevitable improvement over time, of the essential role of the *philosopher* in the development of social justice, and of the critical role of the architect/engineer in the construction of a new and enlightened society. As we know, his architectural hubris anticipated that of the modernists in the 1920s, and seems, from our contemporary standpoint, to be indissolubly linked to the impossible, if not utopian, dreams of modern architects to change the world, dreams shattered by World War II and, despite a brief revival in the Paris of the late 1960s, definitively dashed by consumerism and capitalism. It would indeed be possible to write the history of the disenchantment debate through the reception of Ledoux – in modernism or even in postmodernism (could one find anyone more complexly "disenchanted" in the Weberian sense than Philip Johnson himself?).

I have introduced this abbreviated history of a debate between two historians, heirs to historicism and Weberian disenchantment, not to propose a solution for thinking through the architecture of the new digital era, but rather to expose the rooted nature of our thinking about history, temporality, and change within modernism. If we were to follow the same models of thought for the present fin de siècle, as many have proposed, we will certainly fall into the difficult trap of "ending" or "future," pessimism or optimism, no more or more, posed by the terms in which the question "anymore mores" has been set. I would argue that this trap is only avoidable if we develop alternative approaches toward history and spatiality – approaches already sketched by Gilles Deleuze and others – that refuse to see time and space as distinct, separate, and potentially opposed entities, and that understand the processes and forms of digitization as integral to the development of the very interpretative schema that we need to work with and control these processes and forms. We are, in this sense, bound to think digitally to work digitally. Anymore *mores* in architecture depends on this.

Gregory Volk

The Youngest Country

1.
Iceland, famously, is the world's oldest democracy, dating back to 930 A.D. when the ancient parliament – the Althingi – was established at Thingvellir. For two weeks every summer, people from all over Iceland gathered there to hash out disputes, make plans, make laws, and provide a cohesion for a society scattered loosely about a particularly inhospitable part of the world. Uncommonly homogenous, Iceland is also a place where genealogies can be traced way, way back, and where the language itself, relatively unchanged through the ages, serves as a bridge to the distant time 1,000 plus years ago when intrepid Vikings (and some Celts) first settled there – as you often hear in Iceland, if one of those Vikings were to return right now, he or she would have no trouble conversing with current residents. It is interesting to note that this old, intact society occurs in what is by far the youngest European country, and the last one to be settled, in 874. The land mass of Iceland,

which largely took its present shape 9,000 to 13,000 years ago at the end of the last Ice Age, is bisected by the Mid-Atlantic Ridge which separates two huge tectonic plates, the Eurasian and North American. Half of Iceland is, in fact, on the North American side of these plates, and half on the European side, which gives it a peculiar in-between status. As an American, I grew up believing that the first European to "discover" my part of the world was Christopher Columbus. In fact, Icelanders had landed in what is now Canada some 500 years before.

I won't pretend to be an expert about this country, place, and society, having visited there twice (recently) for a total of just about three weeks. I can say, however, that these were three enormously influential weeks. There is something about this youngest country that insinuates itself into one's mind and even more into one's blood stream, almost as soon as you get off the airplane, when you drive from Keflavik to Reykjavík through bleak yet riveting lava fields that seem altogether otherworldly. There is something that scrambles one's perspective, that rejuvenates one, that baffles one, that makes one unsteady, and that ultimately persuades one to reexamine just how one proceeds through the world. This can happen culturally, but it can also happen physically, and especially in one's relationship with the land and all its forces, which, incidentally, can also happen in the capital city of Reykjavík. I remember going swimming in one of the many warm geothermal pools in the city (there is always an outdoor pool nearby, you go swimming year round) and then taking a sauna, and then lounging around in the hot tubs. After this session, I felt wonderful, and then proceeded to walk down some bleak streets on a gray day in a West Reykjavík residential neighborhood and across the park toward the old town. There was a slanted rain like cold needles, and an impossible, freezing wind that seemed to be occurring on some other planet, on one of Jupiter's moons, perhaps. I remember shaking uncontrollably and thinking I was going to die. Hypothermia in the city park. I also remember thinking, oddly, as I leaned into the wind, how lovely Reykjavík seemed in the distance, like a small harbor town, with the downtown houses blue or russet (they're covered with sheets of colored tin) and the soaring church Hallgrímskirkja rising on the highest hill. It was raining sideways. Sometimes the rain was raining up, or straight, and the wind seemed to be coming from all directions simultaneously. I remember feeling lonely, but really less in a psychological than in a bone-deep physical way: skin and bones in a raw place. I also remember feeling ridiculously happy, keyed up, exquisitely alive. It was early afternoon and twilight and it was possible, inside Reykjavík, to be connected to, and affected by, the kind of rampant forces that are routine in the interior, or along the windswept coasts.

2.

I was lucky to travel with Sabine, and Pétur, and Ragna to one of what Ragna calls her "studios," namely, remote lava fields near the great volcano Hekla, once understood to be the site where luckless souls descended to hell. Ragna's "paintings" are made of lava chips which she applies to the walls. Tiny lava chips on the walls, hundreds of them, instead of paint marks or brush strokes, and indoor wallworks which come with news of a really big and potent outdoors. She gathers her materials in the lava fields: the black lava from Hekla and Katla, and the red lava from Seydishólal, and the fine, black mix of lava and sand from Myrdalssandur (also coming from Katla, through lava flows) which she then brings home to her studio, where she cleans them, sifts them, puts them in bins, and treats them altogether like exquisite jewelry or fragrant spices. Outside, in her "studio," the youngest country seems at once terrifying and lovely. It is pure geology and pure sky – a region of elements and minerals. Lava everywhere. Big chunks and little stones. An index of explosions. The earth turned inside out. No plants, save for a little thin lichen. No trees and no animals. Just the elemental land with its various colors (largely formed out of lava) and a generally spectacular light. There was nothing picturesque about this experience, and in this sense Iceland is not at all a romantic place; on the contrary it is a confrontational place, for you are always being confronted with the otherness of the planet, its pure inhuman geology. Moreover, this confrontation can often seem confusing to the extreme. Perspective, for instance, changes radically. Things far away can seem very, very near, high ridges in the lava fields are disclosed to be small hills, towering cliffs look like polite slopes; the landscape is dizzying. After walking only a hundred meters or so I already felt lost. It was tough to find something to attach my vision to, anything to serve as a marker, for everything seemed to be changing before my very eyes, becoming slippery and elusive. Hills seemed to move, or morph into new shapes, and the sun (when it appeared) seemed to be bouncing around wildly in the sky. For all its rugged beauty, Iceland can be a supremely unsettling place, which makes sense when you realize just how much world-shaping power there is underfoot.

Later we went higher, far higher, walking, essentially moving upward through a fierce lava flow that erupted long ago, and poured down, and hardened, and turned into a fantastical region of looming boulders, figure-like shapes, profiles, outcroppings, outrageous structures, the heaped up scenery left behind by a conflagration (in Iceland there are sculptures everywhere, just ones not made by human hands). Sometimes you smell the sulfur and see the steam and you're at a bubbling warm place that reminds you that this land will explode once again, and maybe soon. Otherwise, snow, and colorful striations of minerals, and a silence so supreme that it leaves one shaken and bewildered. Sabine and I sat on a lava chunk for half an hour or more. When the wind stopped, there was no sound at all, save for the blood in our ears, and the sound of our hearts, and the sound of our breathing. Alone in a very direct and simple sense, with the world. Alone with the stuff of nature which is pure material: lava, light, wind, and air. Steam and distance. Water. Sky.

3.

At the turn of the twentieth century, there were 5,000 people in Reykjavík, which in Icelandic terms was already a huge metropolis. Now there are some 110,000 people, out of a total population of 270,000, and Reykjavík is a thriving city sprawling into the outlying districts, which means into the lava fields, and down along the water across from the famous Mt. Esja, which looms over everything, and up the outlying hills. For centuries, Iceland, way out in the North Atlantic, was absolutely the remotest part of Europe, but all of this has abruptly changed during the past couple of decades, and a new identity has arisen: Destination Iceland, volcanic and exotic, a Scandinavian paradise promoted in glossy brochures and crisscrossed by package tours in the wonderful summers.

Modern Iceland, with all the amenities of middle-class European life, is actually a very recent phenomenon, dating back essentially to World War II and the economic boom that resulted. This was when an overwhelmingly rural society marked by centuries of withering poverty, and hunger, and hand to mouth life, was almost instantly transformed. These days you can meet fairly young people whose parents grew up in traditional dried mud houses somewhere way out in the land. One consequence of relativly new-found wealth is how people tend to travel widely and at length, often times studying in other countries, and living in those countries for years. Iceland was founded by voyaging Vikings who got the idea to drop everything and take off for parts unknown, which were only inhabited by a few mystic Irish priests who didn't last long. The urge to wander has abided, and it includes current Icelanders who tend to leave, but also, eventually, to return. It is my experience that Iceland continues to have a tremendous hold on their consciousness no matter how long they've been away, which goes way beyond issues of homeland, familiarity, family, friends, and the-place-where-one-is-from. A profound sense of connection and also of responsibility – that's what I've been told. A mysterious involvement, a primal bond, based on one's own experience, and the language, and the literature which everyone knows, but also on the generations-long adventure of surviving and flourishing in this distant North Atlantic place. Friends have told me that after a long time abroad, the first thing they hunger for upon returning is seeing Mt. Esja, massive and resplendent, across the bay from Reykjavík. That's when they know that they are truly home.

4.

In 874 Ingólfur Arnarsson, the first settler, arrived in what is now Reykjavík. He had a friend, Hjörleifur Hródmarsson, his de facto neighbor, who, a bit later, settled a hundred or so miles down the coast at Myrdalssandur. I went to this place, a towering, rectangular plateau directly at the ocean, and quite frankly it is impossible for me to imagine anyone actually choosing to settle there. Who on earth could survive in such loneliness? The wind would undo you; the gray ocean would make you insane. Above, in the volcanic mountains, there is the Myrdalsjökull glacier; you can see it from the beach and from the road. Sometimes it releases tons of glacial debris in an instant downhill flood which obliterates everything in its path; this is not a rare occurrence. Whole villages have been lost. The beach is black, and wide, and you can see the ocean in the distance. When I went, it was during a time of warning, namely, that the glacier was about to release one of its periodic floods. The youngest country is, and was, and probably always shall be a precarious place. As we drove across the beach, toward the ocean, it seemed we were making no progress at all, for the ocean didn't get any nearer. Another trick of perspective, another of Iceland's confusions. Vast distances and the near-at-hand were completely compressed, like some kind of invisible Möbius strip connecting what's close and what's far away, what you know and what you know not.

We stopped to make a little picnic, at the edge of a cliff leading way up to Hjörleifur Hródmarsson's former homestead. Once again there was a strange wind, the kind that circles, and undulates, and is entirely unpredictable, and freezes, and whistles through your rib cage. This time it was filled with stinging particles of beach sand (actually ground up lava) which turned the butter black, hurt our eyes, and worked under the bread of our sandwiches: we were eating a volcano. I noticed how there were fat birds on the beach, flapping their wings pitifully, trying to achieve a little lift off, but they were just too heavy. At one point a truck came up, and a man in a uniform got out, and scooped up the wallowing birds. I remember thinking what an advanced compassionate society this is, with government employees out there scouting around to protect the seabirds at a vulnerable time. Pétur told me that the man was scooping up the cute birds to wring their necks and turn them into dinner, for they are a delicacy in that area. They gorge themselves to the point where they're aerodynamically unable to fly and only a few survive. Over several days they lose enough weight so that their wings work. I eyed the glacier up in the mountains, the ocean in the distance which is not exactly friendly, Hródmarsson's high, dark cliffs, all of which, like so much else in Iceland, tend to work deeply into one's psyche, with wonder but also with some fear: bleak beauty, magical severities. Peculiar place, this youngest country, with its peculiar powers. There is a tradition of outsiders who visit once, and then keep visiting. I think that I will be one of these people.

5.

By any European standards, Iceland has the youngest art, an art which pretty much began in the twentieth century. There are a number of reasons for this paradox: geographical isolation, centuries of crushing poverty, a culture-wide focus on literature, and the traumatic effects of the long period of Danish occupation, during which pro-Reformation zealots from the continent decreed that that much of Iceland's visual culture, including artifacts, crafts, icons, and sculptures be destroyed, perhaps to eradicate any trace of Iceland's pagan past. In any event, the notion of the professional artist appeared in Iceland only at the turn of the twentieth century, when pioneering landscape painters like Ásgrímur Jónsson (1876-1958) and Thórarinn B. Thorláksson (1867-1924), returning from study at the Royal Academy of Art in Copenhagen, began to respond to Iceland's unique landforms: its active volcanoes, its glacier fields and its desolate interior regions. Following them was Jóhannes Kjarval (1885-1971), whose pulsating, densely brushed landscapes and "lavascapes" earned him a reputation as Iceland's preeminent artist.

Much has transpired since those origins, as various movements and countermovements coursed through Icelandic art, as influences from abroad were assimilated and explored, and as local approaches developed, spanning painting (both figuration and abstraction) and different kinds of sculpture. Dieter Roth moved to Iceland in the 1950s and helped to start a Fluxus dialogue. Various forms of Minimalist austerity took root, probably not for the same reasons as in the U.S. and Europe, but more because they seem so apt in a place which is itself so elemental. In the late 1960s and early 1970s, during a time when abstract painting ruled the day, the small, at the time notorious, yet ultimately cathartic movement called SUM fundamentally renewed art-making in Iceland, opening it up to performance, socially critical work and pieces made of ephemeral materials. Contemporary artists, now free to pursue their own eccentric aesthetics, owe a debt to SUM, and they know it.

Right now, visual art is flourishing in Iceland, including Icelanders living and working abroad, and a great deal of vivid and distinctive art is being produced, even though there has never been very much attention to, and infrastructure for, the arts, although this is beginning to change. Moreover, this art is diverse, so diverse, in fact, that it might seem pointless to ask what is peculiarly "Icelandic" about it. One thing you do notice, however, is that no matter how internationally minded Icelandic artists are, eventually the country itself comes to figure in their work: as a physical locus, as a trove of images and materials or – more mysteriously for outsiders – as a comprehensive force with which one is perpetually in dialogue. It is not that the compelling work now being produced is about Iceland in any literal sense. Far from it. But Iceland is nevertheless there, in the deep grain of the inquiry, a constant presence that can be approached with a sense of wonder, humor or irony, via poetic engagement or tough-minded criticism. There is a line, in fact, between Kjarval painting Thingvellir, the ancient seat of Icelandic society, and all sorts of current, go-for-broke experimenters who are also dealing with Iceland, its culture and its landscape on their own terms, and in a much-changed time.

Manfred Wolff-Plottegg

Updating Transformating Principles in Architecture

Fake

The fake theory is based on the recent observation that a fake is a media related phenomenon, which today in the world of computers and of the www comes to an ultimate climax.

The nature of the new media makes a fake different from forgeries, deceptions, lies, April fools' jokes etc., which traditionally want something, transmit something. A fake is not conceived in terms of content, therefore isn't, does not have, but offers anyhow.

It is an obvious and generally accepted phenomenon that "persons" in a chatroom on the Web develop several and varied identities. These IDs can be changed rapidly and according to whim; sometimes they are partial, extremely exaggerated or similar. The classic concepts of personal identity and integrity are abolished. From now on, split and multiple personalities are possible and, at least on the www, we are now allowed what up to now was frowned upon "in real life"

(IRL), what was forbidden socially_scientifically_artistically.

This development and differentiation is an indication of the characteristics of a fake.

It follows that the clarity and lack of ambiguity required up to now are being replaced with complexity; that the historical cultural unity of the person_identity_integrity is being erased;[1] that the reliability of an opinion, of the individuality, of a viewpoint, of a character, of handwriting are being relativised; that all rules such as "one man one word" or "what I say in no uncertain terms" and "I stand by my word" are now ending up in the trashcan. "Read my lips!"

The underlying rule of rules on identity and coherence was the mandatory unity of space_time_place (Greek drama). As if we were trapped in a fold of time, this unity is binding even today: the alibi, the elsewhere, the proof, that the accused was in a different place than the scene of the crime at the time of the act and therefore cannot be the perpetrator. This becomes obsolete in the age of dislocation and telemanipulation.

The theories of morphogenesis and behaviour patterns are of course subject to the same change: the theories of representation, the Pygmalion syndrome, the transposition of expression, the total work of art, the world improvements, the derivative procedures, static determinism, etc. Of course in architecture the old Vitruvian rule of unity of function_form_construction corresponds to this.

In fact there were always, nevertheless, in the arts and sciences, attempts to escape these commitments, to escape the prison of space, the limits/transitoriness of time, the obligation that something must be just so and not any other way. The developments in the sciences and especially the dynamics of the twentieth century explicitly require the removal of old rules and parameters. The rule of the "body" is erased by virtuality, the stylistics of the nineteenth century, the functionalism of the twentieth century are being replaced by system controls; that is to say – away from the product (hardware) and towards the metalanguage of control (software): the developments "from expressionism to actionism, from constructivism to deconstructivism, from determinism to relativity"[2] were brought about by various disciplines. Formalisation (methodology) replaces the content approach, the sense of mission. The trail runs from pataphysics (via surrealism, fractal theory, fuzzy logic, chaos, complexity, and "real virtuality") to the fake. The change of paradigm from the monopole of unity was brought about quite decisively by the new media. The differentiation of

1. Fake ID's

2. Exhibition catalogue, *Jenseits von Kunst,* ed. Peter Weibel, Budapest, Graz, Antwerp, Passagen Verlag, Vienna, 1996.

time_place_action, the simultaneity of presence_absence_dislocation, the coincidence of subject_object as system variables are at the beginning of the twenty-first century are no longer delusions as before. The virtual is real.[3] We emancipated ourselves: shift, beam, morph, zoom, fake!

So just as the potential of "real virtuality" throws a new light on "IRL," the knowledge and production of fakes allow us to see what was perceived until now as the "true" non-fake-world in a new way. With fake it is not a case of manipulation of reality (as with deceptions, etc.) but rather the production of new combinations of reality. Primarily, the "content" is erased or shifted. A major step in development lies in the detachment of information from body_object_place as information carrier. The flow of data in computers/www dissolves identities (autochtone, genius loci, ethno, etc.) and so provides a further basic principle of the fake: placelessness – if something is somewhere where it should not be, it has potential to be a fake. And if information as a whole floats freely, a fake is not far away. Capricorn One – ...and no man on moon?[4]

This prototype of shifting can of course also be found in the dimension of time and speed. Dislocation corresponds to Quick and Dirty: it is not that the "rightness_truth" of information counts, but the speed (see the tabloid press or fuzzy logic). The subsequent outcome becomes the primary event: There is no original; even the attitude/intent does not exist.

Quick and dirty/fake architecture:

The world of new media, especially that of the computer and the www has always been virtuality. The tradition of architecture has always been the place and the identity (identity of place, defining/shaping a place/identity).

Even in the "real world" of architecture, shifts have been experimented with for a long time now, e.g. just after the invention of perspective (anamorphoses, anagrams, Borromini/Palazzo Spada, illusionist architecture/painting, etc.). As early as in ancient times the appropriateness of material was in doubt,[5] but we grumble about this less than about PVC imitations of wood. The rules of architecture such as readability (e.g. of construction) were also interpreted differently in Gothic times (Trento Cathedral); the Potemkin City as forerunner of postmodernism, but certainly not of "form follows function;" "coherence and truthfullness" are yet again erased: the fake design not as pretence of reality, but as invention, does not become "true," it becomes a new reality.

3. *Zeichenbau/real virtualities*, exhibition Künstlerhaus Vienna, 1999, curator M. Plottegg.

4. http://www.loq12.at/conspiracy/07_moon/

5. The Doric temple is a fake temple, because a timber construction was built from stone, which is in contradiction to the rule "appropriateness of material." Even the classic "corner problem" is just a fake so that generations would discuss it.

Finally, when generative architecture developed in the late twentieth century, the previously cultivated anthropocentric approach was replaced by external automated events. The computer allowed architecture to get rid of the former intention to represent world-views, and the most essential characteristics of an up-to-date and modern architecture were formulated. Neither the architect's handwritten trademark as an individual signature, the purpose as fulfilment of an aim, nor predefined functions as metaphor for teleologies exist any more. The longlasting predominance of form, body, and material has been overcome; architecture is no longer a signifier; divorced from retrospection, relieved from habits, personal desire and projections, it no longer pays tribute to the powerful. Being no longer derivative, architecture accelerates, becomes autocatalytic.

Within the environment of the CPU, the linear, singular and visual logic of orthogonal projection and perspective are obsolete. Binary lines are strokes devoid of any content, the namelessness of lines leaves them without any functional purpose, whereas the CPU supplies the vocabulary of forms. The binary house is complete in the CPU, without location in an environment, without point of view, a site without standpoint. For the eye, the presentation is immediate, all opened images are equivalent, the CPU condensing the duration of time into simultaneity. The binary house itself has no dimension, it is simultaneous and timeless, non-hereditary, abstract, dematerialized architecture. The plan is dead; perspective is dead. There is no more point of view. The flow in the Net defines architecture as instantaneous and placeless.

By browsing the Net, architecture is further accelerated: as the Net is characterised by rapid access to an enormous amount of data stored side by side which is non-hierarchic, quasi equivalent, architecture manifests itself by browsing or surfing. In conventional thought, each design step was a stage of development, an improvement on the former step. Whereas browsing, because of the huge amount of equivalent coexisting data, now relativizes the illusion of "quality," the idea of truth and thus also the fiction of improvement. The modern architect is no longer an idealistic do-gooder.

The aspect of rightness is abolished and the architect's know-all dogmatism has no more basis. Subsequently, neither appropriateness of material nor of craftsmanship nor of construction exist any longer. As a criterion, appropriateness is now replaced by speed, and as a result of speed, precision is replaced by superficiality. For this ever faster speed and superficiality, the theory of fuzzy logic has been developed. This means that there should be more generosity. A good architect is a superficial surfer.

Static models of architectural production have run their course. Instead, intelligent, interactive surfing in system processes has become important. The formulations of architectural algorithms in the Net will not aime at a better world or any other content or ideology. This architecture without teleology will be autocatalytic, algorithmic and emancipated: quick and dirty.

Speed allows neither time for fundamental analysis nor for checking for correctness (which becomes fiction anyway), nor for questioning the sense, the teleology. As preliminary assumptions, some parameters arise: a fake is deliberately against what is generally accepted, does not need an analysis, does not wait for changes by evolution. Speed makes a fake climax, but it is short-lived, creative and quick – has esprit, but no identity or authenticity.

And this speed guarantees dynamic developments. Planning has always been determinism, designing something today to be built tomorrow and to last as long as possible (today argued with the term "sustainability"). Now we have the tools to escape determinism.

The aim and the product of any architectural transformation has always been the adding of an object, of a form, of aesthetics to the world: something new to the old, something artificial to nature, something domestic to the landscape. So that the world afterwards becomes different from before, "better" according to the corresponding world improvement theory, which presidents speak about at inaugurations. The interesting thing today is that objects, forms, conditions are no longer transformed, but that the "principles of design" are themselves transformed. From object planning (1st order) to the metalevel of systemplanning (n^{th} order): from product to tools, to machine tool, to know-how. The successful architect of the twenty-first century will simulate and control processes not as world improvement but rather out of the pure joy of designing quick and dirty fakes.

Forward planning:

Warning: a long slow fake becomes "true" and must immediately be re-faked! The method of forward planning never looks back, it accelerates architecture. Because architecture is a slow medium, which did not accept the major scientific changes in the twentieth century, it is even more urgent that new browsing systems become part of our design methods. To accelerate architecture, design must be dynamised, the design process simulates/stimulates real-life procedures.

The forward-planning method is not (as is usual) linear from the first sketch to the "finished project," from one scale to the next bigger scale – where the finished project differs, if at all, from the beginning only in terms of details. The forward planning process is permanent modification – not in the sense of correcting errors or of improvement of the world, but in the sense of permanent changes of surrounding variables, growth or changing of functions. As soon as something already known appears, it must be changed.

As seen from the point of view of the theory of architecture, the rigid images (object, proportion, aesthetics) of traditional architecture become abandoned and shifted towards the control, steering of (urban, architectonic, building) processes. Building science is no longer understood as object-related (function, structure, typology), but as mode of procedure, as design method.

The function of "the function in architecture" is not the object/form any more, but rather the process. The object-like built form is not the aim, but might be the result. Buildings are changing (cf. Steward Brand: "How buildings learn") and the history of architecture confirms: after the traditional building_body_architecture (volume, mass) and subsequently structural architecture, we are nowadays designing information-architecture. Built architecture becomes the flesh for the wireframe-model of reality. The theory of mapping_merging_morphing_faking different electronic, physical, and social spaces together as a new "site" of architecture is the basis for the concept of virtual&real-life space. Thus – after the rigid, deterministic design of definite conditions, and after the concepts for the design of developments – the transition to an architecture of process-design is formulated and thus the transition towards architecture-algorithms, towards autocatalytic and genetic architecture takes place.

These dynamic events are simulated by the methodic procedure. Instead of the usual settings (program of functions, location, site, etc.) algorithms for design are provided – and are naturally to be modified while the work is developing.

A straightforward design project demonstrates that it is independent from the site/place, the location may be changed at any time/rapidly. It is free from functional interdependencies, i.e. a project can be connected, overlaid, moved, intersected, merged, displaced, etc. (cf. game of life) with others, thus modifying the preliminary design.

After this merge/morph, the project is treated with the factor of "growth." What is the effect if particular components of the design are growing? What development potential lies in the design? Can it be treated with the process of growth? When does it lose its shape and become something new? Thus the center of interest is not a detached singularity (auratic object, charismatic demiurg), but a dynamic interchange.

Neuronal architecture processor[6]

In a setup for an installation we experimented and demonstrated how to get rid of one´s own creativity, how to generate architecture directly out of neuronal spikes!

Processor 1 simulates 3 biological neurons. The "spike train" output is transmitted to Processor 2. A script, simulating a "DNA-transcription," transforms the incoming spike trains into data sets for 3-D solids: by autolisp the "genes" of the spike train ("DNA") are transformed into autocad commands. Thus the incoming spike-trains permanently generate new solids.

This installation is an experimental set-up to demonstrate a principle and to prove our thesis on digital creativity. The principle is the following equation:

A sequence of pulses (spike trains) in biological organisms = binary streams of signs (bit strings) = data (coordinates, vectors) interpreted as geometric bodies (solids). This equation brings together three spheres of reality that are traditionally considered as distinct:

- the world in our head: information, imagination and ideas in the way they are actually coded in our brain;
- the world of digital data processing, represented by binary streams of signs as communication vocabulary between digital processors;
- the world of generating new images/spaces/architecture.

These three spheres of reality are brought together under the common denominator of information processing. Thus the installation demonstrates that the generation of images/spaces/architecture must no longer be perceived as anthropocentric/expressionistic. Through the use of the computer it is possible to emancipate oneself from established patterns of behavior, evaluation and production.

The installation consists of two digital processors that

6. M. Wolff-Plottegg, W. Maass, *Prototype 1999/update 2000;* Programming: Harry Burgsteiner/Andreas Gruber, University of Technology, Graz, Austria.

communicate with each other, the output of each of them is projected by a beamer.

Processor 1 simulates the atomic units for information processing in our brain: circuits consisting of nerve cells (neurons) that are connected by synapses (shown as blue triangles). The biological neurons that are simulated here communicate with other neurons by sudden increases in electrical potential (spikes): at certain points in time, the voltage rises instantaneously in the soma of the neuron (demonstrated through color changes of the neuron), and subsequently falls at an equal speed, approximately one millisecond later. These sudden voltage changes are transmitted to other neurons through axons (demonstrated in the installation by moving white bars that represent spikes). This constitutes an original version of the digital codes used by nature in our brain: every single spike is indeed such that at any point in time there is either a spike or no spike – there being no such thing as a half or quarter spike. Information is encoded in the distances between the spikes, corresponding to the distances between Ones in a bit string.

Every neuron in our brain receives spike trains as inputs, i.e. sequences of spikes in time, sent by other neurons. In particular, sensorial perceptions – e.g. all built forms visually perceived by us – are coded in the form of spike trains before they reach the neurons in our cerebral cortex. In our experimental set-up, the neural circuit receives 4 spike trains as input. Spike trains Bio 1 and Bio 2 are real spike trains from neurons belonging to the visual region in the brain of monkeys, as recorded by brain researchers (Krueger and Aiple). Instead of a monkey, the data could be taken directly from visitors without a noticeable difference. As for the other 2 spike trains, they consist of streams of pulses (spike trains) by means of which the viewer obtains direct contact with the neural circuit: the viewer can generate these spike trains by pressing keys on a keyboard (instead of being directly wired).

In a biological neuron, some of the incoming spike trains have a stimulating effect (e.g. they increase its readiness to fire) whereas in others they have an inhibiting effect (e.g. they reduce its readiness to fire). Accordingly, in our installation, some spike trains have stimulating effects, while others have inhibiting effects on the simulated biological neuron. The output spike train is recoded as a binary code, i.e. as a sequence of Ones and Zeros (1 = one spike, 0 = no spike), and in this form, which is easily understandable to all artificial computing machinery, it is transmitted to Processor 2. Processor 2 is a form generator, which uses the binary codes coming from Processor 1 to control a chain of commands: by means of a script, the incoming spike trains are, so to speak, transformed into data sets for 3-D solids which are then represented graphically. Processor 2 interprets the incoming data from Processor 1 in order to control a programme, by selecting and fixing the parameters in the chain of available commands. The core software, the mathematical-geometric potential of the 3D vector-program and the controlling script, are not changed by the incoming data from Processor 1. These invariants impose overall patterns on the generated pictures, similar to the way in which the invariants of our individual human visual apparatus and brain impose overall patterns to the world of images which we perceive and reproduce, patterns of which we are not generally aware.

One can compare the interplay of random factors and fixed rules in the generation of images through the two processors with the functioning of a genetic system. Similar to a DNA transcription, Processor 2 offers a chain of genetic elements (= commands), whose reading matrix filters the RNA out of the spike trains as edited information. The traditional procedure of anthropocentric creative design of built form is – according to our theory – shifted to the definition of a genome, which in turn generates new built forms.

The experiment shows that relatively few bits, represented by the stream of pulses of a single neuron, have sufficient complexity to produce designs for extremely diverse and sometimes even astonishingly novel visual creations. The same is true for the operators of the script, based on simple geometric commands: polyline, extrude, union, intersect, rotate, etc.

In this installation, the simulated biological neuron and genome are of an extreme simplicity compared to the information processing capacity of their biological counterpart. A neuron in our brain is not fed with spike trains from only 4 other neurons or sensors, but simultaneously receives 5000 to 10000 spike trains as inputs. Furthermore, the typical frequency of these spike trains is not on the order of 0,1 Hz, as in this installation, but on the order of 50 Hz. The processing of information in a biological neuron is 500 times faster than in this installation, in fact so fast that one could not follow the real spike trains with the naked eye.

This is also the reason why the visualization frequency of Processor 2 is reduced to a perceivable level.

The readability of development/growth/movement becomes

possible as a sequence of single frames (image rate < 15 i/sec). Furthermore, it is not only one neuron that is processing and producing images in our brain, but roughly 40 different brain regions of more than 1,010 (= 10,000,000,000) neurons. These 1,010 neurons are interconnected by means of approximately 1,014 links (axons, synapses, and dendrites). The total length of these "wires" within only one cubic millimeter of grey matter in our cerebral cortex already reaches a length of approximately 4 km. This gives a rough idea of the complexity of the "data processor" in our head. The controlling script of the form processor we have used (which has approximately 20 lines, uses 30 exec_commands, 256 colours/8bit, etc.) is of a similar simplicity when compared to the human genome (100,000 genes, 109 elements, etc.).

Nevertheless, we can already make the following observations from this simple experimental set-up:

1. unforeseen results arise even out of a few elements/small numbers;
2. they lie within a spectrum inherent to the system;
3. different bit-string inputs (be it from monkeys, visitors, keyboard-strokes, light sensors or generated data sets) do not affect the characteristics of the system and the unforeseen nature of its results;
4. modifications of the output can be obtained through modifications of the programme (script).

Despite the relatively low degree of complexity of this Neuronal Architecture Processor prototype, the results are more differentiated than those arising out of a traditional analogue architectural production (under the same base conditions). This has consequences for our understanding of art, architecture and human versus machine/digital creativity. It proves our thesis that creativity (in this case production of architectural images) is the result of a "neuronal machine" and as such can be released from the brain.[7]

7. http://www.cis.tugraz.at/igi/maass/ http://www.cis.tugraz.at/igi/demos/spike_trains.html http://baukunst.tu-graz.ac.at/~plottegg

Fig. 1
Olafur Eliasson, *Moss - wall*,
1994, detail.

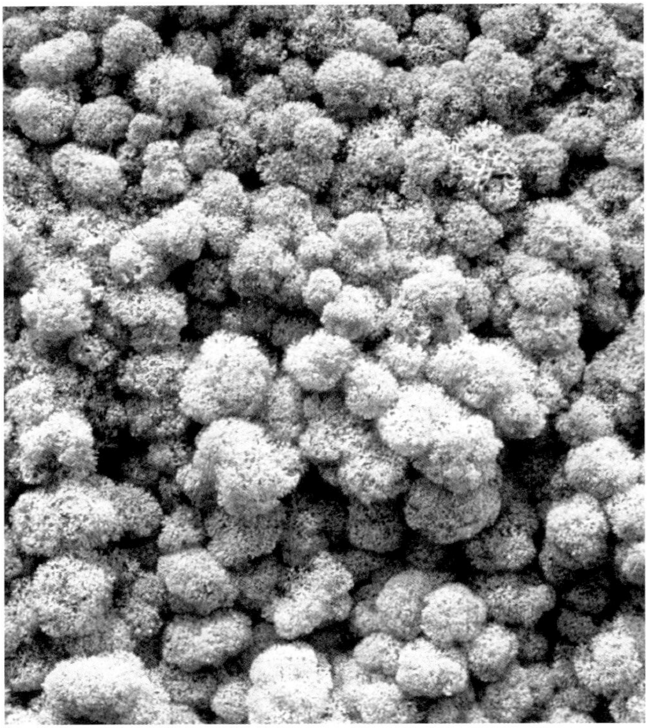

Fig. 2
Olafur Eliasson, *Waterfall*,
1998, Kunsthalle, Cologne.

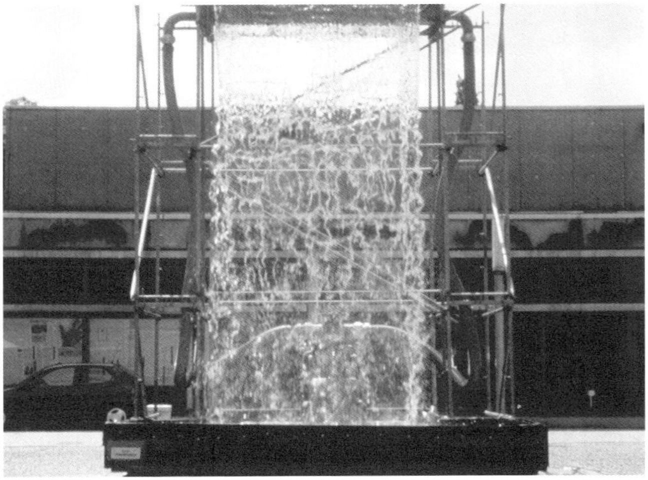

P.S. for Olafur:
Since I have been observing these developments, the arguments have become more and more weak at the knees, and L. Wittgenstein cannot continue to ask himself what the world was. Already before Sokal's Hoax, the reliability of texts was gone. http://www.war-of-the-worlds.org/Radio/... Before, your wall with moss would have shown me the difference between architecture and art, but since – neither in the one nor the other – it is no longer a matter of objects, forms, colors and since I too am disappearing as a subject, it seems to be rather more a matter of transfer. But as gathering for an encyclopaedia has somehow stopped, even the transfer now seems inflationary, because since postmodernism, all forms have been allowed anyway. And thanks to globalisation anything can be anywhere. Therefore nothing exotic remains, nothing is autochtonic anymore, and even the esoteric know-how is faked: the moss could come from Iceland or from the flower market, your waterfall could be a big soundbox that deceives our senses with its roar? http://www.whatisthematrix.com/. What does our friend Schauberger say, that – since your sculpture disappeared from Venice – your waterfall makes Möbius movements! In his case the water also flowed from bottom to top.

Flatland, A Romance of Many Dimensions,[8] without any immigration limits. – Olafur, we should meet there, because my page has been faked – be aware, that you are visiting a faked web site that offers distorted information on my cause – it's all a fucking good fake, cu asap – Plo!

8. http://www.geom.umn.edu/~banchoff/Flatland/

Epilogue

See, this impossible task started when we spoke about what is between you and everything else. The surroundings, you – and the engagement between the two. We spoke about collecting all my favorite matters into one system just like in a studiolo, where the idea of the all-encompassing everything is organized as artefacts and objects in small systems and structures. When our surroundings reflect our engagement in it, orientation becomes a task of both extrovert (radiant) and introvert (absorbent) activity. We very much shared this notion that everything matters even though we never share the same everything.
This is my surroundings surrounded.

I deeply want to thank all the authors in this book. I also want to thank Ursula Frohne and the ZKM editorial staff and graphic designers without whom this book would not exist. Peter Weibel for questioning the sense in everything and in particular Marianne Krogh Jensen for her inspiration and intuition.
Finally, I want to thank my father Elias for sharing the idea that everything matters.

Olafur Eliasson

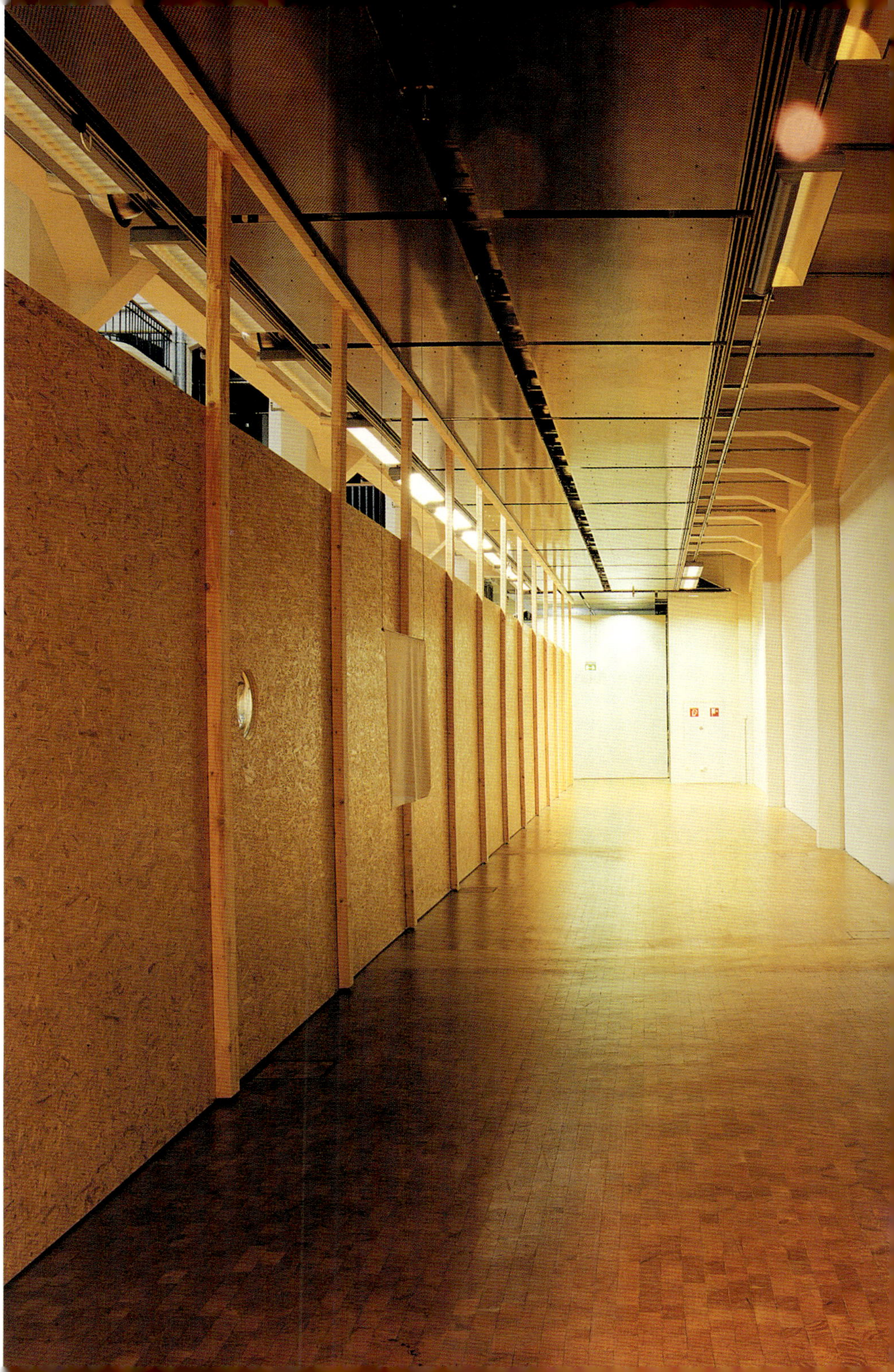

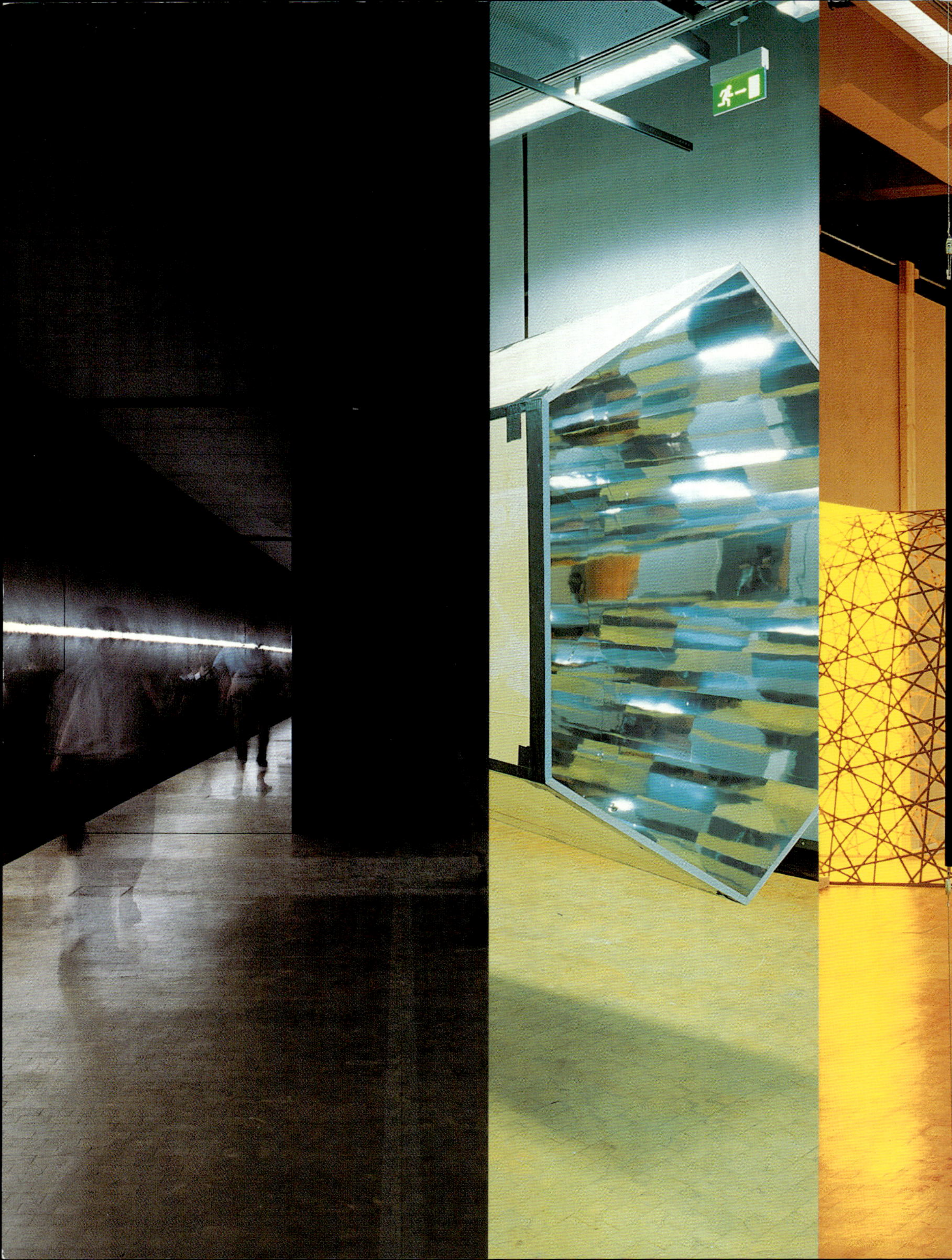

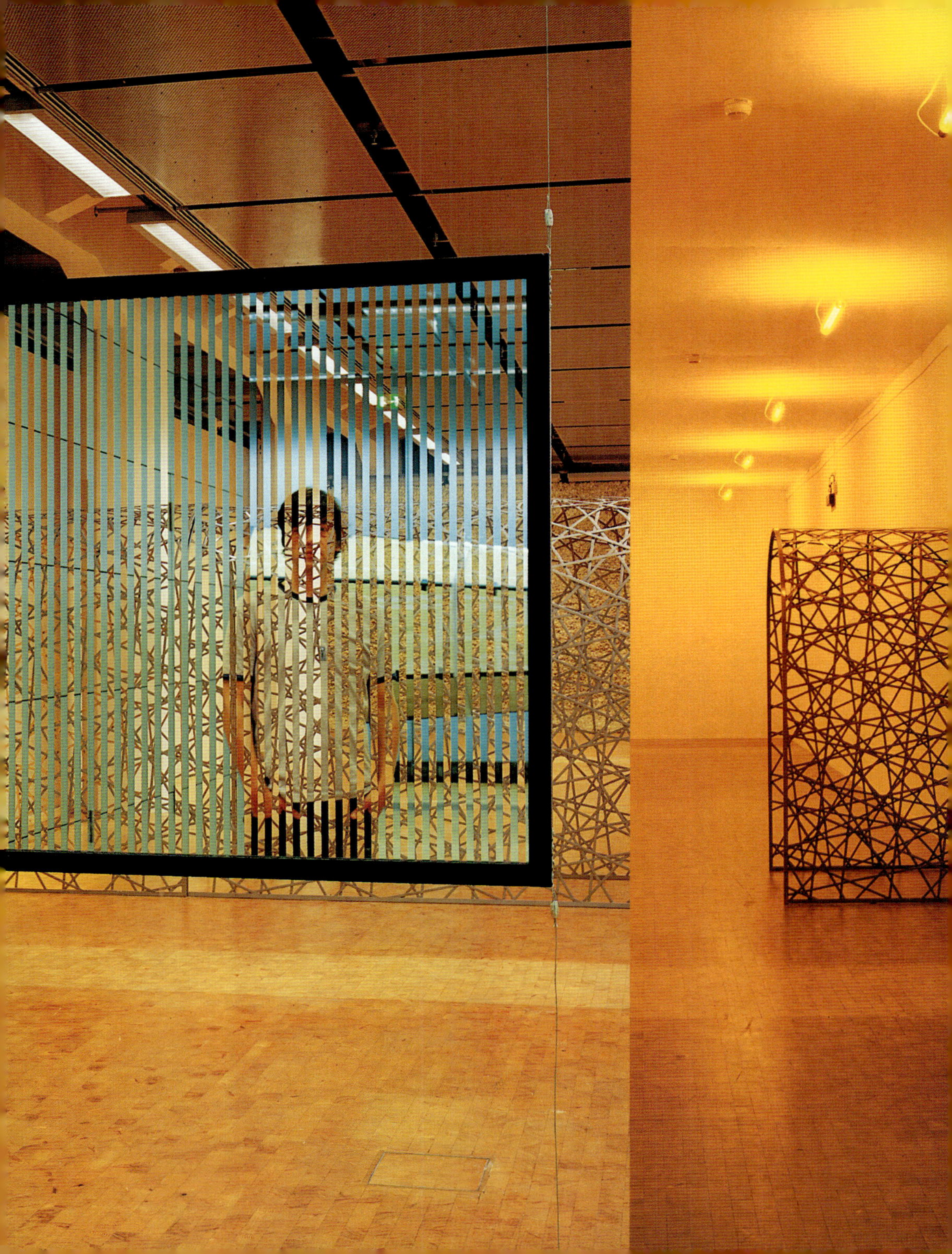

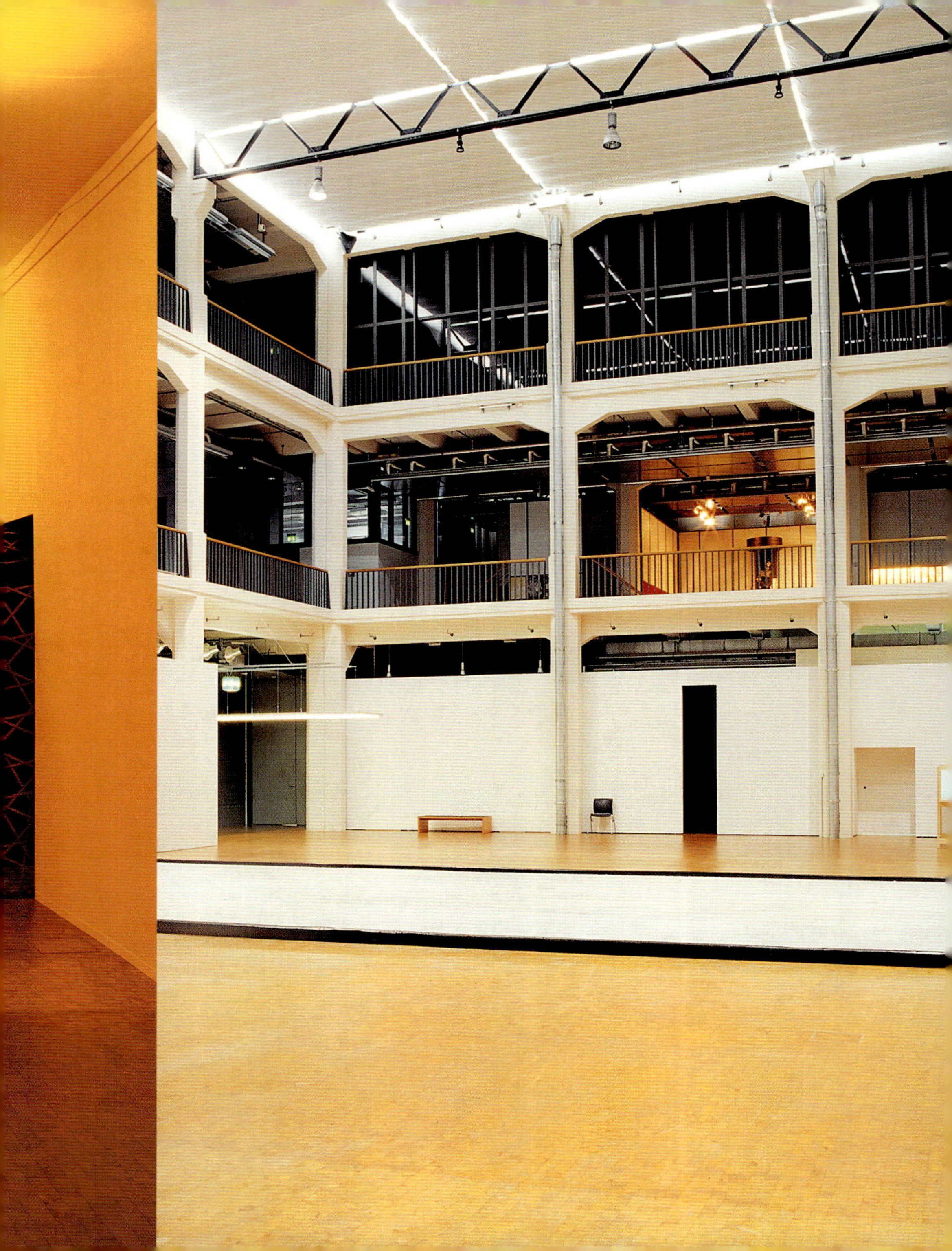

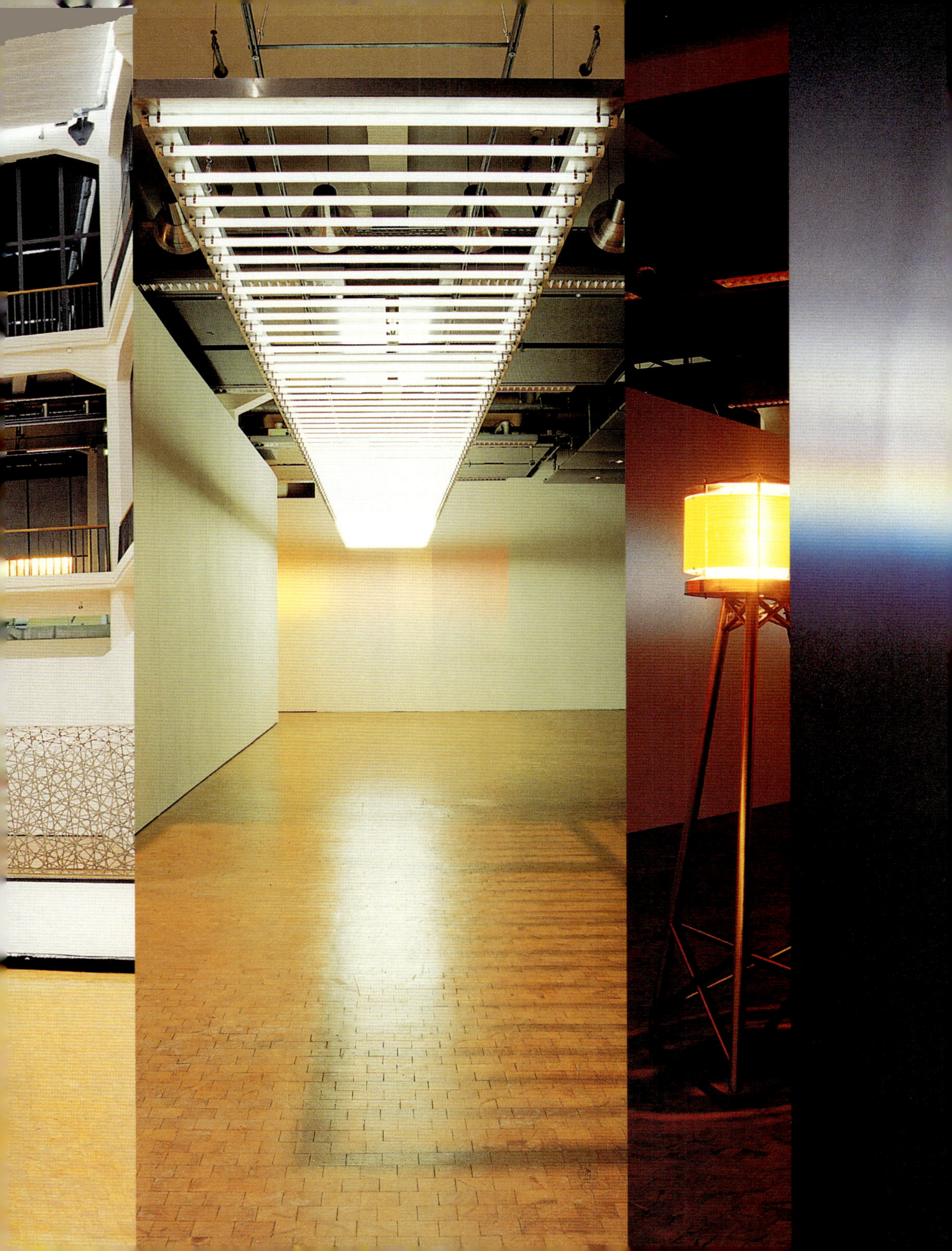

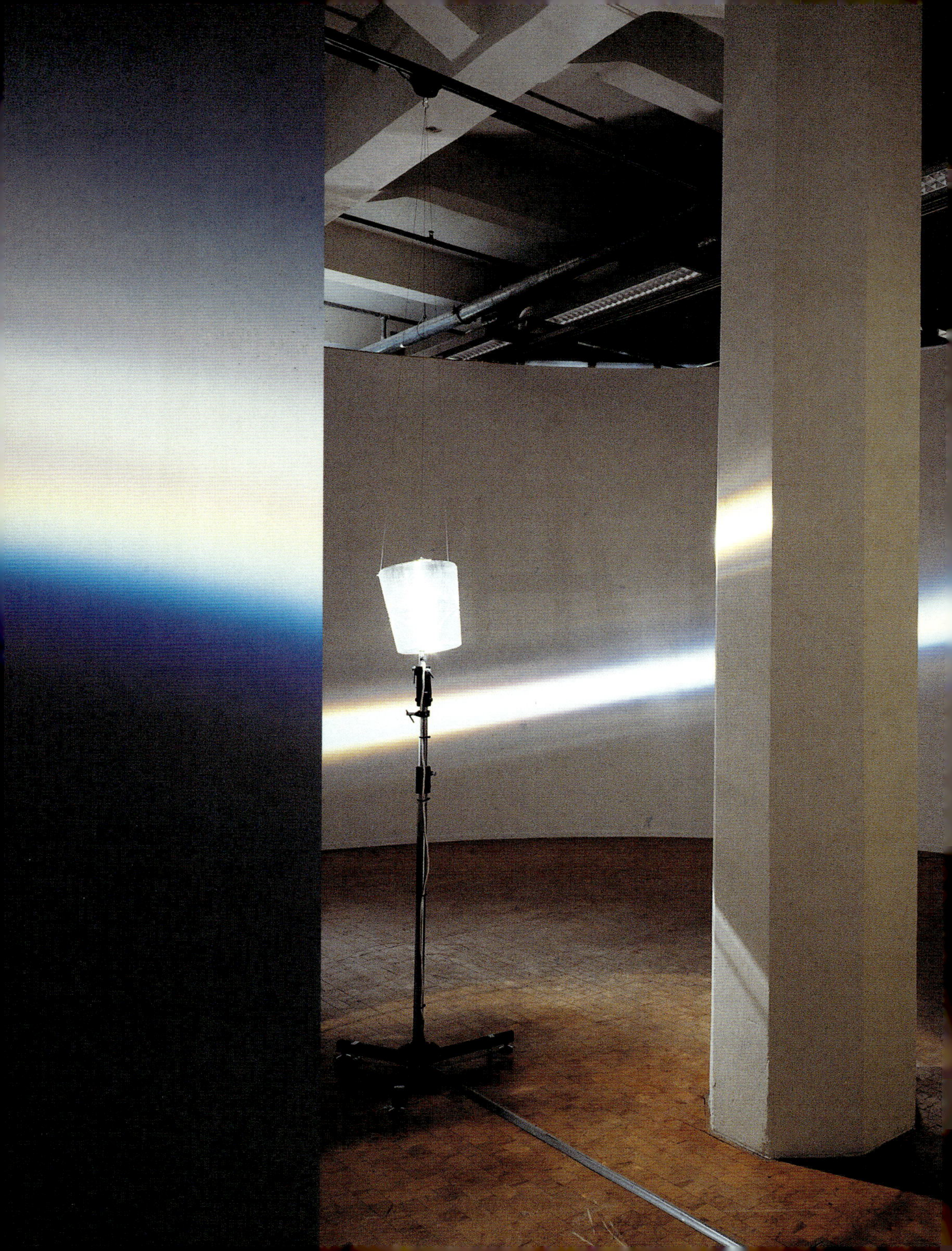

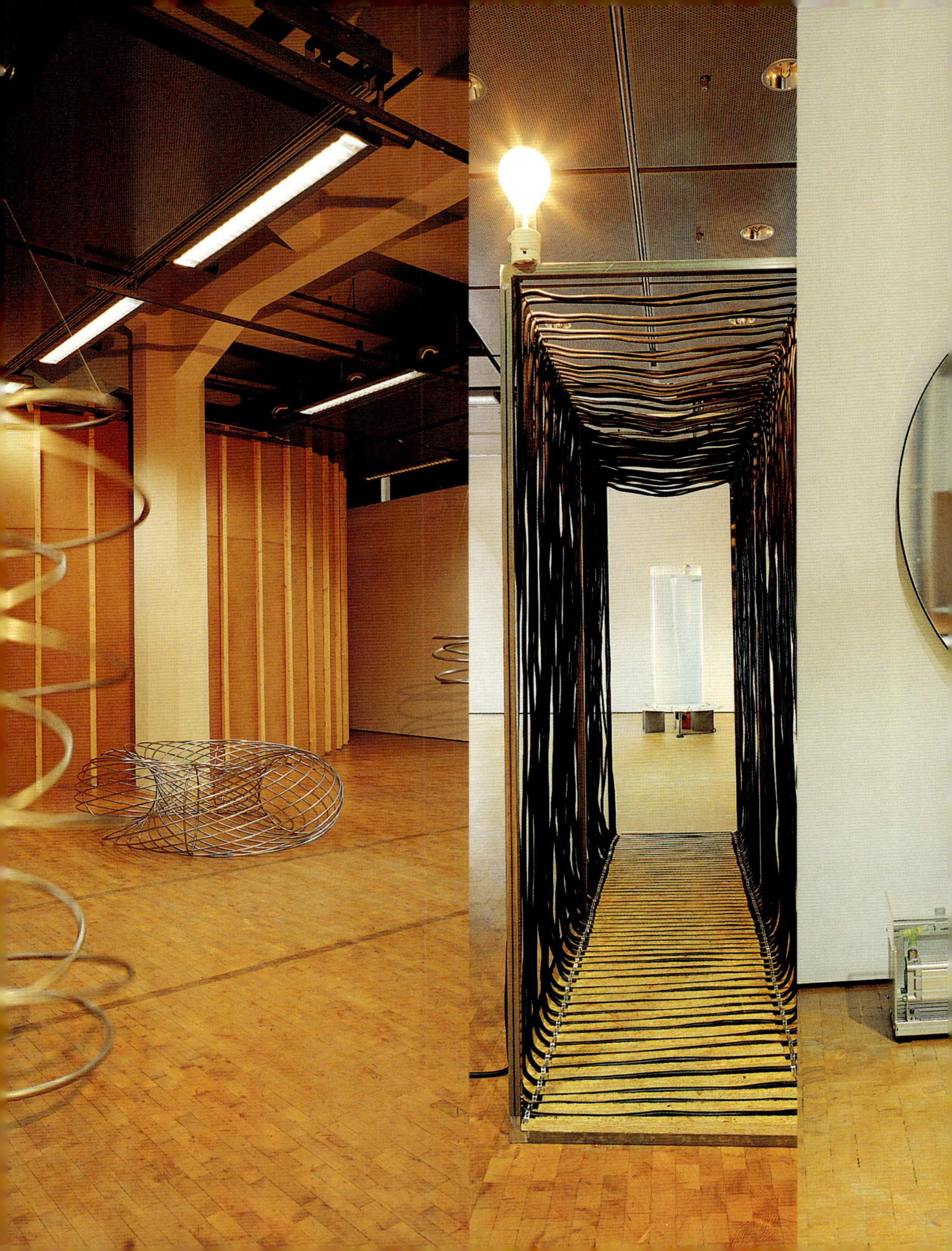

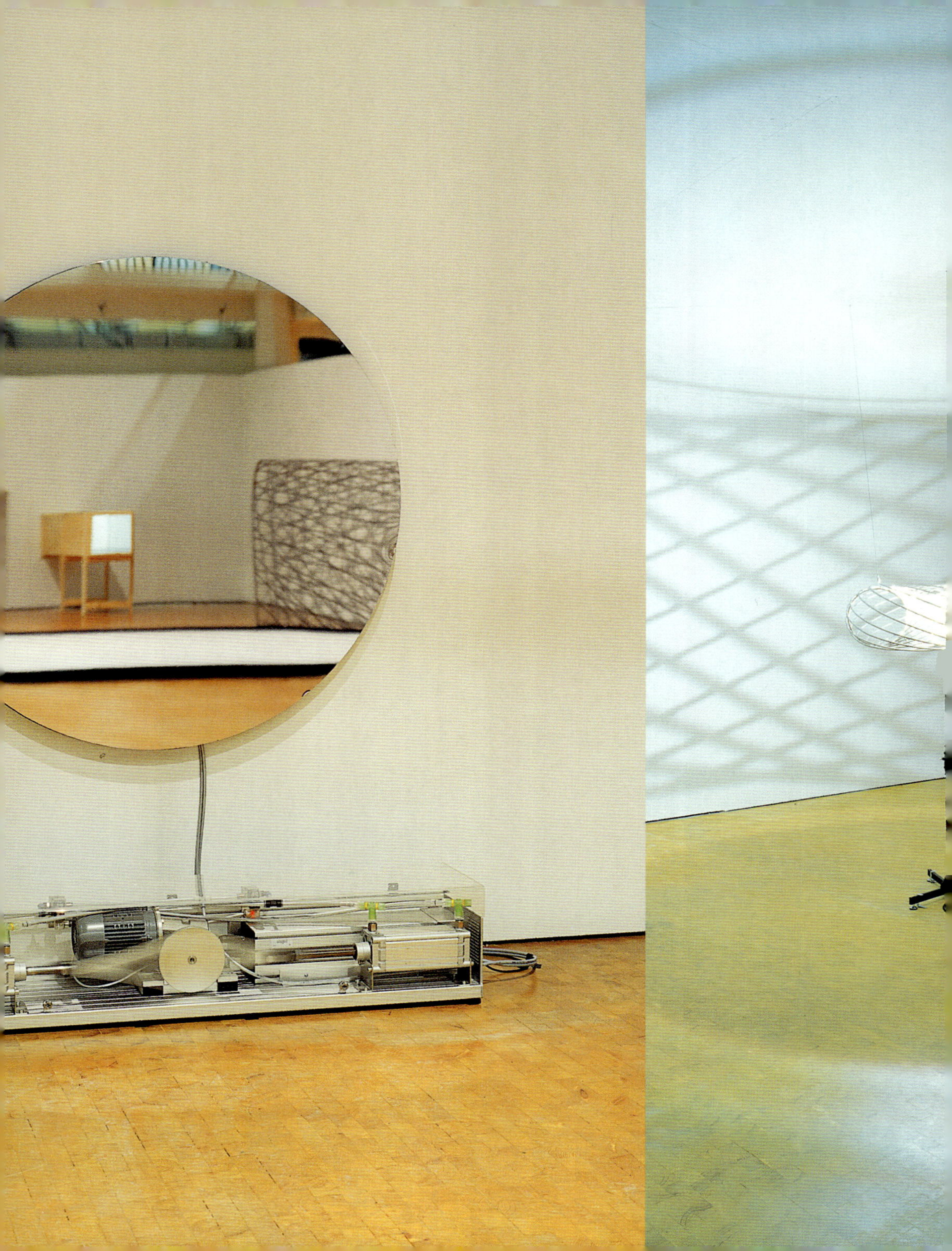

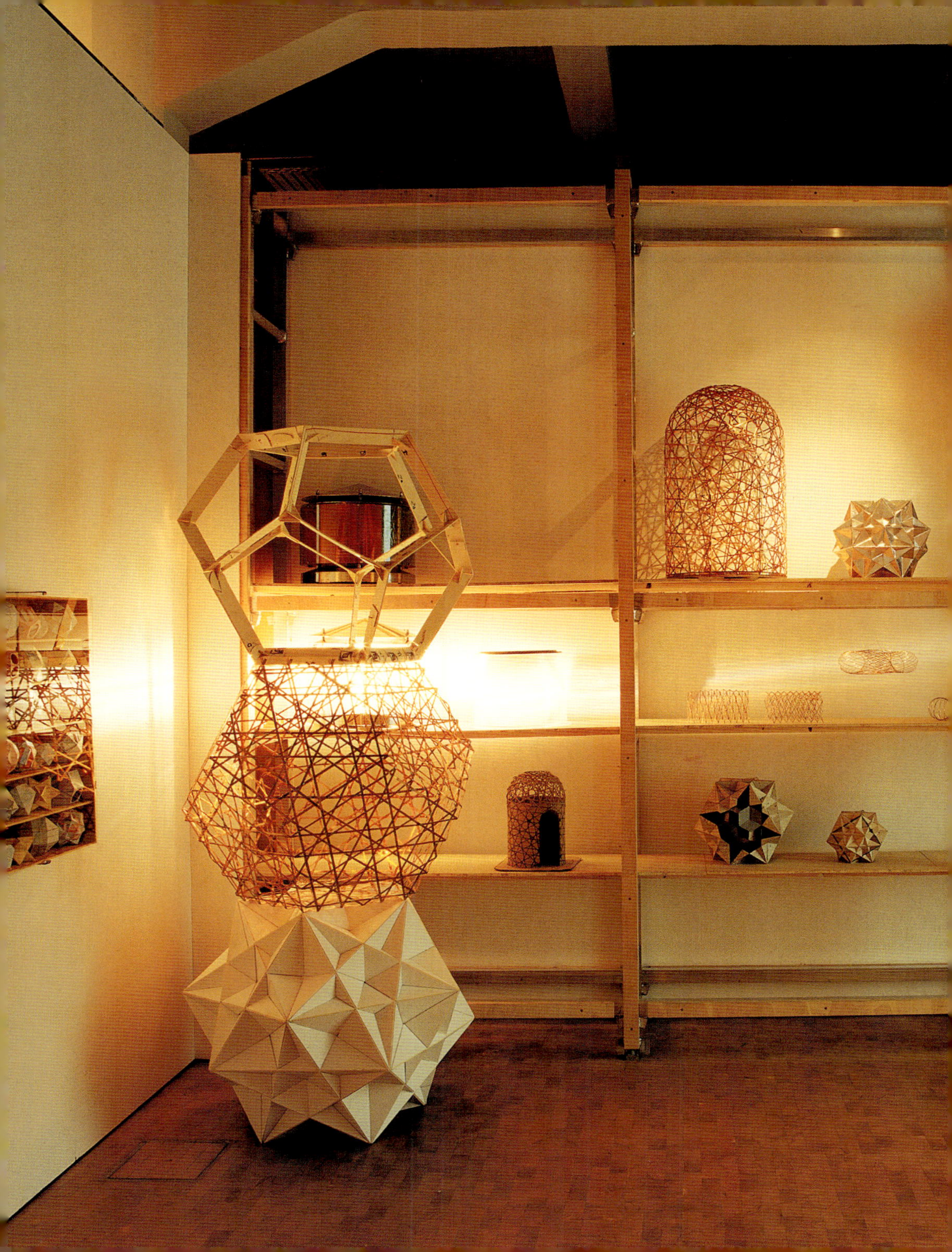

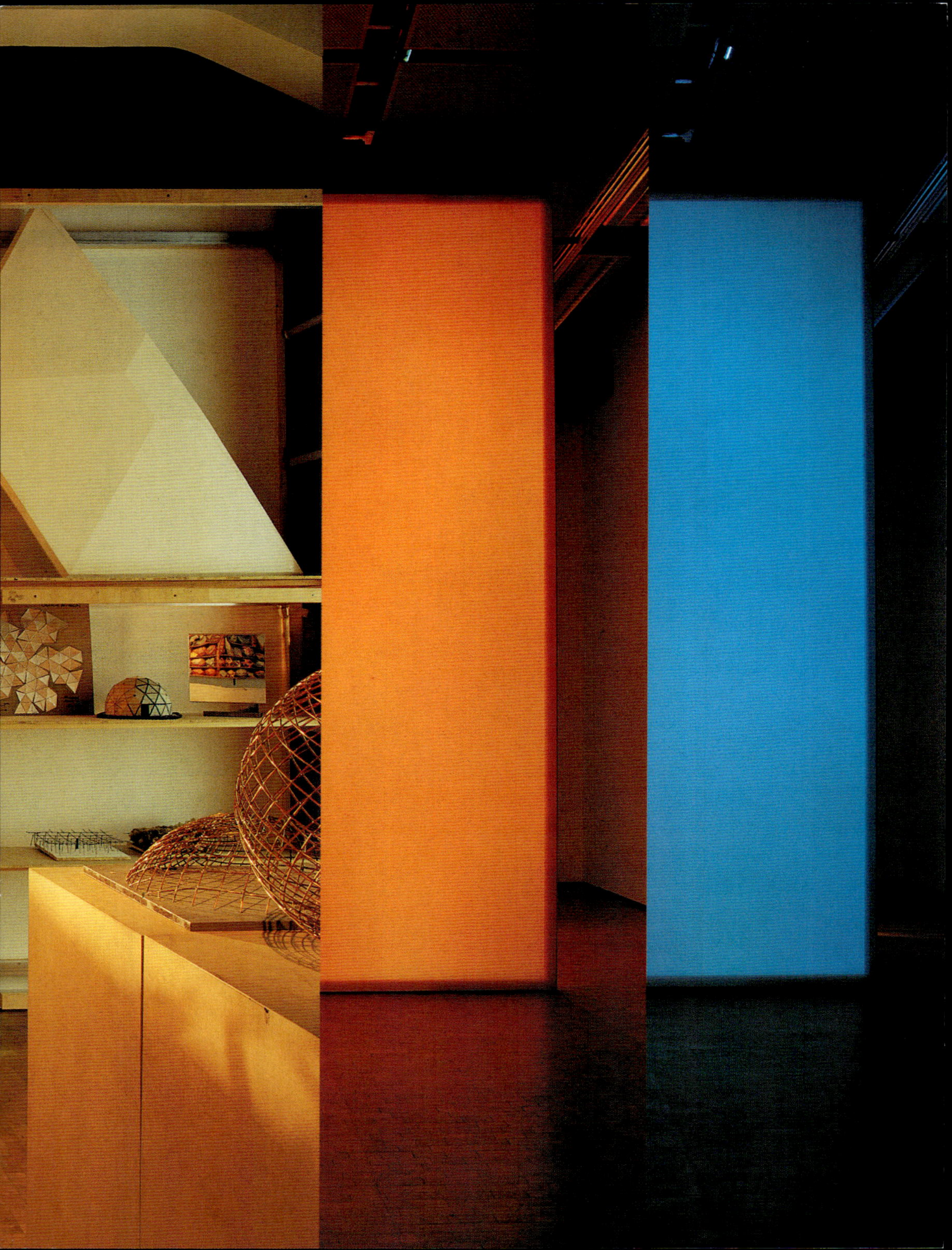

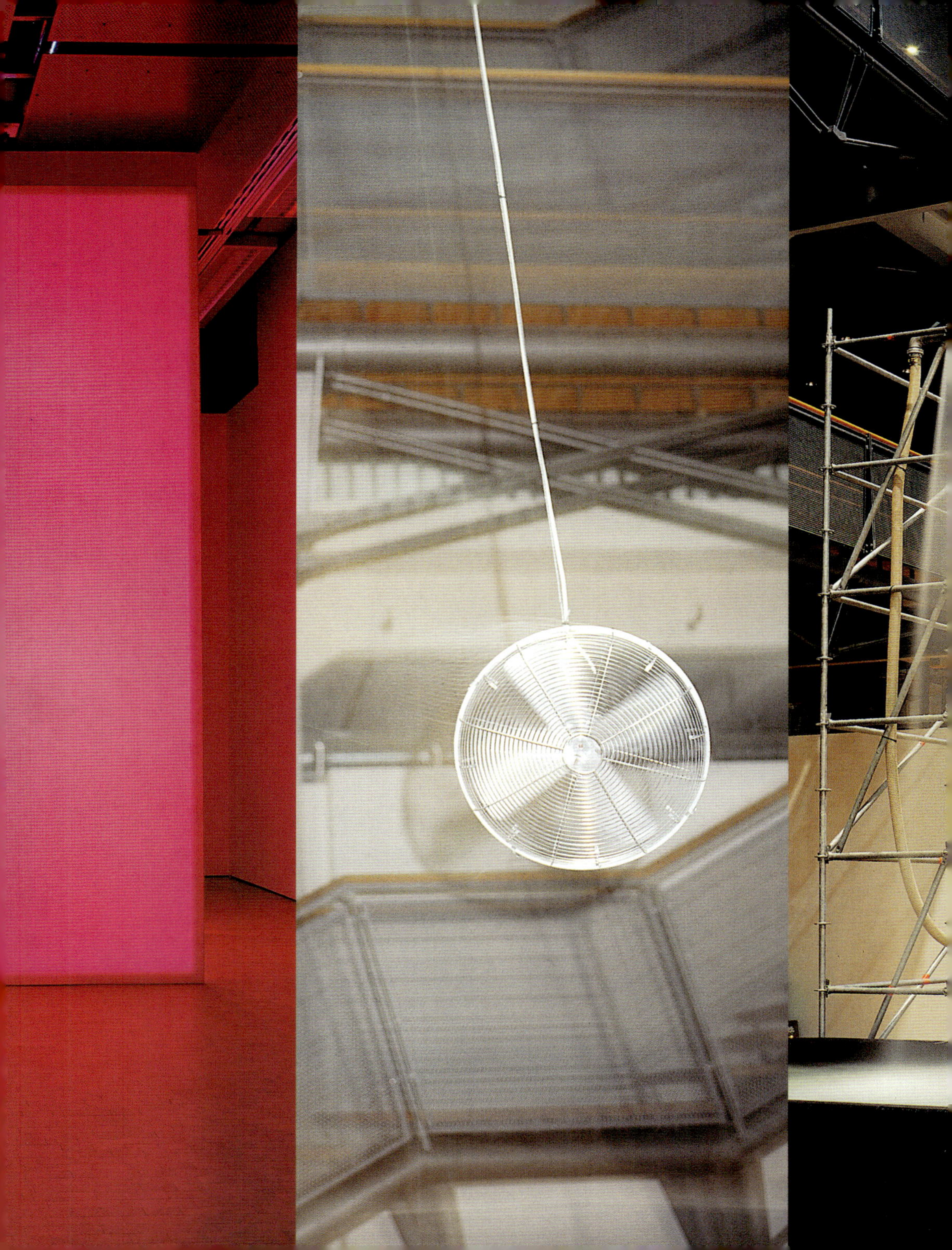

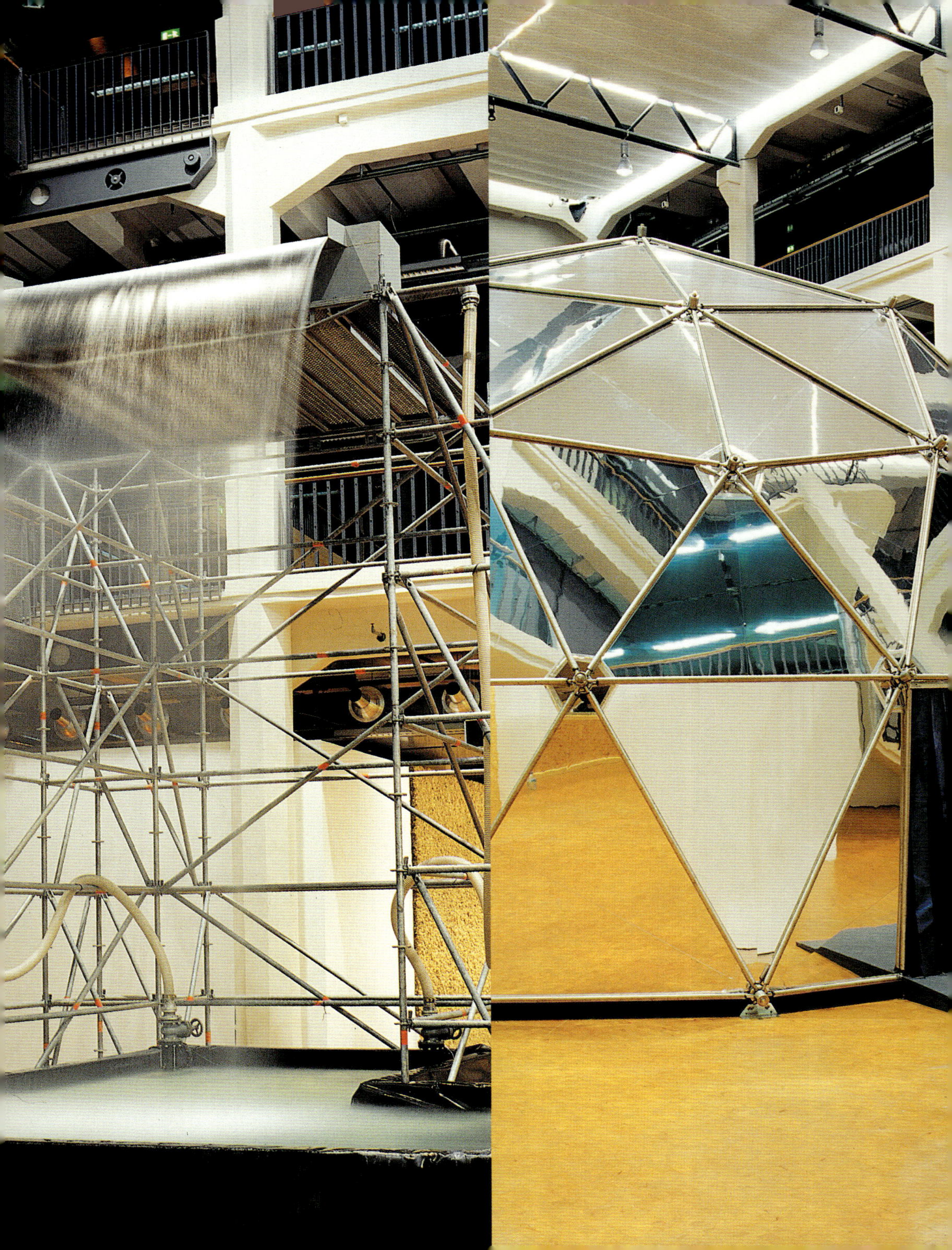

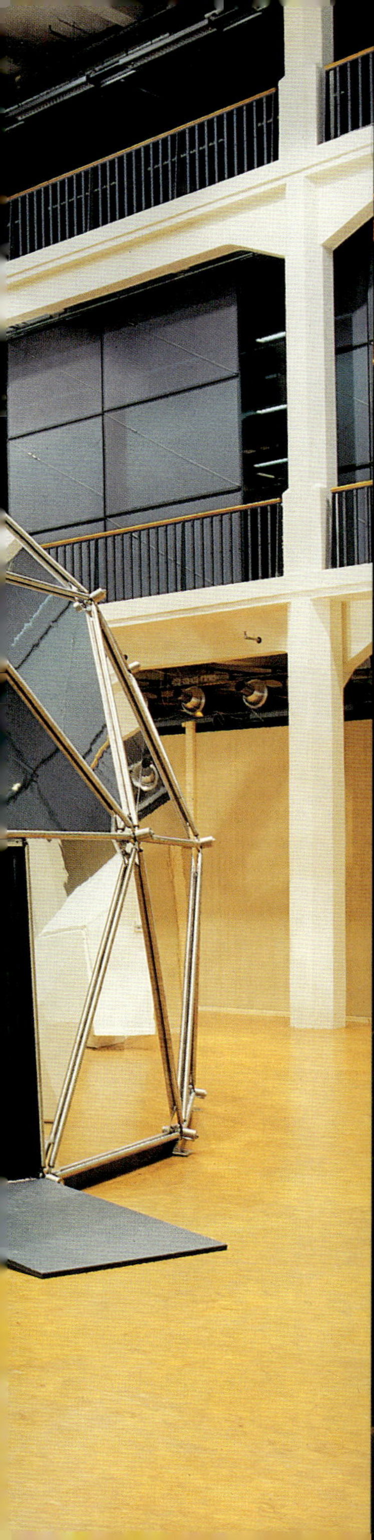
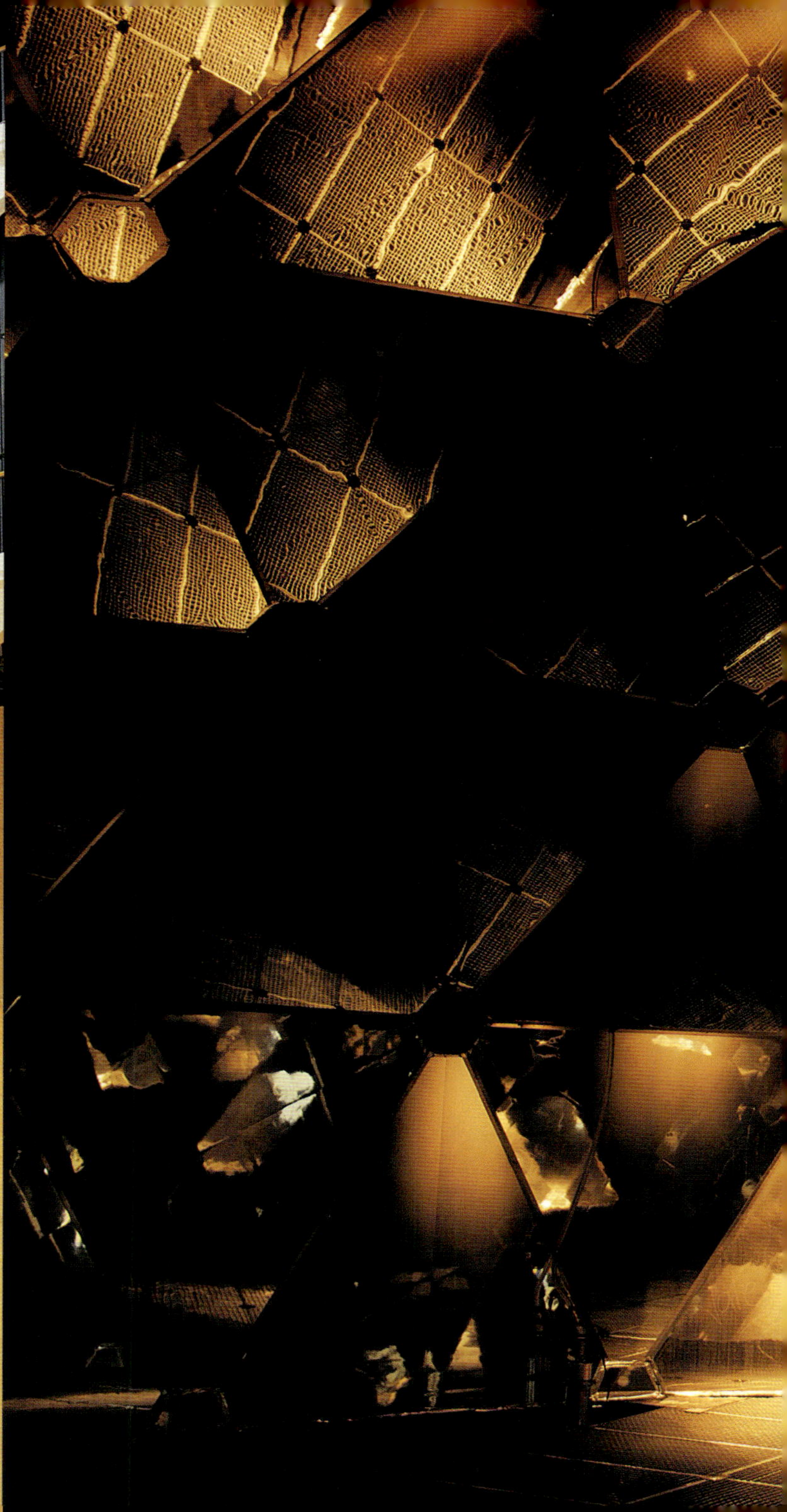

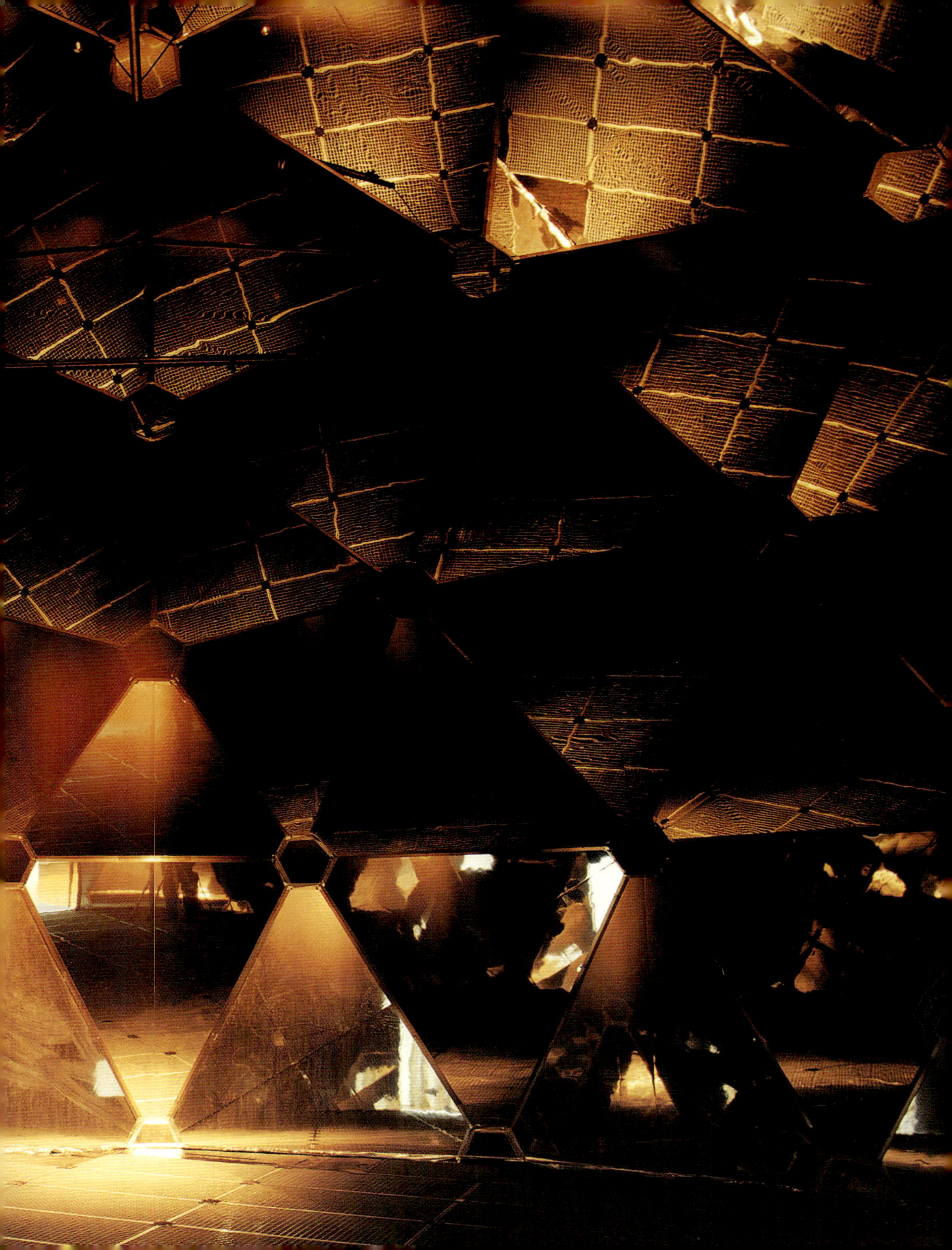

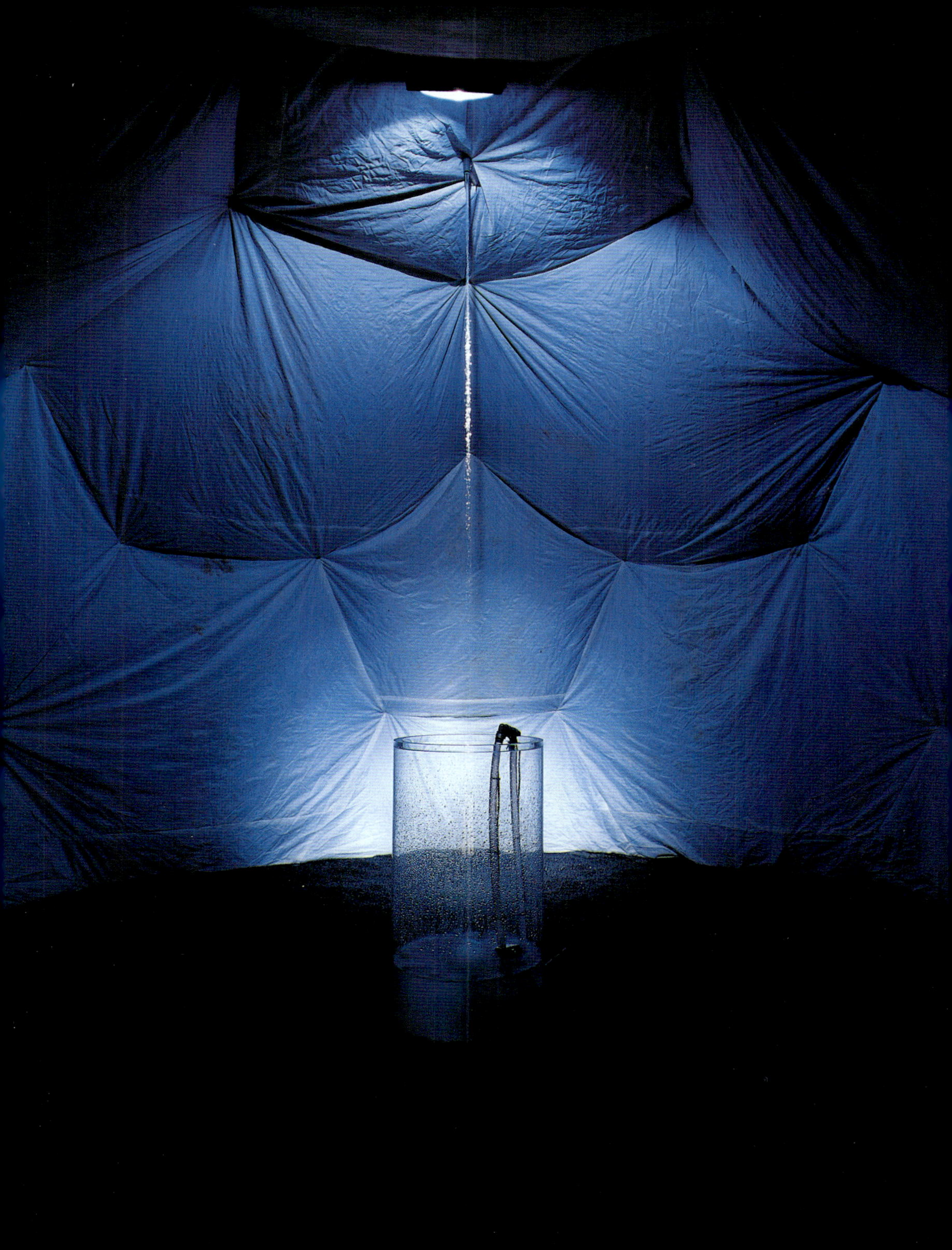

1 **Camera obscura (Your double day diary),** 1999	Size varies with installation; glass lens, metal frame, foil; private collection, Munich, Germany
2 **Surroundings surrounded,** 2001	Size varies with installation; strobelights, mirror; courtesy neugerriemschneider, Berlin; Tanya Bonakdar Gallery, New York
3 **Your compound space,** 2001	7,2 x 1,8 m; aluminium mirror; courtesy neugerriemschneider, Berlin; Tanya Bonakdar Gallery, New York
4 **Seeing yourself seeing,** 2001	1 x 1 m; glass, mirror, wooden frame; collection Dare & Themis Michos, San Francisco, USA
5 **Fivefold tunnel,** 2000	10 x 1,1 m; stainless steel; courtesy neugerriemschneider, Berlin; Tanya Bonakdar Gallery, New York
6 **The very large ice floor,** 1998	15 x 7,5 m (size varies with installation); water, ice machine; courtesy neugerriemschneider, Berlin; Tanya Bonakdar Gallery, New York
7 **Lightwave,** 2001	12,5 x 1,2 x 0,2 m (size varies with installation); neon tubes, aluminium frame, control unit; ZKM, Karlsruhe, Germany
8 **Orientation lights,** 1999	2 x 0,7 x 0,7 m; stainless steel, glass, light, colour filter; collection Patrizia & Juan Vergez, Buenos Aires, Argentina
9 **360 degree expectations,** 2001	ø 10 m (size varies with installation); wood, plastic lens, light, tripod, motor; collection Tanya Bonakdar; courtesy Tanya Bonakdar Gallery, New York
10 **360 degree expectations,** 2001	ø 10 m (size varies with installation); wood, plastic lens, light, tripod, motor; collection Tanya Bonakdar; courtesy Tanya Bonakdar Gallery, New York
11 **Endless doughnut,** 2001	ø 2 x 0,62 m; stainless steel; courtesy neugerriemschneider, Berlin; Tanya Bonakdar Gallery, New York
12 **Induktionsspule,** 2000	Size due to installation; cable; courtesy neugerriemschneider, Berlin; Tanya Bonakdar Gallery, New York
13 **Konvex / Konkav,** 1995/2000	ø 1,5 m; mirror foil, pump; Sammlung Boros, Wuppertal, Germany
14 **Doughnut,** 2000	ø 1,2 x 1.8 m; stainless steel, glass, HMI-lamp, ballast, tripod; Neue Galerie am Landesmuseum Joanneum, Graz
15 **Models (work in progress),** 2000/2001	Various materials; courtesy Olafur Eliasson and Einar Thorsteinn

16 **Room for all colors,** 1999	Frame 3,7 x 3,7 m (size varies with installation); bulps, coloured foil, electricity, screen, computer; Sammlung Boros, Wuppertal, Germany
17 **Room for all colors,** 1999	Frame 3,7 x 3,7 m (size varies with installation); bulps, coloured foil, electricity, screen, computer; Sammlung Boros, Wuppertal, Germany
18 **Room for all colors,** 1999	Frame 3,7 x 3,7 m (size varies with installation); bulps, coloured foil, electricity, screen, computer; Sammlung Boros, Wuppertal, Germany
19 **Ventilator,** 1997	ø 0,6 m; ventilator, steel wire; courtesy Tanya Bonakdar Gallery, New York; neugerriemschneider, Berlin; Sammlung Boros, Wuppertal, Germany
20 **The drop factory,** 2000	ø 10 x 6 m; stainless steel, aluminium, mirror; courtesy Tanya Bonakdar Gallery, New York; neugerriemschneider, Berlin
21 **The drop factory,** 2000	ø 10 x 6 m; stainless steel, aluminium, mirror; courtesy Tanya Bonakdar Gallery, New York; neugerriemschneider, Berlin
22 **By means of a sudden intuitive realisation,** 1996	ø 5.1 x 3 m; water, strobelight, water pump, plexiglass, fiberglass; courtesy neugerriemschneider, Berlin; Tanya Bonakdar Gallery, New York
23 **Waterfall,** 1998	9 x 9 x 6 m (size varies with installation); scaffolding, pump, stainless steel, water; courtesy neugerriemschneider, Berlin; Tanya Bonakdar Gallery, New York

Works in the exhibition

Camera obscura (Your double day diary), 1999
Variable size
Glass lens, metal frame, foil
Private collection, Munich, Germany

Surroundings surrounded, 2001
Variable size
Strobelights, mirror
Courtesy neugerriemschneider, Berlin; Tanya Bonakdar Gallery, New York

Your compound space, 2001
7,2 x 1,8 m
Stainless steel, mirror
Courtesy neugerriemschneider, Berlin; Tanya Bonakdar Gallery, New York

Your repetitive view, 2001
7 x 0,6 x 0,6 m (variable size)
Wood, mirror
Courtesy neugerriemschneider, Berlin; Tanya Bonakdar Gallery, New York

Seeing yourself seeing, 2001
1 x 1 m
Glass, mirror, wooden frame
Collection Dare & Themis Michos, San Francisco, USA

Room for one color, 1998
Variable size
Light, control panels
Collection Patrizia & Juan Vergez, Buenos Aires, Argentina

Fivefold tunnel, 2000
10 x 1,1 m
Stainless steel
Courtesy neugerriemschneider, Berlin; Tanya Bonakdar Gallery, New York

The very large ice floor, 1998
15 x 7,5 m (variable size)
Water, ice machine
Courtesy neugerriemschneider, Berlin; Tanya Bonakdar Gallery, New York

1 m³ light, 1999
1 x 1 x 1 m
Pin spots, smoke machine, tripod
Private collection, New York, USA

Lightwave, 2001
12,5 x 1,2 x 0,2 m (variable size)
Neon tubes, aluminium frame, control unit
ZKM | Karlsruhe, Germany

Orientation lights, 1999
2 x 0,7 x 0,7 m
Stainless steel, glass, light, colour filter
Collection Patrizia & Juan Vergez, Buenos Aires, Argentina

360 degree expectations, 2001
ø 10 m (variable size)
Wood, plastic lens, light, tripod, motor
Collection Tanya Bonakdar; courtesy Tanya Bonakdar Gallery, New York

Double spiral, 2001
ø 1 x 2 m
Stainless steel
Courtesy neugerriemschneider, Berlin; Tanya Bonakdar Gallery, New York

Small double spiral, 2001
ø 1 x 0,6 m
Stainless steel
Courtesy neugerriemschneider, Berlin; Tanya Bonakdar Gallery, New York

Endless doughnut, 2001
ø 2 x 0,62 m
Stainless steel
Courtesy neugerriemschneider, Berlin; Tanya Bonakdar Gallery, New York

Induktionsspule, 2000
Variable size
Cable
Courtesy neugerriemschneider, Berlin; Tanya Bonakdar Gallery, New York

Vortex for Lofoten, 1999
ø 1,2 x 2 m
Plexiglass, water, pump, hose
Sammlung Boros, Wuppertal, Germany

Eine Beschreibung einer Reflexion, oder aber eine angenehme Übung zu deren Eigenschaften, 1995
Variable size
Mirror, projection surface, light
Sammlung Boros, Wuppertal, Germany

Konvex / Konkav, 1995/2000
ø 1,5 m
Mirror, pump
Sammlung Boros, Wuppertal, Germany

Highlighter, 1999
Variable size
Spotlight, control panel
Sammlung Haubrok, Düsseldorf, Germany

Doughnut, 2000
ø 1,5 x O,6 m
Stainless steel, glass, HMI-lamp, ballast, tripod
Neue Galerie am Landesmuseum Joanneum, Graz

Models (work in progress), 2000/2001
Variable size
Various materials
Courtesy Olafur Eliasson und Einar Thorsteinn

Your blue afterimage exposed / Your orange afterimage exposed, 2000
Variable size
Spotlight, dimmer, tripod
Collection Takahiro Matsuura, Osaka, Japan

Tell me about your miraculous invention, 1996
6 x 5 m (variable size)
Mirror, spotlight
Collection Århus Kunstmuseum, Århus, Denmark

Room for all colors, 1999
Frame 3,7 x 3,7 m (variable size)
Projection foil, metal frame, bulps, colour foil, control unit
Sammlung Boros, Wuppertal, Germany

Your strange certainty still kept, 1996
Length 5 m (variable size)
Water, pump, strobelight, foil, wood
The Dakis Joannou Collection Foundation, Athens, Greece

Your windless arrangement, 1997
variable size
Ventilators, motors, metal frame
Malmö Konstmuseum, Malmö, Sweden

Ventilator, 1997
ø 0,6 m
Ventilator, steel wire
Sammlung Boros, Wuppertal, Germany

The drop factory, 2000
ø 10 x 6 m
Stainless steel, aluminium, mirror
Courtesy neugerriemschneider, Berlin; Tanya Bonakdar Gallery, New York

By means of a sudden intuitive realisation, 1996
ø 5.1 x 3 m
Water, strobelight, water pump, plexiglass, fibreglass
Courtesy neugerriemschneider, Berlin; Tanya Bonakdar Gallery, New York

Wasserfall, 1998
9 x 9 x 6 m (variable size)
Scaffolding, pump, stainless steel, water
Courtesy neugerriemschneider, Berlin; Tanya Bonakdar Gallery, New York

Moss wall, 1994
3,9 x 8 m (variable size)
Moss
Courtesy neugerriemschneider, Berlin; Tanya Bonakdar Gallery, New York

Double window projection, 2001
2,5 x 4,5 m (variable size)
Spotlights
Collection Susan & Michael Hort, New York, USA

Chronology

Olafur Eliasson, born in Copenhagen, Denmark, 1967
Lives and works in Berlin, Germany

Education

1989-95 Royal Academy of Arts, Copenhagen, Denmark

Solo Exhibitions

2001
neugerriemschneider, Berlin, Germany
Project for Garden Hall, Museum of Modern Art, New York, USA
Surroundings Surrounded, ZKM | Center for Art and Media, Karlsruhe, Germany (catalogue)
Your only real thing is time, The Institute of Contemporary Art, Boston, USA (catalogue)
The mediated motion, Kunsthaus Bregenz, Austria (catalogue)
Your position surrounded and your surroundings positioned, Dundee Contemporary Art, Dundee, UK (catalogue)
Your now is my surroundings, Bonakdar Jancou Gallery, New York, USA

2000
Surroundings Surrounded, Neue Galeriem, Graz, Austria (catalogue)
The only thing we have in common is that we are different, CCA, Kitakyushu, Japan
Your orange afterimage exposed, Gallery Koyanagi, Tokyo, Japan
Your blue afterimage exposed, Masataka Hayakawa Gallery, Tokyo, Japan
The Curious Garden, Irish Museum of Modern Art, Dublin, Ireland
Your intuitive surroundings versus your surrounded intuition, The Art Institute of Chicago, Chicago, USA; Kunstverein Wolfsburg, Wolfsburg, Germany; IASPIS, Stockholm, Sweden

1999
Your position surrounded and your surroundings positioned, Dundee Contemporary Art, Dundee, Scotland; De Appel Foundation, Amsterdam, The Netherlands; (with Job Koelewijn); Frankfurter Kunstverein, Frankfurt/M., Germany; Kunstverein Wolfsburg, Wolfsburg, Germany; Marc Foxx, Los Angeles, USA; Emi Fontane, Milan, Italy; Castello di Rivoli, Torino, Italy; Galleri Ingólfsstraeti, Reykjavík, Iceland

1998
Museum for Contemporary Art, Leipzig, Germany; neugerriemschneider, Berlin, Germany
Tell Me about a Miraculous Invention, Århus Kunstmuseum, Århus, Denmark
Photoworks, Bildmuseet, Umea, Sweden
Aquarium, Galerie Enja Wonnenberger, Kiel, Germany; Bonakdar Jancou Gallery, New York, USA; Kjarvalstadir Museum, Reykjavík, Iceland (catalogue); Galerie Peter Kilchmann, Zurich, Switzerland

1997
Your sunmachine, Marc Foxx, Santa Monica, USA
The curious garden, Kunsthalle Basel, Basel, Switzerland; Stalke Out of Space, Copenhagen, Denmark
Sonnenfenster, Kunsthalle Wien, Vienna, Austria

1996
Your foresight endured, Galleria Emi Fontana, Milano, Italy
Your strange certainty still kept, Bonakdar Jancou Gallery, New York, USA
Tell me about a miraculous invention, Galeri Andreas Brändström, Stockholm, Sweden; Kunstmuseet, Malmö, Sweden

1995
A Description of A Reflection, or a Pleasant Exercise Regarding Its Qualities, neugerriemschneider, Berlin, Germany; Künstlerhaus, Stuttgart, Germany
Thoka, Hamburger Kunstverein, Hamburg, Germany; Tommy Lund Galerie, Odense, Denmark

1994
Stalke Out of Space, Copenhagen, Denmark
Some People Remember Walking That Night, Lukas & Hoffmann, Cologne, Germany
No Days in Winter, No Nights in Summer, Forumgallereit, Malmö, Sweden

1991
Overgarden Galleri, Copenhagen, Denmark

Group Exhibitions

2001
All-Terrain: An Exploration of Landscape and Place, Contemporary Art Center of Virginia, Virginia Beach, USA
Black Box, Kunstmuseum Bern, Bern, Switzerland
Vrai que Nature, capcMusée d'art contemporain, Bordeaux, France
Freestyle – Werke aus der Sammlung Boros, Museum Morsbroich, Leverkusen, Germany

2000
Preis der Nationalgalerie für junge Kunst, Hamburger Bahnhof, Berlin, Germany
Raumkörper, Kunsthalle Basel, Basel, Switzerland
Vision and Reality, Louisiana Museum, Humlebæk, Denmark
Photogravüre, Niels Borch Jensen, Berlin, Germany
Wonderland, St. Louis Museum of Art, St. Louis, USA
ForwArt, BBL Brussels, Brussels, Belgium
Over the edges, SMAK, Gent, Belgium
The Greenhouse Effect, Serpentine Gallery, London, UK

Wanas 2000, The Wanas Foundation, Knislinge, Sweden
Under the same sky, Kiasma, Helsinki, Finland

1999
Drawings, Bonakdar Jancou Gallery, New York, USA
La Biennale di Venezia, Venice, Italy
To the People of the City of the Euro, Frankfurter Kunstverein, Frankfurt/M., Germany
Photography: An Expanded View, Recent Acquisitions, Guggenheim Museum, New York, USA
Landscape: Outside the Frame, MIT List Visual Art Center, Cambridge, USA
Schöpfung, Diözesanmuseum, Freising, Germany
Photography from the Martin Z. Margulies Collection, The Art Museum at Florida International University, Miami, USA
Gegenwartskunst in Deutschland, Kunstmuseum Wolfsburg, Wolfsburg, Germany
Arte Continua, San Gimignano, Italy
Sommerens mørke og lyse nætter, Århus Kunstbygning, Århus, Denmark
Overflow, Marianne Boesky & D'Amelio-Terras & Anton Kern Galleries, New York, USA
The Midnight Sun Show, Lofoten, Norway
Panorama 2000, Centraal Museum, Utrecht, The Netherlands

1998
Light x Eight: The Hanukkah Project, The Jewish Museum, New York, USA
Auf der Spur, Kunsthalle Zurich, Zurich, Switzerland
Sharawadgi, Felsenvilla, Baden, Austria
The 7th Triennial of Contemporary Art, Cool Places, Contemporary Art Centre, Vilnius, Lithuania
New Photography 14, The Museum of Modern Art, New York, USA
Round About Ways, Ujazdowski Castle, Warsaw, Poland
The Edstrand Foundation Art Prize 1998, Rooseum, Center for Contemporary Art, Malmö, Sweden
The Erotic Sublime (Slave to the Rhythm), Galerie Thaddeus Ropac, Salzburg, Austria
The very large ice floor, XXIV Bienal de Sao Paulo, Sao Paulo, Brazil
Waterfall, Sydney Biennial, Sydney, Australia
Something is Rotten in the State of Denmark, Fridericianum, Kassel, Germany
Brytningstider, Norrkopings Konstmuseum, Norrkoping, Sweden
StadtLandschaften, Sabine Kunst Galerie & Edition, Munich, Germany
Pakkus: Momentum, Nordic Festival of Contemporary Art, Moss, Norway; Villa Medici, Academie de France de Rome, Rome, Italy
Do All Oceans Have Walls? Künstlerhaus Bremen, Bremen, Germany
Mai '98, Kunsthalle Köln, Cologne, Germany
Transatlantico, Centro Atlantico de Arte Moderno, Las Palmas, Canary Islands
Nuit blanche, La jeune scène nordique, Musée d'Art moderne de la Ville de Paris, Paris, France (traveling to: Reykjavík Municipal Art Museum, Reykjavík, Iceland; Bergen Billedgalleri, Bergen, Norway; Porin Taidemuseo and Goteborg Konstmuseum, Goteborg, Sweden 1999).

Warming, The Project, a space in Harlem, New York, USA
Interferencias, Museo de Arte Contemporaneo, Madrid, Spain
Seamless, De Appel, Amsterdam, The Netherlands (catalogue)
Sightings: New Photographic Art, Institute of Contemporary Art, London, UK
underground, kuratiert v. Jacob Fabricius, Copenhagen, Denmark; Stalke Anniversary Show, Copenhagen, Denmark

1997
Heaven, P. S. 1, New York, USA
été 97, Centre genevois de gravure contemporaine, Geneva, Switzerland
Kunstpreis der Bottgerstraße in Bremen, Bonner Kunstverein, Bonn, Germany
On life, beauty, translation and other difficulties, 5th International Istanbul Biennial; (curated by Rosa Martines), Istanbul, Turkey
Trade Routes, 2nd Johannesburg Biennale, Johannesburg, South Africa
Truce, Site-Sante Fe, Santa Fe, USA
Alikeness, Center for Contemporary Photography, Fitzroy, Australia
New Scandinavian Art, Louisiana Museum, Humlebæk, Denmark
3rd Symposium on Visual Arts, LANDART, Amos, Canada
Vilnius Center of Art, Vilnius, Lithuania
The Scream, Borealis 8, Arken Museum, Copenhagen, Denmark
Platser, Public Space Projects, Stockholm, Sweden; Kunsthalle Wien, Vienna, Austria

1996
Manifesta 1, Rotterdam, The Netherlands (catalogue)
Glow: Sublime Projected and Reflected Light, New Langton Arts, San Francisco, USA
Prospect 96, Frankfurter Kunstverein, Frankfurt/M., Germany, (catalogue)
Alles was modern ist, Galerie Bärbel Grässlin, Frankfurt/M., Germany
Provinz-Legende, Samtidsmuseet, Roskilde, Denmark
Summer Show, Bonakdar Jancou Gallery, New York, USA
nach weimar, Kunstsammlungen zu Weimar, Weimar, Germany (catalogue)
Remote Connections, Neue Galerie Graz, Graz, Austria; Wäino Aaltonen Museum of Art, Turku, Finland; Artfocus, Tel Aviv, Israel *Views of Icelandic Nature*, Kjarvalsstadir Museum, Reykjavík, Iceland
The Scream, Nordic Fine Arts 1995-96, Arken Museum, Ishøj, Denmark
tolv, Schaper Sundberg Gallery, Stockholm, Sweden; Museum of Modern Art, Ishøj, Denmark

1995
Landschaft, Mittelrhein Museum, Koblenz, Haus am Waldsee, Berlin, Germany
Campo 95, Venice, Italy, Torino, Italy, Malmö, Sweden (1996); Curated by Francesco Bonami
Kunst & Ökologie, Kunstverein Schloss Plön, Plön, Germany

1994
Europa, Ausstellung Münchner Galerien, Munich, Germany

1993
1700 CET, Stalke Out of Space, Copenhagen, Denmark
Black Box, GLOBE Kuratorengruppe, Copenhagen, Denmark

1992
Overdrive, 10 Young Nordic Artists, Copenhagen, Denmark
Lightworks, Demonstrationslokalet for Kunst, Copenhagen, Denmark
Paradise Europe, Billboard Project, Copenhagen, Denmark

1991
Young Scandinavian Art, Stalke Out of Space, Copenhagen, Denmark

1990
Street Signs (billboards), BIZART, Copenhagen, Denmark

1989
Ventilator Projects, Charlottenborg Konsthall, Copenhagen, Denmark

Projects

1998
Galerie Ingolsstraeti, Reykjavík, Iceland
Raum für eine Farbe, Kunsthalle Bremen, Bremen, Germany

1997
Your windy corner, Galleri Andreas Brändström, Stockholm, Sweden
Erosion, Water-project, Johannesburg Biennale, Johannesburg, South Africa (catalogue)
The very large curve, Chalkline drawing, Amos, Canada

1996
The Mukkepark Project, Huidovre, Copenhagen, Denmark

1994
Beauty, Lukas & Hoffmann, Cologne, Germany

1992
Expectations, Copenhagen, Denmark

1990
31 Days of News, Krasnapolsky, Copenhagen, Denmark

Bibliography

2001
Olafur Eliasson: Surroundings Surrounded. Essays on Space and Science, edited by Peter Weibel, Neue Galerie, Graz, Austria and ZKM | Karlsuhe, Germany; *my now is your surroundings – process as object. Olafur Eliasson,* Verlag der Buchhandlung Walther König, Cologne, Germany; Miriam Bers, "Berlin, from neo pop to cross culture," in *tema celeste,* January/February 2001, pp. 70-75; *Your only real thing is time,* Institute of Contemporary Art, Boston, USA (with texts by Jill Medvedow Plaut, Lars Lerup, Jessica Morgan).

2000
Barbara Hess, "Nase im Wind," in *Texte zur Kunst,* 39, September 2000, pp. 189-196; Katrina Brown, "If the eye were not sun-like, the sun's light, it would not see,"and Russell Ferguson, "Freezing and Melting," in *Your position surrounded and your surroundings positioned,* Dundee Contemporary Art, Dundee, UK; Ralf Christofori, "The Vitality of Non-Orthogonal Abstraction," in *Raumkörper,* Kunsthalle Basel, Basel, Switzerland; Andreas Spiegl, "Olafur Eliasson, Non-Trueness as the Nature of Theatre," in *Afterall,* 2, 2000, pp. 99-106; Gertrud Sandquist, "Olafur Eliasson," in *Afterall,* 2 , 2000, pp. 107-110; Maren Lübbke, "Olafur Eliasson: Surroundings Surrounded," in *Camera Austria,* 71, 2000, p. 61; Markus Wailand, "Olafur Eliasson, Neue Galerie Graz," in *Frieze,* pp. 127-128; Rochelle Steiner, "Wonderland," in *Wonderland*, St. Louis Museum of Art, St. Louis, USA; James Rondeau, The Art Institute of Chicago, Chicago, USA; Edward Leffingwel, "Carnegie Ramble," in *Art in America,* March 2000, pp. 86-93; Joshua Decter, "Panorama 2000," in *Flash Art,* January-February 2000, pp. 43, 112.

1999
Carnegie International 1999/2000, essay by Madeleine Grynsztejn, Curator, pp. 32, 33, 70, 102. Michael Brenson & Madeleine Grynsztejn, "Fact and Fiction," in *Artforum*, September 1999, pp. 67-70. David Birnbaum & Peter Nilsson, *Like Virginity, Once Lost: Five Views on Nordic Art Now*, 1999, p. 74. Burkhard Riemschneider and Uta Grosenick, *Art at the Turn of the Millenium*, Taschen, Cologne, 1999, pp. 144-145; Edward Leffingwell, "Report From Sao Paulo: Cannibals All," in *Art in America,* May 1999, pp. 48-55; *Photography from the Martin Z. Margulies Collection*, The Art Museum at Florida International University, Catalogue, p. 28.

1998
Jan Verwoert, "Berlin Biennale," in *Frieze*, Issue 44, January-February 99, pp. 91-92; Márica Fortes, "XXIV Sao Paul Biennal," in *Frieze*, Issue 44, January-February 99, pp.87-88; Francesco Bonami, "Olafur Eliasson," in *Cream: Contemporary Art in Culture*, London, Phaidon, 1998, pp. 104-107; Simon Grant, "Olafur Eliasson," in *Every Day*, Catalogue for the 11th Biennale of Sydney, pp. 90-91; Christian Haye, "The Iceman Cometh," in *Frieze*, May 1998, pp. 62-65; Sophie Berrebi, "Nuit Blanche, Musee d'Art Moderne de la Ville de Paris," in *Frieze*, May 1998, pp. 88-89; Gregory Volk, "On the Edge. Olafur Eliasson: Fire and Iceland," in *Artnews*, April 1998, p. 200; Daniel Birnbaum, "Openings: Olafur Eliasson," in *Artforum*,

April 1998, pp. 106-107; Jan Winkelmann, "Project: Olafur Eliasson," in *Art + Text*, February/April 1998, pp. 44-49; Olafur Eliasson and Barbara Steiner. "Gegen die Zeit gehen." in *Kunst Bulletin*, January/February 1998, pp. 10-17.

1997
Jonathan Crary, "Visionary Events," in *the curious garden,* Kunsthalle Basel, Basel, Switzerland, pp. 43-49; Roxana Marcoci and Diana Murphy, Eve Sinaiko, eds. *New Art*, Harry N. Abrams, New York, 1997, p. 51; Charles Dee Mitchell, "Reports From Santa Fe: New Narratives," in *Art in America*, November 1997, pp. 43-47; Hans Rudolf Reust, "Reviews," in *Artforum*, Summer 1997, p. 146.

1996
Christiane Schneider, "Olafur Eliasson," in *Frieze*, January/February 1996, p. 77; Francesco Bonami, "Olafur Eliasson," in *Flash Art*, May/June 1996, p. 105; John Rapko, "'Glow' at New Langton Arts," in *Artweek*, July 1996, p. 20; P. C. Smith, "Olafur Eliasson at Tanya Bonakdar," in *Art in America*, December 1996, pp. 92-93.

Biographies

Hans Christian von Baeyer

Hans Christian von Baeyer, Chancellor Professor of Physics at the College of William and Mary in Virginia, was born in 1938 in Berlin, Germany. He graduated from Columbia University in New York and earned his Ph.D. at Vanderbilt University in Tennessee. In recognition of his contributions to mathematical physics he was elected Fellow of the American Physical Society. Mr. von Baeyer has won the principal teaching awards of his university, and in 1990 was selected as one of the outstanding faculty members of the State of Virginia. In recent years he has increasingly turned his attention to science writing for the public. His essays in *Discover, The Sciences, New Scientist*, and other journals from *Reader's Digest* to *The Gettysburg Review* won him the 1991 National Magazine Award in the category "Essays and Criticism." He wrote the script for a one hour film entitled "The Quantum Universe" which aired on the Public Broadcasting Network as part of the series *Smithsonian World* and was nominated for an Emmy Award. In December 2000, he participated in a celebration of the centenary of the quantum on German National Television.
http://www.physics.wm.edu/Faculty/VonBaeyer.html

Per Bak

Per Bak is currently Professor at Imperial College, London. During 1996-2001 he was Professor at the Niels Bohr Institute, Copenhagen and between 1983-1996 scientist at the Brookhaven National Laboratory, New York. As external professor he has been associated with the Santa Fe Institute, New Mexico, USA. He is the author of the book *How Nature Works*, Fellow of APS, AAAs, member of the Danish Academy of Science, and Titular member of the European Academy of Science and Letters.
http://www.ma.ic.ac.uk/mathematical_physics/pbak.html

Cecil Balmond

Cecil Balmond, who was born in Sri Lanka, is a leading structural designer working with several key architects such as Rem Koolhaas, Daniel Libeskind, Alvaro Siza and Arata Isozaki on major international projects. He is a Director of the engineering consultancy firm Ove Arup & Partners in London and teaches at various architectural schools to promote his ideas on complex forms and the overlap of art and science. Cecil

Balmond lives in London with his wife and three children.
http://www.arup.com/press/profiles/Cecil_Balmond_Profile.htm
http://www.jersemar.org.il/balmond.htm

Lise Bek

Lise Bek is Professor in Art History at the University of Århus, Denmark. She has written extensively on space conception in architecture and landscape, particularly from Antiquity to the Renaissance. Some of her major publications include *Towards Paradise on Earth: Modern Space Conception in Architecture: A Creation of Renaissance Humanism*, Odense University Press, Odense, Denmark, 1980, *Virkeligheden i kunstens spejl* (Reality in the Mirror of Art), Århus University Press, Århus, 1988, and *Rumanalyser* (Space Analyses), together with H. Oxvig, B Press, Århus, 1997.
http://www.au.dk/en/

Ben van Berkel and Caroline Bos

Ben van Berkel (born in Utrecht, 1957) studied architecture at the Gerrit Rietveld Academy in Amsterdam and the Architectural Association in London, receiving the AA Diploma with Honours in 1987. Caroline Bos (born in Rotterdam, 1959) studied History of Art at Birkbeck College, University of London.

In 1988 they founded The Van Berkel & Bos Architectuurbureau in Amsterdam, which has realized among other projects the Karbouw office building, the Erasmus bridge in Rotterdam, museum Het Valkhof in Nijmegen and the Moebius House.

Current projects are: a restructuring of the station area of Arnhem, NMR facilities for the University of Utrecht, a music theatre for Graz (Austria) and the design and restructuring of the Wadsworth Atheneum Museum of Art in Hartford, Conn.

In addition to Van Berkel & Bos Architectuurbureau, Ben van Berkel and Caroline Bos established a new firm in 1998: UN Studio (United Net). UN Studio presents itself as a network of specialists in architecture, urban development, and infrastructure.

Ben van Berkel and Caroline Bos have lectured and taught at many architectural schools around the world. Since 2000 they have been visiting professors at Princeton University, leading the unit Public Construction. Central to their teaching is an inclusive approach whereby architectural works integrate virtual and material organization and engineering constructions.

Their major publications are: *Move,* Goose Press, Amsterdam,

1999; *Museum Het Valkhof,* Goose Press, Amsterdam, 1999; *ANY. Diagram Work 23,* 1999 (guest editors Ben van Berkel & Caroline Bos); *Ben van Berkel,* monograph issue by *El Croquis 72.I,* Madrid, May, 1995; *Mobile Forces*, monograph, Ernst & Sohn, Berlin, 1994; *Delinquent Visionaries, a collection of essays*, 010 Publishers Rotterdam, 1993, reprint 1994, *Ben van Berkel, monograph*, 010 Publishers, Rotterdam, 1992.
http://www.unstudio.com/

Aaron Betsky
Aaron Betsky joined the San Francisco Museum of Modern Art as Curator of Architecture and Design in February 1995. He is responsible for exhibiting and collecting designed artefacts and spaces, including those in the fields of architecture, urban design, landscape design, interior design, industrial design, furniture, and graphic design. In 1997, he mounted *Icons: Magnets of Meaning*, a large exhibition of mass-produced objects. He assembles five to six exhibitions a year on subjects in design, and, through the Architecture and Design Forum of the Museum, has helped organize several dozen lectures, public symposia and competitions. In 1995, he cofounded the San Francisco Prize, an annual competition that has elicited designs for the Philip Burton Federal Plaza (1996) and Union Square (1997). In 1997, he organized the first biannual San Francisco Forum, *Architecture of the Imagination.*
Before joining the San Francisco Museum of Modern Art, Aaron Betsky was an Instructor and Coordinator of Special Projects at the Southern California Institute of Architecture (SCI-Arc). He has taught and lectured extensively, and is currently an Adjunct Professor at the California College of Arts and Crafts (CCAC). He is active as a writer on design and is a Contributing Editor of the magazines: *Architecture, Metropolitan Home, Blueprint* and *ID*. Aaron Betsky has published eight books on architecture and design, including *Violated Perfection: Architecture and the Fragmentation of the Modern* (1990), *James Gamble Rogers and the Architecture of Pragmantism*, 1994, *Building Sex: Men, Women, Architecture and the Construction of Sexuality*, and *Queer Space: The Spaces of Same Sex Desire*, 1997.
Aaron Betsky was born in Missoula, Montana, in 1958, but moved to The Netherlands at an early age and received his grade and high school education there. He was granted both a Bachelor of Arts (1979) and a Master of Architecture (1983)

degree from Yale University. Upon graduating, he taught at the University of Cincinnati (1983-1985) before going to work as a designer in the offices of Frank Gehry (1985-1987) and Hodgetts & Fung Design (1987). In 1987, Aaron Betsky set up his own design practice while teaching and writing in Los Angeles. He currently lives in San Francisco with his partner of nine years, the artist Peter Christian Haberkorn.
http://www.sfmoma.org

Daniel Birnbaum
Daniel Birnbaum is the Director of the Städelschule and of Portikus in Frankfurt/M., Germany. He is the author of several books on art and philosophy and a contributing editor of *Artforum.*
http://www.uol.com.br/bienal/24bienal/rot/txt_ing_ensbirn.htm
http://www.artnode.se/artorbit/issue3/i_iaspis/i_iaspis.html

Ina Blom
Ina Blom is an art historian, critic, and writer based in Oslo, Norway. She is an associate professor at the Department of Art History, University of Oslo and has written extensively both on contemporary art and twentieth century avant-garde movements. She has recently published a book on the ambivalence of Joseph Beuys.
http://www.nutscape.com/fluxus/homepage/ina1blom.html
http://www.nordicartreview.nu/

Jonathan Crary
Jonathan Crary is Professor of Art History at Columbia University, New York. A founding editor of Zone Books, he is the author of *Techniques of the Observer (1992)*, *Suspensions of Perception (2000)*, and co-editor of *Incorporations (1992)*.
http://www.columbia.edu/cu/arthistory/htm/ah_faculty_direct_crary.htm
http://www.caareviews.org/reviews/crary.html
http://mh.cla.umn.edu/txtimbw3.html

György Darvas
György Darvas (born in 1948, Budapest, Hungary) has his background in theoretical physics and the philosophy of science. He earned a master's degree at the Eötvös Loránd University in Budapest in physics (Faculty of Sciences, 1971) and in philosophy (Faculty of Arts and Letters, 1974) as well as a Ph.D. (1985). His fields of interest cover many aspects of the

phenomena of interdisciplinarity in the sciences, with special regard to the role played by symmetry in bridging (a) different disciplines, (b) sciences and the arts, and (c) different cultures. He has been working for the Hungarian Academy of Sciences for thirty years, and teaches at the Faculty of Sciences of the Eötvös Loránd University, Budapest. He was founder and directs the specialized institute for symmetry studies, the Symmetrion. He was one of the founders of the International Society for the Interdisciplinary Study of Symmetry (ISIS-Symmetry) in 1989, and has been serving as its secretary general as well as editor of its journal *Symmetry: Culture and Science*. He took part in and led several international projects, has initiated and organized a series of conferences and art-science related exhibitions. He has published eight books, twenty-two book chapters, many periodical articles, and conference lectures.
http://www.mtakszi.iif.hu/darvas.htm
http://hps.elte.hu/oktaeder/atmeneti/darvas.htm
http://members.tripod.com/vismath/isis5.htm

William Day
William Day, a native of Indiana, is a graduate of Indiana University and McGill University in Montreal where he received his doctorate in chemistry. His research and writings deal principally with structural order and origins, including four books on physics: *Bridge From Nowhere I, II, Holistic Physics*, and *A New Physics*. He resides in Oxford, Mississippi, where he researches and writes on scientific problems.
http://www.non-newtonianphysics.com/author.htm

Jørgen Dehs
Jørgen Dehs, a Danish philosopher, was born in 1945. From 1987 to 1999, he taught the history of philosophy at the University of Århus. Since then, he has been associate professor at the Århus School of Architecture, where he is head of the School of Research. He has published books and articles on aesthetics and on Søren Kierkegaard. He is co-editor of the *Nordic Journal of Architectural Research* and member of The International Advisory Board for the Søren Kierkegaard Research Center at the University of Copenhagen.
http://www.a-aarhus.dk/Ny-engelsk/AAA.htm

Diller + Scofidio
Diller + Scofidio is a collaborative, interdisciplinary studio that fuses architecture, the visual arts, and the performing arts. The

team is primarily involved in thematically-driven experimental work that takes the form of temporary and permanent site-specific installations, multi-media theater, electronic media, and print, as well as architectural commissions.

Elizabeth Diller and Ricardo Scofidio are the recipients of the MacArthur Foundation Award, the first fellowship given in the field of architecture. They have recently been awarded an Obie for Creative Achievement in Off Broadway Theater for *Jet Lag*, a James Beard Foundation Award for Best New Design for the *Brasserie*, and a Progressive Architecture Design Award for the *Blur Building*. They have also recently received the MacDermott Award for Creative Achievement from MIT, the Chrysler Award for Innovation in Design, the Tiffany Award for Emerging Artists, and fellowships from the Graham Foundation, the Chicago Institute for Architecture and Urbanism, and the N.Y. Foundation for the Arts. D+S is currently working on *Blur*, a media pavilion for the Swiss EXPO 2002, *Brooklyn Academy of Music Cultural District*, a master plan for BAMLDC, in collaboration with Rem Koolhaas, *evansandwong*, a concept store, Palais de Tokyo, Paris, *Facsimile*, a permanent installation for the new Moscone Convention Center *expansion* in San Francisco, and *Travelogues*, a permanent installation at the new JFK International Arrivals Terminal in New York. A retrospective of their work is planned by the San Francisco Museum of Modern Art for 2002.

Recently completed projects include: The *Brasserie*, in the Seagram Building, New York, *Master/Slave*, an installation at the Fondation Cartier in Paris, *Slither*, 104 units of social housing in Gifu, Japan, *Jet Lag*, a multi-media work for the stage in collaboration with The Builders Association, *EJM1: Man Walking at Ordinary Speed* and *EJM2: Inertia*, two dance collaborations with the Lyon Ballet Opera and Charleroi Danses, all currently touring the USA, Europe, and Asia, *Refresh*, a web project for the Dia Art Foundation; *The American Lawn: Surface of Everyday Life*, an exhibition at the Canadian Centre for Architecture in Montreal, *InterClone Hotel*, an installation at the Ataturk Airport for the Istanbul Biennial, and *Pageant*, a video installation for the Johannesburg Biennial. In the last several years D+S has completed *X,Y*, a permanent installation for a pachinko parlor in Kobe, Japan, *Jump Cuts*, a permanent video marquee for the world's largest Cineplex theater, San Jose, CA, *Moving Target*, a collaborative dance work with Charleroi/Danses, Belgium, *Business Class*, a collaborative theater work with Dumb Type and Hotel Pro

Forma for Copenhagen Cultural Capital, *Indigestion*, an interactive video installation; *Subtopia*, an electronic project for the ICC Gallery in Tokyo, and *Pageant* for the Venice Biennale of Architecture.
Installations of Diller + Scofidio have been commissioned by the Cartier Foundation, the Museum of Modern Art and the New Museum, NY, the Walker Art Center, Minneapolis, the Palais des Beaux-Arts in Brussels, and Gallery Ma in Tokyo, among others. Their work is in the permanent collection of MoMA, SFMoMA, the Fond National d'Art Contemporain, various FRACs in France, the Musée de la Mode in Paris, and many private collections.
Elizabeth Diller is Professor of Architecture at Princeton University and Ricardo Scofidio is Professor of Architecture at Cooper Union. Their bilingual book, *Back to the Front: Tourisms of War / Visite aux armee: tourismes de guerre* was published by the FRAC Basse-Normandie. A book of their work, *Flesh*, was reprinted last year by PAP.
http://www.dillerscofidio.com

Thorleifur Einarsson
Thorleifur Einarsson (†) finished his doctorate in geology from the University of Cologne, Germany, in 1960, after which he spent post doctorate time in Bergen, Norway, and Cambridge, England. After his return to Iceland, he was engaged in varied geological work, both applied and pure research, as well as teaching. As of 1975, he was Professor of Geology at the University of Iceland. In addition, Thorleifur Einarsson was involved in conservation and has written a large number of books and articles on geology.
http://www.ijsland.com/boeken/geology.html
http://www.mm.is/baekur/eng/0306890.htm

Ralph Erskine
Ralph Erskine, a Swedish-British architect, was born in London in 1914. He graduated from the Regent Street Polytechnic in 1938 and moved to Sweden a year later, shortly before the outbreak of World War II.
After the war and after further study at the Academy of Arts in Stockholm, he established offices in Sweden, where he designed a large number of houses, schools, apartments and urban planning schemes. In his work, Erskine has developed an organic and expressive architecture partly inspired by Swedish Empiricism and British community planning.

Erskine has experimented with designs that depend on user participation and environmental compatibility. In his later works, he experimented with climatically controlled building environments. Erskine typically creates an architecture of contrasts in which he uses a variety of forms and materials to juxtapose heavy and light elements.
http://www.GreatBuildings.com/architects/Ralph_Erskine.html

Norman Foster

Norman Foster was born in Manchester in 1935 and studied Architecture and City Planning at Manchester University and Yale University. He founded Foster Associates, now known as Foster and Partners, in 1967. Since its inception the practice has received more than 230 awards for design excellence and has won over 50 national and international competitions.
Major buildings include the Hongkong and Shanghai Bank, Hong Kong, 1985, Stansted, London's Third International Airport, 1991, Commerzbank Headquarters, Frankfurt/M., Germany, 1997 and the new Hong Kong International Airport at Chek Lap Kok, 1998. Recent projects include the new German Parliament, Reichstag, Berlin; the Great Court of the British Museum and the new Millennium Bridge, London.
Norman Foster has been awarded the Gold Medal from the RIBA, the French Academy of Architecture, and the AIA. He was appointed Officer of the Order of the Arts and Letters from the Ministry of Culture in France in 1994. In 1990, he was granted a Knighthood in the Queen's Birthday Honors and appointed by the Queen to the Order of Merit in 1997. In 1999 he became the 21st Pritzker Architecture Prize Laureate and was honored with a Life Peerage in the Queen's Birthday Honours List, Lord Foster of Thames Bank.
http://www.fosterandpartners.com/studio/foster.html

Yona Friedman

Yona Friedman was born in Budapest in 1923. He studied architecture at the Technical University, Budapest (1943), but he left Hungary in 1945, completed his training at the Technion, Haifa (Diploma in Architecture, 1948) and subsequently taught. In 1956 he attended CIAM X in Dubrovnik, which confirmed his belief that requirements generated by technological progress and demographic growth were too great to be solved by traditional social, urban, and architectural values and structures. In 1957 he settled in Paris and founded the Groupe d'Etude d'Architecture Mobile (GEAM) with Paul

Maymont, Frei Otto, Eckard Schultze-Fielitz, Werner Runhau and D. G. Emmerich. The group's manifesto was Friedman's *L'Architecture mobile* (1958), in which he rejected the idea of a static city. In contrast, he developed the principle of "infrastructure," a skeletal metal "space-frame grid" of several levels, on which mobile lightweight "space-defining elements" would be placed. He proposed to adapt these ideas for large cities by superimposing this grid on the existing fabric of London, Tunis, and New York, or by allowing commercial facilities to be built over the network of high speed roads in Los Angeles.
http://www.artnet.com/library/02/0299/T029953.asp

Ursula Frohne
Ursula Frohne earned her Ph.D. in the History of Art at the Freie Universität Berlin 1993. In 1990 DAAD Grant in New York; 1990/1991 Fellow at the Getty Center for the History of Art and the Humanities, Santa Monica; 1994/95 Grant from the American Council of the Learned Societies in New York and 1998 Fellow at the Getty Summer Institute, University of Rochester; 2001/01 post-doctoral Fellowship at the Pembroke Center, Brown University, Providence. Curatorial work for numerous exhibitions on twentieth century architecture and contemporary art. Assistant Professor at the Department for Art History at the Freie Universität Berlin 1988-1995. Since 1995 curator at the ZKM | Center for Art and Media Karlsruhe; she also teaches at the University of Design, Karlsruhe. Latest publications on contemporary art, new media, cultural and museum studies in *Mediascape*, 1996; *Contemporary Art*, 1997; *video cult/ures*, 1999, *KunstSammeln*, 1999; *Afterimage, The Journal of Media Arts and Cultural Criticism*, 1999, *Maler und Millionäre, Erfolg Als Inszenierung: Amerikanische Künstler im ausgehenden 19. Jahrhundert, 2000.*
http://www.zkm.de
http://www.medienforum.org/veranstaltung/2000/london.html
http://www.lag-neue-medien.de/lafontaine.htm

Peter Galison
From 1983-92, Peter Galison taught at Stanford University, where he was in both the philosophy and physics departments. Since 1992, he has been at Harvard University, where he is the Mallinckrodt Professor of the History of Science and of Physics. In 1997, he was named a John D. and Catherine T. MacArthur Foundation Fellow. Galison's main work explores the complex interaction between the three principal subcul-

tures of twentieth century physics – experimentation, instrumentation, and theory. The volume on experiment (*How Experiments End*, 1987 and that on instrumentation *Image and Logic*, 1997) are to be followed by the final volume – *Theory Machines* – that is still under construction. In addition, Galison has launched several projects examining the cross-currents between physics and other fields – these include his co-edited volumes on the relations between science, art and architecture, *The Architecture of Science*, 1999 and *Picturing Science, Producing Art*, 1998, as well as *Big Science*, 1992, *The Disunity of Science*, 1996, and *Atmospheric Flight in the 20th Century*, 2000.
http://www.fas.harvard.edu/~hsdept/faculty/galison
http://www.acls.org/op47-3.htm#galison

Manuel Gausa
Manuel Gausa, Barcelona, born in 1959. Architect. Graduated from ETSAB, Barcelona, in 1986. Member of the editorial board of the magazine *Quaderns d'Arquitectura i Urbanisme* since 1985, and its director since 1991. Co-founder of ACTAR, architectural agency and specialized publisher. From 1994 Professor of Projects at ETSAB and member of the direction board of the Master course "La Gran Escala" (The Big Scale). From 1996, Professor at the School of Architecture of the Universitat Lliure de Catalunya. Author of several books and publications, among others: *Barcelona y su área territorial*, 1988-1990: *Guia de Arquitectura* (with Marta Cervelló), COAC Barcelona, 1991. Berlin, ed. ACTAR, Barcelona 1994; Barcelona Sagrera, ACTAR, Barcelona, 1994; *Viviendas: nuevas alternativas, nuevos sistemas*, ACTAR, Barcelona, 1997.
http://quaderns.coac.net/
http://www.arce.es

Brian Greene
Brian Greene received his undergraduate degree from Harvard University and his doctorate from Oxford University, where he was a Rhodes Scholar. He joined the physics faculty of Cornell University in 1990, was appointed to the position of full professor in 1995, and in 1996 joined Columbia University as a professor of physics and of mathematics. He has lectured at both a general and a technical level in more than twenty countries and is widely regarded for a number of groundbreaking discoveries in superstring theory. His book, *The Elegant Universe*, was a finalist for the Pulitzer Prize in General Nonfic-

tion, won Europe's top prize for a book on science, and spent half a year on the *New York Times* bestseller list.
http://www.columbia.edu
http://www.phys.columbia.edu/faculty/greene.htm

Elizabeth Grosz
Elizabeth Grosz was born in Sydney, Australia and earned her BA (Hons) and Ph.D. in Philosophy from the Department of General Philosophy, University of Sydney, where she taught as a lecturer and senior lecturer from 1978-1991. She moved to Monash University in Melbourne as Director of the newly formed Institute of Critical and Cultural Studies in 1992, where she was Associate Professor and Professor in Critical Theory and Philosophy. She has been a Visiting Professor at University of California, Santa Cruz, University of California, Davis, Johns Hopkins University, the University of Richmond, George Washington University, and the University of California, Irvine.
http://www.gmu.edu/departments/cultural/grosz.htm
http://www.cddc.vt.edu/feminism/Grosz.html

Mika Hannula
Mika Hannula, born 1967, Ph.D. in Political Philosophy, lives and works both in Helsinki and Berlin, is the director of the Academy of Fine Arts, Helsinki, and has also worked since 2000 as the review editor of *NU: The Nordic Art Reviews*. He has published essays, articles and reviews in various languages, and four books, the latest *Why Do I Like Rock Music? – A Theoretical Discourse on Contemporary Visual Art and Culture in the 1990s – A Defense of Postmodern Plurality*, University of Trondheim Press, 2000.
http://www.nordicartreview.nu/
http://www.polarities.net/articles/arts/hannula.htm

Frederikke Hansen
MA in art history and social science, Frederikke Hansen is a freelance writer and a curator at the Shedhalle in Zurich. She has run several exhibitions off-space and has contributed essays to various art magazines and catalogues throughout Scandinavia and Europe. As a curator, her main concerns are questions of gender and sexual politics. Thus, she has conceived projects such as *Tendencies in Love. Trends, joys and dilemmas in contemporary relationships*, 1999; *Automobility. Frauen, Fahrzeuge und die Macht der Mobilität* (Automobility.

Women, Vehicles, and the Power of Mobility), 2000 and the upcoming exhibition project *Pedigree Pal – Neudefinition von Familie* (Pedigree Pal - A Redefinition of Family), 2001. Frederikke Hansen is based in Berlin and Zurich.
http://www.sheldrake.org/
http://www.artnode.dk/inserts/text/hansen/main.html

István and Magdolna Hargittai
István Hargittai is Professor of Chemistry at the Budapest University of Technology and Research Professor at the Hungarian Academy of Sciences at Eötvös University. He has a Ph.D. from Eötvös University, a Ph.D. and Doctor of Science from the Hungarian Academy of Sciences, an honorary Doctorate from Moscow University, and an honorary Doctorate of Science from the University of North Carolina. He is a member of the Hungarian Academy of Sciences, Norwegian Academy of Sciences, and the Academia Europaea.
Magdolna Hargittai is Research Professor at the Hungarian Academy of Sciences at Eötvös University. She has a Ph.D. from Eötvös University, a Ph.D. and a Doctor of Science from the Hungarian Academy of Sciences, and an honorary Doctorate of Science from the University of North Carolina.
They both have done research on molecular structures, lectured in over thirty countries, and authored books in structural chemistry and on symmetry-related topics, including *Symmetry through the Eyes of a Chemist*, Second Edition, Plenum, New York, 1995, *Symmetry: A Unifying Concept*, Shelter Publ., 1994, *In Our Own Image: Personal Symmetry in Discovery*, Kluwer/Plenum, New York, 2000, and *Candid Science: Conversations with Famous Chemists*, Imperial College Press, London, 2000. They have further volumes in preparation in the *Candid Science* series, the next one will be *Candid Science II: Conversations with Famous Biomedical Scientists*. István Hargittai is the Editor-in-Chief of *Structural Chemistry* (Kluwer/Plenum, New York). He is currently working on a new book *The Road to Stockholm: Nobel Prizes, Science, and Scientists* (for Oxford University Press, U.K.). Magdolna Hargittai is Book Review Editor of *Structural Chemistry* and is currently working on a book on woman scientists. The Hargittais have two grown-up children, Balazs, a chemistry Ph.D. at the University of Minnesota and Eszter, a Ph.D. candidate in sociology at Princeton University.
http://www.tki.aak.bme.hu/
http://www.leonet.it/culture/nexus/96/hrgittai.html

Ashley Hunt
Ashley Hunt (1970) is a filmmaker and visual artist currently living and working in New York, USA. His most recent work and debut feature film – a documentary about Prison Privatization, tracing its history and influence on public imagination – was in the official selection in the Slamdance Filmfestival 2001 and has since been screened throughout the country as well as internationally. He was recently a fellow at the Whitney ISP, New York.
http://www.slamdance.com/2001/festival/

Henrik Plenge Jakobsen
Born 1967, Artist. Lives and works in Copenhagen.
http://home4.inet.tele.dk/plenge/index.html
http://www.bremen.com/alloceans/pro_jaco.htm

Marianne Krogh Jensen
Marianne Krogh Jensen has a master's degree in art history from the University of Århus, Denmark. From 1996-1999, she worked as a curator at the Danish Contemporary Art Foundation. She is currently working on a Ph.D. on spatial conceptions in contemporary architecture at the Danish Building and Research Institute in Copenhagen. She lives in Copenhagen and Berlin.
http://www.uol.com.br/bienal/24bienal/nac/inacdinelia02.htm

Rem Koolhaas
Rem Koolhaas was born in Rotterdam in 1944. Educated at the Architectural Association School in London from 1968 until 1972, he produced the *Berlin Wall as Architecture* (1970) and *Exodus, or the Voluntary Prisoners of Architecture* (1972). In 1972 he received a Harkness Fellowship for research in the United States, studied at Cornell University and then became visiting Fellow at the Institute for Architecture and Urban Studies in New York. While in New York, he wrote *Delirious New York, a retroactive Manifesto for Manhattan*, which was published in 1978.
Rem Koolhaas founded the Office for Metropolitan Architecture in 1975 with Elia and Zoe Zenghelis and Madelon Vriesendorp in London and has been involved in building and urban planning projects ever since.
In 1995, he published together with graphic designer Bruce Mau *S,M,L,XL*, a book that documents the work of OMA and Koolhaas' interest in contemporary society, building and urban

development. Since 1995 he is Professor of Architecture and Urban Design at Harvard University. He conducts design research into a focused investigation of current urban-architectural conditions in various parts of the world. Currently he is involved in thesis advising through the ongoing *Project on the City*. The projects include a study of five cities in the Pearl River Delta; *Shopping*, an analysis of the role of retail consumption in the contemporary city and recently a study on Lagos, Nigeria.
The work of the office has won several international awards, including the Pritzker Architecture Prize 2000, and was the subject of a retrospective exhibition held at the Museum of Modern Art, New York in 1995: *Rem Koolhaas and the Place of Public Architecture*.
http://www.greatbuildings.com/architects/Rem_Koolhaas.html

Manuel de Landa
Manuel de Landa is the author of three philosophy books, *War in the Age of Intelligent Machines*, 1991, *A Thousand Years of Nonlinear History*, 1997, and *Intensive Science and Virtual Philosophy*, 2002, and has also written many philosophical essays published in various journals and collections. He teaches two seminars at Columbia University, School of Architecture: "Philosophy of History: Theories of Self-Organization and Urban Dynamics," and "Philosophy of Science: Thinking about Structures and Materials."
http://www.t0.or.at/delanda/

Lars Bang Larsen
Lars Bang Larsen is a critic and a curator based in Copenhagen. He writes on art and culture for various publications. He has lectured at The Arts Club of Chicago, Transmission Gallery, Glasgow, University of Wisconsin and at Fundació "la Caixa," Barcelona. Larsen recently co-curated the exhibition "Pyramids of Mars," which deals with contemporary art in a psycho-social perspective, and is the editor of the anthology *Remarks on Interventive Tendencies*, Borgens Forlag and Verlag Walther König, Cologne, 2001.
http://www.nordicartreview.nu/
http://www.n55.dk/LNuk.html

Henri Lefebvre
French philosopher and social theorist Henri Lefebvre (1901-91) was a deeply political figure. A committed Marxist and

leading intellectual within the French Communist Party, he perceived philosophy not as some isolated and specialized discipline, but as an activity that should be closely related to political practice. Although he became estranged from the French Communist Party in 1958, as it continued to support Stalinist beliefs, he remained committed to the revolutionary cause. Indeed he is regarded as one of the influential figures behind the events of May 1968, and the highly popular lectures which he gave as a professor of sociology at Nanterre are often viewed as one of the factors that helped to ignite the subsequent student uprisings.

Lefebvre set his philosophy in opposition to many of the dominant trends. Although critical of structuralism, positivism, critical theory, and certain strands of existentialist thought, he successfully appropriated elements of each along with aspects of psychoanalysis into his own philosophy, such that it is difficult to locate him within any particular category. Comparisons may be drawn with Situationist thought. Lefebvre developed, for example, the concept of the "moment," a fleeting, intensely euphoric sensation which appeared as a point of rupture which revealed the totality of possibilities of daily existence. This was not dissimilar to the "situation" in Situationist thought, although the Situationists criticized Lefebvre's "moment" as being passive and temporal, in comparison with their active, spatio-temporal "situation."

http://www.notbored.org/space.html

http://www.ukc.ac.uk/secl/philosophy/rp/biog/1lefeb.html

Günther Leising

Günther Leising was born 1952 in Gleisdorf, Austria. After studying Technical Physics at the Technical University Graz, Austria he worked in Applied Physics Research at the BBC, Baden, Switzerland. Ph.D. and habilitation were carried out in Solid State Physics at the TU Graz. He had several visiting professorships e.g. in Nantes, France and Paderborn, Germany and focussed his research and teaching activities on the physics and chemistry of organic solids. He was honored with the 1988 Fritz Kohlrausch Price for his experimental work. Since 1995 he has been Professor at the Institute for Solid State Physics of the Technical University Graz. He is author of over 450 scientific publications and a number of patents. After funding a few start-up companies with former students and an Institute for Nanostructured Materials and Photonics, Joanneum Research Inc. In 1999 (together with his

colleague Professor Walter Papousek), Günther Leising accepted the offer of AT&S, Leoben, Austria, in November 2000 to become Senior Vice President of Technology.
http://www.atspcb.com

Bruce Mau

Born in Sudbury, Ontario, Canada, Bruce Mau studied at the Ontario College of Art and Design. He has been the design director of Zone Books since its inception in 1985, and an editor (with Sanford Kwinter and Jonathan Crary) of Swerve Editions, a Zone imprint. From 1991 to 1993, he served as creative director of *I.D.* magazine. He was the Associate Cullinan Professor at the Rice University School of Architecture in Houston, Texas, from 1996 to 1999. He has been a thesis advisor at the University of Toronto's School of Architecture, artist in residence at California Institute of the Arts, and a visiting scholar at the Getty Research Institute in Los Angeles. He has lectured widely throughout North America and Europe and in 1998 was awarded the Chrysler Award for Design Innovation. With Rem Koolhaas, Mau designed and conceived the award-winning and critically acclaimed *S,M,L,XL*. *S,M,L,XL* marks one of many collaborative partnerships between Bruce Mau and artists and architects including Frank Gehry (Los Angeles), Claes Oldenburg and Coosje van Bruggen (New York), Michael Snow (Toronto), François Girard (Montréal), Terry Winters (New York), Douglas Gordon (Glasgow), Glen Seator (New York), and Meg Stuart of Damaged Goods (Brussels).
Mau's current projects include:
Design of Tree City, a new park to be built on the demilitarized area in the north end of Toronto; the conceptual programming for various cultural and educational facilities including an art museum, a history museum, and a new museum of the Mississippi River, a synagogue, a youth center, and the redevelopment of a central train station; Signage and environmental graphics for the Walt Disney Concert Hall (Los Angeles), the Seattle Public Library, The Ray and Maria Stata Center at MIT, the UCLA Hammer Museum, and Casa da Musica (Porto). Program, art direction and communication strategy for "New Tokyo Life Style Roppongi Think Zone," an information centre on the site of the Roppongi Hills development in Tokyo; identity programs for Access Storage Solutions (London), Vizible (Toronto), and the Canadian Centre for Architecture (Montreal); the identity and publications program for the Gagosian Gallery (London, New York, Los Angeles).

Bruce Mau's book *Life Style*, a book on design culture, was published by Phaidon in autumn of 2000. The second printing will be released in 2001.
http://www.brucemaudesign.com

Anders Michelsen

Anders Michelsen is presently writing a dissertation on technology and the imagination at the University of Copenhagen. He has co-edited and contributed to a number of Danish and foreign publications, books, catalogues, and journals, dealing with design, technology, art, culture, and globalization. He is advisory editor of *Atlantica internacional revista de las artes*, CAAM, Gran Canaria. Since the early 1990s, he has worked as a freelance art critic and curator.
http://www.hum.ku.dk
http://www.cybergeography.com
http://www.biospherics.org

Ove Nathan

Ove Nathan, born 1926, Physicist and Professor. As of 1953 associated with the Niels Bohr Institute, where he worked on experimental nuclear physics. He was awarded a Doctorate of Science in 1964, became a professor in 1970, and from 1982-1994, was the President (Dean) of The University of Copenhagen. In the 1980s he was involved in the international debate on nuclear weapons and human rights on the basis of Niels Bohr's ideas of an open world.
http://www.nbi.dk

Jeff Noon

Jeff Noon was born in 1957. His first novel, *Vurt*, won the Arthur C. Clarke award. Since then, in the novels *Pollen, Automated Alice* and *Nymphomation*, he has further explored the imagined realms that coexist with, and comment on, contemporary Britain. *Pixel Juice* was a collection of avant-pulp stories. Later works such as *Needle in the Groove* and *Cobralingus*, deal with a more lyrical expression of weirdness, often borrowing techniques from the world of electronic music and dance culture. His one avowed hope is that language be set free, to discover new ways of telling stories.
http://www.jeffnoon.com
http://www.needleinthegroove.com

Hans Ulrich Obrist

Hans Ulrich Obrist was born in May 1968 in Zurich, Switzerland, and currently lives and works in Paris. Since 1993 he has run the program *Migrateurs* at the Musée d'Art Moderne de la Ville de Paris, and has been a curator for the museum in progress, Vienna. He was the founder of the migratory Museum Robert Walser (1993) and the Nano Museum (1996). Since 1997 he is editor in chief of *Point d'Ironie*, which is published by agnes b. Since 1991 he has curated numerous exhibitions including *The Kitchen Show* (St. Gallen, 1991), *Christian Boltanski* in the Monastery Library (St.Gallen, 1991), *Gerhard Richter*, Nietzsche Haus, Sils Maria (1992), *Hôtel Carlton Palace* (Paris, 1993), *The Broken Mirror* (with Kasper Kœnig, Vienna Festival, 1993), *Life/Live* (with Laurence Bossé, Musée d'Art Moderne de la Ville de Paris and Centro Belem, Lisbon, 1996), *Do it* (so far 30 versions since 1994, American tour 1997-2001), *Cities on the Move* (with Hou Hanru, Secession Vienna and CAPC Bordeaux, 1997, and Hayward Gallery, London and Kiasma, Helsinki and Bangkok, 1999), *Le Jardin, La Ville, La Mémoire* (with Laurence Bossé and Carolyn Christov-Bakargiev, Villa Medici, Rome, 1998-2000), *Laboratorium* (with Barbara Vanderlinden, Antwerp Open, 1999), *Sogni/Dreams* (with Francesco Bonami, Fondazione Rebaudengo, 1999). *Retrace your steps: Remember tomorrow* (Sir John Soanes Museum, London 1999-2000) *Rumor City* (Fri Art, Fribourg and Mutations, Arc en Reve, Bordeaux, 2000). Obrist is one of the curators of *Seoul Media City*, South Korea, 2000 and of *Mutations: Evenement culturel sur la ville contemporaine* (co-curated with Rem Koolhaas, Sanford Kwinter, Stefano Boeri) Arc en Reve, Bordeaux, 2000/2001. He has edited the writings of Gerhard Richter, Louise Bourgeois, Gilbert and George, Maria Lassnig, and Leon Golub.
http://www.bibliomania.org.uk/contributors/Completed_contrib/Ulrich_obrist.htm

Robert Ossermann

Robert Ossermann has been Professor of Mathematics at Stanford University since 1955. Since 1990 he has simultaneously served as the Deputy Director of the Mathematical Sciences Research Institute in Berkeley, California. He has been a Fulbright lecturer, a Guggenheim fellow, and was the chairman of the Department of Mathematics at Stanford from 1973 to 1979. The author of numerous professional research articles, he is also the winner of a Dean's Award for Outstanding

Teaching.
http://www.msri.org/people/staff/osserman

Franz Pichler

Franz Pichler was born 1936. After finishing an apprenticeship in telecommunications he studied Mathematics and Physics. Since 1973 he has been Professor for Systems Theory (in Information Technology) at the Johannes Kepler University, Linz, Austria, since 1988 head of the Institute of Systems Science there. Visiting professorships in the USA (University of Maryland 1970, SUNY Binghamton 1975, 1982), Italy (University of Napoli 1991) and Spain (University of Las Palmas, Gran Canaria 1992).
http://www.cast.uni-linz.ac.at/People/AcademicStaff/prof.htm

John Pløger

John Pløger, Doctorate of Art, Senior Researcher. Norwegian Institute for Urban & Regional Research, Oslo, Norway. Born 1953, educated as a cultural sociologist in Ålborg, Denmark, 1986 and received a Doctorate of Art in Human and Urban Geography, University of Oslo, Norway, 1996. Currently also guest researcher at the Danish Building Research Institute, Copenhagen, Denmark. Writings on shopping malls, community and urban planning, urban theory, aesthetic philosophy, and aesthetic planning. Recently published the book *Byens språk* (Urban Discourses), Spartacus Forlag, Oslo, 2001.
http://www.pion.co.uk/ep/epb/abstracts/b28/b2669.html

Andrzej Przywara and Adam Szymczyk

Andrzej Przywara (born 1968) and Adam Szymczyk (born 1970) are curators and writers who live and work in Warsaw. They both studied Art History at the University of Warsaw. They work with the Foksal Gallery, a public art space in Warsaw and they co-founded the Foksal Gallery Foundation (with Joanna Mytkowska) in 1997, a non-profit institution which aims to support contemporary art in Poland through publications, exhibitions and various forms of research. They organized the exhibition of Hans Bellmer in Katowice (1996) and are currently working on the show dealing with the Silesian episode in the biography of Robert Walser. In recent years they have worked with artists as curators at the Foksal Gallery, including Susan Hiller, Gregor Schneider, Edward Krasinski, Douglas Gordon, Richard Wright, Piotr Uklanski, Stanislaw Drozdz, Gerda Steiner, Pawel Althamer, Katarzyna Jozefowicz.

This biographical note covers only their common activities.
http://www.nordicartreview.nu/
http://www.aussenstelle.purespace.de/adam_szymczyk.html

John Rajchman

John Rajchman is a philosopher based in New York. He is Visiting Professor of Art History at MIT, Cambridge, Mass., and Columbia University, New York. His most recent books are *Constructions* and *The Deleuze Connections* (MIT Press). Forthcoming is *Post-war French Philosophy*, ed. with Etienne Balibar (The New Press). Currently a contributing editor at *Artforum*, he has been an editor of *October* and a member of the Board of Directors of *ANY* (Architecture New York). He has taught in Paris, and is part of the advisory board of publications in Brazil and Japan. His earlier books on Foucault, Lacan, and on ethics have been translated into many languages.
http://www.sitesarch.org/reviews/Rajchman.html
http://www.columbia.edu/cu/staff/

Otto E. Rössler

Otto E. Rössler was born in 1940. After studying medicine he worked at the Max-Planck-Institute for behavioral science in Seewiesen and at the Center for Theoretical Biology in Buffalo. Since 1977 he has been a Professor for Theoretical Chemistry at the University Tübingen. His research concentrates on deductive biology, chemical robots, chaotic attractions, hyperchaos, and endophysics. He was involved with the formation of chaos research and gave the name to the Rössler-Attraktor, which was his discovery. Published books, e.g.: *Endophysik. Die Welt des inneren Beobachters,* Berlin, 1992; *Endophysics, The World as an Interface,* World Scientific Publishing Co., Singapore, New Jersey, London, Hong Kong, 1998.
http://www.uni-tuebingen.de/uni/c14/Chemie/PC/Profs/roessler.html
http://theonext.itc.uni-tuebingen.de/

Gerhard Roth

Gerhard Roth was born in Marburg in 1942. He studied philosophy, German literature, and musicology in Münster, Germany and Rome, Italy from 1963 to 1969, receiving his degree in philosophy in 1969 from the University of Münster. Between 1969 and 1974 he studied biology at Münster and at the University of California, Berkeley, receiving his Ph.D. from the University of Münster in 1974. In 1975-76 he served as

Assistant Professor at the Kassel Polytechnic, Germany. From 1976 on he was Professor of Behavioural Physiology at the University of Bremen, Germany and Director of the Institute for Research on the Brain; since 1997 he has served as the Founding Director of the Hanseatic Insitute for Advanced Study in Bremen and Niedersachsen, Germany.
http://www.doebe.li/bibliothek/p00064.html
http://kultur.aec.at/festival/1992/roth.html

Jaime Salazar
Jaime Salazar Rückauer, editor. He was born in Bilbao, Spain in 1964 and studied architecture at the Escola Tècnica Superior d'Arquitectura de Barcelona (ETSAB). In 1991 he joined the editorial board of the magazine of the Catalan Association of Architects, *Quaderns*, with Manuel Gausa as editor-in-chief, and has been its main editor since 1996. The collaborative work between architects and designers led to the creation of an interactive team – Actar – devoted to the proposal and diffusion of architecture in the contemporary context. He participates as founding member. Together with the collaboration in several publications and exhibitions, he has recently published the book *MVRDV at VPRO* and co-authored with Manuel Gausa the monography *Single Family Housing. The Private Domain.*
http://adolfo.uai.cl/profesores/jaime_salazar.php
http://www.actar.es

Katya Sander
Katya Sander, born in 1970, is a visual artist currently living and working in Copenhagen, Denmark. Her recent work addresses consumer culture mainly through investigations of the spatial staging of subjects as consumers, and questions how desire drives collective identity. She is the editor of *Øjeblikket* – a magazine for art and visual culture – and a founding member of the women's art and activist collective "Women down the Pub." She was recently a fellow at the Whiteney ISP, New York.
http://www.rooseum.se/curex/curex.html
http://www.location1.org/artists/recorders.html

Erik Scheldon
Erik Scheldon was born 1952 in Copenhagen. He is currently at the Solar Energy Center Denmark, Danish Technological Institute. He graduated as an architect from the Royal Danish

Academy of Fine Arts, 1979. He has more than twenty years R&D experience in the field of solar energy and ecological design, e.g. Danish solar house of the future "villa VISION" in Taastrup, 1994.
Founder and, since 1998, manager of the Danish Solar Energy Center, which is a forum – with approximately 50 employees – that enables all sides of the solar industry to meet and cooperate. The Center brings together representatives for fitters and manufacturers, sales and marketing organizations, and research and development institutions. The Center also houses the Solar Energy Test Laboratories and quality assurance programs for solar thermal and photovoltaic systems. He is a member of ISES (International Solar Energy Society).
http://www.uk.teknologisk.dk/
http://www.solarenergycentre.com

Kurt Schilcher
Kurt Schilcher was born in Linz, Austria, in 1959. Diploma and doctoral studies in the natural science and technology departments at the University of Linz (received his doctorate in 1997), after which he worked as an assistant in the Institute of Biophysics at the University of Linz.
Since 1999, he is managing director of *nanolytics* (characterization and micromanipulation of different surfaces with an atomic force and a scanning tunnel microscope).
Research focal points and interests: scanning probe microscopy, surface physics, physical chemistry, biophysics and bionics. He is also preoccupied with new forms of expression in the fine arts (development of *Mantography* – "*with the eyes of a seer:*" computer-supported processing of high resolution microscopic images). First exhibitions in Düsseldorf, Germany (2000) and Linz, Austria (2001).
http://www.nordico.at/ausstellung/Mantografie.html

Jane Schul
Jane Schul, born 1943, landscape architect, based in Copenhagen, Denmark, where she has had her office since 1995.
http://www.egeskov.dk/english/sightseeing/9.html
http://www.lbh.kvl.dk/uk/uk-samling.htm

Richard Sennett
Richard Sennett, born in 1943, Professor of History and Sociology, Professor of Humanities, Ph.D. 1969, Harvard University; B.A. 1964 (with special honors), University of Chicago.

Selected Works: *The Corrosion of Character*, W.W. Norton & Company, 1998; *Flesh and Stone: The Body and the City in Western Civilization*, W.W. Norton, 1994; *The Conscience of the Eye*, Knopf, 1990; *La Transparence du Pouvoir aux Etats-Unis*, Fayard, 1982; *Narcissimo y Cultura Moderna*, Kairos, 1980; *Authority*, Knopf, 1980; *The Fall of Public Man*, Knopf, 1977; *The Hidden Injuries of Class*, with Jonathan Cobb, Knopf, 1972; *The Uses of Disorder*, Knopf, 1970; *Families Against the City: Middle Class Homes of Industrial Chicago*, 1872-1890, Harvard University Press, 1970; *Nineteenth Century Cities*, with Stephen Thernstrom, Yale University Press, 1969.
Major interests: urban sociology, art/music, family, history of ideas, and history of the body.
Recent Honors: Fellow, American Academy of Arts and Sciences, since 1996, Fellow, Royal Society of Literature, since 1996, Wissenschaft und Gesellschaft Professor, Johann-Wolfgang-Goethe Universität, Frankfurt/M., Germany, 1991.
http://www.nyu.edu/gsas/dept/socio/faculty/#sennett

Simon Sheikh
Simon Sheikh is a critic and curator. He is managing director of Overgaden – the Cultural Ministry's Exhibition Space for Contemporary Art in Copenhagen, Denmark. He is co-editor of *Øjeblikket* – a magazine for visual culture, and is currently editing two books, an anthology of contemporary Nordic artists writings and the compilation *Models of Resistance* on contemporary critical art practices. He lives and works in Copenhagen.
http://www.artnode.dk/features/plumvelvet/plumvelvet1/plum6.html
http://www.hum.au.dk/nordisk/realisme/docs/aktiviteter/produktion.html
http://www.artpublic.ch/fleurycv.html

Michael Speaks
Michael Speaks was born in Jackson, Mississippi in 1959. He completed a Ph.D. at Duke University in 1993. Speaks is the founding editor of Polygraph, and has been the Senior Editor at *ANY* magazine in New York, where he was also the Series Editor for "Writing Architecture" published by the MIT Press. Speaks has taught in the graphic design department at the Yale School of Art, in the architecture departments at Harvard University, Parsons School of Design, The Berlage Institute,

Columbia University, The Center for Contemporary Architecture Studies at the Universidad Torcuato Di Tella, Buenos Aires, and is currently Director of the Graduate Program at the Southern California Institute of Architecture in Los Angeles. He has also been a research fellow in the architecture faculty at TU-Delft in the Netherlands, and heads the Los Angeles-based urban research group, BIG SOFT ORANGE. Speaks has published widely in journals such as *A+U, Assemblage, Architectural Record, Daidalos, Domus, Architecture Design, Architectura Viva, Archis, de Architect, Metropolis*, and *Space and Design*. Speaks serves on the Board of Directors at the Storefront for Art and Architecture in New York, the Southern California Institute of Architecture, and the advisory board of *A+U*.
http://www.sciarc.edu/

Christa Steinle
Christa Steinle studied History of Art and Romance Languages and Literature in Graz, Austria and Perugia, Italy, Ph.D., 1977. Since 1999, Director of the Neue Galerie am Landesmuseum Joanneum in Graz. Curator and author with Alexandra Foitl, *Styrian Window. Bildende Kunst in der Steiermark 1970-1995*, published by Droschl, Graz, 1996.
http://www.stmk.gv.at/verwaltung/lmj-ng/ng/ng02.html

Einar Thorsteinn
Einar Thorsteinn studied architecture at the Technical University of Hannover, Germany 1963-1969 (from which he graduated as Ingeneer), and lightweight structures with Professor Frei Otto at the Institut für leichte Flächentragwerke at the University of Stuttgart, Germany, and at Professor Otto's private studio: Atelier Warmbronn 1969-1971. Post graduate: 1980-1981 a six months research on Catastrophe Safe Housing at the Institut für leichte Flächentragwerke of the University of Stuttgart under the auspice of DAAD in Bonn, Germany. Founder and director of CL (CONSTRUCTIONS LAB) a privately financed research laboratory 1973-1998. Main research fields: tensile structures for the Icelandic climate; geodesic domes as a possible basis for new type of Icelandic residence; sustainable houses/ecological building technology and three dimensional geometry/quasi-crystals. Parts of the last subject supported by the late Dr. Linus Pauling. Thorsteinn has published 250 articles on architecture, city planning, environmental design, sustainable housing, ecological building technology,

biological influences on housing (SBS and HSE), today's medicine and various other scientific fields on the frontiers of science 1967-2001. His books include *Nature's Forms*, 1977, and *Towards a New Reality*, 1997.
http://www.mmedia.is/kingdome/

Anthony Vidler

Anthony Vidler chairs the Art History Department at the University of California in Los Angeles. His books include *The Architectural Uncanny, Architecture, Revolution and Restoration: The Politics of Monumentality, 1799-1989* and *Warped Space. Art, Architecture, and Anxiety in Modern Culture.*
http://www.humnet.ucla.edu/humnet/arthist/cv/vidler.htm

Gregory Volk

Gregory Volk is a New York based art critic and curator who contributes regularly to *Art in America* and other publications. His article "Art on Ice," concerning contemporary art in Iceland, was published in the September 2000 issue of *Art in America.*
http://www.cinemedia.net/bridge/artists/artists_s_z/gregory_volk.htm

Peter Weibel

Peter Weibel studied literature, medicine, logic, and philosophy in Paris and Vienna and wrote his thesis on mathematical logics. From 1976 to 1981 he was lecturer in the theory of form and, in 1981, Visiting Professor of Design and Art at the Vienna University of the Applied Arts and was Visiting Professor at the College of Art and Design in Halifax, Canada. In 1981 he was lecturer in Perception Theory and Professor of Photography at Gesamthochschule in Kassel, Germany. Since 1994 he has been Professor of Visual Media at the University of Applied Arts in Vienna, Austria and Associate Professor of Video and Digital Arts at the State University of New York at Buffalo. In 1989 he headed the Institut für Neue Medien at the Städelschule in Frankfurt/M., Germany. He was Artistic Director of *Ars Electronica*, Linz, Austria, from 1986 until 1995. He is currently the Director of the ZKM in Karlsruhe, Germany. He has published numerous books on twentieth century art and technology.
http://www.zkm.de
http://on1.zkm.de/zkm/personen/weibel

Manfred Wolff-Plottegg

Manfred Wolff-Plottegg, Architect, was born in Schöder, Murau, Styria, Austria, in 1946. He studied at the Technical University of Graz, Austria the Beaux Arts Academie, Paris and Salzburg Summer Academy, graduating in 1974. Since 1983, he has taught at various universities, including the Technical University Graz, Linz Design School, Innsbruck University, and Munich Technical University. He has been a guest lecturer in academies and universities all over Europe and North America. He has taken part in numerous exhibitions and competitions and received prizes such as the Austrian Concrete Construction Prize, the Geramb-Award for good design, the Architecture Prize of Steiermark and the Austrian Aluminium-Architecture-Prize. His books include *Architektur-Algorithmen*, Passagen Verlag, Vienna, 1996; *Das binäre Haus*, 1989 (Architekturgalerie Munich) and *In welchem Style sollen wir Bauen*, 1984 (Schrift Plottegg) together with numerous articles in leading architectural journals.
http://www.baukunst.tu-graz.ac.at/~plottegg
http://baukunst.tu-graz.ac.at/~plottegg/fake_txt.htm

References

Hans C. von Baeyer, "Impossible Crystals," from *Discover*, February 1990, pp. 69-72, 75, 76, 78.

Cecil Balmond, "Powers," from Cecil Balmond, *Number 9. The Search for the Sigma Code*, pp. 141-153, © Prestel, Munich and New York, 1998. All intellectual and pictorial material is the copyright of the author.

Per Bak, "Self-Organization of Earthquakes," from Per Bak, *How Nature Works*, Copernicus, Springer-Verlag, New York, 1996, pp. 88-93.

Daniel Birnbaum, "The Limits of Presentation," from Daniel Birnbaum, *The Hospitality of Presence. Problems of Otherness in Husserl's Phenomenology*, ACTA Universitas Stockholmiensis, *Stockholm Studies in Philosophy*, 20, Almqvist & Wiksell International, Stockholm, 1998, pp. 106-113.

Jonathan Crary, "Visionary abstractions," from Jonathan Crary, *Techniques of the Observer – On Vision and Modernity in the Nineteenth Century*, first published in 1990, The MIT Press, Cambridge, Mass., here quoted from the fifth edition, The MIT Press, Cambridge, Mass., 1994, pp. 137-150.

William Day, "Motion," composed with excerpts from William Day, *A New Physics*, Foundation For New Directions, Cambridge, Mass., 2000.

Thorleifur Einarsson, "Geothermal activity," first published by Mál og menning in 1991, original title *Myndun og mótun lands – jardfraedi*, here quoted from the English version Thorleifur Einarsson, *Geology of Iceland*, trans. Georg Douglas, Mál og menning, Reykjavík, 1994, pp. 81-88.

Lord Norman Foster, *The Rainbow Cloud*, project study for the Royal Academy, March 2000, unpublished manuscript.

Yona Friedman, "Poor World," from Yona Friedman, *Structures Serving the Unpredictable*, eds. Sabine Lebesque, Helene Fentener van Vlissingen, NAi Publishers, Rotterdam, 1999, pp. 60-61.

Manuel Gausa, "Dynamic Time – (In)formal order: (Un)disciplined trajectories," from *Espirales Spirals, Quaderns 222*, Barcelona, 1999, pp. 6-11.

Peter Galison, "Objectivity is Romantic," from *The humanities and the sciences*, eds. Jerome Friedman, Peter Galison, and Susan Haack, *Occasional Papers*, American Council of Learned Societies, ACLS, New York, No. 47, pp. 15-23.

Brian Greene, "The Elegant Universe – Space, Time, and the Eye of the Beholder," from, *The Elegant Universe – Superstrings, Hidden Dimensions, and the Quest for the Ultimate Theory*, by Brian Greene, published by Jonathan Cape. Reprinted by permission of The Random House Group Ltd., New York, 2000, pp. 23-34.

Elisabeth Grosz, "The Future of Space: Toward an Architecture of Invention," from *Anyhow*, ed. Cynthia C. Davidson, The MIT Press, Cambridge, Mass., and London, 1998, pp. 242-251.

Henrik Plenge Jakobsen, "Diary of plasma," first presented in the context of the exhibition *Neutron*, ENSAD/FRAC, Champagne Ardennes, France, 1995, and later in the exhibition *Now Here*, Louisiana Museum, Humlebaek, Denmark as a part of the installation *Diary of Plasma*. Text edited by Dean Inkster. Copyright Henrik Plenge Jakobsen, 1995.

Rem Koolhaas, "Generic City," from *S,M,L,XL*, eds. O.M.A., Rem Koolhaas, and Bruce Mau, The Monacelli Press, Inc., New York, 1995, pp. 1248-1264.

Manuel de Landa, "Meshworks, Hierarchies, and Interfaces," from *The Virtual Dimension. Architecture, Representation and Crash Culture*, John Beckman, ed., Princeton Architectural Press, New York, 1998, pp. 275-285.

Henri Lefebvre, "The Production of Space *(Extracts)* – The Monument," first published in *The Production of Space*, trans. David Nicholson-Smith, Blackwell Publishers, London, 1991, here quoted from *Rethinking Architecture. A reader in cultural theory*, ed. Neil Leach, Routledge, London, and New York, 1997, pp. 138-143.

Bruce Mau, "12 Strategies. Notes," from Bruce Mau, Kyo Maclear with Bart Testa, *Life Style*, Phaidon Press Limited, London, 2000, pp. 317, 319, 321, 323, 325, and 327.

Ove Nathan, "The Quest for the Great Symmetry," trans. Dan Marmorstein, original title "Jagten på den store symmetri," from *Universe*, Berlingske Tidende, 4. Sektion, December 15, 1998, pp. 8-9.

Jeff Noon, excerpt from Jeff Noon, *Pollen*, first edition Ringpull, Great Britain, 1995 here quoted from Pan Books, an imprint of MacMillan Publishers Ltd., London and Basingstoke, 1996, pp. 145-149.

Robert Osserman, "Encompassing the Earth," from *Poetry of the Universe. A Mathematical Exploration of the Cosmos*, by Robert Osserman, copyright © 1995 by Robert Osserman. Used by permission of Doubleday, a division of Random House, Inc., New York, London, Toronto, Sydney, Auckland, 1995, pp. 20-40.

John Rajchman, "The Virtual House," first published in *ANY*, 19/20, September/October 1997, here quoted from John Rajchman, *Constructions*, The MIT Press, Cambridge, Mass., and London, 1998 (The Writing Architecture Series), pp. 115-121.

Otto E. Rössler and Peter Weibel, "Endophysics or Our Rainbow World," from *The World from Within – ENDO & NANO*, eds., Karl Gerbel, Peter Weibel, Veritas-Verlag, Linz, 1992, pp. 13-21.

Gerhard Roth, "Can One Meaningfully Speak of a World Independent of Consciousness?," trans. Ian Balfour and Anna Elkins, original title "Wirklichkeit und Wahrheit. Kann man sinnvoll über eine bewußtseinsunabhängige Welt sprechen?," from Gerhard Roth, *Das Gehirn und seine Wirklichkeit. Kognitive Neurobiologie und ihre philosophischen Konsequenzen*, © Suhrkamp Verlag, Frankfurt/M., 1994, pp. 320-326.

Jaime Salazar, "MVRDV, VPRO," introductory text, from *mvrdv at vpro*, eds., ACTAR, Jaime Salazar, trans. Peter Bijker, Andrew Langdon-Davies, Ozcariz-Lindstrom, Actar, Barcelona, 1999, pp. 7-25.

Richard Sennett, "The Technology of Unity," from Richard Sennett, *The Conscience of the Eye. The Design and Social Life of Cities*, W.W. Norton & Co., Inc., New York, 1992, pp. 103-114.

Michael Speaks, "It's out there. The Formal Limits of the American Avant-Garde," from *Other Spaces. The Affair of the Heteropia*, edited by Roland Ritter and Bernd Knaller-Vlay, Verlag Haus der Architektur, Graz, 1998 (*HDA Dokumente zur Architektur* 10), pp. 156-177.

Einar Thorsteinn, "A mathematical order of polyhedrons – Fourfold to fivefold Symmetry Transitions," excerpts from Einar Thorsteinn, *The Development Pattern of Geometrical Structures*, Reykjavík, 1978.

Anthony Vidler, "Any Mores," from *Anymore*, ed. Cynthia C. Davidson, Anyone Corporation, New York, The MIT Press, Cambridge, Mass., and London, 2000, pp. 244-248.

Photo Credits

Unless otherwise specified, copyright on the illustrations lies with the respective artists, authors, and photographers. Cover and frontispiece: © Olafur Eliasson; p. 13: © Neue Galerie am Landesmuseum Joanneum, Graz; p. 36: from István and Magdolna Hargittai, *Symmetrie. Eine neue Art, die Welt zu sehen,* Rowohlt, Reinbek near Hamburg, 1998, p. 280; p. 44: Copernicus, Springer-Verlag New York, Inc.; pp. 50-52: from D. Stassinopoulos and P. Bak, "Democratic Reinforcement. A Principle for Brain Function," *Physical Review E 51,* 1995, p. 5033; pp. 55-58: all graphics and illustrations courtesy of the author, taken from Cecil Balmond, *Number 9. In the Search for the Sigma Code,* Prestel, Munich, New York, 1998, pp. 140-153; pp. 83-85: courtesy of UN Studio; pp. 128, 131: courtesy Tate Gallery London, including p. 132: from Jonathan Crary, *Techniques of the Observer,* October Books, The MIT Press, Cambridge, Mass., pp. 140, 144, 146; p. 140: © J. D. Watson; p. 142: © Tamás F. Farkas; p. 143: from the internet; p. 145, fig. 5: from Weyl, H., *Symmetry,* Princeton University Press, Princeton, 1952; p. 145, fig. 6: photo: M. Fujitsuka, from G. Darvas, D. Nagy, and M. Pardavi-Horvatheds: *Symmetry, Natural and Artificial,* Symmetrion, Budapest, 1995, p. 734; p. 146: from Y. Ne'eman, Y. Kirsh, *The Particle Hunters,* Cambridge University Press, Cambridge, Mass., 1986, p. 272; p. 147: combined from two figures in J. Rosen, *Symmetry in Science. An Introduction to the General Theory,* Springer Verlag, Heidelberg, et. al., 1995, p. 213 and Y. Ne'eman, Y. Kirsh, *The Particle Hunters,* Cambridge University Press, Cambridge, Mass., 1986, p. 272; pp. 177-180: all pictures courtesy of Diller + Scofidio; pp. 182, 184: all figures courtesy of Mál og menning, Thorleifur Einarsson and Gunnar H. Ingimundarson, here taken from *Geology of Iceland,* Mál og Menning, Reykjavík, 1994, pp. 81-88; pp. 189-193: all sketches courtesy of Lord Norman Foster, taken from his study on the project *The Rainbow Cloud* for the Royal Academy, March 2000, unpublished manuscript; pp. 195-198: figures taken from Yona Friedman, *Structures serving the Unpredictable,* NAi Publishers, Rotterdam, 1999, pp. 60-61; p. 261: figure taken from Elisabeth Grosz, "The Future of Space: Toward an Architecture of Invention," in *Anyhow,* ed. Cynthia C. Davidson, Anyone Corporation, New York, 1998, p. 247; p 281: © Roger Penrose; pp. 282-294: © István und Magdolna Hargittai; p. 290:

photo of Buckminster Fuller © Lloyd Kahn; p. 293: photo of A. Kitaigorodskii © Petr Zorkii; p. 294, fig. 21: © Khudu Mamedov; p. 298: © Henrik Plenge Jacobsen; p. 336: photograph courtesy University of Pennsylvania, School of Engineering and Applied Science; pp. 382-385: © Günter Leising; pp. 391, 392: figures taken from Bruce Mau, Kyo Maclear, Bart Testa (eds.), *Life Style*, Phaidon Press Limited, London 2000, pp. 325, 326; p. 395: from www.orbit6.com/celss; p. 397, fig. 3: from www.orbit6.com/celss; p. 397, fig. 2: from www.ajnpx.com/images; p. 400, fig. 5: from http://www.cybergeography.com/atlas/geographic.html; pp. 399, 401: from http://www.cybergeography.com/atlas/topology.html; p. 400, fig. 6: from *Documenta <10, 1997, Kassel>: Das Buch zur Documenta X = politics-poetics/,* ed. Documenta-und-Museum-Fridericianum-Veranstaltungs-GmbH, Cantz-Verlag, Ostfildern, 1997, p. 190; pp. 443-451: from Robert Osserman, *Poetry of the Universe. A mathematical exploration of the Cosmos,* Anchor Books, Doubleday, New York, 1996, pp. 21-40; p. 455, fig. 1a: Franz Pichler, Linz; p. 455, fig. 1b, p. 461: PKS (Pythagoras-Kepler-Schule) Lauffen/Bad Ischl; p. 493: from http://www.bory.tucholskie.pl/new/www/bory/atrakcje/index.htm; p. 494: published by Panstwowe Przedsiebiorstwo Geodezyjno – Kartograficzne 1992; p. 495: from postcard published by Oficyna Wydawnicza "Pomorze" Gdansk Fot. Bogdan Dabrowski, Layout: Boguslaw Nieznalski; p. 497: from exh. cat. *Pawel Filonow und seine Schule,* Städtische Kunsthalle Düsseldorf, DuMont Buchverlag Cologne, 1990, p. 199; pp. 540-542: courtesy of Eric Scheldon; pp. 544-550: courtesy of Kurt Schilcher, taken from Kurt Schilcher, *Forces due to surface water measured by force microscopy. Consequences for anchoring biological cells to surface,* Linz, 1997; pp. 608-627: courtesy of Einar Thorsteinn; p. 656: courtesy of neugerriemschneider, Berlin; p. 659-673: © Franz Wamhof.

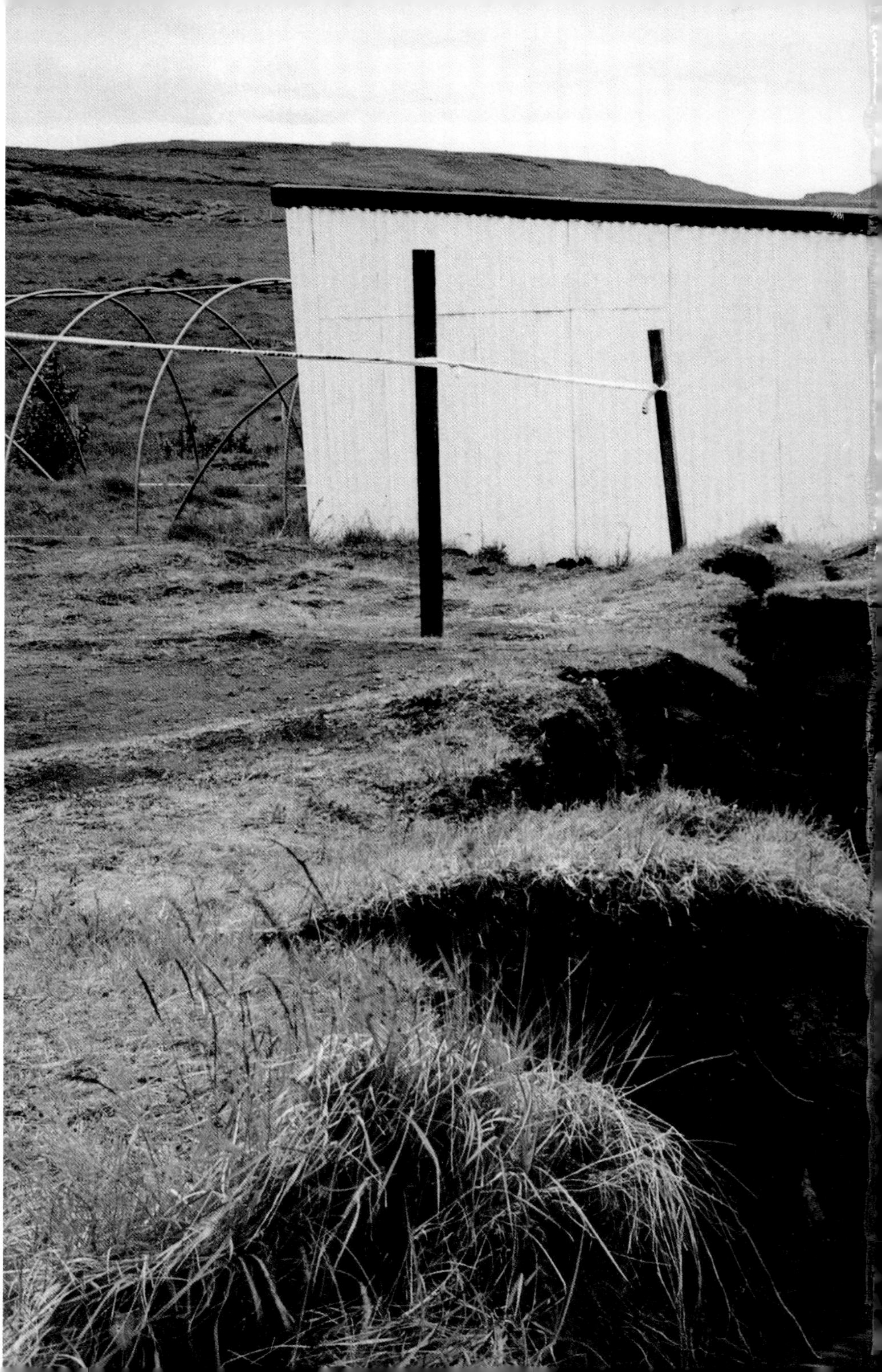